KU-713-920

Fundamentals of Management

Mike Smith

The **McGraw·Hill** Companies

London   Boston   Burr Ridge, IL   Dubuque, IA   Madison, WI   New York   San Francisco
St. Louis   Bangkok   Bogotá   Caracas   Kuala Lumpur   Lisbon   Madrid   Mexico City
Milan   Montreal   New Delhi   Santiago   Seoul   Singapore   Sydney   Taipei   Toronto

Fundamentals of Management
Mike Smith
ISBN-13 978-0-07-711515-9
ISBN-10 0-07-711515-5

Published by McGraw-Hill Education
Shoppenhangers Road
Maidenhead
Berkshire
SL6 2QL
Telephone: 44 (0) 1628 502 500
Fax: 44 (0) 1628 770 224
Website: *www.mcgraw-hill.co.uk*

British Library Cataloguing in Publication Data
A catalogue record for this book is available from the British Library

Library of Congress Cataloging in Publication Data
The Library of Congress data for this book has been applied for from the Library of Congress

Acquisitions Editor: Rachel Gear
Editorial Assistant: Karen Harlow
Marketing Manager: Alice Duijser
Production Editor: James Bishop

Text Design by Hard Lines
Cover design by Rob Duyser
Printed and bound in Finland by WS Bookwell

The *McGraw Hill* Companies

Dedication

This book is dedicated to the many students who have taught me so much. Thank you.

Brief Contents

Detailed Table of Contents

Preface

Over many years I have taught the fundamentals of management to, perhaps, 10 000 students. They have taught me the importance of good information expressed in a straightforward way aided by the right level of illustrations – eschewing distracting effects that look pretty but only serve to increase costs. Unusually for an academic and researcher, I have been fortunate to experience management at first hand: junior manager in a knitwear factory in Leicester, director of a quoted company in London and chairman of a small property company in Manchester. This has taught me the need to focus upon what is practical and relevant. Consultancy assignments in Europe, Australasia, South Africa and Asia have also taught me lessons. In particular, I have learned that whilst the important details, context and expression differ the *fundamentals* of management are amazingly consistent. All of this made me aware of the need for a text that offers good value by combining a broad, classic framework of management with a deeper treatment of contemporary topics.

This book is focused on the need of three groups of readers. First are students embarking on a course of business studies or management at university or college. They face the danger that other courses dealing with specific areas of management become isolated or disjointed. It is hoped that this book provides them with an integrating framework that places other studies within the context of management as a whole. Second are students of other subjects, perhaps engineering, IT or languages, who are taking one or two courses in management as subsidiary subjects. Even if they never choose to become managers themselves they will need to interact with those who do. It is hoped that this book will equip them with a vocabulary and understanding of management that will enable them to relate effectively with managers. The third group of readers are those already working in organizations who have started, or are thinking of starting, a managerial career. Perhaps they have been selected for a training course. This book is designed to provide them with an authoritative, high-quality text. This group also includes people who are about to embark on an advanced course such as an MBA after many years away from education. This book is designed to serve as precourse reading that gives them a head start.

The starting point for a book on fundamentals of management was obvious. It needs to define the essence of management and give some idea of the varieties of managers, their levels, the types of organisation in which they work and their psychological characteristics. In itself, the history of management is not too important. But a brief examination of it serves useful functions. It shows how social and economic thinking shape management ideas. It also gives an appreciation of trends that may shape future management practices. At a more banal level a brief survey of history provides a good opportunity to introduce key ideas such as "scientific management" and "contingency theory".

Students of management need to know the processes which managers use to transform resources into more valuable outputs. The large number of management processes can be bewildering. Consequently an organising framework is needed. Very early in my teaching I found that Fayol's framework (planning, organising, staffing etc.) is better than most. It is widely known, its acronym (POSDCRB) is easy to remember and, above all else, it is very, very widely used and understood by practising managers throughout the world. Sure, it is an old framework but that is no impediment to the inclusion of up-to-date topics. For example, strategy fits perfectly within Fayol's process of planning and it benefits from being placed in this context: it can be seen as an important part of a larger chain of activities that includes, say, organisational visions and MBO.

Most organisations have functions of some kind and it will be difficult for a manager to be effective without some knowledge of them. There are at least 12 functions. It is imposs-ible to describe all of them in a book of this kind. The best solution is to mention all functions, with emphasis on IT, and then devote substantive chapters to each of the "Big Four": marketing, operations, HRM and finance. The distinction between management pro-cesses and management functions is clearly understood by practising managers but it can cause confusion. Sometimes, for example, staffing is wrongly equated with HRM while budeting is wrongly equated with finance. In essence, *processes* are activities performed by almost all managers at an individual level. *Functions* are specialist activities performed by groups or organisations.

Management processes and functions are the bread-and-butter of what students new to management need to know. However, some filling is needed to provide depth and taste. Some topics such as ethics and critical evaluation are self-evidently important but it was dif-ficult to choose amongst the many other topics. Management careers was included at the request of students who said that, even at an early stage, it was helpful to know something about careers in order to guide their long-term thinking and choices. Practically all organ-isations are affected by commercial factors. Consequently a chapter was devoted to two commerical issues, e-commerce and globalisation, as a way of demonstrating the range and variety of concepts involved. Similarly, all organisations involve people. The range and variety of these issues are demonstrated by a chapter dealing with diversity and bullying.

The chapter on ethics is a distinctive feature of the book. Most other management texts include sections on ethics but they are usually dispersed among several chapters. Whilst this arrangement has the advantage of demonstrating that ethics apply to most areas of manage-ment, I always found this approach unsatisfactory. It makes it difficult for students to form an integrated and coherent view of the subject. A separate chapter, on the other hand, allows ethics to be viewed as a whole. Many texts also restrict themselves to describing organisational ethics and social responsibility. However, practising managers around the world have to deal with a wider range of ethical issues. I felt it was important to reflect their experience by including sections on ethics for individual managers and ethics for con-sumers and members of society.

The chapter on "Fads, Gurus, Cons and Science" is another distinctive feature and it was enjoyable to write! Unfortunately, there is a lot of bad management advice and research. Yet many texts ignore the problem. One of the prime responsibilities of educationalists is to develop critical and evaluative abilities. I hope that this chapter enables readers to recog-nise managment fads, evaluate management research and differentiate between good and bad advice.

An introductory text needs to do more than describe facts and outline theories. Readers often ask "what are the implications of theories and research for me?" Many chapters therefore include "toolkits" giving practical advice on how to apply at least some of the ideas in that chapter.

Ideally, I would have liked to include more guidance and information but it would make the book unwieldy and expensive. From the outset I was determined to produce a book that would be within the budget of as many people as possible. This has meant focusing tightly on the key aspects of management. Fortunately, extra material for students and tutors is available on the website associated with this book. I hope that readers find the book and website interesting and that they obtain a good understanding of the Fundamentals of Management.

Mike Smith
June 2006

Guided Tour

Learning Objectives

Each chapter opens with a set of learning objectives, summarising what students should learn from that chapter.

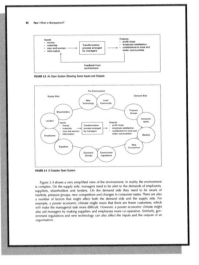

Figures and Tables

Each chapter provides a number of figures and tables to help students to visualise the various ideas, and to illustrate and summarise important concepts

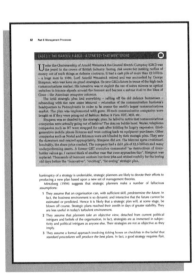

Cases

There are a number of cases featured in the text which help to place theories and concepts into a real life context.

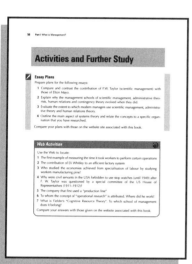

Essay Plans

These are designed to test students' understanding of the key concepts in each chapter by providing the framework for an essay.

Web Activities

These end-of-chapter activities promote increased understanding and further research.

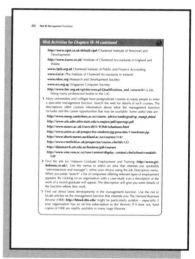

Experiential Activities

These exercises are designed for students to relate what they have learnt to their own experience and help concepts come alive.

Technology to enhance learning and teaching

*Visit **www.mcgraw-hill.co.uk/textbooks/mikesmith** today*

Online Learning Centre (OLC)

After completing each chapter, log onto the supporting Online Learning Centre website. Take advantage of the study tools offered to reinforce the material you have read in the text, and to develop your knowledge in a fun and effective way.

Resources for students include:

- *Essay outlines*
- *Study hints*
- *Material for chapter exercises*
- *Additional activities for further study*

Also available for lecturers:

- *PowerPoint presentations*
- *Suggested course structures*
- *Other course materials*

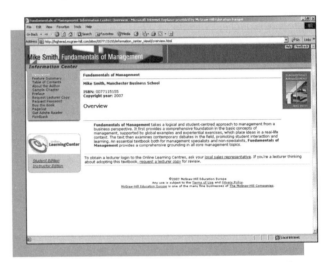

Details of this outline content are correct at the time of going to press and may be subject to change. Please refer to the website for up-to-date information.

Lecturers: Customise Content for your Courses using the McGraw-Hill Primis Content Centre

Now it's incredibly easy to create a flexible, customised solution for your course, using content from both US and European McGraw-Hill Education textbooks, content from our Professional list including Harvard Business Press titles, as well as a selection of over 9000 cases from Harvard, Insead and Darden. In addition, we can incorporate your own material and course notes.

For more information, please contact your local rep who will discuss the right delivery options for your custom publication – including printed readers, e-Books and CDROMs. To see what McGraw-Hill content you can choose from, visit *www.primisonline.com*.

Study Skills

Open University Press publishes guides to study, research and exam skills to help undergraduate and postgraduate students through their university studies.

Visit *www.openup.co.uk/ss* to see the full selection of study skills titles, and get a **£2 discount** by entering the promotional code **study** when buying online!

Computing Skills

If you'd like to brush up on your Computing skills, we have a range of titles covering MS Office applications such as Word, Excel, PowerPoint, Access and more.

Get a £2 discount off these titles by entering the promotional code **app** when ordering online at *www.mcgraw-hill-co.uk/app*

Acknowledgements

Author's Acknowledgements

Acknowledgements are due to John French at the Precinct Library, Faculty of Humanities, University of Manchester. Without his help I would not have been able to locate and check many of the cases, examples and references used in this book. I am also grateful to my son, John Mark, for his insightful help with many chapters, especially those dealing with IT. Finally, I would like to apologise to Bodycheck, Glossop, on whose treadmills and other equipment I vented my frustrations when the writing of this book became difficult.

Publisher's Acknowledgements

Our thanks go to the following reviewers for their comments at various stages in the text's development:

Mags McPhee – University of East Anglia
Annick Willem – University of Ghent
James Cunningham – National University of Ireland, Galway
Andy Sharp – Glasgow Caledonian University
Guy Brown – University of Northumbria
Jacqueline McLean – Manchester Metropolitan University
Stuart Challinor – University of Newcastle

Every effort has been made to trace and acknowledge ownership of copyright and to clear permision for material reproduced in this book. The publishers will be pleased to make suitable arrangements to clear permission with any copyright holders whom it has not been possible to contact.

PART I
What is Management?

Part Contents

Definition and Varieties of Management

❖ LEARNING OBJECTIVES

After studying this chapter you should have a general overview of management that combines both the common elements in management work and the differences in management work. In particular you should be able to:

1 **define*** the essential role of management and differentiate managers from operatives and specialists

2 **explain** the concepts of transformation, added value and organising people

3 **compare and contrast** different types of managers – especially:
- owner managers, entrepreneurs and intrapreneurs
- line, specialist and project managers
- junior managers, middle managers and senior managers
- general managers and specialist managers

4 **list:**
- 12 types of *commercial organisations* where managers work
- 4 types of *voluntary organisations* where managers work
- 3 types of *government organisations* where managers work

5 **define** culture, **explain** its importance to management and **list** the ways in which organisational cultures may differ

6 **identify** 3 general management skills and explain how their importance changes at different levels of management

7 **list** 3 characteristics of management work and 10 management roles

8 **list** the three competences sought most frequently by employers

9 **describe** the main psychological characteristics of typical managers

> 10 **compare** the approach and management style used several decades ago with the approach and management style used today
>
> * Notes on what is meant by terms such as define, describe, describe briefly, compare and contrast, list, analyse etc. are given on the website associated with this book

Managers play a very important role in our society but, unlike many other occupational groups, such as teachers, builders or doctors, managers do not form a single homogeneous group. They work in many different ways, at many different levels in many different types of organisation. One of the first tasks in studying management is to obtain an idea of both the common aspects of the managerial job and the very wide range of forms in which it exists. This chapter aims to achieve this goal by answering, in five sections, the question "What is Management? The five sections are:

Chapter contents

1.1 Definition of Management

The basic transformational role of management

Management has been defined in many ways. A simple definition is "the activity of using resources in an efficient and effective way so that the end product is worth more than the initial resources". This simple definition has the advantage that it focuses upon the crucial role of management to transform inputs into outputs of greater value. This is shown in Figure 1.1.

However, the simple definition has a drawback: it is too inclusive. According to this definition, a cow chewing the cud would be an excellent manager since it eats a cheap resource, i.e. grass, and converts it into a more valuable product, milk. The definition includes practically

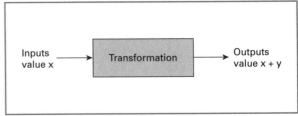

FIGURE 1.1 The Fundamental Transformation Process

every adult: a housewife cooking a meal, a vagrant collecting cigarette stubs, a student working in a library and an operative assembling chocolate boxes would qualify as a manager. A definition so wide is useless because it is synonymous with humankind and does not differentiate a subset of people who are clearly managers. To improve the definition it is necessary to specify the resources a manager uses. Classically (according to Karl Marx) there are three main resources (inputs):

- **capital**: the money to buy machines and raw materials
- **labour**: the people to work the machines
- **land**: where raw materials such as coal, iron ore and cotton can be extracted or farmed

Modern theory has refined Marx's list of resources. Today we tend to think of resources as the four "M's" of management:

- Markets
- Making goods and services
- Men & women
- Money

Even when the resources are specified, a definition of a manager as "someone who uses resources in an efficient and effective way so that the end product is worth more than the initial resources" is still inadequate. It still includes too many people. A person working alone assembling bundles of firewood or an academic reading a book in a library would still qualify as a manager. Many people identify the management of *other people* as the defining characteristic of management. Mary Parker Follett (1941) defined management as:

❛❛ Getting things done by other people. ❜❜

More recently Stewart (1967) described a manager as:

❛❛ Someone who get things done with the aid of other people. ❜❜

This emphasis on the management of other people provides a good way to differentiate between managers, operatives (workers who work directly upon raw materials or information or who directly provide personal services) and specialists (workers who use their skills and knowledge to enable other people to do things). Specialists such as neurologists or financial analysts may have equal or higher status and salaries than managers. However, they will not be managers until they are responsible for the work of other people such as a clinical team or a group of junior investment analysts.

The simple definition of a manager needs a final improvement. It needs to specify what is meant by "more value". Resources can be combined in ways that merely make the workers feel happy or they can be combined in ways that merely give managers pleasure. However, managers work within organisations and the phrase "more value" means "more value" in terms of the organisation's goals. When all these ideas are taken into account management can be defined as:

❛❛ the activity of getting other people to transform resources so that the results add value to the organisation in terms of reaching its organisational goals. ❜❜

CASE 1.1: SIMILARITIES BETWEEN DISSIMILAR MANAGERS

Arthur Darfor is an owner manager of an ostrich farm at Oudtshoorn in South Africa. He is responsible for the work of eight farm hands who need to be allocated work such as feeding or moving the birds to breeding paddocks. At times their work needs to be monitored closely to ensure that the correct temperatures and hygiene standards are maintained in the incubators. Since breeding is seasonal, Arthur needs to plan his flock carefully so that his farm is fully utilised throughout the year. He also needs to plan the supply of "lucerne", which is a key part of the birds' diet. Many of his decisions are routine, but the timing of sending the birds to market is a key judgement as the prices for both feathers and ostrich meat need to be predicted. The income produced must be budgeted carefully to ensure that cash is available to meet labour and other costs until another flock of birds is sent to market.

Karen Bede is the team leader of a group of six computer programmers working for a software company based in Berkshire, near Windsor Castle. Every week she allocates the parts of a larger program to each programmer and checks the code they produce. The work needs careful planning to ensure that the parts fit together and the costs stay within the budget agreed with the client. Karen often needs to juggle demands and prioritise tasks in order to meet deadlines. A considerable amount of her time is spent writing progress reports and attending meetings so that the middle managers in her organisation can integrate the work of several teams like hers.

Despite the fact that Arthur and Karen are working in very different environments (different countries, different industrial sectors and different technologies), the processes they use – planning, organising, staffing, deciding, budgeting – are very similar. The only major difference is that Karen spends time reporting and communicating to others. In both cases, these managers are using other people to transform resources so that the end product has greater value than their inputs.

Indices of managerial effectiveness and types of transitions

This definition has the advantage that it is linked to some standard indices of managerial effectiveness. In the commercial world organisational goals are usually framed in monetary terms. The effectiveness of managers is often gauged by the percentage return on capital. For example, a manager who uses £1 million of resources to produce a product worth £1.2 million will, other things being equal, be a better manager than one who uses £1 million to produce a product worth £1.1 million. Similarly, a managing director who takes over a company that is valued at £50 million and turns it into a company worth £55 million after one year is, other things being equal, a better managing director than one who takes over the same company and destroys value so that it is worth only £45 million one year later.

In many situations financial indices are too crude. They need to be supplemented by other information. For example, the number of people managed is an important consideration. The value added per employee is another common index of a manager's efficiency (see p. 191). For example, a manager who employs five people to convert £1 million of resources to products worth £1.2 million is probably doing a better job than a manager who employs 20 people to convert £1 million of resources to products worth £1.2 million – even though they add the same value (£200 000). Each person employed by the first manager is adding £40 000 value per year while each person employed by the second manager is adding only £5000 – probably not enough to cover their wages and other costs. Unless the second manager is able to obtain a subsidy from government or other parts of the organisation, their unit will not be viable and the 20 jobs will eventually disappear – with enormous consequences for the 20 employees and their families.

These examples have been drawn from the commercial world because they are clear. However, similar indices can be used in other types of organisation. The main difference is that value will be expressed in non-monetary units. For example, in the university sector a unit of performance will be FTE (full-time equivalent) per member of staff, in the theatre the unit of performance may be the number in the audience per performance, while in the health sector a hospital manager may be judged on the number of operations per surgeon per year. Table 1.1 lists some of the transformations where managers can add value to resources they consume.

Industry	Transformation	Means of Transformation
Education	Makes students more valuable by adding to their knowledge, intellectual ability and, perhaps, skills	Lectures, tutorials, practicals, books, etc.
Transport and Communication	Alters the position of physical things to a location where they are more valuable	Air-flights, lorry journeys, courier services, postal system
Media	Transmits information from mind of originator to mind of someone who finds it valuable	Newspapers, radio, TV, computer databases
Manufacturing	Changes the physical form of objects or chemicals into a more valued shape	Bending, cutting, joining, heating, assembling, etc.
Storage and Warehousing	Holds things until a time when they are more valuable	Warehouses, depots
Exchange	Transfers the ownership of an object or commodity to someone who places a higher value upon it	Wholesale organisations, retail organisations, merchanting organisations, exchanges such as the Stock Exchange
Health care	Removing or ameliorating illnesses	Hospitals, clinics
Government	Improving security and infrastructure for the population	Parliaments, councils, armed forces, police services

TABLE 1.1 Examples of Various Management Transformations

Management processes, management functions and other perspectives of management

Management is a very complex activity that can be viewed from several perspectives. The two most common viewpoints are *management processes* and *management functions*:

1 **Management processes** are the *activities* performed by the majority of individual managers in order to transform resources. For example, almost all managers make plans and supervise their staff. The main management processes are planning, organising, staffing and making decisions. Often management processes can be performed adequately without very high, detailed levels of specialist knowledge. For example, a manager may be able to motivate staff without having studied psychology to degree level.

2 **Management functions** are reasonably distinct *areas of management practice* that involve only a fraction of all managers. For example, in most large organisations less than 10 per cent of managers are directly involved in marketing or looking after the organisation's money. The main management functions are marketing, operations, human resources (HR) and finance – although the IT function is increasingly important. People working within a management function will usually need specialised training or experience in order to perform the intricate, high-level tasks within their function. For example, a manager in the HR function will need specialised training in order to devise an appraisal system that will be applied to the whole organisation. Managers working within a function often belong to relevant professional organisations. For example, a manager working within the HR function is likely to belong to an institute of personnel and will have studied for its qualifications. Similarly a manager working within the finance function is likely a member of an Institute of Accountancy.

In principle, management processes and management functions are independent but in practice they are often related. For example, a manager working within the HR function is likely to spend a large proportion of his or her time on staffing processes, while a manager working within the finance function will spend a large part of his or her time dealing with budgeting processes.

Even two, fairly distinct viewpoints do not cope adequately with complex special topics where the interplay of different influences is subtle. For example, bullying at work is a topic of contemporary interest. To some extent it lies within the management process of staffing. However, an organisation's HR function is likely to take the lead in forming and implementing policies to reduce the level of bullying at work. Furthermore, the policies and their implementation are likely to draw heavily on the academic discipline of psychology. The inter-relationships between management processes, management functions and special topics are shown in Figure 1.2, which also serves to show the structure of this book.

Even the complicated structure shown in Figure 1.2 is a simplification. A further perspective is needed – the viewpoint of academic disciplines that underlie many management processes, functions and topics. The main management disciplines are sociology, psychology, economics and quantitative methods. Marketing, for example draws on each discipline. A manager in the marketing function may use economics and sociology to identify unexploited markets. He or she may use psychology to ensure that advertisements have the maximum impact in the minds of customers. He or she may also use quantitative

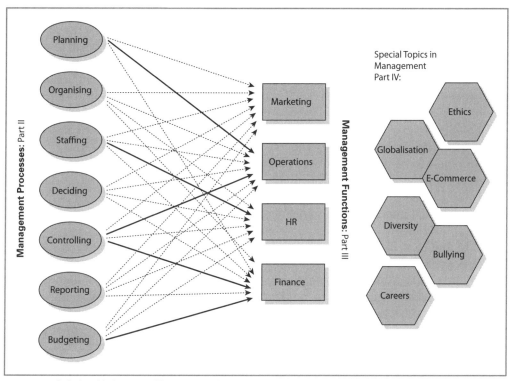

FIGURE 1.2 Relationship between Management Processes, Functions and Topics

methods to predict the number of future sales. Unfortunately, even a superficial treatment of academic functions is impossible in a book of this size. However, textbooks covering academic disciplines are readily available elsewhere.

1.2 Varieties of Manager

Many schools of management tend to assume that all managers are the same. Even contingency theory (see Chapter 2, section 6) tends to imply that all managers in the same kind of organisation will be similar. In fact there are many different kinds of manager. The main types of managers are:

1 Owner managers, entrepreneurs and intrapreneurs
2 Line, specialist and project managers
3 Levels of manager (junior, middle, senior)
4 Functional and general managers

Owner Managers, Entrepreneurs and Intrapreneurs

The concept of an "**owner manager**" is self-explanatory. It is, perhaps, the archetypal form of manager where the management and the ownership of the organisation is the same person or people. The combination of ownership and management was probably the dominant form of management before the Industrial Revolution. However, with the rise of limited companies and government organisations, a specialist cadre of people emerged to manage organisations on behalf of other people. People can own an organisation even when they are patently unsuitable to manage it. Perhaps these people have inherited an organisation from previous generations. Perhaps such people have saved money all their lives and have used their savings to purchase an organisation, or shares in an organisation, in order to provide an income in their retirement. Professional managers, on the other hand, can be selected and trained specifically for the job.

Today most owner managers exist in small firms and will be involved in most, if not all, activities. They can keep their finger on the pulse by walking round the firm and directly observing the state of affairs. As an organisation grows beyond, say, 50 employees the demands and the complexity of communication are too much for one person to control directly and the organisation will tend to hire professional managers.

Many, but not all, owner managers started as **entrepreneurs**. An entrepreneur is someone who identifies a business opportunity. The opportunity may arise from a gap in the market, a technological development or a commercial change. Once the opportunity is identified an entrepreneur will take a moderate risk to initiate a business venture to exploit it, which will involve assembling money, materials and men and women to meet a market need. A classic example of an entrepreneur would be Dyson. He noted that current vacuum cleaners became less efficient as the dust bag filled. He developed a new type of vacuum cleaner that did not need a dust bag. Dyson took a calculated risk and used his own money to fund the early developmental stages. Then he spent considerable time and effort convincing bankers who specialise in funding new developments (venture capitalists) to provide further funds that would pay for later development and the set-up costs for a factory. Other examples of entrepreneurial successes are Amazon book distribution, Last Minute travel and hotel reservations, and Anita Roddick's Body Shop. Perhaps the most successful entrepreneur of all time has been Bill Gates, who founded the software colossus Microsoft. New and small firms (with under 500 employees) account for a disproportionate number of innovations. One survey suggests that small firms are responsible for 55 per cent of all innovations and 95 per cent of radical innovations. Fast-growing businesses, sometimes nicknamed "gazelles", produce twice as many product innovations per employee as larger firms (Birch, 2000). Unfortunately, entrepreneurs do not have a guarantee of success. Small entrepreneurial organisations have a high failure rate. Perhaps 60–80 per cent of small businesses fail within five years.

In recent years the importance of entrepreneurs to the economic well-being of a country has been appreciated. Many large employers have been investing in machinery or moving their factories to countries where labour costs are low. Consequently, many large employers have been shedding (outplacing) workers. Governments have been looking to entrepreneurs to start up new businesses which will replace the jobs being lost from large organisations. Entrepreneurs frequently set up businesses in two sectors: business services and restaurants – presumably because the "entry costs" are low in these sectors. Many entrepreneurs are corporate refugees. They have either been the victims when a large organisation has downsized or they are people who feel uncomfortable with the restrictions imposed by corporate life. Entrepreneurs follow one of five main tactics:

- **Start a new business**: this means the entrepreneur is in total control and can form the business in any way he or she prefers. Starting a new business can take a long time to produce a profit.

- **Buy an existing business**: an existing business can be obtained fairly cheaply if the former owner wishes to retire or sell businesses for other personal reasons. Existing businesses carry much less risk. However, it will be more difficult for the entrepreneur to mould these to their own preferences.

- **Buy a franchise**: in a franchise an entrepreneur buys the right to produce or distribute a product or service which has already been developed. Franchises carry much less risk than marketing a totally new product. However, the person taking on the franchise will have much less freedom because he or she will need to operate procedures determined by the owners of the product. Perhaps the most famous franchises are McDonald's, and some hotel chains such as Holiday Inns.

- **Be incubated**: some venture capitalists, government organisations and universities have incubator units where a number of entrepreneurs are gathered in close proximity, probably in a "science park". The parent organisation provides facilities such as premises and secretarial support in return for a share in the equity. The proximity of other entrepreneurs means that they can share information and business leads.

- **Be spun off**: sometimes good ideas emerge within organisations. However, it may not be appropriate for the large organisation to exploit the idea. The large organisation may therefore produce a spin-off company which is staffed by its former employees. They usually buy their materials and, perhaps, patents from the parent organisation. The parent organisation may provide support such as guaranteed sales for the entrepreneur's output. A typical spin-off situation would be where an employee of a large glass producer develops a new type of double glazing. A doubl-glazing unit or division would provide the glass producer with a distraction that could mean a loss of focus from its core activity. The double-glazing company could, however, be spun off. The new company might use the parent as a source from which to buy raw materials and, maybe, to identify contacts as potential customers.

Obtaining sufficient finance is a significant problem for most entrepreneurs. In essence there are two sources of finance: debt financing and equity financing. In **debt financing** an entrepreneur will approach a bank, other institutions or wealthy individuals and obtain the required capital at a rate of interest. Sometimes the money is borrowed from family and friends. If the money is borrowed from commercial sources, the rate of interest may be high because the risk of failure may also be high. Commercial sources of finance are likely to demand extra surety such as a claim on the entrepreneur's house. In **equity financing** money is obtained in exchange for a share in the ownership of the new organisation. Often the funds are provided by venture capital firms such as 3i. If the firm fails the venture capitalists lose money, but if it succeeds they make big profits. Usually a venture capital company will only provide money if it has reasonable expectations of a high rate of return. This is because the return from successful companies must outweigh the losses they might make from unsuccessful ones. However, using a venture capital company brings the additional advantages of advice, information and other support. (See also Chapter 14, p. 290 onwards.)

It would be wrong to think that all entrepreneurs work in small companies. Some large organisations realise that it is often necessary to act like a small firm. They value the entrepreneurial spirit and give entrepreneurs scope to work (Drucker, 1985). Entrepreneurs who work within a large company are called **intrapreneurs**. Some large organisations take proactive steps to encourage intrapreneurs. They set up small units where groups of people are able to work on new ideas creatively and without formality. Sometimes, these units are called "skunk works". Perhaps the best-known skunk work was a fiercely independent and sometimes anarchic unit set up by Apple Computers that developed the famous Macintosh computer which was state-of-the-art and user-friendly.

Line, specialist and project managers

Line managers are directly responsible for producing goods or services to customers. Sometimes, line managers are called "production managers" or "operations managers" but this title should not be interpreted narrowly since most line managers these days produce services rather than material goods. In a factory, the line manager will be the supervisor, the head of the production department or the head of the manufacturing unit. In a call centre, line managers will be the section supervisor, the floor manager and the call centre manager. The line managers' actions play a clear and identifiable part in the performance of the organisation. Line managers will be responsible, perhaps at second or third hand, for the people who have direct contact with customers. Often line managers have large spans of control. Many line managers regard themselves has being at the "sharp", "front-end" of the management spectrum.

Specialist managers are sometimes called staff managers or enabling managers. Typically they are found in finance, human resources, purchasing or technical service functions. Usually these specialist managers are involved only at the request of the line managers and, in some senses, they have the line managers as their "internal clients". If the line manager believes that a specialist manager is not adding value to the production process, in theory, the line manager does not need to request or follow these specialists' advice. Indeed, in theory, a line manager can often source the required advice from similar specialists outside the organisation.

However, some specialist managers have much more formal authority than the previous paragraph suggests. These are specialist managers in a control function that is designed to prevent errors and wrongdoing. The archetypal specialists who exercise very powerful control functions are managers concerned with environmental health and safety. These specialist managers generally act as a friendly source of advice and guidance to line managers. Nevertheless, they usually have the power to overrule line managers and, if necessary, shut down production if they feel that the line manager is likely to breach legal requirements. Similarly, quality-control managers will generally offer diplomatic advice to line managers in order to ensure high-quality products and services. Nonetheless, when the chips are down they will have a right to overrule line managers if they feel that the output is below the standard that is demanded by customers or regulatory authorities. Human resource managers generally offer advice and guidance which may, or may not, be accepted by line managers. However, if they feel that a line manager is in danger of acting against legislation (such as equal opportunities law) they have a right and obligation to intervene.

New initiatives and major changes are usually developed and brought to fruition by a special project team. For example, a financial services organisation that decides to offer a new tele-banking service would probably set up a team consisting of a line manager from its existing services, an HR specialist, a legal specialist and an IT specialist. This team would meet on a very regular basis to produce plans, organisational structures, procedures and training systems until the new service is up and running. It would then disband. When the organisation undertakes another project or major change a fresh team of different members would be constituted. The person in charge of such a team is usually called a "**Project Manager**". Project managers are usually, but not always, line managers who retain some responsibility for their production line while they are also managing the team which develops the new initiative.

Sometimes organisations hire special managers who are employed by the organisation only for the time (the interim) it takes to finish a project. This usually occurs when the project requires specialist expertise which is not provided by anyone in the organisation. **Interim managers** are also used if there is expertise within the organisation but the person or people concerned cannot be spared from their other duties. They may also be used to substitute for existing managers if they suddenly become unavailable due to ill health or other causes. Interim managers usually have a considerable track record in management which has equipped them with a wide range of experience that they can deploy rapidly and effectively. When they are called into a company interim managers need to "hit the ground running".

Levels of management

Managers may be classified according to their level in the organisation. Typically, managers are divided into first-line managers, middle managers and senior managers.

First-line managers are also called junior managers, supervisors, overlookers, team leaders or foremen. First-line managers are primarily responsible for directing the day-to-day activities of operatives. Usually they have substantial spans of control but their range of responsibility is usually quite narrow. Their responsibility is usually restricted to ensuring that their team of operatives is achieving performance targets. Often first-line managers will be directly responsible for machinery and materials. The objectives of first-line managers are usually clear. Their success in achieving their objectives is clear-cut and apparent within a short period of time (i.e. their time span of discretion is low). First-line managers frequently work at a frenetic pace, often needing to attend to a new issue every one or two minutes. An important part of the role of a first-line manager is to listen to the concerns of the people they manage (their direct reports) and relay these concerns to more senior managers. Similarly, they need to be aware of the wider organisational objectives and translate these into terms that are relevant and understandable by their direct reports. First-level managers are usually recruited from the ranks of operatives. They would be expected to be able to perform the job they supervise as well as managing it.

First-line managers are the most junior level of management. Their contribution is often taken for granted or ignored – especially by Business Schools and theorists who deal with senior managers. However, the contribution that first-line managers make to an organisation cannot be overstated. Recently, the role of first-line managers has expanded. They are now expected to perform many of the activities previously required of middle managers. The main reasons for this change are a tendency to flatten organisational structures, a greater use of computer information systems and a marked trend to better training and recruitment of first-line managers.

Middle managers manage first-line managers. They will have titles such as Head of Department or Head of Human Resources denoting responsibility for a function. One of the major trends in management during recent years has been reduction in the number of middle-management posts. Their number has often been reduced by as much as 30 per cent in many organisations. This has been achieved by using computers to accomplish many middle-management tasks and by training first-line managers to do some (hitherto) middle-management tasks.

The key activities of middle managers are co-ordination and liaison. Middle managers transmit information up and down the hierarchy and across the various functions in the organisation. They convert the strategies and objectives set by senior managers into specific actions and plans which must be implemented by first-line managers. Often they are required to find creative ways to achieve objectives. They will have a fairly wide remit and will spend most of their time on managerial activities rather than operations. Middle managers will spend a great deal of their time in meetings with other middle managers. The pace of middle management work is less frenetic than the work of first-line managers. Typically they will have about nine minutes to concentrate on a problem before they need to attend to another matter. In some large organisations there may be several layers of middle managers.

Senior managers are sometimes called "top managers". They are responsible for making strategic decisions about the direction of the organisation. Senior managers are often called directors, president, chief officer or controller. Generally they will report to the most senior person in the organisation such as the Chairman or the President or the Principal. However, in some very large organisations senior managers may be rather more distant from the peak of organisational power. Senior managers are responsible for the performance of the organisation as a whole. They need to be particularly sensitive to trends and developments in the outside environment. Senior managers are primarily concerned with future strategy and developing a "vision" for the organisation. They then need to communicate their vision effectively so that other people within the organisation are motivated towards its achievement.

Much of the time senior managers are in meetings with other senior managers, middle managers and with important people from the external environment, as well as acting as the figureheads for the organisation.

Functional and General managers

Functional managers are responsible for units or departments that achieve a single functional objective. Their staff will have similar abilities and training. The major functions are usually production, sales, finance and human resources – the four Ms of management: markets, making, men and women and money. However, other functions such as research and development and IT will also be crucial to the functioning of many organisations.

General managers are responsible for units that include many functional areas. For example, the general manager of a manufacturing plant will have some responsibility for the other functions listed in the previous paragraph. Often their title includes the words "General Manager". The term general management is only loosely linked to a person's position in the organisational hierarchy. The manager of a small department store will be a general manager but the person who is in charge of a whole chain of department stores will also be a general manager. Project managers at all levels usually have general management responsibilities. General managers are responsible for establishing the work environment within which other managers operate. They are also concerned with allocating resources and building the unit for which they are responsible into an effective "whole".

1.3 Organisations in which Managers Work

Managers work in many different kinds of organisation. In broad terms these organisations can be grouped into three types: commercial, voluntary and governmental. Below is a list of the main organisations in each group. Many of the types are well known or self-explanatory. Readers familiar with this subject can merely scan the list and perhaps read some of the more unusual entries such as limited partnerships, conglomerates and virtual organisations.

Commercial organisations

- **Sole traders** (often in a shed) are people who run a one-man or a one-woman band. They handle all aspects of the organisation and are responsible to and for only themselves. Often, sole traders work from home. Sole traders are personally responsible for the debts they incur. This type of organisation has expanded rapidly in the last decade. Technically, sole traders are not managers: they are not usually responsible for the work of others – unless of course their trade is organising events and other people.

- A **franchise** is an arrangement between the owner of a product or service and a franchisee who owns the limited rights to make or sell the product or service. The product is usually unique or has a very strong brand image. The franchisee is relieved of much of the risk of developing and marketing the product and often benefits from the advice and supervision given by franchiser. However, the franchisee usually has to pay a substantial purchase price and a continuing proportion of the profits. Perhaps the best-known franchise in the world is the McDonald fast-food chain.

- **Owner managers** were discussed earlier. The main difference between owner managers and sole traders is that the former will employ other people. There are a large number of owner-manager organisations, especially in retailing. Most owner managers employ up to 50 people. Above this limit it becomes increasingly difficult for one person to control all aspects of an organisation. Consequently, when organisations employ more than 50 people, it is likely that professional managers will be employed.

- **Partnerships** involve two or more people who jointly act as owner managers. The key aspect of a partnership is the personal and unrestricted liability of each partner for the debts and obligations of the firm – whether or not he or she specifically agreed to them. One partner can be made personally liable for the business debts incurred by another partner. Partnerships are particularly common in organisations providing professional services in architecture, accountancy and law. Many management consultancies are partnerships and there may be dozens or even hundreds of international partners. Generally, however, the number of partners is fewer than six. The most well-known partnership, the John Lewis Partnership, is quite unusual since all employees who have a substantial length of service are partners.

■ **Limited partnerships** have existed in continental European countries and the USA for some time. They now exist in the UK. In limited partnerships each partner is only liable for the organisations debts to the extent of the capital they may contribute or agree to contribute.

■ **Private companies** are owned by a small number of shareholders and the shares are not traded to the public. Private companies have the advantage that they are not required to make stringent disclosures of financial information. This involves less cost and it gives greater confidentiality of commercial information. Many private companies start as owner-manager organisations that have grown substantially. The original owner manager may have passed some ownership to friends, family and business acquaintances. One of the most famous private companies is the BMW organisation.

■ **Public Limited Companies (PLC)** are usually owned by thousands of shareholders and the shares are traded to the public. In order to protect the public these organisations are required to submit detailed, stringent accounts. Public companies are often traded on national stock exchanges such as LSE (London) and NYSE (New York). Sometimes the stock exchanges specialise in various sectors of the economy such as technology (NASDAQ). Some public companies are set up merely to trade in the shares of other companies. These are usually called Investment Trusts. Large public companies that are usually in the top 100 companies are often referred to as "blue-chip" companies. Obtaining a quotation is a long, costly and protracted procedure that involves establishing a track record and producing Articles of Association that regulate the way a company is governed. This elaborate process inhibits small or medium-sized organisations from obtaining a quotation. Consequently, small and medium companies are often listed on the "Alternative Market". Belonging to the Alternative Market is less onerous and acts as a halfway house to a full listing.

■ **Holding companies** are organisations that own a number of other companies. Often they have assets of many billions of pounds or dollars but they employ only a small number of people since most of the work is performed by the employees of subsidiary organisations. Most holding companies own subsidiaries that are related in some way. Sometimes there is a vertical structure whereby, for example, one subsidiary mines the raw materials, another subsidiary processes the raw material and a third subsidiary retails the product to the public. Sometimes there is a horizontal structure whereby, for example, one subsidiary manufactures a product in the southern region, another manufactures it in the northern region and a further subsidiary manufactures a product in the eastern region.

■ **Conglomerates** are usually large organisations and are often called "corporations" or "groups". They are usually a type of holding company where the subsidiaries are involved in different industrial sectors. Conglomerates are usually formed when one company takes over several other companies in order to diversify risk, improve its marketing position or make additional use of existing plant and machinery. The formation of conglomerates was particularly frequent between 1960 and 1980. Well-known conglomerates include AEG-AG, Agfa-Gevaert Group, Alcan, Lever Brothers and Broken Hill Proprietary Company.

■ **Multinational corporations** are organisations that maintain significant, simultaneous, operations in several countries but are based in one home company. Well-known examples of multinational companies include the Kerry Group (Ireland), Shell Oil (Britain and Netherlands) and Nestlé (Switzerland).

■ **Virtual companies** are a relatively new kind of organisation. They occur when the various departments or components of an organisation are physically divided and separated by distances of several miles. Often the component units may be separately owned. The separate components are linked together by computers and IT connections. These links mean that the separate components can work together as if they were one organisation. For example, a bookseller could set up a central computer that receives Internet orders. The computer could then search the inventories of several book wholesalers to locate a copy of the relevant book. It could then initiate the wholesaler's dispatch of the book to the customer. Finally, the computer could arrange to debit the customer's bank account. As far as the customers are concerned, they would be dealing with a large bookseller holding a huge inventory of books. In fact, they are dealing with a sophisticated computer system that links various components of the process of retailing books. Virtual companies have tended to arise in publishing and other industries where information is the key product.

■ **Mutual organisations and co-operatives** are types of business association which are created for the mutual benefit of members. Often these are trading associations or financial institutions. In the UK they are sometimes called Building Societies or Unit Trusts. In the USA they are often called Mutual Funds. A co-operative is a legal entity that is owned and controlled by those who work for it or use it. There is usually some form of profit-sharing and the directors and managers are accountable to the members rather than the owners of capital.

Voluntary organisations

■ **Charities** are institutions or organisations set up to provide help, money and support to people and things in need. Many charities are small and are staffed by volunteers. However, some charities have huge turnovers equalling those of substantial commercial organisations. Examples of large charities are the National Trust, Oxfam and Médecins sans Frontières.

■ **Clubs and Associations** exist to increase the enjoyment of members who have similar interests. Some are managed by volunteers and are quite small. However, some clubs are large and employ professional managers. Some famous clubs are the MCC, the Garrick, the Liverpool Athenaeum and the Royal Channel Islands Yacht Club. Some clubs become huge commercial successes and convert into commercial organisations. Typical examples include Manchester United Football Club and the Automobile Association.

■ **Trade Associations** and **Professional Bodies** are organisations which seek to protect and foster the interests of certain occupational groups and companies. To some extent they are very similar to political pressure groups since their aim is to increase the power of their members. These organisations can be quite substantial and wield considerable influence. They may also employ numerous managers. Associations fostering the interests of trades are usually called "unions". Typical examples include the Communication Workers Union, the Amalgamated Engineering and Electrical Union and UNISON. Professional bodies tend to be called associations or societies. Typical examples include the Law Society, the British Psychological Society and The British Medical Association. Companies which share similar interests usually form a trade association to protect and foster their interests. Frequently they are called associations, federations or chambers. Typical examples include the Knitting Industries Federation, the Building Material Producers National Council and the Newspaper Publishers' Association. Usually trade associations and professional bodies start off as voluntary organisations but as their reputation and power increase it becomes virtually compulsory for members of the trade to enrol. For example, it is virtually impossible for a doctor or lawyer to practise unless they are a member of their professional body.

- **Political parties and pressure groups** aim to obtain sufficient power to change society. They aim to persuade other people to adopt and support their views so that they are then able to control resources they do not actually own. Senior managers in these organisations usually need a high level of charisma.

Government organisations

- **Government departments** employ many managers. Usually these managers are responsible to representatives who are directly elected by the adult population of a country. The range of government departments is enormous. They include the diplomatic service, the armed forces, revenue collection and the provision of services such as education and health. Usually government organisations are divided into two groups: central government and local government.

- **Public Enterprises** are created by statute to govern nationalised businesses. Perhaps the most famous public enterprise is the Bank of England. Other public enterprises include the German Federal Railway and the Tennessee Valley Authority. These organisations do not have share capital and are owned by the government.

- A **Quango** is a quasi-autonomous-nongovernmental organisation. They are semi-public administrative bodies which are set up by a government to achieve a "public good". Some are financed directly by a government and others are financed by a levy, which is often compulsory. A key feature of quangos is that the members are appointed, directly or indirectly, by the government and thus provide the government with huge powers of patronage. Quangos are often called agencies, commissions or councils. Typical examples of quangos are Health Service Trusts, the Health and Safety Executive, the Arts Council of England, the Boundary Commission, the Commission for Racial Equality and the Equal Opportunities Commission. Some lesser-known and esoteric quangos include the Crofters Commission, the Home Grown Cereals Authority and the Unrelated Live Transplant Regulatory Authority.

1.4 The Cultural Dimensions of Management

The variety of management work is increased by the fact that organisations have different cultures. For example, a manager of a provincial newspaper will have quite a different work environment from that of a manager of a national newspaper based in London – even though they work in the same industry, produce a similar product and use similar technology. A great deal of the difference can be explained by the culture of the two organisations. One of the best-known definitions is given by Schein (1985):

> 66 the pattern of basic assumptions that a given group has invented, discovered or developed and therefore taught to new members as the correct way to perceive, think and feel in relation to problems. 99

In other words, culture is "the way we do things round here". Schein's definition focuses upon the intangible aspects of culture. However, as Figure 1.3 shows, it has both tangible and intangible components.

Tangible aspects of culture include the physical layout of the organisation. For example, an organisation with a culture that emphasises status might have separate canteens for managers and workers. The intangible aspects of culture are usually more important and more numerous. They include shared values, shared knowledge and a fund of shared stories of past events and heroes.

Organisational cultures perform very **useful functions**. They help integrate the organisation and make sure that all members are "on the same wavelength". They help communication and give a sense of purpose. It has been claimed that a strong corporate culture helps to increase performance efficiency. However, research by Kotter and Heskett (1992) suggests that the relationship between corporate culture and performance is weaker than earlier claims suggest.

Corporate cultures do not happen at random and the **main causes** have been identified. Schneider (1987) believes that the main cause of a culture is the personality and style of the person who sets up the organisation. If the founder has a fluid, ethical style with an interest in basics (e.g. Anita Roddick, founder of Bodyshop) the organisation will be imbued with a fluid, ethical culture that emphasises products. This initial culture is then transmitted to future generations by the ASA process. First, the organisation **a**ttracts applications from people who hold similar values. It then **s**elects those who adhere most closely to the cultural norms. Finally, there is a process of **a**ttrition whereby employees who do not feed into the culture are encouraged to leave the organisation. Schneider's ASA theory does not fully explain the transmission of organisational culture. There is a socialisation

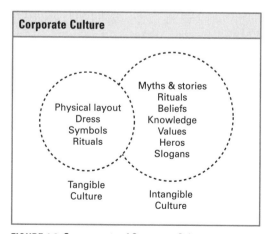

FIGURE 1.3 Components of Corporate Culture

process by which newcomers are taught the appropriate way of doing things and receive rewards, such as promotion, when they perform according to the organisation's culture.

There are many different **types of organisational culture** and most consultants and researchers have their own list. Organisational cultures may differ in the way they deal with *conflict and harmony*. Some organisations, especially those based in Australia and the UK, regard disagreement as a healthy sign. Employees are encouraged to discuss openly their reservations and conflicting views. There is a cultural belief that suppressing disagreements leads to longer-term problems and prevents good ideas from being adopted. Some organisations based in Asian countries have cultures that emphasise harmony. There is a cultural belief in preserving present methods and fostering traditional social relationships. Organisational cultures may also differ in a way that they deal with

- risk-taking
- teamwork
- attention to detail
- people and their needs
- time as a scarce commodity
- a proactive approach to change

Contrasts in organisational cultures may be particularly stark when they come from different countries. Early work by Hall (1976) divided cultures into low-context and high-context cultures. *Low-context cultures* are typified by the UK, Canada, Germany and the USA. Important communication uses verbal media of the written and spoken word. A message will be encoded very precisely in words. To decode the message the recipient needs to listen and read very carefully. *High-content cultures* include Japan and many Mediterranean countries. Only a part of the message is communicated in words. The rest must be inferred from contextual cues such as physical setting, the body language and even previous history. High-context communication takes considerable time. People from low-context cultures may not understand this and they may be perceived as pushy, hurried and even rude.

The best-known investigations of cultural differences were conducted by Hofstede (1984) and Trompenaars (1993). Trompenaars' research was more systematic and involved 15 000 people from 47 countries. He came to the view that cultures differed in three main ways: relationships between people, attitudes towards time and attitudes towards the environment.

Relationships between people was the most complex way in which cultures differed. Trompenaars differentiated five sub-dimensions:

- **Universalism vs. particularism** reflects a culture's emphasis on rules and their consistent application (universalism) or its emphasis on flexibility and bending the rules depending upon the person and his or her circumstances (particularism).
- **Individualism vs. collectivism** concerns the emphasis a culture places upon the individual and his or her rights and responsibilities (individualism) or the interests of the group and achieving a consensus of opinion (collectivism).
- **Unemotional vs. emotional** is the degree to which a culture stresses detachment and objectivity in decision making (unemotional) or whether subjective feelings are a part

of decisions (emotional). This dimension may be related to universalism vs. particularism.

- **Specific vs. diffuse** is the extent to which a culture stresses in-depth, intense relationships (specific) or a wider range of superficial relationships (diffuse). Again this may be an aspect of universalism vs. particularism; universalism is more likely when there are diffuse relationships.

- **Achievement vs. prescription** reflects the extent to which a culture rewards people on the basis of their achievement or their social standing, celebrity and connections.

Trompenaars' second major dimension of cultural differences was the *way that time was viewed* – particularly the way that the present is viewed in relation to the past. Western cultures tend to see time as a linear **synchronic** dimension. There is a clear past, present and future. Present time is precious and must not be wasted. Decisions need to be taken quickly without losing time. In **sequential** cultures, time is a passing series of recurring events where opportunities will recur. Consequently there is a relaxed attitude to time and appointments – a philosophy of "manyana".

Trompenaars' third dimension of cultural differences focuses on the *relationship with the environment*. In **inner-directed** cultures people see themselves as separate from the environment and attempt to control it for their personal benefit. On the other hand, in **outer-directed** cultures people see themselves as a part of nature. They try to live in harmony with nature and are more likely to "go with the flow".

Organisational culture is so pervasive that it affects most aspect of management and it is relevant to many later chapters in this book. For example, an organisation's plans will be influenced by its cultural attitudes towards risk and teamwork. Similarly the appropriate leadership style will be influenced by an organisation's cultural attitude towards conflict and power-distance. In particular, organisational culture has a very important influence on communications within an organisation (see Chapter 8) and its impact is a very clear when dealing with global organisations (see Chapter 16, p. 344).

1.5 Management skills

The skills needed by managers have been studied by a large number of researchers. Probably the most influential studies have been carried out by Katz, Mintzberg and McClelland. Other important studies have centred upon management competencies and the psychometric qualities of managers.

Katz's three broad skills and management level

Katz (1974) was one of the earliest commentators on management skills. He divided management skills into three broad groups:

- **Conceptual skills**: the ability to view situations broadly, think analytically and to solve problems. Often conceptual skills involve breaking problems into smaller parts and understanding the relationships between these parts.

- **Interpersonal skills** involve the ability to work effectively with other people and teams within the organisation. They involve listening carefully to the views of other people and tolerating differing perspectives. Communication is a very important interpersonal skill but others include the ability to motivate people and generate the appropriate psychological atmosphere. Interpersonal skills also embrace political acumen – which is needed to be able to build a power base, establish the right connections and the ability to enhance one's own position.

■ **Technical skills** consist of specialised knowledge of an industry or a process. Technical skills can involve engineering, scientific, financial or legal knowledge. Knowledge of IT systems, markets and commercial procedures are also kinds of technical skill. Often technical skills are obtained initially through formal education and are then developed by formal training.

Figure 1.4 shows the mix of these three skills changes according to a manager's position in the hierarchy.

First-line managers typically require high technical skills. Operatives and their supervisors must have detailed technical knowledge in order to transform resources into more valuable products. The possession of good technical skills is often the basis for a higher career in management. However, as a manager rises in the hierarchy, detailed technical skills become less important. A computer programmer, for example must know the ins and outs of the computer language that is used. However, a chief executive needs a less detailed understanding but he or she must understand the contribution which IT can make to the organisation.

The most important skills for middle managers are the interpersonal ones. Many technically competent people who are promoted into middle management fail because their interpersonal skills are insufficient to harness the capabilities of other people. Sometimes

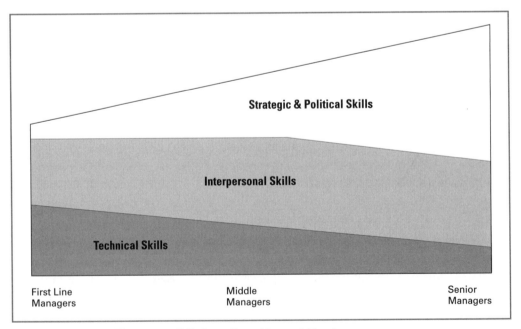

FIGURE 1.4 Changes in Management Skills According to Managerial Level

people with brilliant financial skills rise to high positions within organisation only to then fail because they antagonise so many people that their position becomes untenable. While interpersonal skills assume their maximum importance at middle management level they are still very important at all other levels.

Conceptual and political skills are highly important at senior levels. Managers at the top of the organisation encounter more complex, ambiguous and longer-term problems. They need to be able to understand the many components of a problem and find accurate, long-term, solutions.

The changes in the composition of skills needed at different management levels cause much frustration and heartbreak. First-line managers who have exceedingly good technical ability can become very frustrated when they are passed over for promotion in favour of a colleague who has better interpersonal skills. Similarly, very successful middle managers may be promoted to senior levels only to find that they no longer enjoy their jobs because they do not have the required conceptual skills.

Katz's analysis has important implications for management training and education. It suggests that introductory courses should focus upon technical skills with an appreciation of interpersonal and conceptual skills. Courses for senior managers, however, should focus upon conceptual skills.

Mintzberg and the nature of managerial work

Probably the most famous study of the skills needed by managers was conducted by Henry Mintzberg (1973). His study is a classic example of research using structured observation. He observed each of five chief executives for five days and noted their activities using a carefully worked out scheme. Mintzberg noted that the work of the chief executives was characterised by three features: brevity, variety and fragmentation.

Management work primarily consists of a series of *brief episodes*. Mintzberg carefully recorded the duration of each episode. He found that, on average, each managerial episode would last nine minutes. Less than 10 per cent of managerial episodes last longer than an hour. The average for chief executives included six minutes for each of numerous telephone calls. This was counterbalanced by scheduled meetings which tended to last 68 minutes. By some standards nine minutes is a long time. Previous research into the work of first-line managers (foremen) suggested that they attended to 583 incidents per day – less than one minute for each incident. Indeed, it would seem that the duration of a managerial episode is closely related to the level of management. The more senior the level, the longer the duration of an individual manager activity until at chief executive level the average managerial incident lasts about 10 minutes. This is in sharp contrast to the assumptions made by many management educators who emphasise that managers should spend extended periods of analysis and reflection before they take action.

Management work is also characterised by *variety*. This is in contrast to many other jobs such as a physician. The average time a physician devotes to each patient is, perhaps, about nine minutes. But for each patient the physician will be dealing with a medical problem. However, each nine minute episode completed by a manager is likely to vary from the previous one: the first episode may involve a financial problem; the second episode may involve a customer; the third episode may involve disciplining a subordinate and the fourth episode may involve a mechanical problem that is affecting production. The range of activities which managers need to complete suggests that their education should be broad and multi-disciplinary with a wide range of knowledge and skills.

The third characteristic of managerial work is *fragmentation*. Managers are rarely able to complete a task in one go. Often, they will spend nine minutes dealing with a problem – perhaps by ascertaining the nature of the situation and requesting further information. They will then deal with several totally different issues. Later in the day they may return to the initial problem, absorb the new information and request further clarification. The problem will be revisited, perhaps during the next day, when a decision will be made. This implies that management courses should not be a straightforward linear exposition of the subject. They should involve time pressures and a mix of topics.

Mintzberg also noticed that managers *prefer live action*. Managers much prefer talking to people and observing situations for themselves. They dislike static, formal and written work. Much of this dislike was based upon the fact that formal media are slow. By the time a written report is composed, typed and checked it is likely to be out of date. Furthermore people are more circumspect when writing things down: they are more likely to be diplomatic and disguise the true facts and causes.

Mintzberg noticed that managers routinely perform 10 major roles. He groups the roles under three major headings:

Interpersonal roles centre upon dealing with other people:

1 **Figurehead**: this is probably the simplest and most basic managerial role. Most managers act as a symbol of their unit because they have the formal authority and responsibility for it. They are therefore obliged to perform a number of ceremonial duties such as welcoming guests or presenting retirement presents. In other cases a manager must formally sign documents in order to meet legal requirements.

2 **Leader**: it is a manager's responsibility to induce people to do things they would otherwise let lapse. He or she must inform, motivate and guide subordinates to perform activities that contribute to the organisation's goals. A manager must act as a role model for his or her subordinates.

3 **Liaison**: managers have a vital function in linking their own group to other groups. Their role in vertical communication (forming a channel between their own subordinates and senior management) is demonstrated in most organisational charts. With middle and senior managers the vertical communication role is masked by the importance of horizontal communication. A large proportion of a middle manager's time is taken up by liaising with other middle managers in the same organisation. A large proportion of a senior manager's time involves liaising with senior people from other organisations. Often this is a source of complaint from junior managers who frequently feel that senior managers should spend more time liaising with them.

Informational roles deal with the key management activities of obtaining and receiving information. Once the information has been obtained it is important that it passed on to people who can use it effectively. The informational roles are:

4 **Monitor**: managers are continuously seeking information about the performance of their area of responsibility (AoR). They do this by making frequent, informal tours of

inspection (walking the job), discussions with other people and by reading the trade press. Furthermore, they are bombarded with information from suppliers, customers, regulatory authorities (such as a health and safety) and other stakeholders. They must sift this information and identify the small portion that is relevant. In particular, they must sift information to identify relevant trends.

5 **Disseminator**: once the manager has collected and interpreted all the information that comes his or her way it must be transmitted to the people who can use it effectively. Once factual information has been checked it can be forwarded to subordinates for action. Much of the information will be more ambiguous. It may consist of trade gossip or tip-offs that can help tailor a presentation to a potential client. It may consist of disseminating a set of values the manager wishes subordinates to uphold.

6 **Spokesperson**: a spokesperson is similar to a disseminator but, while the disseminator directs information internally within the organisation, a spokesperson directs information outside the organisation. The organisation is required to keep the general public informed. The chances are it will be a manager, and probably a senior manager, who performs the task.

Decisional roles concern the choices made in the allocation of resources, the direction to follow and how to negotiate with other organisations. Often a senior manager is the only person who is able to commit his unit to a course of action.

7 **Entrepreneur**: a manager often acts as an initiator and designer of change. Often the entrepreneurial roles stem from a manager's ability to authorise action. This allows him or her to spot opportunities and to galvanise their unit into appropriate action.

8 **Disturbance handler**: in an entrepreneurial role a manager is proactive. However, managers sometimes need to react to events that have gone wrong. Unforeseen events may result in progress being off-target. A disturbance handler takes action to get progress back on track. Typical disturbances arise from the sudden departure of staff, accidents such as a fire on the premises or when a major customer takes their business elsewhere. Sometimes disturbances arise when subordinates cannot agree among themselves or when a problem is too difficult for them to solve. Disturbances usually have a sudden onset. Managers usually give disturbances priority and will change their schedules to deal with them. Often the first reaction is to "buy time", which is used to find a solution to the problem

9 **Resource allocator**: usually a manager has more possibilities than his or her resources can match. A manager will therefore exercise judgement and choice when allocating resources to some activities and not to others. The power of authorisation gives a manager ultimate control without the necessity of being involved in the detailed preparatory work. Demands on managers are so great that they are not able to undertake all the tasks themselves: they need to delegate tasks to others. The process of delegation involves considerable power because it contains the authority to choose one individual over another. The choice process communicates to the whole unit the preferences which a manager will reward. The act of delegation is a clear manifestation of power because the manager can give the work to a second person if the first choice does not live up to expectations.

10 **Negotiator**: a manager will nearly always be involved when his or her unit is involved in a major negotiation with an external organisation. Normally the manager will lead the other negotiators from his or her unit. In part the negotiation role flows from the role of figurehead, but it also involves the spokesperson and the resource allocator roles since only a manager can commit the resources that are implicit in the negotiated solutions.

McClelland and managerial needs

David McClelland (1971) was interested in the needs which motivate managers. He was particularly interested in achievement motivation (n ach). Achievement motivation is the need to do something quicker, better or more efficiently. McClelland maintained that if a society had a high proportion of people who were motivated by achievement the society would grow faster. Using an ingenious method of gauging motivation by analysing street ballads he was able to show that the industrial revolution in the UK was preceded, fifty years earlier, by a surge in the level of achievement motivation of the British population. Similarly, the relative economic decline of Britain in the first part of the twentieth century was pre-ceded, fifty years earlier, by a fall in the level of achievement motivation in the British population.

McClelland analysed the level of achievement motivation of executives in companies in the USA, Finland, UK, India and Australia. He obtained a very robust finding. Companies who had executives with high level of achievement motivation made more innovations, filed more patent applications and grew faster than companies whose executives had lower levels of achievement motivation.

McClelland was also interested in the motives for power (n pow) and affiliation (n affil). He found that people who rose to senior levels in large organisations showed a distinct motivational pattern which he called the Leadership Motivation Profile (LMP). People who rise to the top of large organisations tend to have a high need for power, a moderate need for achievement and a low need for affiliation.

Managerial competencies

During the 1980s many organisations were keen to identify the skills, abilities, attitudes and other characteristics which made managers competent at their jobs. Boyatzis (1982) called these attributes "competencies". Organisations tried to determine the competencies which their executives needed so that they could recruit people who already had the required competencies or who could be trained to achieve them. Many organisations produced their own list of competencies. The lists used different words to describe the competencies but often they were referring to the same attributes. Bristow (2001) analysed the lists which were used by over 60 different organisations. Table 1.2 is based on his results.

It can be seen that interpersonal skills dominate the competencies a manager needs. Seven of the top ten competencies concern relations with other people. Communication skills are particularly important and tower above all other competencies. This suggests that the priority in both self-development and management training should be given to inter- and intra-personal skills. Once these competencies have been developed, precedence should then be given to organisational skills, analytical ability and a results orientation.

Competency	Components	%
1 Communication	Written communication, oral communication	97
2 Self-management	Personal effectiveness, self-control, self-discipline, self-confidence, resilience	75
3 Organisational ability	Organisational awareness, delegation, control, structure	68
4 Influence	Impact others, networking, negotiation	67
5 Teamwork	Team membership, team leadership	60
6 Interpersonal skills	Relationships, dealing with individual people	58
7 Analytical ability	Conceptual thinking, problem-solving	58
8 Results orientation	Achievement focus, concern for effectiveness	55
9 Customer focus	Customer service, customer orientation	53
10 Develop people's potential	Enabling others, coaching	53
11 Strategic ability	Vision, breadth of view, forward thinking	52
12 Commercial awareness	Business acumen, market awareness, competitor awareness	48
13 Decision-making	Decisiveness, evaluating options	48
14 Planning	Planning and organising, action planning, task planning	40
15 Leadership	Providing purpose and direction, motivating others	40
16 Self-motivation	Enthusiasm for work, achievement drive, commitment, energy, drive, will-to-win	35
17 Specialist knowledge	Expertise, professional knowledge, functional expertise, operational understanding	35
18 Flexibility	Adaptability, mental agility	32
19 Creativity	Innovation, breakthrough thinking	32
20 Initiative	Proactivity	31
21 Change orientation	Change management, openness to change	23
22 Dealing with information	Information gathering, information processing	20
23 Concern for quality	Quality focus, concern for excellence	20
24 Reliability	Accuracy, disciplined approach, procedural compliance, attention to detail, systematic	18
25 Ethical approach	Integrity, commitment to social and economic equity, valuing people	13
26 Financial awareness	Financial judgement, cost awareness	12
27 Negotiating skills		7
Other		15

TABLE 1.2 Competencies Demanded of Graduates

Psychometric qualities of managers

Managers have been completing psychometric tests for many years. Usually these tests measure intelligence and personality. Managers usually complete them as a part of a selection procedure or career counselling. The present author has available the records for almost 2500 managers and they reveal a fairly consistent pattern.

Managers need to be more intelligent than the average person. Only three of the 2500 managers scored below average. The degree to which they are above average often correlates with their managerial level. The average IQ score for the population as a whole is 100. Typically, a first-line manager will have an IQ of about 109 which would put him or her in the top 27 of the population. A typical middle manager will have an IQ of about 119 (top 10 per cent of the population) while a typical senior manager will have an IQ of about 124 (top 5 per cent of the population). This pattern is not perfect and there will a spread of scores either side of these averages. Nevertheless, intelligence tests (the politically correct term is "tests of cognitive ability") are good predictors of management ability. The exact nature of a person's intelligence is also relevant. Typically managers do best on verbal problems, especially those that involve understanding the reasons behind events and identifying similarities between objects and situations.

The results concerning personality are slightly different. Personality tests are moderately good predictors of managerial performance but there is a wider spread of scores about the averages. Furthermore, personality is more complex and difficult to measure. Research indicates that there are five main aspects of personality. They are:

- extroversion
- stability
- conscientiousness
- tough-mindedness
- openness to new ideas

Typically managers, especially production managers, tend to be *moderate extroverts*. They are lively and sociable without going "over-the-top". Moderate extroverts enjoy jobs involving a variety of tasks and where they need to make quick practical decisions involving people. This is consistent with Mintzberg's work that showed that the managerial job involves brevity, variety and fragmentation. There are, however, some exceptions to this rule. Managers of specialist functions such as R&D, quality control or finance may be less extroverted and perhaps even a little introverted.

Managers are usually also *emotionally stable* people. This enables them to cope with a torrent of emotional situations and gives them the resilience to bounce back after setbacks. Again, there are some exceptions to this rule. Project managers and some managers in the finance function may have average stability and may even be a little "touchy".

Almost all managers are *conscientious*. This means that they show a sense of duty and they have a clear self-image to which they adhere. This often means that they are reliable and their work is well organised and considerate of other people. The few exceptions to this rule are usually seen in managers working in highly competitive, dealing or merchanting situations.

Finally, managers tend to be moderately *tough-minded*. This means that they are prepared to take responsibility, push proposals through and get things done. They will face conflict but they will not actively seek it.

The level of open-mindedness is often related to the industry in which they work. Traditional industries which are "close-coupled" to the market and which produce a fairly standard product with high efficiency and at low cost tend to suit people with a personality that is down-to-earth and focuses on concrete information. On the other hand academia, the media, advertising and fashion industries tend to favour a personality that exults in new ideas.

Writers such as Dumaine (1993) believe that the skills needed by managers are changing in order to match contemporary demands. Table 1.3 shows the contrasts between what Dumaine calls the old manager and the new manager.

Dumaine's work highlights the fact that management and managers are not static. They change over time. In order to have a good understanding of management it is necessary to have a basic knowledge about how it has changed in the past. In other words it is easier to understand current management if something is known about its history.

OLD MANAGER	NEW MANAGER
Thinks of self as manager or boss	Thinks of self as sponsor, team leader or internal consultant
Follows chain of command	Deals with anyone necessary to do job
Works within existing structure	Changes structure according to environment
Makes decisions alone	Involves others in decisions
Hordes information	Shares information
Masters single discipline, e.g. finance or marketing	Masters broad array of disciplines
Demands long hours	Demands results

TABLE 1.3 Differences between Old and New Managers

Activities and Further Study

Essay Plans

Prepare plans for the following essays:

1 Compare and contrast the work of managers and non-managers.
2 To what extent are managers, and their work, the same?
3 What skills do managers need in order to perform their work effectively?

Compare your plans with those given on the website associated with this book

---

Web Activities

1 Go to the website associated with this book and download the spreadsheet containing a sample of 100 activities performed by managers. Use the adjacent column on the spreadsheet to classify each activity according to its management process. Use the initials:

   P = planning
   O = organising
   S = staffing
   D = deciding
   C = controlling
   R = reporting (communicating)
   B = budgeting (money and time)

   Use the sort function to rearrange the activities according to the management process involved. Work out the percentage of time that managers spend on each process and answer the following questions:

   - Which two activities take up most management time?
   - The sample of a hundred activities was obtained from managers in manufacturing. To what extent would you expect the results to differ if the sample had been obtained from managers in a service industry?
   - To what extent would you expect results to differ according to the level of managers involved?

   Compare your answers with those given on the website associated with this book.

2 Use the Web to locate two specific examples, preferably from your own area or region, on the following types of organisations in which managers work. Enter their names onto a table such as the one that follows:

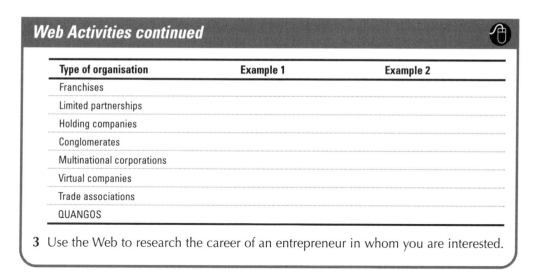

Web Activities continued

Type of organisation	Example 1	Example 2
Franchises		
Limited partnerships		
Holding companies		
Conglomerates		
Multinational corporations		
Virtual companies		
Trade associations		
QUANGOS		

3 Use the Web to research the career of an entrepreneur in whom you are interested.

Experiential Activities

1 Form a discussion group to examine one or more of the following topics:

■ The changes that have occurred in management work during the past 40 years (i.e. during the working life of someone who is just retiring).

■ The changes that are likely to occur in management work during the next 40 years (i.e. during the working life of someone who is just starting a career).

■ The skills needed for management work (start by brainstorming the skills and competencies needed) and writing them on a flip chart. Then list the skills and competencies according to their importance. Finally, compare your group's list with list of competencies from organisations – for example, see the list on page 27.

2 Interview a manager (use your network of friends and relatives to identify someone who would help) and ask about:

■ the people they supervise

■ the people to whom they are responsible

■ the way they spend their time at work

On the basis of this information decide whether they are junior, middle or senior managers. Also decide whether they are general or specialist managers. You should also identify the function (e.g. marketing, operations, finance, human resources, etc.) in which they work. Check your decisions by asking your interviewee to name their management level and their management function.

3 Arrange (perhaps with the help of your college, university or careers service) to observe a practising manager at work for one or two days. In advance of your visit read Henry Mintzberg's book *The Nature of Managerial Work* (or at least a summary of it!). Keep notes on the roles that the manager occupies and the duration of his or her "working episodes". Compare your notes with the findings by Mintzberg.

CHAPTER

History of Management

02

Henry Ford once famously said that "History is bunk". At a superficial level this may be true – except for those people who find history interesting in its own right. History tells us about the past. Most people, especially managers, are more concerned with the present and the future. However, there are three good reasons why most managers need a basic grasp of the history of their subject. First, it is important to learn the terms and ideas that are used by other managers. A brief study of the history of management is a good way to learn what they mean. Furthermore, knowing how the terms arose helps to ensure that they are used intelligently and within their proper context. Second, history allows management to be seen in perspective and in its wider context. This has two advantages. It stops people taking a narrow view of management where their actions are based on limited personal experience. A sense of perspective will also help managers to identify and react to longer-term trends. Third, managers in the past have made mistakes and learned from them. A knowledge of history can mean that some of these lessons can be learned without the hassle of making the mistake. It can reduce the likelihood of wasting time "reinventing the wheel".

The history of management can be described in six sections. The six sections are:

Chapter contents

2.1 Early Beginnings

Management is not a new phenomenon. It has existed ever since humans started to undertake tasks in groups. The hunting of mammoths by groups of Neanderthals required some managerial activity. The high priests of the Sumerian Empire managed agricultural estates and developed writing specifically to record resources for purposes of taxation. The Egyptians used fairly advanced management techniques to build the pyramids. Druids used management skills to build Stonehenge.

The Romans were great and systematic managers. Their soldiers were organised into cohorts, managed by senior centurions, which in turn were organised into legions and armies. Diocletian (AD 248) was perhaps the greatest manager of Roman times. He divided the Empire into 100 provinces. Each province was divided into dioceses, each of which was further divided into four divisions. He also arranged a clear, unbroken chain of command from each divisional governor to himself. The Roman Catholic Church (in terms of longevity, the most effective organisation of the Western world) adopted a similar organisation leading from the parish priest to the Pope. Indeed dioceses under the control of a bishop are an important unit in the organisation of Christian religions today.

Machiavelli tried to improve the management skills of his bosses, the Medici princes of Renaissance Florence. Machiavelli identified four main management principles:

- mass consent for actions – ultimately authority is derived "bottom-up"
- cohesiveness amongst followers by setting expectations and rewarding those who meet these expectations

- the will to survive – being alert and prepared to respond to threats in a prompt and forceful way
- good leadership – wisdom, kindness and justice together with setting an appropriate example to others

One management writer (Jay, 1967) believes Machiavelli's works are "bursting with urgent advice and acute observations for top management of the great private and public corporations all over the world".

2.2 Scientific Management (Rational Goal)

Scientific Management is sometimes known as the Rational Goal School of Management and it emerged with the Industrial Revolution. There were three reasons why management became more important as the Industrial Revolution progressed:

- Larger units of economic activity became more common. Previously the family or a group of families was the predominant unit of economic activity. Large organisations were exceptional and usually associated with government, armies or religion.
- Industry requires greater specialisation of labour. Industrial processes were more complex and required high expertise. Employment in agriculture depended upon a few generic skills which most agricultural workers could perform as and when they were required.
- Factories and machinery were costly and often could only be financed by the combined savings of a group of people. This led to the development of the Limited Company where the person managing the enterprise may or may not have been the same as the person or people who owned it.

Bolton and Watt were pioneers of the scientific management movement. They built a factory to manufacture steam engines in Birmingham in 1800. Existing systems of manufacturing were based on the methods used in craft workshops, which were disorganised and inefficient. Bolton and Watt adopted a scientific, analytical approach to increase productivity by making work easier to perform:

- They made a systematic analysis of the market for steam engines and the rate at which steam engines needed to be produced.
- They designed their factory to provide an efficient flow of work on the basis of these estimates. The speeds of the various machines were studied and adjusted to provide the desired rate of output. Each stage was broken down into a series of minor operations which could be analysed systematically. The basics of time-and-motion study were developed at Bolton and Watt's factory.
- They developed a wage system which was based on the work done. The output for each job was estimated and workers who exceeded the estimate received a bonus while those who did not achieve the estimate received a wage cut. This system can be thought of as the forerunner of later piece-rate systems.
- They introduced an accounting system which kept track of material costs, labour costs

and finished goods. The accounting system also recorded indirect costs. It also allowed management to pinpoint inefficiencies and waste so that productivity could be improved.

F W Taylor – the father of scientific management

The scientific approach was taken up with enthusiasm in the United States, where workers were often seen as mere parts of a large machine. One of the most famous proponents of scientific management was Frederick W. Taylor. Taylor is most famous for his work at Midvale Steel and then the Bethlehem Steel Company. He studied jobs more scientifically than Bolton and Watt. He determined how much work could be expected from an operative each day. Previously management had relied upon tradition and workers had, over time, kept their output low in order to reduce the demands on them. Taylor used time-and-motion study to establish what a good worker should achieve. In one case, Taylor studied men loading pig iron into railway wagons: the average was 12.5 tonnes per day. Taylor calculated that if men worked 42 per cent of the time they should be able to achieve 47 tonnes per day. Taylor then chose a man called "Schmidt" and supervised him very closely, telling him exactly what to do and when. At the end of the first day Schmidt had, in fact, loaded 47.5 tonnes of pig iron. After a short period of training other men on the shift also achieved the target of 47 tonnes. Another experiment at Bethlehem Steel concerned shovelling iron ore and coal. When men were working with iron ore the load was very heavy but when they were working with coal the load was much lighter. Taylor's experiments showed that most material was moved when the shovel load was 21lb. At that time workers provided their own shovels and they tended to use the same one irrespective of the material moved. Taylor provided a series of shovels – a small one for heavy material and a larger one for lighter material – so that the load was always constant at 21lb. The average tonnage moved per labourer per day rose from 16 to 19. At a consequence the number of labourers needed fell from about 400 to 140. Taylor was careful to pass on some of the increased productivity to the labourers. Their wages increased from $1.15 per day to $1.88 – a rise of 63 per cent. In 1911 Taylor wrote his classic book *Principles of Scientific Management* and in 1912 he spoke before a congressional committee investigating systems of management. On the basis of these achievements Taylor was named the "father of scientific management".

Other prominent members of the Scientific Management movement were Frank Gilbreth and his wife Lillian, who was a psychologist. Gilbreth studied the hand movements of bricklayers in minute detail. By eliminating repetitions and movements which served no purpose he was able to reduce the number of movements needed to lay a brick from 18 to 5. Some movements were eliminated by training bricklayers, others by improving materials (e.g. making sure that the mortar was at the proper consistency so that bricklayers did not need to "tap down" each brick) and by providing equipment such as a stand to hold the bricks so that the bricklayers did not need to stoop to pick up each brick. These improvements meant that the number of bricks one person could lay in an hour rose from 120 to 350. The analyses conducted by the Gilbreths were so detailed that they needed to use slow-motion photography. Gilbreth and his wife developed a system which characterised all operative work in terms of 17 basic motions such as "reach", "grasp", "hold" and "position". They called these basic movements "Therbligs".

Writers today tend to minimise or even disparage the contribution of scientific managers. However, the greatness of their contribution is clear when it is set against the context of the times. At that time industry was very labour intensive. Productivity was very low. The scientific managers tackled the most pressing managerial problem of their time – to increase efficiency and productivity. Today we take much of their findings for granted. We automatically assume that workers will be properly selected, trained and equipped. Scientific managers were primarily concerned with the productivity of manual workers in heavy industry. The importance of heavy industry to the economy has decreased substantially in the century since the heyday of Taylor and Gilbreth. Nevertheless, scientific management retains an important role. Equipment manufacturers conduct studies to ensure that their products are suited to peoples' capabilities. For example, designers of computer software will check that screen images are legible. Similarly, manufacturers of mundane military equipment such as boots and socks will conduct studies to ensure that their products are designed in a way that will allow soldiers to march the longest distance without producing foot sores. Designers of control panels for complex chemical plant will go to great lengths to ensure that the control displays are easy to understand and that warnings of danger are unmistakable. Finally, road safety authorities will undertake studies to determine the work and rest patterns a driver of a commercial vehicle must take in order to avoid serious risks of accidents. Today studies in scientific management are usually covered by the discipline of Ergonomics – the Science of Work.

The Quantitative School of Management

Scientific management and the basic ideas of Taylor reached a second peak, in a slightly different form, between 1940 and 1980 and it operated under different names such as the Quantitative School or Management Science. There were, however, important differences. Taylor was largely concerned with physical work, whereas the Quantitative School focused upon managerial decisions. While Taylor used very straightforward analytical techniques, the Quantitative School used very sophisticated methods of analysis. In many areas the Quantitative School is still strong today.

During the Second World War huge quantities of men and material were deployed against an enemy. Governments were anxious to obtain a military advantage by deploying the men and materials in the most effective way. To do this they employed scientists, mathematicians and statisticians to study a problem in a rational, quantitative and scientific way. For example, it was imperative to defeat the U-boats menacing supply convoys. Depth charges were one of the main methods of attack. However, a large number of questions needed to be answered in order for a destroyer to make a successful attack. How many depth charges should be used against a single submarine? Too few might not result in a "kill" while the use of too many might mean there were insufficient to attack other submarines in the pack. At what depth should the fuses be set to explode? What would be the most efficient pattern of scattering the depth charges? Scientists and mathematicians studied the kill rates for various answers and derived an attack plan which would result in the greatest number of submarine kills per depth charge. More recent, civilian problems are illustrated by a retail organisation which wants to know the optimum density for its outlets. If each outlet serves a large area, a large number of consumers will be within the catchment areas and profits will be high – except for the fact that large catchment areas involve high transport costs and management supervision becomes costly and difficult. Furthermore, wide spacing of outlets might allow competitors the chance to establish themselves. On the other hand, if retail outlets are too close to each other the catchment areas are small but transport and management costs are low. The question arises "what is the optimum density of retail outlets". The company might conduct a study and its mathematicians might produce the formula:

$$\text{profit (in millions)} = r \times 2 + (r^2 \times \pi) - (r^3 \times 0.5).$$

It is then possible to construct the following table:

Catchment radius	1	2	3	4	5	6	7	8	9
Expected profits £m	23	49	75	98	116	125	122	105	70

From the table it is clear that the catchment area of retail outlets should have a radius of six miles. Therefore shops should be set 12 miles apart so that the catchment areas touch but do not overlap.

Similar methods are used, mainly by large organisations, to establish the optimum ways of deploying stocks, materials, production schedules and production control. Two very well-known aspects of the Quantitative School of management are queuing theory and "Just-in-Time" production methods. The Quantitative School uses algorithms and game theory to reach conclusions. It aims to provide the best possible decision and it is usually applied to problems that are too complex to be solved by common sense. When managers are asked to solve complex problems without the aid of qualitative models they tend to settle for solutions which are satisfactory rather than the best possible solution.

The quantitative approach is often called operations research (OR). Sometimes the qualitative approach is called the Management Science approach. Typically the quantitative approach is characterised by three features:

- use of mathematical models, linear programs and statistical trend analysis to identify patterns that can be projected into the future to make forecasts
- simulations to determine the impact of different decisions – often these simulations take the form of a computer spreadsheet that is used to examine several "what if" scenarios where the impact of several variables can be studied
- specialised techniques such as algorithms, critical path analysis and Just-in-Time methods to help managers determine key dates and identify likely bottlenecks

The Qualitative School is a far cry from the techniques developed by Taylor. Nevertheless they share the aim of making behaviour more predictable, more productive and more machine-like. The quantitative approach has made enormous contributions to management decisions, especially decisions concerning planning and control.

However, quantitative methods are not perfect. They may be less precise than they seem. They often rely upon data which are estimated by managers and other people who may have a vested interest in providing distorted information. These estimates can be substantially awry and unreliable. Furthermore, the assumptions used in the models developed by the quantitative managers may be wrong. Because these assumptions appear scientific they are difficult to identify and correct. Finally, quantitative methods may place an unreasonable emphasis on economic effectiveness. They may miss more subtle goals such as satisfaction, enjoyment and justice because intangible psychological states are very difficult to quantify.

Some critics go further and complain that the Quantitative School gives too narrow a view of management. Other critics maintain that it is not a school at all. Mathematics and statistics are used in many sciences such as engineering and medicine but they are not elevated to the status of a "School".

2.3 Classical (Administrative) Theorists

Scientific managers were concerned predominantly with managing operatives and labourers. They said very little about management itself. The classical theorists were largely senior managers in large organisations who turned their minds to analysing the processes of management.

Henry Fayol

Probably the most important classical theorist was Henry Fayol. Fayol was the general manager of a large French mining company. He was primarily concerned with "administrative principles" that apply to the organisation as a whole. Fayol identified the key processes which managers needed to achieve. If a manager performed these functions properly, he or she would be effective. The main processes of management according to Fayol were: planning, organising, commanding, co-ordinating and controlling. Since his time Fayol's list has been amended and the main processes of management are now seen to be:

- Planning
- Organising
- Staffing
- Deciding
- Controlling
- Reporting
- Budgeting

The processes can be remembered by the acronym POSDCRB. Each of the processes will be considered in greater depth in Part 2 on management processes. Fayol also identified a number of management principles. They were:

- **Division of labour** – up to a point people should specialise in performing certain tasks so that they can build a high level of expertise.
- **Authority and responsibility** – the right to give orders and expect them to be obeyed. Authority usually arises from the role occupied by the manager. Sometimes, however authority arises from the person's individual abilities such as intelligence, expertise,

charisma or general character. This kind of authority is sometimes known as "informal" or "personal" authority. A good manager should have both formal and informal sources of authority. Fayol was keen to link authority with responsibility. When a manager uses power to issue an instruction he or she is responsible for the consequences. If the course of action leads to success, the manager should be rewarded and if it leads to failure the manager should be punished. Later writers referred to Fayol's concept as the "parity of authority and responsibility".

- **Discipline** – which involves obedience, diligence, energy, correct attitude and outward respect.

- **Unity of command** – everyone should have one, and only one, boss.

- **Unity of management** – efforts and plans should be in pursuit of the same objective.

- **Subordination of individual interests to the common good** – the goals of the organisation should take precedence over the goals of individuals or groups of individuals.

- **Remuneration of staff** – employees should be fairly rewarded for what they do.

- **Centralisation** – concerns the degree of initiative which is left to individuals or groups. Centralisation is neither good nor bad since it depends upon the organisation, its environment and its goals. However each organisation must strike the appropriate balance.

- **Scalar chain of command** – there should be a clear hierarchy which runs from the bottom of an organisation through to the top. This ensures the integrity of the organisational structure and the unity of command. Generally, communications should follow the hierarchical route. However, Fayol recognised that if every piece of information needed to go from the bottom of an organisation to the top and then down again to the bottom the delays would be unacceptable. Fayol therefore introduced the "gang-plank" principal whereby people at the same level within an organisation could communicate with each other.

- **Order** – the correct position for equipment should be determined and equipment should be kept in that position (a place for everything and everything in its place). Furthermore, key posts should be filled by competent people who do not exceed their role.

- **Equity** – managers should be friendly and fair. They should show good sense and good nature.

- **Stability of staff** – staff turnover is disruptive and incurs costs. It should be minimised so that staff can develop required skills and commitment to the organisation (modern thinking is that excessive stability produces rigidity and should therefore be carefully controlled).

- **Initiative** – initiative of employees is a considerable strength to an organisation, especially when times are difficult. Initiative is the ability to conceive and execute a new plan when existing plans are not satisfactory.

- **Espirit de corps** – refers to the harmony among people within the organisation so that morale is high.

Max Weber

Max Weber is another classical theorist who focused upon the administrative processes which managers must perform. Weber was struck by the inefficiencies of the old semi-feudal structure of many organisations where people had loyalties to their patrons rather than the organisation as a whole. This led to conflict and inefficiency. Weber attempted to provide guidelines for a rational organisation which had rules so that the organisation performed predictably and consistently. He envisaged organisations that managed in an impersonal, rational way. He called these organisations "bureaucracies". Weber attempted to improve routine office operations in a way similar to that in which Taylor and other previous management experts had successfully improved labouring operations. According to Weber an ideal organisation would be characterised by six facets:

- Jobs are specialised and have clear definitions of their authority.
- Jobs are arranged in hierarchical order in which each successive level has greater authority and control.
- Personnel are selected and promoted on the basis of merit. Personnel are given adequate training.
- Acts and decisions are recorded in writing. Proper records form the memory of an organisation and the use of precedents ensures the equality of treatment.
- A comprehensive set of rules which cover almost all eventualities. Employees are expected to keep to the letter of these rules and apply them impartiality – irrespective of the ranks and positions of the administrator and that of the person who was concerned. This meant that employees, customers and citizens would not be subject to the whims of individual employees and people would be treated fairly.
- In most bureaucratic organisations, management is separate from the ownership of the organisation.

Bureaucratic organisations have been heavily criticised because they become inflexible. Rules confine initiative and lead to the demotivation of employees. Some writers have identified the phenomena of **bureau pathology** in which unrealistic and irrelevant rules are set. When employees fail to observe these rules, yet more rules are developed to control non-conformance. The additional sets of rules alienate employees further and provoke more non-conformance – which triggers yet more detailed rules and so on, ad infinitum. A further disadvantage is that, over time, the original purpose of the rules is forgotten. The rules become ends in their own right. The strict observance of the rules may serve administrative officials well because it offers security – as long as they obey rules they are safe from criticism. However, the rules may not be in the interests of the organisation's clients.

2.4 Human Relations

Scientific managers tended to think of human beings as machines. In their view management's job was to improve the efficiency of the machines. Even during the heyday of scientific management, some people were not convinced that human beings were like machines. They argued that human beings had special characteristics. The Human Relations

School of Management goes back at least to the days of Robert Owen, the Scottish mill owner, who criticised fellow managers of his day for buying the best machines and then hiring the cheapest labour. He set up a textile mill in New Lanark where he established better working conditions for his employees and noted a rise in productivity.

The work of Robert Owen was influential but it did not employ techniques that were explicitly scientific. One of the first people to use scientific methods to investigate the characteristics of human beings in work situations was a German, Hugo Munsterberg. Munsterberg noted that the scientific managers emphasised physical skills but ignored mental ones. Munsterberg was way ahead of his time. During the first decade of the 1900s he identified the major trend in the nature of work which is still evident today: work is becoming less dependent on physical skills and more dependent on mental skills. Munsterberg therefore developed tests which could identify workers who had the mental skills demanded by a job – especially higher-level jobs. Munsterberg also tried to establish the psychological conditions that produce highest productivity. In many ways Munsterberg was the link between the scientific managers and the Human Relations School of Management.

Elton Mayo and the Hawthorne experiments

Elton Mayo followed Munsterberg's lead and tried to find the psychological conditions that would give higher levels of productivity among workers at the Hawthorn electrical plant near Chicago which, among other things, manufactured light bulbs. The work of Mayo and his colleagues has been described by Roethlisberger et al. (1939) and criticised by Parson (1974), Adair (1984) and Diaper (1990). The company was keen to prove that good lighting improved the performance of operatives. Mayo and his colleagues established two groups of workers. One was a control group. The other was an experimental group and the level of illumination at their workplace was varied. As the level of illumination rose so did productivity. However, most people were surprised when productivity also rose as the illumination was reduced. Evidently the actual levels of illumination were not the key factor in productivity. After a number of other experiments it was concluded that workers were responding not to the levels of illumination but to the levels of attention which management was devoting to workers. These studies are famous for identifying the "Hawthorne Effect". (See p. 395 for some practical implications of the Hawthorne effect.)

The Hawthorne effect was a very important discovery. However, a second finding from the Hawthorne studies was equally important. Mayo and colleagues observed workers in the Bank Wiring Room where connections on electrical equipment were soldered. The time-and-motion department had established that an efficient worker should be able to solder 7312 connections per day. However, workers generally completed about 6300 connections. Mayo and his colleagues wondered why output was lower than expected – was it because the time-and-motion department had set a target that was too high? Mayo came to the conclusion that informal social norms were the reason for the lower output. The men, and indeed their immediate supervisors, believed that 6300 connections was a fair day's work. If anyone made significantly more connections than 6300, they were called a "rate buster" and were punished by sarcastic comments and a hard punch on the top of their arm – a process called "binging". If anyone made fewer than 6300 connections they were called a "chiseller" and subjected to similar sanctions. This was not the machine-like behaviour that scientific managers expected. Machines do not form coalitions to set and enforce their own standards of output. The work of Mayo in the Bank Wiring Room showed that managers need to take account of social and psychological factors such as social norms and group dynamics.

Barnard and Follett

Two other experts refined and developed the ideas which had been demonstrated in the Hawthorn studies. Mary Parker Follett (1941) argued that the management of people was the very essence of management itself. She defined management as "getting things done by other people". She advocated the abandonment of traditional bureaucratic organisations together with their demotivating and reactionary disadvantages. Instead, she argued, we should try to harness the potential of people. She suggested that management's main task is to encourage people to form self-governing groups that are empowered to solve commercial and industrial problems. This advice contradicted the principle of "specialisation" advocated by the scientific managers. Mary Parker Follet also offered advice on conflict resolution. Whereas the scientific managers believed that senior managers should work out the best possible solutions to the problem and then force their employees to implement that solution, Mary Parker Follett suggested that it is better to bring conflicting groups together and allow them to work out their own solutions to the problem.

Chester Barnard was president of the New Jersey Bell Telephone Co. He stressed the need for managers to obtain the co-operation of employees so that they would work towards adding value to the organisation rather than their own goals. Chester Barnard maintained that the best way of obtaining employee co-operation is to communicate effectively and hence create a harmonious working atmosphere. Again, this was in direct contradiction to the mechanistic approach implied by the scientific managers – working atmosphere is irrelevant to the performance of machines.

The Human Relations School has had an enormous, evangelical impact on management practice. Nevertheless, it is open to criticism. Many of the early experiments were less scientific than they seemed. For example, many of the Hawthorn Studies were very poorly controlled and many factors were left to vary at random. In other cases the changes introduced from a human relations standpoint were introduced at the same time as other changes such as higher wages. Consequently, it is not possible to identify with certainty the causes of improvements. Other critics point out that the Human Relations School has too narrow a focus, which excludes aspects such as equipment, planning and organisations that are an undoubted part of management.

2.5 Systems Theory

During the 1950s people became increasingly critical of a series of theories which, while true, only explained a part of the management task. In 1961 Koontz complained that there was "a management theory jungle". Systems Theorists aimed to correct the situation by pointing out that organisations needed to be considered as a whole in the same way that the medics need to consider the human body as a whole rather than a collection of separate functions such as excretion, breathing and thinking. Each part of an organisation would have an impact on other parts and the whole organisation can only work effectively if the individual parts work effectively and co-operate. A system is usually defined as a set of interrelated parts that function as a whole to achieve a common purpose.

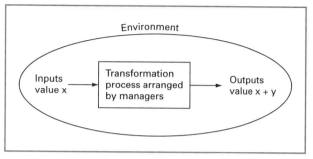

FIGURE 2.1 A Simple Closed System

The simplest system is a **closed** one that operates in isolation to its environment. A closed system is depicted in Figure 2.1. Closed, simple systems tend to be called "linear systems". In linear systems events occur as management plans them without too much interference from the outside environment.

This means that the outside environment is usually stable and, with effort, can be understood and predicted. In a linear system it is usually clear what actions (levers) must be taken in order to achieve a given goal.

Many early management theories tended to operate on the basis that organisations were closed, linear, systems. As an approximation, this was almost true. A century ago technological developments were relatively slow to make an impact on a large organisation. Communications and ideas travelled slowly. Furthermore, physical barriers and tariffs meant that outside competition was often minimal. The ethos of a closed system was typified by Henry Ford's comment that people could have a car of any colour they liked provided it was black: Ford's production plant was a closed system which felt it did not need to respond to the wishes of the consumers in its environment. It was more important that black paint dried faster and that a black car would be cheaper than a car of any other colour. Today the Ford Motor Company is very careful to ensure it has a large range of colours so that it can respond to the wishes of its much more affluent customers.

Modern organisations tend to be complex **open systems.** The defining characteristic of an open system is that it interacts with its environment via a feedback loop. This is shown in Figure 2.2.

Systems theorists spend considerable effort specifying inputs and the outputs in detail. Often the inputs are specified in classical terms of money, machines and men and women. However, information resources are important to most modern organisations and are added as an important input. Traditionally the main output of an organisation has been its profit (or loss).

However, a modern list would also include employee satisfaction and contribution to the local and wider community. A modern systems view is given in Figure 2.3.

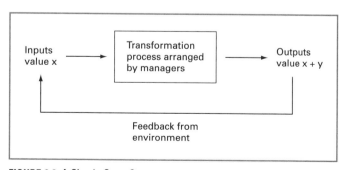

FIGURE 2.2 A Simple Open System

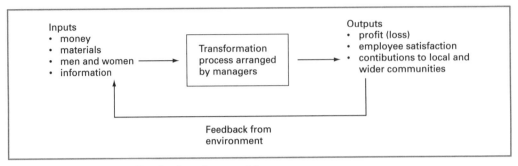

FIGURE 2.3 An Open System Showing Some Inputs and Outputs

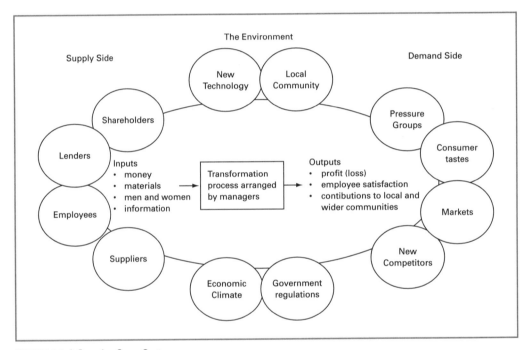

FIGURE 2.4 A Complex Open System

Figure 2.4 shows a very simplified view of the environment. In reality the environment is complex. On the supply side, managers need to be alert to the demands of employees, suppliers, shareholders and lenders. On the demand side they need to be aware of markets, pressure groups, new competitors and changes in consumer tastes. There are also a number of factors that might affect both the demand side and the supply side. For example, a poorer economic climate might mean that there are fewer customers, which will make the managerial task more difficult. However, a poorer economic climate might also aid managers by making suppliers and employees more co-operative. Similarly, government regulations and new technology can also affect the inputs and the outputs of an organisation.

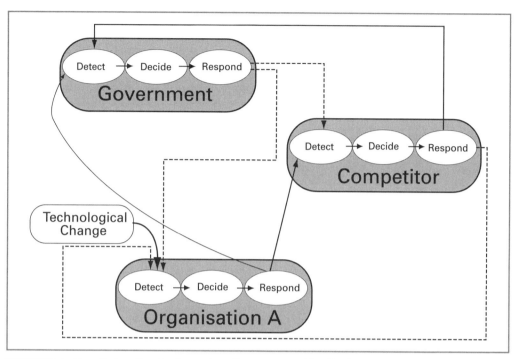

FIGURE 2.5 An Open System Showing Competitors, Government and Feedback

Figure 2.4 also illustrates the concept of **stakeholders**. A stakeholder is any person that is affected by an organisation's decisions, policies and activities. As the diagram shows, stakeholders include employees, suppliers, customers, clients, pressure groups, the local community, competing organisations and government. These are additional to the more obvious stakeholders who have a formal financial interest – the shareholders, lenders and creditors. In many ways managers, especially senior managers, need to achieve a successful balance between the often competing demands of the organisation's stakeholders.

Closed systems tended to be linear systems in which the outcome of any action would be highly predictable. Complex open systems, such as the one shown in Figure 2.5, are generally non-linear systems with less certainty about the outcome of a decision. In a non-linear system managers may be able to predict the short-term consequences within their organisation but it is very difficult for them to predict the wider, longer-term consequences.

Open systems are complex, containing many feedback loops. They are much less predictable and decisions can have quite unexpected consequences. Figure 2.5 represents only a fraction of the complications that exist in reality: it shows only one organisation, one competitor and the government. However, there are feedback loops both within the three organisations and between them.

Suppose that there is a major technological advance. Suppose also that organisation A detects the technological change and uses it to improve production so that quality is increased by 50 per cent and costs are reduced by 50 per cent (not an unlikely scenario in the computer industry!). In a closed system this would bring enormous benefits to organisation A because it would be able to dominate its market with superior goods at a lower price. However, in an open system the situation may be quite different. A competitor would be more likely to monitor web sites, newspaper articles and the promotional literature and to detect organisation A's actions. The competitor might respond in a number of ways. If it was larger and richer it might engage in a predatory price war designed to starve organisation A of funds so that it could not exploit the new product. Alternatively, the competitor could decide to meet the challenge "head on" by embracing the same technological advance and developing a parallel, improved product. Finally, the competitor could abandon hope, exit that particular market and concentrate on its other products. Organisation A is unlikely to know which of these alternatives its competitor will choose.

Government would also detect the increased revenues that organisation A obtains from the new product and it would decide upon some course of action. It might decide to levy a windfall tax; it might decide to write off organisation A's extra capital expenditure on favourable terms. In the interests of greater employment the government could also offer organisation A help in developing export markets. It will be impossible for organisation A to predict exactly which combination of decisions will be made by its competitor and the government in response to its initial decision. Most modern organisations tend to be more like non-linear systems than linear ones.

Feedback mechanisms are generally believed to be good. As organisations put more information on the Internet the rate of feedback both within and between organisations has accelerated. However, excessive feedback and extremely fast feedback can, as any acoustic engineer will verify, be dysfunctional. The feedback mechanisms can amplify the consequences of each decision so that the level of noise in the system is so great that it becomes intolerable. Furthermore, highly sensitive feedback mechanisms often react to a decision before the consequences of that decision are clear. Subsequent decisions are then based upon incomplete information with a result that the system swings ('hunts') violently between extremes.

The systems approach to management emphasises three other concepts: entropy, synergy and subsystems.

Entropy is the tendency for a system to run down, decay and become chaotic unless it receives regular inputs and maintenance. Unless an organisation receives a subsidy from a government or other organisation, the value of its outputs must equal or exceed the value of its input – otherwise it will decay and eventually become extinct. The duration of this decay will be influenced by the organisation's size: small organisations usually reach the point of extinction before larger ones. A key element in ensuring that input is exceeded by outputs is the skill with which managers arrange the transformation process.

Synergy is the extra value that is produced when two parts of a system interact. For example, in isolation even an excellent production department will not generate extra value, because it will have to rely on customers calling in person to buy a product. In isolation even a superb sales team will not generate extra value, because it will have nothing to sell. However, the combination of an excellent production department and a superb sales department can both make and sell products at considerable added value.

Except for one-person concerns, organisations are not amorphous structures where all parts perform the same tasks in the same way. Usually they are split up into **subsystems** which perform specialised functions. For example, some people in an organisation will attend to financial matters, others to purchasing supplies and materials and others still will attend to personnel matters, and so on. Technically subsystems are defined as relatively homogeneous parts of a system that depend on one another for their functioning. Subsystems must be managed and co-ordinated as a whole and the impact that changes in one subsystem have upon other systems must be understood. In many organisations the sub-systems are called departments or functions. The main functions of organisations will be considered in Chapters 10–14.

Specialisation into subsystems brings enormous advantages. A subsystem can concentrate upon a narrow range of tasks and develop a higher level of expertise so that a higher level of proficiency is delivered. Furthermore, subsystems can produce organisational clarity. People know who is responsible for specific tasks. Unfortunately specialisation into subsystems also brings disadvantages. Within a subsystem individuals may develop their own ethos and goals. These may conflict with the ethos and goals of the larger organisation. Even worse, several subsystems may conflict and the conflict may divert so much energy that the organisation is unable to concentrate upon adding sufficient value to the resources it receives.

2.6 Contingency Theory

The systems approach to management emphasises that most modern organisations are open systems which need to respond to their environment. Contrary to the ideas of scientific management, administrative management and the human relations schools (who implied there was one best way to manage – if only it could be identified) systems theory implies that the style of management needs to be responsive to (contingent upon) an organisation's environment.

To an extent the contingency theory of management has its roots in research into leadership. The rise of Adolf Hitler had focused attention upon the impact that a powerful leader could have upon history. There was great interest in discovering the characteristics of leaders so that the armed forces and business organisations could either select people who had these characteristics or send people on training courses so that they could develop the characteristics of leaders. Many research programmes were conducted but they tended to produce different results. It was concluded that there is no one set of characteristics which personifies leaders and that the style of leaders is contingent upon the circumstances of their group. Later re-analyses suggest that, to an extent, this was false. There is a clear tendency for leaders to be more intelligent, stable, conscientious and assertive than most people. Nevertheless, the conclusion exercised a powerful influence upon ideas of management. The topic of leadership will be considered in greater detail in Chapter 5, which deals with staffing. However, the work of Fred Fiedler will be discussed here in order to demonstrate the principles of contingency theory.

Fiedler

Fiedler, Chemers and Mahar (1978) measured whether members of a group had good or poor relationships with each other. They also measured whether the group had a clear task or an ambiguous task. Finally, they measured the extent of the leader's formal power. Fiedler categorised groups into eight kinds. He then looked at the leadership styles that were preferred by each kind of group. The results are shown in Table 2.1.

Group relationships	good	good	good	good	poor	poor	poor	poor
Tasks structure	high	high	low	low	high	high	low	low
Position power	high	low	high	low	high	low	high	low
Situational control	very high							very low
Appropriate leader style	task-oriented style			relationship-oriented style			task-oriented style	

TABLE 2.1 Fiedler's Contingency Theory of Leadership Style

Fiedler's results indicate that when the situational control is either very high or very low a leader should emphasise the task which faces the group. However, when the situational control is in the middle range a leader should emphasise the maintenance of good relationships among group members.

Woodward

Another classic investigation which supports the contingency view of management was conducted by Woodward (1965). She investigated three groups of manufacturing companies. One group was classified as "unit and small batch production". In this group products were made in small quantities – often to the specifications of individual customers. The products included designer furniture, luxury yachts and specialist cars. In some ways these firms were like craft organisations because they relied heavily upon individual skills and employees were very concerned about the quality of the products they were making. The second group was termed "large batch and mass production". Employees in these organisations made large quantities of standard products such as computer disks, standard cars and everyday washing machines. The work was heavily mechanised and routinised. The third group of organisations were termed "continuous process". Highly sophisticated machines did most of the work, which continued on a 24-hour basis. Employees had the task of maintaining and checking the machines. This group included brewers, oil refineries and steel makers. Woodward and her colleagues collected a wide range of data about the organisations. They found sys-

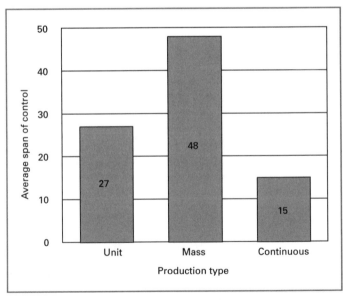

FIGURE 2.6 Span of Control and Type of Production

tematic differences between the types of production. For example they noted systematic differences in managers' spans of control (see Figure 2.6).

The differences in spans of control could be explained readily by the differences in the complexity of information involved. In the continuous process manufacturing work was intricate, of a high level and each worker undertook separate tasks. Hence, managers could only keep track of the activities of a relatively few number of employees. In the mass production most workers were producing similar or identical products. Hence managers could keep track of a relatively high number of employees.

Woodward and other researchers such as Pugh and Hickson (1976) and Burns and Stalker (1961) identified the major contingency factors which managers should take into account. They are:

- **Size**: large organisations tend to have more formal, bureaucratic, hierarchical structures and tighter control systems.

- **Maturity**: young organisations tend to be small, informal and flexible in the sense that people are expected to fulfil a number of overlapping roles. Many young organisations are owned by a single person and hence they tend to be highly centralised.

- **Environmental uncertainty**: organisations operating in an uncertain environment tend to have few rules. They tend to expect staff to use their initiative to solve problems. Communications are usually horizontal rather than vertical.

- **Relationships between subsystems**: if subsystems are largely independent, relationships are governed by standard procedures and a set of rules and regulations. If subsystems are sequential – for example, an assembly line where one department relies upon another for previous and subsequent stages of production – managers rely heavily upon plans, schedules and formal meetings. Specific people will have responsibility for liaising between the subsystems. If subsystems are reciprocal – where the output from subsystem A forms the input to subsystem B, which then returns the product back to subsystem A for further processing – managers use teams, project managers and many unscheduled meetings.

Many of the terms and ideas introduced in this brief history of management are still in use today. For example, most management courses and texts use terms such as "span of control", "open systems" and "stakeholders". The management processes first outlined by Fayol are still considered important – even though the details have been heavily modified and improved. Consequently, the next section of this book is devoted to providing a more up-to-date and detailed description of planning, organising, staffing, deciding, controlling, reporting and budgeting.

Activities and Further Study

Essay Plans

Prepare plans for the following essays:

1 Compare and contrast the contribution of F.W. Taylor (scientific management) with those of Elton Mayo.
2 Explain why the management schools of scientific management, administrative theorists, human relations and contingency theory evolved when they did.
3 Evaluate the extent to which modern managers use scientific management, administrative theory and human relations theory.
4 Outline the main aspect of systems theory and relate the concepts to a specific organisation that you have researched.

Compare your plans with those on the website site associated with this book.

Web Activities

Use the Web to locate:

1 The first example of measuring the time it took workers to perform certain operations
2 The contribution of Eli Whitley to an efficient factory system
3 Who studied the economies achieved from specialisation of labour by studying workers manufacturing pins?
4 Why were civil servants in the USA forbidden to use stop watches (until 1949) after F. W. Taylor was questioned by a special committee of the US House of Representatives (1911–1912)?
5 The company that first used a "production line"
6 To whom the concept of "operational research" is attributed. Where did he work?
7 What is Fielder's "Cognitive Resource Theory". To which school of management does it belong?

Compare your answers with those given on the website associated with this book.

Experiential Activities

1 Draw a timeline stretching from 1800 to the year 2000. Position the following schools of management onto this time-line: contingency theory, operational research, scientific management, human relations and administrative theory.

2 Choose an organisation you know well and identify all the possible stakeholders. Then classify the stakeholders into three types: supply side, demand side and others.

3 Prepare a 14 × 2 matrix. Use the first column to list Fayol's 14 management principles (division of labour, etc.). Then, using a 5-point scale, estimate how relevant they are to present management practices (5 = very relevant, 1 = little relevance).

4 Arrange a debate with other students to discuss the motion "On the whole, observing bureaucratic principles brings benefits to an organisation".

5 Hold a seminar discussion on "the value of studying the history of management".

6 Hold a brainstorming session on "the likely developments in management practice in the next 30 years". In a brainstorming session a small group attempts to generate as many ideas (which may seem zany) as possible. All ideas are written on a flip-chart and no-one is allowed to criticise what others say.

PART II
Management Processes

Part Contents

Planning Processes

03

❖ LEARNING OBJECTIVES

After studying this chapter you should have a clear understanding of the planning process. You should be able to see the topic of "strategy" in its context as a key and early part of a bigger chain of activity. You should also be able to make a balanced judgement on the advantages and pitfalls of planning. In particular you should be able to:

1 **define** planning and **list** the four main stages in the planning process

2 **devise** a mission statement and **itemise** two disadvantages of visions and mission statements

3 **differentiate** strategic plans from tactical and operational plans

4 **explain** the concept of competitive advantage and give **three typical examples** drawn from contemporary organisations

5 **produce** SWOT and PESTEL analyses for an organisation you know well

6 **briefly describe** business strategies concerned with:
- size (7)

- focus (2)
- customers (4)
- adaptation (4)
- other (2)

7 **discuss** the dangers that might arise from the use of strategies

8 **explain** the nature of tactical plans and their place in the planning cycle

9 **draw up** a Gantt chart for a project you are about to undertake

10 **explain** the nature of operational plans and their place in the planning cycle

11 **draw up** an action plan for a project you are about to undertake

12 **critically evaluate** Management by Objectives (MBO)

13 **describe briefly** single-use, standing and contingency plans

14 **explain the reasons** for using PERT charts and **draw** an illustrative example

15 **discuss in detail** the advantages and disadvantages of planning

Classical management theorists (see Chapter 2) identified seven main management processes. The first process is Planning. It can be considered under six main headings:

Chapter contents

3.1 Definition of Planning

A plan is a scheme which specifies the future resources and actions that an organisation needs in order to achieve its goals in an efficient and orderly way. It involves anticipating future requirements and challenges. It also involves sequencing future resources and actions to minimise the delay and waste which could arise if events were allowed to take their natural pace and chronological order.

For example, a student might be set an assignment to produce a report within a week on, say, the impact of computers on marketing. A student who dislikes planning might immediately start work by borrowing a library book on computers and then spend the next two days extracting relevant information. The student may then attempt to borrow a book on marketing only to find that it is on loan and the recall will take two days. After the book becomes available, it takes a day to extract and integrate the relevant information and to word process the assignment. Unfortunately, on the evening before the deadline it is discovered that the printer has run out of ink and paper. By the time ink and paper have been obtained the deadline has passed. By contrast, another student carefully notes the future deadline, anticipates the need for both books and orders them from the library simultaneously. At the same time this student checks the supplies of ink and paper and tops up her stocks in advance. Consequently this student does not waste three days' waiting time. The assignment is submitted on the fourth day and the remainder of the week is spent on leisure activities. This example illustrates the essential features of planning. They are:

- a goal – the desired future states an organisation intends to achieve
- an analysis of resources and stages
- an arrangement of stages to minimise unproductive time and waste

A number of other concepts are related to plans and planning:

- **Policies** – guidelines for decisions and actions. For example, a policy of equal opportunities which will guide the way employees make decisions about selecting, training and remunerating employees. Policies usually require people to interpret what to do in a specific situation.

- **Procedures** – step-by-step sequences of events needed to achieve short-term goals or specific circumstances. Often these are called SOPs (Standard Operating Procedures). Procedures usually involve a sequence of three or more actions.

- **Rules** – specific courses of action which must be followed. They involve little or no interpretation and frequently entail a single action. An example of a rule is, "all accidents must be reported to the Safety Officer".

3.2 Visions and Mission Statements

Many people believe that planning should begin with an *organisational vision*. This is an idealised picture of the future shape of an organisation. It usually reflects the values and aspirations of the organisation's owners, senior managers or governors. Much criticised, but highly readable, research by Peters and Waterman (1988, see section 17.2.3) suggest that a key feature of outstanding companies is that employees share a core ideology or philosophy. Vision statements are usually full of lofty language, superlatives and rhetoric which aim to position an organisation on high moral ground.

Mission statements are usually based upon the organisational vision. They usually specify the goals that form the basis of strategic plans (see section 3.1) Mission statements are marginally more practical than visions. They answer fundamental questions such as:

- What is our business? Mission statements point to the basic position of an organisation within the world of business, public service or other sector.
- What are the key aims and objectives?
- Who are the main stakeholders? Usually this specifies the balance of responsibility to the owners, the employees, the customers and the community.
- What are our values? What is the balance between the value placed on profit and the value placed on contribution to society.
- What technology do we have available?

Mission statements should be succinct, distinctive and have a wide scope. They are statements of good intention. However, they usually contain flowery and grandiose phrases such as:

- deliver ever-appreciating shareholder value via . . .
- being the premier organisation in . . .
- working in partnership with . . . we promote high-quality, cost-effective teaching to meet . . .
- working in harmony with respect for the human spirit . . .

A good mission statement can help motivate employees and gain their commitment. It may also simplify the planning process and organisational decision-making. However, mission statements have been criticised as a managerial fashion of the 1990s. Many mission statements reek of condescension by people who consider themselves "great and good" setting appropriate moral standards for the "lower orders". Boddy (2002a) points out that mission statements can be unrealistic and fail to recognise an organisation's capabilities. Unrealistic mission statements can serve to blind an organisation to commercial realities. Unrealistic mission statements can also induce cynicism in employees.

3.3 Types of Plan

There are many different types of plan: 1) strategic plans, 2) tactical plans and 3) operational plans. These are covered in some detail in this section. Other, more specialised types include standing plans, single use plans and contingency plans.

Strategic plans

What are strategic plans?

Strategic plans specify the major objectives of an organisation. They are derived from the mission statement. Strategic plans may be thought of as an organisation's overall master plan that will shape its destiny. They indicate the direction an organisation needs to take. Indeed, some people call strategic plans "directional plans".

Competitive advantages and strategic thinking

Strategic planners aim to identify the *competitive advantage* an organisation enjoys (see section on Porter in Chapter 18, p. 389–391). A competitive advantage is a medium or long-term factor that works in favour of one organisation or, at least, a restricted number of organisations. Sometimes competitive advantages are called *"core-competences"* or *"critical success factors"* depending upon the consultant giving the seminar! Competitive advantages give an organisation an edge over its rivals. They enable an organisation to transform resources more efficiently than similar organisations. An organisation with a competitive advantage may be able to achieve superiority, if not supremacy, so that they are copied by others. Competitive advantages are usually facets which are costly and time-consuming for others to develop so that the "entry price is high". Typical competitive advantages are *cost leadership, brand recognition, technological superiority* and *uniqueness*. Examples of cost leadership would be the John Lewis Partnership "who are never knowingly undersold" and the DIY chain B&Q who refund 110 per cent of the difference if a local supplier sells the same item at a lower price. Marks & Spencer once had a competitive advantage in the quality of their clothes. IBM also had a competitive advantage in the field of mainframe computers but this advantage evaporated when personal computers became common.

The last two examples illustrate that competitive advantages are not permanent. Companies may seek to sustain a competitive advantage by using patents, trademarks and copyrights. However, the most effective methods of maintaining a competitive advantage are probably improvements and innovations to produce "layers of technological advantage", economies of scale and "strategic alliances" with suppliers which deny raw materials to competitors. All of these approaches seek to make the entry price for competitors daunting. Action to thwart threats to a competitive advantage needs a system of *competitive intelligence* that scans the business environment for information about the activities of competitors. The vast majority of competitive intelligence is available from public sources. The expansion of the Internet means that information on new competitor activities is available much more quickly!

Methods of producing strategic plans

Strategists use several methods to identify an organisation's competitive advantage. Probably the best known is a **SWOT analysis** which covers four main features:

Features internal to the organisation:

1 **Strengths** include closeness to customers, management expertise and other skills, financial strength, branch network, market position and brand image.

2 **Weaknesses** are often the opposite of the strengths. They may include poor reputation, out-of-date equipment, inadequate R&D, difficult markets, poor industrial relations and poor communications.

Features in the external environment:

3 **Opportunities** can arise from either strengths or weaknesses. Often they occur from a change in technology, legislation or markets where there is a gap.

4 **Threats** usually arise from competition – especially new entrants in the market and substitution products, shortage of resources (including skilled labour) and new government regulations.

Another way of identifying an appropriate strategy for an organisation is to conduct a PESTEL analysis. It examines six main factors:

1 **Political factors** such as government stability, privatisation/nationalisation plans, government regulation and control, or health and environmental issues.

2 **Economic factors** such as phases of the business cycle, economic growth, interest rates, inflation, labour costs and unemployment rates.

3 **Socio-cultural factors** include population trends, educational levels, lifestyles and changes in consumer tastes and values.

4 **Technological factors** include new discoveries, new production methods, better communications, speed of technology transfer.

5 **Environmental factors** such as discovery of new supplies of energy or raw materials, shortages of water, etc., climate change.

6 **Legal factors** include changes in the law concerning employment, companies or business regulation.

The aim of any strategy is to guide the organisation to areas where the organisation will find it easiest to achieve its objectives. Often this means directing the organisation towards promising markets. Consequently marketeers have devised additional methods of identifying strategies. More details of the BCG matrix, the GE matrix and the Anscoff matrix are given in the chapter on Marketing (pp. 221–223). These pages should be read as a part of the present chapter. Further, Michael Porter, a guru among strategists, has identified ways of achieving a competitive advantage – as well as five sources of competition which a good strategic plan needs to take into account. Porter has also examined the ways countries can devise strategies to establish national competitive advantages. Porter's important contributions to strategic planning are explained in more detail on pp. 389–390.

Alternative strategies

Once an organisation has analysed its position and its competitive advantages, it must decide upon the appropriate way to accomplish its mission. Many different kinds of strategy are available and have been identified by writers such as Miles and Snow (1978), Mintzberg (1987) and Porter (1996, 2001). Some of the main business strategies are:

Strategies concerned with *size*:

- **Globalisation**: expanding into other countries.
- **Industry dominance**: capturing such a large part of a market that there is little room for competitors.
- **Growth**: to obtain economies of scale and market dominance. Growth can be:
  - organic (natural) growth of present business
  - acquisition (takeover) of other organisations
  - merger with other organisations.
- **Retrenchment** is a defensive strategy aimed at increasing efficiency. It takes several forms including:
  - downsizing – usually by removing middle managers and support staff
  - selling parts of the organisation to refocus on core competences
  - liquidation: closing parts of an organisation to eliminate debt (bankruptcy) or to realise assets (asset stripping).

Strategies concerning *focus*:

- **Core competences**: restricting activities to those the organisation does best. Often this means selling minor parts of the organisation.
- **Geographical focus**: restricting activities to a well-defined area so that regional dominance is achieved.

Strategies concerning *customers*:

- **Product differentiation**: making a product appear different to others.
- **Cost leadership**: offering a product or service cheaper than competitors – by increased efficiency or "squeezing" suppliers.
- **Imitation**: following the ideas of a market leader and not incurring risk or development costs.
- **High speed**: delivering services to customers more quickly than competitors.

Strategies concerning *adaptation*:

- **Prospectors** innovate and follow new opportunities. They bear a risk in return for prospects of substantial growth.
- **Defenders** attempt to hold a position in a declining market by emphasising existing products. This strategy usually ends in terminal decline.
- **Analysers** "follow the leader when things are good". These organisations usually maintain the stability of their key products while expanding a few promising areas pioneered by others. Analysers will also follow the imitation strategy and make goods that are clones of the market leaders' products.
- **Reactors** only respond to competitive pressures when there is a danger to their survival. Often reactor organisations do not have any other strategy and only change as a last resort.

Other strategies

- **Employee talent** involves finding and retaining able people.
- **Strategic alliances** involve collaborating with other organisations – especially in marketing and sales where the same infrastructure can be used to sell non-competing products from different companies.

These strategies are not mutually exclusive. Many organisations, especially large ones, will use a combination of strategies. For example, they may retrench older and less profitable parts of the organisation while expanding more profitable ones.

Criticisms of strategic planning

Some people are sceptical of the need for strategic planning. They suggest that it is only useful with hindsight. They claim that its advocates ignore strategic plans that have gone wrong. For example, one of the biggest business failures in recent decades has been the fall of the Marconi Company. For half a century Marconi had prospered and grown under the name of General Electric Company and its pragmatic chief executive Arnold Weinstock. Under a new chief executive the company was renamed and followed a vigorous strategy of acquisition and expansion into telecommunications using the "cash pile" accumulated by Weinstock. Within a couple of years the strategy had led the company into a serious decline and its shares became almost worthless.

Some people claim that strategies are dangerous things. The development of strategies consumes large quantities of management time and effort that would be better spent elsewhere. Furthermore, strategies can produce a rigidity. The effort expended on developing strategies generates a heavy psychological commitment to them. People feel foolish if they are forced to abandon activities which have cost them dear. Consequently, there is a psychological tendency to hide information which runs counter to the strategy. Instead of reacting to the environment in an intelligent way, strategists are likely to argue that their plans will work if only the organisation will provide more resources. In the face of continued failure they are likely to claim that the strategy is correct and the difficulties are only short-term aberrations. When it becomes clear that the aberration is not short term they are likely to argue that the strategy is fine but it was implemented in the wrong way. When the

CASE 3.1: THE MARCONI FIASCO – A STRATEGY THAT WENT WRONG

Under the Chairmanship of Arnold Weinstock the General Electric Company (GEC) was the jewel in the crown of British industry: boring, risk averse but making oodles of money out of such things as defence contracts. It had a cash pile of more than £2 billion – a huge sum in 1999. Lord Arnold Weinstock retired and was succeeded by George Simpson, who was keen on grand strategies. He saw GEC's future in terms of the high-tech communications market. His intention was to exploit the use of micro mirrors as optical switches to bounce signals around the Internet and become a serious rival to the likes of Cisco – the American computer colossus.

The bold strategic plan had everything – selling off the old defence businesses – rebranding with the new name Marconi – relocation of the communication business's headquarters to Pennsylvania in order to be nearer the world's largest communications market. The plan was implemented with gusto. Hi-tech communication companies were bought as if they were going out of fashion: Reltec & Fore, RDC, MSI, etc.

Simpson was so dazzled by the strategic plan, he failed to notice that communications companies *were* actually going out of fashion! The dotcom bubble burst. Worse, telephone companies such as BT were strapped for cash after bidding for hugely expensive, third-generation mobile phone licences and were cutting back on equipment purchases. Other companies such as Nortel and Ericsson were not blinded by their strategic plan. They saw the downturn and reacted appropriately. Simpson did not. The Marconi spree continued. Inevitably, the share price crashed. The company had a debt *pile* of £2.5 billion and many underperforming assets. A former GEC executive commented "as destructions of shareholder values go, I cannot think of another case that even approaches this". Simpson was replaced. Thousands of innocent workers lost their jobs and wished ruefully for the boring old days before the "innovative", "exciting", "far-seeing" strategic plan.

bankruptcy of a strategy is undeniable, strategic planners are likely to devote their efforts to producing a new plan based upon a new set of management theories.

Mintzberg (1994) suggests that strategic planners make a number of fallacious assumptions:

1 They assume that an organisation can, with sufficient skill, *predetermine the future*. In fact, the business environment is so dynamic and interactive that the future cannot be estimated or predicted. Hence it is likely that a strategic plan will, at some stage, be blown off course. Strategic plans reached their zenith in days of greater stability. They are less useful in today's turbulent environment.

2 They assume that *planners take an objective view*, detached from current political intrigues and beliefs of the organisation. In fact, strategists are as immersed in subjectivity and political intrigues as anyone else. Their strategies are not as objective as they imply.

3 They assume a formal approach involving ticking boxes on checklists in the belief that *standard procedures will produce the best plans*. In fact, a good strategy requires flair,

imagination, insight and creativity, which tend to be stifled by a formal approach. It is necessary to think "outside the box".

Mintzberg acknowledges that organisations may have deliberate, *intended strategies* but these will be buffeted and blown about by forces that subsequently emerge in the environment. The *realised strategy*, the events that actually happen, may be quite different. Perhaps the most sensible approach is an *incremental strategy*. An incremental strategy occurs when an organisation takes sensible, case-by-case decisions that gradually merge to form a strategy. An incremental strategy emerges via unstructured, unpredictable, organic processes rather than a series of clinical steps. This organic approach often produces the strategy that is more appropriate to the environment.

Kay (1996) suggests that strategic planning has a formal impossibility. If good strategic planning can be reduced to a set of procedures and checklists, most organisations would be able to produce a good strategy. If all organisations have good strategies then there is little or no competitive advantage in having one!

Tactical plans

Tactical plans are also called functional plans or intermediate plans. They translate a firm's strategic plan into specific goals for organisational sub-units. For example, a strategic plan may call for a 10 per cent increase in the market share. This needs to be supported by detailed tactical plans for each of the sales, production and finance departments. Tactical plans are usually concerned with *how* things are done whereas strategic plans are usually concerned with *what* is done.

Tactical plans need to be co-ordinated with each other and with the strategic plan for the organisation as a whole. They usually have a timescale of one to five years. This contrasts with strategic plans and visions which generally have a timescale of ten years or more. Strategic plans primarily involve top managers, whereas tactical plans primarily involve middle managers.

One of the main tools of tactical planning is the Gantt Chart. These are particularly useful because they show how related operational plans are progressing. An idealised Gantt chart associated with a marketing department's tactical plan to increase sales by 10 per cent is given in Figure 3.1.

This example is highly simplified but it demonstrates the main features of a Gantt Chart. A complete Gantt Chart would include holidays and other activities. It would also show progress to date and other events. Often each of the main programs shown on a Gantt chart would also be accompanied by a more detailed action plan.

Much less research and thought has been devoted to tactical plans than to strategic ones. The reasons are open to speculation. Perhaps it is because academics, writers and researchers find the heady world of high-level strategy much more exciting.

Operational plans

Definition of operational plans

Operational plans are sometimes called action plans or production plans. They constitute the most detailed level of planning. They specify the actions or results which individuals or small

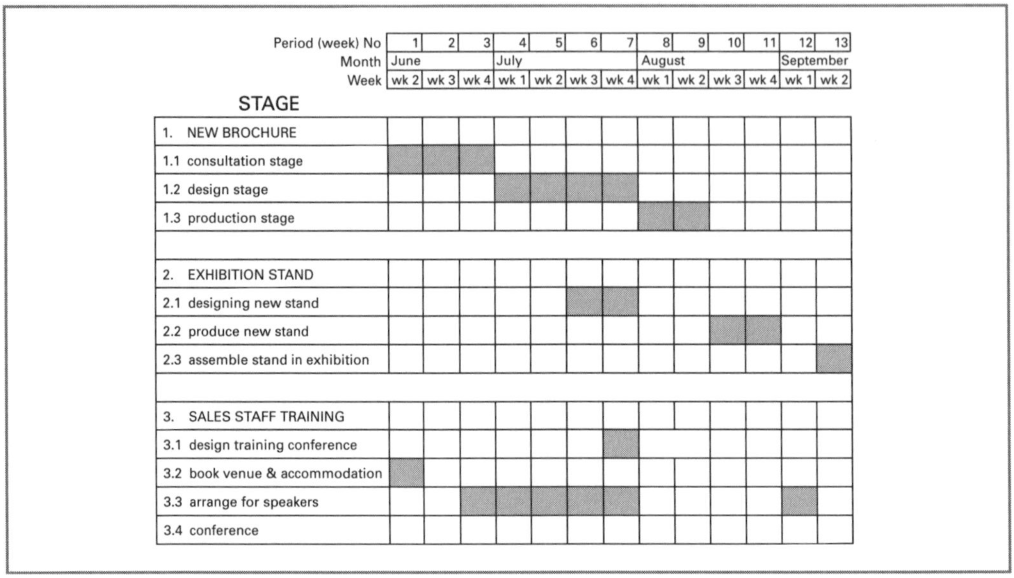

STAGE	1	2	3	4	5	6	7	8	9	10	11	12	13
Month	June			July				August				September	
Week	wk 2	wk 3	wk 4	wk 1	wk 2	wk 3	wk 4	wk 1	wk 2	wk 3	wk 4	wk 1	wk 2
1. NEW BROCHURE													
1.1 consultation stage	▓	▓	▓										
1.2 design stage				▓	▓	▓							
1.3 production stage								▓					
2. EXHIBITION STAND													
2.1 designing new stand						▓							
2.2 produce new stand										▓			
2.3 assemble stand in exhibition													▓
3. SALES STAFF TRAINING													
3.1 design training conference							▓						
3.2 book venue & accommodation	▓												
3.3 arrange for speakers				▓			▓					▓	
3.4 conference													

FIGURE 3.1 An Example of a Gantt Chart

groups must achieve. Operational plans are usually very specific. For example, they may specify that a production line should produce 150 objects per week, a sales representative should obtain orders worth £100 000 per month or that a consultant should recruit two new clients every quarter. Operational plans should be linked to tactical plans, each of which may depend upon the successful completion of several operational plans. Operational plans are short term. They generally have a time span of several months but they can involve time intervals that are as short as a week or less. Operational plans usually involve first-line managers and often incorporate suggestions and input from employees at lower levels.

Good operational plans are essential to the efficient functioning of an organisation. They affect all employees on a day-to-day basis. They state the results which must be achieved so that tactical and strategic plans come to fruition. The clear, unambiguous communication of operational plans is essential. While strategic plans and tactical plans are not altered over long periods, operational plans constantly change – even though much of this change is cyclical. Operational plans usually incorporate rules and standard operating procedures (SOPs). These procedures are often contained in an Operations Handbook.

Action plans

The prime tool for operations planning is the action plan. These are produced by dividing a larger goal into small discreet stages. These are placed in the optimum sequence and completion dates are estimated. Sometimes, action plans allocate responsibility for the completion of the stages. Table 3.1 gives a simplified example of an action plan, starting on 1st June, for producing a new brochure. This was one of the three projects included in the Gantt chart in the previous section. A comparison between the Gantt chart and the Action plan will show that the latter is more detailed and specifies the results that must be achieved by individuals.

Action Plan for New Brochure			
Stage		**Completion Date**	**By**
1	Review present brochure	1 June	MA
2	Discuss needs and ideas with sales force and small number of customers	21 June	MA & MD
3	Discuss needs and ideas with Marketing Director	28 June	MA & MD
4	Produce specifications for new brochure and submit to Marketing Director for approval	7 July	MA & MD
5	Produce draft brochure	21 July	CW
6	Discuss draft brochure with Marketing Director, sales force and small number of customers	28 July	MA & MD
7	Dispatch revised draft to printers	1 Aug	MA
8	Correct proofs	14 Aug	MA
9	Receive copies of new brochure from printer	21 Aug	MA

TABLE 3.1 Example of Action Plan

MA = marketing assistant   MD = marketing director   CW = copywriter

Management by Objectives

Description and examples of MBO

Management by Objectives starts with the goals of a worker's boss. Often these are called "key results". The boss's key results are examined and the ways that a worker should contribute to them is identified. These are developed into key results for the worker. If he or she has subordinates, the worker's key results are examined to identify the subordinate's key results and so on. MBO is therefore a top-down system that ensures clear areas of responsibility where everyone is linked, directly or indirectly, with organisational goals.

For example, an organisation's tactical plan may give a production manager a key result of making 100 machines per month. If there are four production lines, the production manager will discuss this requirement with each of the four first-line managers. Taking other factors such as the quality of the equipment and the availability of operatives into account, the production manager and first-line managers will agree individual targets. For example, the four first-line managers may agree to produce 30, 30, 25 and 15 machines, respectively. The first-line managers with the higher targets may have agreed an above-average contribution because they are in charge of the production line with the most up-to-date equipment and the most experienced staff. The first-line manager with the lowest target may be the one who manages a production line staffed by trainees and where much machine maintenance is needed. However, as a group the four first-line managers will produce the 100 units of machinery the production manager needs to achieve his or her key result.

CASE 3.2: PLANNING AT BOURNE SALADS

Bourne Salads is a subsidiary of the multinational food giant Geest. It is based in Lincolnshire and employs about 500 people to pack salads and vegetables. The company receives raw materials every day. These are washed prepared, inspected and packed and then dispatched. Each day it sends about 2 million bags (70 lorry-loads) of lettuce and other leaf products to top-of-the-range customers such as Safeway, Tesco and Whitbread.

Although this sounds simple, planning such a large operation is very difficult. The main challenges arise from the fact that the materials to be transformed (leaf salads) are very perishable and large stocks cannot be held. Second, demand is very variable and changes drastically on a day-to-day basis according to the weather. Supermarkets send their orders one day and expect them to be executed the next. Third, the product is more complex than it appears on the surface – different customers require different mixes of salads and the raw materials need to be ordered from as many as 30 different suppliers. All this needs to be done at very short notice.

Before 1998, planning was conducted on a manual basis. Plans were drawn up on a piece of paper using standard calculations to determine the amount of raw materials, boxes and trays needed to fulfil an order. These were then transferred onto Gantt charts and sent to production departments.

Today there is a team of planners. They use sophisticated software. Each week the system estimates the material and packaging requirements using a MRP (Material Requirements Planning) program. Another part of the program produces daily schedules that make sure equipment is fully utilised. Works orders are automatically sent to individual production lines. There are feedback mechanisms that can quickly amend and produce new plans. For example if materials are received at 2.00 a.m. and rejected by quality control at 3.00 a.m. new supplies can be ordered immediately and a new production plan can be in place soon after that. The planning system can also incorporate extra activities such as routine maintenance and hygiene requirements. Perhaps the most sophisticated aspect of the planning system is to use "what if" scenarios to identify potential bottlenecks or times when equipment may be under-utilised.

When the key results have been agreed the production manager and each first-line manager consider the methods by which they can be achieved. Each first-line manager will then have similar meetings with his or her supervisors. The supervisors will then have equivalent meetings with operatives.

At the end of the month each manager and subordinate meet to discuss performance. Any shortfall is examined and the reason identified. The shortfall may not be the fault of the subordinate. It could be that the initial target was too ambitious – in which case it will be reduced. It could be the shortfall was caused by an unreliable supplier – in which case the purchasing department would be asked to improve the supply chain. It could be that the subordinate did not have the experience to deal with a problem – in which case training would be arranged. Finally, it could be that the manager omitted to communicate a key piece of information – in which case the manager would seek to improve his or her communication skills.

Key features of MBO

This example demonstrates five major features of Management by Objectives:

1 **Every person's objectives are linked to those of their superior**. *Ultimately, each person's key results are linked to the organisation's strategic plan.* Each person can see the importance of their contribution to the organisation as a whole.

2 **Goals are specific**. There are concise statements of the key results. Usually there is a definite time period and a specific number of outputs. In theory, it is possible to determine objectively whether or not goals are met. In practice, especially in jobs involving a service to others, this may be difficult.

3 **Key results are not unilaterally imposed**. They should be discussed and mutually agreed in a participative way. They should take into account particular skills and the particular working environment. Advocates of MBO maintain that the emphasis on participative goal setting is a major advantage. It is claimed that this increases the organisational commitment.

4 Once the key results have been agreed, a manager and subordinate *co-operate to produce an action plan* which leads to the attainment of the key results.

5 **Performance is reviewed on a regular basis**. It is best if the review period is long enough to minimise very short-term fluctuations. But the review period should not be so long that matters can get out of control or require a mammoth session. Typically, a review period should be between three and six months. Performance reviews should be a genuine, mutual discussion. It should give subordinates genuine feedback and it should not be assumed that any shortfall is the fault of the subordinate. It should take the form of a mutual problem-solving session.

Research results and MBO

MBO is consistent with research by occupational psychologists such as Locke, Shaw, Saari and Latham (1981) which shows people perform better when they are given specific goals that are moderately, but not excessively, challenging. However, many people are unenthusiastic about the effectiveness of Management by Objectives. The research results concerning participation in decision-making are less positive. It would seem that the level of the difficulty of the goals is much more important than the way the goals are set (Latham and Saari, 1979). In general, however, research indicates that MBO is highly effective and is likely to produce productivity gains in over 90 per cent of cases (Rogers and Hunter, 1991). Rogers and Hunter's study also emphasised the importance of top-management commitment. When their commitment to MBO was high the average productivity gain (56 per cent) was higher than the productivity gain when top-management commitment was low (6 per cent).

Disadvantages of MBO

Unfortunately MBO has at least five disadvantages:

1 MBO may distort an organisation by focusing upon the obvious, objective, but not necessarily more important, results that can be easily quantified. When MBO is

introduced the performance of individuals on the narrow range of key performance indicators increases in the way indicated by Rogers and Hunter. However, the gains may be at the expense of equally important, less measurable, general activities such as setting a good example, being courteous and contributing to the common good. Often, these activities are called "corporate citizenship". A major criticism of MBO is that it decreases corporate citizenship. In a nutshell, when MBO is installed, the specific short-term goals set for individuals can become much more important than the wider organisational goals. MBO focuses upon quantitative results such as the number of machines produced or the number of research papers written. These aspects are easy to measure by counting. The quality of production is much more difficult and subjective. When MBO is introduced workers may increase quantity at the expense of quality.

2 Implementation and operation of MBO absorbs a great deal of managerial effort. Sometimes MBO produces excessive paperwork and managers may spend more time devising criteria, drawing up action plans and preparing for appraisal meetings than actually managing their subordinates.

3 In the longer-term, MBO encourages managers to set lower goals. Initially, participative goal setting may produce positive results, but once managers realise that successive cycles of MBO will result in ever increasing targets, they become wise and manoeuvre to set themselves goals that can be achieved more easily.

4 MBO might work in countries such as the UK, USA, Netherlands and Australia where there is a high work ethic and where people are accustomed to working towards goals in an independent way. However, there is doubt whether it works in other cultures that have different values (Hofstede, 1980).

5 Finally, MBO does not work well in situations where rapid change is the norm. Management by Objectives was developed in the 1950s when the business environment and technology changed less quickly. In those days organisations and their managers had time to prepare documentation, devise targets and review performance. Nowadays a dramatic, overnight change can make such plans obsolete.

3.4 Miscellaneous plans and planning techniques

Sometimes it is useful to distinguish between *single-use plans* and *standing plans*. Single-use plans are devised to meet unique situations and are never used again. For example, a pharmaceutical company setting up a new production plant will have elaborate plans covering the construction of buildings, the cash flow and the recruitment of employees. These plans will never be used a second time. Even if another production plant is commissioned, the circumstances will have changed so much that the original plans will be useless. *Standing plans* are used when a task recurs. For example, the pharmaceutical company may make a range of medicines, manufacturing a stock of each medicine on a cyclical basis. Thus, for example, it will have a standing plan for the manufacture of an anti-cancer medicine, a standing plan for the manufacture of a medicine to combat high blood pressure and a standing plan to manufacture a medicine to reduce inflammation of joints. Standing plans have the advantage of ensuring consistent standards and methods.

Because the business environment changes rapidly it is difficult to plan for the future with certainty. Hence, many organisations develop parallel plans to cover likely eventualities. Two or more parallel plans which are in place and activated if certain conditions arise are called *contingency plans*. A company that is extending its production facility may have two contingency plans: one will come into operation if the new plant is ready on time, while the other will be used if there is a significant delay. Similarly, a company bidding to take over another will have two plans: one will be used if the takeover bid is successful and the other will be used if its bid fails. Contingency plans enable organisations to respond to events in a flexible way.

Previous sections have described the two most popular planning techniques, Gantt Charts and Action Plans. However, these simple methods may not be adequate for complicated projects where there are many inter-related activities. *PERT charts* are often used in these circumstances. PERT is an acronym of Program Evaluation and Review Technique. A PERT chart is a flow chart that shows the sequences, durations and timings of events needed to achieve an objective. In some senses, PERT charts can be thought of as complicated versions of Gantt charts. They are usually so much more complicated that a computer program is needed for their construction.

PERT charts consist of activities which have a start, a duration and a completion point. Usually completion points are called "milestones". The start point of an activity is usually governed by the completion of a previous activity. Events which govern the start of an activity are usually called "dependencies". The preparation of a lecture provides a simple example of the process of structuring a PERT chart. The activities are shown in Table 3.2.

A computer can compile the information into a PERT chart such as the one shown in Figure 3.2

A key feature of a PERT chart is the "critical path" which indicates the shortest time in

Activity	Duration	Dependency
A. Check syllabus	½ day	None
B. Order & collect library books	½ day	Activity A
C. Locate own books	½ day	Activity A
D. Read and note relevant material	3 days	Activity B,C
E. Write lecture notes	3 days	Activity D
F. Prepare visual aids	1 day	Activity E
G. Prepare handouts	2 days	Activity E
H. Duplicate handouts	½ day	Activity F
I. Assemble all materials	¼ day	Activities E,F,H
J. Deliver lecture	1 hr	Activity J

TABLE 3.2 Data for a PERT Chart

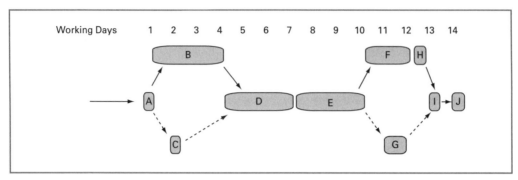

FIGURE 3.2 An Example of a Simple PERT Chart

which the project can be completed. The critical path is usually emphasised by thicker lines or use of colour. Activities along the critical path must be completed to time. If they are not, the project will not finish on time. The timing of activities that are not on the critical path is less crucial. Some delay can be tolerated. The tolerable level of delay is called "the float". In our example, the timing of locating own books is not crucial. It can be performed any time before the library books are obtained. In fact there is a float of 2½ days.

3.5 Advantages and Disadvantages of Planning

Most people agree that the advantages of planning far outweigh the disadvantages. Plans are good because they:

- **Give direction and focus** to organisational activities – provided the plans are well communicated to those who need to know. Without plans people will make decisions in isolation from the actions of others and the goals that need to be achieved. Consequently, plans help people cope with ambiguous situations in a way that increases the co-ordination with the efforts of other people and helps achieve organisational goals.
- **Indicate the standard of performance** that is required.
- **Improve the speed of decision-making**. Instead of referring matters to higher authority and waiting for their reply a manager can consult a plan and make a quicker decision. Plans allow lower levels of staff to participate in making decisions.
- **Give context** and an explanation of many decisions which are handed down from senior management.
- **Minimise waste and redundancy** by foreseeing future difficulties and therefore taking any action to circumvent them.
- **Focus attention on the future** and the way an organisation must marshal its resources to meet the challenges it will face. Without ambitious plans people may be content to "rest on their laurels".

Despite these advantages, plans do not always turn out for the best. They have a number of disadvantages which include:

- **Inducing rigidity**. Plans usually involve a great deal of effort by prestigious members of an organisation. They may become emotionally attached to the plan even if it is based on assumptions that may be out of touch with reality. Further, events may change and render a plan obsolete. Its prestigious author may be reluctant to face reality and abandon a cherished plan. Plans may therefore act as blinkers inhibiting creativity, innovation and adaptation. Like old generals, planners often fight a previous campaign rather than coping with the present commercial battle.

- **The effort needed to develop plans consumes a great deal of management time** which could be spent more profitably by making contacts or communicating to and motivating employees.

The inevitable conclusion is that managers must use plans to their full advantage. Nevertheless, they should beware of devoting too much time perfecting plans to the nth degree and they should abandon plans when there is clear evidence that they are inadequate or if the environment has changed. Plans are excellent servants. They are very dangerous masters!

3.6 Planning Toolkit

- Most of the disadvantages of planning are connected to the inflexibility plans may engender. Hence planners should make a major effort to ensure that plans exist within a flexible environment which values learning and continuous improvement.

- The goals contained in plans are important. Goals should be ambitious but not unreasonable. The goals will be more practical and easier to understand if the people required to implement the plans are involved in setting the goals. Generally speaking, plans should be constructed "bottom-up" rather than "top-down".

- Time-scales implicit in plans should be realistic. They should take into account:
  - illnesses and holidays
  - time for staff training
  - daily, seasonal and other variations in workload
  - the rotation of staff into different jobs so that versatility and motivation are enhanced.

- the role of a planning specialist should not be that of an aloof expert operating in a distant planning department. Rather, the role should be that of a facilitator who assists a group in formulating workable plans, helping to gather data, conduct statistical analysis and do other specialised tasks.

The importance of planning was identified very early in the history of management. However, plans must be communicated to other people and there must be an organisational structure that is capable of executing the plans. The next chapters describe other important management processes such as organising, staffing and communicating.

Activities and Further Study

Essay Plans

Prepare plans for the following essays:

1 Compare and contrast three methods of producing strategies for organisations.
2 Select a local organisation (perhaps your college or university department, perhaps a charitable organisation or club that you know well) and conduct both a SWOT analysis and a PESTLE analysis.
3 Compare and contrast strategic plans, tactical plans and operational plans.
4 Evaluate the benefits and disadvantages of planning.

Web Activities

1 Log onto the website associated with this textbook and access "Web Based Exercise 2: Planning Techniques". Follow the instructions and produce an action plan and a Gantt chart. When you have finished compare your work with the model answer which is also given on the website.

2 Search the Internet for mission statements – perhaps the mission statement of your employer, university or college. To what extent do you think people in the organisation find a mission statement useful in achieving organisational goals? Ask six members of the organisation whether they are aware the mission statement exists. Ask those who are aware of its existence what the mission statement contains.

3 Search the Internet for more information about the Marconi case study (hint: wikipedia.org and news.bbc.co.uk are good places to start).

Experiential Activities

1 Imagine that you are a member of a consultancy group that helps other organisations install Management by Objectives. You have received an enquiry from a small organisation that employs 100 people and has 12 managers. They invite you to give a 20-minute presentation to explain MBO. Prepare this presentation and deliver it to a group of fellow students.

2 Make a list of the six most important goals you wish to achieve in the next year. Examine these goals critically for their technical merit as objectives:

- Are they clear?
- Are they quantifiable?
- Are they realistic, etc?

(hint: it may be useful to visit websites such as ***www.smc.qld.edu.au/goals.htm*** or ***www.goal-setting-guide.com/smart-goals.html.***)

3 Visit the Preactor Website (***http://www.preactor.com/online-demo/data/english/ standard%20demo/online-demo.html***) to gain an impression of the complexity of operational planning. After a wooden introduction the demonstration shows how complex Gantt charts are set up to control production.

04

Organising Processes

❖ *LEARNING OBJECTIVES*

After studying this chapter you should be able to suggest ways of structuring jobs and organising them into an efficient system. You should also be able to suggest techniques for changing existing organisations so that their structures are aligned to contemporary needs. In particular, you should be able to:

1 **define** the organising process and **differentiate** between formal organisational structures and informal ones

2 **explain** how you would design a job using the concepts of:
   – division of labour
   – authority and responsibility
   – span of control
   – ergonomics

3 **describe** the following ways of scheduling work
   – flexitime
   – compressed working week
   – home-working and tele-working

   – job sharing
   – contingency working
   – office sharing and hoteling

4 **briefly explain** the concept of functional organisational structures and differentiate between tall and flat structures

5 **briefly explain** the concept of divisional structures and **itemise** the three main ways of creating divisions

6 **draw a diagram** of a matrix organisational structure

7 **describe** team structures

8 **draw a diagram of** network organisational structures

9 **explain** the concepts of learning structures and itemise their five main characteristics

10 **differentiate** between the concepts of:
   – data, information and knowledge
   – explicit and tacit knowledge

- data warehousing and data mining
- knowledge portals

11 **draw up a substantive table** that systematises the advantages of functional, divisional, matrix and team structures

12 **itemise** four ways of co-ordinating the activities of groups or sections within an organisation

13 **itemise** five main dimensions of organisational structure

14 **explain** the need for organisational change and **explain in-depth** the factors that help and resist change

15 **describe in detail** the methods you could use to bring about organisational change

In a one-person set-up there is no need for organisation: the one person does everything. As soon as more people are involved the process of organising becomes essential – otherwise people will complete tasks at random using whatever resources are at hand and in ignorance of what others are doing. Chaos will ensue. While *planning* determines what tasks need to be done in what sequence, *organising* is concerned with determining who completes the tasks and what resources are required. Usually, planning and organising are inter-related.

For example, many action plans involve a certain amount of organising. The topic of organising can be divided into five main sections:

Chapter contents

4.1 Definition of Organising and Organisational Structures

Many definitions do not make the distinction between planning and organising sufficiently clear. One of the clearest definitions is:

> 66 Organising is the process of determining who will perform the tasks needed to achieve organisational objectives, the resources to be used and the way the tasks will be managed and co-ordinated. 99

Four points from this definition need to be noted. Organising:

- **Is not primarily concerned with specifying goals and tasks**. However, the way in which

CASE 4.1: ORGANISATIONAL RESTRUCTURING AT PILKINGTONS IN AUSTRALIA

Pilkington is a world-renowned maker of glass and is now owned by Nippon Sheet Glass. One of its manufacturing plants is in Dandenong, Australia.

The factory had a very traditional organisational structure with workers at the bottom and senior managers at the top (see Figure 4.2 below). The normal flow of information was from the top downwards. Top management set standards and objectives which were then communicated down the hierarchy. The organisational structure resulted in many employees feeling they were given orders by managers who had little knowledge of things that were happening on the "factory floor". The hierarchical structure was largely responsible for strong divisions between "them and us". Labour relations were poor and at the time the plant was shut down by strike action. Furthermore, the plant was losing its competitiveness against other glass makers.

Pilkington decided to implement major changes in the way that work at Dandenong was organised. Work was organised into three business units: glass making, glass cutting and glass warehousing. Within these divisions employees were structured into work teams which participated in setting standards and working methods. The main information flow was reversed and passed from employees to team leaders to team supervisors and upwards to the plant manager.

An evaluation showed that the changes in organisational structure had resulted in higher morale, greater industrial harmony, higher customer satisfaction and increased employee productivity.

Based on: B. Barrett, C. Cook and M. Williams Pilkington, *An organisation in transition*, (***http://www.thomsonlearning.com.au/higher/management/waddell/2e/media/CaseE_Pilkington.pdf***)

things are organised will have a bearing on the tasks which can be attempted and the degree to which they are achieved.

- **Is fundamentally concerned with the allocation of the tasks** to specific people or groups of people.
- **Is concerned with the coordination of the efforts** of several people needed to complete large tasks.
- **Concerns resources and other people**. It may involve budgets, territories, production facilities or intellectual abilities.

An *Organisation Chart* is a representation of an organisation's formal structure – the official arrangement of work positions within an organisation. The distinction between the *formal* organisation and the *informal* organisation is important. When they are set up, the formal and informal structures may be very similar. In practice the formal structure is soon modified by friendships, the personalities of individuals and the networks which develop. The "grapevine" is an important component of an informal organisation. The informal organisation often allows people to use shortcuts and obtain information and take action which would otherwise be impossible. It is particularly important during times of change and stress. The informal organisation often meets the psychological needs of individuals. However, informal organisations do have disadvantages. They may take on a life of their own and work towards goals which are different from the formal goals. Information "on the grapevine" may be inaccurate or distorted. The informal organisation can be used to exclude certain people and their ideas.

4.2 Job Design

The most fundamental aspect of organising is to decide what people are required to do as part of their job. This process is called *job design*. Five main factors need to be considered: the level of specialisation; authority; span of control; ergonomics; and work schedules.

Specialisation and division of labour

Job design assumes that some workers will specialise in certain activities while other workers will specialise in different ones. *Specialisation* means that each worker only does a part of what is needed. It is sometimes called *division of labour*. Up to a point it leads to greater efficiency and economies of scale because:

- Individuals can quickly develop a high level of skills in certain activities.
- People can be directed to those activities where they have most ability and hence their potential can be exploited more fully.
- Employees do not waste time changing from task to task.
- Jobs are often simplified and can be allocated, at less cost, to workers with lower skills.

Extreme specialisation is seen in some assembly lines where employees are required to do a single task, repetitively but with a high level of speed and efficiency. Unfortunately, high levels of specialisation have disadvantages:

- Highly specialised jobs are boring and tend to de-motivate people. Employees rarely see a finished product so they tend not to have a sense of pride in their work.
- Teamwork and creativity are inhibited.
- Employees will only have a restricted range of skills. They cannot be redeployed to deal with bottlenecks elsewhere. Further, these employees are vulnerable to changes. When changes occur these employees are likely to be dismissed or need retraining.

In general job design seeks to achieve a balance between the advantages and disadvantages of specialisation. Figure 4.1 indicates that optimum productivity is achieved at intermediate levels of specialisation.

A major aim is to design jobs that avoid the negative effects of specialisation by including factors which motivate workers. Research (Hackman and Oldham, 1980) suggests that people will be motivated if a job:

- Requires the use of many, different skills rather than the repetitive use of one or two skills (*skill variety*).

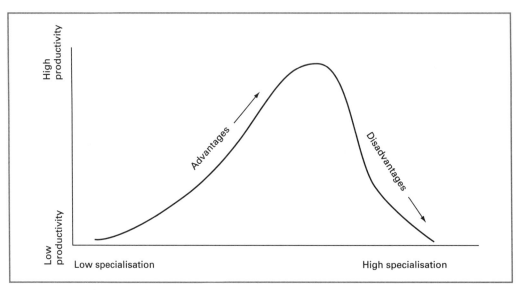

FIGURE 4.1 Specialisation and Productivity

- Allows a person to do a complete job rather than a small part of a job. The worker is then more likely to be motivated by a sense of pride (*task identity*).
- Allows a person to understand the contribution that their work makes to the goals of the organisation or its importance to colleagues or customers (*task significance*).
- Gives freedom, discretion and independence in the way that the work has to be done – providing that the correct results are achieved (*autonomy*).
- *Provides feedback* on a worker's effectiveness. Sometimes feedback is *extrinsic* in the sense that people are told how well they are performing. At others feedback is *intrinsic* because the job itself provides information about success or failure.

Often these principles are applied to improve specialised jobs which are believed to be demotivating. The jobs are examined using a special questionnaire and those areas that are found to be deficient are improved by, say, including new activities or developing a systematic method of feedback.

Authority and Responsibility

Authority is the formal power a job holder has to make decisions, marshal resources and give instructions to others. Authority is mainly a characteristic of a job rather than a characteristic of an individual – it remains the same even if a job is held by a different person. Early management theorists considered authority in depth. They viewed it in a feudal perspective. All authority was held by top management and it was successively delegated to lower ranks. Authority is determined by one's position in a management hierarchy.

The modern view of authority is rather more complicated. Subordinates often refuse to obey the authority of a superior who is disliked or incompetent. Subordinates may join forces to thwart authority of a new or insecure manager. Subordinates who have particular expertise may exercise more authority than those in superior positions. For example, a chief executive may follow the judgement of a human resource manager when choosing key members of staff because the HR manager has a higher level of expertise in that area. Job descriptions usually specify the limits of authority. For example, a job description might state that a manager can only authorise overtime up to a certain level.

Traditionally authority was closely guarded because of an implicit belief that employees at lower levels are idiots and cannot be trusted. Often this means that time is wasted because subordinates repeatedly needed to refer matters to their superiors and then wait for their decisions. Many decisions were made by superiors who had neither up-to-date information nor specialist expertise. The modern trend is to push authority as far down the organisation as possible so that decisions can be more timely and based on better information. This trend is called *empowerment*.

Responsibility is usually linked to authority. It is the duty of a subordinate to perform a task that has been assigned to him or her. However, this duty only exists if the employee, in turn, has authority over the resources needed to do the job. A manager's "area of responsibility" (AOR) is the domain of resources over which she or he has authority. Job design must achieve the correct relationship between authority and responsibility.

Span of Control

Responsibility for the work of other employees is a special kind of authority. The number of employees supervised is called the "span of control". Traditionally it was argued that about six subordinates was the optimum span of control. If a manager is responsible for more employees there is the danger of "communication overload" and delays will occur. However, research has indicated that the span of control depends upon a number of factors such as environmental stability. In highly stable situations with few complexities and exceptions, the span of control can be higher, perhaps extending to 20, 30 or even 50 subordinates. The latter situation occurs on production lines making highly standardised products. In more changeable situations, where different products are made to meet the needs of individual customers, smaller spans of control may be better. High spans of control are possible when an organisation has a clear system of values, where a boss and subordinates work in close proximity, or where there is an efficient computer system that captures and collates key management information. The increasing use of information technology may be one of the reasons why, in recent years, the spans of managerial control have been increasing.

Ergonomics and Job Design

Ergonomics is a specialised area of psychology which aims to ensure that jobs are designed in a way that makes them suitable for human beings to perform. This means that workplaces should be constructed to minimise harmful effects. Machines should be designed in a way which makes accidents impossible. For example, a metal-cutting machine can avoid accidental amputation of a hand by making sure that the cutting blades do not come into operation until a guard is in place and the operative's hands are safely out of the way while pressing two buttons that are placed well outside the danger area.

Ergonomics plays an important role in the design of instrument displays. For example, the pilot of an aircraft must monitor many dials. Many scientific experiments have been conducted to ensure that a cockpit display is laid out to maximise the ease of reading and to minimise the risk of confusion. One of the most recent concerns of ergonomists is the design of computerised workplaces. They should be constructed so that the working position does not create problems from poor posture, glare or repetitive actions that result in repetitive strain injury (RSI) .

Ergonomists try to establish the patterns of shiftwork which do least damage to long-term health. Working very long hours (48 hours or more per week for more than nine weeks) carries long-term health risks. Furthermore, studies conducted as long ago as 1918 showed that the output of people who work very long hours is less than those who work to a more reasonable schedule.

Work Schedules

In traditional agricultural economies work schedules were determined by the natural cycles of night and day and the seasons. With the Industrial Revolution and the invention of artificial lighting, work schedules tended to involve long shifts of 12 hours or more. Such long hours were often counter-productive and shorter hours with more holidays became the norm. In the middle of the last century the stereotypical work schedule followed a "nine to five" pattern – although probably only a small proportion of the working population actually worked that schedule. In the closing decades of the last century work schedules became more varied and included flexible working hours, a compressed working week and home working.

- **Flexitime** is probably the most common variation on the "standard" working week. It allows workers some autonomy and discretion in the hours that they work – provided that the total hours worked is sufficient. Flexitime employees must usually be present for certain core hours such as 10.00 a.m. to 3.00 p.m. It is very popular with secretarial and administrative staff. The growth of flexitime has been helped by the development of computer systems which can easily keep track of the hours an employee works. Flexitime often increases productivity because it decreases absenteeism and lateness. Employees like flexitime because it allows them to balance the competing demands of work and home. However, some managers may question an employee's motivation and commitment if they use flexitime too liberally.

- **Compressed working week** is another variation on the "standard" working week whereby employees have longer working days in return for more days when they do not work. The most common form is for employees to work ten hours for four days in return for having a weekend break of three days. Some employees then choose to take a second job. The compressed working week is ideally suited to the domestic arrangements of some employees. However, it has been claimed that many people are fatigued during the last two hours of the 10-hour working shifts and consequently their concentration and attention may suffer.

- **Homeworking** and **teleworking**. Working at home, or in the fields near to home was once the most common form of work. In many industries, such as assembling small products or packing goods, working from home persisted for many years. The increasing availability of computers has led to a new variety of homeworking –

telecommuting. In telecommuting an employee works at home but is linked to "the office" via computer and modem. In addition, they attend "the office" perhaps one day a week for meetings and social activities. The archetypal form of telecommuting is employees who are engaged in data input. Teleworking has a number of advantages:

- *Low overheads* – a firm does not have to provide office space, heating and lighting. These costs are usually borne by the teleworker.

- *Reduction of labour shortages* – firms can employ people who would otherwise be outside the labour market. Teleworking often allows employers to recruit people with domestic responsibilities or who do not wish to commute to work.

- *Increased productivity* – research suggests that teleworking can increase productivity by 25 per cent. Part of this saving is due to lower absenteeism and labour turnover. Some of the saving may be due to a reduction in time spent on social activities at work and the fact that employees are not fatigued by commuting.

Some people point to the disadvantages of teleworking:

- Teleworkers may feel that they and their *careers suffer* because they are not as visible to important people in the organisation.

- *Home circumstances may interfere* with teleworking and increase the stress placed upon teleworkers.

- Teleworkers may find the *home–work interface* very difficult and will work very long hours in order to complete assignments.

- **Job sharing** – the concept of job sharing is self-explanatory. The duties involved in one job are shared, usually, by two people. Sometimes they work on different days of the week. Sometimes one person works in the morning while the other person works in the afternoon. Frequently the people who share the job are friends. Indeed, job sharers are sometimes husband and wife. If the job is complex, it is important to arrange a short "handover" period where the sharers co-ordinate the jobs in hand. From the employee's point of view job sharing may be an excellent way of combining work with domestic responsibilities or leisure. From the employer's point of view job sharing reduces the impact if an employee needs sick leave. Some people maintain that there is an increase in productivity because each person will achieve more than their proportionate share of the job. Apparently this is particularly true when the job involves creative work: a job shared between two people may well produce 20 per cent or more ideas than a single employee might produce.

- **Contingent workers** – Casual workers who are hired as and when there is sufficient demand are often called contingent workers. There is nothing new about contingent working. In agricultural economies many people were hired during the harvest period and their employment ended once the crops were gathered. In the past, dockyard workers were normally employed when ships arrived with cargoes which needed unloading. Universities employ large numbers of contingency seminar leaders to cope with increased student numbers. Managers who are hired for specific projects are often called "interim managers". The provision of contingent office workers is highly organised and "temping agencies" have developed to meet this need. Many contingent workers are paid low wages but the temporary nature of their work may be a useful way of obtaining convenient short-term employment. The costs of using contingent workers from an agency may be high because an agency usually pays higher wages and charges a sizeable commission to cover its costs of recruiting and maintaining a register of temporary employees. Nevertheless, the costs of employing "temps" may be an efficient way of meeting peaks in demand.

- **Office sharing and hoteling**. Providing employees with a workplace or office is expensive. It is particularly expensive if the workplace requires specialist equipment or if it is located in the centre of a major city. To make matters worse individuals may only use their workplace for a part of the time. For example, a sales manager may only use his or her office during the mornings. During the afternoon he or she may be accompanying sales representatives "on the road". Therefore it may be possible to allocate an office to two sales managers. One uses it in the morning and is "on the road" during the afternoon while the other is "on the road" during the morning and in the office during the afternoon.

Hoteling takes this idea one step further. A firm can have a number of desks or offices. Staff can book a desk or an office when it is needed in a way that is analogous to booking a hotel room when it is needed for a day or for some purposes only an hour! These arrangements are often used by major consultancy firms which have premises in the prestigious but expensive centres of major cities. Providing consultants with their own accommodation would be prohibitively costly. Each might occupy an office for only a few hours each week because most of their time is spent at the premises of their clients. The system of booking an office or desk space for short periods is called "*hot-desking*". Often, a hot-desking employee will be given a trolley to store files and other equipment. It will be stored, relatively cheaply, in a depot. When office facilities are needed they will be reserved, the trolley will be taken from the depot to the allocated desk and a computer will route telephone calls to the appropriate extension. When the task is completed the desk will be vacated, the trolley returned to the depot and the desk space allocated to another consultant. From the firm's point of view, hot-desking is an excellent proposition – it slashes accommodation costs. Furthermore, it inhibits employees wasting time luxuriating in their own office rather than spending time with clients on work that generates fees. However, the impact on employees can be very negative. Hot-desking may involve considerable inconvenience. It hardly engenders a feeling that the organisation has a long-term commitment to its employees. Consequently, hot-desking reduces an employee's commitment to the organisation. After all, if the organisation provides them with so little back-up, they may as well "poach" clients and work on their own account.

Under some circumstances the concept of hoteling can work well. For example, the provision of facilities for researchers in management is very expensive and, often, the facilities lie idle for considerable periods while researchers are planning their experiments and writing up results. A recent innovation is the "*research hotel*" in which researchers plan their investigations and write up their results in their permanent offices at their own universities. However, the actual experiments and data gathering, which require expensive and specialised facilities, are undertaken at regional centres where good facilities can be reserved for the days or the weeks when they are actually needed.

4.3 The Six Main Types of Organisational Structure

Job definition is an important stage of organising work but the process cannot stop there. If it did, jobs would be performed efficiently but they would be isolated and lack co-ordination. Consequently, once jobs have been defined it is vital to devise a structure that relates jobs in a logical and appropriate way. There are many ways of structuring jobs. The main ones are:

- functional structures
- divisional structures (regional, product, client)
- matrix structures
- team structures
- network structures
- learning structures and knowledge management

Functional structures

The most usual way to organise jobs is to group them according to their function. A function is an intended purpose. For example, the purpose (function) of the brain is to think and the purpose (function) of the skeleton is to support the body. Similarly, the function of the production department is to make goods or services while the function of the sales department is to sell those goods.

Most organisations have a number of functions. The major functions are operations (production), sales, human resources and finance. These are covered in detail by later chapters. Here the focus is upon the way an organisation might structure jobs according to functions. For example, the common purpose of selection, training, manpower planning and safety is the management of human beings. Hence, an interviewer, a management trainer, the manpower planning officer and a safety officer might be grouped into the human resource function. Similarly, the common element of paying suppliers, paying employees, raising money on the stock market and obtaining payment from customers all concern money and the people whose jobs involve these activities might be grouped into the financial function. A functional structure brings together people with similar expertise. This means that they can advise and support each other. A functional structure normally engenders considerable loyalty in its members. Organisation by function is depicted by a classic organisation chart of a small manufacturing business shown in Figure 4.2.

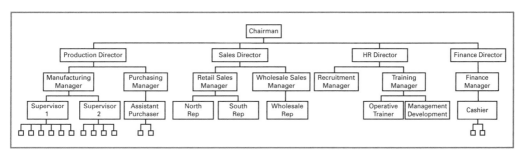

FIGURE 4.2 A Functionally Based Organisation

This organisation has a *flat structure* and is typical of many manufacturing organisations with large spans of control and where a small number of people manage the work of many operatives. Some administrative and clerical organisations also have flat structures. For example, in government departments collecting taxes a few senior officials will supervise the work of many people who process tax returns.

Some organisations have *tall structures* where each manager has only one or two subordinates. Tall structures are found in specialised organisations where the activities of one person are related to the activities of others. A typical tall structure is depicted in Figure 4.3. It would be typical, for example, of a consultancy designing software.

Functions differ from organisation to organisation. A manufacturing organisation will have functions similar to those shown in the first organisational structure. In a large bank, however, the functions might be called retail operations, major accounts, lending and public relations. In a legal partnership the functions might be called commercial property, intellectual property, financial, international, litigation etc. Functional structures work well when an organisation recurrently processes large batches of a few standard products.

Functional organisational structures have a number of **advantages**:

- **Operational efficiency is high**. They give tight, centralised control. Responsibilities are clearly defined and understood.
- **Similar jobs are grouped**. People doing similar tasks can support each other and develop considerable expertise. Work groups are cohesive.
- **Employees have a clear career structure.**
- **Economies of scale are obtained**. Resources are used efficiently. Specialised equipment is located where it is needed most and fewer items of equipment need to be bought.

Unfortunately, functional structures also have one major **disadvantage**. Loyalties develop to the function rather than the organisation. People put the goals of their own groups before the goals of the organisation. Functional groups may develop narrow perspectives that lead to conflict with other functions. For example, the sales function may blame the manufacturing function for producing poor products while the manufacturing function may blame

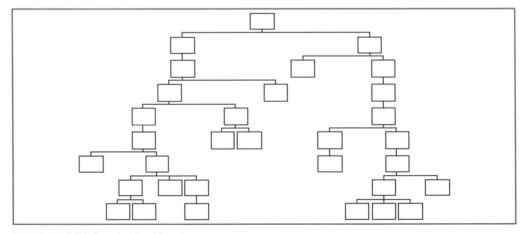

FIGURE 4.3 A Tall Organisational Structure

the sales function for not selling products energetically. The narrow viewpoints of functions are often called "*functional chimneys*" that lead to a "blame culture" and poor communication. Decision-making slows because choices are referred to higher levels where responsibilities for the functions converge.

Functional structures also lead to "*empire building*" by managers. They enhance the prestige of their jobs by expanding the numbers inside their function – irrespective of the contribution extra workers might make.

Divisional structures

Large organisations are often structured into self-sufficient divisions. This has a number of **advantages**:

- **Clear identification** of costs, profits and the contribution a product is making to an organisation's success. The responsibility for poor performance can be pinpointed. Managers of a division are highly motivated to respond to their customers and their environment.
- **Justification of dedicated facilities**. Decision-making is speeded and changes to customer needs can be met quickly. An organisation that is divided into divisions is likely to be flexible and adaptable.
- **Co-ordination within divisions** is usually easy because a division is likely to consist of a small number of units.
- **Divisions can focus on particular areas of business** and build up the specific expertise needed in these areas.
- **Structural changes are easier** when organisations are structured into divisions: failing divisions can be closed and new, profitable, divisions can be established.
- **General managers have a training ground**. Each division will have managers who are concerned with integrating a whole business unit. When a new manager is needed at corporate level, there are likely to be a number of suitable candidates in the various divisions.

Divisional structures also have **disadvantages**:

- **Facilities are duplicated**. For example, a New Zealand organisation structured into regional divisions may have three separate accounts departments: one in the North Island and one in the South Island. Furthermore, there may be a further accounts department at corporate headquarters. It might be more efficient to have one accounts department for the whole country.
- **Divisions may become too autonomous**, following their own vision and strategy rather than those of the organisation.
- **Divisions may also be subject to "empire building"**. "Divisional chimneys" may develop.

In large organisations the advantages of structuring operations into divisions usually outweigh the disadvantages. The divisions can be based upon many characteristics – mainly region, product, customer and process. Usually there is a hybrid structure combining an appropriate mix of divisional structures. However, it is useful to know the pure types:

- **Regional divisions**: activities that occur in geographical proximity are grouped. They are very common in organisations involved in retailing, distribution and transport. They are also common in service organisations such as hospitals, highway maintenance and schools. Multinational organisations are often organised on a regional basis. Organisations structured into regions have a key advantage that decisions can be made at a local level where personnel have first-hand local knowledge. Further, they often reduce transport costs. Unfortunately, regional structures may not give managers the wider, general experience needed to operate at a national or global level: they only have experience of their own region. A typical regional structure is shown in Figure 4.4.

- **Product divisions group** activities making distinct products or services. They have a major advantage that a business unit can specialise in a technology or market and develop a high level of expertise. Figure 4.5 gives an example of a chemical organisation structured according to its products.

- **Client divisions** group jobs and activities according to their customers. This is common in service organisations such as hospitals and prison services. It is also common in consultancies and organisations making sophisticated equipment. For example, a hospital may be structured into paediatrics, accident and emergencies, obstetrics and geriatrics. Organisations supplying a handful of powerful clients will set up a division for each client. Client divisions are able to serve the special needs of customer groups. In a commercial setting, an organisations, may be able to build customer loyalty which gives them a competitive advantage. A major disadvantage of client divisions is that many clients have common needs, yet the divisions duplicate facilities when meeting the needs of each separate group.

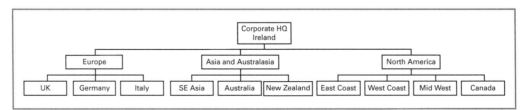

FIGURE 4.4 A Regional Organisational Structure

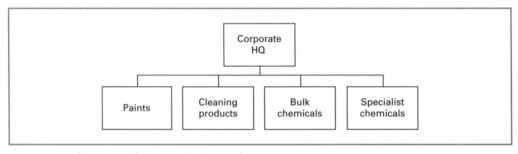

FIGURE 4.5 An Organisation Structured into Product Divisions

Matrix structures

Matrix structures aim to avoid functional and divisional chimneys by making sure that sub-units co-operate. At the same time they try to maintain the advantages of specialisation. In many ways, matrix structures can be thought of as a mixture of functional and divisional structures. They have been defined as "a structure in which the tasks of the organisation are grouped spontaneously along two organising dimensions". Figure 4.6 shows a typical matrix structure where functions are given along the top of an organisation chart while divisions, in this case product divisions, are placed down the side.

A distinctive feature of a matrix organisation is that each person appears to have two bosses. They have an operational boss who is in charge of their function. They also have an operational boss who has day-to-day authority relative to working on a specific project. The function boss will have authority over professional matters such as promotions and salary. The project boss and function boss need to co-ordinate their demands. Some matrix structures are even more complex. They attempt to place employees in a three-dimensional matrix of, say, functions, products and client base. Such complex matrix structures are often impractical.

Many medium and large organisations have adopted a matrix structure. The main **advantages** are:

- **Co-ordination is increased and gross duplication is avoided**. Often a matrix structure enables an organisation to achieve several objectives simultaneously.
- **Employees have varied work and they gain wide experience**. Matrix structures may allow a higher level of worker participation.
- **A cohesive organisation** results from the interaction of employees from different functions or divisions.
- **A more adaptable and flexible organisation** results from the richness of the contacts between employees. It can readily adapt to changes in the business environment.

The major **disadvantages** of a matrix organisation are:

- **Confusion arises** when a functional boss and a project boss fail to cooperate or, worse, when they engage in a power struggle. People in a matrix structure are sometimes confused about where their main responsibility lies.

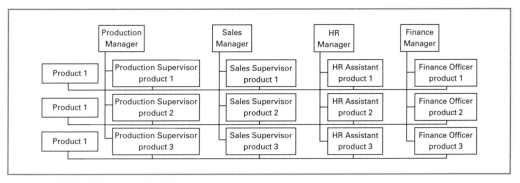

FIGURE 4.6 A Matrix Organisational Structure

- **Much time is consumed** by complexities of co-ordination. Matrix structures may lead to more discussion than action.
- **Employees feel isolated** from the colleagues with whom they have a natural or professional affinity.

Team structures

In traditional structures it takes time for information to travel up and down an organisation in order for a decision to be made. Team structures aim to avoid this problem by pushing responsibility downwards and empowering groups to make autonomous decisions. Sometimes teams are called "self-managing teams". Sometimes the teams are called "cross-functional teams". A team structure is like a matrix structure except the teams are not permanent. A team will consist of a relatively small (about 12) number of managers drawn from relevant functions. Teams are usually multi-disciplinary in order to maximise the available skills and knowledge. Furthermore, teams will have little hierarchical structure. A team has a specific task such as developing a new product or implementing a new piece of legislation. The team will be mutually responsible for achieving the desired results. It will be disbanded when it has completed its task. The members will be reallocated to new teams with a new problem.

Self-managing teams weaken traditional boundaries. Functions still exist and achieve advantages of economy of scale and specialisation. However, functions interact on specific projects so barriers between functions are weakened. Members of a function develop an understanding of problems faced by other functions. They develop workable compromises. This produces the flexibility to respond to changes. It is claimed that teams harness the potential of the skills and knowledge held by team members.

Unfortunately, self-managing teams have disadvantages. Disproportionate time is devoted to meetings. Senior managers, who once knew details of the work of everyone in their function, find it difficult to keep track of the activities of their "subordinates" working in teams. They may find this disorienting. They may not be able to exercise control. This may lead to an additional difficulty. Teams may follow their own idiosyncratic objectives rather than the objectives of the organisation.

Network structures

Network structures are a modern innovation. They are sometimes called "boundaryless organisations". Sometimes they are also called "strategic alliances" and "partnering arrangements".

In a *network structure* (see Figure 4.7), a small core of employees have responsibility for the general organisation, communication, finance and perhaps one function where it excels, such as design. All other aspects are subcontracted to outside suppliers. Core workers co-ordinate outside suppliers so that the final product can be delivered. For example, an entrepreneur may invent a new self-sealing can that prevents fizzy drinks going flat. Instead of setting up a sizeable organisation to manufacture and market the product, the entrepreneur enters an arrangement with an existing Malaysian manufacturer.

This saves expense. There is no need to acquire expertise in the container production. The entrepreneur could also enter into an alliance with a sales and marketing organisation

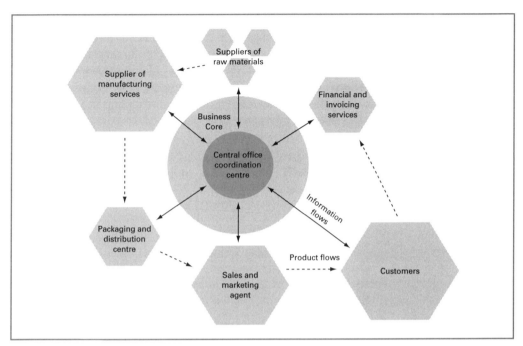

FIGURE 4.7 A Network Organisational Structure

based in New York – saving the time and trouble of setting up a sales organisation. The entre-preneur would also hire three or four core workers who would manage relationships with the suppliers. Naturally, the training and salary administration of the core workers would be outsourced to a specialist agency based in Delhi.

Network organisations are particularly common in the clothing, computer and publishing industries. Network or boundaryless organisations are free to find subcontractors anywhere in the world. The network can be changed rapidly in response to market demand. If a product is not selling, a contract with the producer can be terminated. A new contract can be struck with another producer who makes a more profitable or attractive product. In a sense, a network structure is a modular organisation where the components can be removed or added according to demand.

There are three main kinds of network structures:

1 **Internal networks** exist within large organisations that need to retain full control in order to achieve high quality or to meet statutory requirements. They often set up subgroups with responsibility for supplying various products or services to "internal customers". The subgroups operate like mini-organisations. Usually they act independently as a separate profit centre. They negotiate prices and conditions of supply with their internal customers. However, the organisation maintains sufficient control to prevent them defecting to another organisation or refusing to supply their internal customers. Most of the power is with the internal customers since they are usually free to source their requirements from the open market.

2 **Stable networks** rely on outsourcing. Suppliers are chosen with care. The objective is

to establish strong, long-standing relationships. Suppliers have a high level of loyalty and commitment to the core organisation, which in turn will act in a slightly paternalistic way to ensure the health of their key suppliers. The core organisation may give help with financing and research and development. These relationships may be called "organisational partnerships". But the power lies with the core organisation. When the chips are down, the core organisation switches to a cheaper supplier. The partner supplier, on the other hand, usually becomes too dependent upon the core organisation to resist.

3 **Dynamic networks** are characterised by outsourcing most operations. They consist of many alliances and partners. Partners change rapidly and there is little loyalty.

The physical headquarters of a network structure may be small: in extreme cases it may simply consist of a room with a computer and communications equipment. This type of network structure is often called a *"virtual organisation"*. Virtual organisations can locate and relocate very quickly in any country that suits their temporary requirements.

Small entrepreneurial firms may find that a network structure enables them to match the power of large organisations since they are able to "buy in" facilities and services at will. Other organisations adopt a network structure in order to concentrate on key strengths (core competences) and will leave other aspects to outside organisations which are chosen on the basis of core strengths that complement the strengths of the central organisation.

The main **advantages** of network structures are that they:

- **Enable organisations to manufacture and market globally**. A network structure can often achieve large results from meagre resources.
- **Give flexibility to redefine an organisation rapidly** in the search for markets.
- **Enable efficiency**. A network organisation will have little administration and low overheads. There may be no need for a traditional hierarchy.

The **disadvantages** of a network structure include:

- **Loss of control**. Many decisions will be made by subcontractors. Further, actions will be fragmented amongst subcontractors. Long-term suppliers may be unstable because subcontractors are able to switch to another organisation who can offer better terms. Loss of control often means an increase in uncertainty. Long-term projects may become difficult to plan and organise. Loss of control may mean loss of key components overnight.
- **Employee loyalty may decrease** because there is little identification with the central core.

Learning structures and knowledge management

Management gurus such as Peter Drucker (1997) (see pp. 383–387) suggest that in today's organisations the knowledge they contain is their major asset. This knowledge includes patents, copyrights, trade secrets and contacts. The majority of such knowledge is inside the heads of employees. Senge's (1990) book, *The Fifth Discipline*, emphasised the need to structure an organisation in a way that maximises its ability to increase the capital of knowledge it holds by adopting a "learning structure". A learning structure uses its people, values and systems continuously to change and improve performance-based experience (Senge, 1990). This places a high value on learning from the experience of customers, suppliers, partners and contractors. Learning structures seek out learning opportunities whenever and wherever they can.

A learning structure shows five main characteristics:

- **Employees share the same vision of the organisation**. They will have participated in the formation of the vision and will therefore be willing to consent to the actions needed to bring it about. If the vision is clear, people are able to identify and solve problems in order to achieve that vision.

- **Employees understand how the whole organisation operates**. Understanding how the organisation works as a system helps individuals work in a succession of project teams while maintaining a sense of perspective.

- **Employees are willing to discard the old ways** – in particular, views on controlling staff change. Managers in learning structures think of control as a co-operative process. Rather than having control *over* subordinates, managers exercise control *with* subordinates. People are not a cost which needs to be minimised. Their knowledge, experience and creativity are regarded as the organisation's main asset. An atmosphere of respect and trust creates an environment where it is safe to experiment. Mistakes are accepted not punished. They are an inevitable part of taking necessary risks needed to learn, grow and improve. People are expected to "push the envelope" on the understanding that sometimes things will go wrong and they will not be blamed.

- **Employees feel confident of their position** within the organisation. They are able to discuss ideas openly and frankly, without taking defensive positions. Features which emphasise status differences (car-parking spaces, separate restaurants, and differences in dress) are eliminated.

- **Information is distributed widely**. Everyone can obtain information about budgets, expenses, schedules and other databases. People can see for themselves how their actions and ideas contribute to organisational goals. Communications are fluid. People can email any other person in the organisation.

Learning structures place a high value upon knowledge management. They make a competitive advantage out of the knowledge held by the organisation. Some organisations take knowledge management so seriously that they develop a "knowledge strategy" and may appoint a senior person to the post of "Chief Knowledge Officer" (CKO). This person will be in charge of the organisation's intellectual assets. The CKO will be responsible for a strategy to ensure that the organisation has a portfolio of knowledge that enables it to meet challenges. The CKO will be expected to motivate everyone in the organisation to extend their knowledge and skills. Furthermore, the CKO must make sure the information is shared widely.

Knowledge management means the management of three inputs: data, information and knowledge. *Data* is merely a statement of an event or situation such as "19 analyses conducted" or "20 units sold today". *Information* is a commodity that is derived from data when they are manipulated in some way (collated, compared, analysed) so that they have meaning to someone. For example, when the sale of 20 units is compared to the data, 15 units, 16 units, 18 units for the previous three days it has the meaning that an increasing trend has continued. *Knowledge* is what people understand on the basis of information. It occurs when they evaluate the information against their experience, thinking and learning about similar events. Knowledge allows people to exploit information in order to achieve organisational goals. For example, knowing that a product is in increasing demand might enable a manager to increase its production or raise its price.

Another important distinction lies between *explicit knowledge* and *tacit knowledge*. Systematic knowledge that is written or recorded in some form is called "explicit knowledge". On the other hand, poorly organised knowledge that is contained in people's heads or in ephemeral notes or emails is called "tacit knowledge". It is difficult to capture tacit knowledge in a database. It is also difficult to formalise and transmit. Tacit knowledge is important in doing things smoothly. It is often lost when people leave an organisation or when an organisation is merged with another.

Chief Knowledge Officers (CKOs) will be responsible for looking after both explicit and tacit knowledge. They will be responsible for data warehousing, data mining and maintaining knowledge portals. *Data warehousing* is a fairly straightforward concept. It means storing large quantities of information in a way that enables it to be comprehensively and easily retrieved when it is needed for a report or business decision. *Data mining* involves the use of sophisticated search tools that looks for patterns between items of data. The patterns can be useful: for example, in identifying trends or market segments. A *knowledge portal* is a point that allows employees access to a data warehouse or a data mine. Normally a knowledge portal is a part of an organisation's intranet. It is a single point of access where users can gain access to information contained in various parts of an organisation's data warehouse. The portal will have a simple, unified system of commands so that users do not need to master a series of complicated systems. For example, Cisco, the Internet infrastructure giant, has a portal for newly hired engineers. Once they have mastered a few basic commands they are able to access information they might need in the first 90 days' employment at Cisco.

Co-ordination

Methods of structuring an organisation place people into groups and then arrange the groups into some kind of logical order. On its own, this is not enough. There must be some mechanism that enables the groups to relate to each other so that their activities harmonise in an effective way. This process is called "co-ordination". In this context it refers to the quality of collaboration between groups or departments. All organisations require some co-ordination. In very small organisations this can be provided by one person, usually the owner, who directly supervises all activities. In large organisations, especially international ones, specific methods of co-ordination need to be built into the organisational structure. The main methods are:

- **A hierarchical arrangement of authority** means that someone is available to tell groups what they must do in order to work harmoniously with other groups. The higher authority arbitrates in disputes and issues plans or instructions to ensure that groups work towards the organisation's goals in a mutually helpful way.
- **Standardisation** helps co-ordination by simplifying the situation so that compatibility

and interchangeability are increased. Standardisation covers procedures, inputs and outputs.

■ **Personal contact** where one person speaks to people from other groups allows each group to be aware of events in the other group. This means that they are able to adjust their own activities in a way that helps themselves and the other group. Often this personal contact is formalised and certain people are given the specific responsibility of keeping one group informed of events in another group. These roles are usually called "liaison posts". For example, one member of the engineering department may have an official responsibility for liaising with the sales department.

■ **Computer information systems** are playing an increasingly important role in the co-ordination of organisations. Data from one group can be automatically passed to other groups that need to be kept up to date. Indeed, with automated information-sharing, a receiving department has data almost as quickly as the group that generates it. Moreover, the information on organisational intranets often allows every employee to see the progress an organisation is making towards it production, sales or financial targets.

4.4 The Five Main Dimensions of Organisational Structure

The structure of an organisation can take many forms. The main dimensions are size, role variety, centralisation, mechanistic or organic, formalisation and environmental uncertainty.

Size

Size is a very significant, self-explanatory, organisational dimension. Large organisations tend to have a more formal structure, usually based on functions or departments. Large organisations also tend to have many hierarchical levels.

Role variety

Some organisations are very simple and have only two jobs: the manager and the aides who do all kind of work, as and when needed. Other organisations have many different jobs which are quite distinct. Sometimes, role variety is also called "specialisation". Role variety centres upon interchangeability. If many employees can be substituted there will be little role variety. Tyler (1973) developed a mathematical index of role variety.

Centralisation

Centralisation is the concentration of power. The opposite is called "decentralisation", "autonomy" or "participation". If all power is in the hands of one person the organisation is highly centralised. If members of an organisation have equal power the organisation is highly decentralised. A highly centralised organisation is characterised as follows:

■ Decisions, even quite minor ones, will be referred to senior managers.

■ Plans, even operational plans, will be drawn up without the participation of junior staff.

- Information will be "hoarded" by managers. It will only be given reluctantly to subordinates.
- There will be stringent control procedures to ensure that operations are carried out exactly in the prescribed way. Employees have little discretion.

Mechanistic and organic systems

Burns and Stalker (1961) noted that organisations often operate in one of two ways. Some operate much like an efficient machine devised by scientific managers and administrative theorists. In these mechanistic organisations tasks are divided into small parts that are organised in a logical sequence. Senior levels of mangement exercise downward control using precise instructions and rules which minimise discretion. Boundaries of responsibilities are clearly defined and often related to technical expertise and knowledge. Mechanistic organisations seem to work well in stable situations – especially when products or services are mature and produced in high volume. In the second type of organisation things are less predetermined. In these organic organisations there is a degree of disorganisation and fluidity that is analogous to the flexibility seen in the cells of living material. There are few prescriptive job descriptions, rules and regulations are kept to a minimum and employees are often expected to use their initiative. Communications within these organisations tend to be horizontal between colleagues rather than upwards towards senior management. Organic organisations seem to work best in volatile situations where the market or technology is changing rapidly and frequent adjustments mean that long production runs are infrequent.

Formalisation

Formalisation (see Reimann, 1974) is the extent to which expectations and norms are made explicit. In theory, formalisation applies to both written and oral communication. In practice, formalisation is the level to which rules, procedures, instructions and other communications are written. Formalisation is related to concepts such as routinisation (Hage and Aiken, 1968, 1969) and standardisation. Routinisation is the degree to which roles are structured. Roles are routinised when tasks are simplified and repeated. The degree of standardisation in an organisation can be measured by counting the number of repetitive sequences.

Environmental uncertainty

Lawrence and Lorsch (1969) maintain that a major difference between organisations is the uncertainty of their environments. Organisations, such as manufacturers in the computer industry, operate in an uncertain environment where new developments and market trends can emerge overnight and then completely change the organisation's operations. Ambiguity is often highest in the political arena where political leaders do not spell out their requirements clearly. Public services also suffer from competing demands. A prison service, for example, must strike a balance between the need to restrict the activities of prisoners in order to make the community safer and the need to expand the activities of prisoners in order to rehabilitate them into society. A final component of environmental uncertainty includes the quality and speed of feedback.

Other significant dimensions of an organisation are its attitude towards risk, innovation and rules.

4.5 Changing Organisational Structures

When organisations are founded, their structure is usually suitable to the environment at that time. The environment, of course, is not static but changes. Organisations also change. In most cases the organisation will change at a slower rate than the environment. An organisation's structure is likely to become more and more outdated. Field force analysis helps explain this situation: it identifies factors which push for change and those factors which push to maintain the present situation. If the factors for change greatly outweigh the factors for the status quo, an organisation will change rapidly. If the factors for change are equal to the factors for the status quo there will be little, or no, alteration.

Factors helping change

Factors which push for change include:

- desire to make greater profit
- desire to grow
- new technology
- need to keep customers
- enjoyment of new things

Factors resisting change

A main source of resistance is the belief, which may be correct, that a change will make matters worse and will involve extra effort. This is based upon *self-interest*. Resistance also arises from *misunderstandings*. People are usually comfortable with the present system. Documents, charts, standard operating procedures, personal relationships and even the layout of equipment reinforce the feeling of security with the status quo. A new situation, on the other hand, will be less defined. Employees use their imagination to fill in missing details. Such details may be wrong and provide reasons why the change should be resisted. Misunderstandings arise when there is a feeling of *distrust* between management and other employees. Boddy (2002) identifies a number of other factors which make change difficult and slow:

- Change involves core activities of the organisation
  - it will result in a solution that is unfamiliar or novel
  - it will require rapid action
  - it will be controversial.
- Goals change rapidly.
- Change involves many other companies or organisations.
- Senior management do not support the change.
- Many other things are being changed at the same time.

If forces against change are strong, change is likely to encounter tactics of *counter-implementation*. Opposing change is usually risky. Most organisations wish to be seen as progressive: methods of opposing change tend to be covert rather than open. Keen (1981) identified seven tactics of counter-implementation. They are:

1 **Divert resources** to other projects so that the change has inadequate support. Staff involved in the change are given competing priorities. It can be arranged for essential equipment to be shared with another department – preferably a department in a remote location. Resources can also be diverted by commissioning research, writing long reports, holding many meetings and arranging fact-finding tours (preferably abroad).

2 **Insist enthusiastically that the project is "done properly"**. Everyone's views must be canvassed and reconciled. It is certain that contradictory views will emerge and a heated conflict between rival proponents will slow or kill the project.

3 **Be vague**. Use long, convoluted communications couched in general, grandiose and abstract terms. At all costs avoid giving specific goals with specific timetables.

4 **Encourage inertia** by commissioning research, waiting for the completion of another project, waiting until the "time is ripe" or until an important (and preferably very busy) person is consulted and persuaded to back the project.

5 **Ignore interpersonal issues** during the early stages. This will ensure that misunderstanding and animosities incubate and grow to the point where they can later jeopardise the change project's success.

6 **Damage the credibility of those leading the change**. Spread gossip concerning those who are championing the project. It is particularly important to spread the gossip among those who are supporting the project champion. This can be done most skilfully by pretending to be outraged by a rumour and pretending to defend the project champion.

7 **Avoid overt hostility to the change**. Overt hostility alerts change champions and allows counter-measures to be deployed.

Reducing resistance to change

If resistance outweighs the forces pushing for change, progress will be slow. Managers need to take specific action. Sometimes it includes appointing people responsible for ensuring that change takes place. These people are often called *change agents* or *organisational development* consultants. They may be employed within the organisation or they may be hired as outside specialists. Sometimes the role is fulfilled, on an unofficial basis, by existing employees. Change agents use a number of techniques to increase change so that an organisation's structure does not lag behind the environment.

The most frequently used strategy for producing change was developed long ago by Lewin (1947). It involves three stages: unfreezing, changing and re-freezing.

Unfreezing involves breaking down existing attitudes and positions. Essentially it means emphasising and strengthening the need to change so that the forces for change outweigh the forces in favour of the status quo. The main techniques for the unfreezing stage involve communication. First, as many reasons for the change as possible are assembled. These reasons will then be translated into words, examples and images which are appropriate to particular groups of employees. The reasons to resist change will also be mentioned, because research suggests that giving both sides of an argument is more persuasive and much more effective against subsequent counter-arguments. The reasons for change are then communicated using many media such as meetings, memos, newsletters and presentations. It is important that employees should not be passive recipients. It is better if they play an active part. A standard tactic is to co-opt likely opponents of change to the planning and delivery of the change (provided the opponents are neither numerous nor powerful). Negotiations will be needed with powerful figures who resist the changes. It may be necessary to offer a trade-off or compromise that compensates any negative effects the change may cause. If all else fails it may be necessary to point out the bad consequences if change is blocked. Such explicit or implicit coercion carries enormous risks but may be appropriate where a speedy change is necessary.

Once a situation has been unfrozen, the *actual change* can start to take place. Change agents and organisational development (OD) consultants have evolved techniques to help. The main techniques include: survey feedback, team building and process consultation plus large-group interventions.

Survey feedback

Research suggests that survey feedback is one of the most powerful techniques of organisational development. It has four stages. First, the main worries about the change are identified. Second, a questionnaire is designed to measure people's attitudes. Third, the questionnaire is given, on an anonymous basis, to a large sample. In fact, the questionnaire is usually sent to all employees. This makes it clear that the change will affect the whole organisation. Fourth, replies are analysed and the main results are distributed to everyone. Results are discussed by groups of employees, who are asked to produce recommendations. Survey research has an obvious role in clarifying employees' views. However, survey feedback also has useful by-products. The construction of the questionnaire forces an organisation to clarify the main issues. Further, completing the questionnaire helps to educate employees. In addition, the process emphasises the importance of participation and it allows people to feel that they have been consulted. Survey research works best when the findings of the survey lead to specific actions which can then be reported back to those who took part. Survey feedback is a relatively cheap way of involving a large number of people. Because the effect of survey feedback can be widespread it can lead to a rapid change.

Team building and process consultation

Team building is designed to weld a number of people into a cohesive group, able to work effectively towards a common goal. Team building is particularly important because changes bring together collections of people who have not worked together previously. Indeed, many change processes bring together people who were previously competitors or even enemies. It essential to remove old attitudes or rivalries. Team building involves providing information about the way effective teams function. Also, it will usually include sessions on behaviours that decrease team effectiveness. When participants are taught these skills they are organised into groups that are given a "team task". Each group will be observed by a facilitator. At the end, the facilitator leads a discussion on how well the group operated as a team.

Process consultation is a special aspect of team building. It is generally used where a harmonious, cohesive team exists but where the team works in a way that is inefficient. It involves a small group that aims to analyse and improve the way the team works. It examines how group norms are formed, how the group members perceive each other's roles and how decisions are made. For example, a trainer might start by observing the way that a team tackles a specific problem. Under the facilitator's guidance a team meets to discuss its performance. It is important to note that the trainer will not diagnose the problem unilaterally. The facilitator's role is to help the team diagnose its own problems. However, the facilitator will ensure that the team does not overlook important facts. The facilitator will also help the team recognise and correct its own prejudices. For example, the facilitator might point out that the team spent a lot of time obtaining information which was already known to an unpopular member who was excluded. The team might then conclude that its effectiveness was being diminished because of personal prejudices and informal cliques. An examination of the team's prejudices and social structure follows before deciding on remedial action.

Team building and process consultation are expensive: they require a high number of facilitators. They generally produce permanent changes in specific, but small, areas of an organisation. These techniques often produce gradual, incremental changes.

Large-group interventions

Organisational development works well with small groups of people but with large organisations progress is often slow because it takes a long time to cover everyone. Consequently, OD interventions are often very expensive. In response, OD consultants have developed ways of intervening on a large scale (Dannemiller and Jacobs, 1992)

Large-scale interventions aim to change a whole system in a relatively short period. They bring together, say, 300 participants for three days in a large hotel. Participants are drawn from all sections of the organisation and may also include suppliers or clients. There will usually be a number of set presentations which aim to give as much information as possible about the nature of the change. There will also be a number of group discussions led by facilitators. Often these events finish in activities where participants are required to show their commitment to the change and in the development of personal action plans which will help the change.

Because large-scale interventions involve many people, they can bring about major and profound changes. They can harness pressures to help change because everyone in the organisation will have been involved and everyone will be involved at the same time. Substantial momentum for change can be established.

The management processes of planning and organising are useless unless the organisation has people who are willing and able to implement the plans and fill the roles within the organisation. The management process of "staffing" ensures that the organisation has employees that will do these things. "Staffing" is outlined in the next chapter.

Activities and Further Study

Essay Plans

Prepare plans for the following essays:

1 What are the advantages and disadvantages of work specialisation?
2 Do charities have organisational structures?
3 What are they different ways in which work can be scheduled?
4 What are recent trends in structuring organisations and why have they changed from traditional structures?

Web Activities

1 Search the Internet for organisational structures. You should try a number of organisations including governmental and charity organisations. Some useful examples of organisational structure are given by:

   ■ Parker Pens – a structure very largely based on geographical regions – why? Try www.competition-commission.org.uk.

   ■ Gillette – a complicated structure which uses both product group and geographical regions.

   ■ Nomura Research Institute – a service organisation largely based on customers and products. Try http://www.nri.co.jp/english/company/org.html.

   ■ Serious Fraud Office – a governmental structure based on procedural responsibilities. Try http://www.sfo.gov.uk/about/structure.asp.

   ■ For a really complex organisational structure look at the organisation chart for Microsoft, which can be found at: http://www.directionsonmicrosoft.com/sample/DOMIS/orgchart/sample/orgchart.html.

2 You might also try to locate the organisational structure for a "virtual organisation" such as Amazon or eBay.

3 Log onto the website associated with this book and access the file containing the organisation chart exercise. Examine the chart, locate the errors and a draw a new chart which does not contain errors.

Experiential Activities

1 Draw up a job description for your role as a student. Compare your result with the model answer given on the website associated with this book.

2 With a group of fellow students discuss the different ways that work can be scheduled. Allocate one of the following roles to each member of the group:

- single unmarried worker
- married worker
- married worker with young children
- worker who is a single parent with young children

Each person should then examine the following work schedules and describe the impact it would have on their work and domestic lives:

- traditional 9–5 schedule
- flexitime schedule
- compressed working week
- job share

Staffing Processes

❖ LEARNING OBJECTIVES

After studying this chapter you should be able to **explain** the importance of staffing processes (the way all managers relate to staff) and **make a preliminary distinction** from Human Resource Management (the specialist activities undertaken by a group of experts). You will also be able to **outline** the main ways in which managers recruit, train, motivate, lead and develop positive attitudes in their staff. In particular you will be able to:

1 **list** the four main stages involved in selecting employees

2 **evaluate** the advantages and disadvantages of four scientific methods of selection – especially their accuracy

3 **list** three main categories of training methods

4 **describe briefly** each of six methods of "off the job" training

5 **explain** the difference between training and development

6 **describe briefly** the concepts of learning skills, self-awareness and 360° feedback

7 **explain** the importance of motivating employees

8 **compare and contrast** three theories of motivation

9 **critically evaluate** the concept of leadership

10 **describe in detail** types of leaders and leadership styles

11 **explain in detail** the relationship between leaders and the characteristics of their followers

12 **explain in detail** the relationship between leaders and the situations in which they operate

Most analyses of management work show that dealing with people is *the* main management process. No matter whether they work in operations, sales, marketing or even IT, *all* managers need to deal with other people and it will be a quite exceptional day if a manager does not meet at least one other human being. This contrasts with other processes such as planning, organising and budgeting. At certain times of the year a manager can go for days without performing any of these processes. Staffing may be divided into four main topics:

Chapter contents

5.1 Selection and Recruitment

Recruitment and selection concerns the supply of suitable employees. Poor recruitment and selection will lead to the employment of unsuitable people, productivity will fall and a commercial organisation will become uncompetitive. Good recruitment and selection can easily raise productivity by 10 per cent and give an organisation a competitive edge. Good selection has four stages:

- producing job descriptions
- producing personnel specifications
- attracting a field of candidates
- choosing among candidates

In addition, good selection often involves giving applicants a realistic preview of the job.

The *first stage* of good selection is to define the job that needs to be done. Some aspects of **job descriptions** were explained at the start of the previous chapter on "organisation". It will be recalled that a job description details the tasks which a member of staff is required to perform.

The *second stage* is to consider the knowledge, skills and abilities which a person must have in order to perform those tasks in a competent way. In other words it is necessary to specify the ideal person for the job. A **personnel specification** can take many formats. One very basic method of producing personnel specification uses Roger's Seven-point Plan, which groups requirements under seven headings. On the basis of the job description essential and desirable characteristics of workers are identified. Essential characteristics are those which are central to the job and which would be difficult or expensive to develop by training. Desirable characteristics are those which are important to the job but which might be developed with appropriate training. Table 5.1 gives a simplified personnel specification for a sales representative of a software company.

	Essential	Desirable
1. **Physical characteristics**	– good grooming – clear speech and diction – acceptable appearance	
2. **Attainments**	– 2.2 degree – driving licence	– degree in science or computer-related subject
3. **Intelligence**		– in top 10% of population
4. **Special attitudes**	– good communication, especially listening skills – good visual presentation of materials – commercial acumen	– time-management skills – results orientation
5. **Interests**	– meeting and persuading people – computers and IT	
6. **Disposition**	– high motivation – resilience to setbacks – self-confidence – conscientiousness – enthusiasm and ability to relate to people	– self-organisation
7. **Circumstances**	– no impediment to travel – no impediment to working flexible hours	– membership of appropriate social and professional groups

TABLE 5.1 Roger's Seven-Point Plan

Great care should be taken to avoid unfairness and discrimination. For example, it would generally be unfair to include a candidate's height in a personnel specification. Men are generally taller than women and a height requirement would differentially exclude more women than men. This would normally constitute unfair discrimination. In a famous case in the United States it was declared illegal for a police force to demand that recruits should be taller than 1.75 m (5′ 10″) because this would exclude many women who could be competent police officers. However, the police force *was* allowed to demand that recruits should be taller than 1.65 m (5′6″) since shorter officers might endanger themselves and colleagues because they would not be sufficiently tall to shoot a pistol over the top of a car (this is America!). Similarly, personnel specifications should not imply that women candidates might be unsuitable because they would be responsible for the care of children.

Once a fair personnel specification has been devised, the *third stage* of selection is to **attract a field of applicants** by advertising the vacancy. The aim should be to attract about eight credible applicants for each post. If there are fewer than eight there might not be enough to allow a good choice. If there are many more, it will be difficult to give each candidate full proper consideration. Some ways of attracting applicants are:

- internal notices and emails
- government employment agencies
- private employment agencies

CASE 5.1: SELECTION OF TECHNICAL MANAGERS

Bristol Myers Squibb is a world-famous pharmaceutical company. Recently it made a major investment in a new production plant near Dublin airport, Ireland. This major expansion meant it needed to employ more than 40 technical managers who would be responsible for producing medicines to impeccable quality standards. Because requirements were so high the company decided to engage in a textbook selection exercise in order to obtain the best possible recruits.

First, the jobs of technical managers were analysed in detail in order to identify the precise characteristics the managers would need. This was a substantial exercise involving more than 60 interviews with senior managers and currently successful managers. A selection system was devised to measure the exact characteristics needed to perform the job.

Applicants were first screened on the basis of their application forms. Those who survived were invited to a mini-assessment centre where they completed:

- two tests of high-level mental ability (verbal reasoning and numerical reasoning)
- a personality test to check, among other things, conscientiousness and emotional stability
- an in-basket test to check how well they could handle written administrative tasks
- a group discussion to check their ability to communicate and work in a team
- a situational interview seeking their reactions to realistic situations they might face
- a technical interview with the potential line manager to check their technical knowledge

The system proved very successful and it was used with hundreds of applicants. It was calculated that the improved selection system saved the organisation over €6 million during the time that the cohort of technical managers would work for the company

- headhunters (executive search agencies)
- advertisements in the local press, national press and professional journals
- careers fairs, college visits

The choice of media will depend upon the exact situation. Many senior management jobs are advertised in the national press and professional journals. Very senior management posts will seek applicants using executive search agencies. The use of headhunters is very expensive (about 33 per cent of the first-year salary) but the service is very confidential and it is most likely to locate able people who are not actively searching for the job, because they are successful in their present job. Whichever medium is chosen, care must be taken to ensure that the advertising is fair. Advertising a job solely in a magazine such as *Playboy* or *GQ* is likely to be unfair because, presumably, few women read these magazines. Advertising a vacancy using internal notices or by word-of-mouth of existing employees may also be discriminatory since it is less likely that minority groups will learn that a vacancy exists.

When a field of candidates has been assembled, the *fourth stage* of selection is to **choose the best person** for the job. A large number of selection methods exist. The well-known methods of selection include **traditional interviews**, **references**, **application forms** and **CVs**. Many organisations use more modern methods.

Modern selection methods

Psychometric tests

These are samples of behaviour which are highly standardised so that everyone is given precisely the same instructions and time to complete the same tasks. The answers are also evaluated in a standard way. Thus, psychometric tests are usually more objective than other methods. Broadly speaking, two kinds of tests are used in selection: tests of mental ability and tests of personality.

- **Mental ability** is the ability to process information quickly and accurately. It is fairly stable after the age of about 18. Tests of mental ability have been used for over 100 years. They are highly reliable (a typical reliability correlation is 0.9). Scores of mental ability tests usually correlate 0.53 with future success. In managers the correlation is slightly higher at 0.58. Mental ability is an important factor in job success because it enables people to learn the job more quickly and to respond better to changes or unusual events.

- **Personality** is the style in which things are done. It is moderately stable after the age of about 30. Tests of personality are rather less reliable than ability tests. A typical test–retest correlation will be about 0.75. Personality tests are useful predictors of job performance and correlate about 0.4 with future job success. Personality is less accurate than mental ability in predicting job performance because equal success can result from different styles. Furthermore, up to a point people can mould their jobs to suit their personality. Honesty tests are a particular type of personality test. They attempt to predict whether a future employee will participate in theft or other anti-social activity such as drug-taking. Honesty tests are most frequently used in retail organisations.

Work samples

These are carefully worked out exercises which aim to be mini-trials of the job. For example, an applicant for the job of a carpenter would be provided with a standard piece of wood and a standard set of tools. A set time would be allowed to produce a piece of work entailing a range of joints and cuts. The exact nature of the task would be determined by a prior analysis of the joints and cuts which differentiates between good and bad carpenters. Work samples of management jobs include:

- **Written analysis** of a business problem on the basis of a set of files.
- **A presentation** on a business topic to an audience.
- **A group exercise** which mimics a management meeting. Several candidates would participate in the same meeting and the performance of each one would be observed and

evaluated by neutral judges. Group exercises need to be carefully arranged so that the groups are equal, otherwise the composition of the group can affect the performance of individual candidates.

- **A role play**. For example, a candidate is asked to study an errant employee's file and conduct a disciplinary interview with that employee.

Work samples are among the best methods of selection and usually correlate 0.54 with subsequent job performance.

Structured interviews

These have a more scientific basis than traditional interviews. The structure means that all candidates are asked more or less the same questions and consequently better comparisons can be made. Furthermore, structured interviews are based on an analysis of the job and only ask questions concerning work behaviour. For example, an applicant sales representative might be asked how they would respond to the following, realistic, situation:

> suppose that you have arranged to see an important customer. You arrive at the arranged time only to be told that the customer is busy. You wait for 30 minutes and just as you are about to leave to go to your next appointment the customer emerges from her office with the sales representative from a rival company . . . what would you do?

The applicant's answer would be compared to a carefully calibrated set of model responses and a score would be allocated. An applicant would be asked how they would respond to five or six of these situations. This particular kind of structured interview is known as a "situational" interview. If properly prepared, situational interviews can be good predictors of future job performance and can rival work samples in their accuracy.

Biodata

This is a way of collecting information, usually by a questionnaire, about the course of a person's life. Typically the data would include details of educational qualifications, hobbies, memberships and work experience. The data will then be applied to a carefully derived formula that calculates a person's probability of being successful in a job. Credit scoring and the calculation of insurance premiums are specific varieties of biodata.

Assessment centres

Many organisations, especially large ones, use a combination of methods. Candidates are asked to attend for a whole day when they will be asked to, say, complete tests of mental ability and personality, take part in a discussion group, write a report and participate in a situational interview. Combinations of methods such as this are usually called **assessment centres**. At senior management level they may be more intensive and last two days or even a week. Because assessment centres use several methods, the weaknesses of individual methods have chance to iron themselves out. However, assessment centres are expensive and may cause disruption to both the candidates and the assessors within the organisation.

Because there are so many methods of selection the question arises "which one to use?". A consultant graphologist would probably claim that graphology is best; a firm specialising in interview training would probably suggest using interviews while a pychometrician might recommend psychometric tests. Before an organisation can choose the best candidate, it must first choose the best method of selection!

Fortunately the three main characteristics that a good selection method should possess are well known. They are:

- **Sensitivity**: it must differentiate between different candidates. If a method gives the same score to every person it is useless. References, for example, are often not very helpful because a very large majority of referees maintain that their applicant is very good.

- **Reliability**: it must give consistent results – otherwise the choice of candidate would depend upon the day on which they were present. Reliability is often measured using a correlation. A correlation of 1.0 means that a candidate will always achieve the same score, while a correlation of 0.0 will mean that the scores of a candidate will vary at random. For example, the scores of ability tests are very reliable and achieve a correlation of 0.9 or more. This means that a candidate will achieve a very similar score if they complete an ability test a second time. The reliability of traditional interviews is much less, and a typical correlation would be 0.3. This means that, while there would be a slight trend for candidates to obtain similar scores, far more would depend upon the person who interviewed them.

- **Validity**: does the selection method accurately predict which candidates will be successful? Validity is usually established by collecting scores at the selection stage and correlating them with the later job performance.

Occupational psychologists have been studying the use and accuracy of different methods of selection for over 80 years and are able to provide the general results contained in Table 5.2.

The left-hand side of the table shows the frequency with which companies use the different methods (Smith and Abrahamson, 1992). It will be little surprise that the traditional methods of interviews, application forms or letters and references are the most frequently used methods of selecting employees. There are, however, some interesting national differences. In most countries the use of graphology is fairly rare at about 3 per cent. However, in France approximately 40 per cent of organisations use this technique and the French data have a marked effect upon the average figure shown in Table 5.2. Indeed, the use of graphology outside France is largely restricted to subsidiaries of French companies. Whilst, on average, references are used as a part of selection in 43% of cases there are notable national differences. The use of references in the UK is very prevalent and is used by about 74 per cent of companies, but its use is much less common in other countries.

The right-hand side of Table 5.2 indicates the accuracy (validity) of the methods of selection. It is based largely upon the paper of Schmidt and Hunter (1996). Results gathered over the last 85 years indicate that the traditional and most prevalent methods of selection are not very accurate (valid). Traditional interviews, for example, have a validity of about 0.15.

More modern methods such as work samples, intelligence tests and situational interviews are far more accurate and have validities in excess of 0.50. While this is a big improvement it should be noted that modern methods of selection are still far from perfect and many selection errors are still made.

	Use		Accuracy/Validity	
100%		1.0		
90%	Traditional Interviews 90%	0.9		
80%	CVs & Letters of Application 80%	0.8		
70%		0.7		
60%		0.6	*Intelligence & Integrity*	*(0.65)*
			Intelligence & Structured Interviews	*(0.63)*
			Intelligence & Worksample	*(0.60)*
50%		0.5	Work Sample Tests	(0.54)
			Intelligence Tests	(0.53)
	References 43%		Structured Interviews	(0.51)
40%		0.4	Job Knowledge Tests	(0.48)
			Integrity Tests	(0.40)
			Personality Tests	(0.40?)
30%		0.3	Assessment Centres	(0.37)
			Biodata	(0.33)
			Conscientiousness	(0.31)
20%	Mental Ability Tests 22%	0.2	References	(0.25)
	Personality Tests 18%		Traditional Interviews	(0.15)
	Work Samples 13%		Years Education	(0.15)
10%	Graphology 13%	0.1	Interests	(0.14)
	Assessment centres 8%		Years Job Experience	(0.09)
			Graphology	(0.2)
0%	Astrology 2%	0.0	Age	(−0.01)

TABLE 5.2 The Use and Accuracy of Selection Methods

■ **Fairness**: selection methods should be equally accurate in predicting the success of candidates irrespective of factors such as sex, ethnic group, age or disability. This does not necessarily mean that every group must have the same average score (the egalitarian fallacy).

The selection process should give applicants a *realistic preview of the job*. In other words, at the end of the selection process a candidate should have a realistic picture of what the job involves. If they have an unrealistic picture of their future jobs they are likely to leave within a few weeks and the organisation will have to bear the extra costs of recruiting another replacement. Realistic job previews (RJPs) can be provided by giving applicants information in brochures or handouts. An RJP can also be arranged by asking candidates to watch a video or by providing a tour of the workplace and allowing questions to existing employees.

5.2 Training and Development

Selection tries to ensure that employees arrive with the skills, knowledge and abilities (competencies) that are needed. However, selection is never perfect. Usually new employees have most, but not all, the required competencies. Training and development is one way of making up the deficit between actual and required competencies. The subject of training can be divided into five major topics:

- assessing training needs
- induction training
- on-the-job training
- off-the-job training
- management development

Assessing training needs

An analysis of training needs usually proceeds in three stages. First, the *strategic plan is inspected and the major human resource implications are identified*. For example, a strategic plan may aim for a 20 per cent increase in market share. To achieve the increase it may be necessary to arrange training for existing sales staff, recruit four extra sales representatives and seven production operatives together with two additional administrative staff. Sometimes, this process is called human-resource planning.

Second, the capabilities of existing or new employees are evaluated against the capabilities that will be needed. The difference is often called "*the training gap*".

Third, arrangements are made to *provide the training and development* which will close the training gap. In essence, this training can be divided into on-the-job training and off-the-job training. If the strategic plan requires a large number of new employees, a substantial level of induction training will be needed to close a training gap.

Induction training (orientation training)

Induction training aims to familiarise a newcomer with the organisation. It usually covers details which are taken for granted by existing employees. It may include arrangements for receiving wages, conditions of employment, grievance procedures, refreshment facilities and car-parking arrangements. It aims to remove irritants to new employees and reduce the probability that they leave within the first few weeks. Induction training will usually include information about the company, its history, its structure and products. This information is an important element of fostering company loyalty and ensuring that a new employee becomes an effective one. Finally, induction training usually tries to communicate the culture and ethos of the organisation.

On-the-job training

On-the-job training is probably the oldest and simplest type of training. Since time immemorial new female recruits were told to "sit by Nellie" and watch what she does and male recruits have been told to "stand by Sid" and be similarly observant. On the job training requires little preparation and there are few obvious costs. Furthermore, the training is very realistic and there are no transition problems when a trainee is transferred to production. Nevertheless, this type of training has severe problems: it is inefficient and costly. Costs are, however, hidden and show themselves in terms of low production from Nellie and longer training times. In addition Nellie may teach the trainee bad habits!

Other forms of on-the-job training have more positive outcomes and they are very useful after initial training has been completed. The success of these approaches depends upon careful planning and the availability of a **mentor** who will discuss work with the trainee and ensure that appropriate lessons are drawn. First, the mentor determines what the trainee already knows. Often the mentor will then demonstrate the job to the trainee. In other cases the mentor will arrange for someone else to give instruction. Instruction will cover one point at a time. The trainee will be asked questions to check that learning has taken place. When it is evident that the trainee has fully understood the task he or she will be asked to try it out by themselves. Once the trainee has gained confidence further guidance can be given. Finally, the trainee is left to perform the job unaided. Initially the performance of the trainee should be monitored at regular intervals but later this can be reduced.

This basic approach to on-the-job training is used in two main contexts: job rotation and special assignments. **Job rotation** is useful with new recruits, such as graduates, who have little previous experience of work or the organisation. It involves moving trainees through a series of jobs in different departments. For example, a graduate trainee may spend the first month in the production department, the second month in the sales department, and so on. Job rotation is an excellent way of allowing new recruits to build up knowledge of the organisation. It produces a flexible workforce and it allows trainees to make informed decisions about the direction of their future careers.

Special assignments are used with longer-serving employees. Generally a review of training needs for a specific employee reveals development need. An assignment which is different to present duties and which will allow new knowledge and skills to be acquired is found. For example, the strategic plan of a financial service company may envisage expansion into foreign markets. A review may reveal that an existing personnel manager has no experience of foreign cultures. The organisation may therefore arrange a special assignment in which the individual is seconded for six months to the personnel department in, say, Singapore. Sometimes it is possible to arrange a special assignment in another organisation.

Off-the-job training

Off-the-job training is conducted away from the workplace. This can disrupt the normal flow of work and incur substantial out-of-pocket expenses. Off-the-job training can be delivered in many ways including:

- night school
- day release
- block release
- special seminars and workshops
- correspondence courses
- audiovisual training

The most appropriate method of delivery depends upon circumstances. For example, a day release course for printing machine engineers may be appropriate for trainees who work close to a suitable college. However, commuting and travelling times would make day release inappropriate for similar engineers who work in outlying areas. They might find block release courses more suitable. Similarly, much will depend on the ability and motivation of trainees. Generally, night school courses and correspondence courses are only suitable for people who are very highly motivated.

Off-the-job training may involve a wide range of the instruction methods. The main ones are:

- **Lectures**. Lectures are a very cost-effective method because their size is limited only by the size of the lecture theatre. Lectures can be very good at introducing a topic, identifying the structure of a subject and highlighting the key points. Lectures are not a good medium for consolidating learning of detailed matters. This must be completed by the trainee at a later time using their notes and books. Lectures have an intrinsic difficulty: they are usually boring. Communication between lecturer and learner is usually one-way only. It is therefore vital that lecturers maintain interest by introducing variety and involving the students in some way.

- **Classes and seminars** are costly because their size is usually limited to a maximum of 16 students. Classes are based upon the question and answer technique. They are interactive and are able to maintain interest while consolidating detailed learning. Classes can only make slow progress and can cover only small areas of a subject. Neither classes nor lectures are good at teaching interpersonal skills.

- **Role plays** require trainees to act out certain situations – usually situations involving decisions or interpersonal situations. For example, customer relations training may involve trainees dealing with a succession of "mock" customers who make a range of complaints. Often role plays are videotaped so that the trainee's performance can be discussed and appropriate lessons drawn.

- **Discussion groups** are used when training focuses upon changing or developing attitudes. A relevant topic will be introduced by a skilled leader. The group will then be invited to discuss the topic. The leader inconspicuously rewards positive attitudes and ignores negative ones. For example, a training session on ethnic diversity might include a discussion group on racial prejudice. Whenever a participant expresses tolerant attitudes, the discussion leader signals approval and encourages the participant to amplify their ideas. The contributions of participants with intolerant attitudes are accepted politely, often with minimal comment.

- **Case studies** are a very popular method of in-depth management development. Students are given background data and the details of the specific problem. They are then asked to discuss the situation and recommend a course of action. The actions actually taken and their consequences are then revealed. Students are able to compare their suggestions with the action actually taken. They also try to analyse the situation to evaluate why the organisation's actions did, or did not, work. Case studies aim to extend the experience of students in a short period of time. It is claimed that the process improves students' analytical ability. Although the case study method is used in many top management courses, it also has its critics who maintain that the method results in "shared ignorance". There is an assumption that the person who creates a case study is an objective and knowledgeable expert. In fact, most problem situations involve a number of explanations. The person who creates a case study will choose the explanation which suits her or his purposes and it can never be known whether or not they have chosen the correct one. Students like case studies because they seem realistic. In fact, most case studies are oversimplifications and the solutions proffered rarely have empirical evidence of their effectiveness. Indeed, shortly before its collapse in shame and ignominy, business schools around the world used more than a dozen Harvard Business School case studies that hyped and praised the innovation of Enron and the Enron business model (Curver, 2003). In effect, these case studies were teaching bad business methods. More details of the Enron collapse are given in Chapter 15.

- **Audiovisual training** is a medium that has many potential advantages. Typically, training is contained on a compact disc and trainees can use it at any time convenient to them. The flexibility of audiovisual training means that there is no disruption of the normal workflow. The training is also likely to be cheap since it can be delivered to any workstation or home study which has a personal computer. At its simplest audiovisual training will involve a screen containing text. When this has been read, the trainee completes, say, a multiple-choice test and he or she is immediately given a score which shows whether the material has been learned successfully. Audiovisual training can have more sophisticated features. For example, a video clip can be used instead of text. In some situations, audiovisual training can be highly interactive and the training can branch according to decisions made by the trainee. Audiovisual training is very useful when there is a clear set of objective "facts" that a trainee must learn. For example, audiovisual training is a good way of training computer programmers to diagnose problems and faults. However, the set-up costs are high. This means that it is only appropriate where a large number of people require training. The high set-up costs also mean that this training is appropriate where the material is unlikely to change for a significant period of time. Indeed, critics complain that audiovisual training is inflexible, because the costs of making adjustments are so high. Initially, trainees like audiovisual training. However, the most able trainees quickly become bored and complain that it is too repetitive and pedestrian.

Management development

Training implies learning specific knowledge, procedures or skills to meet existing challenges. Development implies the improvement of a more general capability which can be used to meet unforeseen situations. Management development is therefore a broader concept than management training. In most circumstances people in the first two years of their management career should spend at least four weeks on development courses. Thereafter, experienced managers should spend about two weeks per year on development activities. The two most prominent aspects of management development are **learning skills** and **self-awareness**.

Learning skills are an important aspect of "knowledge management". In a dynamic and rapidly changing world it is impossible to specify and train people to solve all the problems they might encounter. It is much better to train people in ways of solving problems so that they can solve problems themselves as and when they arise. This means that managers need to be aware of their own style and any of their weaknesses in problem solving. Probably the most famous analysis of problem solving was made by Kolb and Fry (1975). They viewed problem solving as a continuous cycle with four main stages:

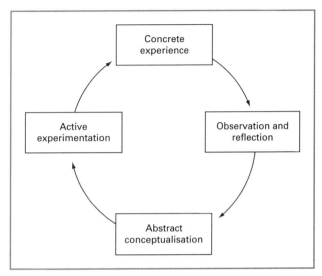

FIGURE 5.1 Kolb and Fry's Learning Cycle

- **Concrete experience** occurs when a person performs an action and then directly experiences the results of that action in their specific situation.

- **Observation and reflection** follow from concrete experience. An individual tries to understand why the result followed from the action in that particular situation.

- **Abstract conceptualisation** involves extending the lessons from a particular situation to a more generalised idea of how the action and the result might be linked in a wide variety of situations.

- **Active experimentation** involves seeking out new circumstances in which to test the general ideas generated in the previous stage.

The active experimentation produces a new set of concrete experiences which set the cycle in motion again. According to this analysis management learning is a continuous cycle in which ideas become more and more accurate. Kolb found that individuals differed in their approach to problem solving. Some would emphasise concrete experience while others would emphasise active experimentation, etc. However, effective learners need to be proficient at all stages of the cycle. A weakness at any one stage will slow down the whole learning process. It is therefore important for managers to locate their area of weakness and develop it to the level of their ability at the other stages. A number of people including Honey and Mumford (Honey, 1982) have adapted Kolb's ideas.

The **self-awareness** of managers can be developed in a number of ways. Sometimes it is achieved by special training courses (*T groups*) where a workgroup sets aside, perhaps, two days to discuss their perceptions of each other. Each group member becomes, in turn, the focus of the training. The other group members give their frank and open views of that person and any inaccurate perceptions are challenged and discussed. Often the sessions are stormy but, it is claimed, at the end of the training the workgroup will have fewer personal misunderstandings.

360° feedback is another way of increasing a person's awareness of their strengths and weaknesses. A questionnaire measuring the competencies the organisation believes are necessary is produced. The questionnaire is then circulated to a person's boss, their colleagues and their subordinates and it is completed anonymously. The results are compiled and fed back to the individual so that she or he will be aware of how they are perceived by other people. The feedback will clearly indicate areas where other people believe they are strong and where they are weak. A manager will then be in a position to take action to improve areas of weakness.

5.3 Motivation

Motivation is the energy which enables people to achieve an organisation's objectives. Motivations are sometimes called drives. An organisation can recruit and select very able people; it can train them so that they have the appropriate knowledge but without motivation they will be ineffective employees. Motivation determines the goals a person attempts to achieve, the energy that is devoted to attaining the goal and the persistence with which the goal is pursued.

Motivation can be increased in many ways. Probably the most effective way is to design a job so that people derive intrinsic enjoyment in their work and are keen to do it. This aspect of motivation was covered by the section on job design in the previous chapter on organisational processes. However, it is often necessary to use other techniques to add extrinsic motivation to a job. Extrinsic motivation can be provided by factors such as pay, recognition or social pressure. Extrinsic motivation can also be provided by a person who is either a formal or informal leader of a group.

Theories of motivation

Many theories of motivation have been put forward. Some popular theories, such as Maslow's Hierarchy of Needs and Hertzberg's two-factor theory, have not been supported by scientific evidence. However, Equity Theory, Expectancy Theory and Goal Setting Theory are particularly relevant to managers.

Equity theory

Equity Theory was put forward by Adams in 1965. It is a very simple theory which states that people try to balance what they put into a job with what they get from it. If the rewards from a job are less than the effort they expend, they will reduce their effort to restore the balance. On the other hand, if the rewards are noticeably higher than the effort they expend then will increase their effort in order to restore the balance. The implications of Equity Theory are straightforward. If an employer wishes to increase motivation, wages should be raised and employees will then increase their effort in order to maintain the balance. Unfortunately, research suggests that the situation is not quite so simple. It would seem that, while balance theory is correct in predicting that a decrease in rewards will be met with a decrease in effort, an increase in rewards does not necessarily guarantee an increase in effort.

Expectancy theory

Expectancy theory is one of the dominant theories of motivation. It starts by noting that different people value different things. In an employment context, some people are motivated by money, some by status while others are motivated by security. This means that one of the first steps in increasing motivation is to identify those rewards which are valued by a specific individual.

Expectations play a crucial role in determining how hard people will work. Two expectations are particularly important. The first is the expected probability of achieving the level of performance demanded. This is called the *"effort–performance expectancy"*. It is the answer to the question, "if I make the effort, how likely is it that I will achieve the performance required?". For example, a sales person might have a target of 100 sales per month. The effort performance expectancy is the chance a sales person believes they have of achieving that target, provided they make the effort. They may believe that their chances are good (high effort–performance expectancy) and consequently they will work hard to achieve that target. However, the sales person may believe that the target is too ambitious or the market is in recession, and consequently no matter how hard they work they will not achieve that target (low effort–performance expectancy). Consequently they will not be motivated to make the required effort.

The second expectation concerns the link between performance and reward *(performance–reward expectancy)*. It answers the question, "if I achieve my target performance what is the likelihood that I will be given my reward?". For example, a sales person might believe that achieving their target is certain to result in a large bonus (high performance–reward expectancy). On the other hand, the sales person might believe that the organisation's word cannot be trusted and that, even if the sales target is achieved, a bonus will not be given (low performance–reward expectancy). The situation is shown in Figure 5.2.

Expectancy theory has clear indications for managers who wish to maximise the motivation of their staff:

- Do not assume that everyone is motivated by money. Work out the rewards that each person values and offer these as incentives.
- Make the performance required absolutely clear. Specify exact behaviours.
- Make sure that employees know that achieving the target performance will be rewarded. Never renege on a promise of a reward – it will lower, probably irrevocably, the performance–reward expectancy.

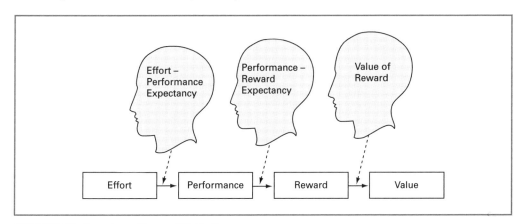

FIGURE 5.2 The Expectancy Theory of Motivation

■ Make sure that performance targets are considered to be reasonable and attainable with extra effort.

Goal-setting theory

The basics of goal-setting theory were developed by Locke (1968) and claims have been made that it has more scientific support than any other approach to motivation (Pinder, 1984). The basics of goal-setting theory are very simple: people are motivated and work harder when they are set difficult, but not impossible, goals. Goals focus people's attention on required behaviour and allow them to mobilise their efforts in a clear direction. Moreover, goals often boost people's commitment so that they will persevere longer in the face of difficulty.

The nature of the goals is a crucial factor in their ability to motivate. People are motivated when goals are:

■ **Difficult but realistic** and within the capabilities of employees. Often, goals should be set using the performance of existing employees as a guide. For example if the top 15 per cent of sales representatives obtain average monthly sales of £80 000, a target of £80 000 can be set for all sales representatives.

■ **Vague goals** such as "work very hard" do not motivate people as much as specific goals that specify quantity, quality and timescale. A specific goal for a lumberjack might be to fell 40 trees (quantity) per day (timescale) with side branches removed and delivered to central logging depot (quality).

■ **People are committed to goals** and regarded them as reasonable. Some researchers say that goals should be set in a participative way but others maintain that delegated goals are just as effective.

5.4 Leadership

Definition and concept of leadership

One way of motivating people is to provide leadership. The central concept of leadership is the power to influence others and get them to do things they otherwise would not do. It is often the ability to get people to follow a vision of a better state of affairs. Probably the best formal definition of leadership is:

 ... a social influence process that involves determining a group's objectives, motivating behaviour in aid of these objectives and influencing group maintenance and culture.

(Lewis, Goodman and Fandt, 1995)

Sources of leadership power

Leaders have power. Managers usually have formal power which derives from their position in the organisational structure. However, there are other sources. The main types are:

■ **Position power** is sometimes called legitimate power and it stems from a manager's position in the organisation. Often this power will be written down and enshrined in job descriptions. Position power may overlap with other sources of power because a position in a hierarchy will usually give a person control of both intellectual and material resources.

■ **Reward power** is the ability to bestow or withhold things that other people desire. Typical rewards are pay and promotion. Rewards also include the allocation of desirable jobs and recognition. Managers can use these rewards to influence behaviour. **Coercive power** is one particular type of reward power. It is the ability to dispense punishments. Typical punishments include verbal reprimands, pay penalties or even dismissal.

■ **Expert power** is based on knowledge and special expertise. It is often derived from possession of a central position within a communication network which provides up-to-date and, often, confidential information. Expert power may not always reside with managers. Frequently, expert power resides with technical specialists. For example, a relatively junior IT specialist may eclipse a senior manager when a problem involving computers needs to be solved.

■ **Referent power** is based on popularity. It is the power associated with interpersonal attraction. It often involves admiration and the willingness to accept someone as a role model.

It should be remembered that power in itself is neither good nor bad. It is the uses to which power is put that matter.

Structure of leadership

At first sight leadership might appear a simple and unitary topic – people are born to leadership and when a situation is in need leaders are able to emerge, take charge and lead people to better things. Consequently, according to this view, it is only necessarily to understand the leaders. However, leadership is much more complex and involves two other major factors: the people who follow the leader and the situation in which the leader operates. The situation is shown in Figure 5.3.

This structure provides a convenient way of organising the many theories of leadership. In many texts they are treated as a "graveyard tour" in which the ideas of dead theorists are described in chronological order. It is better to organise ideas under three headings: characteristics of leaders, leaders and followers and, leaders and situations.

Characteristics of leaders

Many researchers tried to identify the characteristics of leaders. Initially, this research was not very fruitful, because different studies highlighted different characteristics. These differences led researchers to the contingency theory of leader-

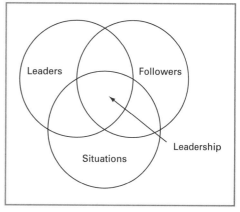

FIGURE 5.3 The Structure of Leadership

ship. However, a re-examination of the results of early studies indicated that leaders tend to show a consistent set of traits. They tend to be more:

- energetic and tenacious
- assertive and proactive
- honest, trustworthy and well organised
- intelligent, verbally fluent
- self-confident, interpersonally skilled
- commercially astute

Possession of these qualities does not guarantee a leader. However, someone who does have these qualities will be more likely to gravitate into a leadership role.

More recently, attention has focused on different types of leaders. Three types have attracted attention. They are charismatic leaders, transformational leaders and transactional leaders:

- **Charismatic leaders** are sometimes called "**visionary**" **leaders** and they include great leaders of the past such as Alexander the Great, Boadicea, Churchill, Mother Theresa, Gandhi and Martin Luther King. Charismatic leaders are characterised by a personal "presence", a vision and the ability to inspire followers towards that vision. Charismatic leaders have a dramatic effect on the lives of their followers, who often regard them with awe. Charismatic leaders were first identified by Weber (1947) who defined charisma as a "quality of an individual personality by virtue of which he is considered extraordinary and treated as endowed with supernatural or exceptional forces or qualities". The notion of charismatic leaders belongs to the "great man" (masculine intended) theory of leadership where great leaders are born and cannot be developed or trained. Often, in the fullness of time, charismatic leaders turn out to have feet of clay.
- **Transformational leaders** are less exceptional and revered than charismatic leaders. According to Bass (1985), transformational leaders form a clear view of the future and they are able to achieve a step change in the performance of their followers. This is often achieved by radically changing the way that followers see a situation and their organisation. Transformational leaders usually raise the self-esteem of individual followers and pay attention to their development needs. This contrasts with charismatic leaders who require followers to sacrifice their own needs in favour of "the cause".
- **Transactional leaders** establish goals and then they guide their followers to pursue their plans – largely by means of giving rewards when the plans are executed properly.

Many researchers have investigated the *style of leaders*. At first, investigators studied a *single dimension* of management style – participation. As early as the 1930s Lewin et al. (1939) experimented with leadership style in boys' clubs and found that democratic leaders were more effective than authoritarian or laissez-faire leaders. In 1958 Tannenbaum and Schmidt refined Lewin et al.'s ideas. Instead of seeing leadership style in terms of clear-cut groups they saw it as a continuum stretching from authoritarian at one end to participative at the other. Furthermore, Tannenbaum and Schmidt gave specific instances of the behaviour of managers at various points on this continuum. For example, a very autocratic leader would tell subordinates what to do; a fairly democratic leader would consult with his or her group and a very democratic leader would engage in joint decision-making. A little later McGregor (1960) suggested that managers could adopt one of two leadership theories. Theory X, held by autocratic managers, maintains that workers are lazy, unreliable and need to be told what do. Theory Y, held by democratic managers, says that workers naturally enjoy work and are most productive when they have made a contribution to decisions. The similarities between the work of Lewin et al. (1939), Tannenbaum and Schmidt (1958) and McGregor are shown in Figure 5.4.

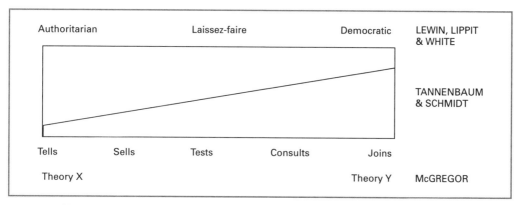

FIGURE 5.4 Similarities between One-dimensional Models of Leadership

Probably the most important studies of this genre were conducted at Ohio State University and the University of Michigan in the middle of the last century. The Ohio studies looked for dimensions of leadership, while the Michigan studies looked for differences between leadership in high-performance units and leadership in low-performance ones. They both came to the conclusion that there were two major dimensions: the emphasis a leader places on *people* and the emphasis a leader places on the *task*. As Figure 5.5 shows, other researchers have located similar dimensions but have used slightly different names. Blake and Mouton (1964) put the two dimensions into graphical form and created the well-known **Managerial Grid**. There they were able to divide the grid into five areas representing five main leadership styles. A leader who stressed both the personal side of the team and the task was called a 9,9 "team manager". A leader who stressed task but ignored the personal side was called a 9,1 "scientific manager" while his or her complement, a leader who stressed the personal side, ensuring that employees enjoyed their work while ignoring the task they were supposed to do, was called a 1,9 "country club manager". A leader who stressed neither the task nor the people was called a 1,1 WIB (weak inefficient bastard). Of course, most managers were somewhere in the middle of the extremes and would be called a 5,5 "average manager".

Leaders and followers

It soon became apparent that even a combination of leader characteristics *and* leader style failed to give a reasonable understanding of leadership in work situations. Something was missing. Sometimes a task-oriented style worked, while at other times a person orientation

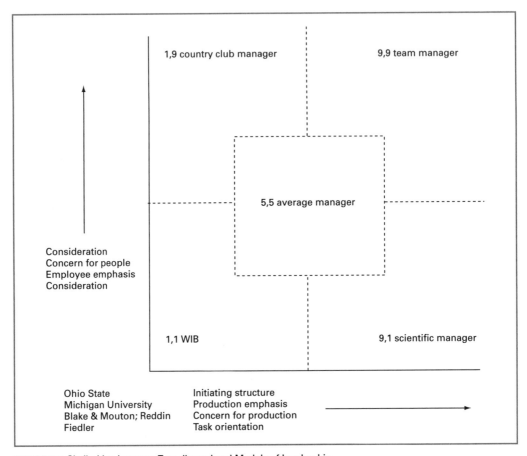

FIGURE 5.5 Similarities between Two-dimensional Models of Leadership

seemed to be better. Some researchers felt that the followers needed to be taken into account while others felt that the situation facing a leader was more important (see next section). Hersey and Blanchard (1982) focused upon the influence of the followers.

They believed that the maturity of the followers was a key variable. Some leaders needed to contend with followers who were not ready to do the task because they were insecure, unable, inexperienced and unaware of what they needed to do. In these circumstances, it would be very appropriate for leaders to adopt an authoritarian style and instruct people what to do. Other leaders might have followers who are ready to do the task. These followers would be able, experienced, willing and confident to perform the jobs that need to be done. In these circumstances, it would be much more appropriate to adopt a participative style where a leader would delegate many things. Hersey and Blanchard divided the followers' readiness to do a task into four segments. As Table 5.3 shows, they then worked out appropriate management styles for each segment.

Table 5.3 also demonstrates how Tannenbaum and Schmidt's work and Blake and Mouton's (1964) scheme can be integrated with Hersey and Blanchard's ideas. Robert House (1971) also investigated the way that the appropriate leadership style depends on fol-

Follower Readiness	Very Low (R1)	Low (R2)	High (R3)	Very High (R4)
i.e. characteristics of followers	unable and unwilling to do tasks or insecure	unable to do job but willing or confident to do tasks	able to do tasks but unwilling or insecure	able to do tasks willing and confident
Appropriate Leadership Style	**Instruct**	**Explain**	**Participate**	**Delegate**
	and closely supervise performance	decisions and provide opportunities for clarification	share ideas and facilitate decision-making	give responsibility for decisions and implementation
Tannenbaum and Schmidt	**Tell**	**Sell**	**Participate**	**Delegate**
Blake and Mouton's Type	**9,1** scientific management	**9,9** team management	**1,9** country club management	**1,1** WIB

TABLE 5.3 Leadership Style and Follower Characteristics

lowers. However, he took a different tack and developed the **path–goal theory**, which has several points in common with the expectancy theory of motivation. In essence, the theory maintains that a leader should adopt a style that helps subordinates attain their goals – provided the goals are consistent with the aims of the organisation. In general, this means that a leader should clarify a follower's *path to goals* and *increase the relevance of rewards* obtained when the goals are reached. Clarification of the path involves:

- helping followers clarify their roles
- helping followers define the goals they should reach within those roles
- increasing followers' confidence that they can achieve the goals

Increasing the relevance of rewards involves:

- learning the followers' needs
- ensuring that a follower receives his or her reward when goals are achieved

House believed that good leaders are capable of different styles and they vary their approach according to the followers' needs. House's ideas are somewhat similar to the idea of **servant leadership** (see Greenleaf, 1977). This rather upside-down view of leadership expects leaders to serve others and the organisation above their own self-interest. Servant leaders are prepared to give away credit for accomplishments, ideas, data and even power in order to fulfil the needs of subordinates. Because they value and wish to enhance their followers they encourage participation and commitment. They encourage creativity and a desire to learn. Servant leaders act as role models and bring out the nobler side of their followers. It is important to note that House also recognised the importance of situations. Although he emphasised helping followers achieve their goals, he acknowledged that the situation was also important. For example, a formal work environment where tasks are highly structured would require a different leadership approach to professional workers in a creative environment.

Leaders and situations

House was not alone in believing that the situation is important in determining the optimum leadership style. Both Fiedler and Vroom and Yetton put situations at the centre of their theories of leadership. Fielder's theory was described in Chapter 2, p. 47 in order to demonstrate contingency theories of management. Fiedler acknowledged that the relationships amongst followers were important, but he also contended that situational variables such as the degree to which tasks were structured and the power of the position occupied by a leader were equally important. Fiedler believed that these three aspects (group relationships, task structure and position power) were aspects of **power** which a leader could wield. According to Fiedler the position power determines the optimum leadership style. This relationship is depicted in Figure 5.6.

Figure 5.6 indicates that when a leader has either low or high situational control they should adopt a style that is task oriented. When they have moderate control they should adopt a style which has high consideration.

Vroom and Jago also considered the importance of situations. Decision-making was the focus of their research and hence their work is considered in more detail in the Chapter 6, Decision processes (p. 137).

Miscellaneous aspects of leadership

A section of this kind can do no more than cover the main themes from the vast topic of leadership. However, it is important not to lose sight of a number of smaller issues. For example, it is interesting to speculate on the differences between men and *women leaders.*

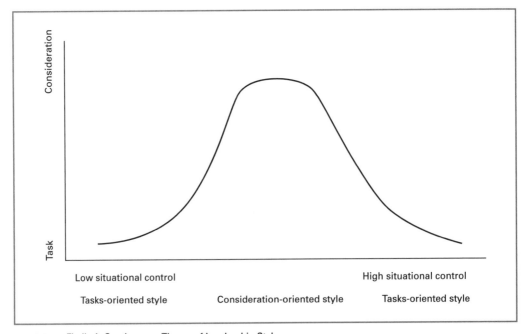

FIGURE 5.6 Fiedler's Contingency Theory of Leadership Style

As more women move into leadership positions, this is an issue of increasing importance. There is some evidence that women leaders are particularly good at motivating and communicating with their teams. They also tend to lead in an interactive, collaborative way. Another up-coming topic is the issue of *virtual leaders* and how they may differ from traditional leaders. Teleworking and other technological advances mean that more people are working away, sometimes continents away, from their leaders. Nobody quite knows how this affects leadership style. Finally, it should be noted that some people are quite cynical about the topic of leadership. They say that it is merely a retrospective attribution. It is very difficult to predict, in advance, which leaders are good and which are bad. They contend that a good leader is merely someone who happens to be on the winning side and who is able to claim the credit for winning.

Activities and Further Study

Essay Plans

Prepare plans for the following essays:

1 Describe how three different theories of motivation can give practical guidance to managers wanting to motivate their subordinates.

2 Define leadership and then describe the main dimensions of leadership style.

3 To what extent are leadership and management the same thing?

4 What is mentoring, how does it work and how effective is it?

Web Activities

1 Look up the local website of Saville-Holdsworth Ltd (SHL), e.g. *www.shl.com/shl/nz*, *www.shl.co.za* or *www.shl.com/SHL/hk* or shl.com. Follow the trail site map … candidate help line … practice tests …; you will then be able to do some of their psychometric tests on line. The site also contains a lot of excellent information about selection and assessment.

2 Look up other sites that give information about recruitment. One good source is the site at the University of Cape Town: *www.careers.uct.ac.za/students/ careering/ articles/selection.pdf*. Often the sites of major employers give details of their selection methods. A good one is Qantas's site *www.qantas.com.au/infodetail/about/ employment/QTests.pdf*. Beware: there are many poor sites offering unscientific tests or which use tests as a part of a sales ploy.

Experiential Activities

1 Write two sentences about yourself under each heading of Roger's Seven Point Plan.

2 Think of a job that you would like to do in, say, three years' time. List the skills and knowledge needed to do that job. Then rate yourself on whether you have the knowledge and skills at present. For each area where there is a gap identify the training you will need and identify a suitable training method.

3 Imagine that you have been asked by your present employer, university or college to develop a one-day induction programme for people joining your organisation. Work out what training you would give.

06

Decision Processes

After studying this chapter you should be able to **explain** why managers need to make decisions, the ideal way in which they should be made and **give some of the reasons** why the ideal is not always attained. In particular you will be able to:

1 **describe in detail** the seven main stages of rational decision-making

2 **describe** five ways of generating alternative solutions to organisational problems

3 **explain in detail** how alternative solutions to organisational problems can be evaluated

4 **draw up** a decision matrix for a major choice you may need to make

5 **describe briefly** six common faults in making decisions

6 **list** two major ways that decisions may vary

7 **distinguish** between programmed and non-programmed decisions

8 **discuss in detail** different styles of making decisions

M anagers never have enough time, money, staff or other resources. If managers obtain what they think are enough resources, they then discover new, more demanding goals which require yet more time, money or staff. This is a good thing. It means that managers are proactive and accept the challenge of continuing improvement. However, the perpetual shortage of resources requires frequent decisions between the available options. Decision-making is therefore an important management process. It can be considered in four main sections:

Chapter contents

CASE 6.1: TO TEA OR NOT TO TEA

Elmwood Fine Teas started in 1990 as tea-room set in a mansion in Kentucky. In a short time it became a local institution and achieved recognition as one of the British Tea Council's best tea places in the world. Thousands of people went to enjoy a formal British tea of sandwiches, scones, cakes and, of course, tea. Two gift shops and an art gallery were added. They did well – visitors usually made purchases after drinking their afternoon teas. The owners diversified. They started wholesaling tea and published books with gourmet recipes (check on Amazon.com). Soon the wholesaling and publishing became bigger than the tearooms and the owners found running all aspects of the business was too much. They had to make a decision whether or not to close the tea-rooms and concentrate on wholesaling and publishing.

Major factors in the decision were:

- The impact on the local community. The tea-room had become a tourist feature, earning money for the local community.
- The tea-room accounted for 40 per cent of the total income.
- Money would be needed for investment in the publishing and wholesale business.
- The tea-room was an important aspect of the brand.

After considerable deliberation the tea-rooms were closed. The mansion was sold (with stipulations that tea-rooms could not be re-opened and the mansion's image could continue as the company logo). The owners are pleased with their decision. The wholesale business is prospering and more books are being published.

Based on Wellner (2006)

6.1 The Rational Decision-making Paradigm

Most organisations wish to make rational decisions and attempt to use the paradigm shown in Figure 6.1.

Each of these stages needs to be examined in detail.

Detect problem

The most crucial step in good decision-making is to recognise a decision needs to be made. It goes without saying that if the need for a decision is not identified then an appropriate action cannot be taken. Most decisions stem from two main causes: a need to correct a problem and a desire to exploit a new opportunity.

Problems are situations where there has been a failure to meet established goals and it is easy to dismiss failures on the basis that they are minor blips which should go away of their own accord. It is easy, and often justifiable, to claim that a failure is the result of someone else's actions and should be resolved by them. Problems arise from five main *sources*:

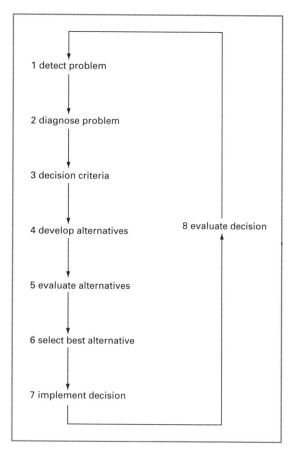

FIGURE 6.1 The Rational Decision paradigm

- **A disturbance** caused by unpredictable factors such as a sudden resignation by an existing employee, the interruption of supplies by bad weather or the discovery of theft and fraud.

- **A decline in performance** such as increased levels of waste, poorer machine utilisation, higher expenses. Gradual, insidious declines often present the greatest difficulties because they are easier to rationalise, overlook or deny.

- **Deviation from plan** such as a delay in commissioning new equipment, failure to achieve planned market share or even an overproduction of merchandise.

- **Competitive threats** such as new competitors, the expiry of patents or the development of substitution products.

- **New opportunities** usually arise from technological developments such as biotechnology or sociological changes including changes in the age distribution of the population and in social attitudes.

Diagnose problem

Once a problem been recognised it must be *defined* and the nature of the problem *diagnosed*. Sometimes a problem is diagnosed at a very superficial level and a decision is made to treat the symptoms of the problem rather than its real cause. For example, a manager may conclude that a decline in sales is due to lack of effort by the sales force. He or she may then decide to retrain sales staff. However, the real cause of the problem may be that the product is out of date and competitors are offering products that are more in tune with the market.

A very simple approach to problem diagnosis is to ask, "*who* is doing *what* to *whom*". A rather more sophisticated method is to ask the following questions:

- What is the evidence that a problem really exists?
- Where does the problem appear to arise?
- When does the problem appear to arise?
- How urgent is the problem?
- Who is most involved with the problem?
- What factors, people, departments, organisations, processes are related to the problem?
- Why did the problem occur?

When a problem has been diagnosed, it is always worth checking the analysis with people who are not involved in the situation and who will not share the same assumptions. This will result in a more robust diagnosis.

Establish decision criteria

Establishing the criteria which a good decision should possess is a vital part of the diagnostic phase. It is often overlooked. Many people do not develop decision criteria until *after* alternative solutions have been identified. This has a major disadvantage. The decision criteria may be distorted to favour one of the alternatives instead of being thought out in a logical way. Examples of some frequently used decision criteria are:

- financial benefits
- financial costs
- physical resources needed
- human resources needed
- quantity (more production)
- quality (better performance)
- certainty of desired outcome (risk)
- acceptability to others
- appropriate timescale
- reliability (e.g. low maintenance)
- compatibility with organisation

The combination of criteria used to decide between alternative solutions will depend on the exact nature of the problem. For example, an organisation deciding which photocopier to purchase may choose to base its decision upon cost, reliability, quantity (sheets per minute) and delivery time.

When decision criteria have been established their relative importance can be assessed. For example, the weight given to the decision criteria for the photocopier might be: reliability 0.4, delivery time 0.3, quantity 0.2 and cost 0.1.

Develop alternatives

The next stage is to develop alternative solutions. Often managers accept the first reasonable solution that occurs. This is called **satisficing** and it is very common. Satisficing means accepting a solution which meets minimum requirements. It is the opposite of **optimising** which is the acceptance of the solution that provides the best possible answer. Research suggests that most managers accept satisfactory rather than optimal solutions.

In most circumstances it is important to generate several alternative solutions which can be evaluated and the best one chosen. If the decision is important, special techniques may be employed to produce enough alternatives. The main techniques are:

- **Employee suggestion schemes** encourage everyone in the organisation to produce new ideas. Many suggestion schemes are moribund and either produce no suggestions or only trivial ones. Good suggestion schemes are usually found in organisations which stress creativity and which give substantial rewards for good ideas.

- **Idea quotas** are used to ensure a steady flow of new proposals. Some companies require each employee to propose at least one improvement to quality, efficiency or service every month. Idea quotas need to be supported by a range of incentives and a commitment by management to implement a large number of the suggestions made.

- **Brainstorming** was a very popular method of generating ideas in the 1970s and 1980s and is still used today. A meeting of, say, six people would meet specifically to generate a large number of ideas. Every member is expected to provide new thoughts, no matter how zany or bizarre they may appear. The number of ideas generated is emphasised. Participants are expected to "freewheel" and build on the ideas of others in a spontaneous and uninhibited way. Criticism, sarcasm or judgemental comments are not allowed. Since written notes appear formal and may slow the process, brainstorming sessions are often tape recorded. Some people doubt the value of brainstorming. They point to findings from social psychology which indicate that true creativity is often a solitary process and that the presence of other people, even in a brainstorming situation, tends to increase the quantity of routine rather than novel ideas. In group situations many people are reluctant to make radical suggestions because they fear the disapproval or ridicule of others.

- **The nominal group technique** attempts to overcome some of the difficulties that arise from group dynamics and is more controlled than brainstorming. Members first write down their individual ideas. During this stage they are not allowed to speak to other participants. Each member then presents one idea to the group. The ideas are not discussed but are merely summarised on a flip chart. In the final stage group members rate each alternative. They are not allowed to speak to each other during this process. Nominal groups are useful when complex, controversial decisions need to be made. They are also useful in situations where assertive members are likely to dominate a discussion. Computer versions of nominal groups in which members communicate by email can also be used. An added advantage of using email is that contributions can be made anonymously.

- **The Delphi technique** is similar to the nominal group technique. However, participants do not meet in person. Instead, participants write out their ideas, which are collated and fed back to the group in an anonymous form. Participants are asked to give the revised estimates which, in turn, are again collated and fed back. The process is repeated until some kind of group consensus is achieved. Initially the Delphi technique used paper questionnaires but today it is more usual to use email.

Evaluate alternatives

The fifth stage of decision-making involves *collecting and collating relevant information*. For example, data concerning reliability, productivity, delivery time and cost of photocopiers could be obtained from rival manufacturers. The accuracy of the information is important. It makes sense to cross-check information from several sources. It would be better, for example, to cross-check the details given by photocopier manufacturers with information from organisations which have already purchased their photocopiers.

More complex decisions such as where to site a factory or whether to develop a new product will require a great deal of information – often more information than a human brain can store. Consequently computers and *management information systems* may be used to assemble, collate and present the information. Generally management information systems track four kinds of information:

- **production data**, e.g. number of units produced, the number of clients processed, machine utilisation or levels of waste recovery
- **financial data** such as present and future cash flow, invoices outstanding, investments
- **commercial data** such as sales, stock levels and perhaps competitor activity
- **personnel data**, e.g. employee numbers, seniority, location and training

Management information systems usually produce routine, monthly or weekly, reports and only alert managers when events deviate from a plan (*exception reporting*). However, managers who are making major decisions are able to request specific reports which contain the information they need. Programmes which produce these specific reports are often called "*decision support systems*". Decision reports have a tighter focus than general reports and they will attempt to filter out routine and irrelevant information. Decision reports need to deliver high-quality information which is up-to-date and comprehensive. Furthermore, the information needs to be presented in a way that is easily understood by the people who are making the decisions (see Chapter 10, p. 207).

Many decisions are made against an uncertain background. The data used by decision support systems often contain estimates containing a margin of error. Decision support systems may therefore include a "*sensitivity analysis*" (sometimes called a "what if" analysis) that will take account of a range of possibilities. Typically, a sensitivity analysis consists of three sub-analyses: first, the analysis is performed on the best estimates available. This will be called the "central prediction"; second, an analysis using optimistic estimates, which assume everything goes well, is performed; third, an analysis using pessimistic estimates, which assume that things go wrong, is performed. Sensitivity analyses are vital if a wrong decision could jeopardise the survival of an organisation or have other very serious consequences. They allow the decision-maker to see whether a decision could send the organisation out of business.

In theory, a decision should be made on the basis of all relevant information. This is often the counsel of perfection – it may take a long time to assemble all the relevant facts. In the meantime, the decision may have been overtaken by events and a competitor may have already exploited the opportunity. Furthermore, there may be so much relevant information that it swamps the memory and the brain capacity of the decision-maker. Unless the decision is very important it may be better to make a choice upon the information that is readily to hand. Some people adopt the *Pareto Principle*, which implies that a decision can be made when 80 per cent of information is available (the 80/20 rule).

Unfortunately, the data on the decision criteria are usually provided in terms of different units. For example, the reliability of a photocopier may be expressed in terms of break-downs per year, productivity may be expressed in terms of pages per minute and the cost of the machine may be expressed in terms of pounds, dollars or euros. It is necessary to convert them into a common unit. The simplest way of achieving this aim is to rank each alternative on each decision criterion. However, ranks can be very deceptive. It is better to use a common scale (usually a 1–9 scale). These ratings are multiplied by the weighting to produce a *decision matrix*. For example, Figure 6.2 gives a decision matrix for the purchase of a photocopier.

In this example it is clear that copier B is the best choice despite its relatively poor delivery time.

	Reliability (0.4)	weighted reliability	Delivery (0.3)	weighted delivery	Quantity (0.2)	weighted quantity	Cost (0.1)	weighted cost	TOTAL
Copier A	5	2.0	1	0.3	9	1.8	3	0.3	**4.4**
Copier B	9	3.6	3	0.9	7	1.4	1	0.1	**6.0**
Copier C	3	1.2	9	2.7	1	0.2	9	0.9	**5.0**
Copier D	1	0.4	7	2.1	3	0.6	5	0.5	**3.6**

FIGURE 6.2 Example of Decision Matrix

Implementation

Even correct decisions are useless unless they are implemented. The first stage of implementation is to communicate the decision to those who need to take action. This is much easier if these people have previously participated in making the decision. One specific person should be made responsible for carrying a decision to fruition.

Evaluation

The implementation process should be monitored to check whether a decision produces good results. Sometimes it may be necessary to adjust the way that the decision is implemented or it may be necessary to adjust the decision itself – in extreme circumstances it may even be necessary to abandon or reverse the decision in the light of subsequent events. The lessons learned during evaluation should be used to improve later decisions.

6.2 Common Problems in Decision-Making

It is rare for the decision-making paradigm to be followed in its pure form. Sometimes certain phases will be omitted. Often it is necessary to cycle through the paradigm several times before the best decision is made. Frequently other factors intervene to create decision-making faults. The most frequent faults are probably bounded rationality, anchoring, procrastination, escalation of commitment and groupthink.

Bounded rationality

The decision-making paradigm is based on the assumption that people are rational and logical. However, experts such as Simon (1955), Bromiley (1999) and Agnew and Brown (1986) have argued that human beings find it difficult to be totally objective and when managers make decisions they do so in a "**bounded rationality**" – in other words a rationality that is limited by human frailty. The rationality of managers can be bounded by a number of factors. It can be bounded by cognitive overload. A decision may involve a great deal of information which is too much for a human being to remember and understand. Under these circumstances the decision-maker may try to simplify the situation and use "rules of thumb" called *heuristics*. Heuristics are simplifications and shortcuts that appear to help complex decisions. Typical everyday examples of heuristics are "never schedule activities for more than two-thirds of the time available" or "always allow a 20 per cent overrun on building projects".

Many other factors may prevent people from behaving totally rationally. Logical reasoning may be distorted by attitudes, emotions and intuitions. The ability to reason logically may also be bounded by pressure and stress (see p. 136)

Procrastination

Procrastination is the tendency to delay decisions without a valid reason. It is sometimes called dithering and is personified as the "thief of time". Procrastination usually results in indecisiveness and may make a problem more difficult because it has extra time to grow. Procrastination often arises from a fear of failure. It is most prevalent in organisations with a "blame culture" where avoiding mistakes is more important than achieving success. Probably the most effective way of overcoming procrastination is to divide a decision into smaller stages and to set a deadline for the completion of each smaller stage.

Avoiding procrastination does not mean that decisions must be rushed. It means that *unnecessary* delays should be avoided. Impulsive decisions are as bad as delayed ones. In most circumstances it is appropriate to allow time to "sleep" on a decision so that it can be subjected to a reasonable period of reflective thought. Procrastination only arises when a decision is delayed for several days without the prospect of new information.

Anchoring

Anchoring refers to a tendency by decision-makers to give undue importance to information that is received early. It is sometimes called the "**primacy effect**". Early information tends to act as the standard by which other information is assessed. If later information is contradictory it will tend to be ignored or dismissed. Unfortunately, early information is often inaccurate because it was assembled in a hurry, without the time to perform cross-checks to ensure that it is comprehensive.

Escalation of commitment

A decision may be made on the basis of early information; but as more facts emerge the original decision becomes untenable. By this time a decision-maker may have invested a considerable time, effort and prestige in the original decision. To abandon it may appear to be a waste of past commitment and be disloyal to their advisers. They may feel that abandoning the original decision would cause them loss of face. Consequently, they may become more and more determined to commit resources to ensuring the success of their initial decision. Up to a point, this may be justified. If a little extra effort is able to produce success then it is reasonable to give a little extra effort. The problem is that a little extra effort may not achieve success – it may require just a little more effort and so on – ad infinitum! There comes a point where it is necessary to cut one's losses and follow another course of action. Some of the worst decisions in history have been the result of the escalation of commitment. In the 1970s America escalated its commitment to the Vietnam war long after it was apparent that the initial decision was flawed. Many government projects have been continued to the point of absurdity because politicians are reluctant to admit mistakes and cut taxpayer's losses. Generally, it is better to avoid these situations by taking a leaf from the book of stock market investors and setting a "stoploss" – a clear point at which they will sell their investment and accept whatever losses they may have incurred.

Groupthink

Participative decision-making has many advantages. A wider range of knowledge or experience and the synergy between members may produce ideas of better quality. However, participative decision-making has a number of disadvantages: it takes extra time, dominant members may distort discussions and the goals of individuals may detract from the goals of the organisation. A further problem with participative decision making is the phenomena of **groupthink**.

Groupthink is a mentality among members of a decision team to suppress their own disbelief in order to show solidarity and maintain agreement at any cost. Members suspend their critical judgements which could lead to a better decision. Groupthink is particularly prevalent in closely knit groups, whose members come from similar backgrounds and who share similar goals. It is also prevalent in groups that have a high regard for each other. Groupthink is partly produced by the desire to conform. Dissenting members may suspend their personal judgement in favour of what they see as the consensus of the group. Unfortunately, other members may be doing the same. An *illusion* of agreement is created. Those who question this apparent agreement may be ridiculed or have their loyalty questioned. Groupthink often impairs a group's ability to generate a wide range of alternatives and to evaluate them effectively. Many disastrous political decisions such as the Watergate cover-up, the Bay of Pigs Invasion and the 1986 Challenger Launch Disaster have been attributed to the negative influence of groupthink.

The effects of groupthink can be so catastrophic that a number of counter-measures have been devised Some organisations only take major decisions after appointing a **devil's advocate** who challenges assumptions and assertions. This forces decision-makers to consider a wider range of solutions. A similar technique is the use of **multiple advocates** where individuals are charged with arguing minority and dissenting viewpoints. Multiple advocacy is used by several governments to ensure that decisions are well argued and take a number of different perspectives into account.

Communication failure

The final fault in decision-making is failure of communication. It is obvious that a decision needs to be communicated to those involved in its implementation. It is slightly less obvious that it should also be communicated to those, such as suppliers, customers and stakeholders, who will also be affected by the decision. Communication should not be confined to the actual decision. The need, the diagnosis and the range of alternatives underlying the decision must be explained. Particular effort is needed to explain the advantages and the disadvantages of the chosen alternative.

6.3 Types of Decision

The previous section outlining the Rational Decision Paradigm was illustrated using a straightforward example of purchasing a photocopier. However, decisions can differ in many ways. In particular, they may differ in the clarity of the situation and the pressure upon the decision-maker.

Clarity

Decisions differ according to their clarity. Some decisions, such as the choice of a photocopier are straightforward. The objective is clear, the decision criteria well known, the information concerning the photocopiers is objective, the problem is well structured and the organisation has procedures for handling this kind of decision. This type of decision is called a "***programmed decision***". Programmed decisions often require little thought and may be delegated to less senior employees. Usually:

- They are repetitive and routine.
- They have existing precedents. Managers do not need to establish new methods and can rely on those which were successful in the past.
- They are well structured.
- They have solutions that are well known or obvious.
- They have a high degree of certainty of the outcome.
- They have most, if not all, of the required information available.

"Non-programmed decisions" are the opposite of programmed decisions. They are non-routine, require original thinking and they are usually taken at a senior level. It has been argued that the increasing uncertainty and volatility of the business environment has increased the proportion of non-programmed decisions. Sometimes, non-programmed decisions can involve unusual or life-threatening situations. Strategic decisions are also usually non-programmed.

In many cases managers cannot be certain of the outcome but they are able to calculate their chances of success or failure with some accuracy. The probability of failure is known as **risk**. Risk is not necessarily a bad thing – it is often associated with higher returns. However, it needs to be managed carefully. It often needs to be spread across different projects or investments so that the failures of some will be compensated for by the success of many others. A cardinal principle of risk management is that the combined level of risk should not jeopardise the fundamental stability of the organisation.

A decision-maker may have clear goals but may not be able to calculate accurately the risks attached to the alternative solutions. These situations are uncertain. **Uncertainty** is usually defined as the inability to calculate the probability of failure. It arises from two sources: the absence of information and the complexity of the environment. For example, a marketing manager may make an uncertain decision because the size of the potential market is not known. An uncertain decision may also be made when the size of the potential market is well established but there are so many factors influencing purchasing decisions that it is impossible to predict the number of sales.

Ambiguity represents the lowest level of clarity. It usually exists when a decision-maker is not clear about the goals. Ambiguity also arises when the alternatives are difficult to define. Sometimes, there is ambiguity in whether a manager should be making a decision at all. Ambiguity means that a manager cannot be clear whether he or she is tackling the right problem or evaluating the right alternatives. Hence it is impossible to even estimate the probability of success.

In general decisions that are clear are likely to be successful. The relationships between the five concepts related to clarity (programmed decisions, certainty, risk, uncertainty and ambiguity) and other factors are given in Figure 6.3.

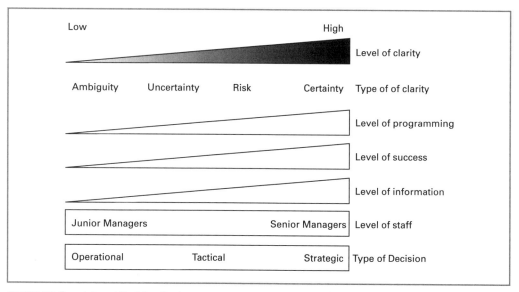

FIGURE 6.3 Correlates of Decision Clarity

Pressure

Decisions also vary according to the degree of pressure involved. Pressure is largely inde-pendent of clarity since a manager can be under pressure whether or not the decision involves a clear, programmed problem or an ambiguous, non-programmed problem. The previous example involving a decision to purchase a photocopier would be a fairly unpressured decision. There are time constraints but conflicts of opinion and political clashes are not present. Pressure in decision-making can be classified under three headings: time, conflict and organisational politics.

Many decisions are made under some kind of **time pressure**. Sometimes the time pressure is caused by a decision-maker's lack of planning and foresight. Managers may simply not foresee problems in time. Sometimes the time pressure is generated by an unfore-seen event such as an accident or the resignation of a key employee. A crisis arises when there is a major threat which must be resolved quickly. Most managers find crises are stressful but many thrive on the excitement and activity. In crisis situations, decision-makers may not be able to consult others. Consequently, they may not be aware of all possible sol-utions and may not be able to reconcile differences of opinions. Many organisations attempt to reduce pressure on the managers in times of crisis by providing *"disaster training"*. This aims to teach decision-makers how to remain cool under pressure and how to deal with the media. It also encourages them to visualise how they would deal with a number of disaster scenarios.

Pressure may also be generated by **conflict** between opposing groups. Conflict may gen-erate strong emotions that interfere with judgement. However, a moderate level of conflict may improve the quality of decisions because it tends to ensure that a wider range of alternatives is considered. Dealing with conflict situations needs a high level of social skill in order to avoid long-term antagonism between contenders.

Conflict is often the consequence of **organisational politics**. Ideally, decisions should be based on a totally objective analysis of facts. In many situations judgements are distorted by favouritism, coalitions, alliances and the desire to please superiors. In these circumstances the pursuit of power and influence may become more important than the correctness of the decision. Organisational politics are more likely to affect ambiguous and uncertain decisions where there are conflicting viewpoints. Dean and Sharfman (1996) found that organisational politics tend to reduce the effectiveness of decision-making. However, it is possible to defend the inclusion of "political factors" on the grounds that, if they are taken into account, the implementation of a decision will be easier because it meets less opposition.

The results of Dean and Sharfman support the generally held view that pressure inter-feres with decision-making. Pressure tends to produce tunnel vision and restrict the number of alternative solutions considered. Moreover, pressure uses up mental capacity so that less is available to diagnose the problem and evaluate alternatives. Other factors which reduce the quality of decisions are described in Section 6.2.

6.4 Styles of Decision-making

Managers approach decision-making in varied ways. Often, the decision-making style adopted by managers will reflect their personality. For example, some managers are cautious and favour solutions that carry little risk, while others are adventurous and favour decisions which carry a high risk. Similarly, some managers are decisive and reach conclusions swiftly while others take a long time and will not come to a conclusion until all the information is available. Perfectionists tend to make decisions slowly. Rigid people often fail to consider all alternative solutions – especially those solutions which include novel elements. Intelligence has a major impact on decision-making. Generally, intelligent people make better decisions more quickly because they process a wide range of information speedily. However, a combination of intelligence and perfectionism can slow down the decision-making process. Such people like to gather vast quantities of information and analyse it exhaustively. Sometimes this can lead to "*paralysis by analysis*".

Rowe, Boulgarides and McGrath (1994) considered all these aspects and came to the conclusion that there are two main dimensions which govern decision style. The first dimension deals with *tolerance for ambiguity*. Some managers like to deal with situations where the objectives are clear, the alternatives are easily understood and the information is objective. These managers dislike ambiguity. They value order and consistency. Other managers are happy to deal with situations that are ill-defined and which can be tackled in a large number of ways. They have a tendency to see problems in a wider perspective and they revel in the freedom which ambiguity may give. The second dimension concerns *rationality*. Some managers are very *rational* and stick to reasoning with objective information. They make their decisions in a logical and sequential way. Others are more *intuitive* and go by their "gut feelings". They tackle a problem from many angles and may use unorthodox, even zany, methods. Rowe, Bulgarides and McGrath used a combination of these two dimensions to identify four decision-making styles.

A manager with an *analytical style* will collect as much data as possible – preferably objective data from a management information system. She or he will consider the alternatives in a clinical, objective way and try to choose the optimum solution. Their decisions will usually be technically very competent. A manager with a *conceptual style* will try to see a problem in perspective and will try to understand the general principles that will give a broad approach. They will collect a large amount of data but they will use information obtained from people as well as that obtained from a management information system. Their decisions will often be unusual and creative. A manager with a *directive style* will often appear efficient and practical. They usually make decisions very quickly because they simplify the situation, deal with a restricted range of information and consider only a narrow range of conventional

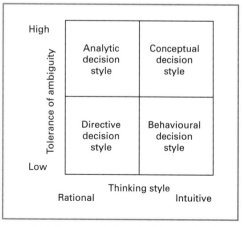

FIGURE 6.4 Rowe et al.'s Four Decision-making Styles

alternatives. A manager with a *behavioural style* is usually concerned with other people's feelings and the impact a decision has upon colleagues and employees. They obtain the majority of their information by talking to others on a one-to-one basis.

It must be emphasised that few people are pure examples of these four styles. Managers may tend towards one of the styles but they will generally adopt other styles when the situation demands. In fact, the situation in which a decision is taken has a considerable influence upon the style that is appropriate. Vroom and Jago (1988) tried to be more specific. Their work involves three main components: an analysis of decision styles, an analysis of decision situations and a procedure for linking styles and situations.

Vroom and Jago did not use the classification of management styles developed by Rowe, Boulgarides and McGrath. Instead they developed their own classification based upon how autocratic or democratic a manager was:

- A **very autocratic** manager (A1) makes decisions entirely on their own using the information available.
- A **fairly autocratic** manager (A2) makes decisions on their own but will obtain information from subordinates.
- A **fairly consultative** manager (C1) discusses decisions with *individual* subordinates and will obtain their ideas. However, this manager will make the decision on their own and the decision may or may not incorporate the views of subordinates.
- A **very consultative** manager (C2) discusses decisions with *subordinates as a group*. However, the decision will be made by the manager on their own and it may or may not incorporate the views of subordinates.
- A **very democratic** manager (G2) is very group oriented. The group will play a major part in identifying the problem, diagnosing the situation, suggesting alternatives and choosing the final course of action. This manager accepts and implements the alternative chosen by the group.

When Vroom and Jago examined decision situations they identified eight important situational variables which are:

- the requirement for decision to be technically correct (DQ)
- the importance of employee commitment (DC)
- the adequacy of the leader's information (LI)
- the structure of the problem (DS)
- probability of employees' commitment to autocratic decision (EC)
- degree to which employees' goals are congruent with those of the organisation (EG)
- the probability that employees will disagree among themselves over the preferred alternative (ED)
- the degree to which employees have enough information to make a good decision (EI)

Note: the abbreviations have been changed from Vroom and Jago's diagram in order to make it clear which factors relate to the Decision (D), the Leader (L) or the employee (E).

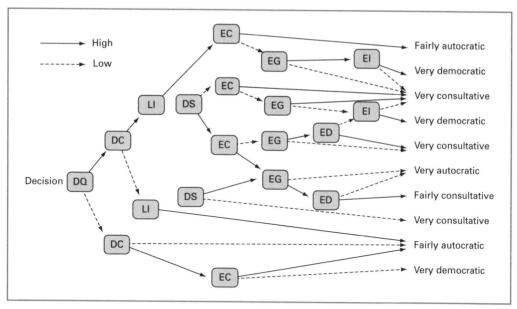

FIGURE 6.5 Vroom and Jago's Decision-making Algorithm

Vroom and Jago simplified these characteristics into two levels: high or low. They were then able to draw up the algorithm shown in Figure 6.5 to identify the appropriate decision style.

Vroom and Jago's diagram is very elegant but it is probably too complex to be of much use to practising managers. Two very general conclusions may be that structured decisions and employee commitment may slightly favour autocratic styles.

Activities and Further Study

Essay Plans
Produce essay plans for the following topics:
1. Why do people make bad decisions?
2. How do decisions differ from each other?
3. What different decision-making styles can managers adopt?
4. Is one decision style better than another?
5. What techniques and strategies would you use to ensure that decisions are properly implemented?

Web Activities

1. Use the web and other sources to find out about the phenomenon of "Risky Shift".
2. Access the following website: ***http://www.mindtools.com/pages/article/newTED_00.htm***. It gives details of the following decision-making tools:
   - Pareto analysis
   - paired comparison analysis
   - grid analysis
   - decision trees
   - PMI (plus and minus implications)
   - Six Hats analysis

   Which tool do you think would be most helpful in making A) simple, easily reversed decisions B) complex decisions with expensive implications?

Experiential Activities

1. Think of three managers (or other people you know well) and try to identify their decision-making style. Evaluate their success as decision-makers and summarise their impact on you and others affected by their decisions.
2. Analyse three decisions you have made in the last year. Identify ways that your decision-making process could be improved.
3. Identify an important decision (such as your choice of course options for next year). Perform a grid analysis to establish the best solution to the problem.

Control Processes

❖ *LEARNING OBJECTIVES*

After studying this chapter you should be able to **appreciate** the importance of control processes in ensuring that plans are effective. You should be able to understand the basic principles of control systems – together with their advantages and disadvantages. In particular you should be able to:

1 **define** control and give at least two examples of the dire consequences to organisations when control is lax

2 **draw a diagram** showing a basic control system

3 **describe in detail** how targets and standards are set

4 **describe briefly** the following concepts:
   – hard outcomes, soft outcomes and distance travelled
   – the characteristics of good standards of performance

   – control variety and the law of requisite variety

5 **describe in detail** the four main requirements of measures of performance

6 **give at least two examples** where measures of performance have been distorted

7 **explain** how actual performance is compared with standards

8 **describe briefly** the following concepts:
   – control charts
   – "six sigma" control systems
   – statistical process control
   – upside risk

9 **explain** how corrective action can be taken to remedy any variance between standard and performance

10 **describe in detail** different types of control system – especially feed-forward, concurrent and feedback control

11 **contrast** the control systems used in different management functions (purchasing, production, HRM, etc.)

12 **explain in detail** the concept of a balanced scorecard

13 **evaluate in depth** the dangers of control systems

Control is an important process because it is the final link in a chain of management. Without some form of control to ensure that end results are achieved, planning, organising, staffing and deciding will have been a waste of time. Control is sometimes called the "terminal" management process because it occurs after the other processes. Control is very closely linked to both strategy and planning. Control ensures that the right things are done at the right time and in the right way.

The consequences of poor control can be dire. Barings Bank is a classic example of an organisation brought to its knees by poor control. It was founded in 1762 and established a venerable reputation until it collapsed in 1995. Nick Leeson, an ambitious securities dealer working in Singapore, decided to obtain outstanding results by using the bank's resources for unauthorised speculation in Japanese securities. Leeson made a small but manageable loss of £2 million in 1992. Inadequate financial controls allowed him to cover his losses with a spiral of further unauthorised speculation until losses reached over £860 million. When the level of Leeson's, and his employer's losses became known, the bank almost collapsed and was ignominiously sold to a Dutch Bank, ING, at a token price. Poor financial control had ended 200 years of banking history. Dire consequences of poor control often arise outside the financial area. For example, in the 1990s poor quality control of its cars meant that Alfa Romeo was forced to withdraw from the American market. A few years ago the giant tyre manufacturer, Firestone, was forced to recall 6 million tyres when its control procedures failed to detect a manufacturing fault. Fortunately, not all control systems are faulty. For years, Perrier had traded on the purity of its bottled water. Then an engineer inadvertently cleaned equipment using benzene. Minute traces of benzene, well within the legal limits, found their way into the water. The control system quickly detected the fault. *All* bottles were withdrawn from shelves and destroyed but good control and response enabled Perrier's reputation to remain intact.

The process of control can be divided into six sections:

Chapter contents

7.1 Definition of Control

One of the best definitions of the control process is given by Merchant (1985) as:

> The systematic process through which managers regulate organisational activities to make them consistent with expectations established in plans and to help them achieve all predetermined standards of performance.

Merchant's definition has two advantages. First, it emphasises that control is a systematic process rather than a haphazard collection of activities that may be started or stopped at whim. Second, it explicitly links control processes with plans and desired organisational outcomes.

7.2 Stages of Control

The control process can be seen as a cycle which contains four main components:

1 setting performance **standards**
2 measuring **actual performance**
3 **comparing** the actual performance with the standards
4 **taking action** to reduce significant discrepancies between standards and actual performance

In fact the situation is more complex and each of these components needs to be covered in greater detail. Furthermore, in reality there are other factors, such as the impact of the environment and the possibility that standards are incorrect. Figure 7.1 illustrates how the components relate to each other.

Setting standards

Standards can take many forms and often they are called *targets* or *outcomes*. They are easiest to set in batch-manufacturing operations such as the production of DVD players. Here a standard might read "each month the Dundee factory will produce 300 000 DVD players that meet quality specifications". Standards are also easy to set in sales environments where a standard might read, "The Canberra store will achieve a turnover of A\$1 400 000 per month with a gross margin of A\$400 000" or "capture 5 per cent of the UK confectionery market by September, 2010". It is usually easy to set standards at a corporate level. Corporate standards might be "Value added per employee will be RMB5000 per year" or "the share price will increase by 5 per cent above the Dow Jones Index over the next three years". Such standards and targets are often called "hard" or "quantitative" standards. *Hard standards* are those which can be checked objectively. The above examples illustrate the fact that hard standards usually have three components:

1 a **quantitative component** specifying how much is produced

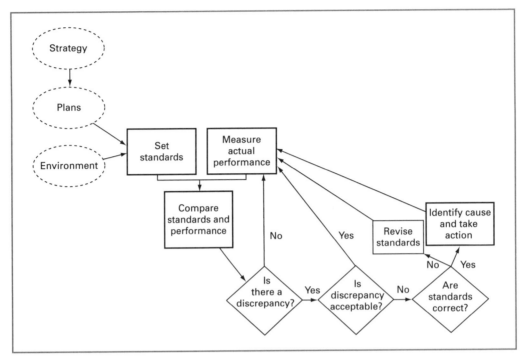

FIGURE 7.1 The Components of a Control System

2 a **qualitative component** specifying the quality of what is produced

3 a **deadline** specifying the **time-frame** of production

Sometimes the standards of performance will have additional components such as the margin of error (i.e. the deviations or random fluctuations that will be tolerated).

In many contexts hard standards are not sufficient. A hospital, for example, may meet its hard target of 100 clinically successful operations per month but it would not be a success if it achieved its target by treating patients in a brutal, inconsiderate and impersonal way. In many situations hard targets need to be supplemented by "*soft-outcomes*" (see Dewson et al., 2000) such as "to the satisfaction of patients". In another situation a local authority in West Yorkshire, UK was awarded a European Union grant for training disadvantaged minority groups. The EU controlled the project by setting hard standards (the number and types of people trained), and soft standards such as participants' self-confidence or their ability to work in a team. In education and training standards are often less concerned with absolute levels of, say, reading ability. A school with a very privileged catchment would find it easy to ensure that 50 per cent of pupils were above the national average for reading whereas a school with a deprived catchment would struggle to achieve the same level. In these circumstances standards are often set in terms of "*distance travelled*" – the actual **change** in, say, reading ability.

The standards employed will depend upon the organisation, its characteristics and the nature of the tasks that it performs. Many *standards will originate* in strategy documents, plans and organisational structures such as MBO. However, a substantial number of the standards will, in effect, be imposed by the external environment. For example, motorists expect a certain level of reliability from their cars. If a manufacturer sets a lower level of reliability it will sell fewer cars and the manufacturer will be faced with the choice between raising their standards or becoming bankrupt. In other instances the standards will be directly imposed by government – in cases of pollution and safety the government will set the standard. For example, a UK molybdenum processing company will be obliged to control its emissions of SO_2 so that they are within the permissible levels set by the British Government. Extra-territorial governments may also set standards. For example, a pharmaceutical manufacturer in the north of Dublin must meet the quality standards of the US Federal Drug Agency because it needs to sell its products in the American market.

Standards of performance may have several characteristics. They should be *clear* and *easy to understand*. Standards need to be written with care so that they are *precise*. For example, a teacher should not set students the standard of being "well prepared" for seminars. The teacher should specify that the student must:

- complete related assignments
- bring materials such as worksheets, books, paper and pencils
- arrive a few minutes *before* the start of the seminar, etc.

Multinational companies also need to take *cultural differences* into account when setting standards – especially when the standards relate to inter-personal relationships and dress codes. For example, it would be inappropriate to set a dress code of a skirt, blouse and jacket for women working in a Muslim country. This illustrates that standards of performance must be reasonable and acceptable to those expected to achieve them.

Another issue is the *number of standards* which should be set. As a very broad generalisation, it is better to limit the number of standards to seven or fewer. This means that people will be able to remember, understand and observe the standards without constant references to books and charts. A small number also means that contradictions between standards are likely to be spotted and eliminated. However, in large or complex organisations more than seven standards are needed in order to give comprehensive control. For example, a handful of standards would not give proper control over a pharmaceutical giant such as GlaxoSmithKline. Such an organisation needs to have standards to cover its research laboratories, its production units, its sales force and its accounting procedures. The number of activities, processes and items that an organisation needs to control is referred to as *control variety*. In general, an organisation needs as many standards of performance as there are components to be controlled. This is known as the *law of requisite variety* (Ashby, 1964). It contends that a simple control system applied to a complex organisation will not be comprehensive and will miss important changes and developments.

Control systems designed by committees are prone to having too many performance measures – each committee member may argue for the inclusion of measures that show their unit in a favourable light. Too many measures cause costs to rise, and people may tend to spend more time measuring performance than performing productive work. Furthermore, a large number of measures is likely to swamp management's ability to interpret the information and important information may be crowded out by less useful data. Generally it is better to decide first upon the number of indices that can be handled competently, then prioritise the potential measures before adopting those that are most important. The top 20 per cent of control measures will probably provide control for 80 per cent of an organisation's activities.

Standards are not permanent or "carved in stone". They can and should be changed. Setting standards, especially "soft standards", is often an art rather than a science. Such standards are often first set by guesswork, and experience may then prove them to be too difficult or too easy. They should then be changed so that they are more appropriate. Thus, many standards emerge by a process of trial and error. In other situations changes in the business environment may require changes of standards. For example, if a government enacts legislation to provide extra safeguards for investors, the added paper work will mean that workers in the back-offices of investment institutions will not be able to process the same number of transactions per hour and consequently their performance targets will need to be reduced.

Measuring performance

Once standards have been set, measures of actual performance are needed. In many cases this is easy and what needs to be measured is obvious from the standard itself. For example, if the standard of performance requires a call centre to handle 3000 calls per hour, it is clear that there should be a system for logging and reporting the number of calls answered. However, the situation is rarely so straightforward. Appropriate measures of performance will depend on five factors: what is to be measured, number of measures, accuracy, reporting and costs.

What is measured by performance standards?

Choosing what is to be measured is more difficult than it seems at first sight. The above example of the call centre illustrates that it is easy to identify quantitative, banal measures but, on their own, they are rarely satisfactory. Often the obvious measures are short-sighted and merely perpetuate the status quo. Instead the *measures should be linked to the call centre strategy*. If that strategy is to encourage callers to find the information they need on the Web, it would be much better for each operative to answer fewer calls and spend more time with each caller explaining the Web resources available. In this case a better index of performance would be the number of callers who subsequently refer to the website.

There is also *a tendency for performance measures to be chosen because they are easy to collect* rather than because they provide useful control information. In fact, while it is easy to count the number of calls, the result is not very useful because a call centre which briskly fobs off each caller with an excuse will seem better than one which thoughtfully resolves the callers' problems. The call centre should collect performance data based on the number of enquiries *successfully* resolved per hour – a task which is much more difficult than simply logging the number of calls. A classic example of measuring what is easy to collect rather than what is important is often seen in education, where a committee will scrutinise a course outline and reference list but never attend lectures or observe a lecturer advising a student.

Sometimes, performance measures fail because they *do not monitor the external environment*. For example, a sales manager may monitor the sales figures of his or her team and discover a 10 per cent fall below target. The sales manager may then fire a large proportion of the team and recruit new sales people. However, data from the environment might show that in the country as a whole, sales had declined by 20 per cent and in relative terms the sales team had been doing a good job. Failure to measure the environment probably led to firing high-performing staff and hiring recruits who would probably perform worse.

Number of measures

Control systems should have enough measures so that the main aspects of a system are included – otherwise something important will be missed. On the other hand, it is also ill advised to have too many measures – otherwise the system becomes too cumbersome, time consuming and bureaucratic, and gets in the way of the actual transformation of resources. Under these circumstances there will be a tendency for people to cut corners by entering false data. In some circumstances the use of too many measures means that unimportant ones distract from, or conceal, important information. As a broad generalisation any individual process should be controlled by 5–15 measures.

Accuracy of performance measures

Accuracy of control information is important. A stock control system which merely gives the total number of items in a food warehouse would not be very useful. It would be much better if the warehouse's contents were itemised by product and classified by the proximity of the sell-by date. On the other hand, some control systems, especially those where data is automatically captured by computer, report actual performance to a ridiculous degree of precision. For example, the ink cartridge for a leading brand of bubble-jet printers contains 6 ml of ink plus or minus 0.05 ml, i.e. 5.95 ml–6.05 ml. However, at one time, the zealots in the quality control department measured the ink in cartridges to five decimal places and the control logs would be replete with figures such as 5.03462 ml. Printing the extra digits possibly consumed more ink than was measured by the last three digits! The unnecessary precision may make the information more difficult to interpret.

CASE 7.1: MASSAGING CONTROL DATA IN THE BRITISH NATIONAL HEALTH SERVICE

An established index of the performance of a hospital is the time patients spend on trolleys waiting to be transferred to beds. In response to such targets, some hospitals merely removed the wheels from trolleys and claimed that patients were lying in beds. Another well-established performance measure is based on the time patients spend on waiting lists. Hospitals developed many techniques to manipulate this control measure. One ruse involved telephoning patients to enquire about their holiday plans and then, shortly afterwards, offering the patient an appointment during the period when they were known to be away. When the appointment was declined, the patient was removed from the list and the hospital's performance appeared to improve (Pitches et al., 2003). A spot survey revealed that about one-third of 41 healthcare trusts in the UK were systematically fiddling their performance data (Audit Commission, 2003).

The accuracy of control data can also be undermined by *conscious or unconscious manipulation*. This is euphemistically termed *"data massaging"* or *"performance optimisation"*. As soon as something is known to be used as a measure of performance, it will distort the actual performance it is supposed to gauge. Indeed, there is a maxim: "an index of performance ceases to be an accurate measure of actual performance within two months of its adoption". The rationale is quite straightforward. Managers are rarely stupid. They are aware that if an index shows their performance is poor they, and their unit, will be penalised. Improving performance will probably involve a lot of hard work. On the other hand, *massaging the performance data* on which the index is based probably involves less work. From a parochial view, the latter is a better investment of time. As the months and weeks go by skills in massaging performance data improve. Hence, after an initial interval, more and more error is added and performance data become less and less accurate until it is a very imperfect reflection of true performance. There are stunning examples of this phenomenon in the British National Health Service (see Case 7.1).

The health sector is not alone, however, in fiddling performance. University departments are another guilty party. One index of performance is the number of research papers written by their academics. Some departments boost their performance artificially by encouraging those with few publications to resign and head-hunting staff from other departments who have published more widely. *Smoothing* is a common form of "data optimisation". It is very prevalent in sales and consultancy organisations. If, say, sales for one month considerably exceed a target, some of the sales will not be registered until the next month. Similarly, if sales fall below the target, some anticipated sales for the next month will be registered early. These ruses manipulate control data so that the bonuses to managers and their teams are maximised. Manipulation is so widespread that it must be taken into account when designing control systems. It is essential either to choose performance measures that cannot be falsified or to install an audit system which will detect malfeasance. In many situations it is better to ensure that performance data are collected by someone who is totally independent of the people responsible for actual performance.

Reports of performance measures

Timeliness is another important feature of control systems. Information should be up-to-date so that prompt remedial action can be taken. In batch production of, say, micro-chips, data need to be collected every few minutes so that, should faults occur, corrections can be made quickly so that only a few minutes' production will need to be scrapped. In other industries such as nuclear power generation, performance measures are instantaneous so that problems can be identified very quickly indeed. However, in many circumstances it is better to base indicators of performance on longer time intervals. They will then be less contaminated by temporary factors. For example, it would probably be wrong to judge a sales force's performance upon a single week's, or even a single month's, sales figures. Such information will be inherently unstable. It will be influenced by exceptional events such as one or two very large orders or a dearth of activity caused by seasonal factors.

The format of control reports requires careful consideration. A report should give the information needed to decide whether standards have been met. Its format should be compatible with performance standards and it should be consistent with the needs of those who will use it. Generally, a report should only contain information relating to factors which a person can change or influence.

Costs of performance measures

Finally, *the costs* of performance measures should be kept within reasonable limits. These costs should certainly include the time of those who collect the information, prepare reports and decide upon appropriate action. It may also be wise to include the opportunity costs – the value of the work which they would otherwise be performing. It is a fundamental rule of control systems that the cost of the system must be less than the cost of deviations which they seek to regulate. The rule can be illustrated by a trite example from libraries: it is wasteful to install a security system costing £20 000 per year when the cost of stolen books is only £5000 per year. A more realistic example can be found in one social service department where an administrator whose labour costs are £22 000 per year is employed to check attendance records of care assistants in order to avoid false travel claims amounting to £5000 per year.

Comparing performance with standards

As the diagram of a control system at the start of this chapter shows, the third stage is to compare actual performance with the standard, attempting to determine whether or not there is a deviation from the standard. In practice, the situation is more complex because many deviations are trivial and insignificant. Consequently, once a deviation has been detected it is necessary to make a further decision whether it justifies action. The situation is clearest with *control charts* that are used in production processes such as radiator manufacture. The nominal size of some radiators is 1 m but plumbers have no difficulty in using radiators that are 5 cm larger or smaller. The radiator manufacturer therefore sets the standard at 1 m but is happy to ignore deviations up to 5 cm. It controls production by measuring every tenth radiator and plotting its length on a traditional control chart.

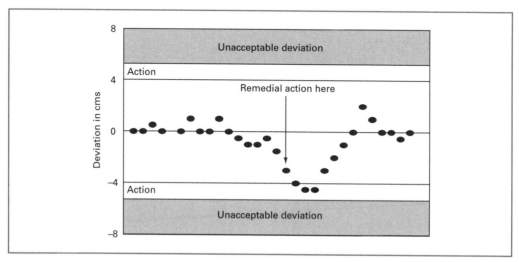

FIGURE 7.2 An Example of a Classic Control Chart

The control charts shows both the target performance and the actual performance (the length of every tenth radiator). It also show the region of unacceptable deviation. In the example of the radiator manufacturer it can be seen that production is proceeding smoothly, well within the region of acceptable performance. Then, for some reason, the radiators begin to get shorter. When they are 4 cm too short, remedial action is taken. However, there is a time lag, and for a while the shortening of the radiators continues but the trend changes just before the deviation becomes unacceptable. The remedial action begins to take effect and the length of the radiators increases until it reaches the standard. As is quite usual, the correction slightly overshoots before settling down at normal levels once more.

The radiator manufacturer set the level at which action should be taken (4 cm) on the basis of its experience. Other companies use "*tectates*" as their level for taking action. A tectate is the level which contains 68 per cent of products when the system is working properly. The tectate equals approximately one-half a standard deviation either side of the performance standard. In fact, the standard deviation is an important statistic in many statistical control processes. Some systems insist that faults occur no more frequently than six standard deviations from the performance standard (approximately three faults per 10 million instances). Such systems are usually called "*Six Sigma*" control systems. They are found most frequently in the manufacturing sector where many thousands of objects are produced and the control process is highly statistical, and in these instances the system will be called "*statistical process control*" (SPC).

It is often assumed that a control process should only protect an organisation against "downside" risk (variation) – such as a failure to meet a production or a sales target. However, in many circumstances, the "*upside*" risk is just as important, if not even more important. A factory that produces too many goods will have had to pay extra costs for raw materials, etc. and then have to pay storage costs until a buyer can be found. It may even turn out that it will need to dump the excess production. Similarly, sales staff who take too many orders may cause an organisation to fail to meet its commitments. Such a sales person may collect his or her commission before moving on to another job – leaving a trail of dissatisfied customers who then turn to competitors.

Corrective action

The first three stages of a control are a waste of time unless some corrective action is taken. Many control systems only trigger action when there are significant deviations from standards. This is usually called *management by exception* – sometimes unkindly dubbed "*wake me if you need me management*". While management by exception is economical and requires the least effort, it is usually misguided. Action should be taken when things are running to plan. For example, people maintaining production at satisfactory levels should be praised for their success. Furthermore, it might be advantageous to analyse why plans are implemented successfully so that they can be held as examples of good practice. In principle, there are three types of corrective action: immediate action, longer-term action and revision of standards.

Short-term corrective action

Immediate action involves accepting a situation at face value and taking short-term measures. It often called "*trouble-shooting*" and it is frequently undertaken by junior management. It is usually clearly defined and it may amount to a knee-jerk reaction. Often appropriate immediate action is stipulated in an operational handbook. For example, a car manufacturer who discovers that cars are leaving the painting department while the paint is still tacky can take immediate action by slowing the conveyor so that cars spend longer in the drying compartment. In many other situations the immediate action is to talk to members of staff whose faulty work has caused the deviation. Short-term remedial action often treats the symptoms of a problem rather than its cause.

Long-term corrective action

Sometimes a control system reveals either a large number of discrepancies or the frequent recurrence of the same discrepancy. It is then necessary to analyse the situation in order to identify the underlying cause or causes. Due to pressure of work some managers are unable to step back and take time to analyse the situation in sufficient depth. They may resort to more and more frequent use of immediate responses. However, it is much more efficient to identify long-term causes and take basic actions. For example, if cars frequently emerge with tacky paint, there could the underlying problems with either the chemical composition of the paint or the engineering specifications of the drying room. Both of these propositions will need to be investigated in depth. In other situations it may be necessary to redesign a job or equipment.

Revision of standards of performance

When neither short-term nor longer-term action can resolve the discrepancy between a standard of performance and the actual outcome, it is usually necessary to re-examine the performance standards. For example, if a railway company cannot meet punctuality standards even after it has purchased new engines and retrained all staff, it would be appropriate to produce new timetables with slightly longer journey times. Unfortunately, revising standards of performance is often a soft option and may be used in preference to making hard decisions about equipment and staffing levels. If standards of performance are revised downwards, the strategic implications must be recognised and the organisation's strategy adjusted in an appropriate way.

7.3 Types of Control System

The stages described in the previous section apply to all control systems. However, the way that they are implemented varies widely. Control systems differ according to their location within an organisation, their orientation in time and the management function.

Control systems classified by location within organisations

A major difference between control systems depends upon whether the control is located in a separate authority within an organisation (centralised control) or whether responsibility for control is widely dispersed throughout the organisation (decentralised control).

Centralised control exercises power along the lines outlined by Weber (see p. 40). It emphasises a hierarchical structure, rules, procedures and the uniformity of their application. Everything is well defined and standardised. Control resides in a formally constituted authority such as quality control or inspectors. Centralised control shares its philosophy with McGregor's Theory X – employees cannot be trusted and they will do things wrong unless they are closely supervised. However, employees can be channelled into doing things correctly using a mixture of threats (e.g. dismissal) and extrinsic rewards (e.g. wages or promotion). Organisations using bureaucratic control tend to be rigid and produce high volumes of standardised products or services. Centralised control is sometimes called "*bureaucratic*" or "*extrinsic*" control.

Decentralised control has a more organic approach. It uses trust and shared values to guide the behaviour of employees. Power is dispersed throughout the organisation. It shares its philosophy with McGregor's Theory Y – employees want to do things right and can be trusted to monitor their own work. Organisations using decentralised control tend to be flexible, adaptive and produce one-off "creative" products or services. Decentralised control is sometimes called "*intrinsic*" or "*organic*" control. Authors such as Ouchi (1980) and Robbins and Decenzo (2003) refer to decentralised control as "*Clan Control*" because control is exercised by the group rather than an external authority. Table 7.1 compares and contrasts bureaucratic and decentralised control.

	Centralised Control	Decentralised Control
Organisational Structure	Top down, formal, many levels, rigid, distrusting	Egalitarian, informal, flat, flexible, trusting
Control Mechanisms	Rules and procedures that are systematically enforced	Socialisation, norms, values and self-control
Enforcement	Quality control, inspectors and auditors	Teams in which everyone monitors quality – especially their own work
Rewards	Extrinsic (e.g. pay, security, status, etc.)	Intrinsic (e.g. pride, satisfaction, work interest, self-development, etc.)
Outputs	High-volume, standardised, mature products and services	Small batch, novel or creative or individual products and services
Environment	Stable or slow changing	Volatile or quick changing

TABLE 7.1 Comparison of Centralised and Decentralised Control

Few organisations are pure examples of either centralised or decentralised control: most occupy intermediate positions. However, the modern trend is to move away from centralised towards decentralised control. Decentralised control is a component of empowerment which means giving junior employees the ability to control their activities, take decisions within prescribed limits and assume responsibility for their actions.

Control systems classified by timing

Control systems are frequently classified according to their timing and are divided into feedforward control, concurrent control and feedback control. Most organisations use a combination of all three types. Figure 7.3 shows how these types of control act upon inputs, the transformation process and on outputs.

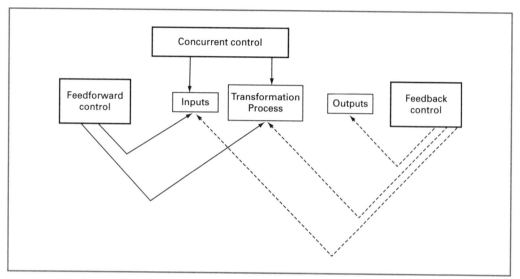

FIGURE 7.3 The Timing of Control Systems

Feed-forward Control (Koontz and Bradspies, 1972) anticipates problems and controls the resources an organisation puts into the transformation process. It attempts to prevent deviations from performance standards before they occur. Generally, this means specifying the correct standards for inputs and then examining them to check that they meet those standards. The exact nature of feed-forward controls will depend upon the nature of the resource being input. For example, manufacturers of Blackberry palm computers will set a high specification for computer chips in order that the chips will perform the required functions reliably over a long period of time. They will then carefully inspect the chips from suppliers to ensure that they meet the specifications. Similarly, top-notch consultancy practices will attempt to control the quality of their future employees by recruiting people with high qualifications from prestigious universities and colleges. Another example of feed-forward control is the screening of potential borrowers by credit agencies to eliminate those who are likely to default on repayments. Feed-forward control is sometimes called *"preliminary"* control or *"preventative"* control. Unfortunately, it is impossible to anticipate all the problems, so concurrent control and feedback control may be needed.

Concurrent control takes place at the same time as resources are transformed. Faults are never given the chance to "build up", and produce waste. A major feature of concurrent control is constant monitoring of the work process. Concurrent control is particularly important in continuous process industries such as refining oil. Instruments constantly measure the process and make adjustments if anything is going wrong. Instruments also alert a human being when any major deviation from standards occurs. Another example of concurrent control is satellite tracking of an organisation's fleet of lorries to establish their progress at all times. Concurrent control occurs in many other situations – especially when a supervisor (sometimes called an "overlooker") works in the same room. The overlooker watches employees at work and, should something go wrong, takes immediate corrective action by steering and guiding the employee. Concurrent controls are sometimes called *"steering"* controls.

Feedback control evaluates products or services after they have been transformed. It focuses upon the end results. The archetypal form of feedback control is when a batch of completed work is sent to a quality-control department, where an inspector checks each item and rejects any that are faulty. Faulty work is then returned to the operative for appropriate rectification or, if this is not possible, the faulty item is scrapped. Feedback control takes many forms. For example, many retail organisations employ "mystery shoppers" who make purchases while posing as members of the general public. They complete a report form on the shop and the service received. The report is then logged and sent to the shop manager and the shop assistant. Other organisations use satisfaction surveys. For example, most colleges and universities use questionnaires at the end of a course to gather data on student satisfaction. Financial reports are also a form of feedback control since they give information on, say, a completed financial year. Feedback control has two big advantages. First, it enables managers to compare actual outcomes with their plans. Hence, it gives useful information on the efficiency of the planning process and allows plans to be improved. Second, it gives employees clear information about how well they are performing. This information may be a powerful source of motivation. However, feedback control has one very major disadvantage – by the time faults have been detected a great deal of damage may have been done and corrective action may be very costly or impossible. A system that relies exclusively upon feedback control will produce a great deal of waste. Sometimes feedback control is called "*post*" control.

Control systems classified by function

Although the principles of control remain constant they are applied in different ways by different management functions.

For example, the *purchasing function* of an organisation will have specialised methods for ensuring the quality of its inputs. In some sectors of the manufacturing industry, such as metal refining, this will involve high-tech equipment and specialists who scientifically test the composition of the ores they use. Most organisations will also have some form of *inventory control* which aims to minimise the cost of maintaining large stocks of supplies. Some organisations, such as a large supermarket, will operate a system of inventory control using *economic order quantities*. They calculate the optimal size of an order in terms of transport and storage costs. They will then set a minimum level of stock and when the actual level of stock reaches this minimum level a new batch of items will be ordered. Because purchases are scanned at checkout, the processes can be automated so that a computer can generate the order which is sent to the supplier. The Argos chain of stores in the UK provides an excellent example of inventory control. Each store holds only a handful of each item in the catalogue – the exact number is determined by the previous buying patterns of its customers. As soon as an item is sold, a computerised system registers the sale and a replacement is immediately requisitioned from the warehouse. Perhaps the ultimate form of inventory control is *just-in-time* scheduling (JIT). These systems, pioneered by Japanese industry, aim to use feed-forward control so that the need for an item is anticipated and an order placed so that the item will arrive "just-in-time" to be used. Just-in-time scheduling needs very careful planning and implementation but it can reduce stocks almost to zero, saving considerable amounts of money.

Production functions usually have highly developed control systems that use both con-current control and feedback control. In some sectors such as the pharmaceutical industry the control will involve high-tech methods where samples taken at each stage of the manu-facturing process are subject to analysis in the laboratory. Even in less high-tech contexts the production function will carefully check its output. Techniques such as *Total Quality Management* (TQM), *Statistical Process Control* (SPQ) and *Quality Circles* are common components of control systems in manufacturing operations.

The *Human Resource Function* has a distinctive set of controls to ensure that people meet performance standards. They may include feed-forward controls which specify the qualifications and licences that people in certain posts must possess. They include concur-rent controls such as arrangements for supervision. The Human Resource Function will also control people's work behaviour through a system of appraisal and reward. Perhaps the final example of control systems concerning people will be disciplinary procedures that will aim to correct major deviations from expected performance.

Sales Function use obvious controls such as sales turnover per month. They may also measure the profitability of sales. However, monitoring the performance of sales represen-tatives presents particular problems: they operate away from the organisation and it is not easy to supervise their work. As noted earlier control of sales staff is made even more diffi-cult because of the high turnover. A sales representative can make all kinds of exaggerated claims to close a sale, collect the commission and then quit before the consequences of her or his technique come home to roost. In the 1990s many UK insurance companies failed to exercise adequate control over their sales staff. As a result many members of the public were sold inappropriate insurance policies. When this was discovered, the insurance companies were required to compensate victims to the tune of £2 billion.

Financial functions are particularly keen on controls to reduce levels of fraud, theft or misappropriation of money. They establish comprehensive accounts which can be audited. The finance function will also control spending commitments to ensure that the organis-ation does not spend more money than it can afford. Furthermore, the finance function will produce financial reports which management can use to control an organisation's financial health. Such reports use indices such as value added per employee, gross profit margin, return on equity and economic value added. These indices are described in more detail in Chapter 9 on budgeting.

7.4 The Balanced Scorecard

The effectiveness of a control system is very dependent on the information used. Obviously, inaccurate data will lead to the wrong corrective action. Less obviously, data from just one aspect of an organisation are likely to skew actions away from the optimum. In the past many control systems at the level of the organisation were based on financial data or data provided by management accountants (see Chapter 14). This situation is quite understandable since money is undoubtedly important. Further, money is easy to measure and quantify. Nevertheless, this emphasis on financial controls meant that many organis-ations were steered away from their true long-term goals.

In 1992 Robert Kaplan and David Norton introduced the idea of the balanced scorecard.

In essence they said an organisation will obtain a balanced view of its progress if it monitors its performance in four main areas – one of which was the traditional financial view. They recommended that organisations examine their vision and goals in order to identify key objectives in terms of:

1 What **financial objectives** must we achieve in order to satisfy our shareholders (or stakeholders)?

2 At what **internal business process** must we excel in order satisfy our shareholders and customers?

3 How do we need to **learn and grow** in order to sustain our ability to change and improve in ways to achieve our vision?

4 How do we need to **appear to our customers** in order to achieve our vision?

It should be noted that the contents of a balanced scorecard are closely linked to an organisation's vision and strategy. It is not necessary to have the same number of objectives in each category but there should be at least two. The total number of objectives should not be more than, say, 15, or complexity could lead to confusion.

On their own, objectives are not enough to create a balanced scorecard. Each objective must be accompanied by a method of measurement (outcome metrics) and a target level that should be achieved. Measures should be taken frequently, perhaps every three months and the results displayed on a series of graphs representing dials (the management dashboard) that clearly indicate whether the objectives are being met. Any under-performance should evoke some action or initiative to bring performance on that objective back to target.

Some organisations, especially local authorities and educational institutions, publish the results from their balanced scorecards on the Internet.

7.5 Dangers of Control Processes

Control processes are a vital part of good management. However, they have their dangers, which should be minimised when designing and implementing any control system. The main dangers are the elimination of good fortune, cost, rigidity, distortion of the organisation and ethical issues.

Controls are used to ensure that plans are properly implemented. However, plans are the products of people's minds and it is not possible for people to anticipate all eventualities. Hence, from time to time, managers will encounter favourable situations produced by *good fortune* (serendipity). If they are working in an organisational climate which has strict and rigid controls, there is a danger that they will eliminate such possibilities or ignore opportunities given by serendipity. For example, a strict control system would have prevented Alexander Fleming from discovering penicillin. Modern quality assurance procedures would have made certain that the laboratory conformed to a sterile environment. No windows would have been allowed to be open. Consequently, dust containing the penicillin fungus would not have been allowed to contaminate the agar jelly lying around in a Petri dish – indeed an open Petri dish would have been disallowed in any modern laboratory with half-decent controls. Furthermore, had Fleming been subject to management controls to enforce a production rate of experimental results, he would not have had the time to ponder the significance of a momentous chance event. In a similar vein many universities have instigated draconian controls over the content of lecture courses. The time and effort needed to obtain consent to deviate from an "approved syllabus" inhibits teachers from making changes in response to contemporary events. Eliminating serendipity has greatest consequences when an organisation's mission involves some kind of creativity.

An earlier selection noted the principle that a control system should save more than its own *costs*. While this principle seems obvious, in practice it is very easy to break. For example, some financial systems try to control fraud by insisting that expenditures greater than £10 are ordered via a central purchasing system. Naturally, such controls are favoured by people in purchasing departments – it ensures their future employment. However, since the labour costs of processing an order via the central system is £17, this control does not make sense for orders under, say, £20.

Control systems may be appropriate when they are first installed. However, as the internal and external environment continues to change, control systems become less aligned with organisational needs. The tendency for control systems to stay the same over long periods inhibits *organisational change*.

Control systems are designed, on purpose, to alter people's behaviour. This would not create problems if all aspects of organisational activity were covered by control systems of equal merit. However, this is rarely the case. Some activities, usually the shorter-term quantitative activities, will be covered by robust controls while other activities will have either poor controls or none at all. This results in people being motivated to perform only those areas with visible controls. The control systems therefore *distort the behaviour* of employees. For example, where sales volume is the only area with controls, sales staff will concentrate only upon achieving high sales figures at the expense of profitability. They may then forsake activities known as *"organisational citizenship"* which includes training colleagues and public relations activities to promote the organisation in general. In universities and colleges there are highly visible control data for research activities (i.e. the number of published papers). Similar data for teaching activities are subjective and harder to collect. Consequently, in some situations there is a tendency for staff to focus upon research to the detriment of teaching. Strict control systems can result in competitive organisations where there is a great deal of stress and tension (Jaworski and MacInnis, 1989).

Ethics is covered in Chapter 15. However, it is important to note here that control systems often raise ethical issues – especially issues of privacy and freedom. For example, some organisations may wish to control the quality of their workforce by requiring all members of staff to be tested for drug use. Other organisations may wish to control the level of theft by insisting that all bags and purses are inspected by security staff when employees leave the premises. Other organisations monitor staff using closed circuit television. Finally, some organisations check emails using work computers. The ethical issues involved are very complex. At a minimum, control systems that invade privacy should be explained to potential recruits at the time they make an application. Surveillance by closed-circuit television should be in the full knowledge of everyone who is observed. It must not be used where decency would be infringed (i.e. toilets and changing rooms). While the courts have upheld the rights of employers to inspect all emails sent from work computers, employees should be made aware of the practice when they apply.

7.6 Control Toolkit

Control is a very important aspect of managers' work. The following suggestions aim to provide useful guidance:

■ Investigate the costs and benefits of controls carefully. Remember to include less obvious costs such as increased workplace tension. Eliminate those controls where the benefits do not exceed the costs by a clear margin.

■ Examine the relationship between the organisation's strategy and plans and the control system. Eliminate those controls which are linked to neither. Introduce new controls where major elements of the plan or strategy are currently unrepresented.

■ Examine existing controls to determine whether they distort the balance of the organisation or if they could be manipulated with ease.

■ Examine cases of failures that have occurred in the past. Consider what extra feed-forward controls, concurrent controls or feedback controls will be needed to eliminate such failures in the future.

■ Reprimands to employees who do not meet standards should:

– Be immediate. Bad practice should not be given a time to establish itself.

– Be applied consistently each time standards are not met.

– Focus upon actions and behaviour rather than the person's characteristics. They should emphasise the correct standards and behaviour rather than dwell upon incorrect and past behaviour. They should provide information which helps the person produce the correct actions.

– Be given in a supportive and friendly way.

Some organisations adopt a policy of *progressive discipline* whereby the strength of any reprimand depends upon the severity of the deviation from standards and its frequency. A minor deviation which is an infrequent occurrence would receive only a light reprimand whereas a minor deviation which is frequent receives a strong sanction. A major deviation from standards or a minor one which has occurred frequently in the past would attract a very strong reprimand.

■ Adherence to standards should be recognised as actively as deviations from standards. People should be congratulated when they have achieved objectives as planned.

Above all, managers must remember that the vast majority of control systems cover less than 80 per cent of the performance of an employee. This 80 per cent of performance is unlikely to be measured with more than 70 per cent accuracy – especially if actual performance is gauged using subjective opinions of supervisors. It is therefore an arithmetical calculation that many control systems are, at best, about 56 per cent accurate!

Activities and Further Study

Essay Plans

Produce essay plans for the following topics

1 What are the characteristics of a good control system?
2 Give examples how feed-forward, concurrent and feedback control could be used in two named organisations of your choice (e.g. college, restaurant, hospital, charity, etc.).

Web Activities

1 Surf the web to find extra reading on the subject of management control. The following sites are excellent places to start your search:

http://www.accel-team.com/control_systems/index.html
http://en.wikipedia.org/wiki/Six_Sigma

2 Surf the web to find information about famous failures of management control. The following sites are good places to start:

http://www.projectsmart.co.uk/avoiding_project_failure.html
http://www.ohnonews.com/perrier.html

Failures you might like to investigate include: failure to control the costs of the Scottish Parliament; the UN's failure to control granting of oil quotas to Saddam's Iraq; failure of insurance companies to control the selling tactics used by their sales forces.

Experiential Activities

1 Choose an important activity of your life. Design a simple system to monitor and control the way it progresses.
2 Talk to two people from different organisations. Ask them about the control processes used in their work organisations and the effect that these processes have on them.

CHAPTER

08

Reporting and Communication Processes

❖ *LEARNING OBJECTIVES*

After reading this chapter you should be able to understand the importance of communication in all aspects of management. You should be able to avoid some of the problems of poor communications. In particular you should be able to:

1 **define** the concept of communication

2 **explain in detail** each of the five main stages of communication derived from the work of Shannon and Weaver

3 **contrast** verbal communication with non-verbal communication

4 **list** and **briefly compare** seven different communication channels

5 **explain** the effect of misuse in communication channels and **list** the changes a message is likely to undergo as it is repeated

6 **draw a diagram** depicting at least three kinds of communication network

7 **briefly describe** five important listening skills

8 **explain** the modifications which have been made to Shannon and Weaver's communication model

9 **give** at least seven practical tips for writing reports and at least seven practical tips for making presentations

People need information to do their jobs. One department needs information about another in order to co-ordinate activities. A supplier requires information about customers in order to anticipate and meet their needs. This transfer of information is called communication. Managers spend more time in communicating than in any other activity. Mintzberg (1973) estimated that managers spend 59 per cent of their time in scheduled meetings. They spend a further 10 per cent of their time in informal meetings and 6 per cent of their time telephoning. Thus, without counting the time they spend on written communication, managers spend no less than 75 per cent of their time communicating.

Definition and Concept of Communication

Communication may be defined as:

> an interpersonal process of sending and receiving symbols that have messages attached to them.
>
> *(Schemerhorn, 2002)*

A similar but less technical definition is given by Miller, Catt and Carlson (1996, p. 71)

> The sharing of meaning between the sender and receiver of a message.

In a managerial and, rather starry-eyed, context communication may be formally defined as:

> An interactive process of providing and passing of information that enables an organisation to function efficiently and for employees to be properly informed about developments. It covers all kinds of information and the channels of transmission.
>
> *(after ACAS, 1982)*

This definition is starry-eyed because a quango such as ACAS would find it politically impossible to admit that, in reality, the purpose of much communication is to obfuscate. Governments, politicians and some industrialists expend a huge effort on communications designed to ensure that the public do *not* appreciate the "real" situation. The ultimate example must be the email by Jo Moore, an information officer in the British Labour Government. When jets had crashed into the twin towers of the World Trade Center in New York on 9/11 she realised that it would monopolise media attention and people would not notice domestic news. Her insensitive and cynical email attempted to obfuscate government policy by advising other information officers that: "It is now a very good day to get out anything we want to bury. Councillors' expenses?" Jo Moore's email is by no means an isolated example. Company communications are awash with disinformation. Presidents and prime ministers routinely express full confidence in colleagues who, backstage, they are forcing to resign. Chief executives of companies about to go bankrupt routinely assure shareholders of the organisation's financial stability (it gives them time to sell their own shareholdings!). Sales representatives routinely promise their managers that a big new order is "certain next month" (it gives them time to jump ship and find another job!).

In the hierarchical days when Fayol first identified the management processes represented by the mnemonic POSOCRB (see page 38), communication was synonymous with reporting. Bosses needed information from subordinates in order to co-ordinate their activities and make decisions. It was also acknowledged that bosses needed to communicate to subordinates in order to give orders and instructions. Nowadays, the situation is much more complex. Furthermore, the increased use of teleworking, part-time staff and fixed-contract or short-term employees has made organisational communication much more difficult.

Communication, good or bad, pervades any organisation. Shannon and Weaver (1949) produced what is probably the most thorough analysis of the stages of communication, but subsequent researchers have modified their model. The remainder of this chapter on reporting and communication in organisations is structured under three sections:

8.1 The Stages of the Communication Chain (after Shannon and Weaver)

In theory, communication can be divided into discrete stages but, in practice, they often occur simultaneously. In fact, communication is a very dynamic process in which the message, the channels and people's perceptions are dynamic and constantly change. Clampitt (1991) identified that one approach to communication can be likened to the flight of an arrow: information flows in a direct line from a sender to a recipient. Based upon the early work of Shannon and Weaver, the flight of information passes through six main stages:

1 **deciding** to communicate
2 **encoding** the message
3 **choosing** a channel and sending the message
4 **receiving** the message
5 **decoding** the information
6 **taking action** and **sending feedback**

Deciding to communicate

People often assume that communication is always good. This is not true. Communicating nonsense merely blocks a communication channel so that other messages may not get through. As Aesop's fable about the boy who sent several nonsense messages about wolves illustrates, wrong or unnecessary messages desensitise a channel so that later, truthful messages are ignored. Some people are "communicaholics". They need to check situations and give instructions so frequently that it distracts others from their work. Communicaholics use their mobile phone on trains and in restaurants incessantly to "touch base" and check "whether anything has happened".

The dangers of over-communication are greatest when likely recipients are deluged with new information. Typical examples are bombarding new employees with the minutiae of long-term information when they are struggling to absorb information that will help them cope with the first week. It is useless to lecture for an hour without a break or change. It is silly to organise training seminars that start at 8 a.m. and continue to 8 p.m. Psychologists know that this is counter-productive. Fatigue inhibits learning and later information tends to block out earlier learning. The latter is called "**retroactive inhibition**". The speed and ease of email has increased the likelihood of irrelevant and unnecessary communication and spam.

However, the probability and dangers of not communicating are even greater than over-communication. People often assume that others know information and do not need to be told. Sometimes, people may not realise that they have information that is relevant to colleagues. Others may realise that their knowledge is relevant but they may fail to communicate because they assume that it is already known to colleagues. When this happens there is a total communication failure that is difficult to correct. In general, the balance of advantage lies in communicating information rather than withholding it.

Traditional models of communication (e.g. Shannon and Weaver, 1949) assume that people are clear about the messages they wish to transmit. In fact, this is often not the case. Holden (2001, p. 257) points out that "the purpose of a communication is not always clear, and communication might have multiple goals for a single message". Multiple and sometimes contradictory goals mean that it is not easy to determine the effectiveness of communication.

Encoding the message

Once the need to communicate has been recognised information needs to be put into symbols that can be transmitted. This is known as "*encoding*". It must be emphasised that information is never communicated directly. It is the symbols that are communicated. If the wrong symbols are chosen, the message may be inaccurate. There are many types of symbols. Generally, they are divided into two types: verbal and non-verbal.

Verbal communication

Verbal communication consists of words, numbers, diagrams or pictures – it includes anything that could be traced or copied with a pen. It is the type of communication that naturally springs to mind when the topic of communication is mentioned. Verbal communication is the primary means by which we convey factual information. This book is conveying facts about management, using words. However, verbal communication can also be used to convey emotions. An example would be a deathbed scene in a novel. Verbal communication usually flows from a conscious decision to transmit information to other people.

Encoding suitable messages with numbers is usually very precise – provided both the sender and receiver are numerate. Encoding with words is less certain. Words have slightly different meanings to different people. Indeed, the difference in meanings can be stark. "Knock me up in the morning" means one thing in Northern England and something quite different in New England, USA. In France the word "demand" is a mild word that means "to ask" while in English it is strong and means "to insist upon". Differences in the shades of meaning frequently involve emotional connotations. For example, the factual meaning of the word "charity" is the free transfer of wealth from one person to another. To a capitalist it conveys the emotions of kindness and humanity. By contrast, to a communist it may convey a sly, capitalist attempt to assuage guilt. These differences in meanings have huge implications for managers – especially those who are managing from a different culture or social group. It is important to use neutral words and avoid those loaded with emotional connotations. For example, it would be unwise for a manager of a multinational company in an Arab country to attempt to galvanise local employees in a "crusade" for efficiency. The scope for cultural misunderstanding is increasing in a world of increasingly diverse work-forces (see Reilly and DiAngelo, 1990). There are well-documented differences in the way that men and women select and encode messages (Borisoff, 1992). Women tend to encode messages with words indicating intimacy (sharing problems and responding to the needs of others) while men tend to use words that have connotations of status and independence. Women also tend to use more qualifying phrases such as "it seems to me" and "I under-stand" (Hirschman, 1975).

Culture and gender are not the only causes why people encode messages differently. Intelligent people such as most managers and specialists will feel the need to give a full and detailed explanation of their ideas. This may mean that the cognitive complexity of their messages will be too high for some other people to understand. Consequently it is a very good idea to observe the KISS principle of communication – Keep It Simple, Stupid. A successful communicator will give concrete examples which show the practical application of their abstract ideas. Personality also determines how people encode ideas. Introverts, for example, will encode ideas in a precise, detailed, accurate and objective way while extroverts will encode the same ideas in grand, colourful, sweeping terms that play upon subjective emotions. There is some evidence that the structure of an individual's brain influences the way a message is encoded. For example, if the left half of the brain is dominant, a message will be encoded in a way that emphasise facts and logic. If the right side of the brain is dominant the message will be encoded in terms of feelings and emotion. Similarly, if the part of the brain that processes visual information is well developed, the message will have lots of visual images such as "I can see your point of view" and the speaker will use lots of diagrams and pictures. If the auditory part of the brain is well developed, the message will eloquent, fluent and contain phrases such as "I hear what you are saying". The study of the way brain structure influences communication is called **Neuro-Linguistic Programming**.

Verbal communication, especially written communication, is under conscious control and is open to conscious manipulation. Verbal communications are therefore frequently mistrusted. People often look for non-verbal cues in order to cross-check to what people say and write.

Non-verbal communication

Non-verbal communication consists of postures, gestures and grunts (para-linguistics) and is usually unconscious. It is almost impossible to avoid sending non-verbal messages. For example, absence from a meeting is likely to convey the message that the meeting is unimportant. Similarly, the lack of a response to a greeting will convey disapproval. Non-verbal communication generally conveys powerful but simple emotional messages. It is the carrier wave that sets the context for verbal communications. If a non-verbal message conflicts with a verbal one, the non-verbal one will prevail. Actions speak louder than words, fine words butter no parsnips and handsome is as handsome does!

Probably the most important non-verbal cue is *eye contact*. Human beings are exquisitely sensitive to the eye movements of others and can identify their direction of gaze to within a few degrees. They can tell whether other people are looking at individual features of their face such as eyes or mouth. Avoidance of any gaze sends the message that a person desires no contact. This is a useful signal of avoidance in crowded situations such as lifts or public transport. Purposefully looking down while listening signals deference, a cycle of fleeting eye contact and looking sideways indicates guilt and shiftiness. Prolonged looking at someone's eyes can indicate confrontation or romance, depending upon the exact context. During a one-to-one conversation, there is a delicate choreography of eye movements. In general, during a sequence in a conversation, the listener looks at either the eyes or mouth of the speaker throughout – looking away signals that they want to end that sequence and perhaps talk themselves, while a steady gaze signals active listener interest. At the start of a sequence, the speaker looks at the eyes of the listener to check that they are paying attention and then they look away while they are concentrating upon delivering the main part of the message. As they end the message the speaker will look at the eyes of the listener once more to check that their attention has been retained and perhaps to obtain tacit approval to continue speaking. Patterns of eye contact differ from culture to culture and this can be the cause of misunderstandings. In some cultures it is considered polite to look away whilst a superior is speaking but a western person might interpret this as shiftiness or insolence.

Facial expressions are keenly observed since they are not usually under total conscious control and frequently indicate a person's true *feelings*. For example:

- Raised eyebrows signal amazement or disbelief.
- Narrow eyes and pursed lips signal anger.
- Frowns signal unhappiness or hostility.
- Biting or trembling lips signal anxiety and worry.
- Smiling signals friendliness, pleasure, happiness and sometimes a desire to please.

A person's *voice* also gives information. A strong, clear, low voice without hesitations signals confidence and certainty. A high-pitched, shaky voice indicates nervousness. Broken, hesitant speech sends the message that the speaker is unsure of him or herself and is unprepared.

Gestures of limbs and fingers often indicate underlying emotional states. Nods are particularly important. They mean a person is paying attention and is in agreement whilst shaking of the head signals strong disagreement. Shrugging shows indifference. Fidgeting, especially with fingers, touching face and hair with fingers and shifting from foot to foot indicate nervousness. Doodling can indicate either nervousness or boredom. Rubbing a finger around the collar is also a sign of guilty nervousness. Finger pointing denotes authority. It also indicates displeasure. Repeated finger pointing in males indicates anger and is often a precursor of a brawl. Gestures can be brought under conscious control and are often used effectively by politicians, celebrities and speakers.

Posture is another important non-verbal cue that is often called *body language*. Sitting upright on the edge of a chair and leaning slightly forward indicates active listening and interest. Sitting with legs slightly apart and arms slightly bent down one's side indicates openness. Hands akimbo on hips signals anger while folded arms indicate a determined unresponsiveness. Slouching generally shows boredom but this can be a source of confusion since some male teenagers use slouching to send a message that they are "cool" and relaxed!

Dress sends non-verbal messages. At one time one's school tie and the colour of one's collar (white or blue) sent crude and often erroneous signals about a person's status and character. Today the signals are more complex, but probably equally erroneous, and are encoded by artefacts such as the exact brand of jeans or the ring tone on a mobile telephone as well as less subtle messages printed on a T-shirt. Most organisations have a dress code that sends messages about the organisation. The egalitarian ethos of some Japanese organisations is often signalled by all levels of the organisation wearing the same design of overall. In the armed forces rank is explicitly signalled by the stars or "stripes" on a person's uniform. In some creative ad-agencies and the media people are expected to conform to the norm of nonconformity!

The *physical setting* (sometimes called *proxemics*) of any communication sends strong non-verbal signals. For example, a meeting with a superior manager in an office where he or she is seated behind a desk will be shorter and more formal and will tend to make a subordinate talk more about their own achievements than, say, a meeting in a pub. Indeed, the layout of offices (open plan or individual offices) sends signals about an organisation's culture. Even the physical distance across which a dialogue occurs has implications. In Anglo-Saxon countries distances greater than 2 m will communicate an impersonal, remote relationship, a distance of 1 m will indicate a working, business relationship, while a distance less than 0.5 m will indicate an intimate, emotional relationship of some kind. These distances may be different in other cultures. For example, they tend to be smaller in Arabic countries – the British are, literally, "stand-offish". Such cultural differences can cause complications, confusion and annoyance.

Communication channels

Once encoded, a message must be transmitted to another person or group via a channel. Many types of communication channels exist. The choice is important. Indeed, Marshall McLuhan (1964) claimed that the channel used can actually alter the message transmitted. He coined the famous phrase "the medium is the message". The form of a message (print, visual, musical, etc.) determines the way in which that message will be perceived – an important message scribbled on a scrap of paper will be perceived as inconsequential whereas a trivial message beautifully typed on a large sheet of heavy paper will tend to be seen as important.

As a rough approximation, communication channels can be divided into two groups: personal communications to one other person or a small group of people and mass communications to large numbers of people.

Personal communication

Personal communication can take many forms such as direct contact, telephone, email, fax and letters. The huge majority of communications involve *"face-to-face contact"* at a one-

CASE 8.1: THE MEDIUM IS THE MESSAGE

The classic example of the medium altering the message was the 1960 presidential election where the two contenders, Nixon and Kennedy, debated the issues. Radio listeners believed that Nixon won the debates with clearer, better-informed, more coherent answers. However, voters who watched the same debate on television believed that Kennedy was better. In addition to hearing his answers they saw his young, handsome, clean-cut appearance. Nixon's suit merged with the studio and he appeared to need a shave. Kennedy won the election but if Nixon had worn a different suit and had had better make-up the result could have been very different. Nowadays, politicians often have "image consultants" in a studio to check the effects of the set, lighting, make-up and clothes before they go on air at a party conference or in a pre-election debate.

to-one level or a one to-several level. Direct contact can also involve the one-to-many level where one person can communicate with thousands with a charismatic appeal to core values. They make each person feel that they are speaking directly to them. The evangelist Billy Graham and the dictator Adolph Hitler were masters at this type of communication. In face-to-face contact both the originator and the recipient are physically present. The latter can hear the spoken words and see or hear all the non-verbal cues. Managers much prefer direct contact because it is quick, has immediacy and offers all the information contained in both verbal and non-verbal cues. Managers tend to dislike formal written documents. They feel that by the time they are written, checked and delivered the information may be out of date. Furthermore, they know that writers of formal documents will be careful and circumspect in what they write – omitting speculation and contentious information. In principle **video-conferencing** should be almost as good as face-to-face contact since participants receive all visual and oral cues. It also allows communication between people who are hundreds or thousands of miles apart without incurring huge travel costs. However, video conferences are more pre-determined, formal and subject to more rigid time constraints. Participants in a video conference may also be suspicious that important things may be happening "off camera".

Managers like the *telephone* as a channel of communication. While there are no visual cues, there are many other non-verbal ones such as enthusiasm, hesitations, etc. that help put the overt verbal message into context. Providing the two people know each other, the telephone has the same immediacy as direct contact. *Letters* and *memos* are excellent channels for transmitting detailed, formal and important information. It has been said that memos are written not to inform the reader but to protect the backs of the writers. The letter heading, the quality of the paper and the format of the letter give important non-verbal cues about the writer and their organisation. A facsimile (fax) combines some of the qualities of a letter (minus some non-verbal cues such as quality of paper) and the immediacy and spontaneity of the telephone. As a channel of communication emails lack the non-verbal cues of the telephone or letter but they have a great deal of immediacy and spontaneity – perhaps too much spontaneity. In the heat of the moment it is far too easy to press the "send" button for an ill-considered and potentially incriminating email.

One of the most popular means to achieve this personal communication is *workplace tours* where, typically, managers walk around their areas of responsibility, surveying the situation and apparently "chatting" to their team. This is often called *"walking the job"* or *"Management by Walk About"* (MBWA). These tours provide a rich source of communication. A manager can grasp the situation in their area of responsibility directly. Tours make it easier for their team to communicate their concerns. They also provide informal opportunities to give the team specific and up-to-date information. Finally, tours are an essential way of building trust between the team leader and team members. Some organisations set up specific ways for managers to communicate with customers. For example, senior executives may timetable one day a month to talk to customers. This provides a communication channel where they can receive direct information about issues such as the reliabilities and capabilities of systems such as invoicing and servicing. Similarly, senior executives at some hotel chains spend time working as porters.

Channels of mass communication

Channels of mass communication have been studied extensively. Some old, but still very valid, studies by Hovland (1957) looked at the way mass messages should be encoded. For example, in general such messages should not try to frighten people into doing things (the technique backfires because people have a tendency to shut out threatening stimuli). Both sides of an argument should be given (this makes the message more resistant to counter-propaganda) and messages should be given by authority figures and celebrities. Hovland also discovered that a **two-step flow of information** operated in channels of mass communication. Mass messages are first detected by a relatively small number of opinion leaders who avidly attend to media in their area of interest. The opinion leaders digest and interpret the information and then pass *their interpretation* to a much larger number of people by informal conversation and other forms of direct contact.

Newsletters and *company newspapers* are the traditional forms of mass communication in organisations. They aim to keep employees informed of new developments and make them feel that they are a key part of the organisation. They are characterised by downward communication, i.e. giving workers the information management wishes them to know. Many try to soften this inevitable fact by "talk back" columns where employees can have their say. Nevertheless, much of the content of newsletters and company newspapers is discounted as "management propaganda". Modern equivalents of newsletters and company newspapers are *company websites* and *ebulletins*. *Podcasts and presentations* by senior figures at "company days" or conferences are other organisational channels of mass, downward communication.

Organisations can communicate to large numbers of workers using meetings. For example, in the 1980s many organisations set up intersecting *quality circles* (see Chapter 12). Information would be passed from circle to circle until it was known by most people in the organisation. *Team briefings* were also popular. The chief executive would brief department heads and the information would be cascaded down the organisation. The department heads would then brief their middle managers who, in turn, would brief their junior managers and the junior managers would brief operatives and so on, until everyone in the organisation had been briefed. A typical team briefing would be held at least once a month and would last for 30 minutes including time allowed for participants to ask questions. *Consultative committees* with trade unions or staff associations are another useful way of transmitting messages to large numbers of workers.

Managers often forget the existence of information channels outside their direct control. In most organisations there are *trades unions* or *staff associations* that communicate to their members on a regular basis. Indeed, some trades unions are better at communicating with their members than the management of an organisation is at communicating with its employees. When this happens management loses a lot of control and influence. It is said that a substantial part of the labour relations problems in the British car industry in the 1970s occurred because union communications prevailed over management communications. The *organisational grapevine* is often overlooked. Traditionally information passes informally by word of mouth or email, from friend to friend or from organisational ally to organisational ally. An organisational grapevine is characterised by two features. First, it is very fast. A whole organisation can get news of an event within 24 hours – long before a newsletter is printed. Second, organisational grapevines are notorious for distorting the information they transmit. *External channels* of communication can also influence the flow of information within an organisation. For example, an organisation can issue newsletters, send emails and organise team briefings until it is blue in the face but claims of financial success will not be believed in the face of a critical article in the London *Financial Times* or the Singapore *Business Times*. Similarly, a petroleum company's eco-friendly assertions can be dented by a well-researched report from an environmental pressure group. *Professional grapevines* operate via informal chit-chat at conferences, meetings and telephone calls. They are largely outside management control yet they transmit information both within and outside the organisation. In general, management communication is most credible when it deals with detailed, operational information. However, when more general and evaluative information is transmitted, managerial channels will often be discounted. Information sent by informal and external channels will have greater credibility. This may even happen in situations where the management version lies closer to the truth!

Channels of communication are also needed to obtain information *from* large numbers of people. They include suggestion schemes and attitude surveys. Often *suggestion schemes* exist in the minimal form of a box on the wall of the canteen to which little attention is paid. However, when they are publicised and when staff receive big awards for suggestions that save the organisation money, they can be very effective. *Attitude surveys* may involve face-to-face interviews, telephone interviews, questionnaires and, nowadays, web questionnaires. Attitude surveys can yield quantitative and "objective" information about employee morale. They can also be used to track changes over several years or to evaluate the success of various projects.

Noise in communication channels

Shannon and Weaver (1949) noted that few channels of communication are perfect. They are subject to events and interference that either obscure or distort a message. This is called noise. In essence noise consists of other signals that break up or interfere with a message and they can be either physical or psychological. Interruptions and mobile phones are prime examples of physical noise. For example, a CEO may be outlining a strategic plan to her board of directors when a business associate phones to check a future appointment. Even though she curtails the call, momentum is lost and the impact of the message is diluted. In a similar vein, many otherwise superb presentations have been ruined by the gauche arrival of coffee and refreshments at a key moment. Another source of noise is distraction – perhaps a loud conversation in the next room or the glare on a computer monitor. Common forms of psychological noise are fatigue, biases and prejudices, daydreaming and not paying attention.

Channels differ in the extent to which they are subject to noise. Written communications are less influenced by noise, while the noise present in an organisation's grapevine can make the original message unrecognisable. Communication where information is passed by word of mouth is especially susceptible to noise. Jablin et al. (1987) note that each individual in a chain filters and interprets information according to their perceptions, thought patterns, motives and attitudes. This filtering constitutes noise that changes the information before it is passed on to others. Jablin et al.'s thoughts were hardly new. They were noted, half a century beforehand, by Frederick Bartlett (1932), a famous British psychologist. As a part of his studies into in the phenomena of "remembering" he conducted a famous experiment on the way that a series of people remembered a spooky ghost story. The tale "War of the ghosts" was narrated to one person who narrated it to another and so on – rather like the party game "Chinese whispers". However, Bartlett very carefully noted the changes to the story as it passed from mouth-to-mouth. He identified three consistent changes:

- with each telling, the message becomes *shorter*. A little of the contextual detail was lost with each rendition (possibly because it exceeded the short-term memory capacity of seven pieces of information that the average human mind can store – which is why it is important to "Keep It Simple Stupid!"). The phenomena of shortening may be responsible for reducing a thoughtful, considerate management decision to a bald diktat by the time it reaches "ordinary" employees. Studies show that the loss in information as it passes down an organisation's hierarchy can be dramatic. Typical figures are:

  - CEO's understanding   100% (perhaps!)
  - director's understanding   63%
  - senior manager's understanding   56%
  - middle manager's understanding   40%
  - junior manager's understanding   30%
  - operative's understanding   20%

  These figures indicate that slightly less than one third of a message's information is lost each time it is transmitted to another managerial level.

- the message becomes *sharper*. The main point of the story is emphasised and minor themes are lost or are distorted so that they reinforce the main theme.

- frequently the message is *hijacked by irrelevant detail*. For example, just one line in a presentation by the CEO (Chief Executive Officer) of a jewellery retail chain might jokingly refer to "crap" products. However, after the speech has been relayed through a series of media interviews it appears that the CEO is confessing that his stores sold only "crap products". A misfortune of this kind forced the UK jewellers, Ratners, into closure.

CASE 8.2: BAD COMMUNICATION – DOING A RATNER

Poor communication skills have been the downfall of many CEOs (Budd, 1993). Perhaps the most spectacular example is the case of Gerald Ratner, head of a chain of jewellers with shops in virtually every major British town. During a speech to the Institute of Directors he joked that one of his firm's products was "total crap" and that some of the earrings it sold were "cheaper than a prawn sandwich" and probably would not last as long. The media seized on the speech. Sales plummeted and £500 million was wiped off the company's value. Mr Ratner was forced off the board and the company had to spend huge sums on rebranding.

Ratner is not the only example of "foot in mouth disease":

- David Shepherd, marketing manager at Topman, was asked to clarify their target customers and commented "Hooligans or whatever". He added "very few of our customers have to wear suits at work … They'll be for his first interview or first court case".

- Matt Barrett, chief executive of the firm that owns Barclaycard said "I do not borrow on credit cards. I have four young children. I give them advice not to pile up debts."

- Dianne Thompson, CEO of the firm that runs the British lottery, said that lottery ticket buyers "would be lucky to win a tenner".

- EMI's CEO, Alain Levy, enraged Finns when he said that he had cut the artist roster in Finland from 49 as he did not think there were that many people in the country "who could sing".

Direction of communication

Many writers classify a communication channel by its direction. Three directions, upwards, downwards and horizontal, are usually differentiated.

Upward communication towards organisational superiors is called reporting and it was identified by Fayol as "R" in the acronym POSDCRB. Information is communicated upwards in reports giving performance data about areas of responsibility and actual or anticipated problems. Managers will also report the performance of their subordinates. Sometimes upward reports make suggestions for scheduling and other improvements. Upward reports usually rise only one level in the organisation because they are integrated with reports of colleagues at the same level before being transmitted higher in a new report. Good upward communication requires an atmosphere of trust where mistakes are accepted and where there is support to help avoid further occurrences. If these are absent, employees will conceal negative facts. Decisions by senior managers are then based on inaccurate information.

Downward communication is how top management let people know the organisation's strategy and the targets they must meet. Typically, downward communication takes the form of meetings, memos, policy statements, operating procedures, etc. Good downward communication helps build employees' organisational commitment. Unfortunately, as noted on p. 170, a great deal of information is lost before it reaches those at the bottom of an organisation.

Horizontal communication occurs between people at the same level. Sometimes it is called *"gang-plank"* communication. Horizontal communication tends to be informal and sometimes lengthy. It often starts with a conversation, telephone call or email which is then followed up by a more formal memo or note. Good horizontal communication is vital if the activities of different departments or people are to be effectively co-ordinated. A large part of a middle manager's job consists of horizontal communication. Quality circles and team-working are specific types of horizontal communication.

Communication networks

Communication channels rarely exist in isolation. They are usually linked to other channels to form a network. As Figure 8.1 shows, there are four main types of network.

In the *star* network (sometimes called a *wheel network*) people at the periphery can only communicate with the person at the centre, who is able to communicate with everyone. Star networks are very efficient when dealing with very simple tasks that amount to little more than collecting and ordering easily understood information. They are hopeless at dealing with complex tasks, because the person at the centre is overloaded and those at the periphery are unable to help. The person at the centre of the star is usually highly satisfied with the group but those at the periphery are not. The *line network* (sometimes called a *"chain"* network) is a little better at complex tasks because people in the middle of the line can share complex processing and they are usually satisfied with the group. People at the ends of the line are usually dissatisfied with the way a group works. A *"Y" network* is a hybrid between a star network and a line network. They are notorious for fostering power struggles between the person at the fork of the "Y" and the person who is next down the "leg" of the "Y". In a *"ComCon"* network (sometimes called an *"all-channel"* network) everyone is completely connected to everyone else. ComCon networks are poor at dealing with simple situations where the choice lies between two obvious actions such as an emer-

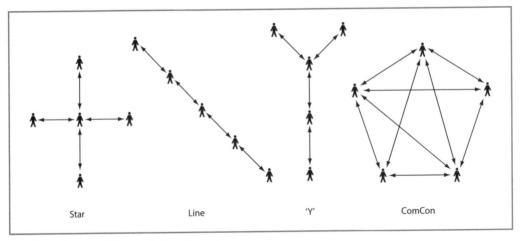

Star   Line   'Y'   ComCon

FIGURE 8.1 Patterns of Communication Channels

gency situation where it is necessary to choose which of two exits is better. In these situations a ComCon wastes time sending messages in haphazard directions while waiting for a consensus to emerge. However, ComCon networks are good in complex situations where a lot of information needs to be synthesised. They are also good at dealing with bottlenecks of information since messages can be rerouted through less-congested channels. In the past organisations tended to adopt star or inverted "Y" networks. Modern organisations tend towards the ComCon model. This development has been assisted by the development of information technology where employees have access to large amounts of information which, previously, was only available to management. The development of organisational intranets has also meant that anyone in an organisation is able to send messages to any other member of the organisation.

Receiving the message

A message may be flawlessly encoded and sent via an appropriate channel but if a part or the whole of a message is not received there will be a breakdown in communication. This is analogous to a broadcaster producing a perfect programme and sending it from a powerful transmitter only to find that the television or radio at the other end is either faulty or tuned to a different wavelength. Sometimes, messages are blocked out of consciousness because they are painful to the recipient or the recipient does not trust the source. This is analogous to a viewer making a snack during adverts because they believe that manufacturers' information is biased and not worth watching.

A message may not be received because a person is attending to other things. To a small extent this problem can be overcome by the sender clearly indicating the relevance and importance of the information. For example, an email can be allotted a high priority and a clear notification of the subject matter. Furthermore, the first few lines of the email should indicate the type of response required and the date, or time, that a response is due. Poor *listening skills* are often blamed for a poorly received message. Actually, the problem is wider and it is better to refer to *receiving skills*. There are five main receiving skills:

- **Setting aside time to receive messages**. Often managers are so intent on sending signals that they leave no time to receive them. It has been said that in face-to-face situations the most important listening skill is to stop talking. The second most important listening skill is to stop talking. The third most important receiving skill is also *stop talking*! Interruptions should be minimised. Eye contact with the other person will signal a wish to listen. Speakers should rarely be interrupted and the listener should give them complete attention.

- **Understanding the overt message**, i.e. comprehending what is actually said or written. Many factors, especially expectations, prevent proper reception of a message. An incoming message is immediately evaluated using our past experiences. This saves time by allowing us to skip detailed parts of the message because we can insert what we expect to hear instead. Unfortunately we may insert wrong data. With small and reversible decisions such wrong assumptions have little consequence. However, whenever a decision has important and irreversible consequences it is vital to check that the overt message has been understood. With written communication this is as simple as re-reading the message or asking others to read it. Where the message is a verbal report of a meeting – especially a report of what a third person did or said – it is well worth verifying the report with an independent source, preferably with the person whose speech is reported. Understanding the overt message may take time, so "snap" judgements and quick responses should be avoided.

- **Understanding the motives** for issuing the message. It is often useful to ask why is *this message* being sent to *me* at this *time* in this *way*? These questions may reveal the sender's motive, which may place the message in context. For example, a notice read out at the end of a very long meeting under "any other business" signifies that the sender hopes the recipient will not place undue emphasis on the information given – either because the information is not, in fact, important or because the sender is Machiavellian and wishes to bury bad news. Similarly, an unexpected memo on the importance of observing proper personal relationships between managers and subordinates probably means that a manager somewhere has been having an improper sexual relationship that might harm the organisation's reputation.

- **Understanding the emotion** behind the message. Often a message might appear to convey no new information but it may be said in an angry voice or a happy voice. Similarly, a letter or memo that contains many underlined or emboldened words often indicates an angry or impatient sender. Sometimes when a communication seems to have no overt point whatsoever, it is carrying a very important emotional message "I want you to notice me and pay me more attention!".

- **Avoiding criticism**, evaluative judgements and arguments before the full message has been delivered.

Receiving messages requires sensitivity to both verbal and non-verbal cues. It also involves paying attention to what a speaker or writer is trying to communicate rather than multitasking by trying to read an email at the same time as conducting a telephone conversation. Fidgeting or thinking about other issues may prevent the accurate reception of a message. Receiving information is not a passive activity – even though one should normally refrain from interrupting a speaker. If a part of a message seems unclear, there should be no hesitation to ask for clarification or for the message to be repeated. A failsafe tactic, to be used if there is any possibility of ambiguity, is to relay one's apprehension of the message back to the sender using phrases such as "I want to be sure I have heard correctly . . . what you have just said is . . .". An active listener will detect and respond to the feelings behind a comment. For example, a colleague may say "we have had many new orders this week". A passive listener might reply "yes, there were 102", whereas an active listener would reply "yes, there were 102 and I guess you are concerned about the extra work load that is placed on you".

Decoding the information

Once a message has been correctly received its meaning needs to be understood. This is called "decoding" and, in many ways, it is the mirror image of encoding described in section 8.1, p. 163. An important principle of decoding is to avoid over-reaction to individual words or phrases. For example, if a single sentence in a document refers to "policing" a regulation, it would be an over-reaction to draw analogies with jackboot authoritarian regimes. Similarly if a two-page email about market competitiveness contains a short para-

Actual Words	Manager's/subordinate's intended meaning	Meaning decoded by subordinate/manager
"How long will it take you to finish the job?"	Please participate in setting your deadlines	He does not know what the job involves
"How are your family?"	I am interested in you as a person, not as a cog in the machine	She is trying to pry into my private life
"We should be able to meet the deadline"	There may be a problem with this deadline	He is confident about the deadline and needs no support
"Have you had a chance to read my report?"	Why haven't you come back to me about the report I worked overtime to write?	She is too arrogant to understand all the things I have to read.

TABLE 8.1 Errors of Decoding

graph about costs it would be wrong to decode it to mean a programme of downsizing is imminent. Triandis (1977) identified a number of errors in decoding messages. Table 8.1 illustrates some of the decoding problems that may arise (see also Chapter 16, p. 344).

The actual example given by Triandis indicates that decoding problems are particularly acute when the sender and recipient of a message are from different ethnic origins.

The final stage in the chain of communication envisaged by Shannon and Weaver is deciding upon appropriate action. The process of decision-making was discussed in Chapter 6. Usually it is appropriate to signal to the sender of the original message that it has been received and acted upon. This feedback completes the communication loop, saves the effort of resending the same information and clears the channels for other messages.

8.2 Modifications to Shannon and Weaver's Model

Shannon and Weaver's "arrow" model of communication has been very influential. It identifies a straightforward series of stages that can be explained easily. The model was based upon an analogy with radio communications where there is a mechanical, non-interactive flow of information from sender to receiver. However, as Schramm (1954) points out, human communication is rarely so simple – it is characterised by feedback. The recipient of a message is not passive like a radio receiver. As soon as a message comes in, a human being starts to react with, say, non-verbal frowns or questions.

Clampitt (1991) likens organisational communications to a *circuit of information* where, in response to feedback, the sender may modify the message she or he initiates. Unfortunately, the situation is still more complex. A radio transmitter simply sends its message and a radio receiver simply receives it. In human communication, both sender and receiver monitor their own activities and adjust their behaviour accordingly. A shy person may become embarrassed on hearing themselves speak and start to stutter. On realising that a message is complex for the listener a speaker may repeat key information. Thus it can be seen that human communications have many feedback mechanisms which generally help clarify messages. The feedback loops in human communications mean there is a constant cycle where messages go backwards and forwards between two people. Clampitt likens this to a *dance* where people need to make complementary moves. These moves are governed by a set of rules such as starting a conversation with a neutral or pleasant topic. For example, many telephone conversations start with the question "How are you?" to which the customary answer is "fine. How are you keeping?". If one partner fails to make the expected steps (for example by giving a long-drawn-out description of their state of health) the communication dance falters.

Herriot (1989) uses the recruitment process as a superb example of the interactive and reciprocal nature of communication. The process is divided into episodes where either the organisation or the potential recruit receives overt verbal, contextual and non-verbal information. At the end of the episode the person or organisation must decide whether to continue the recruitment "dance". For example, at the start of the process the potential recruit sees a job advert. It gives overt details about the job and the organisation. Placement in a quality newspaper, the layout, pictures and general tenor give contextual cues. Using this information the potential recruit decides whether to make an application. The application sends messages to the employer and so on. As Figure 8.2 shows both parties have power and both must choreograph a series of steps for the recruitment process to reach a successful conclusion.

Both the circuit and dance models of communication stress the importance of feedback and it is important to develop a good feedback technique. Some useful guidelines are:

- Give feedback **as quickly as possible** after the receipt of a communication or observing behaviour. However, if the feedback is negative it may be better to wait a little while until a time when the recipient may be more receptive.

- Give feedback in **frequent, short episodes** rather than waiting for a number of issues to accumulate.

- Feedback should be about **specific** communications or behaviour rather than general attitude or approach.

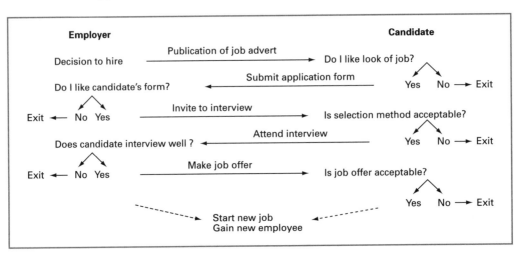

FIGURE 8.2 The Recruitment Tango

- Whenever possible give **positive** feedback on things that people do or say correctly. Often good behaviour is assumed or overlooked. In many circumstances positive feedback is two to three times more powerful than negative feedback. Negative feedback often causes denial and defensive or other emotional reactions. Negative feedback tends to teach people to avoid getting caught rather than doing things right – with the possibility that they may reduce the amount they communicate so that there is less likelihood of attracting criticism.

8.3 Communications Toolkit

The earlier sections of this chapter have many practical implications for managers. However, there are two activities that have a high profile and can have a long-term impact on the career of a manager. They are writing reports and making presentations. The remainder of this chapter is devoted to providing some practical guidance on these two activities.

Writing reports

Reports differ from essays, novels and college assignments because they have a clear purpose – to persuade the reader to *do* something as a result of reading the report. Consequently the first step in producing a successful report is *to be absolutely clear about the action or actions the report needs to initiate*. Some possible actions might be:

- to buy a product
- to make an organisational change
- to incorporate a procedure
- to stop an unwise or unsafe practice
- to approve a budget or staff allocation

The second step is to *identify the readership* and determine:

- what they already know about the topic
- what they are likely to want from the report

The third step is to *collect relevant information and materials*. This should be obtained from as many sources as possible. An Internet search is an obvious avenue but internal organisational sources should not be ignored. It is worth establishing whether there have been any recent reports on the same or similar topics. It is also worth identifying other people who might know something about the topic. It will usually be a good idea to telephone and visit these people: it will prove very helpful in promoting the report at a later stage. Collecting information can take a long time. If it is extensive, it is probably best to index the information on computer files that can easily be re-arranged.

The fourth step is to *arrange the information under five headings*. People can readily cope with things that have seven parts. Since most reports need an introductory section and a recommendations section, the remaining material needs to be organised in five sections.

However, each of these can be split into sub-sections that must be placed in a linear and logical order. The reader should be led gradually from what they already know to what they need to know and feel if the report is to achieve its aims. There should be no backtracking since this bewilders readers. All the information on a given point should be in one place – but it is permissible to refer the reader to its location from other points in the report. Sometimes the conclusions from very detailed information can be mentioned in the body of the report but the details themselves can be placed in an appendix. The material in a report should normally include tables and diagrams.

The fifth step is to *work out the actions that are to be recommended* at the end of the report. These recommendations should be prioritised with the most important recommendations first. In many cases it is also useful to work out the approximate costs and timetable for implementation.

The sixth step is to *write the report*. Except in academia, the key to good writing is to use short words, in short sentences, in short paragraphs. In fact this advice is largely but only partly true. A long succession of short paragraphs soon degenerates into a list; a few long words, sentences and paragraphs provide the reader with some variety and help make a report "flow". Headings help the reader locate information quickly and they help communicate the structure of what is being written. Avoid using block capitals for headings, since they are difficult to read. While the text of a report should be in a serif typeface such as Times Roman, the headings are usually in a sans-serif (without the curly bits on the ends of letters) typeface such as Arial. There should be a consistent system of headings. If all else fails, the system in Table 8.2 can be employed.

Never allow a report to look crowded. Allow ample margins (2.5 cm top, bottom and right but 4 cm left-hand margin to allow for binding). White space helps the reader understand the report's structure. Use one blank line after a heading. Use two or three blank lines at the end of a section, before the next heading. Add one or two extra spaces after a full stop.

Be careful with spelling and grammar. Despite what progressive teachers may have said, friends will be embarrassed, smile and pretend not to notice or make excuses for you. Enemies will use grammatical mistakes to "rubbish" a report as "illiterate" even if the main message is valid. Make sure that the *verb agrees with the subject* – for example, "the man-

Title of Report	**Arial 16 point bold**
Chapter Headings	**Arial 14 point bold**
Section Headings	**Arial 12 point bold**
Sub-section Headings	**Arial 10 point bold**
Sub-sub-section Headings	**Arial 8 point bold**
Main Text	Times Roman 11 point

TABLE 8.2 A Popular System of Headings

agement *is* (singular) concerned that..." not "the management *are* (plural) concerned that..." Do not run the risk that your reader will tolerate *split infinitives*. They make take it as a signal that you are poorly educated. An example of an English infinitive is "to read" or "to use". Never split the two words that form such infinitives. Any additional description goes after the infinitive. For example, write "to read quickly" or "to use badly". Never write "to quickly read" or "to badly use". The same principle applies to other forms of verbs such as "be hit" (intransitive). It would be wrong to write "be hard hit". It would be correct to write "be hit hard". Beware of *misusing capital letters*. They should be used only to start a sentence (after a full stop) and for specific names or titles (of people, places, and titles of books, etc). *Apostrophes* are another major source of problems. They are used to indicate either possession or missing letters. For example a report belonging to a company would be referred to as the "company's report". There are complications when the subject is plural. For example, if a set of plans belong to one subject (e.g. one manager) the expression would be "the manager's plans" (the apostrophe is after the singular form "manager"). If plans belong to several subjects (e.g. several managers) the expression would be "the managers' plans" (the apostrophe is after the plural form "managers"). Reports sometime quote the direct and informal speech of individuals where contractions are used. For example, "cannot" is often contracted as "can't". Here, the apostrophe is used to show the omission of the letters "n" and "o". The most common misplacement of an apostrophe is to write "it's" in a phrase such as "the organisation sold it's assets". The word "its" already denotes possession and nothing is omitted, so an apostrophe is not needed and the phrase should be written "the organisation sold its assets". However "it's" has another meaning – a contraction of the two words "it is". In this case the letter "i" is omitted and an apostrophe is needed to mark the place of the missing letter. For example it would be correct to write "70 per cent of consumers agreed that it's a good product".

Enemies often use the sloppy reporting of percentages to "rubbish" an otherwise sound report. Percentages should always be checked to ensure that the total equals 100 with a small allowance for rounding errors.

The seventh and final step is to *produce (engross) the final version* of a report by adding a title page, an executive summary and, perhaps, a list of contents. The title page should include the name of the author and the date of the report. The title page may also need a list of the people to whom the report will be circulated. The headings in any list of contents should match the heading in the text exactly. Scruffy reports or very flashy ones may attract criticism or sarcasm. A good principle is to examine other recent reports and improve on their appearance slightly.

Making presentations

Presentations have greater impact than written reports. People are physically present and wider range of stimuli (vision, sound, kinaesthetic and, perhaps, olfactory) is used. The audience is also interactive and provides feedback. This interaction means that presentations are less predictable than written reports. They are also shorter and rarely exceed 30 minutes. Hence they must focus on presenting key points in a memorable way. Indeed, highly focused presentations are usually supported by a detailed, logical, written report. Presentations take three main forms:

- **Briefings to two or three people**. An example of this format would be a unit manager briefing the organisation's chief executive during his or her visits to the unit. This format usually involves presentations to well-informed recipients who have more status and power. They are highly interactive and will need to follow the wishes of the recipient. They are also very stressful and require detailed preparation of both the main theme and any subsidiary theme that the recipient might raise. Audio-visual aids are usually restricted to hard copies of diagrams, tables and bulleted lists, perhaps on a lap-top, that can be shared across a table.

- **Presentations to six to fifteen people**. An example of this format would be a departmental manager explaining a new project to other departmental managers. Another example would be a group of consultants explaining their proposals to the management team of a client organisation. The presenter and recipient will have similar status and power. Computer-generated visual aids using Microsoft's "PowerPoint" or WordPerfect's "Presentations" are very likely to be used.

- **Set-piece presentations** to tens, if not hundreds, of people. A typical example would be an address by the chief executive to all members of staff at the organisation's annual conference. They involve little interaction. They will be highly organised using professional quality graphics, video clips or taped quotations.

Each type has its own characteristics. The following suggestions are intended to be used with presentations to six to fifteen people.

The first three stages of preparing a presentation are very similar to the first three stages in writing a report: establishing goals, knowing the audience and collecting information. Usually presentations can convey less detailed information than a report so it is necessary to *be more focused* in identifying five key points.

Thought should be given to the *presentation of essential information*. Generally, each major point will be stated on one slide, with a further slide enumerating the sub-points. Graphics and colour coding can be added to slides to make them memorable. A frequent error is to include too much information on a slide and make the writing too small for the audience to read. If it is absolutely necessary to show a detailed slide with small writing, each member of the audience should be provided with a full-size, hard copy which is easy to read.

The delivery of a presentation needs to be thought through in advance. The *start,* in particular, needs to be prepared with care. Ideally it should commence with a clear statement (perhaps supported by a title slide) of the main subject. This can be followed by an interesting fact, anecdote or rhetorical question that will arouse the audience's interest. Next, the audience can be told the main points and the order in which they will be covered. The bulk of the presentation will consist of explaining the five or so main points. It must be remembered that listening to others for any length of time is boring and the audience will switch off or think of other matters. Great efforts are needed to avoid boring the audience. The two main techniques are *novelty* and *involvement*. Novelty can be introduced by inserting (a few!) jokes or anecdotes. It can also be introduced by involving different senses (vision or movement of props) or by a change in visual aids. A long presentation is best given by two or more presenters where presenters are changed for each major section. Involvement is often achieved by asking members of the audience to help with demonstrations or asking them to provide examples that support the points being made. At the very least, minimal involvement can be achieved by asking a number of rhetorical questions.

An important presentation should be *rehearsed*, say, six times so that the flow of delivery and the use of visual aids is perfected. Rehearsals also allow timing to be fine tuned so that they last within one or two minutes of their target time. Presentations should not be read from a written script. Neither should they be memorised and then delivered by rote. Good preparation and rehearsal aid the *actual delivery*. At the very start it is often useful to pause several seconds in order to establish authority and obtain the audience's attention before speaking. Many presenters make the mistakes of talking too fast, or at a constant and monotonous pace. Speak relatively slowly but speed up and appear enthusiastic in appropriate places. Maintain eye contact with the audience. Glance at each person at least three times. Mentioning people by name helps build rapport. At appropriate points, usually at the end of each major section, it is advisable to pause and ask if there is anything that needs to be clarified. When the main points have been explained, it is often useful to summarise the presentation so far. The final minutes of a presentation are often devoted to outlining the action that the audience could or should take. Indeed, the final shot of many good presentations is to ask members of the audience to state, publicly, what they intend to do as a result of listening to the speaker.

This chapter gives only brief guidance on the development of personal communication skills. Readers should refer to other books such as Caproni (2005) that give more details of these and other management skills.

Activities and Further Study

Essay Plans

Produce essay plans for the following topics:

   1 Draw a diagram of the communication process and then explain each stage.
   2 What are the main barriers to good communication?
   3 What is the importance of the "grapevine" to managers?

Web Activities

   1 Use an information data base such as AIB Inform or ProQuest to obtain longer articles on communication such as:

   Peter Richardson and D. Keith Denton (1996) "Communicating change", *Human Resource Management*, **35**, 2, 203–217 (an excellent article giving specific instances where communication played an important part in changing organisations).

   Dorothy A. Winsor (1988) "Communication Failures Contributing to the Challenger Accident: An Example for Technical Communicators", *IEEE Transactions on Professional Communication*, **31**, 3, 101–108 (a good description of the way failures of communication led to the Challenger Disaster).

   2 Use your search engine to locate extra information on practical aspects of communication. Terms you could use are: communication; listening; non-verbal. A good site is www.mindtools.com.

Experiential Activities

   1 With a group of four friends, each write a topic concerning "communication" on a slip of paper. Allocate one slip to each person at random. Allow three minutes for thought and preparation. Then each person should give a two-minute talk on the subject written on their slip of paper. At the end of each talk friends should nominate three good aspects of the speaker's communication skills and two aspects that could be improved.
   2 Plan a 10-minute presentation to, say, a group of careers advisers on the topic of "me and my future work".
   3 Think of a recent communication (email, letter, phone call, face-to-face comment) which you sent that was misunderstood. Analyse the reasons for the misunderstanding and devise ways of avoiding these problems in the future.

Budgeting Processes

09

❖ *LEARNING OBJECTIVES*

After reading this chapter you will be able to understand the importance of budgeting. You will be able to identify the main types of budget and have some understanding of the budgeting process. You will also be able to understand management ratios that are in common use. In particular you will be able to:

1 **define** a budget and explain the key terms within it

2 **list** four resources that usually need budgets

3 **explain** briefly four main types of cash budgets

4 **draw** and **explain** a cash graph

5 **explain** the following aspects of budgeting:
   – "top-down" and "bottom up" budgeting
   – zero-based budgeting
   – activity-based costing and budgeting

6 **explain** the formulae and use of nine different profitability ratios

7 **explain** the concepts of gearing, leverage and debt ratio

8 **explain** the formulae and use of four different debt ratios

9 **explain** the formulae and use of two different operational ratios

To add maximum value it is necessary to distribute an organisation's resources effectively, plan their use carefully and make sure that they are not wasted. This is usually called budgeting. Budgeting may be defined as:

❝ A single-use, numerical and time-limited plan that commits resources to a project or activity. ❞

This definition has four components:

- Budgets are **plans** for future actions. Furthermore they are **single-use** plans (see Chapter 3) to meet a situation at a given point in time – it is highly unlikely that exactly the same plan will ever be used again. Since budgets are undoubtedly plans, Fayol was technically wrong to identify budgeting as a separate management process. Nevertheless, treating budgets separately has practical advantages: it divides a very large process into two smaller, more manageable, parts and it emphasises the importance of plans involving money.

- Budgets always involve **numbers**. This gives greater precision and enables progress to be tracked and controlled with greater accuracy.

- Budgets have a fixed **time interval** – usually a year but other time intervals of 1 month, 3 months, 6 months or two years are quite common. Sometimes, budgets are automatically refreshed and extended about half-way through their time interval. These are called **"rolling" budgets**.

- Budgets commit resources to **specific projects** (such as an advertising campaign) or specific classes of activity (such as travelling expenses).

Nearly always, responsibility for a budget is formally allocated to one person or **role holder**. For example, the budget for a whole unit will be the responsibility of the general manager. He or she may then delegate part of the budget to, say, the production director or the sales director. Sometimes budget holders are called **responsibility centres**.

In the context of management the word "budget" does not carry the negative connotations of meanness and skimping that are associated with common phrases such as "budget holiday" or "budget jeans". Quite the contrary, some budgets (such as the chairperson's entertainment budget!) might be very generous indeed. Budgets are always closely associated with an organisation's control processes (see Chapter 7). For example, a consultancy organisation will usually compare its budgeted income against its actual income on a monthly basis. It will take action if the actual income is too low. Budgets are used to plan and commit many different kinds of resources such as production, materials, human resources and information.

- A **production budget** is a detailed plan for the output of production units. A production budget is necessary in order to ensure that an organisation's output matches the level of its sales. Short-term production budgets are often called **production schedules**. Some organisations draw up budgets for new products. For example, major drug companies will try to ensure that they introduce several new drugs to the market every year.

- A **materials budget** is a plan for acquiring and storing the parts or supplies which need to be available to the production department.

- An **HR budget** will be a detailed plan for the personnel who will be needed to fill various jobs in an organisation. An HR budget will specify the skills and qualifications that are required by various groups of people. It will need to take into account the likelihood of employees quitting the organisation and the time-lags involved in training their replacements.

- Some advanced organisations produce budgets for their **intellectual capital**. Software developers will draw up a plan to ensure a steady flow of intellectual property such as patents and new ideas. They may also try to quantify and systematically develop the value of the knowledge possessed by its employees, the value of its brands and the worth of its relationships with customers and suppliers. They will draw up a budget to ensure that the intellectual capital of the organisation increases every year.

Money is an important resource in any organisation. It is the means by which resources and products are exchanged with the outside world. It is also the means by which the transformation process within the organisation is evaluated. Managing money usually involves the finance function which is described in Chapter 14. This chapter focuses on the budgets and the way they affect all managers. It is organised into four main sections:

Chapter contents

9.1 Main Types of Financial Budget

Financial budgets attempt to predict and regulate the flows of money to an organisation, within the organisation and from the organisation. There are four main types:

The income budget

The income budget is a plan showing the money an organisation can expect to receive. At the start of the financial year executives will have constructed a plan outlining the income they expected to earn. Indeed, the plan will have probably listed the expected income month by month. They will have made detailed projections of the money that they were likely to receive from sales and from interest on cash at the bank and from any other assets such as rent. The actual receipts each month will have been tracked against this plan. In addition to a detailed income budget for the current year, most organisations have outline income budgets stretching into future years. In some organisations, such as those in the oil industry where lead times are very long, projections and plans for income will be made as much as 15 or 20 years ahead.

The expenditure budget

An expenditure budget is a plan showing the money an organisation can expect to pay out. At the start of a financial year an organisation will try to predict what it will spend. The expenditure will be detailed into various categories such as labour costs, reorganisation costs, sales, materials, etc. In a large organisation the expense budget will show the anticipated and actual expenses for each responsibility centre such as production unit 1, production unit 2, sales, administration, etc. Organisations usually have clearly defined expenditure budgets covering the next 12 months. They will also have outline expenditure budgets for future years. The expense budgets will probably specify the outgoings for each month and the actual outgoings will be compared closely with the plan. If actual expenditure exceeds a budget, action, such as cutting costs, will be taken to eliminate the variance. The major headings for expense budgets are:

- salaries and benefits
- rent
- utilities (heating, light, power and water)
- business travel
- maintenance of equipment and building
- communications (post, telephone, Internet)
- equipment

The expense budget and the income budget are often combined to form the **operating budget** – a good estimate of potential profits. The operating budget is normally used as the **master budget** for the unit or the organisation as a whole.

The cash budget

A profit and loss budget is not sufficient because, although they make a profit, organisations may encounter a cash crisis. While an organisation may make a 10 per cent profit on its products, it will need money to buy raw materials, rent premises and pay workers before it receives any money from sales. A company may be fundamentally sound but if it cannot pay its bills promptly its creditors may foreclose. In a more realistic case, the situation will be less dramatic but there will still be some months where expenditure outstrips income and vice versa. The cash budget is a plan to ensure that money is available when needed to pay bills. Most organisations draw up a cash budget on a monthly basis for a year in advance. Some organisations might budget on a weekly basis and others, especially those in the finance sector, will budget cash very carefully indeed, on a daily basis. The cash flow is sometimes presented as a cash graph. Figure 9.1 gives a cash graph for a holiday company whose cash flow is extremely seasonal.

It can be seen that for the year as a whole, the company will be highly profitable and in most months the cash flow will be positive (colloquially known as being "up north"). However, few people take holidays in November and January. The company's cash flow is likely to "go south" in these months. Indeed, the cash budget indicates that the cash flow will be so negative in these months that it will exceed the organisations' overdraft limit. It indicates that the finance director will need to arrange extra credit facilities and place strong constraints upon purchases during November and January. On the other hand, the strong cash flow between June and September means that major purchases should be made at this time and that arrangements should be made to invest the surplus "cash pile".

The capital budget

The capital budget is intricately related to the cash budget. It concerns the investment an organisation makes in equipment and new buildings. Ideally, these investments are made

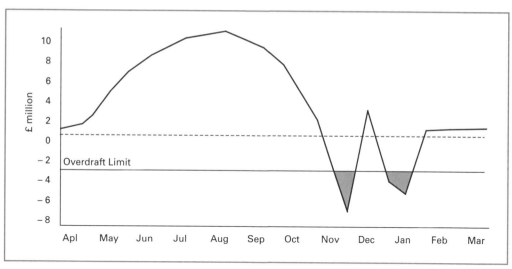

FIGURE 9.1 A Cash Graph

according to a predetermined plan that anticipates future needs and they will be scheduled in a way that maximises the return on the investment. Usually, an organisation will determine the amount of money it can invest in new building or equipment. It will then ask departments for suggestions on how this money can be invested. The most promising suggestions will be chosen for thorough scrutiny to see if they are practical, related to the organisation's strategy and whether they are likely to give a good return on investment. Suggestions that survive this scrutiny and which fit within the money available will be chosen for inclusion in the capital budget. Sometimes, capital expenditure is less controlled. Breakdowns of existing machines, new legislation or unexpected technological developments may force emergency capital expenditure. In this case the existing capital budget is likely to be slashed in order to find money for the emergency spending.

9.2 The Budgeting Process

Budgets can be prepared in two main ways: a traditional "top-down method" and a more recent "bottom-up method". The "*top-down*" method of preparing budgets follows the formal lines of authority described by Weber (see Chapter 2). Senior management set overall budgets which are in line with the organisation's strategy. These overall budgets set out the broad parameters for each department or major activity. Departmental managers then prepare more detailed budgets for each of their sections – and so on until there are detailed budgets for small units of activity or workers. The top-down method has the big advantage of following established lines of command and it usually produces an integrated set of budgets that cover the whole organisation. However, they appear to be autocratic and may alienate junior staff. "*Bottom-up*" budgets aim to remove this disadvantage. Junior members of staff are asked to anticipate their area's income, expenditure and capital needs. Senior management then integrate this information into master budgets which are consistent with the organisation's strategy. The bottom-up approach empowers junior staff. It means that they are more likely to take ownership of the budgets and hence they are likely to apply them more effectively (see Churchill, 1984).

Perhaps the easiest way to prepare a budget is to take last year's budget, increase each entry by a few per cent to take account of inflation and make other adjustments to accommodate foreseeable changes. This method tends to produce budgets that grow needlessly each year irrespective of the organisation's needs or strategy. *Zero-based budgeting* (Pyhrr, 1973) was introduced to counteract this tendency and it has been adopted by most major organisations. In zero-based budgeting all expenditure has to be justified as if it were a new project or activity. The assumption is that any expenditure is unnecessary unless a positive case can be made in terms of efficiency and the contribution towards the organisation's goals. This means that all activities and the priorities allotted to them are reconsidered at the start of each budgeting cycle. Zero-based budgeting is too radical and takes too much time to apply simultaneously to all budgets within an organisation. However, used selectively it does restrain expanding budgets and it reduces the "entitlement mentality" towards budget increases.

Traditionally budgets were produced on a departmental basis with separate budgets for the purchasing department, the HR department, the production department and so on. All of these individual budgets would be co-ordinated by a master budget. Since several different responsibility centres will contribute to a given item of production it is difficult to establish the costs or a budget for specific products or services. *Activity-based costing and budgeting* (ABC) was developed to overcome this difficulty (see Pare, 1993). Activity-based costing traces all the costs incurred in generating and delivering a specific product or service. Armed with an accurate picture of the profits generated by a product, managers can expand production of those goods or services that add greatest value. Alternatively, they can try to increase profits by driving down the costs involved in unprofitable services. In some cases activity-based budgets and costings can point to products or services that should be discontinued. For example, it may emerge that it costs £20 to buy raw materials and manufacture a product that sells for £40. However, activity-based costing might reveal that the product also requires an average of £10 advertising, £4 storage and £9 for customers' support. These additional costs are normally spread among departmental budgets so that the organisation is unaware that it is making a loss on each sale.

A finished budget, replete with columns of figures, looks authoritative and objective. However, budgets are often political and contain hidden assumptions. When preparing and approving budgets it is often valuable to make explicit comparisons with budgets from competitors. Furthermore, it is worthwhile considering previous budgets in the same organisation or industrial sector. For example, in the building industry there is a chronic tendency for projects to over-run their budgets by 100 per cent. It would be prudent to take this into account when preparing a budget for a new building – perhaps by increasing original estimates or by producing a budget with tight controls. Experienced managers are aware that budgets cannot be entirely accurate. When preparing budgets they therefore take a defensive stance: making pessimistic estimates of income and assuming that costs will rise. This conservative approach is likely to give some room for manoeuvre so that the outturn can match the projected budget. However, the total of the "safety elements" inserted by individual managers can represent a considerable amount of money.

9.3 Management Ratios

Financial budgets and outcome figures are usually designed to control individual activities or projects at an operational level. However, the same budgets can be used at a strategic level, to see how well the organisation as a whole is doing. This is achieved by taking information from a budget or set of accounts and combining it to produce *management ratios*. Scores of different management ratios exist. Each has its own purpose. It is important to select the ratio that is most relevant to the situation facing an organisation. The following list contains some of the ratios that are used most frequently by managers. They can be grouped into three main categories: profitability ratios, debt ratios and operational ratios.

Profitability ratios

Profitability ratios are global indices that show how well an organisation or unit is using resources. The global measures of profitability are:

- **Gross profit**, also called **gross profit margin** or **profitability ratio**, is the organisation's mark-up on the sale price. It is probably the best single measure of an organisation's overall ability to add value when transforming inputs into outputs. It is the most frequently used measure of profitability. Gross profit is the difference between income from sales and the cost of the goods sold, all divided by the value of the sales and multiplied by 100 to produce a percentage:

$$gross\ profit = \frac{sales\ income - costs}{sales\ income} \times 100$$

  A comparison of the profit margins over a number of years reveals a great deal about an organisation. *Declining profit margins* mean that the organisation is being forced to lower its prices or is having difficulty in restraining costs, or both. For example, in 2004 the Chinese mobile phone maker, TCL, increased its profit by 30 per cent but its profit margin fell from 27 per cent to 22 per cent. Increased competition had forced it to reduce its prices, hence it was adding less value to each phone it made. Fortunately, TCL was able to sell more phones. *Increasing profit margins* mean that the organisation is able to command higher prices for its products (perhaps by improving them or shifting to more valuable markets) or is better at controlling its costs. The ideal situation is where a company's profitability increases for several years. This indicates a culture of innovation and cost control. Similarly, comparisons on gross profit margins between companies in *the same sector* can indicate which companies have the best management.

- **Profit after tax**, often known as "**net profit margin**", is very similar to gross profit margin except that it takes taxes into account. Sometimes it is called "**net profit tax**". It is a useful index for people who are interested in how much money an organisation is making for itself. It is calculated as follows:

$$profit\ after\ tax = \frac{income - (costs + taxes)}{income} \times 100$$

Profit after tax is an index of how well an organisation is able to transform inputs plus the effectiveness with which it is able to arrange its financial affairs in order to minimise tax. Organisations with high net profit margins will have more money to spend on other business operations such as research and development or marketing, or for distribution to shareholders and others. Comparison of the net profit margin for the same company over several years and comparisons between different companies in the same sector are as useful as those involving the gross profit margin. However, such comparisons need to be made with care where the tax regime differs between companies or financial years.

The previous indices focus on sales and revenue. But, in some circumstances sales and revenue are not the crucial factors. A factory which produces a profit margin of 5 per cent using six machines is probably better than a similar factory that has a profit margin of 8 per cent using twenty machines – the former's margin may be lower but each machine is producing a higher number of goods and more value is being created from the money used to buy the machines. In other words the management of the first factory is making capital work harder. A number of indices measure how efficiently capital is used – i.e. *productivity*. They include rate of return, return on equity, economic value added and, payback periods. There is also the special case of labour productivity.

- **Return on capital** is the traditional, most widely used index of how effectively a company is using its capital resources. Return on capital (ROC), sometimes called **"return on assets (ROA)"** is calculated using the formula:

$$return\ on\ capital = \frac{net\ profit}{total\ assets} \times 100$$

It should the noted that interest on loans is subtracted from net profit and that the index is usually calculated using profits after tax (i.e. net profit). The result depicts the actual benefit to the organisation. However, in some circumstances – when comparing organisations subject to different tax regimes – the index will be computed using the pre-tax figures. Unfortunately, the overall return on capital can sometimes be a misleading index because it includes capital borrowed from other sources. The following index takes borrowing into account.

- **Return on equity** indicates how well the organisation is transforming the resources provided by the owner. It is calculated by the formula:

$$return\ on\ equity = \frac{net\ profit}{owner's\ equity} \times 100$$

For example, the owner of a health club may have purchased a gym with £200 000 of her savings plus £100 000 loan from a bank. After deducting costs (including interest to the bank) and taxes the gym makes a profit of £15 000 per year. This means that the return on equity is 7.5 per cent (15 000/200 000 × 100) which is more than the 5 per cent owner could have earned by leaving her £200 000 in a savings account. However, the extra interest will have been gained by accepting a higher level of risk.

- **Economic value added** (EVA) was developed by Stern Stewart & Co. It compares a company's profitability with a minimum level of profitability elsewhere. It is usually the difference between the return achieved by an organisation and the rate of interest on a standard loan from the bank (other comparators such as a stock index can be used). Economic value added is often used as an index of how well a company is creating wealth for its owners. The formula for calculating EVA is:

$$EVA = net\ operating\ profit\ after\ tax - [capital \times rate\ of\ interest]$$

For example, a computer manufacturer in Singapore spent S$100 million, which it could otherwise invest in securities at 9 per cent, on a new factory. The new factory produced a net operating profit of S$11 million. An S$11 million profit seems most acceptable. However, the economic value added by the new factory is:

$$EVA = 11m - [100m \times 0.09] = 11m - 9m = 2m$$

In other words, taking the opportunity costs into account the new factory added an extra 2 per cent value to what could have been earned by keeping the money on deposit – not a big improvement considering the effort and risk involved.

- **Payback period** is often used to evaluate projects that generate some kind of income. As its name implies, it is the period of time that will need to elapse before the net income received equals the capital invested. Although the concept is simple, the calculations can be quite complex because they involve compound interest. Further, income needs to be discounted to take inflation into account since investment takes place in the present while the income will be received in the future when the money will be worth slightly less. The **net present value** is also based on forecasts of future earnings. Future cash flows are discounted for inflation using present value tables. All the cash flows from a project are then added. If the sum is greater than the initial investment the project goes to the next stage of consideration. If the sum is less than the initial investment, the project is abandoned.

- **Labour productivity** is a partial and specialised aspect of profitability. It indicates the effectiveness with which the efforts of employees are harnessed. There are two main indices: value added per employee and labour productivity. **Value added per employee** is:

$$value\ added\ per\ employee = \frac{net\ profit}{number\ of\ employees}$$

Labour productivity is calculated by the formula:

$$labour\ productivity = \frac{gross\ profit}{labour\ costs}$$

Usually indices of labour productivity are considered alongside indices of return on capital.

Employees who have lots of capital and equipment at their disposal should be expected to be more productive.

Debt ratios

Debt ratios are very important budget considerations because a large number of organisations operate on credit. This is true of governments, charitable organisations and commercial companies. In itself, debt is not a problem – it increases productivity. For example, a government may realise that a new school will improve literacy and, in the long run, the welfare of the population. However, it may not have sufficient funds in its current budget and it may be unable to increase taxes. In these circumstances it may make sense to borrow money and make repayments in future years when the benefits start to feed through to the community. This basic idea lies behind the current use of the **Private Finance Initiative** (PFI). Similarly, a bio-tech company may calculate that a new laboratory will be able to obtain a return of 17 per cent on capital employed. A bank may be prepared to lend the capital at 11 per cent. Again, in these circumstances, it would be sensible to borrow money to build the new laboratory. However, debt has its dangers. The greatest danger is that organisations borrow more money than they can repay (service). If this happens the creditors will foreclose and a non-governmental organisation will be forced into bankruptcy. Debt ratios aim to provide information to help organisations avoid taking on too much debt and to warn lenders when loans might be unsound. There are four main ratios concerning debt: gearing, interest cover, liquidity and "the acid test".

- **Gearing** is also called "**leverage**" or "**debt ratio**". The basic principles of gearing were described in the previous paragraph: organisations may be able to generate a higher rate of return than the interest they would be required to pay. Gearing indicates the proportion of an organisation's assets which have been purchased on credit. The most usual index of gearing is:

$$gearing = \frac{long\text{-}term\ debt}{shareholder's\ equity}$$

The level of gearing shows considerable variation from industry to industry. Organisations that operate in very stable, predictable environments, such as public utilities or brewing, can service high rates of debt. On the other hand, lenders will be wary of loans to organisations operating in dynamic but turbulence environments, such as the building industry. A high gearing ratio means that an organisation will experience a greater profit in favourable times. Conversely, high gearing means that an organisation will suffer disproportionately when times are hard and interest rates increase.

- Sometimes, the level of debt is evaluated using an index known as "**interest cover**" or "**times interest earned**". This ratio portrays the interest needed to service a debt as a proportion of the organisation's income. The formula is:

$$interest\ cover = \frac{profit\ before\ interest\ \&\ tax}{total\ interest\ payments}$$

Obviously, if the income of an organisation is much greater than its interest payments it is a good proposition for potential lenders.

- **Liquidity** is a property that allows material to flow between one point and another. In financial terms, it refers to the ability to transfer money. Some assets, such as cash, are very liquid and can be transferred from one owner to another in a matter of hours or days. Other assets, such as property, may take years before a buyer is found and its value can be liberated for transfer. An organisation's liquidity is very important to its debtors because it indicates the organisation's ability to meet its short-term debts. There are several ratios showing an organisation's liquidity. The most important is the **current ratio**:

$$current\ ratio = \frac{current\ assets}{current\ liabilities}$$

Current assets include cash, invoices that have yet to be paid (accounts receivable) and the inventory of goods that lies waiting to be sold to customers. Current liabilities include invoices from suppliers that are waiting payment (accounts payable), accrued expenses and tax liabilities. The current ratio for commercial organisations varies from industry to industry but for manufacturing organisations it is generally about 2.

- Some organisations apply a stricter liquidity ratio. It is generally called the "**acid test**" but also the "**quick ratio**" because it indicates how quickly an organisation can make payments. It indicates how well an organisation can meet its short-term liabilities without selling its inventory of goods waiting to be sold. The acid ratio is:

$$acid\ test = \frac{current\ assets - inventory}{current\ liabilities}$$

Operational ratios

Operational ratios try to gauge how actively an organisation is using its assets. They deal primarily with the inventory of finished goods that a firm holds. The main operational ratios are the activity ratio and the asset turnover ratio:

- The **activity** ratio is sometimes called the "**inventory turnover ratio**". It is an index of how frequently completed goods or services are replenished ("turned over"). The formula is:

$$activity\ ratio = \frac{sales\ turnover}{average\ inventory}$$

Usually the average inventory is obtained by combining the level of stocks at the start and end of the accounting period and dividing by two. A company that reports a yearly activity ratio of 1 is extremely poor since, on average, finished items languish in stores a full year before they are sold to customers. In general, a high activity ratio is good. However, the nature of the market needs to be taken into account and organisations producing high-priced durable products tend to have lower ratios than producers of low-price non-durable ones.

- The **asset turnover** ratio shows how effectively an organisation is using its assets to generate sales. It is calculated by dividing sales revenue by total assets. The formula is:

$$asset\ turnover = \frac{sales}{total\ assets}$$

A high figure indicates that the organisation is using assets in an intensive way (Brigham, 1985). However, there are substantial differences between industries. Low-tech operations often yield a high asset turnover because they are labour intensive rather than capital intensive.

9.4 Disadvantages of Financial Budgets

Budgets are essential to good management and all managers will need to master the art of preparing and operating a range of budgets and management ratios. However, managers must also be aware of their disadvantages. Three particular disadvantages are costs, manipulation and restricted view. A good budget will take a *long time to prepare* – especially if the budget is zero-based. The budget for a medium-sized department can easily consume four weeks of a manager's time which she or he could be spending on transforming resources rather than paperwork. Unwise implementation of a budget can also lead to *manipulation*. If a manager has an unspent proportion of a budget at the end of an accounting period, there is a strong temptation to spend the residue on unessential purchases in order to make sure that the budget is not cut in future years. Finally, budgets have the disadvantage that they might produce *tunnel vision* and become an end in themselves. In fact, budgets never account for more than 80 per cent of an organisation's activities. They are a tool to help achieve goals rather than goals in themselves.

Activities and Further Study

Essay Plans

Write essay plans for the following questions:

1 What are the main types of budget used by organisations?
2 Explain one of each of the following types of management ratio and outline its advantages and disadvantages A) profitability ratios, B) debt ratios, C) operational ratios.
3 Explain in detail the main disadvantages of using budgets within an organisation.

Web Activities

1 Most organisations view their budgets as commercially sensitive and do not publish them. However you should spend 15–20 minutes trying to locate sites containing some kind of budget. You are most likely to achieve success with international, national and local government sites. These organisations often have a legal obligation to divulge some budgetary information. A good site is: ***http://www.joint-reviews.gov.uk/money/Financialmgt/1-23.html#1-231-councils***
2 Locate sites that give guidance on the preparation of budgets. A good site is: ***http://www.duncanwil.co.uk/cash.html***
3 Locate and examine a website with a complicated budget. One possibility is: ***http://www.enzt.co.nz/~yesweb/_files/Student%20Resources/Finance%203%20Cash%20Budget.doc***

Experiential Activities

1 Obtain budgets for an organisation you know (college, workplace, club, charity). Examine the budgets and compare the range with that given in the chapter.
2 For an organisation you know well list the management ratios that would be relevant if you were managing that organisation.
3 Draw up your personal income, expenditure and cash budget for each of the next 12 months.
4 Talk to someone you know well and who trusts you. Ask them what impact budgets have on the way that they work and the methods they use. Enquire what methods they would use to ensure budgets work to their own and their team's advantage.

PART III
Management Functions

CHAPTER 10

Introduction to Management Functions – especially IT

Introduction to Management Functions

The previous unit was devoted to *management processes*: related activities performed by practically all managers as a part of managing their own areas of responsibility. Management work can also be described under a different set of categories: *management functions*. A management function consists of a specialised area performed only by some managers. It usually involves a specialised group of knowledge and skills and it has an impact on people in the organisation as a whole – an impact outside a manager's direct area of responsibility. For example the Human Resource Function will be responsible for ensuring enough recruits, enough trained workers and workers who are motivated in production, marketing and quality. Similarly, the finance function will be responsible for ensuring the proper control and supply of money to all functions in the organisation.

Management functions and management processes frequently overlap. The main distinction between functions and processes is that management processes are day-to-day activities which are performed by most managers. Management functions, on the other hand, often require a higher level of expertise and may be the preserve of specialists. For example, there is apparent overlap between staffing processes and the Human Resources Management (HRM) function. However, examination reveals important differences. The staffing process involves everyday activities such as leading and motivating subordinates. The HRM function (outlined in more detail in Chapter 13) concerns specialist activities that are performed by a much smaller sub-set of managers who have relevant professional qualifications such as membership of the Chartered Institute of Personnel and Development. The HRM activities will include issuing employment contracts, succession planning and aspects of employment law. Similarly, there is apparent overlap between budgeting and the finance function. Again, however, closer examination reveals significant differences. Most managers will engage in the process of forming and monitoring budgets. The finance function, on the other hand, will involve a special cadre of people who will be accredited to an organisation such as an Institute of Chartered Accountants. They will be involved in specialist activities such as raising finance, the preparation and auditing of accounts and devising financial systems.

Figure 10.1 shows it is possible to identify at least 14 different management functions – although not all will be found in many organisations. The 14 functions can be grouped into three main groups: line functions, enabling functions and control functions.

Line functions are those that take a direct part in producing the goods or services. They usually operate in a strict sequence. The enabling functions provide services and support which help line functions to operate more effectively. Controlling functions ensure that standards, regulations and laws are kept. However, this distinction is not exact. The finance function, for example can act as an enabling function (making sure money is available and producing reports) and as a control function (checking for fraud and ensuring budgets are kept). The diagram also shows that functions are not the same size. Some are bigger, more important and found in more organisations. The "Big Four" functions are:

- marketing and sales (which are usually considered together)
- operations
- human resources
- finance

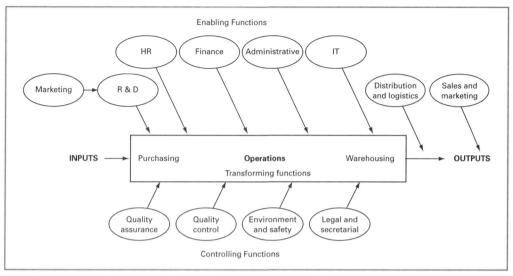

FIGURE 10.1 Management Functions

These four functions are so big that a later chapter is devoted to each one. This chapter outlines the remaining 10 functions – grouped into line, enabling or controlling functions. This chapter gives special attention to the IT function because its importance is growing so rapidly. The three sections are:

Chapter contents

10.1 Line Functions other than Operations

Line functions are those that play a direct part in making a product or service. They include two of the Big Four Management Functions – marketing (see Chapter 11) and operations (see Chapter 12). The remaining line functions are: research and development, purchasing and distribution.

Research and Development (R&D)

The end results of the research and development function are new products or services or better ways of producing old products and services. The R&D function does this by harnessing technological innovation and science. The function is generally traced back to the 1790s when the revolutionary government in France set up laboratories to devise new weapons to defend itself against hostile European neighbours. Their inventions included explosive shells, semaphore telegrams and observation balloons. The tradition was continued by gifted individuals such as Bunsen (of the laboratory Bunsen Burner fame and who helped German companies devise blast furnaces) and Alexander Graham Bell.

By 1900, mainly German firms such as Krupp and Siemens had established laboratories employing several hundred people to conduct scientific research that would lead to new production methods. During the First World War American companies such as General Electric and DuPont set up dedicated R&D departments. In small companies the function may rely upon one or two ingenious people who think up innovations for products and their manufacture. At the other end of the scale are organisations such as GlaxoSmithKline or Hutchinson Communications that have large, dedicated R&D establishments. While R&D exists predominantly within the manufacturing sector, it is also present within the service sector. For example, Barclays Bank conducted considerable research and development before they introduced the world's first credit card.

Governments usually fund a large proportion of R&D activity – especially in the development of weapons and defence systems. Laboratories in organisations that have a large R&D function can usually be divided into three types: *research laboratories* which carry out basic and applied research – they are often situated away from manufacturing units; *development laboratories*, which are more closely related to particular products or services and act as support functions to local units; *test laboratories*, which are usually responsible for monitoring the quality of chemicals, energy and materials bought by an organisation. The latter laboratories may be subsumed under the technical services function. Smaller organisations that cannot afford large resources may either manufacture goods that are licensed from research laboratories or they may outsource their R&D function.

Purchasing

The purchasing function's job is to ensure that the operations function has a timely supply of raw materials of an appropriate quality and at a reasonable price. Sometimes the purchasing function may be responsible for transporting the raw materials from their suppliers. The purchasing function may also be responsible for storing raw materials in the right conditions. The purchasing function needs to identify potential suppliers and investigate their suitability. They then need to negotiate fair contracts. There is often a close relationship

---

CASE 10.1: R&D AT GLAXOSMITHKLINE

The pharmaceutical industry invests heavily in the R&D necessary to discover new medicines and treatments. One of the industry leaders is GlaxoSmithKline which supports a huge R&D effort. It has 16 000 people working in 24 research and development laboratories in seven countries spending an annual budget of £2.4 billion developing new medicines and treatments. The R&D function has responsibility for managing an organisation's resources for keeping up-to-date. It usually conducts background research, product design and modification and testing.

between purchasers and suppliers and this may involve some degree of integration of the two organisation's IT systems. Purchasing is sometimes called "*Procurement*" or "*Supply-Chain Management*". The purchasing function has a very close relationship with the operations function and in some organisations it is viewed as a part of operations.

Distribution

The aim of the distribution function is to store goods that have been made in conditions which maintain the goods' quality and then to move them efficiently and at low cost to the customers. It includes the physical handling and movement of goods. People in the distribution function are usually involved in route planning, stock rotation and the efficient use of warehouse space. Distribution of utilities such as electricity, water and public transport are special cases that involve unique challenges. The distribution function is particularly important in manufacturing industry, but is also important in the delivery of some services such as social care and information industries.

10.2 Enabling Functions

Enabling functions provide the line functions with specialist services so that they can operate more effectively. For example, the HR function will help a production manager recruit new workers. This means that less of a production manager's attention is diverted to activities outside his or her main task or area of expertise. The two largest enabling functions, finance and human resources, are considered in later chapters of this book. Most organisations have three further enabling functions: IT, technical services and secretarial services.

IT (Information Technology)

The classical view that there are the big four functions – Marketing, Operations, Finance and Human Resources – is becoming less accurate each year. There is now a fifth large function, the IT function. Its importance is growing and it may soon be necessary to talk of the "big five" management functions. The influence of the IT function is very widespread. Practically all organisations have at least one computer and use IT in some way. In comparison, there are organisations with no operations function or sales function. For example, DABs.com, the Internet computer supplier is purely a retail marketing organisation. It does not manufacture or provide a service except for selling things. Similarly, tax collectors do not have a marketing and sales function. It is also possible to envisage organisations that have minimal HR or finance functions.

The IT function is more distinctive than the "big four" management functions in two main ways. First, as its name implies it is more heavily dependent on one specific technology (computing). Hence, it is heavily loaded with technical terms and knowledge, which this book does not even attempt to cover. Second, it encounters a rate of change which is many times faster than that encountered by the next most changeable function – operations. The following brief overview of the IT function is organised into three sections:

- historical perspective
- basics of IT systems
- structure of the IT function within organisations

Historical perspective

The first thing to note is that the IT function is not very old – it started only slightly more than 50 years ago. The exact start of the IT era depends upon the definition of "computer" that is used. One contender would be the Colossus machine built by the British intelligence services in 1943. Colossus could be programmed to search intercepts of German codes for certain words which, if located, would enable that day's codes to be deciphered. Some people define a computer in terms of its ability to store programs – in which case the Small-Scale Experimental Machine (SSEM) at the University of Manchester was the first true computer. Thus the start of the IT function might be dated quite precisely as 21 June 1948, when the SSEM stored the world's first computer program. Within a year the SSEM's successor, the Manchester University Mark 1 (MU1) machine had a high-speed magnetic memory drum and was available for calculations. The MU1 formed the basis of the first commercial computer, the Ferranti Mark 1, which was delivered in February 1951 (see Malcolm, 2000).

The first truly commercial computer was called Leo and was owned by the Lyons' chain of tea shops in the UK. It was used keep track of stock and sales in the various tea houses in the UK. Leo's free time was hired out to the Ministry of Defence.

The *first-generation computers* were based on electronic valves which generated a great deal of heat. By today's standards they were not very powerful but they were huge. They were called "main-frame" computers and were usually housed in purpose-built accommodation. First-generation computers were mainly used in scientific research and were based in universities and government establishments. However, a few large firms also used computers for commercial purposes and nascent IT functions started to develop. At this time the IT function was usually a fairly self-contained unit that handled, at arm's-length, routine clerical activities such as calculating payrolls, maintaining inventory lists and keeping ledgers of financial transactions. IBM (Big Blue) used its marketing might to build a company that, for three decades, dominated the market for main-frame computers.

Second-generation computers (about 1960) used individual transistors instead of valves and were much smaller. They became available to medium to large organisations who used them to perform repetitive commercial activities. The means of inputting and outputting information from second-generation computers was very crude and usually consisted of punchcards, punched tape and hard printouts. A large computer of this time would have a memory of about 32K!

Third-generation computers (about 1970) integrated many transistors onto one microchip (large-scale integration) and a mainframe computer was much more powerful than an average computer of the second generation. Large-scale integration also meant that mini-computers (smaller, more limited, computers) could be produced fairly cheaply.

Fourth-generation computers (about 1980) were characterised by very large-scale integration whereby many thousands of transistors could be squeezed onto a single chip.

Mainframes became still more powerful. However, probably the main impact was the development of cheap personal computers that could be provided for individuals or small groups of individuals. Since that time computers have become still more powerful and more readily available. However, the big changes arose from better methods of input and output (computer screen, mouse, etc.) and the development of the Internet. The Internet arose from military requirements for an efficient way of communicating between computers which would withstand an atomic bomb or two.

By the mid-1980s the technical aspects of connecting computers and sending messages had been settled and the Internet had begun. At the start in 1986 there were slightly more than 2000 networks in the USA. By the end of 1987 there were over 30 000. However, many of the networks could not communicate very effectively because they used different methods of encoding the signals.

In 1989 Sir Tim Berners-Lee developed a hypertext system that could be used across the Internet and the World Wide Web was born. Since that time dial-up systems and broadband have been developed which mean that computers can connect to the Internet using the telephone system. These developments and the latest use of wireless technology to interconnect computers have transformed the IT function in most organisations. It was a small, expensive function concentrating on performing routine tasks with speed and accuracy and directly involved only 1 or 2 per cent of people in very large organisations. Now it is a vital function that influences an organisation's strategy, control and operations as well as performing routine clerical tasks in practically all organisations, big and small.

Basics of IT systems

The process starts by identifying the organisational goals, tasks and procedures needed. This is often called *systems analysis*. These tasks and procedures determine the type of the hardware and the software (programs) installed in the computer. In *very* simple terms a computer has two main parts: memory, where it stores programs and data, and a processor where it manipulates the data according to the procedures set out in programs. A computer's primary memory is limited so secondary storage, such as discs, must be used for files that are used less frequently. When data is input it is processed by software to produce information that is valuable to the organisation. An IT system can be used in five main ways:

- Providing quick and efficient **processing of routine transactions** such as payroll, invoicing and bookkeeping.

- **Monitoring** systems reliably and frequently so that deviations from the optimum state can be detected and remedial action taken quickly. For example, IT systems can be used to monitor the temperature, pressure and output of an industrial retort to ensure that medicines are produced exactly to their specifications.

- **Communicating** with other computers by a network or facilitating communications between people using emails or the Internet. Intranet networks allow computers in the same organisation to communicate and share electronic databases.

    Networks can be enterprise-wide. For example, a customer may contact the organisation with a request for a bespoke product. After entering the request the customer service department transmits it to the design section who will prepare plans, etc. which are returned to the customer service department to check that they meet customer

CASE 10.2: CISCO'S CIO RE-ORGANISES THE IT FUNCTION

Brad Boston is global CIO of networking giant Cisco. He heads a global team of around 1800 to 2000 employees plus, depending on workloads, a further 2800 to 4000 contract workers. The team operates from four major IT sites in the US, another four in Europe plus locations in Sydney, Singapore, Tokyo, Beijing and Bangalore. He was a legend in the IT world before joining Cisco four years ago: he played a key role in spinning off the technology arm of American Airlines to become Sabre Holdings, the owner of Travelocity. Memorably, Sabre went on to become worth more than the airline from which it had been spawned.

He took a look at Cisco's existing worldwide business and decided the IT function should match its global vision. Until then, IT had been organised in what Boston calls a "theatre structure" – regional CIOs would run their own shows in different regions of the world.

Boston decided to abandon the theatre approach in favour of a truly global organisation of IT resources. Now, instead of people reporting into their theatre, they report through a global organisation. "This has enabled us to realise that we have very talented people in a number of locations around the world and I can leverage them on a global basis much more effectively than I could before."

Boston sees three main responsibilities for Cisco's IT function. The first is to support the business strategy with IT technology. The second is to help a business drive to improve productivity (again using technology as an enabler). The third is to act as a test-bed for some of Cisco's products.

Developed from "Going Global", *CIO-Connect*, Autumn 2005, p. 49. The full article is available from: ***http://www.cio-connect.com/magazine/articles/CIO12_p49.pdf***. The Asian "sister" magazine has published an idealised Person Specification for a Chief Information Officer. It is available at: ***http://www.cio-asia.com/ShowPage.aspx?pagetype=2&articleid=3148&pubid=5&issueid=76***

needs. Revised plans are then forwarded to the production department. When the product is manufactured, details are sent to the dispatch department and finance department so that they can prepare invoices, etc. Extranets are computer networks that allow people outside the organisation to communicate with it. Often the extranet will use the World Wide Web. In some cases commercial extranets require security provided by firewalls, digital certificates and encryption. Companies use extranets to exchange large volumes of data, share product catalogues or collaborate on joint development efforts.

■ Providing information to **guide decisions**. In many circumstances computers can model the business process and indicate likely outcomes. The computer can also calculate "what if" scenarios which can indicate the sensitivity of outcomes to external buffeting. Decisions may be improved in two ways: decision-makers may be given more accurate and timely information or computer modelling may help a decision-maker understand the problem.

- **Expert knowledge systems** simulate the judgements of high-level experts. Typically, such a system contains a knowledge base and a set of rules which are used to apply the knowledge base to particular situations. A classic example of an expert system is a computer program that plays chess. Another good example is a computer program used to diagnose an illness from a list of symptoms input by a patient. A further example is given by the British Council, which uses an expert system developed by LogicNets to help students, especially overseas students, navigate the complex process of applying for a university place in the UK. Many expert systems use *fuzzy logic* to solve problems. Fuzzy logic is needed because information is often unclear and incomplete. Moreover, there may be several possible answers to a managerial problem. Fuzzy logic is an approach developed by Dr Lofti Zadeh in the 1960s (Zadeh, 1965). It computes "degrees of truth" rather than coming to a clear-cut true or false conclusion. Rather like the human brain, fuzzy logic aggregates to arrive at partial truths. A number of partial truths are averaged to form higher truths until the conclusion is strong enough to warrant action. When an expert system approximates the operation of a human brain it is usually called a neural network. A **neural network** is trained by inputting large amounts of data and rules. Once trained, advanced neural networks can extend rules to new situations and perhaps, even, develop new rules of its own. Neural networks are widely used in oil exploration and weather forecasting.

Information systems

Management Information Systems (MIS) use information technology to collect, collate and report information so that routine, structured and day-to-day activities can be performed more effectively. They record basic transactions. Using simple analytical tools they produce routine reports. Management information systems (see Chapter 6, p. 130) may also use simple rules to solve straightforward problems. MIS is usually thought of as most useful to operatives and first-line managers. **Decision Support Systems (DSS)** are computer applications that analyse business data which are presented so that users can make business decisions more easily. For example a DSS might produce a report comparing sales figures between one month and the next or it might project the likely quarterly income. Decision support systems are thought to be most useful for middle managers. **Executive Information Systems (EIS)** are very similar but the term is usually reserved for systems that support senior management. An Executive Information Systems often contains more data concerning the external business environment – such as information about competitors, legislation and market trends. EI systems are less likely to report raw data. They are more likely to summarise information and present it in graphical form so that the main points can be understood very quickly.

IT installation failures

Information systems can be very useful but there is often no picnic and many, perhaps a half, fail. Businesses often keep their IT failures secret but examples of colossal failures in the public sector are available. For example, a new IT system for the Ministry of Defence, which cost more than £40 million, was obsolete a year after its completion and was never used. A new system for the British Passport Agency was an operational failure and resulted in a five-week backlog in processing passport applications. The National Insurance Recording System encountered problems which meant that an estimated 170 000 pensioners may have been underpaid by up to £100 a week (*The Times*, 1999). Some of the reasons why information systems fail are (Cringely, 1994):

- Users who do not understand their own requirements.
- Technical teams that fall in love with a technology and are determined to apply it – no matter who needs it.
- Business changes during the design phase – such as the sale of a division or a merger of the entire company.
- Project duration is underestimated. The rule of thumb is to double the expected project duration.
- Organisational politics cause project delays while departments slug it out.

Structure of the IT functions within organisations

The head of an IT function is often called the Chief Information Officer (CIO) who, like the head of other functions such as marketing, operations, finance and HR, reports to the organisation's Chief Executive Officer (CEO) or sometimes the finance director.

A manager in charge of *IT operations* will be responsible for making sure that the IT system works. Colloquially this is know as "keeping the lights on". In some organisations this can be an immensely important task. Reuters, for example, is totally dependent on the smooth and uninterrupted operation of its IT system. Reuters is a global company specialising in the selling of on-line financial and other information to 327 000 financial market professionals working in the equities, fixed income, foreign exchange, money, commodities and energy markets around the world. Reuter's IT system enables its customers to search, store and integrate information from its data base. If its IT system failed there would be a risk that stockbrokers throughout the world would make huge losses which they would seek to recover from their information supplier. If Reuter's IT system was even suspected of being unreliable, its customers would rush to competitors, such as Bloomberg. IT managers in most organisations are responsible for having a plan and mechanism to deal with the risk of a malfunction or calamitous disaster such as a terrorist attack.

The *Head of IT Solutions and Applications* will usually be responsible for specific projects such as the development and maintenance of computer programs that manage an organisation's supply chain. A team of *Relationship Managers (RM)* will report to the Head of IT Solutions and Applications. Their title indicates that these people have to manage the way the system relates to groups of either internal or external customers. For example, a large catering company may have a Hotels Relationship Manager whose job is to ensure that the hotel division has appropriate IT systems compatible with the IT system of the organisation as a whole. The Hotel Relationship Manager will be responsible for liaising with senior management in the hotel division and identifying the IT requirements. He or she will then determine whether the requirements should be met by a bespoke program or by the purchase of an existing package. The Hotel RM will establish project teams to write or install the programs. In this organisation there would probably be similar IT staff managing the relationships with restaurants, pubs, clubs and bistros, and relationship managers for headquarters departments such as HR and Finance. Some organisations provide IT services for external clients. In this case the Relationship Managers are organised according to types of client and have titles such as RM Internet Organisations, RM Retail Organisations or RM Wholesale Organisations.

A *Head of IT Infrastructure* will be responsible for the hardware (i.e. the computers, peripherals such as printers and networks). She or he may also be responsible for installing intangible infrastructure such as access rights, passwords and security. The rate of change in computers makes it very difficult to keep an organisation's computer system up to date. On the one hand, a Head of IT Infrastructure will need to keep up with nascent technologies and the most up-to-date equipment on the market. On the other hand, in reality, a great deal of money will have already been invested in equipment that cannot be jettisoned each time there is a new technical development. Consequently a Head of IT Infrastructure will often face the task of grafting new equipment on to a "legacy system" in a way which meets the organisation's needs. As the historical perspective at the start of this chapter implies, there was an upheaval in IT infrastructure when desktop computers became available and there was another upheaval with the introduction of the Internet and the World Wide Web. Currently most IT functions are grappling with the practical problems of grafting wireless technologies and Blackberry devices onto the existing wired infrastructure.

Technical services

The technical service function can take many forms. It can include the maintenance of buildings and equipment – especially where it is of a specialised or scientific nature. In these situations the technical services function will be responsible for testing, calibrating equipment and maintaining its usability. For example, an oil refinery might have a technical department that tests pilot plants before they go into service. In a chemical company the technical function may be responsible for neutralising dangerous chemicals before handing them on to external disposal contractors. The technical function often includes design and drawing office work. Where an organisation's product has a technical element the technical service department may be called on to solve problems encountered by customers. For example, paint manufacturers usually have a technical service department to investigate why paint may not have worked on the surface chosen by a customer. The technical service function is particularly important in the manufacturing sector. Sometimes, the technical service function is subsumed under the operations function.

Secretarial function

The secretarial function is self-explanatory and it is found in most organisations. However, it is usually dispersed among the other functions and may not have a clear identity. In some large organisations there will be a single department that is responsible for servicing meetings by producing agendas and publishing minutes. With the advance of word processors and photocopiers the secretarial function as a separate entity has contracted and other employees have absorbed this work into their jobs. In the past many large organisations would have a "typing pool" of considerable proportions. The secretarial function is sometimes called "administration". Essentially, it is concerned with the production and supervision of correspondence and committee work. The secretarial function is most relevant to financial institutions and government bodies. The classic example of a secretarial function is the Registrar's Department in a large university.

10.3 Controlling Functions

The controlling functions have a responsibility to prevent misuse of the organisation's resources and systems. There are three main controlling functions: quality assurance, quality control and legal services.

Quality assurance

This is a proactive activity to arrange things in a way that ensures products and services are produced according to standards. It involves a series of systematic procedures that are designed to prevent the occurrence of nonconformities. Quality assurance is a continuous process undertaken by all employees playing a part in producing goods or services (see p. 255).

Quality control

This is a retroactive activity whereby production is checked after various stages have been completed to detect and extract products or services which fall below standards. It is usually the responsibility of a team of inspectors who may constitute a separate department within the production function (see p. 255).

Legal and administrative functions

The legal and administrative functions are also control functions. They exist to stop employees, and the organisation, from performing undesirable acts. In a large organisation the *legal function* will be "in-house" but in a medium or small organisation the legal function will be outsourced. The function will generally be staffed by a small number of highly trained and highly specialised staff. Their job will be to ensure that the organisation complies with external laws and regulations and it does not enter into unfortunate contractual obligations. The legal function may also undertake litigation to advance and defend the organisation's interests. Legal functions are particularly important in government organisations and quangos. Most large organisations have some kind of legal department to defend its intellectual property such as patents, trademarks and copyright. The *administrative function* is responsible for ensuring that internal regulations and procedures are upheld. The administrative function is very important in governments and educational organisations and in bodies that award permissions, allowances and grants.

Finally, some organisations will have other control functions. For example, a chemical company may have a small unit to control the rate of noxious emissions from its chimneys and ensure that pollution laws are respected. Often, these specialised control functions are contained within a technical service function or the operations function.

Activities and Further Study for Chapters 10–14

Essay Plans

Write essay plans for the following:

1 Compare and contrast the way that two named companies organise their R&D function (hint: choose one large pharmaceutical company, usually known as Big Pharm, or a company from aeronautics as one example and choose a smaller local engineering company as the other example).

2 Should IT be regarded as one of the "big" functions in modern-day industry and commerce?

3 Compare and contrast the controlling functions found in modern organisations.

Web Activities for Chapters 10–14

The web activities for gaining knowledge about managerial functions are similar for all functions. For each function that interests you:

1 Look up the function in free encyclopaedias, e.g. ***http://en.wikipedia.org/wiki/ Management***

2 Most management functions have close associations with a professional body or institute. Use the web to locate relevant institutes. Some useful sites are:

http://www.iomnet.org.uk/ (Institute of Operations Management)

http://www.esc.auckland.ac.nz/organisations/orsnz/ (Operations Research Society of New Zealand)

http://www.sapics.org.za/ (Professional Society for Supply Chain Management)

www.logistics.ust.hk (Hong Kong Logistics and Supply Chain Management Institute)

http://www.mis.org.sg/ (Marketing Institute Singapore)

http://www.ami.org.au/ (Australian Marketing Institute)

http://www.mrsa.com.au/ (Australian Marketing and Social Research Society)

http://www.marketing.org.au/ (The Marketing Association of Australia and New Zealand)

http://www.shri.org.sg/ (Singapore Human Resources Institute)

Web Activities for Chapters 10–14 continued

http://www.cipd.co.uk/default.cipd (Chartered Institute of Personnel and Development)

http://www.icaew.co.uk/ (Institute of Chartered Accountants in England and Wales)

www.cipfa.org.uk Chartered institute of Public and Finance Accounting

www.icai.ie (The Institute of Chartered Accountants in Ireland)

www.rdsoc.org (Research and Development Society)

www.scs.org.sg (Singapore Computer Society)

http://www.fssc.org.uk/cgi-bin/wms.pl/Qualifications_and_careers/61 (a site listing many professional bodies in the UK)

3 Many universities and colleges have postgraduate courses to equip people to enter a specialist management function. Search the web for details of such courses. The descriptions often contain information about what the management function includes and the career opportunities that may be available: Some useful sites are:

http://www.mang.canterbury.ac.nz/course_advice/undergrad/op_mangt.shtml

http://www-afa.adm.ohio-state.edu/u-majors/pdf/opermgt.pdf

http://www.sussex.ac.uk/Users/dt31/TOMI/whatisom.html

http://www.aston.ac.uk/prospective-students/pg/pros/abs/11markman.jsp

http://www.shortcourses.auckland.ac.nz/courses/114/

http://www.cranfield.ac.uk/prospectus/course.cfm?id=123

http://datasearch.uts.edu.au/business/gsb/courses

http://www.vms.vuw.ac.nz/vuw/content/display_content.cfm?school=vms&id=520

4 Find the site for Hobsons Graduate Employment and Training (*http://www.get.hobsons.co.uk/*). Use the menus to select an area that interests you (probably "administration and manager"), refine your choice using the Job Description menu. When you press "search" a list of companies offering relevant types of employment appears. By clicking on an organisation with a case-study icon a description of the work of a recent graduate will appear. The description will give you some details of the function where they work.

5 Find out about latest developments in the management function. Use the net to locate articles on the management function that interests you. The *Harvard Business Review* (HBR) *http://hbswk.hbs.edu/* might be particularly suitable – especially if your organisation has an on-line subscription to the *Review*. If it does not, hard copies of HBR are readily available in many large libraries.

Experiential Activities

There are few experiential exercises concerning management functions. It is possible to gain some first-hand experience by choosing vacation work in a function or, perhaps, joining a management training scheme involving short periods of work in different functions. The latter are often called "Cooks Tours". The only other practical possibility is to interview or talk to a manager who has experience of a function. In any event it is worth while getting detailed answers to the following questions:

- What is the type of organisation, what are its goals, size, how does it achieve the transformation process?
- How does the function fit into the organisation, how does it help the transformation process?
- How is the function structured, how is the same function structured in similar organisations?
- What other functions are closely related to it?
- What type of people work in the function, what experience and qualifications do they need?
- What are the future challenges the function is likely to face?

The Marketing Function

11

❖ LEARNING OBJECTIVES

After reading this chapter you should understand some of the purpose and position of the marketing function within organisations. You should be familiar with ways of analysing markets and understand the ideas behind the marketing mix. You should also be familiar with some of the general criticisms of the marketing function. In particular you should be able to:

1 **define** both markets and marketing and be able to explain key terms within the definitions

2 **explain** concepts such as market size, niches, market segmentation and relationship marketing

3 **explain** at least two ways of categorising people into market segments

4 **explain** concepts such as competition, barriers to entry and exit and market dynamism

5 **discuss in detail** market strategy and market positioning

6 **draw** both a BCG matrix and a General Electric Matrix which might be useful for strategists in an organisation with which you are familiar

7 **draw** an imaginary product lifecycle for a consumer good that interests you

8 **contrast** briefly the difference between markets research and marketing research

9 **list** seven uses and four methods of market research

10 **discuss in detail** each of the five main components of the marketing mix

11 **explain** the concept of a "brand" in marketing

12 **differentiate** between marketing and public relations

▶
13 **explain** the concepts of guerrilla marketing and cause-related marketing	15 **evaluate** at least four criticisms that have been levelled against the marketing function
14 **outline** some of the techniques and methods used in advertising	

Definition and Introduction to Marketing

In theory at least, marketing has prime place in the sequence of management functions because it is concerned with identifying a need the organisation can exploit with a product or service. Once this need has been recognised, the other functions – operations, HRM, finance function – can work together to actually produce the product or service. In fact, the marketing function also plays an important part at the end of the process – selling the finished product. Some people find it difficult to distinguish between marketing and sales. As a simplification, marketing is "having something you can get rid of" while selling is "getting rid of what you have!" Many people have attempted to define marketing in more formal terms. Typical definitions assert that marketing is:

> An organisational function and set of processes for creating, communicating and delivering value to customers and for managing customer relationships in ways that benefit the organisation and its stakeholders.
> *(American Marketing Association, 2004)*

> Responsible for identifying, anticipating and satisfying customer requirements profitably.
> *(Hannagan, 2005)*

> A management function which identifies, anticipates and supplies consumer requirements efficiently and effectively.
> *(Chartered Institute of Marketing [UK])*

Unfortunately each of the definitions has its disadvantages. The first is so megalomanic in its scope that it includes practically everything in an organisation. It does not differentiate between marketing and other essential functions such as production or finance. Two of the definitions imply, quite wrongly, that marketing only applies to commercial, profit-making, organisations. A definition which escapes these problems and which commands some consensus is:

> A product or service's conception, pricing, promotion and distribution in order to create exchanges that satisfy consumers and organisational objectives and the interest of other stakeholders.
> *(see, for example, Pride and Farrell, 2000; Health Advantage, 2004; Quintessential Careers, 2004)*

This definition has a number of advantages.

- It is centred upon the exchange relationship between consumers (in the broadest sense) and organisations.
- It emphasises that these exchanges should be satisfactorily to all parties.
- It specifies the activities which constitute marketing.
- By implication it accepts that other functions in the organisation play an important part in a satisfactory exchange.

Many writers emphasise the importance of organisations adopting a marketing orientation. They contend that everyone in the organisation has a marketing role. For example, when a driver of a company van parks discourteously it tarnishes the company's image and affects its relationship with a customer. Similarly, an operative making a poor-quality product, an off-hand customer service assistant, a tardy accounts clerk and an arrogant chief executive all reflect badly on the organisation and affect its relationship with customers and clients. The management guru, Peter Drucker (1999) takes the view that:

66 The purpose of business is to create and keep customers ... it has only two functions – marketing and innovation. The basic function of marketing is to attract and retain customers at a profit. 99

This view is probably overstated. It means that marketing and the organisation are almost synonymous and that one of the terms is therefore redundant. Furthermore, there are many non-profit organisations where the satisfaction of customers is not the only objective of the organisation. Nevertheless, most organisations need to have a *market orientation*. This is also called being *"consumer centred"* or being *"consumer driven"*. The marketing function can be discussed in five main sections:

Chapter contents

11.1 Markets

A *market* (in contrast to *marketing*) may be defined as:

66 The actual or potential buyers of a product. 99

This means that a market is wider than individuals and it includes private and public sector organisations, supplier groups and purchasing groups. It is also wider than present or past buyers. It includes anyone or any organisation that is reasonably likely to buy a product in the future. Kotler (1986) defined a product broadly as:

 ... anything that can be offered to a market for attention, acquisition, use or consumption that might satisfy a want or need. It includes physical objects, services, persons, places, organisations and ideas.

An organisation that hopes to sell its product in a market needs to study the market very carefully and may commission extensive market research (see section 11.3). It will need to examine the characteristics of the market such as:

- the **people** and **organisations** that make up the market
- the **product** that it is bought
- the **purpose** for which it will be bought and the **needs** it will satisfy
- the **times** and **occasions** (e.g. birthdays, setting up a new home or everyday purchases) when the product is bought
- the **method** used to buy the product (e.g. visit to retail outlet, regular order, telephone order or Internet shopping)

It should be remembered that people and organisations do not buy products for their own sake. Products are bought because they *solve a problem* or confer *benefits* upon their owners. For example, organisations do not purchase a car for a sales representative because it is a good thing in itself. The car will be purchased because the organisation believes it will benefit from the sales representative's ability to visit more customers each day and because it can be sure that its image will not be damaged by the representative arriving at customers premises driving a clapped-out banger.

Markets can differ in many ways. The main differences are size, competition, barriers and dynamism.

Size, niches and market segmentation

Markets differ markedly in their size. Some markets, such as detergents and cleaning materials, are vast and international. Global companies such as Proctor and Gamble have developed to meet the needs of such markets. In principle, large markets are good and lead to very cost-effective products, because development costs are shared among millions of customers. However, these benefits accrue only if the large market is homogeneous and customers have similar needs. However, it is difficult to mount an effective marketing campaign for a large, heterogeneous market. It is usually better to target a smaller but more homogeneous group. A market can be made more homogeneous by focusing upon a restricted range of either products or consumers.

A market which focuses upon a restricted range of specialised products is generally called a *"niche market"*. A niche market may be defined as "a portion of a market whose needs are met by a restricted range of specialised products". A classic example of an organisation that caters for a niche market is the Tie Rack chain. It operates within a wider market for clothing. However, it sells only ties, scarves, handkerchiefs and other accessories. Appropriately enough, many of Tie Rack's outlets are physical niches at airports or railway stations. WesternGeco, a subsidiary of the American company Schlumberger, also operates within a niche market. It provides seismic imaging services for oil companies. It operates on a worldwide basis from large, technically sophisticated premises. Catering for a niche market means that an organisation can develop highly specialised expertise and project a clear, distinctive image.

Another way to produce a homogeneous market is *market segmentation* where a wider market is divided into subgroups whose members have similar needs. Typical methods of market segmentation divide customers according to factors such as loyalty, age, gender, neighbourhood or social economic status.

Perhaps the most important way to segment a market is to divide it into *past customers* (i.e. loyal customers) and new customers. In the late 1990s there was a craze to focus upon past customers. The craze arose from the realisation that with the development of the Internet, customers had a much greater ability to "shop around" and become "promiscuous consumers". Many organisations therefore concentrated on establishing a dedicated base of existing customers and developing a long-term relationship that would prevent loyal customers switching to other suppliers. This is called *"relationship marketing"*. It was supported by claims such as:

- Costs of acquiring a new customer are ten times higher than keeping an existing customer.
- Loyal customers spend more than new customers.
- Past, satisfied customers tell others about their satisfaction.
- Past customers are more profitable because they are willing to pay a premium for a service they know.

Such principles were embraced by organisations that traded with other organisations. So, for example, a computer software company would develop a close marketing relationship with its customers. Specific programmers would be devoted to clients so that personalised help would be available if needed. It would hope that this would establish a deep, long-term and profitable relationship. Initially these concepts were applied to business organisations (*B2B transactions*). However, their relevance to retail transactions was quickly appreciated. Very successful examples of *customer management* and relationship marketing include the Tesco Clubcard scheme and Airmiles. A fundamental aspect of customer management is the concept of **client life-cycle**. A new client needs to be welcomed, perhaps by email, and assured that they have made the correct choice of supplier. An established customer needs to be told that they are important and that the organisation wishes to attend to their needs. A long-established client needs to be made aware of new products. Unfortunately, some of these basic beliefs have not withstood scrutiny. For example, Werner and Kumar (2002) provided data that indicates loyalty is not as profitable as the gurus of the 1990s suggested. There are some advantages of encouraging customer loyalty but they are not as great as their advocates imply. Werner and Kumar note, for example, that long-term customers tend to demand more favourable contracts. Furthermore, many long-term customers make disproportionate demands in terms of customer support.

Market segmentation by *age* is also very common. Classic examples are the UK travel organisation Club 18–30 which markets lively Mediterranean holidays to youthful consumers, and the SAGA Group which markets holidays and financial products to people aged 50 years or more. Market segmentation by age is widespread in the fashion and entertainment industries.

Market segmentation by *gender* is widespread in the publishing industry. For example magazines such as *Woman's Weekly* and *Cosmopolitan* are marketed for women whilst *Playboy* and *What Car* are marketed for men. Similarly, the range of cars offered by major manufacturers will include at least one car designed to appeal to women and other cars that are designed to appeal to men.

Market segmentation by *neighbourhood* is very common. For example, billboards in prosperous areas will depict luxury goods purchased out of discretionary income whilst billboards in less affluent areas will advertise basic products. Probably the most extensive classification of residential areas is the ACORN system (CACI, 2005). Readers in the UK can obtain the ACORN classification of where they live by visiting the Internet site http://www.streetmap.co.uk . The ACORN classification starts with five major categories:

1 Wealthly Achievers
2 Urban prosperity
3 Comfortably off
4 Moderate means
5 Hard-pressed

These are then subdivided into 17 major groups. For example, the wealthy achievers are subdivided into groups such as wealthy executives, affluent greys and flourishing families. The hard-pressed are divided into four groups: struggling families, burdened singles, high-rise hardship and inner-city adversity. The groups are further divided into subgroups. For example, the affluent greys, who comprise 7.7 per cent of the British population, are subdivided into older affluent professionals (1.8 per cent), farming communities (2.0 per cent), old people in detached homes (1.9 per cent) and mature couples (2.0 per cent). The high-rise hardship group is subdivided into old people in high-rise flats (0.8 per cent) and singles in high-rise estates (0.9 per cent). A manager marketing sophisticated financial products such as shares or annuities would target neighbourhoods containing many affluent greys whilst a government department trying to ensure proper take-up of welfare benefits might target neighbourhoods containing many people experiencing high-rise hardship.

Markets are often segmented by *socio-economic status*. This system classifies markets according to the work performed by the head of the household. The categories are:

■ A upper middle-class (e.g. directors, senior managers and senior civil servants)
■ B middle-class (e.g. lawyers, doctors, middle managers and higher professional workers)
■ C1 lower middle-class (e.g. teachers, nurses, junior managers and lower professional workers)
■ C2 skilled workers including technologists and many engineering workers
■ D working-class
■ E subsistence workers and unemployed people

Market segmentation by socio-economic status is far from exact but it does help to group consumers who have similar spending power and preferences. This discussion covers only the most popular ways of dividing a large market into homogeneous groups. Many other methods exist. Markets are often segmented according to lifestyle using categories with cute acronyms such as "YUPPIES" (Young Upwardly Mobile Persons), "DINKIES" (Dual Income No Kids) or "GRUMPIES" (Grown Up Mature Persons)

Competition

In a totally captive market there is only one supplier and customers must purchase from this supplier or do without the product. From a supplier's viewpoint a captive market is ideal and very little effort is needed to sell products at a high price. Unfortunately, captive markets are very attractive to other organisations who then set up in competition. Captive markets are very rare. A market is generally regarded as being a captive when there are fewer than four suppliers. Sometimes captive markets are called *monopolies* or duopolies. A market which has, say, more than 12 suppliers is generally called a "*fluid market*".

Barriers to entry and exit

Captive markets tend to exist in situations when it is difficult for others to enter the market. For example, in the aerospace industry there are often only one or two suppliers. Few organisations can afford the immense costs of setting up huge and complicated factories or build up the technical knowledge and expertise needed. Barriers to entry also exist in the form of laws and regulations such as patent laws, copyright laws and planning permissions. Distribution channels can also constitute entry barriers. Commercial practices by competitors may present further entry barriers – especially the practice of *predatory pricing* (OECD, 1989). Predatory pricing occurs when a large, established business cuts its price below its costs so that new competitors must sell at a loss and are therefore eventually driven from a market. *Exit barriers* prevent organisations withdrawing from markets. Usually they wish to exit from a market because it is either unprofitable or it is no longer central to the organisation's strategy. Typical exit barriers include loss of capital already invested, the cost of making staff redundant, loss of prestige or government pressure.

CASE 11.1: ROCKEFELLER'S PREDATORY PRICING

A classic case of predatory pricing is given by John D. Rockefeller's oil interests (Tarbell, 1950). A new entrant, the Pure Oil Company, was driven out of business when Rockefeller's Standard Oil Company drastically lowered its price, knowing that its vast reserves could survive a short-term loss in order to reap a long-term benefit. Another example of predatory pricing is the way established airlines cut the price of their air fares in the 1970s to force a new entrant, Laker Airways, out of the transatlantic passenger market.

Dynamism

Markets differ in the rate at which they change. A growing market is called an *"expanding market"*. A market that is shrinking is called a *"declining market"* and one that stays the same is called a *"static"* or *"stagnant market"*. It is generally easiest to operate in an expanding market. Organisations operating in a declining market need to pay very close attention to costs in the hope that they will be able to drive less efficient competitors from the market.

These characteristics are not the only factors that differentiate markets. In order to predict and anticipate markets it is necessary to understand six further influences. They are the political, environmental, societal, technological, legal and economic (PESTLE) factors outlined in more detail when strategy was discussed in Chapter 3, p. 60. **Cultural factors** are also important characteristics of markets. For example, the French culture and traditions made it much more difficult for the McDonald's hamburger chain to penetrate the French market.

11.2 Market Strategy and Market Positioning

Once there is a clear understanding of market characteristics it is possible to choose the type of market an organisation would prefer to serve. This is called *"market strategy"*, *"market positioning"* or *"portfolio planning"*. Organisations and consultancies have devised schemes such as PESTLE analysis to aid market positioning. Additional schemes include the Boston matrix, the General Electric matrix and the Anscoff matrix.

The *Boston Matrix* (also known as the *BCG* matrix) focuses on two aspects of a market, its *dynamism* (growth rate) and a product's relative *share of a market*. This allows products, services or production units to be categorised into the four types shown in Figure 11.1.

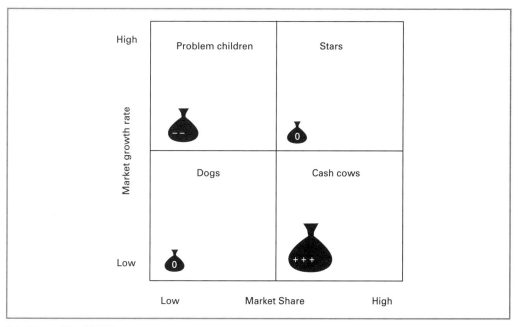

FIGURE 11.1 The BCG Matrix

If a product has a low market share in a slow-growing market, the product is classified as *"a dog"* since it is doing poorly in a weak market. The outlook for the product is poor and an organisation might be well advised to consider eliminating the product from its range – preferably by selling it to someone else, or in the worst case, shutting the product line down. If the product has a low market share but operates in an expanding market, the organisation has a problem because the outlook is mixed. The expanding market bodes well but the low market share implies a struggle to keep up with market leaders who will be able to obtain greater economies of scale. In these situations an organisation must decide whether to inject substantial resources to develop and promote the product. This may involve considerable risk. A product in this quadrant of the market is therefore categorised as *"a problem child"*. Sometimes, products categorised as "problem children" are called *"cash hogs"* because, while their profit potential is uncertain they often require large injections of cash to keep up. A product that commands a high share of a slowly growing market is categorised as a *"cash cow"*. Its high market share means that economies of scale are achieved and a lot of money is generated. This money can be used to promote other projects such as "a problem child" or a "star". Organisations may become complacent about their "cash cows" and pay more attention to new products (stars). Because of lack of investment the "cash cows" lose their competitiveness and turn into "dogs". A *"star"* is a product that has a high share of an expanding market. Generally, it will generate most of the funds needed for its own development and promotion but, from time to time, this may need supplementing by injections of resources from a "cash cow". The Boston Matrix provides a reasonable basis for the allocation of development funds. However, it has its disadvantages (Morrison and Wensley, 1991). It oversimplifies markets by focusing upon just two aspects: market growth and market share. This may lead an organisation to ignore other important aspects (Haspeslagh, 1982). Moreover, the Boston Matrix simplifies the two dimensions into just two crude categories; high and low.

The *General Electric Matrix* is also known as *"The Industry Attractiveness/Business Strength"* Matrix or the *"Directional Policy"* Matrix. It overcomes some of the disadvantages of the Boston Matrix by incorporating more factors and allowing three levels for each dimension. The General Electric Matrix has two composite dimensions: "industry attractiveness" and "business strength". *Industry attractiveness* is an amalgam of the following five characteristics of an industry:

- market forces – size, growth, price sensitivity and bargaining position
- competition – as types of competitors or substitution by new technology
- financial and economic factors – economies of scale, profits, entry and exit barriers
- technological factors – the maturity of the market, patents and copyrights together with the manufacturing technology needed
- socio-political factors – pressure groups, legal constraints and unionisation

A product is evaluated on a similar set of factors to arrive at a measure of *business strength*. Using these two measures the product is located on a matrix and an appropriate strategy is determined. In practice, this process is quite complicated because an intricate system of weights is applied to the characteristics of the industry and the strengths of the business or product. Figure 11.2 indicates the appropriate strategy for products or organisations positioned in each cell.

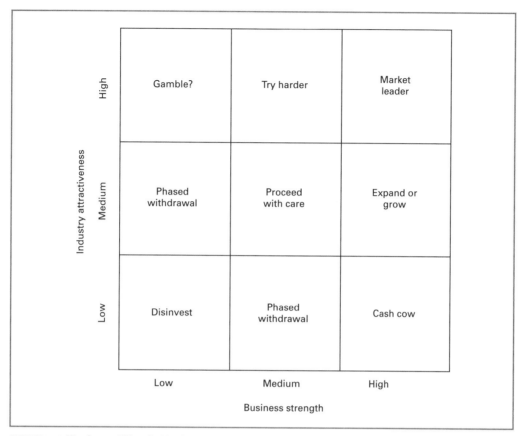

FIGURE 11.2 The General Electric Matrix

For example, a weak product in an unattractive market should be discontinued as quickly as possible, preferably by its sale to another organisation. A strong product in similarly unattractive market should be milked for all the cash it can generate. The case of a weak product in an attractive market is interesting. The organisation should either quit or take a gamble and invest many resources in the product's development in the hope that it can be made a market leader. It is similar to the "problem child" category of the BCG matrix.

Unfortunately, even a system as sophisticated as the General Electric Matrix does not capture the full complexity of positioning a product in a market. For example, a product which is an established market leader can be developed in a number of ways. Efforts could be made to obtain an even greater share of the market. Alternatively, the product can be adjusted so that it appeals to a new market. Ansoff (1989) developed a matrix to aid such decisions. This matrix focuses upon whether both the markets and the products are new or established and, as Figure 11.3 shows, it indicates an appropriate strategy for each combination.

Once a suitable market has been identified it is necessary to decide the organisation's role within that market. It is often assumed that organisations should aim to be market leaders or *pioneers*. In this role an organisation will devise new methods and campaigns

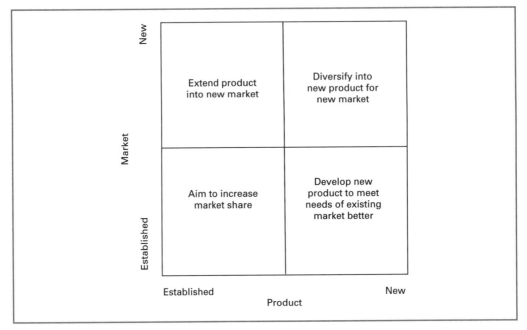

FIGURE 11.3 The Ansoff Matrix

(Pettinger, 1997). Pioneer organisations also open up new markets and devise new products. They frequently have a high esteem. However, being a pioneer can be risky because there may be unknown difficulties. Pioneers will need to carry substantial development costs. If the ideas are successful they can be copied more cheaply by other organisations. An alternative, and often more successful, marketing strategy is to adopt a *"follow the leader"* approach: keeping a keen eye on developments and maintaining a capability to quickly exploit the advances made by others. Other organisations adopt a strategy of building up *technical excellence*, or the *quality of their staff*, and they deploy these assets when and where an opportunity arises.

Organisations must also consider the maturity of their products or services and try to ensure their portfolios contain goods at different stages of the product life cycle. In general, product life cycles have five main phases as shown in Figure 11.4.

The continuous line shows the "natural" progression of sales. As a new product or service is being introduced, there is a period of slow growth. This is followed by rapid increase in sales as the product or service is adopted by opinion leaders and then a wider range of consumers. At maturity, growth is either slow or there is a small decline as the product loses some of its "novelty value". At this point the product has wide acceptance in the market. During the saturation phase, sales may decline somewhat because, although the market may be expanding, new competitors emerge. Finally, the product declines until sales are so low that they generate little cash. This pattern is an idealised generalisation. In practice, it varies greatly. In some cases, usually fashion items and children's toys, the whole life cycle is less than a year. In other cases such as "big ticket" items (e.g. televisions) the life cycle can be more than a decade. Organisations will try to predict the life cycle of their products or serv-

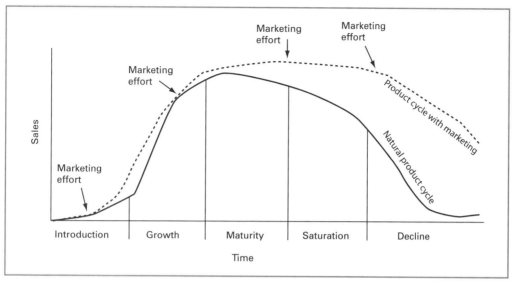

FIGURE 11.4 Product Life Cycle

ices to ensure that they have new products "in the pipeline" to replace the products that are in the saturation and decline phases. Predicting the life cycle of products is particularly important in industries such as pharmaceuticals where it can take years to develop new medicines. The marketing function will monitor the life cycles of products for a second reason. By mounting a marketing effort, such as advertising, new packaging or restyling at key times the marketing function can boost sales and extend the product life cycle. The effect of a marketing effort on a product life cycle is demonstrated by the dotted line in Figure 11.4.

11.3 Understanding Markets (Market Research)

Marketing decisions require a lot of information. The process of collecting and collating this information in a systematic and objective away is called **market research**. It is defined by the American Marketing Association as:

> 66 ... the function that links the consumer, customer and public to the marketer through information – information used to identify and define marketing opportunities and problems; generate, refine and evaluate marketing actions; monitor marketing performance; and improve understanding of marketing as a process. 99

The terms "market research", "markets research" and "marketing research" sound very similar and are often used interchangeably. Technically, however, market research refers to *any* information about markets. *Markets research* is a part of market research and looks at the characteristics of markets. *Marketing research* deals with information relevant to marketing a specific product or service. To avoid confusion it is therefore helpful to divide market research into two main categories: *markets research* and *marketing research*.

Markets research

Research on markets is sometimes called "market intelligence". It obtains information, usually quantitative, on many of the market characteristics such as the size of a market, growth, use of technology, dynamism and level of competition (see Section 1 of this chapter). Often markets research is based on existing (secondary) data compiled by government and industry sources such as census figures, the retail price index and the value of certain imported goods. It may also use journal and newspaper articles to build up a picture of competitors.

Marketing research

Marketing research focuses upon the information that will be useful to organisations who wish to sell specific products. It is the research which, say, the brand manager for Coca-Cola would use to devise a campaign to increase Coca-Cola's market share. While marketing research has some overlap with research on markets, its focus is narrower and it is closer to the actual point of sale. Marketing research can, perhaps, the best considered under two headings: its uses and its methods.

Uses of marketing research

Marketing research can play a vital role in bringing to market a product that is valued by customers and which is presented to them in an enjoyable way. Marketing research's main uses include:

- **Product generation** – marketing research can be used to identify new products. These ideas can be obtained by listening to consumers or by holding brainstorming sessions with designers and marketing executives.
- **Product improvement and embellishment** – existing products can be improved or made more attractive. Again, the source of suggestions can be obtained from consumers or brainstorming sessions. Ideas may also be generated by examining competitors' products or even products and services in other markets.
- **Product testing and refinement** – prototypes of products and services can be tested on small groups of consumers. Their reactions and comments are usually incorporated in a modified product.
- **Consumer targeting** – marketing research can help pinpoint the people who are most likely to buy the product or use a service.
- **Sales forecasting.**
- **Packaging and advertising design** – various suggestions for packaging can be tested out on samples of consumers and the most effective packages or adverts chosen.
- **Point-of-sale displays and procedures** – marketing research can be used to develop and then refine point of sale displays, brochures and other factors that might influence the experience of a buyer.

Marketing research methods

Marketing research uses a wide range of techniques to collect data on customers and products. Some of the main methods are:

■ **Existing internal data** – such as sales records, call reports from sales representatives and especially quotations for work that have been not been taking up by customers. Customer loyalty schemes such as Tesco's Clubcard routinely gather vast amounts of information on specific consumers. This information can give very detailed data on individuals and groups of customers.

■ **Surveys** can take many forms. Perhaps the simplest is a questionnaire returned by a purchaser when she or he registers a guarantee. Many organisations also use questionnaire surveys. Archetypally, questionnaire surveys are administered by market researchers who approach customers, whose characteristics appear to meet their *quotas*, as they visit shopping malls or go about their daily life. Alternatively, questionnaire surveys may be administered in a slightly more rigorous way to a *random sample* of people in their own homes. Unfortunately, random samples are more expensive than quota samples. Questionnaires may also be distributed via the post but this method may result in a very poor response rate. The telephone and the Internet may also be used to administer questionnaires. However, the sample responding to this type of survey may not be representative of the whole market. Questionnaire surveys need to be constructed with care to ensure that the questions are "neutral". Sometimes a series of questionnaires are administered to the same group of people. Often these are called *consumer panels*. Consumer panels have the advantage that they can track changes in customer preferences over time. Unfortunately, the repeated questioning of the same people can sensitise them to issues so that they gradually become unrepresentative. Some unscrupulous organisations use questionnaires as a way of introducing themselves to people, getting them to divulge information and then attempting to sell them a product directly. This is called "SUGGING" (selling under the guise). Charities sometimes use surveys as a ruse to raise funds. This is called "FRUGGING" (fund raising under the guise). Both practices are unethical and should not be used.

■ **Focus groups or group discussions** are frequently used in market research – especially when customers' underlying attitudes to new or changing situations are relevant. Focus groups consist of, say, eight people representing different types of consumers plus a leader who ensures they cover the required topics. Sometimes, focus groups attempt to assess "emotions" and "deep attitudes" towards a product or service. Some of the techniques are exotic and perhaps silly. Group members, for example, might be asked to nominate a type of tree that they associate with a certain public figure. In other situations, a focus group will be asked to taste a new drink and compare it to existing beverages. Focus groups can also be used to evaluate the clarity and impact of different ways of packaging a product.

■ **Experiments** are used infrequently. Usually they are employed to study the impact of advertisements and packaging. For example, the technique of *pupilometry* may be used to monitor a consumer's eye movements and determine the parts of an advert that a consumer selects for attention. Sometimes experiments are used to observe buyer behaviour. For example, a supermarket may stock shelves in a different ways and videotape the behaviour of customers. The videotape will then be analysed to establish which shelf lay-out generates most purchases.

11.4 The Marketing Mix

Successful marketing of a product or service involves an appropriate combination of five main factors. This combination is called the marketing mix and is based on the "5 Ps" of: product or service, price, packaging, promotion and place of purchase.

Products

Section 2 of this chapter discussed the strategic marketing issues but many other factors must be taken into account. A product can be either a physical entity or a service. The main difference is that ownership of a physical entity changes hands when a *product* is purchased. When a *service* is purchased ownership is not transferred. From a marketing viewpoint, the most important feature of either is the *benefit* it bestows upon the customer. An engineer, a technologist, a production manager and a design specialist may eulogise about the product's features, its technical sophistication or its aesthetic appeal. However, these are only important if the consumer believes that they confer some benefit. The benefits may be a saving in time, the ability to perform a previously impossible task, a feeling of well-being and attractiveness or an increase in status. In other words a product or service must solve or ease a problem for the consumer. For example, consumers do not buy computers because they can add up numbers quickly or because they are an example of high technology. They buy computers because the machines solve problems such as communicating with others, keeping accounts or storing information. If a product or service confers benefits its competitors do not, the product has a "*unique selling-point*" that may increase sales.

Consumers frequently judge products on the basis of their *quality* – a freedom from imperfections and an implication of exclusivity or "class". Marketeers imply quality when they offer "fine wines", "prime beef", "select cheeses", "high-calibre education" and so on. Generally products must also offer *durability* – the ability to function satisfactorily for an acceptable time. However, there is a range of products (razors, pens, cameras, gloves, live entertainment, etc.) where durability is not expected.

A product's *brand* is an important feature. The marketing functions of organisations give their brand close attention. Brands started when farmers would burn distinctive marks into the flesh of their cattle so that they could be identified easily should they stray or be stolen. Farmers who produced good cattle were particularly keen on branding because their brand would be recognised at a market and their cattle would command a higher price. In early days of mass production good producers of products such as soap would mark their bars of soap with a distinctive mark so that consumers would know they were buying a better product. As the brands of soap became better known, manufacturers took steps to ensure other people could not use the same mark. They also began to promote brands via advertising that made them instantly recognisable and invoke positive associations in consumer's minds. Kellogg's, for example, developed a brand which is associated with freshness, sunshine and vitality. Today, most major products carry brands, some of which are so well-known that they are very valuable. Some of the most famous brands in the USA include Coca-Cola, Ford, McDonald's, Microsoft and GAP. Other world-famous brands include BP, Cadbury, IKEA, Mercedes, Myer, Nintendo, Qantas, Rip Curl and Toyota.

The major advantage of brands is that they add additional benefits to a product. A classic experiment by Penny, Hunt and Twyman as long ago as 1974 neatly demonstrates the point. They asked consumers who normally used brand B to try two products without knowing their brand. A majority (61 per cent) preferred brand A while 39 per cent preferred brand B. Another group also tried the same two products. For this group the brands were known. 35 per cent were found to prefer brand A while 65 per cent preferred brand B. A brand may be defined as:

> A symbolic construct created by a marketeer to represent a collection of information about a product or group of products. This symbolic construct typically consist of a name, identifying mark, logo, visual images or symbols or mental concepts which distinguish the product or service.

A brand has connotations of a product's "promise" and differences from its competitors. A brand may attempt to give a product and a "personality" (Free-definition, 2005a). To be successful, a brand must have several characteristics (see iboost, 2005). These include:

- **Simple, clear messages**. A campaigning message or one which seems to go against the "Establishment" (e.g. the themes of the Bennetton and FCUK branding) are often a "cheap" way to success.
- **Projections of credibility** – so claims are believed.
- **Motivation of customers** which increases the enjoyment of purchasing products with the brand. This makes it more likely that purchases will actually take place.
- **Creation of strong user loyalty**. This is, perhaps, the most important aspect of branding.

Once a brand has been established, it can be extended to other products. This reduces the cost of a new project gaining a place in the market. However, the extension to weak or inappropriate new products can cause significant damage to the initial brand image.

Price

As a very broad generalisation, a marketing function will set the price of its goods at a low level but slightly above its costs so that it will sell many items, reap the economies of scale and deter competitors from entering the market.

Exceptions to this rule are almost as many as its adherents. The ability and willingness of consumers to pay for a product is important. It is pointless marketing a product or service at a price beyond the means of customers – unless the producer is willing to subsidise its manufacture for strategic reasons. The variation in supermarket and petrol prices from region to region or town to town is a clear example on how the ability of the consumer to pay influences prices: in affluent areas prices are usually higher than in poorer areas. Luxury goods are a classic example where people are willing to pay substantially more than the production costs. The price of diamonds, for example, has, for over a century, been maintained at an artificially high level. Superb branding (a diamond is forever) and a superb cartel (DeBeers) meant that the price of diamonds could be controlled so that the very affluent and starry-eyed people would pay very high prices (see *The Economist*, 2004).

The sales of some products respond very quickly to changes in price while the sales of other products change very little if the price increases or decreases (this is called *price sensitivity* or *elasticity of demand*). The price of vegetables such as broccoli is very price sensitive because people will switch to another vegetable such as cauliflower if there is even a small price increase. On the other hand, many medicines are price insensitive since people will cut back on other purchases in order to have money to buy medicines that save their lives. If a product or service has an inelastic demand, the marketing function of an organisation can engage in *price-skimming* – supplying only the upper fraction (those who can afford high prices) of the market. They can charge very high prices which quickly recover development and production costs. Price-skimming enables an organisation to build a considerable surplus so that, should a competitor enter the market they can afford to engage in predatory pricing (see p. 220).

Branding can also raise a product's price significantly. Classic examples are the pharmaceutical industry where branded, well-advertised products supported by an excellent sales force can cost several times more than an equally effective generic medication. For example, the branded drug Valium, which benefited from the usual periods of exclusivity provided by patents, is used to treat anxiety. It costs more than the equally effective generic drug Diazepam. However, the generic drug Diazepam does not have to bear the marketing, sales and advertising costs incurred by the branded version.

The price of products is heavily influenced by marketing strategy. For example, new products, such as plasma screen TVs, are introduced at a very high price to establish an aspirational position at the top of the market. This confers prestige that will help sustain a higher price among naive and impressionable consumers.

The price of a product or service may be concealed. For example, people can visit many tourist attractions such as museums, parks or educational "lectures" without any fee. However, someone – somewhere – will be paying higher taxes to sustain their enjoyment. In fact, a marketing function's dream is to separate the consumer from the person or organisation that pays for his or her consumption.

Packaging

Often packaging is not considered as a separate aspect of the marketing mix and it is usually subsumed under the heading of "promotion". It is described separately here because, in practice, the marketing function of most organisations will pay considerable attention to the way that their goods are packaged. Indeed, an item's packaging can make a very substantial difference to its sales. An item whose packaging is poor is less likely to be selected from among its competitors on a supermarket shelf. Packaging has the important functional value of ensuring that the product is delivered to the customer in prime condition. However, packaging can also be used to increase the perceived benefit to the consumer. For example, many items are packaged in an oversized box in an attempt to make the customer believe that the product is bigger than its actual size. Similarly, some products such as jewellery and watches, are packaged in grossly expensive cases made of embossed leather and silk in order to enhance the perceived value of their contents.

In general, an organisation's marketing function will try to ensure that the packaging of its products:

- Is distinctive from that used by its competitors.
- Uses colours appropriate to the product's benefits. For example, the packaging of a

valuable item is likely to be coloured in gold and silver while the packaging of a fun item is likely to be coloured in vivid reds, oranges and yellows.

- Displays the brand name in a prominent position.
- Contains a flattering picture of the product where happy people (or sometimes, animals) clearly enjoy the benefits of a purchase.

Promotion

Promotion is also called *"marketing communications"*. It may be defined as:

> Any type of persuasive communication between the marketing function and one or more of its present customers, potential customers or stakeholder groups which aims, directly or indirectly, to increase the likelihood that time, product or service will be purchased.

This definition has four important components. First, it emphasises that the central concept of promotion as a persuasive communication. Second, the aim of communication is to increase purchases. Third, the communications are directed at a target that is wider than the organisation's present customers. Finally, some communications may be closely linked to the sales process in the short term whilst other communications may be designed to have an indirect, longer-term effect. This definition also covers a wide range of activities which include public relations, internal marketing, advertising and personal selling.

Public relations

Public relations is also known as *"Perception Management"* and its critics such as Chomsky (2002) have called it *"Manufacturing Consent"*, *"Media Control"* and *"Spin"*. It may be defined as:

> A part of the promotional mix that communicates with stakeholders, the media and the public in general in order to achieve broadly, favourable and supportive attitudes towards a product, organisation or cause.

A shorter and less technical definition for public relations might be "the management of an organisation's image". Both definitions emphasise that public relations is a general activity and is only loosely tied to the sale of a specific product. It aims to obtain a generally favourable attitude so that subsequent, more specific communications are likely to succeed. Often, an organisation's marketing function will employ specialist public relations consultants to maintain its image. Public relations experts use six main methods (see Free-definition, 2005b):

- **Press conferences** are public or quasi-public events where speakers provide information on newsworthy items. Usually they are attended by selected journalists and TV reporters.
- **Press releases** are also called "news releases" and may consist of short fax statements that are sent to the media.
- **Publicity events** are contrived situations designed to attract media attention. Outrageous publicity events are sometimes called "**guerrilla marketing**".

- **The circuit** refers to the "talk-show circuit" where PR consultants attempt to get their clients or spokespersons to appear on these programmes.
- **Books, brochures** and other writings are sometimes commissioned and published on behalf of clients.
- **Press contacts** are developed assiduously so that they can be fed information about the organisation in the hope that the reporter will write a favourable story.

Public relations experts often identify opinion leaders and powerful people ("movers and shakers"). They then attempt to develop friendly relationships by offering corporate hospitality at events such as the Chelsea Flower Show, the Happy Valley racecourse in Hong Kong or Australia's prestigious Telstra motor rally.

The marketing function in some organisations also engages in "**cause-related marketing**". They undertake to give a certain proportion of their profits to a good cause in the hope that their generosity will reflect positively on their organisation.

Internal promotion

Internal promotion aims to alter the attitudes of the organisation's own workforce. It is particularly relevant when new products are being launched. Internal communications tend to foster the "team spirit" within an organisation. In addition, the staff of an organisation

---

CASE 11.2: GUERRILLA MARKETING

A good example of guerrilla publicity occurred in August 2002 when Vodafone arranged for two men to "streak" at an international rugby game with the Vodafone logo painted on their backs. The men's magazine *FHM* provides another good example of guerrilla marketing. The magazine cover featured a nude photograph of a former children's TV presenter. After doctoring the photograph to remove any suggestion of her nipples, FHM projected it onto one of the towers of the Houses of Parliament. Both stunts earned considerable free publicity (including in this book!).

CASE 11.3: CAUSE-RELATED MARKETING

A classic, and clever example of cause-related marketing is Tesco's "Computers for Schools" campaign in which shoppers are given vouchers to pass to their local school, which is then able to redeem them for computer equipment. This scheme is particularly ingenious because its customers are involved frequently and directly. Furthermore, the recipients are local and are clearly identified. However, such schemes can backfire. In 2003 Cadbury sold chocolate bars with tokens which a school could exchange for sports equipment. The scheme caused uproar and was criticised by the Food Commission since it was seen to encourage obesity rather than a healthy, sporty lifestyle.

become an unofficial sales force who talk about the new product with their relatives, friends and acquaintances.

Advertising

Advertising is a major method of *promoting specific goods and services*. It may be defined as:

> 66 Attracting public attention to a product, service or issue using non-personal methods of communication with a view to persuading the targets to adopt certain behaviours or thought patterns. Usually the desired behaviour is to purchase a product and the advertising organisation usually pays for the advertisement to be put before the target audience. 99

It should be noted that advertising is impersonal. There is no one-to-one contact between buyer and seller. This distinguishes advertising from selling. Moreover, advertising concerns specific products or services. This distinguishes it from public relations.

An advertising campaign can have a number of objectives which will depend upon a product's position in the product life cycle. If the product is new, the campaign is likely to focus upon making target customers aware that the product exists. It may also try to establish the new product's position in the market and its brand. Advertising a new product is also likely to draw attention to its unique benefits and try to appeal to people's needs for novelty and the status of being an early adopter. During the growth stage, advertising may seek to reassure tentative purchasers and boost confidence in the product. In the maturity and saturation stages, advertising will seek to differentiate one brand from another. At this stage the main objective will be to increase, or at least preserve, market share at the expense of competitors. Organisations may engage in either defensive or offensive advertising. Offensive advertising (sometimes called "*knocking copy*") may point out disadvantages of competitors' products.

Advertisers use a very wide range of media which includes: billboards (also known as "poster hoardings"); posters on the sides of lorries, taxis and buses; leaflets (also known as "flyers") distributed in the street; direct mail leaflets; magazines and newspapers; skywriting; web-banners; radio, cinema and television. The exact choice will depend upon the product and the target audience. For example, luxury goods are unlikely to be advertised using leaflets distributed in the street. They are more likely to be advertised in posh magazines.

An advert's first job is to **a**ttract attention, then develop the **d**esire for the product and finally to encourage consumers to take **a**ction and purchase the product (ADA). Methods used to achieve these aims include:

- **Repetition** is very important with new products where the aim is to make people remember the name.
- **Bandwagon** campaigns imply that everyone is purchasing a product and to be without one would be odd. This tactic is frequently used during a product's growth stage.
- **Testimonials** appeal to people's propensity to obey authority. They may quote sources of authority such as "five out of six doctors eat product X".
- **Pressure** campaigns often take the form of "buy now, before stocks are gone" or "buy now, before a tax increase". This tactic is frequently used during a product's maturity stage.

■ **Association** campaigns try to link products with desirable things and attractive or famous people. Association campaigns are often used in conjunction with testimonials.

Place

Place is the fifth and final component of the marketing mix. It is the location where the ownership of goods is transferred or where a service is performed. The place where a product is marketed depends on two main factors: distribution channels and customer expectations.

Distribution

Transporting goods to a market place, storing them until requested by a customer, employing sales staff and providing a setting which the customer finds conducive can cost almost as much as the production of an article or service. Few organisations can afford to provide these facilities on a national or regional basis; hence they need to rely upon other people, wholesalers and retailers, to provide them. Since wholesalers and retailers act on behalf of many producers the costs can be shared. Moreover, wholesalers and retailers develop specialist expertise which enables distribution costs to be minimised. Historically, the location of the transfer of goods and services happened in marketplaces at the centre of ancient towns and cities. Then it took place in shops in the centre of towns and cities. The rise of motor transport has meant that, nowadays, the location of the exchange of goods and services is often in purpose-built *shopping malls* and *retail parks* situated on the periphery of large towns – often at strategic points on a ring road.

However, a traditional *shop* or a *department store* is not the appropriate or most convenient place to sell all goods and services. *Catalogue sales*, for example, are more appropriate for people in isolated communities or those who are confined to their homes by disability. Some organisations have deliberately developed alternatives to the traditional chain of retail distribution. For example, Tupperware developed a new distribution structure by *selling its products in people's homes* at Tupperware parties. This gave a product a unique selling point, it reduced costs and it harnessed social pressures and friendships to increase sales. Catalogue showrooms, pioneered by Argos, reduce the need for space to display merchandise. Consequently *catalogue showrooms* can offer a wider range of products at a keen price. They do, however, require superb logistics to ensure that a replacement article is replaced from a central store on the same day that an item is sold. Since the development of the Internet a growing number of transactions take place in *cyberspace*. This is described in greater detail in Chapter 15.

The customer experience

Customers have clear images and expectations about where they will buy goods. If these expectations are not met they will make fewer purchases. They expect to buy cabbages at a greengrocer and not at a newsagent. They expect to buy expensive jewellery in a plush setting where they receive a great deal of personal attention. Such factors are carefully considered by retail stores who pay great attention to developing an appropriate image. A major factor determining a store's image is the range of goods it sells. This is known as the "*merchandise assortment*". The merchandise assortment must be consistent with the ideas of the consumer otherwise they are unlikely to enter the store to find out whether a suitable article is in stock. Another important factor in determining a store's image is its *location*. People expect stores to be located among other stores selling similar or complementary products. For example, it is expected that a store selling chairs and tables will be near a store that sells carpets, which in turn will be near a store that sells curtains. Stores arranged in a line next to a large parking area are usually called a "*strip*". Stores that are arranged around a central area designed for sitting, strolling and perhaps taking light refreshments are called, especially in America, a "*mall*".

The interior of a store will be laid out with care so that it gives a customer a certain experience which is consistent with the image of the store and its products. The physical characteristics of a store's environment such as its decor, its displays and its layout are called "**atmospherics**" or "**ambiance**". Atmospherics indicate the merchandise assortment within the store. Most important, the exterior atmospherics exert a strong influence on a potential customer's willingness to enter. Interior atmospherics, which may include choice of music, influences a customer's movement and mood. A primary concern of a retail organisation's marketing function will be to draw potential consumers to the back of a store by using a particularly attractive display or moving image. Once drawn to the back of a store a customer will be encouraged, perhaps by appropriate music or exotic displays, to tarry. As they tarry, customers are more likely to make a purchase. A way for supermarkets to draw customers to the further reaches of their stores is to place essential items such as bread at the furthest distance from the entrance. Supermarkets have long appreciated the importance of layout. For example, sales are increased if items essential to customers are positioned either on high shelves or on low ones. Discretionary items are placed on shelves at eye level. As consumers reach for essential items they are likely to see, and purchase, discretionary products. Similarly, supermarkets have learned that the ends, between aisles, are positions where products are most likely to be selected.

11.5 Criticisms of Marketing

Marketing is more controversial than other management functions. Its intentions, interpreting and fulfilling customer demand, are impeccable. It also plays an undeniable role in creating mass markets which bring economies of scale that in turn drive prices down to the benefit of most people. However, its critics also have a strong case. The main charges include misleading advertisements, manipulation, encouragement of antisocial behaviour, creation of false markets and dumbing down.

Use of *misleading adverts* is a frequent criticism. The malpractice seems to be particularly prevalent in the pharmaceutical and food industry where adverts may claim that products provide spurious health benefits. In some countries the problem seems endemic. The marketing function is often accused of *underhand manipulation*. Adverts may not openly state a product's benefits. They may be implied by information of which the consumer is unaware. In other words, consumers are induced to buy products by messages outside their awareness or logical control. This reflects an imbalance in power and resources. A consumer buying an everyday product can only devote seconds to their choice. A multinational organisation marketing the same product can devote a team of a dozen or more experts for several months to devise ways to induce a consumer to make a purchase. One tactic is to target people with fewer evaluative powers. For example, makers of a breakfast cereal may *target adverts at children* knowing that, in turn, they will pressurise their parents.

Another tactic might be to use subliminal advertising. *Subliminal advertising* involves projecting a message at a very low level so that people are not conscious the message is there. For example, an advertiser might project a very faint advertisement during a soap opera programme. The advertisement is so faint that the viewer does not realise it is there but over the period of half an hour the message is subconsciously registered. Initial experiments showing subliminal advertising could be effective were seriously flawed. Modern research shows that subliminal advertising does not work. Furthermore, subliminal advertising is illegal in most countries. Underhand manipulation is not limited to the use of children or subliminal adverts. It can arise from non-verbal messages. An advertisement may not explicitly state that a product will bring wealth and power. However, it may imply these benefits by including images of wealthy and powerful people. For example, a business school might include photographs of successful business people boarding an aeroplane en route to a meeting to discuss international strategy. However, it may know, full well, that most of its MBAs work within the domestic economy. One of first people to note the manipulative aspect of the marketing function was Packard (1957).

Some people criticise marketing for *encouraging antisocial behaviour*. Attracting attention is a major problem for marketeers. There is so much advertising and so much media coverage that an organisation's message may get lost. One of the easiest solutions is shock tactics, but many shock tactics involve antisocial behaviour. For example, an organisation

CASE 11.4: MISLEADING ADVERTS

In 2002 the Chinese State Drug Administration estimated that 89 per cent of advertisements for drugs and medical services were illegal. Specific examples of misleading advert are found throughout the world. In 2003 the American Federal Drug Agency (FDA) ordered Purdue Pharma to withdraw its ads for a painkiller OxyCotin because they omitted to mention fatal side effects if the tablet was chewed rather than swallowed. A rather different criticism was levelled against the American milk industry's campaign "got milk" which featured celebrities with "milk moustaches". Physician groups complained that the advertisements ignored data linking high milk consumption with heart disease and prostate cancer. Their complaints were supported by the Department of Agriculture (USDA).

Criticisms of the marketing function for using misleading advertisements are by no means restricted to the pharmaceutical and food industry. In 2004 the British Advertising Standards Authority ordered the Internet service provider, Wanadoo, to withdraw its adverts for "full speed broadband", because the ads could mislead consumers into believing it was the fastest on the market. The travel industry, especially companies selling airfares, is frequently admonished for misleading, *bait and switch* tactics. Hectares of Sunday newspapers are covered with offers of cheap flights. Yet, when even the nimblest consumer telephones, there are no remaining seats at the cheapest rates. They are encouraged to switch to more expensive, and presumably more profitable, flights

producing crisps (chips) might draw attention to its product with an advert depicting a pupil successfully deceiving a teacher during a mathematics lesson to eat crisps. The advertisement would probably increase the sales of the crisp manufacturer. However, it would make classroom discipline more difficult. The impact on the skill base of a country might mean a significant reduction in its ability to provide social goods such as transport or healthcare.

The marketing function will usually seek to maximise the benefit for its own organisation rather than the community. It may benefit the organisation to develop and market a new product that is unnecessary and which will, in the long term, damage people and their society. In essence, this criticism accuses the marketing function of *developing and exploiting an unnecessary and dangerous* consumer need. For example, the market research of the company Masterfoods (MARS) revealed a marketing opportunity for a large wafer, chocolate caramel cream confectionary bar for women. It developed a product, Mars Delight, which was launched in Ireland. A marketing spend of £15 million was devoted to promoting this product. However, in the light of increasing obesity in the developed world, Mars was criticised for developing a needless and possibly dangerous product.

Perhaps the most important criticism against the marketing function is its impact on society. Because of its economic power and its expertise the influence of the marketing is very widespread and very pervasive. This leads to two further criticisms. First, it promulgates a capitalist, market ethos which ignores other social, cultural and aesthetic considerations. Probably more important is the impact on the intellectual standards – *dumbing down*. A manager in a marketing function of an individual organisation will wish to appeal to as many people as possible. This means that she or he will calculate the lowest common denominator of the market. Hence public standards will be diminished. This trend, combined with the tendency to encourage antisocial behaviour might lead to a society without standards.

Many of these criticisms may be unfair because they are directed at the image of the marketing function. The marketing function may be partly responsible as a victim of its own hype. Furthermore, many countries have enacted legislation that curb marketing's worst excesses.

Activities and Further Study

Essay Plans

Write essay plans for the following questions:

1 How might markets differ from each other?
2 What models might organisations use to locate a profitable market? To what extent are these models consistent with each other and how useful might they be in practice?
3 Why do organisations undertake market research? What methods could they use?
4 What is meant by "The Marketing Mix'?
5 What are the main criticisms against marketing? To what extent are these criticisms valid?

Web and Experiential Activities

Suggestions for Web exercises and experiential exercises for all functions are given at the end of Chapter 10 (p. 211).

CHAPTER

12

The Operations (Production) Function

CASE 12.1: A DAY IN THE LIFE OF AN OPERATIONS MANAGER OF A THEME PARK

Thorpe Park is a large leisure complex near London. The operations manager signs on before 9.00 a.m. in time to check the estimated number of visitors for the day. Next, costumes and appearance of "cast members" are inspected to ensure that they meet standards. Then there is a discussion with the admissions supervisor to check that the pay kiosks are ready. If all is well, the operations manager gives the signal for the park to be opened – all this must happen before 9.30 a.m. Once admissions are going smoothly it is time for a "management walkabout". During the walkabout the operations managers chats to "cast members" receiving and giving information and, probably more important, maintaining their motivation and reaffirming standards. The walkabout also provides other supervisors with the chance to brief the operations managers on aspects such as the cleanliness of certain areas. The walkabout is liable to frequent interruptions. 100 of the 600 cast members have a radio and any incidents can be reported, and receive a response, almost instantly. Often the response involves a visit to the site of the incident. Walkabouts occur several times a day. In between, there are times in the office. An important task is to monitor the number of visitors in the park and compare them with those of the day before, the previous week and the previous year. The information from the walkabouts and the computer provides a continuously updated picture of the activities of visitors. The deployment of "cast members" and other resources is frequently adjusted to ensure that visitors encounter as few queues as possible and have an enjoyable experience at the park.

Adapted from Hannagan, T. (2005), 'Management Concepts and Practices.' 4th edition, Pearson Education (p. 41). With thanks to R. Boaden.

Concept and Definition of the Operations Function

Two hundred years ago the industrial revolution was in full swing but most people were living a utilitarian life, making do with very basic, meagre possessions. Labour and capital were readily available. Under these circumstances the production function was the dominant function. If a product could be manufactured, it could be financed and would be bought by a ready market. Since then, many things have changed. Scientific advances have made available new products such as cars, vacuum cleaners and radios. There is also greater competition both at home and abroad. Furthermore, labour is now less compliant. Financiers demand a high return from their capital. In advanced countries manufactured goods such as cars no longer account for the bulk of economic activity. Instead, the majority of products now involve some element of service. These changes have wrought major alterations in the production function. In particular, its name has changed to "operations" in order to encompass both physical products and services. The operations function may be defined as:

66 The function that manages the part of an organisation that is directly involved in the transformation of resources into higher value goods or services. 99

This definition emphasises that the operations function involves the people who do the actual transformation of the main input into the organisation's output. Operations is a central part of any organisation. The aim of many organisations is to make the transformation process as efficient as possible. This is known as *lean production*. Organisations will also try to make the transformation process as flexible as possible so that it can adapt or change its product should customers' needs change or if the organisation can find a more profitable product. This is known as *agile production*. In a successful organisation the whole of the transformation process is geared to the needs of the customer. Generally, customers make the following demands, often known as *critical success factors,* on the operations function (Slack et al., 2001):

- a **keen price** requiring a tight control of production costs
- **high-quality** requiring quality assurance and quality control
- **fast and flexible** *delivery* requiring either high (and costly) stocks or speedy production
- **reliable delivery** requiring a reliable production system, free from breakdowns
- products and services that offer **variety and innovation** requiring a creative and flexible production system
- the **right volume** of goods or services requiring a production system with the appropriate capacity

Except in very small organisations the customer can be another department or section – often the next step in the production process. In many organisations departments are encouraged to purchase goods and services from other organisations if they can be supplied at the same quality but lower costs. This is called "**outsourcing**". It means that **internal customers** are as important as external ones and an inefficient section is unable to survive by relying upon a "captive market" in its own organisation. Treating each stage of production as a customer of the last also means that a value can be placed on each stage of production. It helps identify stages that add little value and these activities can be eliminated. In other words, the production process can be seen as a chain of events that add value to the "raw materials" and which culminate in a product or service that is purchased by a consumer. The idea of a "**value chain**" was advocated by Porter (1998) as a means of creating and sustaining a superior production system. Indeed, a technique called "**process value analysis**" (Hammer, 1997) may be used to streamline the central processes of an operations function.

In many organisations the operations function is the largest one and employs the most people. Further, the operations function may involve dangerous tools such as metal cutting equipment and chemicals such as acids which can harm employees, the general public or the environment. Consequently, an organisation's operations function must be aware of, and heed, regulations and laws dealing with safety and employment. A more detailed consideration of the operation function can be considered in six main sections:

Chapter contents

12.1 Types of Operations (Manufacturing and Services)

The operations function may vary widely from organisation to organisation – depending largely upon the nature of the transformation that is performed.

Comparison of operations functions in service and manufacturing

Probably the greatest differences lie between operations in the manufacturing organisations (production) and those in service organisations. In a nutshell, there are six main differences:

■ **Manufacturing is more physical**. Transformations in the manufacturing organisations always have a tangible product (i.e. it can be touched, seen and perhaps heard). As a generalisation, products in the service sector are not tangible. It is, for example, impossible to touch or see the learning that has taken place in the mind of a student. However, there are many exceptions to this rule. For example, it is possible to touch and see the transformation which a hospital brings about when it cures a patient.

■ **The product in services is less standardised and more varied**. For example, a large organisation manufacturing cars may have 200 000 employees and produce a range of 50 different cars in a year. On the other hand, a hospital employing, perhaps, 2000 people may perform 500 different surgical procedures in the same year. Similarly a gourmet restaurant with, perhaps, a staff of 20 may produce 1000 different dishes during the year.

■ **Production and consumption are usually simultaneous in service operations**. Transformation in manufacturing organisations is usually clearly separated from consumption. For example, an MP3 player may have been manufactured several months before it is purchased. On the other hand, the provision of a massage occurs at exactly the same time that the massage is enjoyed by the customer. The *simultaneous production and consumption* in service transformations has three important consequences. First, it makes it very difficult for service organisations to stockpile its products in order to even-out peaks and troughs of demand. The products of a service organisation are therefore very perishable. The ultimate example is given by air travel. If a seat it is not sold at the close of check-in, a part of the airline's product is lost forever. On the other hand, the manufacturers of Christmas cards can continue to print cards during the summer and stockpile them until they are needed in December. Second, the simultaneous production and consumption found in service operations usually means that the consumer is present when the service is produced, will play an interactive part and can help to make the product a success or failure. For example, a responsive audience can help to make a theatre production a success. Similarly, lack of preparation and participation by students can ensure that a seminar is a failure. Third, the simultaneous production and consumption found in service operations usually means that the service must be provided in a place close to the location of the consumers.

- **Operations in service organisations usually involve a higher level of personal ability and judgement**. Operations in manufacturing organisations are usually systematised and controlled to the point where the identity of the exact employee performing the transition does not matter and a plasma screen produced in Scotland by Ivan Robertson will be identical to one produced by in China by Yuan Zi. However, this is not the case with services. A song performed by Mike Smith at a party in Glossop will be quite different from the same song performed by Robbie Williams at a nightclub in Dubai! High personal judgement and ability are important ingredients in service organisations such as legal advice, film production, cooking, hairdressing and nursing. The personal factor in service operations is even more significant because service operations are usually much more labour intensive than manufacturing operations.

- **Demand in manufacturing is more predictable**. For example, the monthly demand for mobile phones is fairly predictable and rarely differs from the average by more than 20 per cent. "Spikes" in demand, such a Christmas, are predictable and can be managed by building up and drawing upon stocks. In contrast, a service industry such as package holidays needs to cope with huge swings in demand. Some of this, such as seasonal variations, is easy to predict. However, a great deal also depends upon random factors such as weather, exchange rates and fashions in destinations. To make matters worse, the travel trade cannot draw up on reserve stocks of flights and hotel rooms.

- **Operations in manufacturing are easier to evaluate**. Physical output in manufacturing can be checked against very detailed specifications concerning size, reliability and other technical qualities. In service organisations, this is much more difficult. For example, it is very difficult for an accountancy organisation to measure the quality of its auditing of a set of accounts. It can show "due diligence" – that appropriate steps and procedures have been followed, but the ultimate check on quality is the fairly crude measure of whether the accounts are accepted by the tax authorities. Similarly, surgeons may be evaluated on the percentage of patients who die in their operating theatres. However, the judgements may be very faulty since the best surgeons are usually allocated cases that are more difficult and have severe complications!

Operations functions in service industries

Operations functions differ even within the service industry. For example Schmenner (1986) noted that products in the service industry differed on two major dimensions: the degree of labour intensity and consumer orientation (consumer interaction and customisation). The notion of *degree of labour intensity* is self-explanatory: it means the number of people needed to provide a service. Low labour intensity is often characterised by the use of expensive equipment and tight scheduling to ensure the service is delivered on time and the use of management techniques to smooth the peaks and troughs of demand. High labour intensity is often characterised by human resource issues such as hiring, training and scheduling large numbers of staff. It also involves issues of controlling of large numbers of staff working in widely dispersed locations. The notion of *consumer orientation* is less intuitive: it means the degree to which customers deal, face-to-face, with the staff providing the service and the degree to which the service must be changed to meet the needs of individual customers. Low customer orientation is characterised by an emphasis on marketing and inflexible sets of rules, and an emphasis on good, but standardised, physical surroundings and ambience. High customer orientation is characterised by issues of controlling costs and maintaining high quality while at the same time motivating employees by providing a reasonable career structure, a sense of pride and a lack of a rigid organisational structure. These two dimensions allow the operations function of service organisations to be placed in one of four categories, as shown in Figure 12.1.

Operations functions in manufacturing industries

There are huge differences between the operations functions in manufacturing industries. A great deal depends upon the type of process. These are also divided into categories such as projects, small-batch, large-batch and continuous production.

- A **project** is a one-off product involving a series of activities that are unlikely to be repeated. Since projects are one-off situations they are difficult to automate and they incur high costs. Sometimes this is called project management. Project management is typical in industries such as construction and film making. It is appropriate for situations that require flexibility and a quick response in a dynamic environment. It is also appropriate for temporary situations where there are clear deadlines and where specialised skills are needed. In many projects people with the appropriate skills are assembled as a team, on a temporary basis under the control of a project manager.

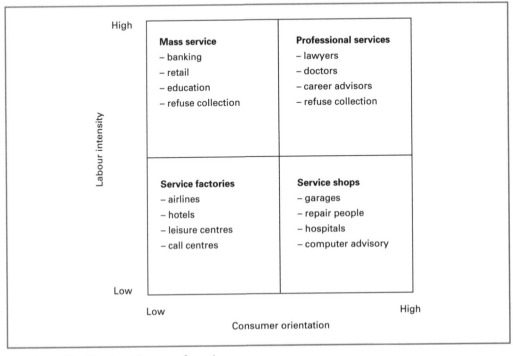

FIGURE 12.1 Classification of Consumer Operations

- **Small batch operations** are sometimes called jobbing, unit or one-off production. They are characterised by smaller orders and units than projects: for example, a small-batch operation may be to supply a hotel with 50 chairs, 10 settees and 10 tables in the hotel's chosen colour scheme. Another example of a small-batch operation would be to configure computers to meet the specialised requirements of a leisure centre. Small-batch operations often have a "craft" quality about them. While there is a small element of standardisation, the requirements are labour intensive and individual employees make a significant contribution. They can see the end result of their work and they take pride in their achievements. Indeed, because the pride of employees is involved, they may devote too much time to the latter and budgets may be exceeded. Often, small-batch operations require the resetting and calibration of equipment between each batch. Small-batch operations offer great flexibility but costs are high. Furthermore, they depend upon the supply and co-operation of skilled employees.

- **Large-batch** operations are typified by mass production. A classic example might be a factory that makes mince pies. During a year, the factory might make 10 million pies that are almost identical. The factory, which is usually large, will contain expensive, technologically advanced equipment that is specially designed for making a narrow range of products (for example, during the summer months the equipment might be able to produce apple pies). Other examples of large-batch operations include the manufacture of glassware, underpants or weighing machines. Because many identical items are produced, the operations function will have reduced the costs of each item to an absolute minimum and it will have clear standards. Large-batch operations are usually very efficient and easy to control, but they are often inflexible. It takes a great deal of time and money to obtain other specialised machines, train workers in new,

CASE 12.2: MANUFACTURING OPERATIONS AT PATAK'S FOODS

Patak's manufactures a wide range of products including fresh breads, frozen ready meals and snacks. It is perceived by consumers as being the most authentic brand of Indian food available in mainstream grocery outlets. Patak's is also a significant supplier of products to Indian restaurants throughout the world and its products are available in more than 40 countries worldwide, including Continental Europe, Japan, Australasia and North America.

Pataks' manufacturing plants are based in Dundee (frozen foods), Glasgow (breads and chilled snacks) and Wigan (products packaged in jars, cans and packets). The Wigan factory is believed to be the largest factory in the world manufacturing solely Indian food and it employs c. 350 employees, out of the 700 who are employed in total by Patak's in the UK. Within the UK factories, nearly 50 per cent of the workforce are employed in direct manufacturing activities. They are managed by dedicated and focused management teams. At each site there are strong technical functions, which work closely with manufacturing to ensure the highest possible standards of housekeeping, hygiene, etc. Within each production facility, considerable autonomy is given to individual manufacturing lines, but clearly defined ambitious Key Performance Indicators are established and performance is measured against these indicators on a consistent and hourly basis.

specialised tasks and to work out a system that produces a new product within great efficiency. Sometimes large-batch manufacturing is also known as "*repetitive production*" or "**the assembly-line system**".

- **Continuous process** operations are typified by oil refining where there is a continuous flow of crude oil into the bottom of a distillation column. As the raw material passes through the process, which usually involves heat and/or treatment by chemicals, it is transformed into more valuable commodities such as refined oils and, say, butane gas, which are continuously extracted from the top of distillation column. Other excellent examples of continuous process operations are provided by the glass industry, steelmaking, electricity generation and water supply. Continuous process operations are characterised by a high use of energy and technology. Since high costs are involved in heating up the process, operations are continued on a 24-hour basis, seven days per week. This implies a considerable use of shift workers. Often the processes are highly automated and they are controlled by a relatively small number of highly educated employees. The input to the system and the output from the system need to be planned very carefully in order to ensure that there are no interruptions.

Different types of operations function reflect an underlying dimension. At one end the focus is on the *products* made. Functions at this end make a small range of goods in high volumes using special-purpose machinery. At the other end, the focus is on the *processes* used. Functions at this end of the spectrum make a wide range of goods but in low volumes. Process-focused functions are usually flexible. Figure 12.2 shows how the different types of production can be located on this dimension.

12.2 Designing Operations

Designing an operation from scratch is a rare event. It is more likely that a facility will need to be grafted onto an existing function. Nevertheless, it is useful to follow the ideal paradigm where a function is being established on a green-field site. The design of an operation system involves three main stages: product definition and design, system definition and design, choosing a suitable location and organising the work layout. The following outline of these stages focuses upon the manufacturing sector. However, the stages are equally relevant to services such as developing a new type of bank account.

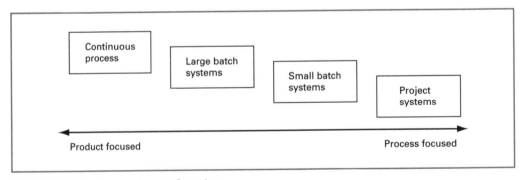

FIGURE 12.2 Product versus Process Operations

Product definition and design

Defining and designing a new product starts with the organisation's mission statements and strategic plans. They are developed as the result of decisions about market positioning into a more specific decision about the exact products. Several products may be considered and each evaluated on their likely demand, the resources they will need and the type of management structure that would be appropriate. Much of the information needed is available from existing employees. Further, consultations with all levels of staff improve communications and help build commitment to the new product. The activities of competitors must also be taken into account. Their successes should be examined in order to learn positive lessons. Whenever possible new products which competitors would find it difficult to make are chosen. Only a small number of potential products are likely to survive this examination. Each survivor is then submitted to the **product development cycle** in the knowledge that several will be abandoned when problems emerge. The product development cycle follows five stages:

- development of a prototype
- testing of a prototype, evaluation and modification
- piloting of revised prototype – with market research
- evaluation of revised prototype and adjustment
- trial production of fully functioning product

Co-ordination between departments at each stage of the cycle is an important ingredient of success. For example, it is argued that the close co-ordination and consultation between departments in Japanese organisations enables them to develop new products 30 per cent faster than comparable American organisations. Each activity involved in producing the new product is examined in fine detail so that unnecessary actions and features can be eliminated and the most efficient **work process** identified. Often this results in **re-engineering** the product. During trial production, fully-functioning workflow will be set up. **Workflow** is the movement of work from one point to another in a production system. An examination of workflow establishes the most efficient order of performing tasks.

Development of a new product can take months or years. The process can be accelerated with **Computer Aided Design** (CAD). CAD speeds the process by drawing designs more quickly. Sophisticated computer packages incorporate information such as physical constraints, government regulations and the properties of materials. A good system will alert designers to features that are impossible or illegal. It may be able to construct large parts of the design from a few basic instructions. A good CAD system will build a model of the new product. Variations of the model can be tested with computer simulations so that the optimal design can be identified. Computer aided design is usually followed by some form of Computer Aided Manufacture (CAM), which is discussed on p. 249.

Production methods and design

As soon as the broad details of a new product or service are known, the ways in which it can be produced must be considered. Product definition and methods of production are very closely related. Design has a crucial influence on the product but often the product is changed to make it easier or cheaper to produce. The main factors influencing production methods are product flow, capacity and the level of automation.

Products and services *flow* at different rates. Some, usually those produced by continuous processes, flow at a steady rate and differences in demand are dealt with by maintaining extra stocks. This is a sensible approach when the costs of closing down and starting up are higher than the cost of maintaining stocks. In other situations the flow is predictable but uneven. For example, there are more letters to be collected, sorted and delivered during the Christmas period and there is more soft fruit to be picked during summer months. In these cases the system will need to carry either a high level of surplus capacity or hire equipment or employees on a temporary basis at periods of high demand. Some production functions maintain lists of temporary workers. Often these include recently retired employees or relatives of current employees. In many cases agencies are used to recruit people on a semi-permanent basis so that they can be seconded to organisations needing to meet a peak in demand. The demand for some products and services escalates at times of crises. Typical examples are the armed forces, firefighters and police. Organisations that need to meet crisis demands often maintain high levels of staff but deploy them to non-core activities when demand is low. For example, during wet weather when there are few fires, firefighters will spend their time maintaining machinery and advising on fire prevention. Another tactic is to train a large reserve of people, on a part-time basis, whose main employment is elsewhere. For example, mountain rescue organisations rely on trained volunteers to cope with a major crisis. A final way of dealing with a peak demand is to pool resources with other organisations that have complementary requirements – on the basis that they are unlikely to need to draw on the pool at the same time.

The likely flow of work has an important influence on the *capacity* of operations. This should be estimated accurately since it is expensive to upgrade inadequate capacity or carry surplus capacity. Capacity that returns the lowest average cost for predicted output should be chosen. In practice, however, a slightly higher capacity is set to allow for breakdowns, maintenance or contingencies. Often, different parts of the transformation process have different capacities. For example, a factory may be able to assemble 2000 units per week, store 2500 units a week and distribute 1800 units per week. In this case the capacity of the whole operation is 1800 units because total capacity is determined by the sub-process with the lowest capacity – the bottleneck.

The *level of automation* is a further major factor in the design of an operational facility. A high level of automation brings advantages. Machines are more reliable, accurate and consistent than human beings. Furthermore, they can be used in environments too dangerous for employees. In some cases equipment must be specially designed and commissioned. This is appropriate in mass production where equipment costs can be set against the income from millions of items. There remains, however, the danger that circumstances may change and that expensive, specialised equipment will not be needed. Generally, it is better to purchase multi-functional equipment.

Fortunately, developments in robotics have meant that it is practical to design very flexible equipment that can be reprogrammed quickly to produce other products. This is called *flexible manufacturing*. Computers may be used to plan and control operations. They may receive information from people or machines. They may then monitor the transformation process and provide alerts (when things go drastically wrong) or provide reports. In some situations a computer will be able to initiate action that corrects a problem. These systems are usually very efficient – provided there is no dramatic change from the scenario envisaged by the programmers. When computers are highly involved in operational systems the process is usually called *Computer Assisted Manufacture* (CAM). This is a misnomer because computers may have an equally high involvement in the provision of services. A better term might be *Computer Assisted Operations* (CAO).

The use of computers by the operations function was often controversial because it appeared to dehumanise organisations and deprived people of their jobs. This may have been true in the short term but its veracity in the longer term is very questionable. Automation has relieved humans of the burden of many tedious, repetitive, alienating and debilitating activities (see Pettinger, 1997). In the short term individuals may have lost their livelihoods but in the longer term the community had benefitted from cheaper goods and greater prosperity.

Computers confer another benefit. They make it easier to share information throughout an organisation. In the past, an individual, even the Chief Executive, could only be aware of a small fragment of the information generated. However, information technology means that all employees can have access to the organisation's order book, the progress of major projects and major financial indices such as an organisation's share price. Sharing information produces a greater "team spirit" and "empowers" people at all levels. It encourages people to take responsibility and it reduces the need for more formal methods of control.

IT technology and robotics usually involve high "set-up" costs. The operations function will become dependent upon the calibre of a small number of systems analysts and computer staff. Moreover, high investment in current IT systems produces a reluctance to adapt to changes in the environment. New and nimbler competitors who depend upon the wit, ability and adaptability of human systems may be able to gain a competitive edge while the programmers and analysts are still researching the situation and testing new programs.

Selecting a suitable location

The estate agent's mantra "location, location, location" is often attributed to Lord Sieff, chairman of the Marks and Spencer organisation (Slack et al., 2001). Location is particularly important in many other kinds of organisation besides retailing. In an ideal situation an organisation will take a long time to decide where to position new premises. In practice the choice will be constrained by existing premises. Nevertheless, large changes in the position of markets or supplies well as expansion or contraction may force an organisation to relocate. The nature of the product or service will be a major factor in selecting a suitable position. The received wisdom that services need to be in close proximity to the market is still largely true but telecommunications have weakened the link. A TV programme may be bounced around the globe from satellite to satellite before it reaches a distant viewer. Similarly a resident in Brisbane may have her enquiry about her electricity bill answered at a call centre in Bombay.

A major consideration will be the cost of land. In turn this will reflect a number of other factors such as the proximity to a city centre. The price of land is also affected by the prestige and image of the neighbourhood (land within 1 km of Buckingham Palace is much more expensive than land within 1 km of the marshalling yard to the rear of London's Euston station). There are many local variations to these trends. The classic example is the location of organisations offering logistics services. They prefer premises that are located at the centre of motorway networks. Transport companies are prepared to pay higher prices for land at the hubs of the UK motorway networks in, say, Northampton or Warrington than for land in the centres of London or Manchester. Minimising transport costs is important for many other organisations – especially true when they transform heavy raw materials or heavy finished products. Organisations that use a lot of energy value need to be near to energy resources. A host of political and cultural factors also impinge upon location decisions. Organisations prefer to site their operations facilities where there is:

- political stability
- freedom to move capital in and out
- lower taxes
- fewer regulations such as planning permissions

A classic example of the importance of these factors is the decision of many American pharmaceutical and electronic corporations to site facilities in the Irish Republic; which is politically very stable, has a convenient transatlantic position and relatively few restrictions on capital moments. The Irish government also offered several years "tax amnesty" to certain types of incoming investment.

Culture, language and the availability of *skilled labour* are other significant factors that determine location. A classic example was the choice by Japanese companies to site factories in the UK. Other governments offered equivalent tax incentives. However, the UK is an island nation similar to Japan and has the advantage of capable of skilled labour which speaks English. The Japanese companies were, however, careful to site these operations away from traditional UK centres of car making in order to avoid "inheriting" bad labour relations and restrictive practices.

Since so many factors can influence the suitability of a site a decision of where to locate an operations facility is usually very complex. These decisions may be made on an intuitive basis but many organisations use more scientific methods. If transport costs are important, an organisation may use the *centre of gravity* method – identifying the midpoint of journeys its supplies, products and people will make. Other organisations use a *weighted scoring system*. A shortlist of, say, six sites is identified and then each site is rated according to the degree to which it possesses the relevant requirements. The ratings are multiplied by the weights. The results for each short-listed site are added to give a total "suitability score". This procedure is very similar to the procedure outlined on p. 131 in the chapter on decision-making.

12.3 Work Layout

Machines, workstations and office space can be configured in many ways. Some configurations will be efficient. Others will waste space and time. A poor physical layout can mean that communication is confused, processing takes longer and larger stocks are needed.

There are four main types of work layout: fixed position, process layout, cell layout and product layout.

- **Fixed-position** layout is where the objects to be transformed are not mobile and must therefore be processed "**in situ**". This often causes confusion because the name may be misinterpreted to mean an operations facility that is fixed. The objects that must be transformed *in situ* are usually static because they are too large or too fragile to move. For example, most houses must be constructed *in situ* where the house will stand. The equipment and construction facilities need to be taken to the building site. Similarly, some medical cases are too dedicate to move and a surgical equipment needs to be brought to the patient. Often, the layout of these sites is fraught with problems: there may not be enough space to receive and store materials and equipment; there may not be enough space to carry out a transformation efficiently. Furthermore, there may be problems of access so that vehicles bringing supplies cause congestion and it is necessary to develop schedules so that only essential materials are on site at any given time. It is not uncommon for these schedules to be disrupted by random events. Fixed-position layouts have the advantage that the product and customer are not moved or disturbed. Unfortunately, fixed-position layouts also have strong disadvantages. Every job is unique so unit costs are usually high. Scheduling can be very difficult and there is often a continual movement of equipment and staff (Slack et al., 2001).

- **Process layout** is where location is determined by the transformation process. It is also called "**job-shop layout**" or "**layout by function**". Similar processes are grouped, usually into departments. For example, a small manufacturing firm may make components for hydraulic pumps. The components may vary significantly but they are all made from small blocks of aluminium that need to be shaped, drilled and then polished. The company adopts a process layout whereby, once the blocks are received, they pass to the grinding department where they are turned on lathes until they are the correct shape. The blocks then pass to the drilling department where the appropriate holes are bored. Finally they are sent to the polishing "shop" where the appropriate finish is applied. Although the shapes, holes and finish may vary from batch to batch, all components pass through the same sequence of departments. The optimal sequence can be established by counting the number of moves that a product makes between processes. The layout is then designed so that processes with a high number of moves are adjacent. Process layout has a number of advantages. It can be very efficient since employees have a chance to specialise in a narrow range of tasks. Moreover, the utilisation of equipment is good since it is concentrated in one specific area where its use can be maximised. However, it does suffer the same disadvantages as functional organisations: operations can become parochial and employees often find that the work is monotonous and demotivating.

- **Cell layout** is also called "**group technology layout**" or "**team layout**". Cell layout is where the raw materials are bought to a closely defined area where all the resources needed are available for the transformation. For example, a beauty salon might devise an operational structure to transform ugly ladies into beauties. One layout would be for customers to arrive at the manicure department to have their nails polished. After this, they would walk to the to the hairdressing department for colouring and tints. Finally, they would walk to the facial department for a make-over. The workflow in this salon would be a process layout. Another beauty salon might arrange things differently. A lady would arrive and be allocated a cubicle where she would be attended by a team who would polish her nails, tint her hair and provide a facial without the customer having to move. In a really efficient beauty salon a client would receive all treatments simultaneously! Within this cell there are the same processes as those in the former salon, but they are organised for the convenience of the product being transformed. The advantages of the cell layout include good team spirit and fast through-put – the product does not waste time being transported from one place to another. The main disadvantages are the high set-up costs and lower utilisation of equipment (the manicurist and other staff waste their time moving between customers).

- **Product layout** occurs when each input to the system follows an identical pre-arranged path in which each transforming process is performed in a logical sequence. A product is usually transported along the sequence using a mechanical material handling device such as a conveyor belt. Product layout is also called "**line layout**" and "**assembly layout**". Classic examples include traditional car assembly and slaughterhouses where carcasses are processed in a strict sequence. Often product layout will entail several "production lines" that are literally parallel. Product layouts are notoriously sensitive to bottlenecks. The activities of workstations must be carefully calculated to ensure that the tasks can be completed before, say, the conveyor moves on. Otherwise backlogs or uncompleted items will occur. If an operation cannot be completed at the rate of the conveyor belt, it will be necessary to allocate more employees or machines. This is called *line balancing*. A number of statistical methods are available to help organisations achieve balanced lines. Product layout has distinct advantages. If the volume of product is high, a product layout is likely to yield lower costs, often because equipment is very specialised. However, product layout is not very flexible and any disruption can cause severe problems. Furthermore, from an employee's perspective, the work is a monotonous and demotivating (see Slack et al., 2001).

There is an approximate relationship between the type of operational function and work layout as shown in Figure 12.3.

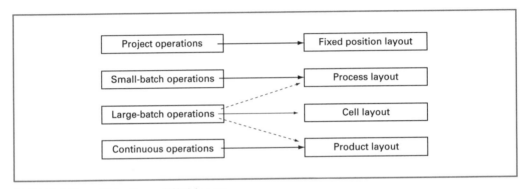

FIGURE 12.3 Type of Operation and Work Layout

The characteristics of all good work layouts include:

- an easily understood flow of work
- the need for storage between stages or, where this is impossible, waiting areas should be adequate
- a straight line flow of products where backtracking is minimised
- open planning so that the overall situation is clear to everyone
- space between workstations is minimised
- rehandling of materials is minimised
- flexibility permits adjustment to changing circumstances

The layout in most operation functions does not follow any one pure type. Usually a hybrid of several types is used.

12.4 Managing Operations

Once an operation has been established it must be maintained and managed. This involves three main components: *scheduling, cost control* and *quality issues.*

Scheduling

A schedule is a kind of plan (see Chapter 3) and planning, especially critical path planning (PERT and CPM), is a major activity of an operations function. However, this planning has several distinguishing features.

Two crucial concepts are "demand lead time" and "supply lead time". *Demand lead time* is the time that a customer is prepared to wait between ordering a product and receiving it. In many situations, especially retailing, the demand lead time is zero – if a product is not on the shelf, a competitor's product will be purchased instead. In other situations, such as white goods (e.g. washing machines and refrigerators), the demand lead time will be about one week. With specialised goods such as furniture the demand lead time is, perhaps, three months. In engineering and infrastructure, such as a nuclear submarine or new motorway, demand lead time may be several years. Demand lead time for services is less than that for goods but there are some spectacular exceptions. For example, people are prepared to wait years for certain kinds of education and health care. *Supply lead time* is the time between a decision to produce something and its delivery. Supply lead time also varies considerably but it is always longer than demand lead time. The whole point of scheduling within the operational function is to reduce supply lead time so that it approximates as closely as possible to demand lead time. Figure 12.4 (after Boddy, 2002) shows the relationship between the two.

Most organisations have "forward plans" which are sometimes called "aggregate plans" and cover a long period – as far ahead as the organisation can usually see. In oil prospecting the planning horizon can be 20 years – the supply lead time between deciding to prospect for oil in an area and a time when petrol will be sold to a customer. More frequently, forward plans have a time horizon of 1–3 years. These plans are not very precise but they

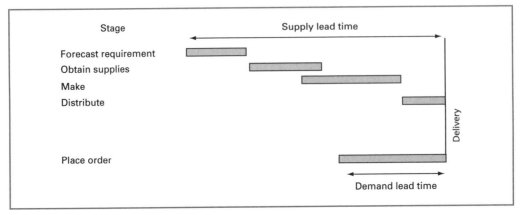

FIGURE 12.4 Demand Lead Time and Supply Lead Time

do have general goals which ensure an organisation does not take on too many commitments, and they signal points when more detailed plans must be produced. Forward plans often concern product groups rather than individual products.

Master production schedules are drawn up for relatively short periods of time. Often they cover only a week but more frequently they cover three months, six months or a year. A master production schedule will be very detailed and it will specify exactly how many items of each kind need to be produced in a time interval (e.g. per day, per week or per month). In many organisations the master production schedule will be subdivided into a production schedule for each department, unit or line which must be integrated with each other.

Despite great care and effort, it is impossible for schedulers to anticipate every possibility. It is inevitable that production is disrupted by events such as non-delivery of supplies or problems with employees. Consequently, most experienced planners overestimate (sometimes by a factor of 100 per cent) the time needed to achieve production goals. This extra time, which is available to cope with emergencies, is often called *"float time"*.

Controlling costs

Controlling costs is particularly important to the operations function. Its high use of energy, materials and equipment means that it is likely to be one of the largest cost centres in an organisation. The importance of controlling costs can be established by glancing at the financial press. There will be numerous articles such as "Nokia, the world's largest supplier of mobile phones, benefited from 'prudent cost-control'" (*Financial Times*, 10 September, 2004). Poor control of costs can have expensive consequences. An organisation may need to borrow or it may need to increase its prices and risk losing customers. For example, poor cost-control forced Network Rail to borrow an extra £10 billion (*Financial Times*, 18 October, 2003).

Organisations usually have clear and accurate information concerning direct costs such as raw materials, wages and energy. They also have good data on indirect costs such as administration, buildings, insurance, etc. However, it is notoriously difficult to apportion indirect costs to specific products. This is particularly important because, in recent years, direct costs have fallen while the proportion of indirect costs has increased. Many organisations have therefore adopted a cost control procedure called "**Activity Based Cost Management**" (ABC) which aims to specify and control the costs of each stage of a manufacturing process.

12.5 Quality and the Operations Function

Definition and concept of quality

Quality, like motherhood and apple pie, is a good thing. Most texts and learned journals accept this axiom. Quality alone is believed to be the reason for Japan's success since 1945 (the industriousness of its population, its strategic position, import controls and a favourable exchange are, apparently, incidental). However, it is a difficult concept to define. One straightforward and objective definition might be:

> 66 Of high standard and free from defects. 99

This is generally taken to mean that a quality product or service should:

- Conform to high expectations of consumers.
- Be safe to use or consume.
- Be reasonably priced and give the impression of a higher-priced product – but without signs of cutting corners.
- Be durable for a reasonable period. "Reasonable" is very dependent upon the product. A reasonably durable bouquet of flowers should last, say, ten days whilst a reasonably durable set of cutlery should last a lifetime.
- Be aesthetically appealing. However, "aesthetics" is a very subjective term.
- Be delivered intact at the appropriate time and place.

Delivering a quality product or service can incur extra costs because organisations must invest more money in equipment and procedures to prevent failures. Further, extra costs will be involved in checking goods or services for defects. However, it is generally believed that the savings from reduced waste, reduced effort in rectifying defects and greater customer loyalty outweigh these extra costs. Indeed, Crosby (1979) contended that "quality is free". It is getting things wrong that costs money. Quality control may be viewed as a special case of "controlling", which was discussed in Chapter 7. From the viewpoint of the operations function, quality can be considered under five headings: quality control and quality assurance; continuous improvement; quality circles; benchmarking and Total Quality Management. The criticisms of the "quality movement" are also important.

Quality control and quality assurance

Traditionally, organisations would attempt to give customers a quality product using **quality control**. Finished items, or a sample of finished items, would be sent to the quality department for checking. Any unsatisfactory items (or batch) would be sent back to the production department for remedial work. In extreme cases, bad work would be scrapped. When samples of work are inspected for defects, it is often called "**statistical quality control**".

Quality control has a number of undesirable features. First, it does nothing to prevent defects occurring in the first place. Second, a quality control department is rarely able to detect all faults. Some get through to the customer and cause dissatisfaction. To counter these problems many firms take a preventative approach and install a quality assurance system. **Quality assurance** is a systematic set of activities to ensure that quality is built into products. It operates throughout the whole process of producing goods or services and is not confined to the end product. Quality assurance tries to ensure that each stage of the transformation process (raw materials and the processes used) is adequate so that a satisfactory end product is guaranteed. Quality assurance is usually the responsibility of all workers who perform the transformation rather than of an external department. Quality assurance is an advance over quality control but it can be interpreted in a very static way. In the worst situation, quality assurance on its own would merely help to churn out the same product that would eventually become obsolete.

Continuous improvement

In a competitive environment it is not sufficient to use the same (perhaps, initially, very efficient) process endlessly to produce the same (perhaps, initially, very innovative) product or service. Other organisations will try to capture a market by adopting better processes to make a better product or service. Consequently, organisations and the people who work in them must adopt an attitude of constantly seeking ways to enhance quality. The idea of continuous improvement became prominent in Japan in the middle of the 20th century and was known as "*Kaizen*".

Quality circles

Quality circles are a small groups of eight to ten employees and their supervisor(s) who work in the same work area or department. They were first developed in the 1960s by Kaoru Ishikawa in Japan. The aim of the group is to identify, analyse and solve quality-related issues. The members of a quality circle first attempt to identify the problems. These problems are taken in turn and examined in detail. The last step in a quality circle is to identify solutions. The solutions are then presented to management for action. Quality circles increase communication in the organisation and motivate employees. Quality circles were very popular during the 1980s but their use has since declined – partly because management failed to take up many suggestions and partly because some managers felt that they undermine their authority.

Benchmarking

The technique of benchmarking was developed at the Xerox Corporation and it consists of comparing operations against the operations of organisations that are recognised as leaders in their industry. The technique developed by Xerox took the traditional practice in which companies had informally compared themselves with others and developed it into a more rigorous process. A benchmarking team first identifies the key processes of its operations. Next it establishes ways of measuring the effectiveness of the processes. Finally, it enlists the co-operation of leaders in its industry and obtains results for its own and their effectiveness.

If the results show that one of its processes is noticeably poorer than that in comparable organisations, the cause of the poor performance will be identified and corrective action taken.

Total quality management (TQM)

Total quality management is not a precise technique. It is a philosophy, which aims to produce zero defects and 100 per cent customer satisfaction. It is often associated with the phrase "doing the right thing at the right time". It is also associated with phrase "getting things right first time". An earlier form of total quality management was *Statistical Process Control* developed by W.E. Deming in America in the early 1950s. He visited Japan to explain his ideas, which received an enthusiastic reception, and they were implemented widely by Japanese industry. Deming's approach was much more than a statistical method – it was a philosophy which pervades a whole organisation. The ideas of Deming were developed and expanded by others such as Juran and Crosby. According to Deming, everyone in the organisation – from top to bottom – must be committed to providing goods or services of the highest possible quality. The approach stretches even beyond the organisation. Suppliers, wholesalers and retailers must also share the commitment. The relationship with customers consists of a chain of events (called *"quality chains"*) to deliver a high-calibre product or service. This, like all chains, is no stronger than its weakest link. Hence, everyone in the organisation needs to be conscious of the quality of the contribution they make. Employee involvement in the quality system is vital. TQM aims to prevent defects rather than detect them at a later stage. The exact nature of TQM will vary from organisation to organisation. It will, however, have six common features:

- Absolute priority, throughout the organisation, to providing the customer with a quality product.
- Top management strongly supports the TQM programme.
- An ethos of continuous improvement.
- Fast responses to the changing needs of the customer. This implies a short product-development cycle.
- Actions based on facts rather than opinions, i.e. measurement, the collection of statistics and interpretation of trends.
- All employees are involved in a TQM programme.

Some organisations such as The US Department of Defense adopt an approach to Total Quality Management approach that has seven stages:

- Establish a management and cultural environment that has vision and long-term commitment to quality.
- Define the mission of each unit within the organisation.
- Set performance-improvement goals and priorities and provide opportunities for improvement.
- Establish projects and plans to detect and devise improvements.
- Implement the improvements.

- Evaluate the improvements.
- Review the situation and start the cycle again.

Perhaps the culmination of the "quality movement" was the development of ISO 9000. It is an international standard that shows an organisation has a "quality" quality system. In order to have ISO 9000 accreditation an organisation must subject its quality system to auditing by an external and totally independent organisation whose own competence in the quality field has been verified externally. An organisation that has ISO 9000 accreditation can supply other organisations, such as large car manufacturers that are themselves accredited. Hence, ISO 9000 offers enormous commercial advantages. Nowadays, when most organisations have ISO 9000 accreditation, an organisation without it operates at a huge commercial disadvantage.

Criticisms of the quality movement

Most organisations still value quality highly – although possibly less highly than in the heady days of the 1980s and 1990s. This is the result of critical examination of the practical impact of quality programmes. There are three main criticisms: too much emphasis on documentation; a lowering of standards; and failure to produce benefits.

Many quality systems such as ISO 9000 depend upon *documentation* to prove that standards have been met. They rarely involve an evaluation of the actual product or service. Hence, organisations will pour enormous resources into improving their documentation rather than improving their product or service. For example, schools may cancel classes and extra-curricular activities so that staff have time to prepare a perfect paper submission for its inspectors.

Quality systems worked well in production environments where the outcome was an objective, measurable product. However, they are more difficult (but not impossible) to implement in personal services where there is an interaction between the provider and the customer. For example, a quality system may evaluate a teacher partly on the basis of questionnaires from students. Hence, a teacher will have a vested interest in giving high marks so that students will rate them highly. Unfortunately, this may lead to the quality of education being driven downwards rather than upwards as the designers of the system intend. *Standards may be driven* down even in manufacturing. An experienced production manager may have witnessed the sacking or humiliation of colleague who has failed to meet quality standards. Therefore, a savvy manager is likely to set lower standards that he or she knows can be met.

The value of TQM has been questioned very severely. A survey by Arthur Little indicated that only 36 per cent of 500 companies implementing TQM felt it was having a significant impact on their competitiveness. Another survey by A.T. Kearney of 100 British firms indicated that only 20 per cent believe their quality programmes have achieved tangible results. A further survey of 30 quality programmes by McKinsey & Co found that two-thirds had not yielded the expected improvements (Hendricks and Singhal, 1999). Singhal and Hendricks surveyed the financial results of 3000 companies and compared their performance before and after obtaining quality awards. They found that companies obtaining quality awards had better stock market performance, better sales, better operating income and higher total assets in the period after implementing quality programmes than in the previous period.

12.6 Measuring the Effectiveness of Operations

The effectiveness of operations is vital and it is no surprise that productivity indices have been devised to measure performance. Fundamentally, productivity is the ratio of inputs to outputs in a given period of time. It should be noted that production is not the same as productivity: production is the number of units made, productivity is a comparison of inputs to outputs. The latter is an index of how effectively resources are transformed. For whole organisations, productivity is relatively easy to measure:

$$productivity = \frac{system\ outputs}{system\ inputs}$$

However, the system outputs, such as number of cars, are in different units to the inputs, which themselves may vary from tonnes of metal to days worked to kilowatts of power. In practice it is therefore necessary to convert each resource and output into common financial units. The basic formula for productivity then becomes:

$$productivity = \frac{value\ of\ sales}{cost\ of\ materials + labour + capital}$$

This formula works well for the organisation as a whole but it is less easy to establish the productivity of a particular part of the organisation such as the operations function. Some of the value of sales will have been contributed by marketing, distribution and others. When judging the operations function, the inputs and outputs of others need to be removed from the equation. Often this is a subjective process that leads to debate.

An alternative approach is to use the number of hours that workers need to spend making an object. These are called "indices of labour productivity". In principle the procedure is very simple. A record on the number of hours worked is kept and the following formula applied:

$$hours\ per\ unit\ produced = \frac{total\ hours\ worked}{number\ of\ units\ produced}$$

For example, if a computer manufacturer employs a group of people for a total of 400 hours and they produce 100 computers, the hours per unit produced will be four. Such indices are particularly useful because they permit comparisons across time and across facilities. If an earlier calculation had shown that a year previously it had taken five "person hours" to produce a computer, the managers of the production unit can congratulate themselves on having raised productivity in the last year. Similarly, they can compare their performance with computer makers in other countries. If they find that their competitors in Taiwan produce computers in three hours, they can be less sanguine about their performance. However, such comparisons need to ensure that like is being compared with like. The increase in productivity in the previous year could have occurred because the company had invested in more advanced equipment. Similarly, competitors in Taiwan may be making computers to a lower specification. The use of hours worked as an index can also lead to problems when work is performed by teams. A skilled circuit designer earns considerably more than the person who packs the computer and it is wrong to count their work per hour as equivalent. To overcome these difficulties many organisations use a further index of labour productivity – the "*added value index*". First, they calculate the added value by subtracting all costs from sales revenue. Next, they compute the index using the formula:

$$added\ value\ index = \frac{sales\ revenue - materials\ and\ service\ costs}{employment\ costs}$$

This is a very useful index of labour productivity. The result is a ratio of the value added to the labour resources used. The added value index should be greater than 1, otherwise the people employed in an organisation are destroying value rather than creating it. The differences in specifications are taken into account, because a higher specification should be reflected in the prices of computers. Furthermore, the use of employment costs automatically adjusts for the fact that one firm might be using a lower-calibre, but cheaper, source of labour.

All indices, including the added value index, should be used with care since they can be affected by factors outside the control of the operations function. For example, productivity can be affected significantly by government regulation, sudden changes in customer demand and new entrants to an organisation's market.

Activities and Further Study

Essay Plans

Write essay plans for the following questions:

1 What is an operations function? How could it differ between organisations – especially between those making a tangible product and those providing a service?

2 What considerations would you take into account if you were asked to set up an operations function for a social work department of a local council?

3 What considerations would you take into account if you were asked to set up an operations function for a factory producing LCD television monitors?

4 Compare and contrast "quality control", "quality assurance", and TQM (Total Quality Management).

5 What criticisms are levelled against quality systems? Are these criticisms valid?

6 How would you assess the effectiveness of an operations function?

Web and Experiential Exercises

Suggestions for Web and experiential exercises for all functions are given at the end of Chapter 10 (p. 211).

The Human Resource Function

13

After you have read this chapter you will have an understanding of the Human Resource Function and the crucial role it plays in many organisations. You will know the main methods employed by the HRM function to produce an effective workforce. In particular you will be able to:

1 **define** HRM and **differentiate** this function from the process of staffing

2 **cite** empirical evidence demonstrating HRM's contribution to an organisation's productivity

3 **draw a timeline** containing six "milestones" in the development of the HRM function

4 **explain** how the HRM function should be linked to an organisation's strategy

5 **draw a diagram** showing an idealised HRM system

6 **list** six areas (and give a specific example of each) where there are legal requirements the HRM function must obey

7 **explain in detail** the concept of Human Resource Planning and **give** two ratios of employee turnover

8 **explain** the HRM function's contribution to recruitment and selection and training and development

9 **explain in detail** how an HRM function might organise "performance management" and appraisals

10 **explain in detail** HRM's role in organising pay and compensation

11 **explain in detail** HRM's role in employee relations

12 **describe** the welfare role of HRM

The Human Resource Function (HRM) is one of the four major management functions. It is certain to be found in any medium or large organisation. Some aspects of HRM are dealt with elsewhere in this book – in Chapter 5 (staffing), Chapter 15 (social responsibility and business ethics) Chapter 17 (diversity and bullying) and Chapter 19 (careers). This chapter focuses on the organisational dimension of HRM. It is divided into six sections:

Chapter contents

13.1 Definition and History of Human Resource Management

Human Resource Management (HRM) is "the human side of enterprises and the factors that determine their relationship with their employers" (Hannagan, 2005). It is a very wide-ranging function that includes the recruitment, development, deployment and motivation of people at work. Other writers point out that HRM is not concerned with *any* relationship at work. It focuses on those between employees and organisations that add value and help attain goals. Just as there are two main parties to the relationship there are at least two sets of goals and they may or may not be compatible. They are the goals of the organisation and the goals of the employees. Human Resource Management may be defined as:

> The productive recruitment, development, deployment and motivation of people at work in order to achieve strategic business objectives and the satisfaction of individual employees.

Since people are an integral part of the definition of management, it follows that the function that deals with the human side of the organisation is a pivotal function. All managers play a part in the productive use of people. Chapter 5, "Staffing", dealt with the aspects of managing people that involve all managers. The HRM **function** involves a higher level of technical expertise that is only required by *some* managers. In particular the HRM function provides a high-level input to the organisation's *infrastructure for managing people.* In other words:

- It formulates policies, strategies and plans concerning the workforce – especially strategies to help organisational change.
- It devises the style and standards of managing people.
- It provides rules and procedures for implementing the two previous activities.
- It provides a service (advice) function for maintaining and improving a workforce.

HRM is one of the enabling functions in an organisation. Its primary mission is to help other functions – especially the line functions – achieve their goals. Since all other functions employ people, HRM is, unlike some other functions, concerned with the whole organisation. HRM managers tend to be generalists because they need to know about all parts of the organisation, its strategy, market position, operations, legal requirements and so on. While the HRM function is primarily a support function, it also has a minor role as a control function. It will usually monitor key indices such as absences, turnover, wage costs and compliance with employment legislation.

There is plenty of evidence that HRM is a function crucial to an organisation's prosperity. There are plenty of CEOs who make comments such as "people are our most important asset". These assertions are backed by empirical research (see Baron and Kreps, 1999; Pfeffer,1998). One of the best studies was conducted by Paterson et al. (1997). They visited 67 UK manufacturing companies and looked at five management functions: human resources, quality, R&D, strategy and technology. They spent two days talking with directors and managers and inspecting documents. At the end of the process they gave a rating to each of the five functions. Patterson et al. returned a year later and collected data on productivity from each company. Finally, they compared the ratings for the functions with productivity during the year. The results for productivity are given in Figure 13.1.

CASE 13.1: THE HR FUNCTION AT MEDIA 24

Media24 is Africa's biggest publishing group. It provides entertainment, information and education 24 hours a day. Newspapers (including South Africa's largest, the *Daily Sun*), magazines, books and web publishing complemented by printing and distribution for private education businesses. Media24 employs about 7100 people in over 60 subsidiaries and divisions.

Each division has an HR function. Typically it has one specialist for every 150 employees who will implement HR policy and provide operational HR support to line managers in fields including recruitment, selection, performance management, employee relations, salary administration and employee relations. The Corporate HR function, based in Cape Town, has about 22 specialists. They set the strategic direction and best-practices management across the group. They give specialist HR expertise in the fields of talent management, recruitment, assessment, selection, training, mentoring, succession planning, transformation (specifically black economic empowerment through affirmative action and skills development), remuneration management, payroll administration, employee relations and employee assistance (some of which is outsourced).

The HR function in Media24 is slightly atypical, because Media24 is operated in a strongly decentralised fashion and approaches to HR may differ from business to business within the group. A major challenge is recruiting and developing talented specialists needed to meet a strategy of rapid growth within South Africa and elsewhere on the continent, as well as in Asia.

We are grateful to Shelagh Goodwin of Media24 for providing this case.

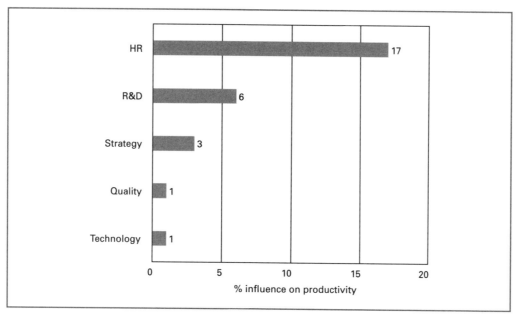

FIGURE 13.1 Influence of Five Functions on Productivity

Such clear-cut results were a surprise. The contribution of HR management to *future* profitability and productivity was much greater than that of the other four functions included in the study. R&D and strategy also made a significant contribution to the future performance of an organisation. The authors were surprised that the contribution made by the quality function was low and they believe that the results arose due to a ceiling effect – the quality in all firms visited was already so high that it did not differentiate between them.

HRM has a long history dating back at least as far as such caring industrialists such as Robert Owen and the Rowntrees. Their philosophy of enlightened self-interest led them to provide decent conditions for their employees on the basis that a well-cared-for worker would be more productive. Often the wives of the industrialists would take an interest in the welfare of employees – especially the welfare of women and children employees. They would visit them when sick, arrange accommodation and supervise their moral welfare (Cannell, 2005). These efforts were often called "industrial betterment". In 1900 there were about a dozen "professional" welfare workers in the UK, but by 1913 there were a sufficient number to form a Welfare Workers' Association. There was a considerable interest in the productivity of munitions workers and an act of Parliament in 1915 made welfare services obligatory in munitions factories. The number of welfare workers grew to about 1300. In the interwar period negotiations with unions became a major issue and these were often conducted by "labour managers" or "employment managers". Large companies such as ICI, Pilkingtons and Marks & Spencer formed specialist personnel departments to manage recruitment and absences among hourly paid workers. During the Second World War the Ministry of Labour insisted that all establishments producing war materials had a welfare worker or personnel officer.

By 1945 personnel management had taken the form that is just recognisable today.

Employment legislation enacted from 1960 onwards added further emphasis to the personnel function. Furthermore, new management techniques for improving worker productivity were suggested by behavioural scientists such as McGregor in the USA. However, personnel management was often seen as a low-status function better suited to amateurs and women! The term "Human Resource Management" began to be used in the USA. The term had useful connotations. It emphasised the fact that human resources were just as important as financial and physical resources. It implied that the people who managed these resources were as important as other organisational "gods" – production managers and finance managers. In addition, the term "Human Resource Management" clearly required personnel managers to take on a strategic role within their organisations. Many people regarded this change of name as superficial spin – "old wine in new bottles!" Others resented the term because it implied that the people in an organisation should be used, manipulated and discarded when necessary like other resources such as metal, machines and a mortgage. As the field of personnel management grew, specialisms started to arise. Larger HR functions may now have special groups devoted to diversity, recruitment, industrial relations or pay.

The HRM function of a large organisation can be structured in two main ways. In the mid-twentieth century many HR departments were highly *centralised*. They formulated a set of procedures that were imposed throughout an organisation. However, this could mean that policies and procedures would be applied where local conditions made them inappropriate. Moreover, other managers often felt alienated by procedures and decisions in which they had played no part. It was easy for them to blame their own shortcomings on, say, a subordinate appointed largely at the behest of the centralised HR function. The HR function in many of today's organisations is decentralised and operates in a "devolved" way with general guidelines and advice from the central HR function. This structure has its dangers too. Devolution may mean that complicated procedures are set up and operated by non-specialist staff – some of whom deliver a poor-quality service. The image of the organisation may suffer. Furthermore, devolved units may duplicate the work of other units.

CASE 13.2: A DAY IN THE LIFE OF . . . A SENIOR RESOURCE EXECUTIVE

Grace works in the HR function of ACNielson in China. Her job involves all aspects of recruitment, staff training and development plus employee relations. A typical day would include: 9.00 a.m. check and reply to emails, 10.00 a.m. interview candidates, 12.00 noon meeting with headhunter (Executive Search Consultant), 2.00 p.m. conference call with colleagues in Shanghai and Beijing, 4.00 p.m. discuss staff development plans with several departments. The things Grace likes about her job are meeting different people every day, gaining people's trust and influencing them.

A day in the life of a number of management jobs can be seen at http://www.careers.manchester.ac.uk/finding/dayinthelife/

13.1 The Scope of the Human Resource Function

The previous section noted that the HR function is very broad in the sense that it plays a part in the operation of all other functions within an organisation. It is a very broad function in another sense too – it covers a wide range of different activities. These activities cannot be undertaken in a haphazard way. They need to be fitted within a logical framework. Figure 13.2 gives an idealised paradigm of the way that the HRM function should be organised in order to achieve a workforce that will give a competitive advantage.

An HR strategy starts with organisational goals that are influenced by both market conditions and government legislation. The HR function must interpret the organisational goals in terms of the numbers of employees needed in various occupations and the skills that will be needed. This interpretation is sometimes called the *"People Requirement"*. The HR function will then need to establish its present complement of staff. The gap between the future requirements and the present complement is the demand that the HR function must fill. The gap can be filled in three main ways: ergonomics and job design, recruitment and selection

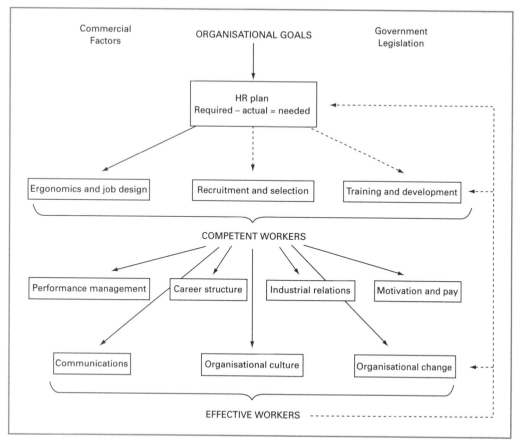

FIGURE 13.2 An Idealised HR System

and training and development. Very generally it is better to redesign a job ergonomically so that it can be performed by most people – there will then be little need for selection or training and the results are more certain. However, it may be impossible to redesign a job to this extent. The HR department should then attempt to select people who already have the skills and competences needed. This will mean that there is no delay while recruits are trained and there will be no need to worry about whether the training will be successful. Unfortunately, selection is not perfect so some of the people offered jobs will turn out not to have the skills they claimed. In many situations the ideal person for a job may not exist and it will be necessary to employ people who have only some of the skills and develop the rest by training.

Well-chosen, well-trained people working in a well-designed job are *competent workers*. They are *able* to do the job. But this does not mean that they *will* do the job. There are a wide range of techniques available to transform competent workers into effective workers. Some of these techniques, such as organisational climate, motivation and communication, have been covered elsewhere in this book (Chapters 4, 5 and 8, respectively). However, the human resource function will also need to consider performance appraisal, career structure, industrial relations and remuneration in order to transform competent workers into effective workers. There are, of course, feedback loops. The success or failure of the HR function to produce effective workers will feed back into the organisation's aims and goals and other aspects of its own function.

13.3 The Legal Background to Human Resource Management

Governments have passed laws concerning the employment of people for almost 200 years. Initially these laws concerned the basic contract between employer and employees such as how wages must be paid (in cash, not in kind) and about the rights of workers to belong to trade unions. Broadly, between, say, 1900 and 1950 governments passed legislation concerning health and safety at work. Since 1960 they have passed legislation concerning social issues and the rights of individuals. Today, as the following list shows, there is a raft of legislation concerning workers.

Categories of employees

- employment of minors – to prevent employment and exploitation of children
- part-time workers – to ensure they not exploited because of their part-time status
- fixed-term employees – to ensure there are not exploited because of their status

Health and safety

- place of work – must be safe, clean and at a reasonable temperature
- working hours – must not be excessive
- injuries to health

Benefits

- form of payment – should not be in the form of tokens to be exchanged at employer's shop
- minimum wage act – to ensure workers are not exploited
- holidays – granting minimum statutory (bank holidays) and other leave
- parental leave – paid and unpaid time off work for mother and father
- pension benefits – to ensure that people have retirement income
- time off for study – to allow people the opportunity to gain qualifications

Redundancy or dismissal

- reasons for dismissal – clear, written notification is required
- consultation on closure – to ensure that workers' viewpoints are heard
- redundancy – to prevent victimisation at times of closure or redundancy
- period of notice – to give some stability of employment
- continuation of employment if organisation changes hands (TUPE)

Anti-discrimination (all aimed to ensure fairness for women and minority groups)

- race, ethnic origin, colour
- gender
- disability
- age
- pregnancy
- rehabilitation of offenders – relatively minor offences need not be disclosed after five years (usually!)

Miscellaneous

- trade union membership – gives the right to belong or not belong to a trade union
- picketing – identifies the circumstances under which picketing may take place
- written statement of wage calculations – so employees can check payment is accurate
- written employment contracts – to ensure everyone is clear about the nature of the work they are expected to perform

Clearly this is not an exhaustive list. Legislation may vary from country to country and from time to time. It is usually the job of the HR function to check the legislation that is in force in the territories where they operate. Usually, they maintain a file with this information. They will also give guidance to other managers in their organisation, perhaps as oral advice, memos on specific cases or advice that might take the form of periodic guidance notes. Failure to observe the legislation can have serious consequences. Infraction of safety regulations, for example, might result in a temporary closure of the organisation. The organisation might also be fined and its senior managers imprisoned. Failure to uphold employment law may involve an appearance at a tribunal which has the power to fine the organisation, award compensation or order an employee's reinstatement. Cases of this kind are nearly always attended by unfavourable publicity.

13.4 Human Resource Strategy and Manpower Planning

A human resource plan is often a very complex document. It is often produced in four stages. First, the *future staffing requirements* must be established. The process starts by examining the organisation's strategic plan in a systematic way to establish the personnel impact of any changes such as:

- new equipment
- new legislation
- new working procedures
- expansion or contraction
- centralisation, decentralisation, reorganisation or mergers

This establishes the kind of job the organisation will need to fill together with the skills and competences that will be demanded. Next the number of people in each type of job is estimated. An organisation may wish, at this stage, to specify the number of various groups such as men, women, ethnic minorities, disabled people it would like to have on the payroll at a future date. At the end of this stage the organisation will have a *Future Staffing Requirement*.

The second stage is to establish similar information for the *present staffing levels*. This is sometimes called a *Human Resource Audit* and the result is sometimes called a *Workforce Profile*. Many organisations conduct HR audits on a systematic basis so that the information will be to hand if it is needed. Usually the information can often be obtained from the organisation's IT system and can be used to calculate various indices of labour turnover. The simplest is the crude **percentage turnover** which is calculated according to the following formula:

$$per\ cent\ turnover = \frac{number\ holding\ posts\ in\ year}{number\ of\ posts}$$

Another index of turnover is the **average length of service**. Both the crude index of labour turnover and the average length of service have the disadvantage that a poor result can be produced by the rapid turnover by a few individuals in a few posts. A more sophisticated index that does not suffer this disadvantage is the "labour stability index" (LSI) which is calculated by the formula:

$$LSI = \frac{number\ of\ people\ with\ more\ than\ a\ year's\ service}{number\ of\ people\ employed\ 12\ months\ before}$$

Very low labour turnover can indicate problems. It might indicate a stagnant organis-ation that is not receiving enough new people and ideas. The problem of a high turnover is even less desirable and more common. An organisation with high turnover will be spending a lot of money recruiting and training people, which is then wasted when they leave. Furthermore, a high turnover disrupts the work of the people who stay with the organisation. A high turnover is often a symptom of problems elsewhere in the HR function, such as monotonous work, poor communications, poor management style or poor wages. However, labour turnover must be interpreted in the light of information from other comparable organisations. Some industries such as hotel and catering have a notoriously high labour turnover. It is difficult to determine the exact reason why people leave the organisation unless exit interviews are conducted. *Exit interviews* should be held within a day or two of an employee's resignation. It is no use waiting until the last day when attitudes have mel-lowed by fond farewells, mending of fences and anticipation of appreciative ceremonies and presents. Exit interviews need to be as close as possible to the point at which an employee decides to leave. They should be conducted by an independent and sympathetic person from the HR function. They *must not* be conducted by line management or people associated with them.

The third stage is to subtract the actual staffing levels from the future staffing require-ments to produce an estimate of the number of new employees that will be needed – the gap between the personnel that will be available and the personnel that the organisation's strategic plan will need. Sometimes the comparison of actual and required staffing levels indicates a surplus. This can occur if, say, a branch is to be closed or if new equipment will require fewer workers. Identifying surpluses is as important as identifying gaps: it often takes longer to resolve and needs early detection.

In the fourth stage gaps or surpluses are carefully inspected and appropriate action taken to ensure that the future supply of workers is equal to the number of workers demanded by the organisation's strategic plan. This is sometimes called *"right sizing"*.

It is often possible to fill gaps for junior jobs by recruiting people from outside the organ-isation and the time needed to train new employees must be taken into account. Recruitment for jobs with long training times needs to be scheduled ahead of recruitment for jobs with short training times. Senior jobs are often filled by promoting people from within the organisation. This is often a long-term process and it requires careful planning. It is called *succession planning* and almost all large organisations use it. Ironically, succession planning is more important for small organisations. In large organisations there is a much greater probability that someone suitable can be found. Simple arithmetical probability means that this is much less likely in small organisations, which can be reduced to chaos if a senior member of the management team resigns and no-one is ready to take his or her place. A succession plan starts with the organisational chart and works on a "falling under a bus" basis. This asks the question "who would take over if the CEO fell under a bus tomorrow?". When the successor is identified, other questions are asked: "how ready would the successor be?" and "what extra experience or knowledge would they need?". Of course, there would then be the problem of filling the post vacated by the person promoted to the CEO. Consequently, the process would be repeated for every position within at least two levels of the CEO. A succession plan is completed by drawing up schedules for the training and development of successors. Succession plans are fraught with problems – which is why they are shunned by many small and medium-sized organisations. If they become public, as they probably will, they become organisational dynamite. The putative successor develops an initial mein of a "crown prince". Rivals to the succession may not acquiesce in their fate. They may set out to undermine the crown prince. They may tear the organisation apart in an attempt to seize the succession.

Staff surpluses often result in retrenchment, which is much less pleasant to deal with than organisational expansion. However, ignoring worker surpluses is great folly. A delay will mean an organisation will decline further, a bigger surplus will accumulate and a further round of unpleasant measures will be needed. Further, delay may mean that probably emergency, traumatic, action will be needed later. It is much better to deal with surpluses promptly. Potential surpluses can be managed by "freezes on recruitment", early retirements or redundancies. Short-term surpluses can be managed by "overtime bans" or short-time working. A freeze on recruitment may mean that the organisation is cut off from new people and new ideas. Furthermore, unfilled vacancies may accumulate in certain departments that are already overloaded. Bottlenecks that impair the organisation's effectiveness may develop. Early retirement schemes can cause a haemorrhage of valuable expertise. Redundancy schemes can cause great disruption and cause the motivation of workers to plummet. The HR function may seek to mitigate the effect on morale by offering voluntary redundancy. This too has great dangers. It is virtually certain that the majority of those who volunteer are those the organisation can least afford to lose. Some organisations manage redundancy situations by adopting a policy of last in – first out. At a superficial level this seems fair but it may be that people who have been recruited recently have competencies that are a better match to the future needs of the organisation. Needless to say, all of these problems are easier to solve if they have been detected early and there is plenty of time available to find a solution.

13.5 Components of Human Resource Management

Human Resource Managers employ a range of techniques. They include recruitment and selection, training and development, performance appraisal, industrial relations and championing the employees' corner.

Recruitment and selection

Recruitment and selection (inplacement) is a substantial HR activity and it is also covered in Chapter 5 (Staffing). The HR function must remember that, except when recruiting its own staff, it is offering a service. Responsibility for selecting an employee must lie with the head of the department where he or she will work. So, the main recruitment and selection responsibilities of the HR function are:

- establishing a system for approving and filling a vacancy
- training staff in selection techniques and legal aspects
- advising on a job description and other information for applicants
- preparing and placing advertisements

- approving and liaising with recruitment agencies
- corresponding with applicants (invitations to interview, etc.)
- making arrangements for an interview or other selection methods
- assisting with interview or other selection method
- advising on starting salary and conditions of employment
- communicating the formal job offer and writing to unsuccessful candidates

Training and development

Training and development will be another major activity of the HR function. Again it must remember that, except when training and developing its own staff, it is offering a service. Responsibility for training and developing an employee lies with the head of the department where she or he will work. So, the main training responsibilities of the HR function are:

- establishing and maintaining a system that monitors and ensures that all employees are fully developed and properly trained
- advising on the training needs of specific individuals
- monitoring and maintaining a list of training providers
- co-ordinating the training offered to employees within the organisation
- developing and providing training courses on topics specific to the organisation or where there are advantages in providing training "in-house"
- evaluating the effectiveness of the training

Performance management

Competent employees are generally motivated to perform well and are capable of learning. If sub-optimal behaviour is noted and discussed, most workers will improve their behaviour. This impeccable logic has led to many forms of performance appraisal.

Methods of performance appraisal

In the archetypal appraisal system, a subordinate and his or her boss meet at regular, say, three-monthly intervals to discuss performance. Ideally the meeting will have no other purpose than improving performance; the boss will have an intimate knowledge of the job and the subordinate's actions. Moreover, an ideal boss will be completely objective and not preoccupied by other problems which will distract from the appraisal process. Again, ideally, the subordinate will be totally open, prepared to accept that his or her performance is less than perfect and be willing and able to make substantial changes in the way that they work. After "deep and meaningful discussion" the subordinate and the boss will be able to identify the correct way forward and produce a realistic plan that the subordinate will implement with assiduity.

It will be no surprise that these ideal conditions are rarely met. Performance appraisals are linked, or perceived to be linked, to other important organisational activities such as pay rises, promotion, demotion or sacking. Such links are less than helpful to an open and frank exchange of information. In addition, a boss will not usually have sufficient time to conduct a comprehensive appraisal. A thorough appraisal, together with the attendant paperwork, might involve a boss in two day's effort. A boss who has, say, eight subordinates will therefore spend 16 days per quarter (about 20 per cent of available time) on performance appraisals during which time they need to ignore production crises and other "marginal" matters. Bosses are rarely fully informed about their subordinates' jobs and their performances. The jobs may have changed quite dramatically since the bosses were promoted from them. The average boss spends less than 10 per cent of their time with any single subordinate. Furthermore, it is difficult for a boss to be objective. They have their own styles and preferences.

Subordinates share some blame for inaccurate appraisals. They are not stupid. They know that, even with assurances that "our conversation will only be used for purposed of your development", information will leak into decisions about pay rises, promotion and, perhaps, dismissal. They will spend time preparing for the appraisal rather than doing their normal work. They will pursue their own targets rather than being a good organisational "citizens". Consequently, many appraisal systems fail. Employees almost always attribute good results to their own skill and effort. On the other hand bad results are attributed to other people or to unfavourable circumstances.

Organisations have tried to minimise such problems in three main ways: using rating scales, behaviourally anchored scales and 360-degree feedback. *Rating scales* (sometimes wrongly called "ranking scales") attempt to reduce the problems arising from free descriptions. The first step is to identify the qualities (competencies) to be rated. Initially these were *personal qualities* (traits) such as "likeable", "energetic" or "persuasive". The judgements were often very subjective, so many organisations started to rate *observable behaviours* such as "is able to establish rapport with customers" or "communicates ideas convincingly". The modern trend is to rate *results* such as "customers with a problem would have no hesitation in approaching this person" or "people are likely to be persuaded by this person's presentation". The second step in producing a scale is to provide a list of alternatives that indicate an employee's position in comparison to other workers. For example an appraisal form might contain the following scale:

To what extent would a customer with a problem be likely to approach this person?

- very likely – in the top 20 per cent of people doing this job
- likely – in the top 40 per cent of people doing this job
- as likely as not – in the middle 20 per cent of people doing this job
- unlikely – in the bottom 40 per cent of people doing this job
- very unlikely – in the bottom 20 per cent of people doing the job

Behaviourally Anchored Rating Scales (BARS) are a special kind of rating scale that aims to remove the ambiguity from the judgements. Specific example(s) of observable behaviour by someone at that level of the scale are provided. For example, the behavioural anchor for the top position in the previous scale might read:

- Very likely – in the top 20 per cent of people doing the job. He or she stands where they can be seen by customers and greets them with eye contact and a smile. Uses non-verbal gestures such as nodding to indicate empathy.

Although rating scales, especially Behaviourally Anchored Rating Scales, look scientific, there is a problem when they are used in appraisal systems. They lack discrimination, because most employees are placed in the top two positions. This is partly because superiors may wish to be kind to subordinates. It may also occur because superiors do not wish to admit that they manage their unit in a way that tolerates average or below-average performance. Furthermore, some managers want to save their time for other activities they consider more productive. They know that any subordinate who receives an average or below-average rating is likely to contest the judgement and they will need to spend hours justifying their view and placating the aggrieved subordinate. Moreover, the aggrieved subordinate will continue to work in their unit. It may be a more cost-effective use of time to give an acceptable rating and invest the time saved in solving another problem.

Problems with superior ratings led to the development of a technique called 360-degree feedback. 360-degree feedback gets its name from the fact that feedback is provided from all directions. Questionnaires are distributed to a range of people including the boss, colleagues, subordinates and perhaps customers. The questionnaire is completed on a confidential basis and analysed by someone with no vested interest in the results. The average of the ratings will then be fed back to the employee and her or his boss so that they can be discussed and appropriate lessons learnt. 360-degree feedback is not without its own problems. People generally dislike rating their colleagues. The actual rating that they give can be distorted in many ways. Sometimes colleagues come to a mutually advantageous agreement that they will not give each other poor ratings. In other cases rivals for promotion can seek to improve their own chances by giving poor ratings to their competitors.

Consequences of performance appraisal

With luck, a performance appraisal will reveal that a person is working competently and adding value to the organisation but there will be some points that can be improved or developed. The boss and subordinate should note the generally favourable appraisal and produce an action plan to address the development points. This plan should be reviewed after, say, three months to check that the plan has been, or is being, fulfilled. In a minority of cases, an appraisal might reveal problems. This always causes rancour and a great deal of emotion. The subordinate is likely to contend that he or she has been the victim of misunderstandings, bias or stereotyping. These claims may be true and they should be considered fairly.

If the claims are groundless, it is important to tackle the reason for poor performance. If the problem arises

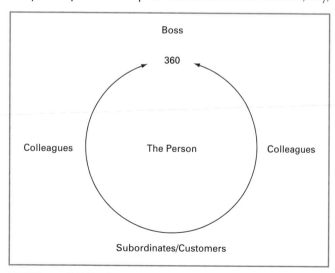

FIGURE 13.3 360° Feedback

from lack of training, additional training can be provided. If the problem arises from a mismatch between a person's abilities and those required by the job, the person can be moved to a more suitable position. A *transfer* that is perceived as demotion will be resented and it is likely that the person will resign from the organisation within a short time. If they remain within the organisation they are likely to experience frustration and a loss of confidence. They may also transfer their discontent to other workers. Transfers may offer a solution when poor performance arises from relationships within the working group. For example, if there are frequent personality clashes between colleagues or with a boss it may be better to transfer the person to another job of equal status.

It is quite rare for people to be dismissed for poor performance. Usually *dismissal* only takes place when there has been a clear failure to perform the job. For example, people may be dismissed for *gross misconduct* such as dishonesty, a clear neglect in duty or a blatant refusal to obey an instruction. Dismissal may also occur if a worker *breaches* their *contract of employment* by going on strike, or disrupting the work of others or putting other workers in danger. Dismissal is a major step and normally only taken after considerable thought. The employees should be notified (preferably in writing) of their poor performance, warned of the potential consequences and given reasonable opportunity to make changes. Dismissal procedures and legal requirements must be followed to the letter. In some circumstances, such as theft, drunkenness, the imminent threat of damage to property or the safety of others, it may be possible to *summarily dismiss* an employee without any notice. If an employer obstructs an employee and makes it difficult for him or her to do their job, the employee may resign and claim a *constructive dismissal*. This means that the employer has shown that they have no intention of fulfilling *their* side of the employment contract. The employee may then claim compensation for *wrongful dismissal*.

Pay and compensation

Pay and job difficulty

The HR function plays a key role in determining the compensation packages for employees. It will establish a salary structure that other departments must operate. If a salary structure is not in place, different departments will pay different salaries for equivalent work. There will be a great number of anomalies and a lot of time and effort will be spent dealing with complaints. Furthermore, the lack of a sound salary structure is likely to lead to an infringement of employment legislation where different groups are paid different salaries for equivalent work. Most pay structures are based on some form of grading or job evaluation. In the past the *tasks* involved in a job would be evaluated and allotted points. The number of points would determine the salary band appropriate for the job. Someone's salary would be within that band but other factors such as experience, seniority or recognition for good work would determine the exact placement. Probably the best-known points system for job evaluation is the Hay-MSL system for evaluating senior management jobs.

In the past, a salary system of a large organisation would have many, perhaps seven or more, narrow bands. People would sometimes start employment at the bottom of the lowest band and work their way up to the top of the highest band by the time they retired. **Narrowband** salary structures give workers the sense of progression but they have their disadvantages. First they are complex to administer; every little change in a job's content means the job needs to be re-graded. Every time someone moves to a slightly different job they might change salary bands. Because small changes could make a difference to an employee's pay, the HR function was forever wrangling with people who contested the positioning of their job. In recent years there has been a trend towards **broadbanding** where there are fewer, wider bands. As Figure 13.4 shows **broadbanding** produces a simpler and more flexible salary structure. Some organisations maintain that it is less divisive and more motivating for employees.

Today it is more likely that jobs are evaluated in terms of the *skills* needed to perform the tasks. Again there is usually a point system. Jobs that demand higher skills, more experience or higher physical demands are generally higher paid. The labour market will also play its part. People in occupations that are in short supply will generally be paid more.

Many firms have moved to a system whereby people are paid according to their *performance*. Such systems are often called *incentive schemes* and they can take many forms. Some jobs are paid on a strict commission basis where there is a direct relationship between salary and output. These schemes produce high motivation for ambitious people who are not concerned about security. However, they have the disadvantage that they encourage selfishness and discourage organisational citizenship. They also encourage people to exploit short-term possibilities and then move onto another job before the long-term consequences are apparent. A less aggressive regime entails a reasonable basic salary plus commission when performance exceeds a pre-set limit. These systems often attract better employees than those solely working on commission. However, they too tend to encourage selfishness and discourage teamwork. Performance-related pay has many conceptual advantages: in theory, it ties remuneration to the contribution an individual makes to organisational goals. In practice the achievements of performance-related pay are much less impressive. Outside sales and other readily quantifiable occupations, it is very difficult to assess accurately an individual's contribution to organisational goals – most jobs are too complex and multifaceted. Performance related pay often engenders distrust. A survey by Towers-Perrin (1999) revealed considerable dissatisfaction in companies that had tried to install the system. Indeed, 84 per

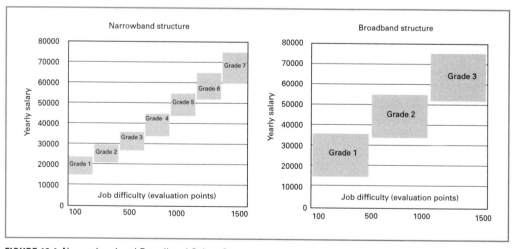

FIGURE 13.4 Narrowband and Broadband Salary Structures

cent of companies had experienced problems ranging from union opposition, employee distrust and poor communications.

A third system is to pay a basic salary plus a bonus that is based upon the performance of the *team*. In principle, this should promote teamwork whilst still providing motivation for individuals. Unfortunately, some members of a team may decide that it is better to provide a moderate performance and rely on other members of the team to earn bonuses for them. Another system involves a profit-sharing scheme of some kind. Individuals are given a reasonable basic salary but there is an additional element based upon the profit an organisation makes in the preceding year.

Other benefits

Employee benefits are the non-cash rewards that a person receives. They can form a substantial proportion of the total remuneration package. For example, when contribution to state schemes are included, most employers pay employees an additional 15 per cent over and above salary in terms of medical, sickness and retirement benefits. As the following list indicates some organisations offer many more *"benefits in kind"*:

- employee share schemes
- membership of professional bodies
- travel accident insurance
- company car (especially in the UK)
- free car parking
- personal training (e.g. pre-retirement courses)
- counselling
- subsidised childcare
- life insurance
- tuition fees for employees and dependents
- recreational clubs
- subsidised canteens and catering

In total, benefits can add 30 per cent or more to an employee's total remuneration package. Organisations offer these benefits because they help attract and retain people of the calibre they need. Many employees value these benefits more than a marginal increase in salary. They are, therefore, an economical way of motivating employees – especially when benefits receive favourable tax treatment. Some employers offer *"flexible benefit packages"* where the value of the total remuneration package is fixed but employees have considerable choice about how it is distributed between salary and their own mixture of benefits.

Pay and organisational maturity

The pay system is often related to the organisation's stage of development. In a young organisation the core salary and benefits will be just enough to compete with other companies but executives will be offered extensive share options so that they will have a high stake in the organisation's future success. As an organisation passes into adolescence core salaries will increase and, while share options will be retained, they will tend to be supplanted by a bonus structure. Employees will also start to receive benefits and perks. When the organisation reaches maturity, core salaries and bonuses will be good. Other benefits will be comprehensive. Executive perks may be lavish. As the organisation starts to decline, salaries will remain high but pressure for reductions will mean that they remain static. Bonuses will be reduced – except bonuses for reducing costs. Benefits will be limited or frozen. Executive perks will be cut.

Employee Relations (Industrial Relations)

Definition and concept of Employee Relations

The topic of Employee Relations (ER) is more widely known as *Industrial Relations* (**IR**). It is also known as **Labour Relations** and **Staff Relations**. The term "employee relations" is preferred because in most modern economies only a minority of people work in industry. Similarly, "labour relations" has strong and possibly misleading connotations with physical labour which now forms only a small part of economic activity. The term is more frequently used in the USA. Staff relations implies that the topic is only relevant to people employed in "staff" positions. The term "employee relations" makes it clear that the topic is relevant to everyone who is employed in an organisation. ER may be defined as:

> 66 The study of institutions and processes controlling the mutual dealings between an organisation and its employees – especially the mutual dealings between an organisation and collective worker groups. 99

In many situations employee relations concerns the mutual dealings between an organisation and a trade union but it also encompasses dealings with staff associations and informal groups. The nature of employee relations within an organisation is usually a feature of the management style and the industrial or commercial sector. Generally three main philosophical approaches to ER are distinguished: confrontation, unitarian and pluralist:

- The **confrontational approach** is characterised by beliefs that organisations and employees have irreconcilable objectives. There is a great deal of mistrust between the two parties. Employee relations is often seen as a battleground in which the employees or the organisation seeks supremacy in dictating terms of employment, etc. Such conflicts can be mutually destructive. For example, workers may strike and picket an organisation with such success that the organisation is forced into bankruptcy and closes, leaving the employees worse off and without employment. The confrontational approach tends to be seen in traditional organisations where there is a long history of poor employee relations. It is also seen in traditional and declining industries where competition, perhaps international competition, is fierce. The confrontational approach to ER is based on a *radical philosophy* derived from Marx. It contends that there is a fundamental conflict between employing organisations (capitalists) and the workers (the proletariat). According to this view employers will maximise profits at the expense of the workers. Since employers have more power than an individual employee, workers need to band together so that their collective power is equal to or greater than the power of the employer. The ultimate goal will be for the workers to own the organisation collectivity or to control it by controlling government. This philosophy was once very prevalent in some trade unions – albeit in a watered down and more sophisticated form.

■ The **consensus approach** is the mirror image of the confrontational approach. Employees or their representatives form a genuine partnership working towards mutually beneficial solutions. In practice, a fully consensual approach is very rare and is, perhaps, only seen in co-operatives and small organisations. The consensus approach is based upon a *Unitarian philosophy* which believes that there is a set of goals and objectives which serve everyone's interests. The well-being of the organisation is therefore paramount and everyone must work towards pleasing its customers. There will be a distinctive working ethos and standards which everyone should uphold.

■ The **conformity approach** focuses on achieving harmony between various subgroups of employees – avoiding demarcation disputes whereby one group of workers take industrial action in order to pre-empt another group trespassing on its traditional territory. The conformity approach to ER tries to set objectives and procedures that allow different groups to rise above their own vested interests. The conformity approach is based on a *pluralistic philosophy* that acknowledges that different workers and groups of workers will have a variety of objectives that may not be totally compatible. Since potential conflict between these objectives may be mutually harmful, it is necessary to have a system of rules and procedures to resolve it. Workers must conform to the system so that the organisation remains productive. Employee relations in public service and government are usually based on a pluralistic philosophy.

Employee relations usually involves a sophisticated interplay between *formal* and *informal* systems. The formal part of the system will consist of "official" documents, meetings, agendas and timetables. The formal part of the system legitimises and crystallises the situation and the solution. However, the formal system is often inflexible and prone to developing into "stand-offs". The informal part of the system consists of networks of respected people in both camps. It often operates via informal meetings in corridors and "off-the-record" telephone conversations. The informal network oils the informal network and helps it function.

Employee relations usually involves the most senior managers in an organisation. The head of the HR function will have a very important advisory role but final decisions will be made by the CEO or the board of directors. The HR function will play an important role in setting up and maintaining the employee relations system. It may be given executive powers with regard to minor decisions.

Parties to bargaining

Employee relations involves a great deal more than the negotiating. Nevertheless, this will be a major part of the HR function's work. Superficially, bargaining involves two main parties: the employing organisation and the employees. In practice, other parties may be involved. They include:

■ **Trade unions** which represent workers by proving advice and political and financial support. Trade unions may encourage workers in a particular organisation to take up a grievance if they feel they can win the dispute and set a useful precedent that can be used elsewhere.

- **Other employers** and **employer associations** in the same sector or industry may provide an organisation with advice and financial support. They may encourage a particular organisation to resist claims which they believe would set a bad precedent for them or their member organisations.

- **Governments** are often involved in negotiations and disputes. They may be involved as employers themselves or they may become involved in order to support their political philosophy. Sometimes public opinion compels governments to play an active part in the belief that a dispute is against the national interest.

- The **media** are usually involved in high profile disputes because it may improve their ratings or circulation figures.

In general, negotiations are more difficult when they generate a lot of publicity and when they involve many different parties. Bargaining can take place on many levels. These include national, regional and unit level. Sometimes bargaining takes place for a whole industrial sector.

Subject of negotiations

The subject of negotiations can be grouped into three categories:

- The **employment contract** – especially wages, working hours and fringe benefits such as pensions. Negotiations on these topics are often called **substantive negotiations**.

- **Procedures for the regulation of workers** such as working rules, consultation mechanisms and grievance procedures. Negotiations of these topics are often called **procedural negotiations**.

- Resolving **individual situations, problems and crises**. For example, a union may be called in by one of its members to argue its case in a dispute with his or her boss. Negotiations of this kind are often called **troubleshooting negotiations**. In terms of volume and time involved most negotiations are troubleshooting negotiations at unit level. The great majority are resolved with reasonable success. However, the minority of unsuccessful troubleshooting negotiations have great potential to escalate into major confrontations where they transmogrify into major substantive or procedural issues.

Of course, real negotiations are rarely so clear-cut. In practice most bargaining will involve some element of all three kinds.

The bargaining process

To some extent bargaining is a ritual and follows a set pattern. Usually both sides wish to avoid conflict which will cost them money and damage their interests. Both sides will wish to achieve an agreement that costs them least but gains them most. As Figure 13.5 illustrates, solutions in a negotiation will be on a spectrum that may be divided into three areas: delight, acceptance and rejection. In most negotiations the areas of acceptance will overlap and the function of negotiations is to find a point in the common ground where both parties can agree.

There are two main difficulties to finding an acceptable solution. First, the employer or the trade union, or both, will define their positions in an aggressive way so that there is *no common ground*. When this happens a deadlock arises and both sides will apply pressure

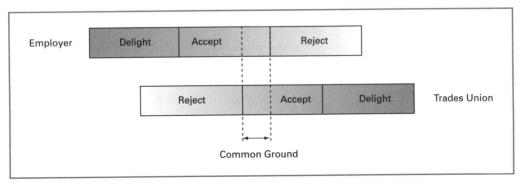

FIGURE 13.5 Common Ground in Negotiations

on the other to soften their position and move towards their own position. Unions may strike, work to rule or impose a "go slow". The organisation may threaten dismissal, withdrawal of benefits or arrange a "lock-out". Eventually, one or both, will modify their positions so that an area of common ground emerges. The second main danger to finding common ground is a misunderstanding of the position of the other party. Emotion can create formidable barriers. If these arise, the informal network and communications are indispensable for correcting misunderstandings.

Usually, collective bargaining follows a clear pattern that involves four phases:

■ First there is the **initial offer** that is usually an opening formality. It is universally expected to be rejected. If by some strange chance it happens to be accepted, problems will arise in future because it will cause resentment. The more usual course is for the initial offer to be rejected out of hand.

■ Second, both sides of the negotiation **adopt postures** designed to persuade the other party of the seriousness of the issues and the weakness of their case. At this stage there may be a number of rituals such as breaking off negotiations or accusing the other side of bad faith or violating agreements. These are attempts to put the other side in a defensive position.

■ Third, **substantive negotiations begin**. The sides start to explore the real objective of their opponents. Usually this starts by exploring possible areas of agreement. Difficult areas are usually tackled last. The aspects that opponents are willing to trade in return for concessions elsewhere become apparent during this stage. The negotiations can be blocked if one side misreads signals or is determined not to reach an agreement. There may be a number of cycles involving a final offer, a final-final offer and, perhaps, a final-final-final offer. Towards the end of this stage the ultimate agreement will be offered on a very tentative basis.

■ Fourth, if the tentative agreement is positively received it will be transformed into the **real final offer** that will be set down in formal terms. The formal offer will then need to be accepted on a formal basis.

Sometimes negotiations stall in the third stage and deadlock results. One way forward is to proceed to *arbitration* where independent people judge the merits of each case. Often it is difficult to find an arbiter that both sides consider independent. The side that genuinely believes its case is stronger may be reluctant to go to arbitration because it feels that the arbiter will compromise simply in order to resolve the conflict. In these cases *pendulum arbitration* may be used. The dispute is referred to an arbiter but she or he must choose one of the cases in its entirety. It is believed that pendulum arbitration encourages parties in a negotiation to be more moderate and reasonable in their demands.

Types of unionisation

The workforce of an organisation can be unionised in many ways. At the bottom of the scale are *non-union organisations*. This may have disadvantages for the organisation. Either it must negotiate separately with each employee or it must ignore employees' wishes. Non-union organisations usually occur in small, recently established businesses which are experiencing favourable trading conditions. If the organisation encounters difficulties and employees feel they are ignored they will either join a union en masse or leave the organ-isation en masse – at a time when the organisation needs to be devoting its attention to other things. Some non-union organisations establish a *staff association* to represent workers and to conduct negotiations on their behalf. Some organisations try to avoid the problems of demarcation disputes between unions by coming to a *single-union agreement*. This means that the whole workforce is represented by one union. It drastically simplifies employee relations and often means that a more logical and systematic approach to ER can be built up. Single-union agreements may be accompanied by *no strike agreements*. Both union and organisation agree a method, usually arbitration, of resolving conflicts without strike action.

Many large organisations with a workforce that is very diverse in terms of its skills and trades and which has long history of unionisation are, necessarily, *multi-union*. Multi-unionism can require a great deal of effort managing rivalries between unions. Organisations are usually keen to avoid a sequence of never-ending negotiations where each trade union attempts to impress its own members and poach members of other unions by "*leapfrogging*" earlier agreements. In these circumstances the organisation may attempt to instigate *single-table* negotiations where all the unions are present and where one com-prehensive agreement can be made. Needless to say, single-table negotiations are often very protracted and complicated.

13.6 The Welfare Role of Human Resource Management

At the start of the chapter it was noted that HRM had some of its roots in the welfare movements of the nineteenth century. The intervening sections of this chapter may have given the picture that HRM is now a mere management tool for controlling and manipu-lating workers. In fact, HRM has never totally lost its welfare role. In most organisations the Human Resource Function has a genuine concern in improving the lives of its employees. The welfare actions an HRM function might take are:

- Helping employees **solve personal problems**. Employees encountering problems often go to the HR department for help. At its simplest this help might consist of a sympath-etic ear plus some commonsense advice. In other situations it might take the form of a transfer, a change in working hours or a modification of the job. At its most sophisticated level the help might take the form of an employee assistance programme (EAP). In an employee assistance programme the workers are given the telephone number or other contact details of a counselling service they can consult if they have personal problems. While the company will pay for the service, the counselling will totally independent and conducted on a confidential basis. It is argued that the independent nature of an EAP will encourage people to seek help at an early stage before a problem becomes difficult to solve. An EAP is usually able to help employees who have problems involving debt, marital and family relationships, a poor work–life balance and drugs.

- **Help employees' careers**. Many HR functions try to structure jobs in their organisation into patterns that provide careers for their employees. They may also offer training that has no direct or immediate relevance to an employee's current job but which will enhance his or her employability. In many cases an HR function will liaise with schools to provide work experience for scholars. Sometimes, the HR function will create temporary posts in order to help unemployed people make the transition into work.

- When an employee encounters a serious and acute crisis such as illness or bereavement, it is usually the HR function that instigates and **co-ordinates the organisation's compassionate response** such as arranging extra leave or sending condolences. In some countries where there is inadequate healthcare the HR function may take the lead in raising money to pay for treatment.

- The HR function usually makes an above average contribution to the **social life of an organisation**. It often manages an organisation's sports and social clubs. Generally, it also organises social events, parties and celebrations. Furthermore the HR function will usually have responsibility for the organisation's catering services.

All of these contributions are usually considered peripheral activities but their sum total improves the quality of people's working lives.

A final aspect of the HR function – *its advocacy on behalf of employees* – is often overlooked. In a majority of organisations HR personnel act as a buffer between the demands of other functions and employees. For example, a production manager may, perhaps to further his or her personal career, wish to instigate a very demanding schedule that involves high targets and a great deal of overtime. The marketing and financial functions may lend their support to the changes. It is likely to be someone in the HR function who draws attention to the impact these changes will have on employees. Similarly, the HR director will be present at board meetings where an organisation's strategy and tactics are first discussed. He or she is almost certain to make a significant contribution to ensure that the strategy and tactics are as "employee friendly" as possible.

Activities and Further Study

Essay Plans

Write essay plans for the following questions:

1 What are the main laws that affect employment of people in your country? What steps can the HR function take to ensure that they are observed within an organisation?

2 What is Human Resource Planning and how does it contribute to achieving an organisation's goals?

3 What is the role of an HR function in *recruitment and selection* and how does this differ from the staffing procedures performed by managers in other departments?

4 What is the role of an HR function in *training and development* and how does this differ from the staffing procedures performed by managers in other departments?

5 Outline some of the factors that need to be taken into account by an HR function when it sets out to devise a salary and remuneration structure.

6 What are the main approaches and components to Employee Relations ?

7 To what extent does the HR function, in an organisation you know well, still perform its traditional welfare role?

Web and Experiential Exercises

Suggestions for Web exercises and experiential exercised for all functions are given at the end of Chapter 10 (p. 211).

The Finance and Accounting Function

❖ LEARNING OBJECTIVES

After reading this chapter you should be able to appreciate the contribution to an organisation made by the Finance and Accounting Function and the way it maintains systems concerning money. You should be able to identify the four specialist activities that the function performs – over and above the budgeting processes undertaken by all managers. In particular you'll be able to:

1 **describe** how the Finance and Accounting Function:
   - records transactions
   - manages theft and fraud
   - tracks commitments
   - manages information
   - controls costs
   - raises money

2 **explain in detail** the difference between debt financing and equity financing

3 **list** five major considerations, including depreciation, that affect investment decisions

4 **list** four ratios used to evaluate potential investments

5 **interpret** a company's profit and loss account

6 **interpret** a company's balance sheet

7 **interpret** a company's cash flow statement

8 **differentiate** between financial reporting and management accounting

9 **describe** different ways of categorising costs and **give examples** of each category

Introduction to Finance and Accounting

The finance and accounting function looks after an organisation's money but is sometimes bitterly resented. Accountants in particular may be castigated "as knowing the cost of everything and the value of nothing". Others dismiss people working in the finance and accounting function as mere "bean counters", implying that they have a narrow and myopic view. Nevertheless, the function is found in all organisations because *all* organisations need to look after their money. This chapter aims to give non-accountants or non-financial experts a general understanding of the function. The work of the finance and accounting function is very extensive and often involves taking the lead role and training other managers in the preparation and use of budgets (see Chapter 9, "Budgeting"). The other activities of the Finance and Accounting Function can be can be described in five main sections:

Chapter contents

14.1 Managing the Organisation's Money

Most people in the finance and accounting function will be involved with managing its day-to-day cash. This involves a wide range of activities such as managing credit, recording transactions, tracking commitments, etc.

Managing credit

Most customers obtain goods on credit – either short-term credit (30 days from invoice) or long-term credit where interest is charged and special arrangements are made. One of the main reasons why organisations fail is that a customer goes bankrupt owing a substantial amount of money. In turn, this loss may force the organisation itself into bankruptcy. Consequently credit control is a vital activity. The finance and accounting function will be responsible for establishing a system that will enable a customer's credit rating to be checked quickly but unobtrusively with credit reference agencies such as Experian or Equifax. Credit reference agencies provide information about individuals. Similar organisations exist to provide information on the financial standing of companies and other organisations. On the basis of this information, a sensible credit limit will be set. If this limit is exceeded the customer will only be supplied if cash is provided at the point of sale. In some industries, such as the building industry (which is notorious for its bankruptcies), supplies may only be provided in return for cash.

Recording and expediting transactions

The finance and accounting function will also need to keep records of its transactions with customers and suppliers. Nowadays, probably all of these records, except petty cash, will be maintained on a computer. An organisation must have mechanisms for claiming money from its customers by sending invoices and bills. This must be a systematic process that operates quickly. Another way an organisation can get into financial difficulty is to focus on output but ignore collecting "money due" until there is a cash crisis. Then it may have difficulty obtaining supplies or it may need to borrow money at a high rate of interest. Invoices for payment therefore need to be sent to customers either at the same time as or shortly after they have been sent goods. Some organisations calculate the following ratio to check whether it is paying its bills faster than it is receiving payments from customers:

$$DebtCredit\ Ratio = \frac{Debtors}{Creditors}$$

Similarly, the finance and accounting function must make arrangements to make payments to suppliers (disbursements). If these payments are not made promptly the organisation may be refused supplies. In particular wages of employees and taxes must be paid promptly.

Managing theft and fraud

In some organisations, such as supermarkets, large amounts of cash need to be stored and transported. The finance and accounting function needs to ensure the security of cash while it is stored and in transit. In many organisations, the prevention of theft and fraud is a major issue. A key element is the fidelity of the staff within the function itself. References and other checks must be made to establish their trustworthiness. Some organisations take out insurance to guard against embezzlement or fraud by employees who handle money and who have access to financial records. This insurance is often called a *"fidelity bond"* or *"dishonesty bond"*. The finance and accounting function must also control access to documents such as cheque-books and to computer systems. The use of the Internet by customers and the growing practice of allowing customers and suppliers access to selected parts of an organisation's information system have made computer security particularly important. Key security principles are:

- No-one in an organisation should be able to authorise payments to themselves.

- Large payments must involve authorisation by two independent people.

- Financial records need to be checked (audited) by independent people. *Internal audits* will be conducted by people from the same organisation but who work in a different department or branch and who have no connection whatsoever with the person responsible for maintaining the cash or the records. Internal audits are conducted relatively frequently, say, once every three months. *External audits* are usually conducted by personnel from an accountancy firm or organisation. External audits will be conducted, say, on an annual basis and the external auditors will be required to state whether they believe the accounts and records are an accurate reflection of the true situation.

Tracking commitments

The finance and accounting function is usually responsible for checking that the organisation's commitments are within its ability to pay. Large projects will be tracked individually and require specific authorisation. Smaller, more routine acquisitions will be delegated to managers who will have strict limits of authority. A junior manager, for example, may be permitted to authorise expenditure up to £500 whereas a director may be able to authorise expenditure up to £10 000.

Financial information and budgets

All managers in an organisation will be involved with budgets and the whole of Chapter 9 was devoted to the topic. The finance and accounting function will give individual managers and departments guidelines and advice. They will also have responsibility for co-ordinating and collating departmental budgets into a master budget. Finally, the accounting and finance function will play the lead role in collecting key financial information and preparing reports for management.

Controlling costs

Organisations must contain costs. In some organisations there is a separate sub-function to look after *"cost accounting"*. When organisations were small costs were originally considered as *"fixed costs"* in the sense that they did not vary with the volume of work – they were much the same during quiet or busy times. For example, a blacksmith's costs of staffing and managing a forge did not change very much according to the number of horses that were shod. However, as organisations became more complex, the importance of *"variable costs"* was recognised. A workshop producing 20 railway carriages per year would incur more costs than the same workshop producing ten carriages per year: it would use more materials, consume more power and employ more staff. As organisations, particularly service organisations, became still more complex, a method of **"standard costing"** was developed. In standard costing, the fixed costs are divided by the number of items produced and the result is then added to the other variable costs to arrive at a cost per item. The method works particularly well when the organisation has only one product or service. Where there are several outputs the allocation of costs is more complicated and requires estimates such as the time spent to produce an item or the percentage of resources used. Some people prefer the terms *"direct costs"* and *"indirect"* costs to the terms *"variable"* and *"fixed"* costs. The main variable costs are wages for casual workers and raw materials. A final development in costing has been the use of activity-based costing.

This section has outlined the "bread-and-butter" work performed by the finance and accounting function. There are, however, other more specialised activities performed by smaller numbers of more senior staff.

14.2 Raising Money for an Organisation

Often an organisation can profitably use more money than it has at hand. When this occurs, the finance and accounting function will be asked to raise money. This is often called "Financial Management". It generally involves raising capital plus the creation and management of an organisation's financial structure. Capital can be raised in two main ways: as debt or equity. The main distinction between them is that debt must be paid a back at some time and it increases the organisation's liabilities, whereas equity is not paid back but some of the ownership of the organisation is transferred to the person owning the money.

Debt financing

Debt financing involves a loan for a fixed period at the end of which the principal is repaid. The lender usually receives interest during the loan. However, the lender does not gain any ownership rights and debt financing is therefore favoured by people who have strong proprietorial feelings about their organisation. Debt is often classified into short-term debt (up to one year – often to cover operating costs such as rents and salaries), medium-term debt (between one and five years – often to cover the purchase of new equipment or other medium-sized assets) and long-term debt (which is usually used to purchase buildings). Normally, lenders will need to see a credible business plan, a cash-flow forecast and a projection of the financial position in future years. A lender also needs to have confidence in the organisation's senior management team. A lender will need to charge an interest rate higher than that which could be obtained by leaving the funds on deposit in a bank. Generally lenders are "risk averse" and will ask for higher rates ("*a risk premium*") if they believe the risks greater than leaving their money in a bank. Some of the main sources of debt finance are:

- **Loans from other parts of the same organisation** which have a positive cash-flows. These are often the easiest types of loan to arrange because there is a commonality of interest and the parties to the loan will know each other well.

- **Loans from individuals**. These may be wealthy people who have assets they do not need for their immediate purposes. These lenders are sometimes called "*Angels*" – especially when they are lending money to fund a theatrical or cinema production. Individuals making substantial loans are likely to require a formal agreement and guarantee or collateral that, should things go wrong, they can sell to recover their loan. The most usual form of collateral is a claim on buildings or land but it may take other forms such as securities. The owners of small companies are often required to offer their private residence as collateral. Often, very small businesses are set up using loans from family members or friends. In some parts of the world the extended family is *the* main source of funds for small organisations. Loans from family are likely to be informal and impose less rigorous conditions.

- **Loans from finance companies** are also available. Perhaps the most famous finance companies are Warren Buffett's Berkshire Hathaway investment company (that, in 2002, loaned Wal-Mart $125m to restructure its finance) and General Electric Capital

Fund. Often finance companies specialise in certain industries where they have particular expertise. Finance firms may also specialise in lending to companies at various stages of development. *Venture capitalists* specialise in lending money to business start-ups that have little or no trading history. Others, *mezzanine capitalists* have developed expertise in lending to companies who are likely to seek their stock market quotation in the near future.

- **Loans from banks** are a traditional source of finance and are available in most localities. However, banks have a reputation for being very conservative lenders.

- **Loans from governments** may also be available for organisations in certain areas that meet policy criteria such as maintaining a rural economy or offering work to groups of people who find it difficult to obtain employment.

- Government, local government and very large organisations may be able to **raise loans from the public**. Typically, they are for terms of ten years or more. Because these loans are usually safe, the interest payable (the coupon) will not be high. Government loans are called "*gilts*" or "*consols*" (*consol*idated annuities – an old form of indefinite loans to the British Government). Such loans to large companies are often called "*debentures*".

If the money is needed to acquire a tangible asset such as land, buildings or equipment it can be financed in a rather different way. It can be *leased* rather than bought outright. The organisation never owns the asset but it pays the lessor a regular rent. This means that it does not have to find the whole cost "upfront" and the rent can be paid out of current earnings. The length of a lease varies considerably. For equipment such as a photocopier or a computer the lease may be as short as one year. Buildings and land, on the other hand, frequently involve leases as long as 25 or 99 years. The finance and accounting function may prefer leasing rather than outright purchase for two reasons. First, it reduces the risk of obsolescence. The risk is transferred to the lessor since, if the machinery becomes outdated, it is returned to the lessor and the lease is terminated at the earliest opportunity. Second, there may be tax advantages in leasing a building or equipment rather than outright purchase.

Equity finance

With equity finance the person or organisation providing the money does not receive interest and there is no promise that it will be repaid. Instead a proportion of the ownership of the organisation is obtained. If the borrowing organisation is a success there will be a share in the increased value. This may consist of some combination of an increase in dividends or the value of the share which, ultimately, can be sold to someone else. If the borrowing organisation is a failure, dividends will be cut and the value of the share (equity) will decrease. In equity finance, the lender is taking a risk on the success of the borrower. Consequently, a lender will look for substantial returns. In equity finance, lenders frequently exercise considerable hands-on control of the company. When shares of the company can be bought by members of the public, individual shareholders are often passive investors but their interests are protected by legislation. Many of the shares of public companies are held by financial institutions such as pension funds. These institutions will watch their investments carefully and may insist on being represented on the organisation's board of directors. A public company must send investors accurate reports and hold a meeting at least once a year in order to appoint directors, approve accounts, approve major changes and appoint auditors. Equity finance has a number of advantages. It limits an organisation's exposure to financial risks such as changes in interest rates. New equity partners often bring useful contacts and wider expertise. However, equity finance also has disadvantages, especially loss of control. In a private company with only a few equity partners there may be personality clashes between the original owner and investors. There may also be acute difficulties when one equity partner wishes to realise their assets and sell their share of the company.

Equity financing is often provided by venture capitalists who will seek to achieve high returns within, say, five years. 3i is a classic venture capital organisation.

Larger companies have the option of raising money on a stock market. Usually, these are companies that have outgrown mezzanine finance and their *"initial public offering"* (IPO) is for the *Alternative Investment Market,* which is specifically tailored to the needs of a growing company. The AIM provides the benefits of a public quotation but it has a more flexible approach and fewer formalities than a full stock market listing. When a company joins a stock market the accounting and finance function together with its advisers issue a prospectus that states the maximum number of shares (*the share capital*) and the basis of its existence. In the UK the latter consists of its *Memorandum* and *Articles of Association.* These set out the company's constitution and the rights of shareholders. The shares are given a "nominal value" which is usually £1. The actual value of a share will change immediately they are traded and will be determined by market forces.

It should be noted that different types of share exist. *Ordinary shares* are closest to the common understanding of shares. They confer ownership of a small part of a company and they carry full voting rights. If the company fails these shareholders are the last to receive proceeds from its break-up and may receive nothing at all. There is no promise that the shares will ever be redeemed and their value will depend upon what a buyer is prepared to

CASE 14.1: 3i THE DOYEN VENTURE CAPITALIST

Before 1945 it was difficult for small, growing companies to obtain credit. In 1946 the government joined forces with major banks to form "Investors In Industry", subsequently known as 3i. Its job was to lend money to small, promising organisations that were too high a risk for commercial sources of lending. Because it involved several banks and lent to a large number of organisations, the risk of an overall loss was minimised. Indeed some of the investments were huge successes. 3i bought a share in the ownership of British Caledonian Airways for £4.5 m and later sold its share for £100 m. Generally 3i was a huge success and it was floated on the Stock Exchange. It is now a world leader in private equity and venture capital. It has a team of over 250 investment professionals whose work spans three continents. Examples of organisations obtaining venture capital from 3i are give on the company website www.3igroup.com/shareholders/about/business/venture/venture.pdf.

pay. *Preference shares* are a safer investment because there may be a redemption date and they may receive higher dividends. Furthermore, should the company fail, the holders of the preference shares will be paid before ordinary shareholders. However, preference share-holders are not usually entitled to vote at general meetings unless there has been a failure in paying their dividends

The accounting and finance function of a publicly quoted company will monitor its share price very closely since it is a reflection of the market's opinion of the company's per-formance. If the share price "underperforms" the market, the company may become a target for a takeover in which the senior management, including those in the accounting and finance function, may lose their jobs.

When an organisation needs to raise money the finance and accounting function will consider the advantages and disadvantages of each source and, with outside specialist help, select the type that is most appropriate. It will then seek to locate a short-list of specific indi-viduals and organisations. The exact mix of equity finance, long-term debt and the organisation's reserves is known as the *"capital structure"*. Probably the most important aspect of an organisation's capital structure is its *gearing (leverage)*. As noted on p. 192, gearing is a ratio of long-term debt to equity.

14.3 Investing an Organisation's Money

Types of investment

When an organisation has more money than it needs to meet running expenses, it needs make sure the surplus is spent wisely on projects that will add value. The finance and accounting function will, therefore, be deeply involved in judging possible uses. This is often called *"investment appraisal"*. Investments may be made in a wide range of activities which may include:

- new plant and equipment
- marketing and brand development
- improved systems, especially IT systems
- stocks of materials or land
- staff training, selection and motivation

Four major investment considerations

Investment projects sometimes arise from current operational demands such as the need to replace existing equipment or move to larger premises. They can also arise from reviews of marketing strategy (see p. 221). The initial screening of any investment project will involve four major considerations. Probably the first is whether the investment will further the *stra-tegic vision*. Those that lie outside the vision and do not fit current activities will cause the organisation to lose focus: it may not have the necessary expertise and it may not be able to concentrate on a number of disparate activities. The *likely rate of return* on the new investment (ROI – see pp. 190 and 294) will be another early consideration. Most organis-ations set target rates of return for investments. If early calculations show that a new investment cannot achieve this target it is likely that the project will be abandoned. The *level of risk* is the third major consideration. The finance and accounting function will be asked to forecast outcomes based on three sets of assumptions: unfavourable assumptions, likely assumptions and favourable assumptions. If the results of projections based upon the unfavourable assumptions are dire and suggest that an investment project may endanger the whole organisation, it is likely that the project will be abandoned unless some of the risk can be offset by insurance or other means. Finally, initial considerations of any project will take *affordability* into account. An investment should fit comfortably within the reserves of the organisation – or at least within its borrowing powers. Furthermore, it should not place an unreasonable strain upon the organisation's working capital and cash-flow.

Depreciation

The finance and accounting function will also estimate the rate at which a proposed investment will depreciate. Equipment will not continue working for ever: it may wear out or become obsolete. The rate at which this occurs plays a crucial role in investment decisions: the costs (which include set-up costs and training, etc.) must be written off by the time the asset comes to the end of its working life. Assets depreciate at hugely different rates. A computer system, for example may need to be written off within three years while agricultural land may not need to be "written down" at all – indeed, it may appreciate. The rate at which an organisation depreciates its assets is, to some extent, a subjective decision based upon the predicted life of the asset. There are usually regulations governing the rate at which assets can be set against tax liabilities. The level of depreciation is shown on a balance sheet and this may affect an organisation's financial standing.

Ratios for evaluating investments

The accounting and finance function will probably use a number of ratios to evaluate proposed investments as well as monitoring the performance of current investments. Usually, the ratios are discounted for inflation. In other words the calculations will take into account the fact that investments will be paid for in today's money but the income will accrue in the future when money might be worth less. Discounting for inflation makes relatively little difference in today's economy where inflation is a few per cent but it was a vital refinement in the 1970s and 1980s when inflation reached 15–20 per cent.

The simplest ratio for evaluating an investment is the **payback period**: the time it takes for net income from an investment to equal the net cost. It is a very straightforward ratio which requires little specialist knowledge. In almost all cases investments with short payback periods are better than investments whose payback period is long.

There are several ratios based upon the rate of return (sometimes called **yield**). They evaluate the average income over the life of the project and divide by the costs of the project. The *simple rate of return* is sometimes called the "*profitability index*". It is useful because it enables organisations to compare the value of a product with the options of either leaving the money on deposit in a bank or the cost of borrowing an equivalent amount. It is also useful for comparing projects that maybe quite dissimilar. It takes the present value of the net income from an investment and it divides it by the costs. Although this method does not take inflation into account, this does not matter when two projects are being compared since it is likely that both projects will be equally affected by inflation. The *discounted rate of return* takes the effects of inflation on both income and costs into account. It indicates the value of an investment in terms of constant prices. Rates of return are often used in conjunction with the internal rate of return – an internal policy which stipulates the yield that must be anticipated before an investment is made. This is usually higher than the available interest rate because it will take *"opportunity costs"* into account. An organisation may be able to borrow capital at, say, 10 per cent but it may know that most of its investments have a yield (opportunity cost) 5 per cent higher. It will therefore set its internal rate of return at 15 per cent. The organisation will not support a project which seems likely to yield 13 per cent even though this is higher than the rate at which it can borrow money – it knows that there are likely to be other opportunities where it can achieve a yield of 15 per cent or more.

The final index, the *net present value (NPV)* attempts to put a cash value on the total project. All streams of likely income from a project are discounted and added together. The cost of the project is subtracted from the total to give an estimate of how much money the project is likely to generate for the organisation. The net present value does not take the size of the project into account and is therefore most useful as a tool for comparing projects of roughly equal size.

14.4 Reporting an Organisation's Finances

The finance and accounting function will play the lead role in preparing reports on the state of an organisation's finances. Many of these reports are legal requirements. They include taxation returns and returns for sales tax or value-added tax. These must be completed correctly and to a deadline otherwise the organisation will incur heavy financial penalties. Reports also need to be made to the owners of the organisation so that they can check that the organisation is being managed effectively. For private organisations these reports will be sent to a small number of people who have a stake in the organisation and they can be almost any format that these owners consider proper. Charities will need to prepare reports for their trustees. Public bodies will need to prepare reports for the appropriate authority. Companies must prepare reports for their shareholders and potential investors. Generally, all reports, except those for the owners of private companies, are publicly available. The financial reports of an organisation usually include three specific sets of accounts: the profit and loss account; the balance sheet; and the cash-flow statement.

The profit and loss account

The profit and loss account (sometimes called an *"income statement"*) is arguably the most important of the three main accounts. It shows the extent to which an organisation is adding value to the resources it consumes. If an organisation is making a healthy profit the chances are that it will also have a healthy balance sheet and cash flow. The profit and loss account also gives some insight into how a company is making its money. A profit and loss account is best explained with a specific example. Case 14.2 gives the profit and loss account for Tesco, the UK's largest retailer. The format has been changed slightly and some minor simplifications have been made.

Tesco's profit and loss account is fairly traditional. There is a clear title, date and a statement of the period covered and the units used – millions of £. There are then three columns of figures: the present year, the previous year and the percentage change. There are also reference numbers to a series of notes contained elsewhere in the accounts.

The profit and loss account shows that in 2005 Tesco made a healthy and growing after-tax profit of £1369 million (five lines up from bottom of table). This is probably the most important conclusion to be drawn from the profit and loss account. It is also important to note that Tesco contributed £593 million to the community in taxes.

CASE 14.2: TESCO PROFIT AND LOSS 2005

TESCO PLC	2005	2004	
PROFIT AND LOSS ACCOUNT			
53 weeks ended 26 Feb 2005	£m	£m	increase
Notes			
Sales (income)	37 070	33 557	10.5%
Turnover including share of joint ventures	34 353	31 050	
2			
Less share of joint ventures' turnover	(379)	(236)	
Turnover excluding value added tax	33 974	30 814	10.3%
2			
– Normal operating expenses	(31 845)	(28 925)	
– Employee profit-sharing	(65)	(57)	
– Integration costs	(53)	(45)	
– Goodwill amortisation	(52)	(52)	
Total expenses	(32 025)	(29 079)	10.1%
Operating profit	**1949**	**1735**	**12.3%**
– Net loss on disposal of fixed assets	(53)	(9)	
+ Share of profit on joint ventures & associates	130	97	
Profit on ordinary activities before interest & taxation	**2132**	**1823**	**16.9%**
– Net interest payable	(170)	(223)	*(23.8)%*
Profit on ordinary activities before taxation	**1962**	**1600**	**22.6%**
– Tax on profit on ordinary activities	(593)	(498)	
Profit on ordinary activities after taxation	**1369**	**1102**	**24.2%**
– Minority interests	(3)	(2)	
Profit for financial year	**1366**	**1100**	**16.3%**
– Dividends	(587)	(516)	13.8%
Retained profits for the financial year	**779**	**584**	**33.3%**

The profit and loss account starts with Tesco's income, its sales of £37 070m. This is then adjusted to take account of activities in joint ventures so that the turnover for Tesco's main activity is £33 974m. The profit and loss account then details the expenses that were paid out of income. The largest expenses were the normal operating expenses of buying and distributing goods, maintaining stores, paying staff, etc. These operating expenses were £31 845 million and the operating profit was 6.1 per cent, i.e. £1949 million. In other words Tesco was transforming goods and adding 6.1 per cent value on its inputs.

The profit and loss account shows that Tesco shares some profit with its employees and that it decided to write down (depreciate or amortise) some of its goodwill. The integration costs probably rose from absorbing stores it had taken over (e.g. changing fitments, layout, staff training and possibly redundancy payments). However, Tesco's total profit was influenced by two other factors. They had decided to buy some assets and this had incurred a cost of £53 million. This relatively small sum was handsomely offset by an income of £130 million from joint activities with other organisations and people. Tesco had clearly borrowed a lot of money because it had paid £170 million in interest. While Tesco can easily service this level of debt, it is significant that it has reduced its interest payments compared to the previous year. In general, Tesco is generating plenty of money to finance its own growth. When these factors are taken into account, Tesco made a profit of £1962 million in the year ending 26 February 2005.

The remainder of the profit and loss account shows what Tesco did with its profits. Its taxes of £593 million (30 per cent of profits) have already been noted. The company distributed £587 million (30 per cent of profits) to shareholders and retained £779 million (40 per cent of profits) in its coffers to fund, no doubt, further expansion.

The balance sheet

The balance sheet is an essential tool for understanding the financial position of an organisation at a specific time, usually at the end of an accounting period. It is like a snapshot of the health of an organisation. In essence a balance sheet shows what an organisation has and what it owes. It indicates whether an organisation is in a position to expand, whether it can handle the normal ebbs and flows of revenues and expenses and whether it has sufficient cash reserves. It also indicates whether it is collecting debts quickly or whether it is slowing down its payments to others in order to avoid a cash shortage. Together with profit and loss accounts, balance sheets are the most important reports the accounting and finance function of an organisation will need to prepare. Balance sheets are best explained using a specific example and again the balance sheet from Tesco PLC has been lightly edited to make it suitable for this book. Most balance sheets have a similar format. The balance sheet itemises the company's assets, then it itemises the liabilities.

An asset is any item of economic value owned by an individual or organisation, especially those which could be converted to cash. Examples are cash, securities, accounts receivable, inventory, office equipment, a house, a car and other property. The balance sheet shows that Tesco has lots of assets, especially tangible assets such as land, buildings and vehicles (£160 953 million). It also has £1044 million of intangible assets such as goodwill, intellectual property and brand image. In addition, it has investments, joint ventures and a share in investments made by associates. All these assets would be difficult to sell in

CASE 14.3: TESCO BALANCE SHEET

TESCO PLC
GROUP BALANCE SHEET
as at 26 February 2005

		2005 £m	2004 £m
Fixed assets			
—Intangible assets		1044	965
—Tangible assets		150 495	140 094
—Investments		7	6
—Investments in joint ventures			
Share of gross assets	4208		
Less: share of gross liabilities	(4037)		
Goodwill	(145)		
Total		388	309
—Investments in associates		21	21
Total fixed assets		**160 953**	**150 423**
Current assets/Liabilities			
Stocks		1309	1199
Debtors		1002	826
Investments		346	430
Cash and bank and in hand		800	670
Total current assets		**3457**	**3139**
Creditors falling due within one year		(6072)	(5618)
Net current liabilities		**(2615)**	**(2479)**
Total assets less current liabilities		**140 338**	**130 004**
Creditors falling due after one year		(4531)	(4368)
Provision for liabilities and charges		(750)	(586)
Total net assets		**9057**	**7990**
Capital and Reserves			
Called up share capital		389	384
Share premium account		3704	3470
Other reserves		40	40
Profit and loss account		4873	4104
Equity shareholders' funds		**9006**	**7945**
Minority interests		51	45
TOTAL CAPITAL EMPLOYED		**9057**	**7990**

a hurry, say in less than a year. They are called "**fixed assets**". Tesco has a total of £160 953m fixed assets. Tesco also has assets (£3457 million) that could be realised quickly, in less than a year. These are called "**current assets**". Current assets include stocks, debtors, short-term investments and cash in the bank. A note in the annual report explains that the stocks consist of goods held for resale and development property. The £1002 million of debt consists of money owed to the business by customers and other people.

However, Tesco also owes a lot of money (£6072 million) to other people – mainly suppliers of goods. When this is taken into account Tesco owes other people a balance of £2615 million. So, if Tesco closed down and sold everything it would have a cash pile of £140 338 million. It would not have all this money for very long because organisations such as banks which have provided long-term lending would want their £4531 million to be returned. Furthermore Tesco would have to pay £750 million liabilities and charges. Consequently, Tesco would end up with "only" £9057 million – and that is what the company was worth on 26 February 2005.

Cash-flow statements

A cash-flow statement indicates how an organisation obtains funds and how it spends them. They are sometimes called "*funds flow statements*", "*Sources and Uses of Funds Statements*" and "*Statement of Changes in Financial Position*". They should conform to accepted standards such as IAS7 (International Accounting Standards 7) developed by the International Accounting Standards Committee (IASC).

Reasons for cash-flow statements

Cash-flow statements are needed because a simple balance might not give a useful picture of an organisation's cash position. It is not uncommon for very healthy companies to have a negative cash-flow – spending more than their income. These companies may be spending a lot of money developing new products and buying new machines. This spending will generate cash in the future. Very unhealthy companies may also have a negative cash-flow. They may be wasting resources on opulent offices, champagne receptions and private jets. Without a cash-flow statement it is difficult to differentiate between the two types. Cash-flow statements have two other major uses:

- Indicating whether an organisation is likely to have **enough money to pay future expenses**. If there is more than enough money the organisation should consider how it can use the surplus to add maximum value. If a deficit is likely, the organisation will need to cut costs or arrange extra finance – probably a bank loan or a loan from another unit in the same organisation.

- Helping **business planning and control**. A cash-flow forecast can be compared with the cash outcomes. This may provide an early warning that things are going wrong. It also helps future planning. The reasons for deviations from the forecast can be identified and incorporated in future plans.

It is sometimes claimed that cash-flow is a better gauge of profitability than reported income. The latter depends on many arguable accounting decisions such as when revenue is recognised and how much to allow for depreciation, etc. Cash-flow is more objective –

it is the amount of money "in the bank" (and other places) on one specific date minus the money "in the bank" on another specified date. Cash-flow is much harder to fudge than reported income.

Types of cash-flow

Cash-flows can happen in two directions: inwards and outwards. Both inflows and outflows can take many forms such as profit from selling goods and services, interest paid to a bank on loans, money that comes as a part of the purchase of another business, tax paid and so on. It is customary to organise these flows into three categories: operating activities, investing activities and financing activities:

■ **Operating activities** usually comprise the largest single flow of cash. The main exceptions to this rule arise in financial organisations such as banks and investment companies. In a healthy company the operating activities should provide a positive inflow of cash. Many details concerning the financial side of operating activities are usually given in the profit and loss account and the balance sheet. Consequently, it is customary to give only the net cash-flow from operations in a cash-flow statement. The figure of cash-flow for operating activities is very important and offers three clear signals that an organisation may be heading for trouble:

  – If operating cash-flow (OCF) is negative the organisation is eating more money than it is creating. This may be justifiable during short periods of expansion and investment. A sustained negative OCF is bad. The organisation may be reporting an income but it may not be making any "real" money.

  – If income exceeds cash-flow or if income is increasing while OCF is falling, the organisation is piling up assets that may not be worth what is claimed. For example it may be counting stocks of unsold goods or income due from customers that have not actually been collected.

  – It is often useful to look at OCF alongside sales and accounts payable (the money owed to suppliers). If sales and OCF are static or declining while accounts payable are increasing, the organisation may be attempting to ward off difficulties by delaying payments to its suppliers.

  Some companies such as Amazon.com emphasise a variant of operational cash-flow, the "**free cash-flow**". Ordinary operating cash-flow does not usually include capital investments a company must make in premises and equipment in order stay competitive. Furthermore, for many retail organisations, such as Tesco, growth is mainly in the form of opening up new stores – which takes a lot of cash. Free cash-flow takes these factors into account. In essence free cash-flow is what is left over from OCF when funds for expansion and continuing operations are subtracted. In Amazon's case, free cash-flow is the OCF minus operating interest and the costs of software and website development.

■ **Investing activities** include cash received or spent on purchases or sales of land, subsidiaries or equipment. Most companies have some form of long-term investments which are often called "financial instruments". The cash spent when these are bought or received when they are sold is also categorised under investing activities. Monies that arise from participation in joint ventures are also usually reported under this heading.

CASE 14.4: TESCO CASH-FLOW STATEMENT 2005

CASH-FLOW STATEMENT

	2005		*2004*	
	Inflows	*Outflows*	*Inflows*	*Outflows*
OPERATING ACTIVITIES				
Net cash flow from operating activities	3,004		2,942	
Balance Operating activities		*3,004*		*2,942*
INVESTING ACTIVITIES				
Dividends from joint ventures	135		60	
Interest (received [+] or paid [−])	83	−346	41	−337
Financial instruments (sale [+] or purchase [−])			235	
Fixed assets (sale [+] or purchase [−])	875	−2,561	115	−2,564
TOTAL INVESTING ACTIVITIES	1093	−2,907	451	−2,901
Balance Investment activities		*−1,814*		*−2,450*
PAYMENTS				
Tax		−483		−326
Dividends to shareholders		−448		−303
Payments [+] or to [−] short-term deposits	97			−220
TOTAL PAYMENTS	97	−931		−849
Balance Payments		*−834*		*−849*
FINANCING ACTIVITIES				
Share issues [+] or purchases [−]	146	−143	868	−51
Other loans decrease [−]		−18		−180
Leases (granted [+] or capital repaid [−]	128	−348	75	−73
TOTAL FINANCE ACTIVITIES	274	−509	943	−304
Balance Finance Activities		*−235*		*639*
INCREASE OR DECREASE IN CASH		**121**		**282**

■ **Financing activities** usually include cash obtained by long-term borrowing from the sale of bonds, stocks, shares and preference shares. If these are redeemed payments are shown as a negative cash-flow.

As an example, a substantially edited version of Tesco's 2004 cash-flow statement is given in Case 14.4.

It can be seen there was a healthy inflow of cash (£3004 million) from operating activities. Tesco also had an inflow of £1093 million from investments. This was largely the result of £856 million from sale of assets and also dividends from joint ventures. However, the cash inflows from investments were dwarfed by the £2907 million investment outflows. In the year to February 2005, Tesco spent a huge sum of £2561 million investing in fixed assets (presumably, opening new stores and buying equipment such as vehicles). The company also paid a further £346 million in interest. The company also made two large payments. It paid £483 million in tax and £448 million in dividends to its shareholders.

The result of all these financial ebbs and flows was a healthy net inflow of cash which it used, partly, to restructure its finances. The company used its healthy cash flow to restructure its finances. It made extra cash (£146 million) from the sale of shares and a useful £128 million by selling leases it no longer needed. On the other hand, it purchased shares of £143 million for trust funds and it paid £348 million due on leases. Taking everything into account, in the year to February 2005 Tesco had a healthy positive cash flow of £121 million to cope with the cash demands of the coming year.

14.5 Management Accounting

The financial reports discussed in Section 14.4 are primarily designed to inform the people outside the organisation so that they can decide whether their investments are used correctly and efficiently. However, a great deal of the work of the finance function is concerned with providing people *within* the organisation with information that helps them make day-to-day decisions and manage the organisation in the short and medium-term. This latter work by the finance function is usually called "**management accounting**". Management accounting is internal to the organisation and is usually confidential. It is therefore subjected to a lower level of external auditing and legislation. Management accounting often includes subjective data. Because managers need to take frequent decisions, management accounting reports are produced more frequently than financial reports – perhaps on a weekly or monthly basis rather than a yearly or half-yearly basis as is the case for financial reports. Management accounting data has many uses which include:

- developing business strategy
- controlling
- using resources efficiently
- improving performance and enhancing value

Management accounting is closely related to **cost accounting**, which is the process of tracking, recording and analysing costs associated with the activities of an organisation. The quantification and control of costs is a key element in ensuring that managers add value to the resources they use. Often, the first stage of cost accounting is to classify costs. One very simple classification involves dividing costs into materials, labour, power, rent, etc. This information can be collected for individual products and it can be compared with equivalent costs in the past or the equivalent costs incurred by competitors. These comparisons frequently point to areas where practical savings can be made. Many situations benefit from a more sophisticated classification where the obvious costs are subdivided and then grouped according to abstract criteria:

- **Direct costs** are those costs that can be *specifically* and *exclusively* associated with a particular product or service (a cost object). For example, the direct costs for a TV remote control will include the costs of components (raw materials), the labour costs of the people that assemble the control and the costs of packaging, etc. Generally direct costs are objective and easy to measure with great accuracy. **Indirect costs** cannot be identified specifically and exclusively with a cost object (Drury, 2005). Indirect costs are often called "overheads" and they include things like marketing and general expenses such as telephone bills and secretarial costs. Indirect costs also include a special category of **facility maintaining costs**, which are expenditures on the organisation's infrastructure such as property taxes, lighting and heating. They are completely independent of business volumes but are necessary if the organisation is to stay in business. Some organisations allocate indirect costs to products or services using a **blanket overhead rate**. They may calculate the total indirect costs and the total of direct labour hours for the whole organisation and then divide the former by the latter. For example, a large organisation may have indirect costs of £30 million and the direct production of its services may involve 2 million labour hours. Consequently, each labour hour will carry an overhead charge of £15. A service which involves three hours direct labour will incur a charge of £45 in addition to the direct costs. Blanket overhead rates are sometimes unfair and give a distorted view of true costs – especially where the indirect costs of departments differ drastically. For example, science departments in universities and colleges have much higher indirect costs than arts departments because they require more premises for laboratories, more support staff and higher insurance premiums. It would therefore be wrong to allocate the same blanket overhead rate to each hour of teaching in both faculties.

- **Fixed costs** remain the same irrespective of the number of units produced. They are often closely associated with indirect costs. For example, if the rental of an assembly machine is $1000 a month, the same rent is paid irrespective of whether it is used to produce one unit or a hundred units. **Variable costs** change with a number of units produced. They are often closely associated with direct costs. For example, if the components for a TV remote control cost $1, the variable costs will be $1000 in a week where 1000 remote controls are produced but will be $5000 in a week where 5000 remote controls are produced.

- **Incremental costs** are the extra amount needed to produce (one) extra item(s) and they are closely related to the variable cost of each item. They are sometimes called **marginal costs**. If something can be sold for the same price and variable costs are low, extra production will mean a substantial increase in profits. Sometimes, however, incremental costs can be so high that extra product will result in a loss. For example, if an assembly machine can produce a maximum of 5000 remote controls a week at a total cost of $6000, the production of 5001 remote controls would cost $7001 (6000 plus $1000 to hire another assembly machine plus $1 variable cost). The marginal cost of $1001 indicated by the management accounting system would probably dissuade managers from producing the extra unit.

- **Opportunity costs** are the value sacrificed when one choice is sacrificed in favour of another. Opportunity costs only apply to the use of scarce resources. For example, an organisation may consider selling a vacant plot of land for a profit of €4 m. However, other things being equal, it could use the land to build a factory worth €6 m, if the opportunity cost of the decision to sell would be €6 m. Management accounting information of this kind would help managers make the right decision.

Management accounting involves much more than cost accounting – although more sophisticated forms of cost accounting often form the basis of these other activities. Management accounting is frequently involved in cost–volume–profit analysis, determining product mix, forecasting profits and outsourcing decisions. Horngren et al. (2002) give further information on these and other uses.

This chapter has only provided a brief introduction to the finance and accounting function. However, it has shown that the function is vital to any organisation and the people working in it contribute far more to an organisation than "just counting beans"!

Activities and Further Study

Essay Plans

Write essay plans for the following questions:

1 What measures can an organisation take to protect itself from the risk of bad credit and fraud?

2 What is the role of the finance function in raising money for an organisation?

3 How can the finance function guide an organisation in the investment of its resources?

4 Using the published accounts of an organisation that interests you, explain the organisation's profit and loss account, its balance sheet and its cash-flow statement.

Web and Experiential Activities

Suggestions for Web and experiential exercises for all functions are given at the end of Chapter 10 (p. 211).

PART IV
Special Topics in Management

Social Responsibility and Business Ethics

15

❖ LEARNING OBJECTIVES

After reading this chapter you should understand the main aspects of ethics and social responsibility that should guide managers, their organisations and individuals in the community. You should be able to quote specific examples of unethical behaviour. In particular you should be able to:

1 **define** the concepts of ethics and social responsibility

2 **list** five philosophical approaches to ethics and for each one **briefly describe** the main concepts involved. **Give** the name of at least one person associated with each approach

3 **name** and **give at least one example** of three ways in which managers may act unethically

4 **list** nine ethical principles that should guide the behaviour of managers

5 **prioritise** the rights of individuals

who may be involved in ethical dilemmas

6 **describe** in detail strategies for upholding ethical principles

7 **name** and **give at least one example** of three ways in which organisations might behave unethically

8 **list** eight ethical principles that should guide the actions of organisations

9 **explain** the actions organisations can take in order to ensure they behave in an ethical and socially responsible way

10 **name and give at least one example** of four different ways consumers and citizens may act unethically

11 **list** four ethical principles that should guide the actions of consumers and citizens

Managers occupy positions of power. That power can be used for good or ill. Its should not be without restrictions. It must be socially responsible. The rules that define social responsibility are called "ethics". The different aspects of social responsibility and ethics are considered in six main sections:

15.1 The Nature of Social Responsibility and Ethics

Definition and concept of social responsibility

The basic idea behind social responsibility is that organisations exist within a community or social structure and therefore should contribute to wider activities to help those communities to flourish. Social responsibility means that an organisation should play more than an economic role. It may be formally defined as:

> 66 An organisation's voluntary activities which go beyond formal laws, regulations and economic goals and which help their community or society meet longer term or wider needs in fields such as the environment, arts, education and health. 99

The inclusion of the term "voluntary" is important. Organisations must already observe regulations which protect the environment and safeguard people's health. These actions are not classified as social responsibility – they are merely complying with the law.

Social responsibility is not a new concept. Many of the Quaker firms in Victorian England were seriously committed to the contribution they made to their communities. The chocolate maker Cadbury built a village, Bournville, where its workers could enjoy good living conditions. The soap manufacturer, Lever Brothers, established a similar village at Port Sunlight near Liverpool.

Some people such as Milton Friedman (1970) argue that social responsibility is not necessary for commercial organisations. He argues that the main social responsibility of managers is to operate their organisations efficiently so that they add the greatest value to the resources they consume. He argues that they are not well equipped to make decisions about the wider society. Whenever managers are using the organisation's resources for

d" they are adding to costs which must either be passed on to the consumer or
ꭓm the dividends paid to shareholders, such as pension funds.

trary view contends that organisations are not independent entities and have
ꜱ. If an organisation helps its community it is likely to flourish. If a community
   will be more able to buy the goods produced by the organisation and so the
      will flourish too. An organisation will have many kinds of stakeholder (see
   ꞑ addition to consumers and shareholders. Wider stakeholders, such as poli-
      government bodies, will control legislation or trading conditions which the
      ꞑ may need. If an organisation behaves in a socially responsible way, the wider
      ꜱ are more likely to grant access to these resources.

and concept of ethics

finition of ethics is:

> code of morals that set standards as to what is good or bad, right or
> ⸴g, in the decisions made by individuals and groups or organisations. 99

This simple definition implies that right or wrong are universally agreed properties that are
either inherent or given by God. However, ideas of right and wrong differ from person to
person and from culture to culture. Hence, ethics can only apply to those notions of right
or wrong which are shared between people or groups. On a global scale ethics may therefore be defined as:

> 66   The established customs, moral and human relationships which people in
>   general believe are right. 99

Ethics are about people's ideas of goodness. They are inextricably linked with values.
Values are relatively permanent and deeply held beliefs of the ideal states of affairs.
They play a great part in shaping our attitudes and they govern many of our personal
choices.

Brief history of ethics

The earliest surviving ethical codes are a list of rules, learned by rote by the Egyptian ruling
class in about 3000 BC. Probably the oldest philosophical literature in the world is the Indian
writings, the Vedas. They date from approximately 1500 BC and they propose an ultimate
principle, the *Ritam* from which the Western notion of "right" is developed. Western ethics
are generally derived from writings of ancient Greek philosophers who attempted to construct moral codes via logic. Jewish, Christian and Muslim ethics are essentially based upon
the interpretation of God's law.

The major philosophical approaches to ethics can be arranged under four headings:
Sophists and Sceptics, enlightened self-interest, utility and rights.

Sophist and sceptic views of ethics

Sophists were a group of philosophers who wandered ancient Greece giving talks and
instructions for a fee. Sceptics too were philosophers from ancient Greece but they questioned the grounds of accepted beliefs. Sophists and Sceptics noted that ethics have a

substantial subjective element. What is considered ethical by one person may be regarded as unethical by another. Usually the division of opinion is along the lines of self-interest: while a lower-paid worker might consider an income tax rate of 50 per cent ethical, a higher-paid worker might consider the confiscation of half of his or her hard-earned income by other people as unethical. In addition, ethical standards can change dramatically over time – even within a generation or two. Each successive generation is convinced that their ethics are better than those of previous generations.

Modern-day sceptics and sophists consider that received ethics are often a little more than the values held by committee members of a professional body at any one point in time. Indeed, a cynic might define ethics as a mechanism by which an influential group of people seek to impose their values on others.

Kohlberg (1976) believed that moral development passes through three stages. The first centres upon avoiding pain and achieving pleasure. The second involves meeting the moral standards of others and society. The best stage, only achieved by some people, is the post-conventional stage where behaviour is centred upon personal, abstract and carefully considered ethical principles.

Cynics are not impressed with such reasoning. They retort that an action can be either unsuccessful or successful. Successful behaviour puts a person in a position to impose their values on others. Accordingly, ethics follow the law of might is right. If you have the power, you determine what is and is not ethical and you get to write the history books that prove your view is justified. If the cynics and sceptics are correct, stop bothering about the nature of goodness, find out what the dominant people think is good and follow their ideas!

Enlightened self-interest

Many other philosophers claim that there is a set of universal principles which should guide human behaviour. An ethical principle that appears in many codes is "Do no harm". One should not leave the world a worse place than one found it. Improving the world a little is a bonus.

Enlightened self-interest is another ubiquitous ethical principle. It is often associated with the philosopher Hobbes and his notion of the social contract. It is based on the idea that we live in a community and many beneficial communal activities would be impossible if everyone followed their own short-term goals. For example, long-term self-interest means that we should not steal books from libraries. If everyone did so, libraries would cease to exist and we would all be deprived of their benefits. Confucius identified the principle of *reciprocity* as an important aspect of ethics. Unless, perhaps, you are dealing with a masochist, you should not do things to other people which you would not like them to do to you. This rule of thumb is often a good guide. When making a decision about other people it is worth pausing to ask the question, "would I think it reasonable if this were done to me?".

Many business ethics such as honesty, integrity, keeping one's word and ensuring the safety of employees are based on enlightened self-interest. If such ethics are followed, business and commerce prospers and an individual will have more opportunities to make a profit. Enlightened self-interest is not served by activities such as:

- giving wrong or misleading information

- refusing to honour a freely agreed contract or agreement
- giving or accepting a bribe to secure a business deal
- stealing the property of others – including intellectually property

Many commercial laws are based on the principles of enlightened-self interest and tend to punish behaviour which would disrupt orderly trading.

Milton Friedman, famous economist and Nobel Laureate maintains enlightened self-interest should be interpreted quite narrowly. He argues that the only responsibility of a manager is to maximise profits, within the rules of the game. Companies who devote resources to other activities are being unethical because they are jeopardising their competitiveness and exposing themselves to the risk of bankruptcy, where shareholders lose their capital and workers will lose their jobs. It can also be argued that companies have no mandate (Stone,1990) or special ability to make decisions except on the basis of long-term profits. Friedman (1970) wrote: there is only one social responsibility of business – to use its resources and engage in activities designed to increase profits so long as it stays within the rules of the game, and engages in free competition without deception or fraud. Friedman takes the view that corporate social responsibility beyond enlightened self-interest is a subversive form of taxation. Shaw (1991) goes further and points out that the demands of social responsibility may represent a covert attempt by government to shift its own responsibilities to commercial organisations.

Writers such as Mintzberg (1983) and Carr (1968) argue that organisations should take a much broader view of self-interest. They should be socially responsible in order to head off government legislation. Socially responsible behaviour enhances an organisation's public image and this has a direct impact on long-term viability. Organisations do not operate in a vacuum. They draw resources from the wider society and business decisions may have an impact on many people. Consequently business decisions always have ethical implications.

Utilitarian approach

The utilitarian approach is probably the dominant approach towards organisational ethics today and it is used to justify many management decisions. It emphasises efficiency and effectiveness. The utilitarian approach is linked to the religious belief that right and wrong stem from the will of God. God wills the happiness of his creatures. So, whatever increases the sum total of happiness is right and whatever decreases the sum of total happiness of God's creatures is wrong.

The utilitarian approach is often associated with philosophers such as Bentham and John Stuart Mill. Bentham made a radical claim for his time when calculating the net effects of good or bad. Each person (male or female, black or white) should be counted equally. Bentham's ideas are fundamental to democracy. Majority interests are always paramount because this produces the greatest good. The majority can therefore bestow or extract whatever it wishes from a minority. Stuart Mill demurred in an aristocratic way. He introduced the notion of the quality of happiness. He suggested it was better to be a Socrates dissatisfied than a fool satisfied. The utilitarian approach is fundamentally concerned with the consequences of behaviour.

Many management decisions are made in a utilitarian way. An organisation may decide to shed 10 per cent of its workforce in order to protect the jobs of the remaining 90 per cent.

A government may decide to promote a vaccination programme by which the health of the majority will be safeguarded, although it might make some people ill. Utilitarian ethics imply that the ends justify the means. If six million people need to be exterminated in order the safeguard the health of 60 million people then, according to an extreme utilitarian, so be it – the six million people need to be exterminated. Some people may consider such ethics as *the tyranny of the majority*.

Utilitarian ethics can be criticised on two grounds. First, it is usually very difficult indeed to perform an accurate cost–benefit analysis. The calculations may be too complex. The data may be unobtainable or may consist of inaccurate estimates. There is also the question of who may legitimately perform the calculation and what weight they attach to the valuation of various outcomes. Second, the harm to the individuals of the minority may be so great or so intense that it may be unacceptable.

Rights

Philosophers such as Locke took up the idea of rights which were incorporated in the English Magna Carta of 1215. The rights of the Magna Carta benefited barons. Locke extended rights to all people and the concept of human rights has become a bulwark against the tyranny of the majority. According to Locke an individual is born with certain rights and she or he does not surrender all of these to the community. Jefferson, a major contributor to the American Declaration of Independence, listed the main unalienable human rights as: life, liberty and the pursuit of happiness. Since then scores of additional rights have been claimed, discovered or invented. Two of the most important codes of human rights are probably the UN Declaration of Human Rights (www.un.org/overview/rights.html) and the European Convention on Human Rights (www.hri.org/docs/ECHR50.html).

Large sections of employment law are based on the concept of rights. The right of workers to have a safe working environment was recognised almost 100 years ago. More recent legislation covers the right to be consulted before a major redundancy, the right to compensation after a redundancy, the right to belong to a trades union and rights to protect workers from unfair dismissal. Equal opportunities legislation is based on the principle that the rights of women and minorities needs protection. More recently, the right to privacy has become an ethical issue.

Often individuals or minorities use the idea of rights to extract benefit from other people without offering reciprocal responsibilities. In some circumstances the idea of human rights can lead to "the tyranny of the minority" where a minority can extract unreasonable concessions on the basis of its own perception of human rights. Many people claim that a right reflects an inherent quality. In fact we have no inherent rights. They are granted by others who are in power. Rights can change when others cease to believe in them. In the past monarchs and their subjects believed in the Divine Right of Kings – until, that is, parliament decided otherwise and beheaded one of them.

Justice

Ethics are often bound up with perceptions of **justice**. Some people regard justice as a special human right but it is often treated separately in the literature. Gilliland (1993) identified two main aspects of justice: procedural and distributive.

Procedural justice concerns the consistency with which rules are implemented. It is often relevant to selection systems. It is unethical to treat some people in a favourable way because, say, they are relatives of senior managers. All candidates should be treated in an equivalent way and asked only for information which is clearly relevant to the performance of the job (Smither et al., 1996). Procedural justice is also involved in promotion decisions, setting salary levels and disciplinary matters.

Distributive justice concerns the correctness of the final decision in terms of a balance between what a person puts into a situation and the rewards they receive. Distributive justice inevitably involves placing a value on these inputs and outputs and these evaluations will vary from person to person. Distributive justice is, therefore, often based on subjective decisions. Notions of fairness and equity are heavily dependent upon cultural norms. What is fair in one society is unfair in another. An hourly wage of £4 is regarded as unfair exploitation in the UK in the year 2007 but, even allowing for inflation, it was a very equitable rate of pay in the UK in the year 1907. Today, an hourly rate of £4 would also be regarded as very fair payment in Angola. A cynic might contend that fairness is whatever you can fool others into believing.

Many ethical dilemmas depend upon notions of fairness. For example, a worker may have exceeded targets every month for 10 years until the last year when he has consistently failed to achieve them. His boss is also under pressure to achieve his goals by firing his subordinate. What, in this case would be the fair course of action? The outcome would probably depend on the tenure of the boss. If the boss has been in post 11 years and has benefited from previous high performance, the subordinate would probably keep his job. If the boss had been in post for a year it is probable that the subordinate would be fired. Is it fair that an individual's future should depend on the tenure of his or her boss? Procedural justice and distributive justice are, in fact, highly correlated (Brockner and Wiesenfeld, 1966; Sheppard and Lerwicki, 1987; Leck, Saunders and Charbonneau, 1996).

15.2 Business Ethics for Individual Managers and Professional Workers

Examples of bad ethical behaviour by individuals

Bad ethical behaviour by individuals can take many forms. Perhaps the three most frequent problems involve bribery, conflict of interest and abuse of authority.

Bribery

Bribery is unethical because it is a secret pact that is not open to examination (rights) and it undermines fair competition (enlightened self-interest). It may result in either excessive costs or the purchase of inferior goods or services (utilitarianism). Examples of bribery concern voting for Olympic venues, Lew Rywin (Case 15.1) and some local authorities.

Bribery is not confined to individuals or commercial organisations. Government and quasi-government officials have also been mentioned in media reports of bribery. Local governments in the UK such as Barnsley and Lambeth were once involved in scandals where officials were bribed to award lucrative contracts to certain businesses. In New York, court officials were bribed to ensure that certain cases were assigned to a judge who was known to be favourable. The anti-corruption organisation, Transparency International, surveyed the

CASE 15.1: BRIBERY AND THE OLYMPIC GAMES

It was alleged that an attempt was made to bribe certain members of the **International Olympic Committee** (IOC) to vote in favour of Salt Lake City as the venue for the winter Olympics, 2002. In August 2004 a BBC programme, *Panorama*, set up a sting operation where its reporters posed (unethically?) as promoters and filmed a Bulgarian member of the IOC, Ivan Slavkov accepting a bribe. He was immediately suspended by the International Olympic Committee. It was suspected that more than 30 of the 124 committee members were open to bribes. Ivan Slavkov explained that he only accepted the bribe in order to uncover the identities of corrupt sports promoters.

Another high profile example of bribery involved **Lew Rywin**, a co-producer of the Oscar winning film *Schindler's List*. He solicited a £10 million bribe from a Polish newspaper in return for a promise to influence legislation on the media. In fact, Lew Rywin was rewarded with a two-and-a-half-year prison sentence.

propensity of companies from various countries to offer bribes. A score of 10 indicates no bribery whilst a score of 1 indicates ubiquitous bribery. The results for the 2002 survey are shown in Figure 15.1.

Bribery is most rampant in construction and public works, arms and defence and in the oil and gas industries. Some people regard bribery as the biggest obstacle to world economic growth and there have been attempts to reduce its extent. The OECD has produced an Anti-Bribery Convention (ratified by those countries in the table marked with an *). However, only 19 per cent of people responding to the survey were familiar with the Convention.

Country	Ratified	Score	Rank	Country	Ratified	Score	Rank
Australia	*	8.5	1	Spain	*	5.8	11
Sweden	*	8.4	2=	France	*	5.5	12
Switzerland	*	8.4	2=	USA	*	5.3	13=
Austria	*	8.2	4	Japan	*	5.3	13=
Canada	*	8.1	5	Malaysia		4.3	15=
Netherlands	*	7.8	6=	Hong Kong		4.3	15=
Belgium	*	7.8	6=	Italy	*	4.1	17
United Kingdom	*	6.9	8	South Korea	*	3.9	18
Singapore		6.3	9=	Taiwan/China		3.6	19/20
Germany	*	6.3	9=	Russia		3.2	21

FIGURE 15.1 Prevalence of Bribery in 20 Countries

In many circumstances the situation is less clear. Part of the problem lies in the difficulty of defining bribery in a way which distinguishes it from a legitimate business fee. Bribery often masquerades under other names such as "a success fee", "an introduction fee", "an arrangement fee" or even "a gift". Nevertheless, a gift may place the recipient in a situation where he or she feels an obligation to respond favourably. For example, a medical practitioner who accepts free flights and accommodation for a conference at an exotic location from a pharmaceutical company may, at a subconscious level, be more likely to prescribe one of that company's medicines.

Bribery has a cultural aspect. In some cultures giving gifts is a routine activity denoting respect. Under these circumstances refusal to accept a gift causes offence. In other cultures a small bribe to a lowly paid government employee is an accepted method of "expediting" the progress of a form. Pressure from developed countries to abandon these practices is often viewed as ethical imperialism. Furthermore, companies from countries where giving bribes to foreign officials is illegal complain that their commercial activities, and hence jobs at home, are being handicapped because they are not competing on a "level playing field".

Despite such protestations, large gifts and bribes should not be sought or accepted. They damage free competition and trade. Consumers do not get the best goods or services at the best price. Bribes can also have major consequences for the donor. For example, the Lockheed Martin Corporation – renowned for its space and aeronautics equipment – was set to buy the Titan Corporation in a lucrative deal for Titan's owners. When, however, Lockheed Martin discovered that Titan was under investigation for suspected overseas bribery they called the deal off. Accepting small gifts is a matter of discretion. Generally it should be avoided. Where exchange of gifts is necessary in order to maintain friendly relationships the gifts should be open and their value should be proportionate. Usually a gift which costs more than a good lunch should be declared in an appropriate register. It may also be both prudent and tactful to donate such gifts to other people or charitable organisations.

Conflicts of interest

Organisations or clients must be sure that the people they are paying are working for their best interests and not the best interests of someone else (rights and justice). People have a right to be told the truth rather than misrepresentations which suit other interests. People and organisations bidding for work expect procedural justice – the same rules apply to everyone. People and organisations paying for goods and services also expect distributive justice – effort will be expended on behalf of those who are paying the bill. Examples of conflicts of interest are given in Case 15.2.

Transactions involving land or property seem particularly prone to conflicts of interest. For example, in December 2002 Allan D. Grecco, a local authority real estate director in Long Island, New York, was forced to resign after accusations that he had brokered a land purchase at an inflated price to someone with whom he had business connections. In another instance a member of Manhattan City Housing Authority was fined $2250 after admitting that he had used his office to help his daughter get a job with a contractor working for the city. Estate agents (realtors) seem to attract many complaints of conflict of interest. For example, some estate agents have been known to refuse to pass on offers made by purchasers who will not provide commission from buying services such as insurance.

CASE 15.2: CONFLICTS OF INTEREST

Ex-cabinet minister, **Peter Mandelson** was the minister in charge of the Department of Trade and Industry which, at the time, was investigating the business affairs of a Mr Robinson. However, Mandelson, had already accepted a substantial loan from Mr Robinson in order to buy a house in a chic district of London. Mandelson foolishly omitted to declare his interests to either the organisation providing the rest of the mortgage or to Parliament. The affair resulted in Mandleson's dramatic resignation.

Kojo Annan is the son of Kofi Annan the head of the United Nations. In 2004 Kojo was investigated over an alleged role in a company that negotiated the sale of millions of barrels of Iraqi oil under the discredited UN oil-for-food scheme. The question arose whether Kojo unwittingly lent his name and influence to a company that was awarded a contract. The Secretary-General categorically stated that neither he nor his son had any connection with the awarding of (the) contract.

Stock analysts belonging to the merchant bank **Merrill Lynch** wrote reports recommending whether investors should buy or sell shares. Merrill Lynch also had an investment banking division which, for a fee, helped companies sell their stocks to investors. The large salaries of the analysts depended upon the fees earned by the investment division. In 2003 the Securities and Exchange Commission complained that the analysts' reports were not independent and that the analysts had allowed their banking colleagues to influence their advice to clients. New York State Attorney Eliot Spitzer said that the investment advice was biased and distorted in order to secure and maintain lucrative banking contracts. Emails emerged which indicated that the analysts "said" one thing in public and another thing in private. These comments were angrily rebutted by Merrill Lynch, which was outraged that emails were taken out of context. Without admitting wrongdoing, it later paid $100 million and agreed to apologise and sever all links between analysts' pay and investment banking activities.

The best defence against conflicts of interest is *avoidance*. For example, many law firms will not accept instructions if they already have any legal dealings with people already in a legal dispute with the prospective client. Another mechanism, often used by politicians and public officials, is to place assets in a *"blind trust"*. For example, it is quite permissible for the Prime Minister to hold shares – even though the decisions he or she makes can directly affect their value. Trustees of a blind trust act without any communication or information from the Prime Minister. Since he or she will not know the composition of his or her portfolio the Prime Minister can make decisions without any conflict of interest. Some companies avoid conflicts of interest by constructing *Chinese Walls* and *Cones of Silence*. After the Merrill Lynch affair, many financial institutions separated their research analysts from their investment bankers and do not allow information to pass between them – as though the Great Wall of China has been extended through their organisation. A "cone of silence" exists when an organisation forbids contractors or their lobbyists to contact its officials (whether they are a few important people at the top of the cone or many people lower down), when they are bidding for new work. Often, a cone of silence is imposed once a shortlist of contractors has been drawn up. In many cases a cone of silence may be enforced by fining organisations or summarily dismissing their bid if they attempt to break through the cone. Conflicts of interest in public life can be mitigated, but not avoided, by *recusal* – abstaining from voting on any issue where one has a conflict of interest. In some circumstances a stronger form of recusal, *physical absence*, is needed. For example, in university examination boards, if a candidate is a relative, friend or business associate of an examiner, that examiner is required to leave the room. If all else fails, a conflict of interest can be mitigated by a *declaration of an interest*. For example, had Peter Mandleson declared his loan from Mr Robinson, he would have probably escaped the need to resign.

Improper use of authority and power

Managers and people in professional positions have considerable authority and power which may play a decisive role in the lives (and deaths) of other people. This power should be used in an ethical way. There are many examples of improper use of power. They include the Challenger Space Shuttle Disaster, abuse of professional trust and taking credit for other people's achievements.

The Challenger episode (Case 15.3) raises major issues about the improper use of managerial authority. Was NASA justified to press for a launch decision? Were the four members of Thiokol management justified in reversing their initial decision and excluding the engineers from the crucial vote? Did the engineers fail to use their authority by allowing themselves to be over-ruled by management?

Consequences of improper use of authority are rarely as dramatic or as well documented as the Challenger case. However, unethical use of authority arises quite frequently. Some managers may use their authority unethically to divert resources for their own benefit. For example, one headmaster abused his authority by ordering school technicians install a new kitchen at his home. Another common abuse is to deny subordinate staff proper recognition for their work and claiming their staff's achievement's for themselves. This occurs in academic life where members of staff publish student work without giving appropriate credit.

Principles of business ethics for managers and professional workers

Many professional bodies have developed their own ethical codes. Managers should be familiar with the relevant ethical codes of their vocation and country. Most ethical codes cover nine main points:

1 fair advertising
2 competence
3 self regard
4 informed consent
5 freedom to withdraw
6 confidentiality
7 respect for social codes and multicultural sensitivities
8 professional relationships between colleagues
9 principles of fees and financial arrangements

CASE 15.3: ABUSE OF POWER AND THE CHALLENGER SPACE SHUTTLE DISASTER

The US Government inaugurated the Space Shuttle Programme in order to beat the Russians in space. The contract to build the booster rockets was given to a company called Morton-Thiokol. Between 1980 and 1984 45 launches were planned – but the actual outcome was only 17. Moreover, NASA was facing unforeseen commercial competition from the European Space Agency. In November 1981 potential weaknesses were found in seals that contained the gases of the booster rockets. A launch in 1985 provided actual evidence that the vital seals, the "O rings", could actually fail – especially when the outside temperature was low. NASA management was told about the problem.

In January 1986 a launch was delayed three times due to bad weather conditions – putting the programme further back. Another launch was scheduled but the weather forecast was again bad: an outside temperature in the region of −3°C was predicted. The Thiokol rocket programme director asked engineers for advice and a three-way telephone conference was held between Thiokol in Utah, Cape Canaveral in Florida and the Space Flight Control in Alabama. The presentation by Thiokol engineers lasted over an hour and ended with the recommendation that the launch be delayed. The project manager at flight control centre said that the evidence was inconclusive. He bypassed the actual engineers and referred the matter to the most senior manager at Thiokol. He supported his engineers and did not recommend a launch. In a heated discussion NASA staff said they were appalled by the recommendation not to launch. The conference was interrupted for five minutes while the evidence was reviewed by Thiokol personnel. Despite continued opposition by the engineers, the managers (the engineers were excluded from the vote) decided that the launch should go ahead. NASA accepted the new decision.

Fifty-nine seconds after the launch the seals failed. The rocket exploded. Seven crew members died.

Principle of Fair Advertising

There is nothing wrong with advertising and promoting goods and services. Indeed advertising increases market size, which eventually leads to economies of scale and less expensive products. However, advertising needs to be fair, accurate and socially responsible (see Chapter 11, pp. 231–237). In general:

- Qualifications, training and affiliations should be represented accurately.
- Information should not be withheld in order to promote misunderstandings.
- Employees of the press, radio television or other media should not be paid in return publicity. Paid advertisments should be clearly identified as such.

The principle of fair advertising extends to the statements of others – especially those who are paid to promote the service or product. If they make a deceptive or full statement on behalf of an organisation the organisation must make reasonable efforts to issue corrections.

Principle of competence

The principle of competence means that managers should operate to high technical and professional standards. Difficult decisions are often necessary and cannot be shirked. The managers who make them should be competent and qualified. They should not get involved in situations where they could not cope should things go wrong. This means being able to cope with the worst case. A key to observing this principle is to recognise one's own limits and operate within them.

In a changing world, this principle also imposes the need to extend competence. It is relatively easy to extend *personal competence* by training and development. The main difficulty is obtaining experience in a way that does not harm others.

Principle of self-regard and welfare

Human dignity should be upheld. People should not be harmed except in very exceptional circumstances. This includes psychological harm. Actions involving *humiliation*, embarrassment and harm to people should be avoided. If such tactics seem *absolutely* necessary *a second opinion should be obtained*. This may be provided by an impartial senior colleague or by an "ethics committee". In this context, degradation or embarrassment must be seen through the eyes of lay people, not through the eyes of managers or professionals who may have become blasé or burnt out after years of work in the field.

Principle of informed consent

People have the right to know what they are letting themselves in for before they make any significant comment. They should have reasonable information on:

- the processes to be used
- the uses to which the information will be put
- the "ownership" of information
- the identity the people and organisations involved

Freedom to withdraw

People are expected to keep agreements that have been willingly agreed. However, there may be a problem over the definition of the term "willing". For example, is a parent taking out a second mortgage in order to buy medical treatment for their child a willing vendor? However, rather different rules apply to professional services and participation in experiments. People are free to withdraw from a professional relationship after giving due notice and paying appropriate fees. People are free to withdraw at will from experiments.

Principle of confidentiality

In the vast majority of circumstances, information obtained on a confidential basis should not be divulged to others without explicit, preferably written, consent.

There are, however, some situations where the principle of confidentiality should be breached. They include situations where people are likely to be a danger to themselves or others. They also arise when people are involved in illegal activities. Even in these cases a second impartial opinion should be sought. Information should only be disclosed to authorities when there is clear legal authorization. In almost all circumstances the law must be obeyed – even if you have formed your subjective opinion that the law of the land is silly!

Respect for social codes

People should show sensible regard to the *social codes* and *moral expectations* of the community in which they work. For example, an atheist doing maintenance work in a monastery should not engage in blasphemous behaviour that causes gratuitous offence. If one cannot be tolerant and courteous to the people in an organisation it is better not to accept work in that organisation in the first place.

Relationships with others

A final set of ethics covers relationships with others. Many aspects of relationships with others are covered elsewhere. However, it is worth pointing out that managers and professional workers should avoid body contact with employees or clients other than customary greetings such as shaking hands or giving "a pat on the back". Any form of activity with clients which could be construed as sexual or likely to reduce objectivity must be avoided.

Ethics relating to professional colleagues usually concern boundaries and roles. A general principle is to agree, in advance, an orderly, explicit arrangement concerning roles, rights and obligations. Harassment of other people, especially junior colleagues, should be avoided. A professional worker should avoid interfering with or inhibiting the work of another professional. While the ideas, theories and data of another person can, and should be, scrutinised, personal "*ad hominem*" attacks should be avoided.

Fees and financial arrangements

There is a cardinal ethical principle concerning fees: *fee structure and terms of payment should be made clear during, or immediately after, an initial meeting or consultation* (Francis, 1999). Sometimes broaching the matter of fees can be "delicate" and it is often appropriate to send a short letter confirming acceptance of an assignment together with a sheet setting out the fee rate, the estimated length of the assignment and the terms of the payment. A client should be notified immediately if it is apparent that costs are likely to exceed the initial estimate. Fees for missed appointments and cancelled meetings often need clarification. As a general rule, some level of fee is appropriate for second and subsequent cancellations.

Up to a limit, "*pro bono publico*" work should be encouraged. "Gift work" serves two main purposes. It provides a way of returning to society the gifts and benefits that have been received. This is in addition to paying taxes and levies. A clear policy of giving, say, 5 per cent of one's time as "gift work" avoids ambiguities and helps defend against unreasonable demands. Sinclair and Pettifor (1991) give a useful guide to the work that can be undertaken on a *pro bono publico* basis. Other ethical aspects of financial ethics include prompt payment of bills and, whenever possible, the avoidance of arrangements involving barter. Where barter is absolutely necessary, the items bartered should be translated into monetary terms and recorded.

Ethical dilemmas

Many, possibly the majority, of ethical problems are not a simple question of right and wrong but arise from a dilemma between two sets of ethical rights. Such dilemmas can often be resolved by placing ethical obligations in order of precedence.

The rights of a **client** (i.e. the person across the desk) have the highest priority. In this context the client may not be the person who commissions the work or pays the bill. For example, an HR director of an organisation may commission an outplacement organisation to offer careers guidance to managers whose job is redundant. The outplacement organisation may employ a consultant psychologist to administer and interpret tests. In this case, the outplaced manager is the psychologist's client, not the outplacement organisation or the previous employer.

The interests of **the profession** are generally placed in second position (see Francis 1999). This may give rise to acute problems in organisations such as the army where a person might be ordered by a senior officer to divulge information. Such dilemmas can be resolved by creating a specific corps of, say, doctors. A senior officer within the specialist corps may, for example, demand information whereas a senior officer outside the specialist corps may not.

There is much less agreement on the precedence of other rights. Much will depend upon the precise circumstances. Perhaps the rights of the person commissioning the work and paying the fee should generally rank third and the rights of the manager or professional should rank fourth. Other generalised or unspecific rights will normally rank fifth or lower.

Upholding ethical principles

The most obvious way of upholding ethical principles is to avoid violating them oneself. You should also set an example to junior colleagues and members of the public by being seen to be ethical – *without* behaving like a sanctimonious prig! Difficult situations can arise when unethical behaviour of others is witnessed. Much depends upon the seriousness of the ethical breach. The main objective must be to ensure that the unethical behaviour is discontinued.

Minor ethical breaches

With minor and occasional infractions it is best to take low-level, informal action. Many, probably most, minor unethical acts arise from enthusiasm or ignorance of the ethical implications. Here a light-hearted and informal comment will often be a sufficient remedy.

Significant ethical breaches

In more serious cases the appropriate action is a substantive conversation. The dangers of the unethical act can be explained in a helpful way. It is often easiest to emphasise the dangers to the perpetrator (the victim might complain to professional body – certification might be withdrawn – the organisation will suffer from bad publicity, etc.) The intervention will be more effective if positive hints about how the ethical principles *can* be maintained are given. It is also possible offer a copy of the appropriate code of ethical conduct.

Serious ethical breaches

Where unethical behaviour is pre-meditated, mendacious, frequent or serious, stronger action must be taken. The perpetrator should be told, point-blank, preferably in writing, to desist forthwith. For example, one personnel manager in an organisation where interviewers had received equal opportunities training would bluntly tell erring interviewers, in front of colleagues and interviewees that "You know you cannot ask that or similar questions – stop now". A violent reaction must be expected. The unethical person is likely make accusations of unreasonableness, nosiness, bossiness and attempting to put them down!

Whistleblowing

Revealing unethical or illegal behaviour of one's employer is called "Whistle-blowing" (Miceli and Near, 1994). It raises big issues because the whistle blower, acting in the interests of the wider community, can bring serious sanctions upon themselves. Whistle-blowers may be fired or their promotion prospects blocked. In some countries there are laws protecting people against such retaliation but they are hard to enforce and financial awards by the courts are usually small. Whistle-blowing is particularly difficult in organisations with ambiguous priorities, with a strict chain of command that makes it difficult to bypass an immediate superior and where there are strong group affiliations. Some organisations view whistle-blowers as assets (Near, 1989) who help identify problems at an early stage. The problems can then be rectified before becoming a major issue that could threaten the organisation's future.

If an organisation does not have "whistle-blowing" procedures, it is probably wise to confide in a third person who can take the matter further. If the unethical behaviour has caused, or is likely to cause, serious damage, it should be reported to the appropriate professional organisation or victims. Except in emergency situations a whistle-blower should make absolutely sure that they understand the situation and that their viewpoint is accurate. In most situations it is preferable to wait two days between observing an unethical act and reporting it to others; the delay will help to put the facts into perspective. When making formal complaints, a whistle-blower should make sure they stick to specific observations that they can prove. They should beware of hearsay evidence and should ensure the complaint is not libellous or slanderous. Whistle-blowers should not assume that the law will protect them even if they are proved to be correct. It may be advisable to take legal advice before reporting major ethical breaches. It is important to make accurate notes and gather other documentary evidence which should generally be stored outside your organisation. Although it may be very tempting, it is usually a mistake to involve the media as a first step in revealing serious ethical breaches.

15.3 Business Ethics and Social Responsibilities for Organisations

Ethics is not just a matter for individuals. Organisations sometimes make unethical decisions.

Examples of questionable organisational ethics

Unethical organisational behaviour includes giving misleading information, exploiting less-developed countries and exploiting emotions.

Misleading or untrue information

Perhaps the most serious types of unethical behaviour is misleading shareholders, clients and employees. Issuing misleading financial information by concealing debt from the balance sheet is particularly heinous. It has caused spectacular problems for organisations such as Polly Peck, Maxwell Communications and Enron (Case 15.4).

Exploiting undeveloped countries

Some multinational companies have been accused of unethical exploitation. Nike, for example, has been accused of employing children in Pakistan at a very low wage to stitch footballs. Nike is not alone. GAP has been accused of employing child labour in Cambodia and Benetton has been accused of paying low wages to children employed in Turkey.

Unethical and socially irresponsible activities in underdeveloped countries are not restricted to the use of child labour – as Case 15.5 shows. The issues involved in these cases are complex. In many countries child labour is traditional and is an essential contribution to family budgets. Sometimes the children provide fake evidence of their age so that they can work in a factory. A wage of 50 pence per hour may not buy many luxuries in a country where the average wage is £25 000 but it buys a lot of essentials in a country where the average annual wage is £250! Furthermore, unethical activity is often conducted by indigenous subcontractors and is discontinued when drawn to the attention of the multinational company. Nike, for example, withdrew contracts from their Cambodian sub-contractor. It stipulated that other contractors must check birth certificates more carefully and enforce a minimum age of 18.

CASE 15.4: HEINOUS ENRON

Enron was a national gas pipeline company based in Houston, Texas. In 1985 it had assets of about $12 billion – not enough to be included in the top 500 US companies – a significant but not outstanding organisation. Under aggressive new management that emphasised results and which used sophisticated financial structures it experienced phenomenal growth. By 2001 it was the seventh largest US company with assets of $33 billion and a share price of $90.

It was an illusion. The sophisticated financial structures involved partnerships and special arrangements under which any losses were kept out of Enron's main accounts. When the stock market fell, losses started piling in. Enron's concealed losses became common knowledge. In 2002 it filed for bankruptcy. The share price plummeted to zero. One senior executive committed suicide, others are serving long prison sentences. The chief executive has been indicted on fraud charges carrying a prison sentence of 30 years and a fine of $5.75 million. The grief of Enrons's concealed debts did not stop there. Its auditors, probably the most prestigious auditors in the world, were deemed negligent. They were caught shredding evidence and have since gone out of business. Perhaps the people who suffered most were private shareholders – including Enron employees who had loyally invested their retirement savings in the company.

Emotional exploitation

Some organisations use shock tactics and exploit emotions in pursuit of their goals. This is sometimes called *"shock and awe"* advertising. It is used by charitable and political organisations who are passionately convinced of their cause. Sometimes shock and awe techniques are used for profit by celebrities, the media and commercial organisations for their own benefit.

The use of shock tactics by charities is easy to understand: so many people die of lung cancer it may be justified to use graphic TV adverts portraying diseased lungs or putrid blood vessels. Nonetheless, a larger number of innocent non-smokers may feel bad when they are bombarded by these images. The charity values their feelings as zero. Furthermore, the majority of cigarette smokers do not die of lung cancer and the shock campaigns may have caused them unnecessary anxiety which has detracted from their sense of well-being. Children and other relatives of occasional smokers may become unnecessarily unhappy and anxious. The charity, for very laudable reasons, believes it is justified in causing such distress.

The cynical use of shock tactics by celebrities and the media is less ethical. They may use the misfortunes of others to increase their own reputations. When the spotlight fades and the media circus leaves town there may be little improvement in the underlying plight. Indeed the publicity may have made the plight worse – leaving a divided community with a poorer image. An analogous situation sometimes occurs with emergency aid. The aid may make local farms or businesses uncompetitive and they may cease to exist. When the aid stops, the community may not be able to support itself. Sometimes organisations are accused of exploiting ethical issues for commercial gain. Case 15.6 identifies some of the problems encountered by Benetton.

CASE 15.5: BENETTON'S LAND GRAB AND NESTLE'S MILK

Benetton has become involved in an affair known as the "United Colours of Land Grab". The Mapuche people live in Patagonia, Argentina, and believe they have acquired ancestral rights to some of the land. Benetton "Compania" is the largest landowner in Argentina and uses it to raise sheep for wool to make sweaters. In 1991 Benetton acquired more land in Patagonia and in 2002 it evicted a Mapuche family who had started to cultivate a farm on unused land. An Argentinean court has ruled that, in fact, Benetton was the legal owner.

Nestlé have been accused of exploitation by marketing baby milk in undeveloped countries. Artificial milk may lead to deaths because, unlike mothers' milk, it needs to be mixed with water, which is often contaminated. Moreover, giving mothers free initial supplies of baby milk causes their breast milk to dry up. Thereafter they were forced to buy the artificial milk at prices they can barely afford. Nestlé claims that the statistics used by its critics imply that all babies who die from diarrhoea do so as the result of bottle feeding – whereas, in fact, few mothers in developing countries use artificial milk. Nestlé supports the World Health Organisation's code and does not now give free samples or advertise its infant formula to the public. It has set up an "ombudsman system" so that any transgressions of its policies can be reported and acted upon.

CASE 15.6: THE UNITED EXPLOITATION BY BENETTON

Advertising campaigns by Benetton have been heavily criticised for using images that evoke powerful emotional responses. The images have included emotive pictures of pictures of AIDS victims on their deathbed, horses copulating, newborn babies covered in blood and a priest kissing a nun. Benetton justifies their use because, as a socially responsible company, it is interested in the social conditions in which its employees and customers live. It is therefore socially responsible for the company to use controversial adverts to raise important issues about society.

Not everyone agrees. A court in Frankfurt concluded that Benetton tries to appeal to compassion in order to earn money. A number of Benetton adverts have been banned in the UK and elsewhere. Some magazines have refused them. Some assert Benetton has cynically exploited controversies in order to draw attention to their brand name, their products and to obtain hectares of free press and media coverage. The ethics of Benetton's "Death Row" campaign attracted a particularly high level of criticism. The campaign featured pictures and interviews with 26 convicted murders awaiting execution. The men were featured in a sympathetic way, focusing on their regrets and their plight but giving few details of their crimes. They included serial murders. One murderer featured by Benetton tortured a child victim in horrible ways. Benetton said it wanted to contribute to the debate on the death penalty. Some viewed the campaign as ethical imperialism whereby an Italian company was trying to impose European, anti-capital-punishment, views on the USA. The campaign caused much distress to the families of victims. The families viewed the ads as callous exploitation. One family member commented "I could not believe that someone would sell clothing using the suffering of the families of the victims."

Many members of the public were also sceptical and doubted Benetton's motives. Some commented that the company could have made a better contribution to the debate by making a large contribution to a campaigning charity such as Amnesty International. The State of Missouri started a lawsuit alleging that the campaign glorified convicted murderers and that Benetton had misrepresented the reasons why it had asked for access to some of the inmates of Death Row. The outcry was so intense that the Sears retailing chain cancelled a $100 million order for Benetton Clothes. Eventually Benetton, without admitting wrongdoing, apologised to the families of victims and agreed to pay $50 000 into a fund for victims of crime in Missouri.

Principles of ethics for organisations

About 90 per cent of organisations with over 500 employees have a formal code of conduct. In many, employees are required to sign that they have understood the document (GAIN, 2004). However, most of these codes concern employee's behaviour. Few spell out the ethics and social responsibilities of the organisation. Moreover, organisations are diverse. It is difficult to provide an authoritative list of ethics and social responsibilities that apply to, say, a financial services company in London, a government office in Beijing and a health-care organisation in Sydney. The following list contains eight, but not all, principles which organisations should follow:

1 adding value

2 transparent governance

3 accurate reporting and information

4 contribution to the community

5 environmental sustainability

6 fair trade

7 just employment

8 whistle-blowing and non-retaliation

Principle of adding value

Organisations exist to add value. If they destroy value, by making unwise acquisitions or wasting resources, they should end their ownership or have it transferred to another organisation that is able to add value. Organisations that destroy value often exist on subsidies from government or other units in the organisation. They may be organisations undergoing long-term contraction. Drastic retrenchment must not be applied too quickly or ruthlessly. It is normal for a healthy organisation to encounter a "bad patch" that will justify, say, three years of support while it reorganises. Furthermore, the social contribution an organisation makes must be taken into account. For example, it might be proper to provide a long-term subsidy for activities such as health or education. However, such exemptions should not be used too widely – otherwise the community will be handicapped by inefficient public services.

Principle of transparent governance

An organisation's governance should be clear. At the very least people should know the identity of its owners, senior managers, its location and the nature of its business. The level of transparency in public companies needs to be higher. People should know the position of its finances, its assets such as equipment, its performance, income, debts, outlook and the remuneration of senior officials. One of the issues in the Enron debacle outlined earlier was payments of $50 million to top employees to prevent them from leaving the company and so revealing its dire financial straits. Transparency needs to be greatest in government organisations.

Principle of accurate information

An organisation must give accurate information. Its annual reports must be accurate. Public statements should contain the truth, the whole truth and nothing but the truth. The information provided about products must be realistic. Further, communications with the community, suppliers, employees and their representatives must be sincere.

Principle of contribution to the community

At the very least organisations must obey international agreements, the laws of the land where they operate and any local regulations. This also involves paying taxes when due. Many organisations choose to do more than the minimum by supporting cultural activities. Benetton, for example, makes an extra contribution to the culture of Argentina by supporting the Leleque museum in Patagonia "to narrate the culture and history of a mythical land". Many other organisations support theatres, operas, orchestras and sporting events. At a more mundane level other organisations support community projects, landscaping of highways and roundabouts and local charities.

Principle of environmental sustainability

The resources of our planet are huge but not infinite. The resources of a region or city may be large but they may be exhausted in a couple of decades. Organisations must therefore consider sustainability. The concept of sustainability is not difficult. It may be defined as "development that meets the needs of present generations without compromising the ability of future generations to meet their own needs" (Brundtland, 1987). The classic example involves ocean fishing. It may suit today's fishing fleets to catch as many fish as the market will buy, but this would mean that too few fish are left to breed and that in future the fishing industry will collapse. Other examples relate to sustainability involve forestry, the extraction of minerals and the emission of gasses. Fortunately, there are many instances where technology and control systems mean that organisations are making fewer demands upon the environment. For example, thanks to technological advances, today it takes less water and electricity to make a car than it did five years ago.

Principle of fair trade

Fair trade has two main aspects. Trade with customers and trade with suppliers. In both cases trading should be transparent with prices and specifications. Bribery, cronyism and other unfair processes should be avoided. Customers should be given accurate, rather than exaggerated, information. The product or service should be fit for the purpose intended. Agreements must be honoured in full. Suppliers should be treated with respect and given sufficient information about the organisation's requirements for them to provide appropriate goods or services. Specifications should not be changed without consultation and costs of changes to specifications should be met. Organisations with a powerful market position should avoid "bullying" smaller suppliers and should set prices at a level that offers small suppliers a degree of long-term security. Invoices from suppliers should be paid promptly – normally within 30 days. Finally, organisations should not thwart open competition by participating in price rigging or cartel.

Principle of fair employment

An organisation should seek to create jobs which have reasonable security and which enhance the quality of employees' lives. Health and safety of employees is paramount. Employees should be treated with respect irrespective of their ethnic background, gender, age or religion. Employees should be consulted or, at the very least informed, of any major changes affecting their work–life balance.

Whistle-blowing and non-retaliation

"**Whistle-blowing**" (informing appropriate authorities when unethical or socially irresponsible actions are observed) should be encouraged. It is one means by which an organisation can become more ethical. Whistle-blowers should be protected from retaliation.

Managing organisational ethics

Detecting ethical problems

Probably the most difficult step in dealing with ethical problems is to recognise they exist. Unethical practices evolve slowly and become an accepted way. One way to identify unethical problems is to ask:

- Would I wish this to be done to me or my family?
- Would I be ashamed if my family or friends knew of this?
- Is this against my long-term self-interest?
- Will an individual or group of people be harmed rather than helped?
- Will the rights of any person or group be diminished?
- Will the majority of people regard the act as unjust or unfair?

If the answer to any of these questions is "yes", an ethical problem probably exists. If the answer to any three questions is "yes", it is certain that an ethical problem exists. Once an ethical problem has been recognised, the next stage is to collect facts which can form the basis of generating alternative corrective actions. Alternative actions can then be evaluated. If possible, the decision should be discussed and checked with a senior colleagues, an ethics officer or an ethics committee.

Creating an ethical organisation

Many, probably most, organisations wish to be ethical. However, it is not always clear how this can be achieved. Probably the most vital stage is to ensure top management understand the importance, nature and practicalities of social responsibility. Top management can be role models for other employees. A section on ethical values can be included in a vision statement. Finally, managers can establish systems that reward ethical values. With top management support an organisation can employ some of the following tactics.

Code of organisational ethics

Major organisations often develop a formal code of ethics. Good examples can be located readily on the Internet. Codes of ethics often start with a statement of general ethical principles which are sometimes called organisational "credos". Generally, organisational credos have three main sections:

- organisational and **social citizenship**, which covers behaviour such as fairness, courtesy, honesty, integrity, altruism and respect
- **compliance** with appropriate laws, directives and regulations
- emphasis on **serving** customers and other stakeholders

The credos of some organisations also include preserving the environment, using resources economically and reducing waste.

The second section of many ethical codes often focuses upon specific situations and outlines specific ways of dealing with activities such as bribes, kickbacks, political contributions, hiring employees or harassment. Unfortunately, an organisational code is no guarantee of socially responsible behaviour. Enron had an excellent code of ethics – which the board of directors decided to suspend it when it became inconvenient!

Ethical structures

Some organisations create structures specifically tasked with managing ethical issues. The three most common structures are: ethics committees, ethics officers and whistle-blower protection schemes.

Ethics committees

An ethics committee or ethics ombudsman will be responsible for taking proactive steps and drawing up an *ethics strategy* to ensure the organisation meets high ethical standards. It may also arrange *ethics training*. Ethics training might coach managers how to resolve ethical dilemmas. An *ethics audit* may be made. This systematically examines the organisation to identify latent ethical problems. *Action plans* may be devised to monitor the implementation of ethics programmes. Finally, the ethics committee or ethics ombudsman will devise ways to detect violations of the code and impose *penalties* on their perpetrators.

15.4 Business Ethics for Citizens and Consumers

Managers are citizens and consumers who deal with other organisations as a part of their private lives. This relationship is also governed by ethics. Business ethics for consumers and citizens is barely recognised by academics and writers (individual consumers rarely offer lucrative consultancies or research grants!). However, the information that does exist is less than reassuring. It would seem that to make the world more ethical one should not focus solely on the inadequacies of managers or organisations. Infringement by consumers is a big issue.

Vitell and Muncy (1992) developed a scale to measure people's acceptance of unethical behaviour. They found that in the USA rich, young and well-educated people tend to have the *lowest* standards of consumer ethics. Babakus et al. (2004) modified Muncy and Vitell's scale to make it internationally appropriate and collected data in six countries. Their scale included situations such as "drinking a can of soda in a supermarket without buying it", "not saying anything when a waitress (*sic*) miscalculates a bill in your favour" and "jumping a queue". On a scale where 0 per cent represents no tolerance and where 100 per cent total tolerance, the average score was 36 per cent. The results, from lowest to highest tolerance to unethical consumer behaviour were: USA (26 per cent), Brunei (28 per cent), Hong Kong (36 per cent), France (37 per cent), Austria (37 per cent) and UK (49 per cent). Older people were more principled than younger people and people with religious affiliation, especially Muslims, had higher standards than those without religious affiliation.

Examples of bad business ethics by citizens and consumers

Perhaps some of the most frequent ethical abuses by citizens involve CVs, insurance claims, benefit fraud and abuse of free services and plagiarism.

CVs and application forms

CVs and application forms are almost always the first sieve in the process of getting a job (Smith and Abrahamsen, 1992) and they frequently lie. It has been said that there are "lies, damn lies and CVs" (Walley and Smith, 1998). Typical inaccuracies involve the manipulation of dates of employment, exaggeration of work experience, false qualifications or hiding a criminal record. Meanwhile innocent people are duped, colleagues are subjected to the extra strain of providing cover and consumers may get a poor service – an outcome no utilitarian would recommend.

Unethical insurance claims

Insurance fraud seems to be an international occupation. Possibly the biggest insurance scam of all time was attempted by twelve Russian businessmen – mainly accountants and solicitors in New York. They helped stage car accidents in order to make claims on medical insurance policies. It is estimated that their activities cost US insurance companies up to $500 million. On a slightly less impressive scale an old Etonian, Lord Brocket, dismantled four vintage cars, hid them in a garage, said they were stolen and then claimed £4.5 million from his insurance company. Lady Brocket was a heroine addict. When she was caught forging prescriptions she informed police of her husband's fraud. Lord Brocket was sentenced to five years' imprisonment. His prison experiences should be a salutary lesson. Because of his assumed wealth he was a target for prison thugs and came close to having a lavatory brush inserted, somewhere, into his body.

A celebrated example of insurance fraud is given by a psychology professor in California who claimed her car was vandalised with ethnic slurs while she was lecturing on racism. Students on campus demonstrated on her behalf against such "race crimes". However, wit-

---

CASE 15.7: LIES, DAMN LIES AND CVS

A good example of a deceitful CV is the nutritionist who advised the England football captain, Alan Shearer, for two years. When she tried to negotiate a sponsorship deal with Lucozade, a sharp-eyed executive noted that her documents were false. Due to ill health she had dropped out of a degree course and subsequently forged degree and diploma certificates. She obtained work at *two* private health clinics before joining Newcastle United.

Another example is an eye surgeon who was sacked on the spot when it was discovered that his application had omitted to mention a disciplinary offence and had covered it up by supplying two false references. Medical and allied professions seem particularly prone to this problem. One organisation that vets the applications of nurses found 24 bogus claimants within a period of nine months.

In 2002 a leading English clergyman, dean of Portsmouth Cathedral, had resigned because he had falsely claiming a PhD. Lies on CVs and application forms are tragic. They are discovered by reference checks. The perpetrator is disgraced and suffers the financial penalty of unemployment and subsequent reduction in earning power.

nesses later came forward to say that Kerri Dunn, who had a previous record of petty crime, had damaged the car herself.

Insurance frauds are often justified on the grounds that they do no harm. In fact the cost is borne by other policy holders. It increases the cost of insurance so that it is beyond the reach of the poorest and most needy members of society. Insurance scams are widespread and some insurance companies use voice analysis, developed by the Israeli secret service Mossad, to screen the telephone calls of lying claimants.

Benefit fraud

A classic example of benefit fraud is given by a lady from (ironically) the Bay of Plenty, New Zealand who claimed NZ$40 000 in unemployment benefits while earning NZ$640 per month in a job. A more extreme example is given by a Londoner who won £1.5m on the National Lottery. He kept his winnings secret whilst continuing to draw income support. Benefit fraudsters are often caught when relatives, friends and associates inform the authorities. In 2004 the National Benefit Fraud Hotline in the UK received 211 054 calls. An amazing example is given by a builder receiving £37 000 per year in benefits to support himself and family. He appeared on a TV programme explaining how he had been unable to work due to a nervous complaint. Unfortunately, one viewer recognised him as the man she had paid to repair her chimney and she reported her suspicions to the authorities. People making fraudulent claims always have a rationale such as: "everybody does it"; "I am entitled to it but the rules are stupid" or "it is only government money". Nevertheless, benefit fraud is unethical. It increases taxes (which damages the economy) or it means that people in genuine need receive less help.

Cuckoo working bears some resemblance to benefit fraud but the victims are employers, co-workers and consumers rather than taxpayers. In cuckoo working, someone does another job, often a freelance sideline, while they are paid by an employer.

Abuse of free offers

Commercial organisations often make free offers to give a risk-free opportunity to evaluate whether their products are suitable. Consumers often exploit these offers. A clear example of this abuse is where a company's representatives sell the free offers rather than giving them away. Many organisations offer free quotations and it is common for consumers to obtain three estimates. However, consumers may obtain more estimates. Worse still, they may waste resources by asking for estimates out of curiosity, say, for the value of their house. Earlier in this chapter the practices of estate agents were castigated. Perhaps they would not resort to dubious practices if they did not need to bear the burden of consumers who want a valuation without any intention to sell their house. These consumers are unethical. They waste resources and the costs are paid by others. Similarly, it is unethical to ask consultants to prepare proposals and then use the ideas in their brief to perform the work oneself.

Plagiarism

Plagiarism is unethical. It involves copying other people's work and pretending that it is one's own. Students must not do this. Anything copied from books, the Internet or other sources must be acknowledged and referenced. Many universities and colleges have sophisticated methods and software to detect plagiarism. Students caught plagiarising the work of others are humiliated and often forfeit their qualifications.

Ethical principles for citizens and consumers

The area of ethics and social responsibility for citizens and consumers is not well developed. The following list of moral principles can only be a tentative one:

Principle of fair trade

Individuals should interact fairly with organisations that provide goods and services. At the most basic level this means that any information given should be truthful. For example it is wrong, and illegal, to tell lies in order to obtain benefits from a charity or government welfare system. It is also wrong to tell lies to an employer during a job interview. Moreover, in some cases it is wrong to make purchases (e.g. agricultural fertilisers) on one pretext while intending to use them for another nefarious purpose (e.g. making explosives!). The principle of fair trade means:

- Appointments should be kept.
- Questions should receive frank and honest answers – even if the answer is "I am sorry I cannot reveal that to you".
- Payments should be made promptly and at the agreed rates.
- Trivial, facetious or mendacious complaints should be avoided.

Consumers should ensure that they give their custom to ethical organisations. Organisations such as Save the Children believe that individual consumers can make a difference by asking questions in shops, or on Internet sites, about the brands they buy. The questions should include:

- Where are the goods made and how do you check the welfare in factories?
- What do they do when they find underage workers – fire them or pay for schooling until they reach working age?

To make ethical shopping easier, Fairtrade Labelling Organisation (FLO) has established a system whereby crops and products produced and traded in ethical ways can exhibit a Fairtrade logo on its label.

Principle of respect for property rights

The need to respect property is obvious and stems from the utilitarian view of ethics. If property were stolen on a widespread basis, no-one would have the incentive to work, build new facilities or invent new processes. Everyone would suffer. Respect for property is especially relevant to intellectual property. It is wrong to steal other peoples ideas, writing or creations. It is unethical to make "pirate copies" of computer programs, video games and music tracks.

Principle of respect for others

Business transactions frequently involve frustration where one cannot get the deal, product or service to which one feels entitled. It is a well-known psychological fact that frustration often boils over into some form of aggression towards the nearest target – usually a representative of the organisation with which one is dealing. However, it is both unethical and often counter-productive to use physical or verbal aggression. While it is permissible to state a case forcefully and eloquently, physical and verbal abuse must be avoided. Even in the fraught situation of an Accident and Emergency Department it is irresponsible to abuse staff. Similarly, it is unethical to abuse check-in staff if a flight is cancelled.

This does not mean that redress for an error should not be sought. What it does mean is that any redress should be sought from the organisation responsible. The same holds true for "political" protests such as Animal Rights. Everyone has a right, within the law, to express their views and bring pressure to bear. However, it is totally unethical to subject employees of the organisation – or worse, their families – to abuse. It is also wrong to intimidate employees of suppliers or customers.

15.5 Rights of Managers and Professional Workers

Managers and professional workers have rights too. They deserve proper respect. They have a right to expect colleagues, employees and members of the public to:

- Make and keep appointments.
- Behave with courtesy and dignity.
- Give frank and honest replies to questions.
- Avoid making trivial, facetious and mendacious complaints.
- Avoid commissioning two managers or professionals for the same assignment. If this is absolutely necessary both parties should be informed.
- Avoid altering specifications of work without renegotiating fees.
- Pay promptly and at agreed rates for products and services received.

15.6 Ethics Toolkit

Ethical problems are usually complex. This chapter is long but does not cover all complexities. Proposed actions to deal with ethical problems can be evaluated against the following questions:

- In the long term, is this action against my own interest (Enlightened Self-Interest)?
- Would this action add to or subtract from the well-being of human beings or other living things (Utilitarianism)?
- Would this action infringe the accepted rights of any individual or group (Rights)?
- Would this action involve unjust methods (Procedural Justice)?
- Would this action involve an unjust outcome (Distributive Justice)?

It is hoped that everything in this book satisfies these standards.

Activities and Further Study

Essay Plans

Write essay plans for the following topics:

1 To what extent does the study of its philosophical roots help our understanding of social responsibility and ethics?

2 What are the ways in which both profit and not-for-profit organisations behave unethically?

3 What are the ways in which individuals, both as employees and private consumers, behave unethically?

4 What measures can senior managers take to ensure that their organisations are ethical and socially responsible?

5 How should individual employees react when they encounter a breach of ethics by other people at work?

Web Activities

1 Surf the Web to locate the ethical code of the professional body for the management function that interests you most. Compare this with the equivalent ethical code for a similar professional body in another country.

2 Use your search engine to locate the annual reports of four organisations. Find out how they report their commitment to ethics and social responsibility. At least one of these organisations should be renowned for its ethical approach (e.g. the Co-op). Another of the organisations should be not-for-profit (e.g. your local authority).

3 Use the Web to locate as much information as you can about ethical controversies involving one of the following organisations:

- Bennetton
- Haliburton
- Nestlé
- Authorities organising major events such as the Olympics

Experiential Activities

1 Write out your own code of ethics.

2 Locate an ethics statement for your place of work or study. In addition identify the ethical structures that exist in your place of work or study.

3 Think of a socially irresponsible or unethical act that you have witnessed in the past and ask yourself the following questions:

- What was it that made the act socially irresponsible or unethical?
- Which philosophical principle of ethics was involved?
- Who was involved?
- What were the results?

4 Imagine that there was a major ethical breach by a senior person at your work or place of study and that you were the only witness. Work out ways that you would handle the situation.

16

Globalisation and E-Commerce

After reading this chapter you should have some insight into current commercial issues facing managers. You should understand the way that these issues are structured and studied. You should be prepared to generalise these approaches to other commercial issues. In particular you should be able to:

1 **define** globalisation and list four reasons why it is increasing

2 **briefly explain** seven ways in which an organisation may globalise

3 **discuss in detail** the cultural dimensions of globalisation

4 **explain** the implications of globalisation for both managers and their organisations

5 **define** e-commerce and specify its main areas of use

6 **give one example** of a failure of an organisation involved in e-commerce

7 **list and describe in detail** three categories of e-commerce

8 **discuss** in detail the concept of e-fraud and suggest ways it can be reduced

9 **speculate** upon future developments in the field of e-commerce

10 **list** at least three other commercial issues facing managers

Management is not static. The environments of organisations evolve and change so managers must adapt. Sometimes the changes are new developments and sometimes they are the ebb and flow of cyclical trends. For example, changes flowing from the use of the Internet were totally new developments while issues involving the motivation of employees seem to be cyclical. However they are caused, managers must respond. This chapter aims to introduce two current commercial issues requiring adaptation: globalisation and e-commerce. Chapter 17, which follows, considers two further current issues of a slightly different genre. They involve people and those topics are: managing diversity and bullying. This chapter considers Globalisation and e-commerce in three main sections:

Chapter contents

16.1 Globalisation and International Management

Definition and history of globalisation

Globalisation is a major current concern. It is estimated (Globalisation Guide, 2002) that in the year 1998 alone almost 3000 academic papers and 600 books were devoted to the subject. Many of these papers offered their own definitions. Some writers believe that globalisation is:

> A de-coupling of space and time, emphasising that with instantaneous communications, knowledge and culture can be shared around the world simultaneously.

Others define globalisation as:

> A process in which geographic distance becomes a factor of diminishing importance in the establishment and maintenance of cross-border economic, political and socio-cultural relations.

Some people believe that globalisation is a capitalist phenomena and define it as:

> A worldwide drive towards a globalised economic system dominated by supranational corporate trade and banking institutions that are not accountable to democratic processes or national governments.

All three definitions are very broad and refer to the general impact on society. They are useful because they highlight the strong influence of communications, the shrinking of geographical distances and the flow of resources across national boundaries together with globalisation's impact on political systems. These wide definitions reflect the impact that globalisation has on virtually every person on the planet. As early as 1962 McLuhan recognised that the world had become *"a global village"*. In the past, humankind existed in villages where they had personal knowledge of other people and events. McLuhan, considering the spread of radio communications in the 1920s, claimed that with the new media we could have the equivalent knowledge of people on the other side of the world. We learn of far-off events, such as a *tsunami* in the Indian Ocean, almost as quickly as we learn of events in our own community. In this sense, the world is now one large village.

However, these considerations are too wide to be useful to managers. A more restricted and intelligible definition is:

> 66 The growing integration of national economies and societies, so that no society is isolated or remote from changes and developments in other 99 societies.
>
> *(Fitzroy, 2001)*

The growing integration of economies is demonstrated by the development of **trading blocs**. The *European Union* founded in 1957 and subsequently enlarged in 1973, 1995 and 2004 is the world's largest trading bloc. It includes 25 countries and over 445 million people. In 1994 the USA, Canada and Mexico signed the *North American Free Trade Agreement* (NAFTA). The *liberalisation of China and India* are also significant events. Both countries gave up many restrictive trade practices and tariffs and subsequently their economies have blossomed – indeed they are often quoted as examples of the benefits that globalisation can bring. It would seem that the world has organised itself into three major trading regions, North America, Europe and South-East Asia. Many people therefore talk about **regionalisation** rather than globalisation. While this term might be useful in some contexts, globalisation is generally a better term because it includes a substantial volume of trade between the three regional blocks and also includes world trade with Australia, New Zealand, Norway and the countries of the Persian Gulf. Furthermore, the trade in many products such as consumer electronics, clothing and food is truly more global than regional.

These factors have produced a situation where globalisation and world trade are stronger than ever before in history. World trade today is not only stronger but its balance is changing. In the nineteenth and early twentieth centuries world trade was centred on Europe. From about 1914 the centre moved progressively westward towards America. At the end of the twentieth century it was balanced on the American side of the Atlantic. In the early years of the twenty-first century it is shifting to the East as India and China join Japan and Australasia as important international economies.

Reasons for and advantages of globalisation

The basic reasons for globalisation are simple. Different countries have different advantages that allow them to make things more cheaply and better than other countries. For example, Saudi Arabia can produce oil, Australia cannot. Australia can graze cattle, Saudi Arabia cannot. Hence it makes sense for Saudi Arabia to concentrate on extracting oil cheaply and to give up rearing sheep. If all countries focus upon what they do best and trade with other countries for things they do less well, the whole world is better off: petrol gets cheaper and so do lamb chops! Barriers to trade make the world less efficient. While these principles are true, the real situation is more complex.

The reasons for globalisation at the *organisational level* are similar but they show themselves in the form of economies of scale, bigger markets and exploitation of resources:

- In many situations there are **economies of scale** if a service or product is made in high volumes. Often the market in one country is not big enough to reap the full benefits of scale so organisations try to get the extra customers in other countries. Indeed, in some industries it would not be economic to attempt *any* production on the basis of national demand. For example, despite the fact that it is situated the USA, the biggest single market for aircraft, Boeing would not have developed the 747 if other markets were closed. Even if it captured 100 per cent of the American market it would not have sold enough aircraft to cover development costs.

- Other organisations expand their global capacity in search of **bigger markets**. This usually occurs when they have saturated their home market. McDonald's is a classic example. It had fully exploited the economies of scale when there were, say, five or six restaurants within a 50-mile radius of any sizable town and the American market was saturated. The only alternative to stagnation was to establish restaurants abroad in the UK, Australasia, Hong Kong and even, eventually, in France and Russia.

- Some companies globalise in search of **cheaper resources**. The colonial powers established their empires in order to have cheaper access to gold, sugar, cotton, tobacco, tea or rubber. A few companies still establish overseas operations in order to have cheap access to physical resources such as gasoline, aluminium or timber. However, today's firms usually establish "offshore" or "extra-territorial" operations, such as call centres and software development, to gain access to cheap labour.

Relocations are usually greeted warmly by recipient countries. Although the wages paid by multinational companies are usually much lower than organisation's "home" country, they are usually significantly higher than wages in the recipient country – bringing advantages for both workers and their country. In other cases organisations have moved production facilities to less-developed countries because they have less onerous regulations. For example, Union Carbide has been accused of having lower

CASE 16.1: FOOTLOOSE AND IN SEARCH OF CHEAPER LABOUR

In the last few decades firms such as Nike, Benneton, GAP, Motorola and Dyson have moved manufacturing units to places such as Taiwan, the Philippines, Mexico and Malaysia in search of cheaper labour. In the last decade many manufacturing organisations have moved their production plants to China where labour costs are only a fraction of those in the developed world. Another example of an organisation seeking lower labour costs is Volkswagen's decision to move the production of its Polo cars to Bratislava, Slovakia. Years previously it moved production of Ibiza cars to Spain in order to avoid the high costs of labour in Germany. By 2002 Spanish labour costs had risen. Volkswagen then decided to move some production to Bratislava. Similarly, many American corporations such as Microsoft sited administrative centres dealing with billing and issuing licences in Ireland in order to take advantages of lower labour costs and government inducements. However, now that Irish labour costs have risen, these companies are relocating their administrative centres in Asia. Indeed, in 2004 Ireland became the second largest exporter of technology jobs worldwide.

safety and environmental standards at its plant in Bhopal than in a similar plant in West Virginia

■ Some organisations globalise in order to **provide a 24-hour service**. By siting offices in each of the three main time zones (London, New York and Tokyo) they will be able to trade or offer services throughout the day.

Stages of globalisation

Organisations rarely jump from domestic operations to operations on a truly global scale. Usually a company's path follows a discernible pattern with four main stages but companies do not necessarily pass through all four stages.

The first step is usually **importing** supplies from another country. Nowadays, this is very easy. A simple Internet search is likely to identify a source of raw materials at a very keen price. The main, but not very onerous, difficulty is to arrange transportation and agree responsibility during transport. Some supplier's terms may specify *"cargo insurance and freight (cif)"*, which means that they are responsible until the goods are delivered to the buyer's door. Other supplier's terms may specify *"free on board (fob)"*, which means that they will be responsible up to the point where they are delivered to the carrier (on board a ship). The difference between the terms may be substantial. In the latter case, the purchaser will need to pay for onward transportation and insurance.

Later an organisation may **export** goods. If it takes a passive stance it can merely set up a web site or advertise in another country. More proactively, it can employ agents. Employing an agent needs to be managed with care so that the agent is motivated towards selling the organisation's products rather than promoting a large number of other products – including those of a competitor!

In a **licence agreement** another company is allowed to use specialised knowledge and processes, often in the form of a patent, to make a product or produce a service. Licensing agreements offer a relatively easy method of global expansion. Licences are operated by people from the second country who use their own resources and capital. However, the main problems with licence agreements usually arise when the agreement expires. The second company may have acquired considerable knowledge and expertise that will enable it to set up as a competitor. A *franchise* is a special kind of licence. The franchising organisation usually provides foreign franchisees with the marketing, services and, sometimes, materials needed to operate within a specified geographical area. Perhaps the best known franchise is the chain of McDonald's hamburger restaurants. Upon paying a substantial fee of about £350 000 a franchisee receives details on how to equip and run a restaurant.

Joint ventures represent the next stage of internationalisation. They are particularly relevant when an organisation needs to develop a new product or service.

Joint ventures have a number of advantages. They often give companies quick access to new markets because they can use existing distribution channels. They also provide quick access to increased production capacity. Possibly the main advantage of a joint venture is sharing a risk. Joint ventures are not as final as a takeover, merger or partnership. They give participants considerable flexibility – even the ability to sell their "share" to other organisations. Unfortunately, about half of all joint ventures experience difficulties. These usually

CASE 16.2: EXAMPLES OF JOINT VENTURES

Airbus is a classic example of a large-scale joint venture. The American giant, Boeing, was so dominant that companies outside the USA were not be able to mount an effective challenge. However, large aircraft manufacturers in France, Germany, England and Spain formed a joint venture that would be able to build a new series of aircraft (such as the super jumbo A380) and overtake Boeing in world markets. Bilateral joint ventures, where one company finds one partner in a host country, are more usual. For example, in 2004 Siemens Mobile signed a contract with Shenzhen Huawei Technology Co., one of China's leading telecommunication equipment manufacturers, to develop wireless-based communication products.

arise if there is a large imbalance in the expertise, where one partner's contribution is disproportionate or where integration and control is poor.

Acquisition is a very bold globalisation strategy. It involves buying an existing organisation in another country. For example, a relatively small UK oil exploration company Paladin PLC was able to expand into the Timor Sea off northwest Australia by purchasing existing interests from the Australian multinational BHP Billiton. Acquisitions provide very speedy and full control over resources in another country. These include trained personnel, their tacit knowledge, an existing customer base and, perhaps, well-known brands. Unfortunately, acquisitions frequently fail. It is very difficult to establish a proper price for an organisation in another country and the subsequent management of those facilities may encounter substantial cultural problems.

Finally, an organisation may expand by starting and **developing their own foreign operations**. For example, when, in 1911, the Ford Motor Company wanted to expand outside the USA it set up an entirely new manufacturing operation at Trafford Park in Manchester. In the subsequent years Ford established manufacturing plants in many other countries. Today such developments are often called *"greenfield ventures"*. Greenfield ventures have the advantage that the new organisation can be set up in exactly the way the parent organisation wishes. Often governments will offer substantial inducements. The main disadvantage with a greenfield venture is that it takes a considerable time to mature.

When more than 25 per cent of an organisation's sales are derived outside its country of origin it is known as a *multinational corporation* (MNC). Technically, a multinational corporation is the same as a *Transnational Corporation (TNC)*. However, the latter term tends to be used with large organisations operating on a truly global scale and where the majority of their income is outside the country of origin. A classic example of a transnational organisation is Nestlé, where over 98 per cent of its income is generated outside its country of origin, Switzerland. Phillips is another example of a transnational company. It is estimated that Phillips earns over 94 per cent of its income outside the Netherlands. Transnational corporations are so big and their reach is so wide that their country of origin is not a major consideration. They are economic giants. Their income may well be higher than that of medium-sized countries.

Problems of globalisation

Organisations that operate in several countries encounter difficulties. They may arise because countries have different *legal systems* and effort may be needed to translate and harmonise agreements. Furthermore, in many countries the *infrastructure* of roads, telecommunications and education may make production difficult. In parts of the world such as some Middle-Eastern and African countries *political instability* can pose a threat. A change in the composition of the ruling faction can wipe out a huge investment or make trading difficult. An unstable government may freeze assets and make it impossible for a multinational to return profits to the parent company.

Languages can cause problems – especially in marketing and advertising. Some excellent examples of linguistic in advertising gaffes are given in Table 16.1.

Differences in verbal and non-verbal communication can plague meetings where people from different cultures are present. Some examples (see Dubrin, 2003) are:

- UK managers understate positive emotions. The comment "not bad at all" is likely to be interpreted by Americans as lack of enthusiasm.

- UK managers dislike personal questions and tend to stand further from people during business meetings.

- French managers expect to be greeted by formal titles for a number of meetings until everyone is well acquainted.

- The American "okay" symbol using the thumb and fourth figure is a vulgar gesture in Spain and many other countries.

- Attempts to impress Brazilian managers by greeting them in Spanish will be counterproductive. The language of Brazil is Portuguese!

- Shaking hands or embracing at the start of the meeting is considered offensive by the Japanese.

- Presenting small gifts when conducting business with Japanese managers is acceptable but it is offensive behaviour when conducting business with Chinese managers.

The importance of cultural differences is often exaggerated. The context of any social interaction is always very important. Most people understand that people from different cultures have different ways of expressing themselves. They make allowances for, and forgive, inci-

Product	Intended message	Translated message
Coors Beer	"Turn it loose"	"Drink Coors beer and get diarrhoea"
Budweiser Beer	"Drink Bud light"	"Filling, less delicious"
General Motors car	"Body by Fisher"	"Corpse by Fisher"
Nova car	Nova	"Doesn't go" (Non Va)

TABLE 16.1 Unintended Cultural Misunderstandings
(see New Mexican, 1994; Ricks and Mahajan, 1984)

dental transgressions of local protocol. However, individual national differences may indicate deeper trends.

16.2 Globalisation Toolkit

Managers need skills in doing business with people from other cultures. They cannot afford to adopt an ethnocentric view that their own country's business methods are superior. The best approach is to retain the best from their own culture but also benefit from the good things in other cultures. This requires judgement and intelligence. Other implications of globalisation can be considered under three headings: implications for organisations, implications for managers abroad and implications for negotiations.

The implications of globalisation for *organisations* divide into opportunities and challenges. A major opportunity is the ability to source raw materials from around the world. This gives greater choice and possibly higher-quality inputs at a lower price. Another opportunity is access to markets in other countries. This results in larger production runs and brings economies of scale. An organisation that operates in another country must:

- Choose the **correct form of presence**: licensing, franchising, joint ventures, acquisition or greenfield development. It is important to recruit the most able people available and then train them in the ethos of the organisation and its goals.

- Be familiar with **local customs, beliefs and laws**. In particular, organisations must be familiar with the local law governing workers. In other countries, workers often have drastically different rights to security employment, holidays and trade union membership.

- Use the organisation's **networks of contacts** to obtain informal information about the destination country, e.g. neighbouring organisations that are already operating in the destination country.

- Be prepared to **modify** the organisation's management style to provide a better fit with the culture of the host country.

- Provide existing employees with **language training**. Managers should be given *acclimatisation training* to minimise "*culture-shock*". These training programmes have three main components. First, the potential "*ex-pat*" managers should be taught about the culture of the host country and its similarities and differences with the culture of the home country. Second, acclimatisation training usually covers culture shock and the ways that a manager can recognise the adaptations that need to be made. Usually acclimatisation training gives guidance on the methods of making these adaptations. Some organisations provide acclimatisation training for members of the manager's family. The third main component of acclimatisation training focuses upon practical aspects such as communicating back home, emergency services procedures and the etiquette of things such as giving gifts or removing shoes before entering a Muslim home.

- Significant public announcements or advertisements in another language should be **checked with at least two local speakers** who do not know the ex-pat manager's home language. This is to ensure that translations do not contain a *double entendre* or unintended meaning.

The *implications of globalisation for managers* sent to a host country mirror many of the implications for organisations. Managers should attend acclimatisation training to learn about the culture of the host country. It is important that ex-pat managers adapt to the local culture rather than try to recreate their home culture in the host country. An individual manager will need to adapt his or her management style to take into account of differences on the dimensions identified by Trompenaars and Hofstede (see pages 19–21).

Implications of globalisation for negotiators are fewer but more acute since they have only a relatively short time to achieve success. They must remember that other cultures have different perspectives on time. Negotiations in a host country will probably take longer than equivalent negotiations at home. There may be a protracted period of establishing friendship and rapport that is punctuated by ceremonial occasions such as giving gifts or formal meals. It is vital that negotiators familiarise themselves in advance with local custom and the formalities of introductions, visiting the homes of their counterparts and closing negotiations. Negotiators should also familiarise themselves with the local euphemisms that their counterparts may use to say "no" or to decline an offer.

16.3 E-Commerce

Definition and some background

The US Economic Census defines **e-commerce** (**electronic commerce**) as:

> " Any business transaction whose price or essential terms were negotiated over an online system such as an Internet, Extranet, Electronic Data Interchange network, or electronic mail system. It does not include transactions negotiated via facsimile machine or switched telephone network, or payments made online for transactions whose terms were negotiated offline. "

It is sometimes called "**e-business**". It is a very new form of economic activity. In the past ten years it has grown in excess of 50 per cent per annum but it is still much smaller than traditional "bricks and mortar" trading in conventional buildings. E-commerce typically uses desktop computers but it can also use personal digital assistants (PDAs) and pagers that distribute information such as stock market prices. The latest Web-enabled cell-phones which can perform most of their functions will also be important tools.

Main areas of e-commerce

The earliest developments in e-commerce tended to involve trading between two *business organisations* (*B2B*) because most computers were then owned by organisations. The recent expansion has been business organisations selling directly to retail customers. This is called *B2C* trading. The classic example of business to customers trading is Amazon.com – the Seattle-based company that started Web trading in 1995. Amazon has been so successful that it has expanded its range of products to include clothing, electronics, toys and hardware. Indeed, Amazon now sells the B2C systems it developed to companies such as the Borders Group, Toys 'R' Us and Target. Amazon's example attracted competitors such as Wal-Mart into retail e-commerce (**e-tailing**). Other early adopters were in the travel industry. Firms such as Expedia (American), Lastminute (British) and eDreams (Spanish–Italian) were well established before the turn of the millennium. *E-booking* is another sector where e-commerce has flourished. Tickets for many theatre, film or sporting events can be purchased over the Internet and this method is now rivalling traditional methods. For example, in 2004 43 per cent of ticket sales for the Edinburgh Festival were via websites. In one day the National Theatre in London issued e-tickets worth £270 000 for the play *The History Boys*. Another major user of e-commerce is the *recruitment industry*. Perhaps the best-known recruitment website is the "Monster" board that operates on a global basis. Most countries have similar websites. In Australia, for example, the government offers a website jobsearch.gov.au while the private sector offers sites such as seek.com.au. E-commerce has also been used for less savoury transactions – especially unauthorised *pharmaceutical* sales and *pornography*. In 2003 Americans spent $700 million buying cut-price Viagra and prescription drugs from across the border in Canada. In the same year over $2 billion was spent in the USA on e-porn! (Markillie, 2004).

Use of e-commerce

E-commerce first emerged in the USA but was quickly adopted by European countries – especially the UK and Germany. At the time of writing the UK was Europe's largest e-commerce economy and had already overtaken the USA in pioneering some developments. Tesco, for example is the world's largest online grocer (Cave, 2004). In 2003 online trade was worth £39.5 billion in the UK. America's Department of Commerce calculates that online retail sales in the USA in 2003 exceeded $55 billion. These figures need to be seen in context – they amounted to only 2–3 percent of all trade: the vast majority of commerce still takes place in the old "bricks and mortar premises" (Markillie, 2004). However, e-commerce is growing very rapidly. E-tailers such as KarstadtQuelle (Germany) and Tesco (UK) have experienced annual growth rates in excess of 25 per cent. This large increase has been the result of two main factors:

- **More people are making purchases using the Internet**. In 2003 it was estimated that about 40 per cent of Europeans who had access to the Internet had made purchases on line, whereas, in 2000 the proportion was about 20 per cent.
- **Ebuyers are purchasing a wider range of goods**. In the early days, buyers used the Internet to buy standard products such as CDs and books. As consumer confidence in e-commerce has grown, they are prepared to purchase more complex products.

E-fiascos

Recent reports of increasing volumes of e-commerce do not mean that Internet trading is risk free. E-commerce has had a roller-coaster ride since the mid-1990s. For about five years it experienced a meteoric rise where venture capitalists flocked to finance quite zany ideas such as pyjamas for pets. The shares in many .com companies rose to astronomical levels despite low earnings. Investors, apparently, could see growth potential and future earnings in a "new economic paradigm" centred upon e-commerce. In 2000, however, reality set in and the valuations of many .com companies were seen to be ridiculous. A classic example of a .com disaster is given by Boo.com. Venture capitalists drew four main lessons: ensure that some senior managers have experience; avoid a concept that is too advanced; avoid oversophisticated technology; control costs strictly – especially champagne, caviare and Concorde (Case 16.3).

The .com bubble burst. The level of e-commerce contracted. Investors and customers became wary. However, with better management and a more considered view of the possibilities, the advantages of e-commerce re-emerged. Within three years e-commerce was expanding rapidly again.

Industry structure

The industry structure supporting e-commerce is very complex and only three aspects can be covered here. They are domain names, aspects of B2B and aspects of B2C.

Domain names

Domain names are a vital part of the Internet. They allow search engines to locate the websites. A domain name has several parts separated by dots. For example, much of the

---

CASE 16.3: BOO.COM DISASTER

Boo.com company was launched in November 1999 by two Swedes, Kajsa Leander, a model, and Ernst Malmsten, a 28-year-old poetry enthusiast. They found it easy to persuade venture capitalists to provide hundreds of millions of pounds for an Internet company selling designer clothing and accoutrements. They targeted a market of trendy young people who had lots of money but relatively little spare time. Their website was very advanced. In fact, it was so advanced that many PCs of the time had difficulty gaining access. On entering the site, shoppers were greeted by Miss Boo, a virtual shop assistant in trendy clothes and a funky hairstyle. Shoppers could also see their purchases displayed on a 3D virtual model of themselves. Leander and Malmsten adopted a very high profile approach to promoting the company and themselves: lavish parties, private jet and transatlantic trips on Concorde to meet further venture capitalists.

The lavish lifestyle (fuelled by the three Cs – champagne, caviare and Concorde) plus the huge advertising campaign and advanced technology were consuming $1 million each week and sales languished far below this level. In May 2000 the company went bust, having spent £178 million of investors' cash achieving very little. Subsequently Boo has been held as an example of how *not* to set up a .com company.

Boo's collapse was not an isolated event. Other .com companies such as Pets.com and Webvan.com also went into liquidation. As its name implied, Pets.com sold pet supplies. It was so heavily advertised that it was spending $179 to acquire each customer and, unfortunately, each new customer spent far less! Webvan.com offered an on-line delivery service and lost $35 million on sales of only £395 000 in its first six months.

information in this section was obtained from an organisation, Business Link (a part of the Department of Trade and Industry) which has the domain name www.businesslink.gov.uk. Similarly, the Institution of Engineers in Singapore has the domain name of www.ies.org.sg. The names of Internet sites could be quite similar and a great deal of confusion would arise if they were mixed up. Consequently, somebody, somewhere must ensure that each website has a unique name.

The most general parts domain names are the *generic top-level domains (gTLDs)*. They indicate the type of sponsoring organisation. Typical examples of gTLDS are .net, .com, .org .gov and .info. They are handled by the *Internet Corporation for Assigned Names and Numbers (ICANN)*. ICANN appoints organisations (usually American organisations!) that check there is no duplication and then issue an Internet address (Internet Protocol) which allows users to access the web address. For example the .com domain and the .net domain are administered by VeriSign.

There are also *country code top level domains* such as .au, .ie, .hk, .nz, .sg, .uk and .za. The official .uk domain name registry is managed by an organisation called Nominet. Nominet manages second level domains such as .co.uk; .org.uk; .net.uk and .ac.uk. The third part of a domain name, such as "manchester" is the name of an individual site. So the address of the University of Manchester is www.**manchester**.ac.uk while the address of McGraw-Hill in the UK is www.**mcgraw-hill**.co.uk.

B2B e-commerce

While B2B trading shares many characteristics with B2C (business to consumer) trading, there are notable differences. In many areas of B2B trading a website is less important. Customers know their suppliers. Therefore they are much less likely to use a search engine to locate the domain addresses. They are also less likely to be impressed by clever, eye-catching designs that may take time to download. B2B customers are more likely to be attracted by a straightforward system that functions effectively. In many cases, there is an even closer link between customer and supplier in B2B trades. There is a growing tendency for orders to be generated automatically and sent to the supplier's own computing system. These advantages produce considerable cost savings which either improve profits or enable them to offer lower prices. One disadvantage of integrated supply systems is that an extra burden can be placed upon suppliers, who are forced to adopt in its customers' systems. For example, all suppliers to Wal-Mart must conform to its computerised ordering system.

Argos, the world's biggest catalogue distributor, maintains tight control of its supply chain. It recently introduced a "track and trace" system for high-value goods. A "tote" (i.e. a bag) of, say, jewellery is given a *Radio Frequency Identification (RFID)* tag and a barcode label. Radio sensors at various stages of the production and transport system automatically log the movement of each consignment. In addition, hand-held sensors can track goods at other points. Tracking information is stored on Argos's database. This allows Argos to locate valuable assets precisely and ensure that products are available when needed by customers. These systems require sophisticated supply-chain management programs. A specialised sector of the computer industry, including firms such as i2 and Manugistics, has developed to provide such systems.

CASE 16.4: B2B INTEGRATION

Recreational Equipment Inc (REI) is a major retailer of sports and outdoor equipment. It sells goods made by many suppliers. In the past, it would send an order when stocks of a product fell below a certain level. It now uses an integrated supply chain where orders are generated and sent to suppliers over the Internet, more or less automatically. Furthermore, approved suppliers can log into certain areas of REI's computer system and view information such as the current stock levels, buying trends and the profit margin made by REI on the products they supply. Suppliers, such as Cascade Designs, makers of tents and snow equipment, can anticipate REI's needs. They can start the production process in advance and ensure that goods are available when they are ordered. Cascade Designs can plan their production programme more efficiently. It also means that they can carry less stock.

B2C e-commerce

Business to Consumer e-trade depends heavily on an organisation's *website* and the ease with which it can be located and navigated. One, costly, way of aiding location is to sponsor links on search engines such as Google. A more subtle approach is to include key words likely to be detected by search engines. The design of the website is crucial. It must be distinctive, yet convey an appropriate image. It must offer relevant information that can be reached with only three clicks of a computer mouse. Simplifying the buying process is a major challenge for B2C commerce. A well-designed webpage should:

- Focus on the target customers and their preferences rather than those of the organisation. It needs to answer the question "what need of the potential consumer does this page meet?" Introductory pages should have a "skip intro button".

- Enable a potential customer to understand the main message of a page in under four seconds.

- Be simple and avoid irrelevant graphics that take time to download.

- Not overlook the importance of text. However, the message of the text should be straightforward and not presented in a very small font (7 point or less).

A website has inbuilt advantages in reaching some groups of consumers. For example, teenagers and young men spend more time online than watching TV (Markillie, 2004). In theory a website should mimic the experience of seeing and entering a "bricks and mortar" retail outlet. Amazon's "Local Yellow Pages" attempts to simulate this experience. In the USA it has used trucks equipped with digital cameras and global positioning systems to capture images, matching them with businesses and the way they look from the street. Yellow Pages lets potential customers see organisations the way they look from "the parking lot".

E-commerce finds it difficult to emulate the psychological experience of customers entering a "bricks and mortar" store. In many cases websites are little more than catalogues with an ordering mechanism. Despite valiant attempts, websites find it difficult to mimic a customer's state of mind when entering a store emblazoned with "sale" signs and littered with bargain bins. E-tailers also find it difficult to emulate the opulent trimmings of up-market shops selling Gucci and Channel. The ultimate website will use anecdotes, pictures and other alluring content to attract people to the site – many of whom will make a purchase. The on-line retailer will always have to do something interesting and different in order to attract and keep the attention of potential purchasers. In bricks and mortar retailing a potential purchaser has to make the effort to walk or drive to a competitor. In e-tailing a competitor is only three clicks away. Some *good* examples of e-tail websites include Galeria-kaufhof.de's system that tells shoppers when products are unsuitable for children (this promotes trust) and Fnac.fr system that allows users to order books or CDs in advance of their release. Fnac.fr's system also notifies customers of authors' and artists' visits to stores. Tesco's otherwise excellent web site is marred by the fact that consumers need to register before they can browse the site to research products.

E-tailing has a role to play in bricks and mortar shops. For example, it is a common experience to visit a store and find a desired garment in the wrong size. In some stores it already possible to take the wrong-sized garment to a scanner, scan its tag and order a garment of the correct size. The process can work in the other direction. The Internet is used to lead customers to bricks and mortar shops. Computer users already ask search engines such as yell.com to locate, say, plumbers, tailors or grocers in their vicinity. In some areas Global Positioning Systems (GPS) are already able to deliver similar information, automatically, to users of mobile phones.

E-fraud

Fraud is a major threat to e-commerce. If customers feel that they will be tricked they will resort to traditional shopping. The problem of *Phishing* (sending a fraudulent but official looking email requesting details such as passwords) is particularly threatening. In October 2004 there were over 1000 known phishing sites. In 2005 fraudsters extracted $2.6 billion. This represents about 2.5 per cent of Internet sales – an increase of 37 per cent over the previous year (Tedeschi, 2004). AOL and eBay already provide software that alerts customers when they enter a known fraudulent site. AOL has developed "Chrome Mail" that allows subscribers to differentiate its official emails from fraudulent ones. *Spyware* is a program surreptitiously placed on a PC to capture and send back information that includes passwords. Many financial institutions are considering using *dynamic passwords* to defeat spyware. Dynamic passwords change each time they are used. One system is a version of a spy's "one-time pad". The bank sends customers a series of four-letter codes that are added to a static password. Once a code is used it is discarded and the next in the series is used. Since the bank also knows the correct series it can identify unauthorised attempts to access an account.

Overpayment Scams are another type of Internet fraud. The buyer sends a cheque or bankers' order for much more than the purchase price of the goods. The buyer then asks the seller to wire back immediately the excess amount which the buyer withdraws immediately. When the seller presents the original cheque, it turns out to be false. By then the buyer will have disappeared and it will be impossible to claim back the money sent for the apparent overpayment. Some people are duped by *chain emails* that promise big returns but are very unlikely to return even the original investment. In some countries it is illegal to start or send on a chain email. In the *Domain Name Scam* a fraudster obtains the details of a site's owner. Just before the renewal date, they send an official-looking invoice asking for the renewal fee – hoping that it will be paid.

E-fraud survival toolkit

Holiday periods are particularly prone to Internet fraud because scamsters know that the higher volume of e-commerce makes it more difficult for organisations. Medium-sized companies are more vulnerable to Internet fraud because they are less able to afford expensive counter-measures. People combat Internet fraud by:

- Being suspicious of any email that requests verification of information that has already been provided.
- Avoiding clicking on links embedded in email messages even from known organisations. It is better to open a new browser window and independently type in the address of the organisation that appears to be requesting information.
- Being wary of attractive offers from unknown organisations. Avoid clicking links in their emails until their background has been researched. Sometimes such emails contain spyware that will install itself on a PC (Tedeschi, 2004).
- Refusing cheques for more than the selling price. Do not part with money or goods until funds have actually been transferred to your account – at the very least telephone a bank to verify that their draft is genuine.
- Not replying to chain emails or enter unknown foreign lotteries. In some countries it is illegal to play foreign lotteries by mail, telephone or Internet.

One form of Internet duplicity is perpetrated by some search engines. They may give undue prominence to sites in return for payment. This is no problem where they are clearly separated under a clear heading such as "Sponsored Links". Indeed paid inclusion programs may give consumers better choice by allowing quicker and more focused searches. However, paid inclusion sites may be concealed by less transparent headings such as "featured listings", "recommended sites" or "search partner" (Federal Trade Commission, 2005).

Wider influence and the future of e-commerce

E-commerce is changing consumer behaviour. A substantial proportion of customers research products on-line before visiting a bricks and mortar outlet to make the actual purchase. In the USA, one in five customers of electrical goods research products on-line and will know the exact price. Seventy-five per cent of Americans research car purchases on line before buying from a traditional dealer (Markillie, 2004). Customers are better informed and more able to negotiate a keen price. They routinely compare prices in their local stores with on-line prices. They may even compare domestic prices with those abroad and then use a Web-based service to import them at a lower price. The process can work the other way around. Consumers frequently visit a bricks and mortar store to see and touch a product before returning home to buy on-line. This may mean that some shops become little more than showrooms. Both trends signify a decoupling of product information and the actual purchase itself. They also encourage consumers to be less loyal.

Some e-tailers, especially catalogue retailers, have adopted a strategy of using multiple channels by allowing customers to complete different parts of a transaction in different ways. Argos is a superb example. It has used its well developed competencies at distance selling and knowing its market to allow customers to, say, check prices and availability on-line and have goods delivered to the customer's home.

Other excellent e-tailers include Amazon(USA), Laredoute.fr, Alaplage.fr, Screwfix.co.uk and Otto.de. This list is interesting since, with the exception of Amazon, none are traditional .com companies that caused all the early razzmatazz. The largest group are catalogue retailers (Argos, Laredoute, Screwfix and Otto). They already had relevant skills, brand strength, distribution systems and customer service departments. Traditional organisations such as Tesco.com, Fnac.fr and Bahn.de are also having success with e-commerce. It would seem that in the longer run success in e-commerce requires an evolutionary approach by large stable companies with experienced management rather than innovative start-ups by young caviare-eating and champagne-drinking entrepreneurs.

Of course, globalisation and e-commerce are only two of current commercial issues. Some others, which could not be included in this chapter, are environmental management, sustainable growth and the management of technology. An excellent introduction to the issues involved in the management of technology can be readily obtained from Broers's (2005) Reith Lectures on "The Triumph of Technology".

Activities and Further Study

 Essay Plans

Draw up plans for the following essays:

1 Describe the history of globalisation and the stages an organisation might pass through on its progress towards full globalisation.

2 What training and development can be given to employees in order to prepare them to cope in a globalised economy?

3 What are the main types of e-commerce? For each type give detailed, specific examples and compare and contrast each type of e-commerce.

Web Activities

1 Use the Web to locate current examples of: (a) phishing, (b) Internet scams, (c) chain-emails and (d) spam.

2 Many organisations run competitions or give awards to applications in e-commerce. Use the web to locate the winners of competitions. Browse the entries to obtain a long list of different uses of e-commerce. Some useful websites are:

- *http://www.ecommerce-awards.co.uk/winners_2005/index.html*
- *http://www2.news.gov.bc.ca/news_releases_2005-2009/2005EMPR0047-000959.htm*
- *http://www.weather.gov.hk/apicta/APICTA2003_PressRelease_e.pdf*
- *http://www.iol.ie/~kooltek/ibias.html*
- *http://www.ird.govt.nz/news-updates/liketoknow-06-04-10-netguide.html*

Experiential Activities

1 Locate a successful e-commerce organisation operating in your area. Trace its history in e-commerce and identify the factors that led to its success.

2 With a group of, say, six fellow students or colleagues hold a brainstorming session on e-commerce applications that might be successful in the next five years.

3 List at least four types of e-fraud to which you might be vulnerable. For each fraud on your list identify at least two measures you can take to minimise your vulnerability.

Diversity and Bullying

17

❖ *LEARNING OBJECTIVES*

After reading this chapter you should have some insight into "people" issues facing managers. You should be able to understand the way that such issues are studied. You should be prepared to generalise these approaches to other "people" issues. In particular you should be able to:

1 **define** managing diversity and explain the importance of the subject

2 **list** the four main characteristics of a multicultural organisation

3 **list** the main characteristics of a workforce's diversity

4 **explain** the main issues involved in managing a workforce that is diverse in terms of gender, ethnic origin, age and disability

5 **explain** the problems encountered by women and minority groups

6 **outline** some of the legal aspects involved in managing diversity

7 **compare and contrast** the advantages and disadvantages of a diverse workforce

8 **define and explain** the concept of bullying

9 **give one example** of bullying within an organisation

10 **list** at least 10 ways people can be bullied at work. **Categorise** this list into four groups

11 **briefly describe** the main types of sexual harassment

12 **assess** the extent and importance of bullying at work

13 **analyse** the main features of bullying

14 **indicate** ways organisations and witnesses can help minimise bullying

The previous chapter illustrated two current commercial issues in management: globalisation and e-commerce. This chapter focuses on current issues involving people. These issues are important because "people" are a key element in the definition of management. This chapter introduces two "people management" issues of current concern: managing diversity and bullying.

Chapter contents

17.1 Definitions and concepts of managing diversity

When Richard Arkwright started the first factory in the world (cotton spinning at Cromford in 1773) he had little cause to worry about managing the diversity of his workforce. There was little geographic mobility. The overwhelming majority of his employees will have been recruited from Derbyshire farm-workers living within 20 miles of his factory. They shared a common language and a common culture. Given the isolated nature of the Matlock area of Derbyshire in those days, they also shared a relatively common genetic pool! Today things will be very different. A major aspect of globalisation (see Chapter 16) has been the movement of people across countries and continents. The owner of a garment factory in Bradford will need to manage workers from England, Scotland, Poland, Ukraine, India, Pakistan, Bangladesh and several other countries. Moreover, the social climate and legal system will be drastically different. Women and groups such as the disabled and senior citizens will expect their views and needs to be respected. Workers will have a wide range of religious convictions. If the manager is to achieve the full potential of the factory in Bradford, he or she will need to manage this diversity skilfully.

The concept of *workforce diversity* is very straightforward and there is a high level of consensus for its definition. It may be defined as:

> 66 The heterogeneity of the workforce in terms of gender, ethnicity, age and other demographic variables and the consequential differences in the abilities, attitudes and beliefs of people at work. 99

Thus, the workforce in Arkwright's Masson Mills in Cromford would be very homogeneous and have little diversity. The overwhelming majority of workers would be men. There would be a very narrow range of skills, experience and beliefs. In contrast, employees in the garment factory in Bradford would be very heterogeneous. There would be a many ethnic groups, a wide age range and believers in several very different religions. Women workers would slightly outnumber the men.

The concepts of multiculturalism and multicultural organisation are relevant to the idea of diversity. A **multicultural organisation** may be defined as:

> 66 An organisation that respects diversity and where a range of different social groups are able to make substantial contributions to the setting and execution of key values and policies while maintaining their own traditional culture or special interests within the confines of a common organisation. 99

A multicultural organisation is likely to show four main characteristics:

- **A low level of intergroup conflict** – there will be harmony between the groups. Groups will form on the basis of the skills needed rather than demographic variables such as age, gender, etc.
- **The absence of prejudice and discrimination**. "*Prejudice* is an opinion or leaning that is formed without just grounds or before sufficient information is available." Technically, a prejudice can be held about things, ideas or people and can be positive or negative. In fact, especially in the area of managing diversity, the term is usually used in the context of negative ideas about people of different groups. Therefore, the term "prejudice" is often taken to mean "irrational attitudes of hostility directed at a group of people on the basis of erroneous beliefs about their race or other characteristics". *Negative discrimination* arises when someone is treated less favourably because of an incorrect negative prejudice.
- A system of **informal networks containing people from different backgrounds** that mentor and support all groups in the performance of their work and progression of their careers.
- **Fair representation** where there are appropriate proportions of members of minority groups in most jobs and at most levels.

Managing diversity is the process whereby the different skills, knowledge and culture of people with different backgrounds are used to further the goals of the organisation and to help individuals maximise their potential. A useful definition is given by Kandola and Fullerton (1994):

> 66 The basic concept of managing diversity accepts that the workforce consists of a diverse population of people. The diversity consists of visible and non-visible differences, which will include factors such as sex, age, background, race, disability and personality and work style. It is founded on the premise

that harnessing the differences will create a productive environment in which everybody feels valued, where their talents are being fully utilised and in which organisational goals are met.

Managing diversity is a fairly new concept. "During the 1970s, in most Western countries, much emphasis was placed on achieving equal employment opportunities and reducing discrimination in organisations" (Herriot, 2003). The idea at that time was to ensure that women and people from minorities would be taken into the organisation and while they were there they would be assimilated into the organisation's culture. The aim was to make an organisation a melting pot in which women and people from minorities were accepted, melted down and mixed with the existing elements to make a uniform soup. Since that time thinking has changed. Women and minority groups are accepted in their own right, adding variety and richness to the existing situation – rather like the addition of new vegetables enriches an existing salad and brings out the flavour of existing ingredients so that the new salad is a more fulfilling dish. Organisations that are "diversity mature" are able to turn the diversity of their workforces into a competitive advantage. The basic building block of a diversity mature organisation is a "diversity mature employee" – someone who understands themselves, is able to cope with tensions inherent in diversity and who understands the complexity of harnessing different viewpoints (Roosevelt-Thomas and Woodruff, 1999). Roosevelt-Thomas (1991) saw this development as a series of overlapping stages leading from taking affirmative action to valuing differences and finally managing diversity purposively. Figure 17.1 is based on Roosevelt's ideas.

Sometimes diversity is viewed in terms of *cultures*. An organisation that consist of one very dominant culture is often called a **monoculture**. Monocultures are sometimes very effi-

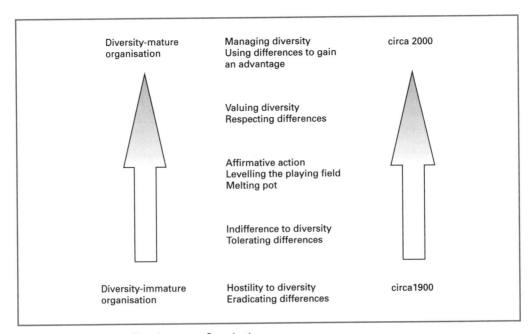

Diversity-mature organisation

Managing diversity
Using differences to gain an advantage

circa 2000

Valuing diversity
Respecting differences

Affirmative action
Levelling the playing field
Melting pot

Indifference to diversity
Tolerating differences

Diversity-immature organisation

Hostility to diversity
Eradicating differences

circa 1900

FIGURE 17.1 Transition to Diversity-mature Organisations

cient in the short term since they need to spend less effort in resolving communication and interpersonal issues. However, they are very vulnerable to changes in the environment because they cannot adapt. People working in monocultures have a tendency to believe that their way doing things is the only approach and that their organisation is at the epicentre of commercial life. Sometimes they develop a kind of *ethnocentrism*. At the other extreme lie organisations that believe all groups and *sub-cultures* are inherently equal. This is called *ethnorelativism*. An extreme ethnorelativist might argue that the police culture of Stalin is inherently equal to the liberal democratic culture of a country such as the Netherlands. They might also argue that the culture of a feudal hacienda is inherently equal to the culture of consultation that exists in many German companies. Extreme ethnorelativism and organisational monocultures are rare. Most organisations contain a wide variety of sub-cultures of more or less equal value. Perhaps the most obvious sub-cultures are based on ethnic background. However, many organisations have *occupational* sub-cultures (especially among professional employees) and *functional* sub-cultures, which can cause large-scale disputes between, say, the production department and the sales department. In addition there may be *generational* and *gender* sub-cultures.

17.2 Dimensions of Diversity

Groups can differ in many ways. Loden and Rosener (1991) organised these differences into two main categories. As Figure 17.2 (based on Loden and Rosener) shows, **Primary**

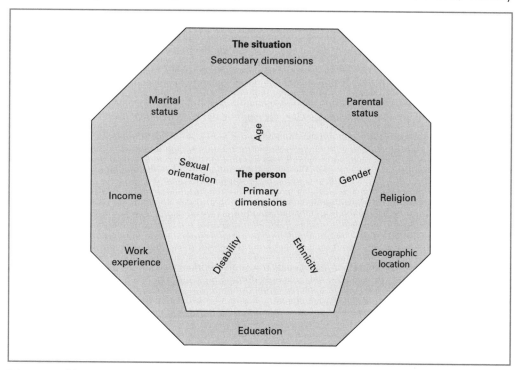

FIGURE 17.2 Primary and Secondary Dimensions of Diversity

Dimensions of Diversity involve inherent and unchangeable characteristics. **Secondary Dimensions of Diversity** involve acquired characteristics that can change during a lifespan.

Figure 17.2 includes only the main factors of diversity such as gender, age and ethnicity. Many other dimensions exist. For example, in some circumstances, physique or military service might be relevant.

17.3 Demography of Diversity

One of the first steps in managing diversity is to collect data about the people in an organisation. The statistical study of the way that characteristics such as age and gender are distributed is known as **demography**. Most organisations conduct **workforce audits** to obtain demographic information about their employees. The results of a workforce audit would be too specific for a chapter of this kind. The following section gives general information that is likely to be of interest to a wider readership. However, it does indicate the type of information and issues that a workforce audit might reveal. Generally, the demographic information about an organisation's workforce is organised under five headings: gender, ethnic origin, age, religion and disability.

Gender

Women are in a slight majority of the population of most countries, but generally they form rather less than half a country's working population. For example, in New Zealand in 2001, women formed 51 per cent of the population and 47 per cent of the working population. The difference is largely due to two factors: women live longer than men and they often interrupt their careers for child bearing. The formal economic activity of women may be less than such figures indicate because many women work part-time. For example, in 1993 about 46 per cent of women workers in Great Britain worked part-time.

Women are not distributed evenly across occupations. There are usually few women working in hard, dangerous occupations such as mining, construction work and heavy transport. Women predominate in lighter, "indoor" occupations such as financial management, teaching assistants and customer services. For example, in the USA in 2003 1 per cent or less of structural ironworkers, brick masons or roofers were women. On the other hand there was a predominance of women secretaries and administrators (96 per cent), receptionists (93 per cent) and nurses (90 per cent) (US Department of Labor, 2003a, b).

It is often said that there are too few women in higher jobs where they can exercise authority. For example, Table 17.1 gives the proportion of women at ministerial level in a selection of countries (World Bank, 2005).

Women earn less than men. For example, in April 2003 the average male worker in the UK earned £536 per week while the average female worker earned £401. Perhaps this is a consequence of prejudice, part-time working, a career break for child bearing, the occupations in which women work and, more certainly, the seniority of their jobs.

Ethnic origin

The issue of ethnic origin has very different proportions and format in various countries. At one extreme are countries such as Iceland where close to 100 per cent of the population

Country	1994	1998	Country	1994	1998
Australia	13	14	Belgium	11	3
China	6	–	Finland	39	29
France	7	12	Germany	16	8
Greece	4	5	Ireland	16	21
Japan	6	0	Malaysia	7	16
Netherlands	31	28	New Zealand	8	8
Russian Fedn.	0	8	Turkey	5	5
UK	9	24	USA	14	26

TABLE 17.1 Proportion of Women at Ministerial Level
All Selected Countries 12.2 (1994) 14.1 (1998)

originate from a common stock. At the other extreme are countries such as India whose vastness contains a wide variety of ethnic groups that include Australoids, Caucasians, Dravidians, Mons, Negitos and Tamils. In the middle of the spectrum are countries such as Malaysia where there are three large ethnic groups – Malays, Chinese and Indians. The UK is towards the end of the spectrum where there is one ethnic group. The percentage ethnic composition of the British population of the UK in 2003 was:

White	92.0	Caribbean	1.0
Indian	1.8	African	0.8
Pakistani	1.3	Bangladeshi	0.5
Mixed	1.2	Chinese	0.4

(EOC, 2004)

A great deal of research concerning ethnic diversity has been conducted in the USA. However, the results of this research should not be generalised carelessly to other countries. The cultures of the USA and the UK are fairly similar. However, there are three major differences that could render the results of ethnic research in one country inapplicable to the other. First there are considerable differences in the *size of the ethnic minority*. In the UK the ethnic minority is about 8 per cent while in the USA it is about 18 per cent. This means that organisations in the USA are likely to have more employees from ethnic minorities. Therefore, it is easier to justify measures to maximise the benefit from ethnic diversity. Second, the *origins of ethnic minorities* in each country are different. The ethnic minority in the USA has a predominantly African origin – with a rapidly growing number of people with Hispanic origins. In the UK, the origins of the ethnic minorities are much wider. As the previous table shows the largest group originates from the Indian subcontinent but there are substantial proportions of people with Afro-Caribbean backgrounds. Third, and perhaps most important, there are huge *differences in the historical background*. The main black immigration to the USA took place predominantly between 1700 and 1860. The black Africans were taken involuntarily to the USA and found themselves in an economic system built on slavery, subservience and rigid segregation. Slavery was abolished in the USA in 1863 but there were segregation laws until 1954. The main wave of arrival of ethnic groups to the UK took place long after the British had abolished the slave trade in 1807 (France abolished slavery in 1848). There have never been segregation laws in the UK. Almost all of the ethnic groups in the UK arrived voluntarily.

Age

There are very large differences in the age structures of the economically active people in different countries. In general developed countries such as the UK and France, USA and Singapore have older age structures than developing countries such as Thailand, China and Brazil. This is illustrated by Figure 17.3, which compares the projected age structures (ILO) of the economically active populations in 2010 in Italy and India.

Figure 17.3 shows India has a higher percentage of workers under the age of 35 whilst Italy has the higher percentage over the age of 35. Italy has one of the oldest workforces in Western Europe but it is not exceptional. The UK labour force is slightly younger than most West European countries. The "greying" of the workforces of developed countries has important consequences. In the past, employers have sometimes favoured younger workers because they were perceived to be stronger, brighter, quicker and more creative. However, these ideas are not well supported by empirical evidence. There is very little difference between the intelligence of a 20-year-old and a 50-year-old. A 50-year-old may also have other attributes such as experience and reliability. In fact the correlation between age and job performance is very close to zero (see p. 108, Figure 5.2)

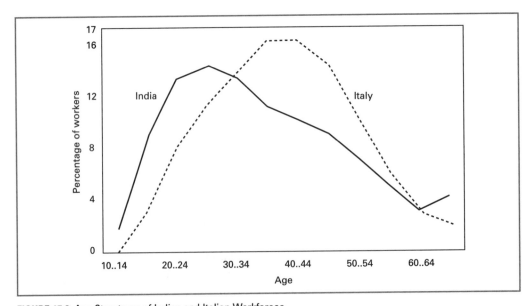

FIGURE 17.3 Age Structures of Indian and Italian Workforces

Religion

In many countries, such as the Russian Federation, the Netherlands, France and Germany religion is not a major issue and managers do not need to worry greatly about the religious beliefs of their employees. However, in other countries such as Israel, Belgium and Ireland religion plays a great part in the culture and politics of the nation. Religious sensitivities are usually most acute when there is either one very strong predominant religion (e.g. Ireland) or where there are a number of strong religions (e.g. Belgium, Israel, India). Figure 17.4, as an example, gives the percentage of the population with various beliefs (derived from the Central Statistics Office Ireland, 2005)

The chart clearly shows that in 2002 religion was an essential part of Irish culture and that the Roman Catholic church held a very dominant position. Sometimes, beliefs held by a small proportion of the workforce can make diversity difficult to manage. For example, the West Midlands police force, around Birmingham in the UK, has only a small number of Sikh officers. In this religion, wearing a turban has an immense significance of men. The West Midlands police force needed to change its regulations about officers' uniforms and redesign crash-helmets so that officers on motor-cycles could wear their turbans and be protected in the event of an accident.

Disability

It is inaccurate to use the term "disabled people". In an occupational setting it is highly improbable that an employee is totally afflicted and unable to do anything. A better term is "people with a disability". This emphasises that these are, first and foremost, people. It also indicates that there will be many areas where they are as competent as others. In general terms, about one in five people of working age have long-term disabilities (see EOC, 2004; Australian Bureau of Statistics, 2004). Disabilities can take many forms: the most obvious involve vision, hearing and movement. Other disabilities, such as psychological ones, are less obvious and more difficult to manage. The incidence of disability increases with age. In general, people with a disability are more likely to be unemployed or work in a part-time

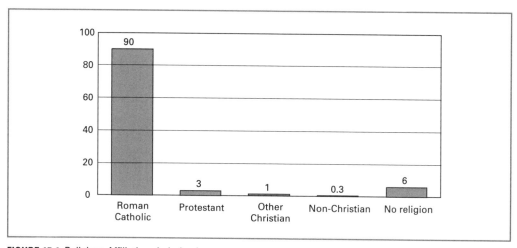

FIGURE 17.4 Religious Affiliations in Ireland

job. In the UK about 3.5 million of the 7 million people with disabilities are in employment. Often, very simple and inexpensive measures can mean they can work as effectively as others. People with movement difficulties can be allocated desks or workstations nearest doors and ramps can be provided to help them negotiate inclines. Similarly, extra lighting, magnification or voice synthesis of documents can be provided for people with vision problems.

17.4 Problems Encountered by Women and Minority Groups

Organisations and societies tend to be shaped in the image of the majority group or those in powerful positions. Hence many organisations present alien environments to less powerful groups such as women or minorities. It is often difficult to establish empirically the exact nature of the disadvantages because they may be subtle or covert. For example, the myth that older workers are less creative is likely to have an indirect impact on subconscious choices involved in assigning older workers to traditional rather than cutting-edge work. It may also exert a subconscious influence when supervisors appraise workers. Few managers are likely to show direct discrimination in public. They are more likely practice bigotry behind closed doors. Nevertheless, there are sufficient good studies to identify a list of possible obstacles faced by women and minority groups. They include:

- The **absence of role models** or **mentors** which they can use to guide their behaviour. Consequently, minority groups may appear to take longer to think things out and there is a much greater risk that they behave in an inappropriate way.

- Similarly, minority groups may be disadvantaged by the **exclusion from informal communication networks**. Because they do not have the same information or contacts, it will be harder to perform the work and get noticed.

- Minority groups are often employed as temporary workers or **part-time workers whose status may be emblazoned** with a distinctive badge or uniform. This may subconsciously influence other people's judgements of the value of their work.

- Members of minority groups often need to adopt a strategy of **biculturalism** in order to be valued by their organisation. In other words, they need to adopt the cultural ambience of their workplace in addition to their own "natural" culture. This requires additional effort.

- **Promotion systems based on seniority** often work against minority groups. Minority groups are often the most recent members to join an organisation. Hence, even if they are of equal merit, they are less likely to obtain promotion when it is based on a queuing system.

- Minority groups and less powerful groups of employees are more likely to suffer **harassment and bullying**. This topic is discussed in great detail in the next section of this chapter.

- A whole range of factors may combine to produce a "**glass ceiling**" or "**glass walls**" that confine women and minority groups to a narrow range of jobs. A glass ceiling is an invisible barrier, made up of myths, suppositions and unfriendly systems which limit the advancement of women and minorities. A glass wall is a similar barrier which confines people to certain areas of work. For example, the belief that women are unable to cope with stress may contribute to a glass walls that keep them away from functions such as production and restricts them into functions such as personnel.

These factors may combine to produce unfairness which hinders inclusiveness. Many governments have enacted legislation, regulations and directives to redress the balance.

17.5 Legal Aspects of Managing Diversity

Laws relevant to the management of diversity vary from country to country and, in the case of the United States, from state to state. It is not possible in a book of this kind to give an authoritative account of the legislation of even one country such as the UK. What follows is a general guide which should be supplemented by more detailed and specific information from other sources such as Earnshaw (2003 – UK), Wilson (2003 – India) and Barrett and Hede (2003 – Australia)

Most countries have legislation to protect women and minorities from discrimination. It usually covers discrimination on the grounds of gender, ethnic origin and age. In some countries it will also cover discrimination on the grounds of disability. In a few countries there will also be legislation covering discrimination on religious grounds. Most legislation makes the distinction between direct and indirect discrimination. *Direct discrimination* is where there is an obvious attempt to exclude certain people or given favourable treatment to other groups. Direct discrimination is usually the most repugnant form. A clear example would be a notice outside a restaurant saying "women not welcome" or "men only". Similarly, it would be illegal in the UK to advertise the job "Scottish chef wanted". However, it would not be illegal to advertise for a chef able to cook Scottish foods since, say, a chef from Hong Kong who was able to prepare a satisfactory dish of haggis would not be disqualified. *Indirect discrimination* occurs when there may not be an overt intention to discriminate but there is, nevertheless, an adverse impact. For example, the dispatch department of a motor manufacturer may be very prepared to employ people from the minorities. By tradition, however, it has always recruited new staff by recommendations from existing staff. Despite good intentions this company would be guilty of indirect discrimination. Members of a minority group might be disadvantaged because they were not included in the informal recruitment networks. Similarly, a publicity brochure that contained only pictures of male employees might constitute indirect discrimination because it might imply that only male candidates should apply. Another common example of indirect discrimination concerns the placing of notices and adverts. For example, placing an important notice in an advert in *Playboy* would be discriminatory because it is less likely to be seen by women.

Governments often set up commissions to enforce legislation and help people comply. In Great Britain the *Race Relations Act 1976* (amended 2000 and 2003) makes it unlawful to discriminate on the grounds of race or colour. The *Commission for Racial Equality* (CRE) was established to help employers understand and comply with the law. The CRE holds seminars, publishes guidelines and will often give organisations advice. Occasionally it enforces the law by taking wayward organisations to court.

Discrimination on the basis of gender is covered by the UK's *Equal Pay Act* and the *Sex Discrimination Act*. In Australia, The Equal Opportunity for Women in the Workplace Agency (EOWA) has a similar role with regard to Australian legislation. The *Disability Discrimination Act, 1995* has a wide remit and protects disabled people against discrimination in areas of employment, access to goods, facilities and services, buying or renting land and property and education. Under this act, organisations have a duty to adjust the way they provide services and make reasonable changes to their practices and procedures. The Act allows the government to set minimum standards of access to facilities such as websites and public transport.

Although the legislation concerning diversity of employees is very important, recourse to the law is often an admission of failure. It is better to persuade organisations to manage diversity effectively by demonstrating that the advantages of a diverse workforce outweigh the disadvantages.

17.6 Advantages and Disadvantages of Organisational Diversity

There are six main advantages in managing diversity correctly. They are:

- The **working lives of many people are improved**. This is an end in itself.
- The **quality of decision-making is improved**. Different backgrounds bring a rich and diverse set of perspectives that result in more creative solutions.
- The organisation will avoid the damaging effects of **bad publicity**. Indeed, the organisation might increase its reputation for social responsibility.
- An organisation with a high reputation for treating it employees fairly will find it **easier to attract able recruits**. This effect may spill over and help recruit good people who belong to the majority group.
- A company known to have a fair employment policy will find it easier to **market goods and services to minority group** members.
- A fair employment policy may enable an organisation to **obtain funds and contracts from government and other organisations**. Many governments encourage the adoption of fair employment policies by stipulating that their suppliers have positive ways of managing diversity.

However, managing diversity also has disadvantages. For example, *communication often takes longer* in a diverse organisation where groups have different languages, experience and cultures. There is much greater scope or misunderstandings and confusion. The communication difficulties sometimes result in the second disadvantage of a diverse workforce – *slowing down the rate of change*. It takes extra time to analyse the needs of different groups and answer several sets of concerns and worries. One feature of good management of diversity is the use of teams that contain a mixture of groups. However, mixed teams take *longer to develop effective relationships*. Finally, a diverse workforce incurs *extra costs*. Setting up extra consultation or making modifications for people with disabilities inevitably involves additional outlays.

17.7 Toolkit for Managing Diversity

Effective management of diversity does not happen by accident. Managers need to take a range of measures to bring it about. Probably the most important measure is to have a *clear policy*. The policy needs to cover most of the situations where diversity might cause difficulties. It then needs to be translated into specific actions and goals. A system that monitors whether the diversity goals have been achieved needs to be established. If the organisation operates a pay system which includes bonuses, the bonuses should, in part, be conditional on managers achieving their "diversity goals". Finally, the policy on diversity needs to be communicated widely and given visible support by top management. Methods of implementing the policy include:

- **Mentoring and network groups** which aim to provide minorities with systems of personal support that are "naturally" available to majority groups. In mentoring, junior members of staff are allocated a senior member of staff outside the normal line of command. They normally meet, say, three or four times per year and the junior member from the minority group will have an opportunity to review, in confidence, her or his progress, air worries or concerns and obtain guidance. The mentor may, or may not, belong to the same minority group. Network groups aim to fulfil much the same function but in a more cost-effective way. Typically, a group of six minority members plus a contributor from the majority group will meet, say, monthly to discuss issues and problems and to share information.

- **Recruitment and selection practices** are often a key part of a policy on diversity. First, jobs will be structured in a way which enables them to be performed by a wider range of people, especially people with disabilities. The way that vacancies are advertised might be widened to include those that are likely to be used by minorities. Selection methods may also be scrutinised to ensure that they do not disadvantage any particular group of applicants.

- **Training and development** plays a key role in implementing a policy on diversity. The instruction can be either embedded in an existing training programme such as introduction programs for graduate recruits or they can be developed into a special training course. Diversity training will cover most of the material given in this chapter. However, it will also attempt to develop positive attitudes and skills in dealing with people from non-traditional backgrounds. It will give participants a chance to reflect on their own attitudes and to examine whether these are supported by established facts. The aim of this process is to help participants understand their own feelings and attitudes. Another important strand of diversity training is to help participants empathise with members of minority groups. This can be achieved in a number of ways such as role-plays, case studies or by inviting members of minority groups to describe situations they have faced. Finally, diversity training attempts to impart helpful skills such as the ability to detect and clarify misunderstandings. It may also try to develop skills in harnessing the characteristics of minority groups in a positive way that adds to the organisation's overall performance.

CASE 17.1: BULLYING AT THE LAW SOCIETY

In 1999 Kamjitt Bahl was elected as vice-president of the Law Society. However, within months, two members of staff, subsequently joined by more than six others, complained that she was a bully. It emerged that in her previous post as chair of the Equal Opportunities Commission she had also been accused of bullying (Clement, 1996). The Law Society set up an inquiry under an eminent lawyer who subsequently found that she had subjected some staff to "verbal onslaughts" or dealt with them in an "unwarrantedly aggressive manner" so that they were humiliated or demeaned. The report said that she had introduced an atmosphere of fear and confusion. On advice from her legal team, which included the Prime Minister's wife Cherie Blair, Ms. Bahl launched an appeal and accused the Society of victimisation and racism. The whole affair, which involved three civil cases and four employment tribunals, culminated in July 2004 when an appeal Court dismissed these counter-claims. The legal fees were estimated to amount to almost £3 million and the bad publicity arising from the bullying incidents damaged the reputation of both Ms Bahl and the Law Society.

17.8 Definition and Concept of Bullying

Many people associate bullying with schooldays where an older boy like Flashman would terrorise a younger pupil such as Tom Brown. Others may also associate bullying with rough treatment of women and minority groups. In fact, most bullying occurs at the workplace and it can cost an organisation many thousands of pounds. For example, in 1998 the police force of Hampshire in the south of England paid a six-figure sum to a female detective who had been bullied by her male colleagues (Marks, 1998). Another high-profile example of bullying involved no less a person than a vice-president of the British Law Society.

It is little wonder that, these days, many organisations are making efforts to eliminate bullying at work.

Bullying is also known as "harassment", "victimisation" and "psychological terror". Sometimes, especially in the USA, it is also called "mobbing" but this word carries connotations of harassment by a number of people. Bullying may be defined as:

> 66 Bullying at work means harassing, offending, socially exploiting someone or negatively affecting someone's work tasks. In order for the label "bullying" ... to be applied to a particular activity, interaction or process it has to occur repeatedly and regularly ... over a period of time ... bullying is an escalating process in the course of which the person ends up in an inferior position and becomes the target of systematic negative social acts. A conflict cannot be called "bullying" if the incident is an isolated event or if two parties of approximately equal "strength" are in conflict. 99
>
> *(Einarsen et al. 2003)*

This definition contains four key phrases that require a little further explanation (see Hoel, Zapf and Cooper, 2002): repetition, negative effect, imbalance of power and negative acts.

Bullying takes place *"repeatedly and regularly"* – a single incident of negative behaviour would not constitute bullying unless it was so intense that it permanently "cowed" the target. Often the distinction between whether an action or is bullying or not lies in the frequency of its occurrence rather than the action itself. One joke at a person's expense would not be bullying – hourly jokes of the same kind would constitute bullying. The definition implies that the bullying process tends to involve the series of stages – aggressive behaviour, bullying, stigmatisation and severe trauma (Leymann, 1990; Einarsen, 1999). The first stage of aggressive behaviour is often characterised by indirect aggression that may be subtle and devious. Confrontation may be difficult because a person may not even realise he or she is being targeted. The second, bullying stage, often involves humiliating, ridiculing and isolating the targets. Victims become aware that someone is out to get them and they may feel hounded. The stigmatisation stage then begins. The victim becomes unable to defend themselves and often their work begins to suffer. They thus become even more vulnerable and, in some ways, seem to "deserve" their treatment. In the final stage, the victim may become withdrawn and reluctant to communicate in case it exposes them to further attack. They may become erratic and obsessive about details.

If an action does not have a *negative effect* on the target person then, even if it is repeated, the action does not constitute bullying. This negative effect is usually a subjective reaction – such as anxiety or low self-esteem. However, in some cases the viewpoint of other people may be important. The final part of the definition centres upon an imbalance of power between the bully and his or her target. Often, the *imbalance in power* is formal – the bully may be the victim's manager. Sometimes, the imbalance in power is informal and is derived from the bully's physical strength, social popularity or specialist expertise. The exact *nature of the negative acts* can vary considerably. A large survey of 5288 British workers by Hoel, Cooper and Faragher (2001) identified 28 negative behaviours. The following list contains the 12 that occurred most frequently:

1 withholding information that affected victims' performance
2 unwanted sexual attention
3 humiliation or ridicule
4 allocation of menial or lower level of work
5 removal of the areas of responsibility and replacement by trivial or unpleasant tasks
6 spreading gossip and rumours
7 being ignored, excluded or being "sent to Coventry"
8 insulting and offensive personal remarks about background, attitudes or private life
9 shouting and being target of spontaneous anger
10 intimidating behaviour such as finger pointing, invasion of personal space or barring the way
11 hints or signals the victim should quit
12 threats of violence or physical abuse

Negative behaviour can be put in four major categories. *Work-related harassment* involves criticism of the quality and quantity of the victim's work. *Personal harassment* is directed at features of the individual and it is used to humiliate or exclude the target. *Managerial harassment* includes things such as withholding important information, being given trivial work or allocated impossible deadlines. *Intimidation* covers threats of violence, rage and shouting.

Sexual harassment is a particular type of bullying and it is illegal in many countries. In essence, it consists of any unwanted activity of a sexual nature that creates an intimidating, offensive or hostile environment which interferes with an individual's work or their employment opportunities. While all sexual harassment should be avoided, there is a spectrum of seriousness. At one end is a *generalised unpleasantness* in the form of sexual comments and actions which are clearly not intended as a sexual overture but which make some people feel uncomfortable at work. Typically, this might consist of displaying nude posters which might make some women feel uncomfortable. Often, this escalates to the point where the victims avoid contact with the people or places involved. Much more serious is the *solicitation of sexual favours*. This might be indirect or direct. Sometimes the solicitation is made with the promise of other favours in return – it amounts to purchasing sex. Sometimes solicitation is even more serious because it is accompanied by coercion or threat of punishment. The threats may be in terms of academic grades, blocking promotion or other ways of damaging the victim's career. The most serious kind of sexual harassment involves *assaults and crimes* such as rape. In most countries rape is second only to homicide in seriousness.

Sexual harassment may involve members of the same sex as well as members of the opposite sex. About 10 per cent of complaints of sexual harassment in the USA in 1991 were complaints by males (Carton, 1994).

17.9 Extent and Importance of Bullying

It is very difficult to arrive at an objective estimate of the extent of bullying. Data on the number of official complaints will vastly underestimate its extent since some victims will be reluctant to report incidents for fear of retaliation. Large-scale survey data based on individuals' subjective perceptions is likely to overestimate the incidence of bullying. Such estimates are likely to be inflated by several per cent because paranoiacs will be prone to see bullying where none exists. Furthermore, such surveys often contain a high-level of response-rate bias – those who believe they have been bullied are more likely to return their questionnaires. Finally, estimates from surveys are likely to capitalise on chance. Respondents will make errors when reporting whether or not they have been bullied. As the next chapter shows this can inflate estimates. For example, suppose that the true incidence of bullying is 10 per cent but there is a 10 per cent error (a small margin in social science) in people's judgements of bullying. This means that one person who was genuinely bullied will have replied that he or she was not bullied. However nine people who were not in fact bullied will have reported that they were bullied. Consequently, this survey would show that bullying occurred in 18 per cent of cases (10−1+9) when in fact the scientific answer would be 10 per cent.

Consequently it is no surprise that estimates of bullying vary dramatically from 38 per cent of respondents to 7 per cent of respondents (see Hoel, Cooper and Faragher, 2001 p. 444;

Queensland Government, 2002, pp. 18–19). Much of the discrepancy can be explained by the use of differing definitions – especially the time-span. Some surveys report occurrences of bullying during a working life while others use a period of six or 12 months. The results of Hoel, Cooper and Faragher appear to be representative and are based on a large sample of over 12 000 employees drawn from 70 organisations in the UK. The response rate was 43 per cent – 5288 questionnaires were returned. 10.6 per cent of respondents claimed that they had been bullied in the last six months and 50 per cent of those who responded reported seeing incidents of bullying. A survey of over 1000 workers by the Institute of Personnel and Development (IPD) in 1996 indicated that about 12 per cent of people had been bullied in the previous five years.

Bullying can have important consequences for organisations. Tribunals consistently find against organisations where there has been tacit acceptance of an atmosphere conducive to bullying. The Bahl case at the Law Society shows that instances of bullying can generate huge costs and cause great damage to an organisation's reputation and credibility. However, there are many other consequences that may have even greater importance (see Hoel, Einarsen and Cooper, 2003). First, bullying frequently reduces the *productivity of the victim*. Second, victims of bullying frequently seek respite by taking days off work. Victims of bullying took, on average, seven days more *sick leave* per year – equivalent to about 18 million lost working days in the UK per year. Third, bullying may lead to *increased labour turnover* with all its associated costs of recruitment and training. However, much of the evidence to support this claim is based on anecdote and "stated intention to leave" rather than the number of victims who actually leave. Bullying can also cause considerable *disruption*. It is likely that the bully will be suspended for the duration of an investigation and someone else will have to be paid to do their work. Often an investigation into bullying results in a change in the place of work of either the bully or, more likely, the victim. Again, this will cause extra disruption and costs. The Australian Institute of Management calculated that in an organisation which has 100 employees on an average salary of $35 000 per year, bullying would cost that organisation $175 000 per year in terms of absenteeism, turnover, legal fees and disruption.

Finally, the important consequences for individuals should not be overlooked. Victims can lose substantial sums of money if their performance suffers and pay is linked to productivity. They may incur extra costs of changing jobs. Perhaps more important is the impact of bullying on the physical and psychological health of victims. Einarsen (2000) suggest that 75 per cent of victims suffered symptoms that are similar to post-traumatic stress disorder and that bullying could lead to social maladjustment, psychosomatic illnesses, depression, anger and despair. Indeed, it has been calculated that one in five suicides is linked to bullying in the workplace (Battles, 2003).

17.10 Anatomy of Bullying

The anatomy of bullying can be examined under three main headings: the bullies, the bullying situation and the victims.

Bullies

Since there is usually a differential of power in a bully's favour it is not surprising that most, but not all, bullies are superiors of the victim. Hoel, Cooper and Faragher (2001) report bullies have the status shown in Table 17.2 (the total exceeds 100 per cent because some victims are harassed by more than one bully).

■ Managers or supervisors	75%
■ Colleagues	37%
■ Clients	8%
■ Subordinates	7%

TABLE 17.2 The Status of Bullies

There is research that indicates most bullies are men. However, this is believed to be largely because men tend to hold positions of power within organisations. Consequently, the proportion of bullies who are male could change as more women reach senior positions. There is some research which suggest that younger workers are more likely to be bullies than older ones.

There is a great deal of speculation about why people become bullies. It is possible that during their childhood or youth bullies receive some kind of positive reinforcement when they harass. Consequently the behaviour pattern is learned. Randall (1997) believes that "bullies are created, not born. They are the product of complex social processes which, through faulty learning, create an antisocial personality characterised by the aggressive manipulation of others.". It has also been suggested that bullies harass other people because it boosts their self-esteem. Some people suggest that many bullies do not understand that their behaviour is wrong and cannot understand why the victims become upset. They may believe that their behaviour is justified in terms of helping the organisation attain its goals. Bullies may often have a strong sense of self-righteousness and conviction in what they are doing. Some researchers have suggested that harassment takes place because the bully is dissatisfied with their job and workplace. Consequently they take out their anger and frustration by bullying others.

The situation

Bullying does not occur randomly. It is concentrated in various places. *Type of occupation* is a major determinant. Health service workers and those in higher education are the groups most likely to be harassed. Indeed, many people believe that bullying is endemic in these sectors. Bullying also seems to be prevalent in many helping professions, construction, business services, transport and communications. *Type of employment* is another factor. Bullying occurs more frequently when workers are not full-time employees but are apprentices, casual workers, temporary workers or subcontractors. Jobs that require people to work in isolation without much contact with others seem to be favourite targets for workplace harassment. There is a clear link between *organisational change* and bullying. It is more likely to occur when there is a new manager, a new owner, new technology, a company reorganisation or budget cuts. There is some evidence that when organisations undergo restructuring, 60 per cent of employees will experience some workplace bullying.

Sometimes several of these factors combine to produce a workplace *culture of harassment*. The values, beliefs and norms of the organisation may lead both workers and employers to accept bullying. This may be reinforced by rites, rituals and patterns of communication. "Robust behaviours" by supervisors may be encouraged by a tradition of hierarchical management or military management style which may be condoned by the employer (Queensland Government, 2002). When individuals challenge this culture they are likely to be considered out-of-line.

The victim

The common stereotype of a victim may be an inadequate individual who brings harassment upon himself or herself. In fact, this stereotype is far from the truth. Bullying behaviours are usually directed at *groups* of people rather than individuals. For example, Hoel, Cooper and Faragher (2001) found that 31 per cent of bullying was directed at individuals whilst 69 per cent was directed at a group of workers. There is a tendency for the victims of bullying to be workers aged under 24 – although older workers are more likely to lodge formal complaints (perhaps because they have higher expectations and have more confidence in stating their own case). There is a perception that some people have a history of victimisation so researchers have tried to determine whether certain types of people are more likely to be victimised than others. In a nutshell they have found weak tendencies for people who have been bullied to be introverted, worrying, submissive and conscientious (Seigne, Coyne and Randall, 1999). However, this personality profile could be the *result* of being bullied rather than its *cause*.

17.11 Prevention and Coping with Bullying

An employer has responsibility to provide a workplace that is safe from both physical and mental hazards. That includes safety from bullying. Consequently an employer must take reasonable steps to prevent victimisation or harassment. Dereliction of this duty is punishable by substantial fines and compensation awards. It may also damage the organisation's reputation.

Prevention by organisations

Organisations can do a great deal to reduce bullying. Most of the measures require few physical resources – although they usually involve additional staff. The main actions an organisation can take to minimise bullying are:

- The most important action is to **create a climate** in which bullying is not tolerated. It should be made clear that the organisation's philosophy, values and norms have no place for the harassment and victimisation. Organisations do have a right to impose standards and to discipline those who do not attain those standards. However, the standards must be reasonable and enforced impartially in a way that is proportionate. It is usually helpful if the organisation's vision statement makes it clear that it has a "zero tolerance" of bullying. As the chapter on communication made clear, non-verbal communication is more powerful than policy statements. Senior managers should act as role models and ensure that they do not bully their own subordinates.

- The second most important action involves **training staff**, especially managers and supervisors. In the event of a dispute, tribunals usually look favourably on organisations that have provided training. Typically the training alerts people to the possibility that their behaviour might constitute bullying and gives them guidance on alternative ways of achieving objectives. Normally it also includes details of those who are most at risk, the sources of bullying and ways that it might be managed.

- Third, an organisation should establish a **mechanism to deal with any bullying** that might occur. An easy step is to nominate a member of staff to whom allegations of bullying should be reported. Another easy step is to guarantee that anyone reporting bullying would, initially, have complete confidentiality. Furthermore, there should be support mechanisms for people who feel that they have been victimised. Complaints of bullying should always be processed sympathetically, promptly and in an impartial way. Indeed, prompt and impartial action usually leads to a speedy resolution of the problem. However, in a protracted situation there should be mechanisms to support both the person making the complaint *and* the alleged perpetrator. It is imperative that there is no possibility of continued bullying whilst a complaint is investigated. However, it must be recognised that automatic suspension of the alleged perpetrator might impose unreasonable stress and other disadvantages – for which compensation might be claimed at a later date – the alleged perpetrator has a right to "natural justice" too.

- The fourth most useful step an organisation may take is to **monitor obvious signs of bullying**. For example, it should monitor increases in absences or deterioration in levels of performance.

Prevention by witnesses

Bullying can also be prevented by witnesses. Research suggests that a substantial proportion of bullying takes place when other people are present. If the witnesses take no action, it is tantamount aiding and abetting the bully. History provides a very useful lesson. One, very worthy German living in the middle of the last century rued his complicity with the Nazis – "when they persecuted gypsies I did not protest; when they persecuted homosexuals, I did nothing; when they started deporting the Jews I looked the other way; when they came from *me*, there was no-one left to give *me* support". Witnesses can take a number of actions, depending on the severity of the bullying. Minor infractions can be dealt with by a humorous comment. More severe infractions should be dealt with by a substantive conversation with the perpetrator outlining the impact they have on others and the impact bullying may have on the perpetrator and his or her career. A severe infraction warrants a clear statement that the bullying should cease and the incident should be reported to the appropriate authority.

17.12 Toolkit for Dealing with Bullying

Victims must first reflect whether they are truly subjected to bullying or whether they have just received insensitive treatment on a vulnerable day. The definition of bullying at the start of this chapter might help clarify whether their treatment actually constitutes bullying. A confidential conversation with a friend, trusted colleague or mentor may also help. If after a period of reflection of, say, three days it still seems that bullying has taken place, a series of actions should be taken.

1 Concerns should be **discussed with a credible and trusted source**. This may be an official from a trades union or professional body.

2 Keep a **detailed log of interactions** with the alleged bully. This includes preserving documents and noting the identity of witnesses.

3 Attempt to **ignore the bully's behaviour**. Proceed on a "business as usual" basis. In some situations, it might be useful to walk away whenever the bully commences his or her harassment.

4 Check on **previous appraisals**. Assemble any memos, voice mails or letters that have lauded your performance.

5 It may be worth checking on the **legal** position – again your union or professional body may be able to help.

If these stages have been followed the victim is then, at a time of their choosing, in a good position to take their allegations to the appropriate person. The objective at this stage should be to stop the bullying rather than extract revenge or denigrate the bully. The combined action of employers, witnesses and victims should ensure that Flashman and his acolytes are confined to history and the pages of *Tom Brown's Schooldays*.

Activities and Further Study

Essay Plans

Draw up plans for the following essays *and* identify three sources of useful information that you might use:

1 Why should managers take an interest in topics such as diversity or bullying? Illustrate your answers with specific examples.

2 Explain what is meant by a multicultural organisation and describe ways that managers can bring one about.

3 What kinds of problems may be encountered at work by women and minority groups?

Web Activities

Use the Web to

1 Locate up-to-date details of anti-discrimination legislation in your country. Some useful sites may be:

- *www.womenandequalityunit.gov.uk/legislation/key_legislation_1003.doc*
- *http://www.hreoc.gov.au/legal/links.html*
- *http://www.lbr.nl/?node=2008*
- *http://www.ldac-taac.ca/LDandtheLaw/ch03_Law-e.asp*

2 Locate sites giving resources and advice that might be useful in combating discrimination at work. Some useful sites may be:

- *http://www.agediscrimination.org.uk/*
- *http://www.seekful.com/indx.cfm?q=Discrimination*
- *http://www.info.gov.hk/hkfacts/eoc.pdf*
- *http://www.lawlink.nsw.gov.au/lawlink/adb/ll_adb.nsf/pages/adb_how_to_deal*

3 Locate sites giving resources and advice that might be useful in combating bullying at work. Some useful sites may be:

- *http://www.ccohs.ca/oshanswers/psychosocial/bullying.html*
- *http://www.workershealth.com.au/facts027.html*
- *http://www.bullyonline.org/workbully/worbal.htm*

Experiential Activities

1 Think back over your recent experiences at college or work and try to identify three incidents where you experienced or witnessed discrimination or bullying. In each case:

   ■ Describe the situation that led up to the incident, including background and organisational factors.

   ■ Describe what happened and what you did.

   ■ Work out, with the benefit of hindsight, the actions you should have taken.

   Compare the incidents and identify common elements.

2 Talk to managers and other people at work. Ask them to identify issues, problems and commercial opportunities that involve people. List at least two other issues in addition to diversity and bullying. Research these extra issues using an electronic database (provided by your college or other library) of current newspapers stories (e.g. Custom Newspapers).

Fads, Gurus, Cons and Science

❖ LEARNING OBJECTIVES

After reading this chapter you should have improved your ability to criticise and evaluate the merits of different claims by researchers and experts. You should have a framework for analysing evidence and you should be more resistant to a passing fads and confidence tricks. In particular you should be able to:

1 **define** fads and give examples of two classic historical fads

2 **decide** whether Business Process Re-engineering is a recent management fad

3 **define** what is meant by a management guru and the **list** the three main types

4 **list** at least six management gurus

5 **critically evaluate** the work of Peter Drucker

6 **critically** evaluate the work of Tom Peters

7 **critically evaluate** the work of Michael Porter

8 **briefly describe** five techniques used to support false claims for management techniques

9 **compare and contrast** three main approaches in management research

10 **describe** two main measurement problems encountered by management researchers

11 **list** three main characteristics of good management research

12 **compare and contrast** a research study in management with a research study in medicine, chemistry, physics, psychology or engineering

Management is an ill-defined and open-ended task that may produce anxiety (see Huczynski, 1993) in the job holders. Managers can never be sure that they are discharging their duties adequately. They are always faced with the possibility that they have ignored some new idea that would improve their organisation's competitiveness. At a more personal level, ambitious managers will want to show that they are more worthy of promotion than their colleagues by being more up-to-date. Managers also tend to be moderate extroverts who are easily bored and who like change even when change is not strictly necessary. The heady concoction of angst, ambition and craving for change leads many otherwise commercially savvy managers to be gullible consumers of fads and gurus. Shapiro (1998) coined the phrase "Fad Surfing" to describe the penchant of managers to latch on to ephemeral fashions and "flavours of the month".

Management fashions can be avoided or ignored. It is usually dangerous: most fads have powerful advocates who interpret any non-conformance as a sign of inability to keep up-to-date. This chapter aims to outline some aspects of management "fashions" so that they can be identified and handled appropriately. It is organised into four main sections:

Chapter contents

18.1 Fads and Crazes

Definition and general characteristics of management fads

A *fad* is "a craze or a peculiar, senseless, idea that is adopted capriciously and uncritically – perhaps because others have recently adopted it or perhaps because it satisfies some temporary psychological need". Fads are not new. Some of the earliest known fads involved finance. This is probably because financial records often survive for future generations. Two well-known examples are "Tulipomania" and the "South-Sea Bubble".

Tulipomania and the South Sea Bubble demonstrate a classic recipe for a speculative craze. The main ingredients are:

- an unfamiliar or new product that seems scarce
- liquid assets (perhaps borrowed money) available to fund purchases
- a widespread belief that demand is infinite
- individuals who believe that they are among the first to know of the opportunity

One of the first signs that a bubble is about to burst is that the general public start buying. The basic dynamics of speculation are seen with depressing regularity. For example, they underpinned the speculation that led to the 1929 stock market crash in Wall Street,

CASE 18.1: CLASSIC FADS

Tulipomania occurred in Holland in 1637. Tulips had been recently introduced to Europe and were a status symbol. Their price rose inexorably and people bought tulip bulbs at high prices, not because they valued tulips but because they believed that someone else would pay a much higher price in the future. Many borrowed money to buy ever-more expensive tulips. Bulbs reached such giddy prices that very few people could afford to buy them – other "mugs" could not enter the market. At that point people realised that the price of tulip bulbs was way above their intrinsic value. There were lots of sellers and very few buyers. Many sellers, especially those who had borrowed, feared that they would not be able to obtain even a fraction of their original purchase price. In fear, they panicked and unloaded tulip bulbs onto an already glutted market. Prices dropped like a stone. Many speculators "had their fingers burnt" and cynics were again able to claim that markets are driven "by greed and fear".

The "South Sea Bubble" took place in England in 1720. The government of the day decided to wipe out some of its debts by creating and selling shares in the South Sea Company, which would have a monopoly of English trade with Spanish Colonies in South America. There was no shortage of investors, because they were promised dividends of 30 per cent in the first year and 50 per cent in subsequent years. The shares were so attractive that demand became a stampede. Between February and July the price of shares in the Company rose ninefold. A valuation in August, however, showed that the assets of the company were far below the value of the shares. The "buy stampede" became a "sell stampede" and by October the shares were back to a price similar to that in February.

Poseidon (an Australian nickel mining company), and Polly Peck bubbles of the 1970s and 1990s, respectively. They also underpinned the .com boom and bust of the 2000s.

Some of the major critics of fads are Collins (2000), Huczynski (1993) and Micklethwaite and Wooldridge (1996). They suggest the main fad of the 1980s was TQM and the fad of 1990s was "empowerment" while Business Process Re-engineering is another example of a more recent management fad.

Business Process Re-engineering: a recent management fad?

Description of Business Process Re-engineering

Business Process Re-engineering (BPR) established itself as the first great management fad of the 1990s (Micklethwaite and Wooldridge, 1996). It first analyses the processes an organisation must perform in order to deliver its product or service. Next, in a way that would find favour with Taylor's scientific managers and latter-day time-study engineers, it breaks the organisation down into its component parts and examines the contribution each unit makes to the key processes. Finally, it reassembles the units so that the process is performed as efficiently as possible. For example, a retail bank may identify opening new customer accounts as a key process. It may then discover that the application is handled by five different people who carry out one part of the process, for example, checking whether there is an existing account, checking creditworthiness, establishing a computer file, issuing credit cards and sending security information. As the application joins the bottom of each person's in-tray the complete process might take a week. Information technology and the use of computers mean that the process can be re-engineered so that one person completes all the stages in one session, taking a single day.

In many ways Business Process Re-engineering reverses the trend of 150 years where workers were given more and more specialised tasks. This is made possible because computers can provide help so that one individual can complete many different tasks. This has two consequences. First, it eliminates the "organisational chimneys" that were described in Chapter 4. Second, it greatly reduces the need for middle managers whose main organisational role is to integrate the activities of the different functions. Indeed, BPR usually results in the loss of many middle management jobs. However, BPR often resulted in the loss of jobs at all levels when whole business units were "obliterated". BPR became associated with the downsizing of major organisations and downsizing became associated with corporate health. A company's share price would often rise immediately a downsizing exercise was announced. One analysis by Mitchell & Co (quoted by Micklethwaite and Wooldridge, p. 35) indicated that downsizing companies outperformed the stock market for six months after their downsizing was announced. Cost–benefit analyses generally showed that BPR usually exceeded the corporate's needed rate of return of 12 per cent, or so.

Criticisms of Business Process Re-engineering

In the mid-1990s opinion began to turn and BPR met increasing criticism. The large consultancy CSI Index (which has close links with the Sloan School of Management at the Massachusetts Institute of Science and Technology) offered a service that quantified the need for, and success of, BPR. A CSI Index consultant, Fred Weirsema and his associate Michael Treacy published *The Discipline of Market Leaders* that extolled the virtues of BPR. Their book shot into the best-sellers list. Demand for the book, the services of the authors and CSI Index was buoyant – until malpractice was revealed. It emerged that the consultants, their employers and some of their business associates were buying tens of thousands of copies of the book themselves – especially from bookshops thought to be used by the *New York Times* to compile its best-seller's list. BPR ran into trouble from two other directions. First, the cost benefit of BPR was questioned. Clients were reluctant to reveal the exact details of the cost–benefit analysis and such analyses were conducted by people who had a vested interest in proving the technique was a success. Hammer (1995) admitted that 70 per cent of efforts at BPR had failed. Furthermore, an independent analysis showed that, while the shares of downsizing (sometimes called "rightsizing") organisations outperformed the market in the short-term, in the longer term (three years later) they underperformed the market. Second, authorities started to point out the dysfunctions of "anorexic downsizing". They are:

- While downsizing cuts the salary bill and shows short-term cost benefits, it diverts resources from longer-term developments and innovations. The organisation becomes an efficient but inflexible machine excellent at making a static product. Inevitably, that product will become out-of-date and the organisation may have engineered-out the capacity to adapt and devise a better product (Dougherty and Bowman, 1995).

- During the downsizing process a great deal of management time is spent discussing who will lose their jobs and who will not. This demotivates top management. Junior and middle management are demotivated when they realise their career ladder has no middle rungs.

- Experienced managers leave and the company is then forced to spend money on training to teach new managers to do jobs that the previous managers knew by heart. Many re-engineered organisations were forced to hire back their previous middle managers – as more expensive consultants.

Advocates of BPR complain that these criticisms are unfair. They first defend BPR's record by using a standard ploy of claiming that the principles are right but the implementation is wrong. This tactic wins little support – a characteristic of a good idea is that it should be easy to implement. Despite these criticisms, some successful examples of BPR engineering exist – especially in areas of logistics and customer delivery. In these areas BPR does usually produce improvements – as the earlier bank example shows – in speed of delivery and the level of service that the customer is given. The advocates of BPR note that companies, such as France Telecom and Bull computers which are protected from the competitive need to re-engineer, are in worse shape and deliver poorer service than British Telecom and IBM who extensively re-engineered.

The example of Business Process Re-engineering demonstrates that evaluating latest trends and fads is a tricky business. They are often surrounded by a mixture of hype, dodgy analyses and gurus with inflated egos but they often contain an element of truth. Wristwatches originated as a fad. So did sandwiches, trousers and many other essential aspects of modern life.

The trick is to identify the fads that are useful and lasting from those that are here today and gone tomorrow. The remainder of this chapter aims help winnow the wheat from the chaff. The next step is to examine the contributions of well-known management gurus.

18.2 Management Gurus

Concept and types of guru

The term "guru" is derived from Sanskrit and means "venerable" (Pattison, 1997). It is applied to spiritual leaders who able to able to solve problems by discerning fundamental truths. A guru has power and authority over his or her devotees. In Europe, the term "management guru" can be used in a pejorative way to imply someone who makes lofty pronouncements that do not take account of the practical constraints that apply to ordinary people. Some people (for example, Collins, 2000) believe that management gurus are the managerial equivalent of *carpet-baggers*. Huczynski (1993) noted that gurus fell into three types:

- **Hero-managers** are gurus with first-hand, practical experience of managing an organisation and who have achieved outstanding things. They have no systematic approach or theory. They often "fly by the seat of their pants" and "dabble" in the running of organisations. Classic examples of hero-managers who have become gurus include Sir

John Harvey-Jones, former chairman of ICI, and Anita Roddick, the founder of the Body Shop.

- **Consultant gurus** have usually worked as a senior member of a major firm of consultants such as McKinsey & Co. Unlike hero-managers, consultant gurus are members of a profession and they will have had specialist training. Their prestige and intellectual power is often derived from their work with many of the world's leading organisations. They intervene in the running of organisations in a purposeful and deliberate way. Classic examples of consultant gurus are Tom Peters, Robert Waterman and Richard Boyatis.

- **Academic gurus** are the products of prestigious universities such as Harvard. They may have specialist training in organisational analysis, but they may lack substantive experience of first-hand management of anything other than a small-scale research group. Their advice and suggestions may be based on theory and high-level abstractions which, while generally true, may have little relevance to the work of a manager facing specific challenges in specific work settings. Classic examples of academic gurus include Peter Drucker, Michael Porter and Charles Handy.

Gurus specialise in different fields. Drucker offers advice on (among other things) the knowledge society, Peters's early work involved the search for organisational excellence whilst Porter offers advice on organisational strategy. Nevertheless they have three common characteristics – vision, research and action (Huczynski, 1993). In keeping with the Sanskrit notion of a guru as a far-sighted religious leader, most gurus have a *vision* that offers salvation. Often it is salvation from foreign competitors operating in low-cost countries. The vision must appear to have clear, simple benefits for followers such as identification of new markets, a faster rate of innovation or improved quality. The vision will be more attractive if it overturns some cherished or commonly held idea (Clarke and Salaman, 1993). Management gurus usually promote *active research* in the sense that they encourage managers to experiment with new ideas and methods. Another common feature of management gurus is their tendency to suggest standard recipes involving short-term *actions* that bring success. A specific example of short term, standard recipes would be Blanchard and Johnson's (1983) *One Minute Manager*. Sometimes actions suggested by gurus are outrageous and "over-the-top" (Collins, 2000).

It is impossible to describe the contribution of all of these gurus in this book. However, as a sample, a brief description of the works of Drucker, Peters and Porter is provided. Drucker is given pride of place because his writings have exercised influence on management thinking over many decades, Tom Peters is a good example of a flamboyant guru from a background of management consulting, while Porter is a classic example of a serious academic guru.

Peter Drucker

Background to Drucker

Few people have had as much influence on the theory of management as Peter Ducker. Indeed, he has been so influential he has been called "the guru's guru". (Micklethwaite and Wooldridge, 1996). Some people regard Drucker as the person who established

CASE 18.2: TOP GURUS

In 2002 Accenture ranked management gurus on the basis of the number of Google enquiries, the number of times they were cited by academics and the frequency with which they appeared in the media. The top 10 gurus were:

Rank	Name	Specialty	Example Publication
1	Michael Porter	Strategy	*The Competitive Advantage*
2	Tom Peters	Excellence	*In Search of Excellence*
3	Robert Reich	Worker's Rights	*Work of Nations*
4	Peter Drucker	Management	*The Effective Executive*
5	Gary Becker	Behavioural Economics	*Human Capital*
6	Peter Senge	Organisational Learning	*The Fifth Discipline*
7	Gary Hamel	Strategy and Innovation	*Competing for the Future*
8	Alvin Toffler	Futurology	*Future Shock*
9	Hal Varian	Information Systems	*Information Rules*
10	Daniel Goldman	Emotional Intelligence	*Primal Leadership*

"management" as a discipline in its own right. (Taylor would probably not agree.) Nevertheless, Ducker has changed the managerial world with his ideas of privatisation and knowledge work. Drucker was born in Austria in 1909 and tried a number of jobs in his twenties. In 1942 he became an academic teaching politics, philosophy and economics at an American university.

Drucker's ideas

Drucker's writings can be grouped under three main themes: management as a discipline, managing organisations and comments on the shape of society.

Perhaps Drucker's greatest contribution has been his focus on *management as a discipline*. Before Drucker management was a hodgepodge of different themes and disciplines. Drucker forged many of these disparate components into a more coherent whole. He emphasised the importance of rational and clear management. In *The Practice of Management* Drucker (1954) pointed out that organisations are not ends in themselves but exist for a purpose – producing a product or service that is valued more highly than the resources the organisation consumes. Consequently, organisational structures should not be allowed to simply happen. Instead, they should be designed carefully so that the organisation can fulfil its purpose in the present, the mid term and the longer term. Drucker also played a large part in developing the technique of Management By Objectives (MBO). He emphasised the importance of outputs rather than inputs – management by results rather than management by supervision.

Drucker urges managers to view labour as a resource rather than as a cost. *People* are the source of ideas for new products. *People* choose or develop machines and production systems. *People* assemble parts into finished goods. *People* identify and exploit markets.

People collect money and prepare accounts. If the people in an organisation are good, they do these things well and the organisation prospers. Drucker argued further that people are not machines. Many have talents that are not utilised. The assembly line, he argued, was inefficient because it could only move at the pace of the slowest individual. It demotivates people and prevents them from using their talents to the full. Drucker suggested that in many situations properly trained workers can manage their own activities better than a remote expert or manager. He emphasised the idea of "a responsible worker". These ideas are now obvious and commonplace. They were not so obvious in America in the 1940s and 1950s where many managers viewed employees as a difficult and troublesome kind of machine that should be replaced by a mechanical device whenever possible. Drucker urged managers to spend more time engaging employee's minds rather than devising ways to control their hands. It can be argued that these ideas of Drucker were the beginnings of "empowerment" and "team-manufacturing".

Drucker has also made a large contribution to our view of *managing organisations*. His second book emphasised the social aspects of organisations. He attracted the attention of the General Motors corporation. They asked him to write a book describing General Motors and he was able to interview people at all levels. In 1946 *The Concept of the Corporation* was published and it quickly became a best-seller. It dealt with both the economics of General Motors and its sociological aspects – especially "the corporation as a social institution" and "the corporation as human effort". These sections of the book focused on the non-economic aspects of the way that people interacted at work. *The Concept of the Corporation* noted that people in General Motors were organised in a decentralised structure and that this had made it easier for GM to find solutions to changes as they moved from wartime to peacetime production. Drucker maintained that decentralisation works because it creates small pools of workers who feel that their contribution matters. Decentralisation into smaller units creates places where young managers can experiment and, perhaps, make mistakes without endangering the whole company. He called these places "farms for growing talent".

Drucker (1969) commented extensively on the *future shape of society*. He came to the conclusion that in the future organisations will be totally different. He envisaged that traditional organisations would cease to cope with the demands of their environment and that they would either perish or metamorphose into entirely different structures. New ways would not quietly evolve from the old. They would be drastically different. He identified three main sources of **discontinuity**: the growth of the knowledge society, globalization and disenchantment with government:

- In 1959 Drucker noted the growing importance of "**knowledge workers**" – employees who collect, synthesise and evaluate information and who create new ideas. He believed they were a country's key assets. Societies and governments should not shore up old industries against cheaper competition abroad. Instead, they should ensure that the knowledge and expertise of its workforce is as high as possible so that they can invent and produce better, higher value, products and services. Drucker believed that the increasing importance of knowledge workers would change management in significant ways. A large part of the information that knowledge workers manipulate is in their own brains. Therefore, this asset is owned by employees, not the organisation.

Knowledge workers are often at liberty to change jobs and use their knowledge on behalf of another organisation. Knowledge workers have a high responsibility to develop their own skills and abilities. The freedom of knowledge working can be both liberating and destabilising. New patterns of employment, training and even pension provision have had to be developed.

■ Drucker acknowledged that **globalisation** is not a new phenomenon and that before the First World War a very large share of manufacturing was conducted on a multinational basis as companies such as Fiat, Siemens and Ford expanded outside their native countries. However, today we have an economy where an organisation's suppliers and their customers can be located all over the world. Drucker's vision has largely been realised and the same goods are offered and bought in very similar shopping malls in Manchester, Miami, Melaka, Melborne and Xian. The Internet, especially its auctions, is perhaps, the epitome of a global market. Globalisation is considered in greater depth in Chapter 16.

■ He predicted that the third source of discontinuity would be people's **disenchantment with government**. Drucker despaired of governments' ability to run any business – except, perhaps, war. He felt that governments should stop meddling with the economy and that a government's job was to govern by [some] legislation, regulation and the occasional provision of funds. Government should leave commercial and economic activities to others. Drucker believed that governments had no business managing telecommunication companies, airline companies and utilities. Indeed, he was sceptical about government's role in managing educational institutions such as universities. Drucker talked about re-privatisation. Some of these ideas of "privatisation" were taken up by British governments in the 1980s and they were later copied throughout the world.

Drucker's discontinuous society would thrive on innovation and entrepreneurship. Change would be risky. However, all economic activity involves an element of risk – "and defending yesterday – that is, not innovating – is far more risky". The new "discontinuous society" would bring great rewards for the successful but it would not offer the security previously given by large organisations. Many individuals might not be able to cope with the greater "information loads" and the instability of working for a small organisation. Drucker feared that society might be starkly divided into the rich and the poor. A new "apartheid society" would be intolerable without a strong "social-sector" consisting of non-profit organisations that would be charged (but not run by) governments to deal with the social problems that might emerge from a post capitalist society (Drucker, 1994).

Criticisms of Drucker

Despite his pre-eminence Drucker's work has been criticised – especially by academics. They complain that, after *The Concept of the Corporation* he does not argue his ideas with sufficient rigour or support them with detailed evidence. Many academics regard him as a journalist rather than a scholar. They may complain that he only states the obvious in a very readable way. This is unfair. His observations only seem obvious because they have been so influential that they have been adopted widely. However, some of Drucker's dictums are clearly silly. For example, he exhorts organisations to avoid an over-emphasis on profits and that: "There is only one business purpose – namely to create a customer". In which case anyone can be a tycoon: millions of customers can be created overnight by offering £10 notes at a cost of £5! Finally, Drucker has few insights about small businesses and yet these are the types of organisations that he himself expects to flourish in a discontinuous, post-capitalist society.

Tom Peters

Background to Peters

Tom Peters, the management guru, has nothing to do with the "Peter Principle" which states that "people tend to be promoted to their level of incompetence". This well-known principle is based on the fact that people are promoted into a higher job on the basis of their competence in a lower one. Eventually they are promoted into a job they cannot do. Since it is difficult to fire or demote people they tend to remain there performing in an incompetent or indifferent way. The Peter Principle was espoused by Laurence Johnson Peter and his colleague R. Hull (1969). The principle explains why higher levels in bureaucratic organisations are filled with incompetent people who were quite good at doing other jobs.

Tom Peters the "management guru" obtained a PhD in organisational behaviour from Stamford University and was a consultant with the prestigious consultants, McKinsey and Co. He rose to prominence in 1985. McKinsey & Co. commissioned two major projects to identify the common features of successful organisations. Peters and Waterman interviewed executives from 32 organisations such as IBM, Atari and Wang Laboratories and they published their findings in a book *In Search of Excellence* (1988 – *ISOE*). The book was a best-seller. It appeared at a time when Japanese industry was making great inroads into the American market. Managers in their hundreds of thousands read the book hoping to find a way to halt or even reverse the Japanese advance. As we shall see later in this chapter, both the methodology and the conclusions of *ISOE* have been heavily criticised. Nevertheless, the book was very readable and has had enormous influence. Tom Peter's other books include: *A Passion for Excellence, The Pursuit of Wow* (1995) and *The Circle of Innovation: You Can't Shrink Your Way to Greatness* (1997). Tom Peters has also given hundreds, if not thousands, of seminars to halls. He is reputed to be the highest-paid management guru with an income in excess of $6 million per year.

Peters's ideas

Although many of Peters's ideas have been discredited they still circulate widely and it is important to know the main concepts. *In Search of Excellence* identified eight common characteristics of excellent companies:

- **Bias for action**: excellent companies are willing to take swift action, try out new ideas and take some risks. Often this action is taken by "ad hoc" project groups who enjoy novelty and innovation. This is in direct contrast with organisations that place excessive reliance on planning and the analysis of "hard" data before they take a decision. Excellent companies avoid "paralysis by analysis". They also avoid forming committees that have a brief to "*talk*" about action.
- **Being close to the customer**: excellent companies link all their activities (e.g. strategies, organisational structure, procedures and systems) identifying customer needs and the

fulfilling or exceeding them. In particular, they establish ways of detecting instances where customer needs are not met and feeding this information to the people who are able to ensure they are met in the future.

- **Autonomy and entrepreneurship**: excellent companies encourage key members of their organisation to act as entrepreneurs. Often this means that excellent companies avoid huge departments that hinder informal networking, contact and alliances.

- **Productivity through people**: excellent companies go beyond lip-service to the idea that people are an organisation's biggest assets. They invest heavily in employee development. They make employees really valued. They are careful to recognise and reward the contributions made by individuals.

- **Hands-on, value driven**: in excellent companies senior staff act as leaders rather than managers. They keep a high profile and lead by example. Leaders in excellent organisations try to foster a common system of values.

- **Stick to the knitting**: excellent organisations have a clear idea of their key skills and markets. They stay within their key competencies. They understand and build up on their strengths rather than trying to master all products and all markets.

- **Simple structure, lean staff**: excellent organisations have a clear sense of purpose and employ skilful and committed people. Consequently, they do not need a complex organisational structure to monitor and control their employees. They have few people checking others or attending to the formalities.

- **Loose-tight controls**: excellent organisations allow their employees considerable freedom and discretion – especially the freedom to innovate with the means to achieve goals. However, the values and the aims of the organisation will be strictly enforced – albeit, in an indirect way. This means that the creative abilities of employees can be harnessed.

Later, Tom Peters focused on the *chaos and uncertainty* of modern times. Apparently, current corporate life is less certain than during the Black Death, world wars or the scramble to "colonise" Africa! Peters believed that the world was changing so fast and so frequently that organisations needed to re-invent themselves at regular intervals. He believed that the pace of change was so fast that it was impossible to predict the future with any certainty. Indeed, the rate of change has produced a business environment that is close to chaos. Peters set out to stop organisations complaining, accept chaos and learn to flourish in the opportunities it presents. He counselled organisations "if you aren't reorganising, pretty substantially, once every six to 12 months, you're probably out of step with the times". He also counselled managers to reappraise their work methods on a continuous basis. At the end of each day they should ask, "what exactly and precisely and explicitly is being done in my work area differently from the way it was done when I came to work in the morning?". Peters asserts that the modern business environment is crazy and not susceptible to rational and purposeful management. Management in crazy times requires crazy actions such as "getting fired", "racing yaks", "taking off one's shoes", "making mistakes" and "taking breathing-relaxation exercises".

Criticisms of Tom Peters

Tom Peters is possibly the world's most criticised management guru. At an emotional level he has been called "a professional loudmouth", "hype-meister" and "Prince of Disorder". Some employees dread the possibility that their boss may attend a second Tom Peters Seminar – fearing that it will produce a trail of chaos, confusion, inanities and lack of consideration for others (Wade, 2003). Other critics point to Peters' own confession that he faked data for the book *In Search of Excellence* (Kellaway, 2001). Peters' work has not stood the test of time. His later books are not based on research. They consist of anecdotes, "war stories" and personal views (Collins, 2000). The latter books are often inconsistent with his earlier writings. Indeed, Micklethwaite and Wooldridge (1996) exclaim that he has "contradicted himself even more often than the average politician". The research underlying Peters and Waterman's *In Search of Excellence* was far from rigorous. Perhaps the most damning criticism is that about two-thirds of the firms that *ISOE* extolled in 1982 have fallen from grace and became corporate basket-cases.

Michael Porter

Background of Porter

Michael Porter has been called the world's most famous business academic (Handy, 2005). Porter specialises in business strategy. His work is academic, carefully argued and supported by evidence. Michael Porter has played a part in creating the *Global Competitiveness Report* (Porter et al., 2004) which ranks countries according to their ability to defend their competitive position against other nations. He has advised many governments including those of the UK, Ireland, Portugal and New Zealand. Porter began in the 1980s by examining the individual organisations. Then, like Drucker, he widened his scope and went on to study the *Competitive Advantage of Nations* (1990) before looking at the problems of specific areas such as inner cities.

Porter's ideas

Porter draws a clear distinction between strategy and efficiency. Modern organisations, he suggests, have focused exclusively on the latter and have used techniques such as Total Quality Management and Business Re-engineering in an attempt to be more efficient than their competitors. However, if an organisation is doing essentially the same thing as its competitors, it is unlikely to be more successful in the longer run: it would be arrogant to believe that it could perpetually outsmart others. Strategy is about choices and setting limits on what an organisation aims to accomplish. The ideal strategy is to position an organisation in a market where there are few or no competitors and where other organisations will find it difficult to start operations. Porter suggests that the underlying principles of strategy are independent of technology and the rate of change. If an organisation is in an industry where customers have power and there are no barriers to entry, it will be difficult to make a profit – even if the organisation makes a huge investment in technology.

Porter suggests that there are three basic strategies an organisation can follow in order to gain a competitive advantage. The choice between them is particularly influenced by current industry and the nature of the competition. In essence, there are five main types of industry and five main competitive forces. The *industry types* are:

- **Fragmented** where there are many suppliers, none of which have a dominant position. Fragmented markets are usually very competitive.

- **Emerging** markets which have considerable potential for growth and may be very profitable – at least for a short time. However, they are attractive to domestic and foreign investors.

- **Mature** markets where control of costs is vital.

- **Declining** markets are best avoided. However, they can sometimes be managed with a strategy of innovation or developing a brand that achieves "cult status". A particular challenge of trading in a declining market is to retain the best employees. A declining market may call for end-game strategies such as divestment or downsizing.

- **Global** markets often provide economies of scale and they can extend the life cycle of older products, which are sold to less-developed countries.

Porter's *five forces of competition* are:

- **Existing competitors** can provide intense rivalry especially when there is no clear market leader and there are high fixed costs or where there are exit barriers such as a high cost of closing down a factory. The strategies of existing competitors are also important. When competitors are following an aggressive growth strategy in a mature market, rivalry will be intense. When competitors are simply "taking profits" rivalry will be less.

- **New companies** entering an industry always raise the level of competition – especially when high exit barriers prevent existing competitors leaving. Some industries, such as motorcar production, have high entry barriers which deter new entrants.

- **Substitute products** lower the attractiveness of an industry because their competition reduces prices. However, the impact may be low if costs of switching are significant. For example, some manufacturers of industrial gases have beaten off the challenge of substitute products because their customers find it too expensive to change the connections, meters and regulators of their canisters.

- The **bargaining power of suppliers** can make an industry unattractive. Suppliers usually have high bargaining power in an industry where there are many small customers but a few dominant suppliers. Sometimes large suppliers can exert considerable bargaining power by threatening to set up their own brands or retail outlets – thereby bypassing their customers.

- The **bargaining power of customers** is the mirror image of supplier power. It too can also make an industry unattractive. Customers usually have high bargaining power when products are standardised and when there are a few dominant customers. For example, the British supermarket, Tesco, has a great deal of bargaining power when it negotiates fresh food products from farmers.

Porter urges organisations to consider these factors and choose one of the three generic strategies that provides the best trade-off of advantages and disadvantages. The three competitive strategies are:

- **Cost leadership** where an organisation makes things cheaper than its rivals.

- **Product leadership** where an organisation makes a product that has special features for which customers will pay a higher price.

- **Market leadership** where an organisation operates in a particular market or niche and dominates that market so that the organisation's position cannot be challenged.

In many cases Porter suggests that the strategy might be one of focusing upon a particular niche market and achieving dominance – perhaps by evolving a distinctive product. In general, Porter is least enthusiastic about the strategy of achieving cost dominance.

Gaining a competitive advantage involves more than determining the appropriate industry. Organisations need to examine their operations to establish which are efficient and adding value. Porter called this "**value chain analysis**". In essence, value chain analysis systematically takes each step in the production of a product or service and determines what it adds to the final product. The value of individual steps culminates in the total value added by the organisation. Porter divided organisational activities into two groups: primary activities and support activities. The primary value chain shown in Figure 18.1.

The secondary value chain consists of support activities such as purchasing, HRM, technology development and the firm's infrastructure. Infrastructure includes both physical assets such as building and machinery and intangible assets such as knowledge, systems and financial procedures.

In the 1980s Porter was a member of a commission set up by President Reagan to consider the competitiveness of the USA. He focused his attention on the strategies for countries rather than organisations and wrote *The Competitive Advantage of Nations*. In essence, Porter believed that a competitive country would have four main factors that can be fostered and encouraged by governments. Probably the most important factor in the competitive advantage of nations is a tough-minded *rivalry between organisations*. Competition drives firms to innovate and improve. Second, a country that has *demanding consumers* will develop rapidly because they force organisations to innovate and improve. Third, a *country's resources* (also called "factor conditions") can take many forms. They include the availability of money to finance new ventures and the general educational quality of its workforce and physical infrastructure such as transport. Traditional resources such as raw materials (coal, iron, timber, etc.) are not as crucial as many people believe. Perhaps the most intriguing is the fourth factor, the *cluster phenomenon*, which is sometimes called "Related and Supporting Industries". It refers to the proximity of suppliers (downstream industries or facilities) and customers (upstream). These facilities need to form a critical mass that can bring four advantages:

- Customers are attracted by the concept that they will be able to contact several potential suppliers in one location.

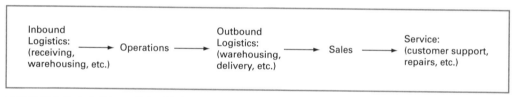

FIGURE 18.1 Porter's Primary Value Chain

- Suppliers collaborate in their dealings with governments, local authorities and educational establishments.
- Suppliers are able to pool resources to commission basic research.
- A cluster of related organisations is able to attract a pool of highly-skilled staff.

Classic examples of the cluster phenomenon include computer design in Silicon Valley, financial services in the City of London and the knitwear cluster of Tiruppur in India.

Since 1995 Porter has tried to devise ways to revitalise run-down *inner-city areas* and give them a competitive advantage. He notes (Porter, 1995) that governments and authorities have poured aid and welfare into inner-city areas without much success. He recommends that, instead, they should try to foster viable economic communities whose products can compete in the marketplace. A sustainable inner-city economic base can only be created through private, for-profit initiatives and investment based on economic self-interest and genuine competitive advantage – not through artificial inducements, charity or government mandates. Past attempts to solve the problems of inner cities have fallen into the trap of *redistributing* wealth. The real need – and the real opportunity – is to *create* wealth. Governments can play a role in developing wealth-creating companies by relaxing some regulations and by keeping local taxes low. Inner-city taxes tend to be high in order to pay for welfare programmes. This produces a vicious circle in which employers re-locate elsewhere, jobs are lost, the need for welfare increases and local taxes are raised to even higher levels.

Criticisms of Porter

Despite high-quality work that is revered in many circles, Porter's ideas have been criticised. Porter rarely takes people into account. He focuses too tightly on strategy and market forces and assumes that the required behaviour will follow quite naturally. In over 500 pages of *Competitive Strategy* he devotes only two paragraphs to the management of people (Handy, 2005). One of the most serious criticisms of Porter's work is that it is out-of-date. Downes (2005), for example, claims that Porter's theories may have worked in the 1980s when despite strong competition the structure of industries was relatively stable and business cycles were fairly predictable. However, Porter's assumptions are no longer accurate in an information age of the Internet where three new forces require new business strategies. For example, the power of *information technology* means that all players, even those from outside an industry, have access to more information. This results in hyper-competition where things change very fast. Those who analyse the situation in the method recommended by Porter would react too slowly and be overwhelmed. In other words organisations that follow Porter's advice would suffer "paralysis by analysis". The nature of *globalisation* has also changed the way that companies determine strategy. Rather than obtaining competitive advantage from cost leadership or quality leadership, competitive advantage today may stem from an ability to develop long-lasting relationships with more mobile customers. Finally, Downes points to the influence of *deregulation*. Deregulation and privatisation mean that government influence in many industrial sectors and countries has shrunk. They are less able to influence organisations than they were.

18.3 Witchdoctor's Cons

Some writers such as Micklethwaite and Wooldridge (1996) liken some management gurus to witchdoctors. They have tricks and cons that allow them to appear effective without actually being so. Some of the main tricks are: hindsight, the fortune-teller and Barnum effects, self-fulfilling prophecies and capitalisation on chance. Knowledge of each of these tricks will help readers avoid falling into the hands of gurus, academics and consultants who offer poor advice.

Hindsight

Gurus often build a reputations upon hindsight – subjective and selective hindsight at that! A corporation experiencing difficulties may consult a leading authority who examines the recent facts and then diagnoses why the organisation is in trouble. These gurus are acting like a death-bed doctor pronouncing the reason for an imminent death. What corporations really need are hygienists that help them avoid trouble in the first place. Examples of death-bed witch doctoring occurred in the USA and Europe during the 1980s when organisations were awash with consultants explaining why they were in imminent danger of losing their markets to Japanese firms. Their explanations varied according to their area of expertise: sometimes it was team-working, sometimes it was quality procedures and sometimes the explanation involved just-in-time delivery systems. Very few consultants had given warning of the Japanese threat in advance during the 1960s. Furthermore, few alerted their clients to the impending slow-down and stagnation of Japanese organisations during the 1990s. This illustrates the subjectivity of *"post hoc"* explanations. Unless they have had chance to confer, gurus often give very different reasons for an organisation's problems. To be fair, some gurus do try to anticipate events. Drucker, for example, did predict the rise of knowledge workers and an information society. However, the predictions of gurus are often overrated or wrong. For example, the past 30 years have been nowhere near as shocking as Alvin Toffler predicted in his book, *Future Shock,* written in 1970.

Case studies are frequently contaminated by subjective hindsight. They may be produced by people who have a vested interest in an area such as finance, logistics, HR or quality. They visit an organisation and, as human beings, can only access a small proportion of relevant information. They then sift this information – often in a subjective way according to their own mental filters, coloured by their own motives and training. The case-study writer then interprets the selected range of information and arrives at a diagnosis. Other diagnoses may be equally valid but case study writers rarely test alternatives in a scientific way. Because case studies are so full of subjective hindsight, they are often characterised as "shared ignorance" and they must be evaluated carefully. Questions which should be asked of any case study include:

- Who is the person(s) conducting the case study? What are their qualifications, expertise and motives?

- What range of relevant information was actually available? Was the information filtered in some way?

- To what extent does the diagnosis follow from the data? Were alternative diagnoses given proper consideration?

Case studies *are* a useful tool in management education. However, they should usually be developed to reflect prior research so that they have some quantitative and objective basis.

The fortune-teller effect

The fortune-teller effect occurs when someone predicts the future using vague comments that are likely to happen. For example, after a display of hocus-pocus involving crystal balls or Tarot Cards, a fortune-teller may inform clients that, "you will be going on a journey", "you will hear from an old friend" or "you will experience sadness". A talented fortune-teller will then use subtle cues in the client's facial reactions to embellish the statements with more and more specific detail. At least some of the statements will come true. Gullible clients will then feel they have proof of the fortune-teller's mystic power. Similarly, after displays of hocus-pocus involving a flurry of flip charts, discussion groups and consultations with senior people a management guru will make predictions such as "the times ahead are going to be difficult", "innovation will improve the organisation's competitiveness' or "government legislation needs to be watched". A talented adviser will then use verbal and non-verbal cues from the audience to make further comments.

Self-fulfilling prophecy

Sometimes a self-fulfilling prophecy is the reason why a guru or an adviser may succeed. A self-fulfilling prophecy occurs when the actual making of a prediction helps determine events that bring the prediction to fulfilment. In management, self-fulfilling prophecies are most clearly seen in the financial securities market. For example, the stock of a company may be progressing in line with that of similar companies in the same industry. It might then attract the attention of, say, Warren Buffett – one of the greatest stock market gurus and investors of all times. He founded the very successful Berkshire Hathaway investment company. If Buffett were, by chance, to suggest publicly that the stock of this random company would rise, it is virtually certain that the stock of that company *would* increase dramatically. Buffett has such a powerful reputation that others would be sure to buy the stock and the price will rise as a result of the prediction rather than any improvement in the value of the company. Self-fulfilling prophecies can also operate within organisations. For example, the strategy department may predict that the sales of a certain product will decline. It is likely that this would result in a cutback in the replacement budget and goods would be produced on progressively older machines. Moreover, the organisation's advertising budget is likely to be switched to other products and sales staff will be less likely to promote the product. Thus, it is almost certain that sales of the randomly chosen product will decline. The strategy department will then crow and to quote it as evidence of their prowess of predicting the future!

The results of self-fulfilling prophesies involving people are often called the "*Pygmalion effect*". This is when an arbitrary judgement about someone sets of a train of events that makes the person conform to those judgements. In a famous experiment, Rosenthal and Jacobson (1992) arbitrarily divided pupils into two groups and told their teachers that one group was bright and the other group was dull (even though the two groups were allocated at random and scored about the same). After a while the groups were measured again and the "bright group" had made more progress than the dull groups. The false information had influenced teachers at a subconscious level. They gave more attention and set more demanding tasks to the "bright" group and this had caused that group to improve and shine. The Pygmalion effect operates in many business organisations. A manager may arbitrarily decide that a subordinate is not very able. He or she may then subconsciously make decisions that cause their expectations to be fulfilled. For example, a low-expectation employee may find that he or she is:

- Located in a low-prestige office far from the manager.
- Given less attention in business meetings. This will include fewer smiles and less eye contact. He or she will be given less time to state their opinions and will be interrupted more frequently.
- Given less information about what is happening in the department and infrequent feedback about their own performance.
- Less likely to be called upon to work on special products or conduct high-profile activities such as giving presentations.

The cumulative effect of these actions will handicap the subordinate and prevent him or her making progress – thus confirming the manager's original arbitrary judgement.

The Hawthorne Effect

The Hawthorne Effect is a well-known friend of charlatans. It enables useless changes to masquerade as important. It was discovered (see Chapter 2) during famous "lighting" experiments at the Hawthorne factory (Mayo, 1933, Chapter 2). They showed that *any* change is likely to bring about an improvement in productivity – not because the change is any good but because employees are motivated by the extra attention that they receive. Managers and social scientists need to be very careful to take the Hawthorne Effect into account. The unwary manager or researcher might conclude that *any* new project causes an improvement. The Hawthorne Effect has enormous implications. Every claim for a management innovation or system must prove that benefits really are due to the innovation and not just to the Hawthorne Effect. The Hawthorne Effect also has enormous implications for medicine and the pharmaceutical industry. It means that any treatment, even a wacky, way-out, therapy is likely to produce *some* positive results. Consequently, any drug or management innovation needs to be evaluated carefully. At the very minimum an evaluation needs to have two groups. One group (the control group) should receive exactly the same attention and consideration. This group is called the *placebo group*. In medical contexts they take a tablet which has the same colour, shape and size as the other group but it lacks the active ingredient. The other group (the experimental group) is treated in the same way except the tablet contains the active ingredient. Scientifically, it is important that these studies are conducted on a *double-blind* basis. This means that neither the subjects nor the people who evaluate their progress or productivity know to which group they belong. Unfortunately, these conditions are very difficult to obtain in studies of management.

Capitalisation on chance

Charlatans and witchdoctors often capitalise on chance to produce evidence that seems to support their theories. They use three main tactics: the numbers game, regression to the mean and riding piggy-back.

The first way to capitalise on chance is to play *the numbers game*. This strategy depends upon the fact most things *could* happen as flukes. For example, it has often been stated that if enough chimpanzees tapped at random on a typewriter one of them would reproduce a Shakespearean sonnet. More probably, if a hundred orang-outans chose between bananas upon which are written the ten alternatives to a marketing decision, it is highly likely that ten urang-utans would choose the banana with the decision that would prove correct. If the ten "successful" urang-utans were then faced with a second, similar, marketing decision, it is likely that one would choose a second banana containing the correct decision. A henna-haired chief executive, ignorant of the background but influenced by the "like me" effect, might then appoint the lucky orang-outan as a marketing vice-principle on the basis of its proven track record! Slightly more realistically, imagine a firm of management consultants based in Boston but with branches in Birmingham, Brisbane and Beijing. It encounters hard times when its consultants' times are not fully filled. A couple of its wayward employees come up with a spurious management technique called "a New Post Porter Paradigm for a Lean, Customer Driven Organisation" (NPPPLCDO or N–O for short). Impressed, the partners write personal letters to the CEOs of 120 world-class organisations saying that their N–O model predicts that their corporation will beat the industry average in the next three months. After three months the partners write to the 60 corporations who have, by chance, beaten the industry average and predict that they will continue to beat the industry average in the following three months. After that three months, the partners write to the 30 corporations who have, by chance, beaten the average and predict that they will beat the industry average in their next three months. They can then write to the 15 corporations who have beaten the industry average for a year and point out that their consultancy has a solid track record of identifying success factors. The partners could then offer consultancy services at £2000 per day to guide the corporation to continued success. If only a few gullible corporations took up the offer, the rewards would be great. Capitalising on chance would have produced a handsome income for the cost of producing and posting just 225 letters!

Witchdoctors frequently con their prey by *misinterpreting chance events*. If, by chance, the chief of a tribe gets a disease, it will be interpreted as a sign of the anger of the gods. Incantations and sacrifices will be made in appeasement. In all probability the chief recovers naturally. This will be interpreted as clear evidence that the witchdoctors were accurate. In modern organisations chance events are misinterpreted in more subtle ways. Two particular cons concern minority positions and regression to the mean. They both depend upon the fact that practically all measures in social science and management are subject to some random error. As Case 18.3 demonstrates, the margin of error is often very large.

Such high levels of random error mean that *minority positions are often overstated* (Paulos, 1998). For example, suppose that it is known for certain that 5 per cent of workers are clinically depressed about their work. Researchers do not know this, however, and a benevolent sponsor arranges for a sample of 100 workers to meet a doctor who will diagnose whether each one is depressed. Suppose that the doctor's diagnoses are 80 per cent correct (which, in the light of Viswesvaran et al. (1996) is a generous assumption). There will be five people who are genuinely depressed and because of the errors of measurement the doctor will only identify four (true positives). There will be 95 people who, actually, are not

CASE 18:3 LARGE RANDOM ERRORS IN MANAGEMENT JUDGEMENTS

An example of measurement error in management is given by Viswesvaran, Ones and Schmidt (1996). They studied the evaluations that bosses make of their subordinates. They obtained data for a total of 14 650 subordinates, each of whom had been evaluated by two independent superiors. Viswesvaran et al. then correlated the two sets of ratings and obtained a correlation of 0.52. This indicates that the consistency between two superiors is only 27 per cent true and the remaining 73 per cent is caused by random error. (Note: to obtain a percentage agreement from a correlation, square the correlation and multiply by 100.)

depressed, but because of the errors of measurement, the doctors will say that 19 are depressed (false positives). Thus, the result of the investigation is that 23 percent of workers are depressed when, in fact, the true figure is 5 per cent! Random error has produced a result that is almost five times the true figure! The managers of this imaginary organisation could well waste a million dollars buying valium and paying for unnecessary counselling. Managers should be very wary of results based upon subjective judgements and where results suggest that less than 25 per cent of people experience problems.

Regression to the mean is a con frequently used by those who promise to rescue organisations from a bad situation. It is a con that is particularly relevant to "before and after" studies. Regression to the mean is another con which depends on measurement error. When any group is chosen, some people are selected by mistake. For example, suppose an organisation selects 100 of its poorest for a training course to improve their performance. Possibly 60 of those chosen are genuinely poor workers and the other 40 are chosen by mistake – a fairly conservative assumption in the light of Viswesvaran et al.'s results. Suppose further that the training is useless. When the 40 initial mistakes are evaluated a second time, 24 are correctly classified (the remaining 16 suffer the misfortune of double injustice (40 per cent of 40 per cent = 16 per cent). However, this evaluation of the useless course would prove that it was worthwhile because it had reduced the percentage of poor workers by 24 per cent. "Before and after" studies in commerce and industry are equally susceptible to "regression to the mean" – especially when the study involves a selected group of any kind.

The final con that is sometimes used by management witchdoctors does not, technically, involve capitalising on chance but, since it may affect "before and after" studies, it is considered here. Riding *piggy-back* involves taking credit for an improvement, caused by other factors, that would have occurred in any event. For example, an ingenious traffic engineer might invent some device, say a new kind of speed hump, and claim that it will reduce accidents. The engineer might well persuade a local authority traffic manager to install the humps in a certain district. When the figures are compared a year later, it might be found that the number of accidents has decreased by 2 per cent. Given that the human consequences of an accident can be dire, an improvement of 2 per cent is well worth having. Consequently, the gullible local authority is quite likely to install the speed humps willy-nilly throughout its area. However, the local authority might be wasting money. There has been a consistent decline in the rate of road accidents over many years. It is probably caused by better design of cars (especially brakes and tyres) and greater driver awareness. In fact, it would only be worth the local authority investing in speed humps if the traffic engineer could show a change that is significantly greater than the trend.

18.4 Science and Management Research

Types of scientific research in management

Scientific research into management can take three main forms: observation, experiments and surveys.

Observation is often used in management research. For example, the marketing function of a museum might want to know which exhibits are most popular. It could conduct a survey but people may not give accurate answers. It might employ someone to count the number of people who visit the different zones in the museum. At a slightly more sophisticated level, it may use closed-circuit television to log the time visitors spend looking at an exhibit – but this would be very labour intensive. More ingeniously, some museums gauge the interest in an exhibit by counting the number of fingerprints on an exhibit at the end of a day. Observation is widely used in market research. For example, supermarkets keenly monitor the way customers progress through aisles and the points at which they are most likely to pause before making a purchase. Observations of actual behaviour give very realistic information that is relatively free from bias.

Experiments are rarely used in management research. Occasionally an organisation will commission *laboratory research* into, say, the safety features of a machine or, perhaps, the way that customers open different types of packaging or, use different computer interfaces. Laboratory research is very good at determining between the factors that are causes and those which are effects. For example, a company supplying the seats to passenger trains might ask a local university to assess the ergonomic qualities of seats. The University department will then set up a laboratory mock-up of a passenger carriage where many factors, (temperature, journey time, age of passengers, etc.) are controlled. They would then assess passenger fatigue at the end of a journey and subsequently recommend an optimal design of seat. The results of experiments tends to be artificial and may not be generalisable to operational situations. The artificial situation in a laboratory usually overemphasises the factor under investigation – because other influences are cancelled out. For example, a laboratory experiment may ask people to sit in a seat for an hour and then complete a questionnaire. In practice, however, few passengers sit in a seat for as long as an hour without a break – after 30 minutes, or so, most move, stand up, annoy other passengers by using a mobile phone, walk about or visit the toilet.

Field experiments overcome some of these problems. They are more realistic and produce results that are more applicable to "real life". For example, an operations function may vary the production system in half of their units and assess the effects objectively. Sometimes a finance director will vary a payment system to check whether it motivates staff. Field experiments are better than laboratory experiments in the sense that they yield more realistic effect sizes and produce results that are generalisable. However, field experiments are not very good at distinguishing between cause and effect. In the field, so many uncon-trolled factors may operate that it may be impossible to distinguish whether a change is due to the differences investigated or other, unknown, influences.

Surveys are widely used in management research. They are relatively quick and cheap to conduct and they are good at exploring a wide range of factors. For example, a single survey would be able to investigate employee satisfaction with pay, working conditions, hours worked, job security and several other factors. In contrast, an experiment into job sat-isfaction would be able to measure just one or two of these factors. Most surveys suffer from the crucial problem that they investigate epiphenomena (what people say about a subject) not the phenomena themselves (the real situation and what people actually do). Often there is a gap between the truth and what people say. For example, 85 per cent of the population claim that their sense of humour is better than average and 80 per cent of men claim that their penises are bigger than average! Similarly, more people claim to vote in elections than the actual turnout. The results of surveys can also be strongly influenced by the exact wording of the questions.

Special difficulties faced by management researchers

Research into many management phenomena is not straightforward. Management researchers are challenged by two particular difficulties: measurement problems and the interactive nature of the subject matter.

Measurement problems in management research arise because many of the variables are intangible and difficult to manipulate. For example, if an engineer believes that a machine will work faster at a higher voltage it is relatively simple to vary the voltage and measure the speed of the very machine accurately. However, a manager who believes that workers will be more productive if they are more motivated will find it very difficult to measure people's level of motivation. The situation with regard to outputs is similar: they too are sometimes difficult to measure in a reliable and objective way. For example, even if it were easy for a manager to measure the motivation of receptionist, it would be difficult to establish whether increased motivation leads to increased productivity. It is very hard to measure the extra care and civility with which a visitor is welcomed. It would be possible to ask the receptionists' supervisors to rate them on, say, a 1–9 scale but, as Viswesvaran et al.'s study (see p. 397) shows, supervisory ratings are not very objective. Alternatively, it might the possible to devise a questionnaire that is completed by visitors. However, the questionnaire could be faulty and merely substitute the subjective judgement of visitors for the subjective judgement of supervisors. These considerations mean that management researchers need to check the accuracy of their measures – especially their reliability and validity:

- **Reliability** assesses whether a measure gives consistent results. For example, large corpo-rations often use intelligence tests to select new employees; but if a test gives different results when a person is tested a second time, the test would be useless and it would not be sensible to rely on the scores it produces (in actual fact, intelligence tests are *very* reliable. The scores from two administrations, separated by a month, would correlate about 0.9).

- Unfortunately a measure can be very reliable but still useless because it does not measure what people may mistakenly think it measures. For example, verbal fluency can be measured fairly reliably (0.9) but, contrary to some stereotypes, it would be useless in selecting salespeople because it would not measure a key sales skill – listening to customers in order to establish rapport and determine their needs. The degree to which a measure gauges what it is supposed to measure is called validity. The validities of some measures used in personnel selection are given on p. 108 in Chapter 5.

The concepts of reliability and validity are not restricted to measures in psychology and human resources. Researchers in economics, marketing and organisational analysis should also ensure that their measures are reliable and valid. The difficulties in obtaining accurate measures mean that the results of research into management are much less certain than many results in the physical sciences such as biology and chemistry.

The *interactive nature* of the subject matter in management research (i.e. other people) also makes scientific analysis more problematic. For example, a sheet of glass does not change its refractive index simply because a physicist uses it as a part of his or her study. However, there is ample evidence that people change their behaviour when they know that they are a part of an investigation. Subjects often try to please the researcher. They try to guess the purpose of the investigation and then behave in a way that they believe will help. For example, a manager may invent a new way of delivering pizzas and decide to assess any improvement by interviewing 50 clients. Although the manager is careful not to state her or his vested interest, non-verbal cues that indicate enthusiasm will be given. The subjects detect these cues and some interviewees will decide to help by overemphasising the advantages of the new delivery system. When the results are collated an unduly favourable picture emerges and the new system may be adopted even when it might be slightly less effective than the existing one. In some cases, the *demand characteristics of an investigation* work in the opposite direction and subjects try to obstruct the purpose of the researcher. Demand characteristics of research were extensively studied by Rosenthal and Rosnow (1969).

The fact that people are the subject matter in a great deal of management research can produce yet further problems. For example, most management research depends upon *volunteers*. A typical response rate for a management survey is about 30 per cent. The minority who reply are a self-selected group who may not be typical of the "population" as a whole. This might bias the results and mean that conclusions from an atypical minority are wrongly applied to a majority. The use of people, rather than objects, in management research also raises a large number of ethical issues (see Chapter 15).

Characteristics of good scientific design in management research

Good scientific investigations into management will pay close attention to the following five characteristics: choice of variables, choice of sample, good measures, good analysis and good reports. A more detailed knowledge of each of these characteristics is very useful. Critical appraisal of research articles, papers and gurus' advice should be based on how well these characteristics are handled. This will help clarify whether findings have scientific credibility or whether they are a fad or a con. A knowledge of the five characteristics of good scientific design may help student earn higher marks by writing critical and incisive essays. Three topics, choice of variables, choice of sample and analysis of results, need to be discussed in more detail.

Choice of variables

A variable is any attribute or characteristic that can be measured and which yields a range of different values. For example, in a study of employees, the variables might be: number of widgets they produce per hour, their age, their educational qualifications, their IQ, their personality or the number of brothers and sisters they have. In a study of an organisation, the variables might be number of employees, the turnover, the type of industry, the level of centralisation, the levels in the management hierarchy and level of innovation. A good scientific study will ensure that all relevant variables are included. If important variables are neglected, investigators can never be sure their findings are true or whether they are the result of variables they have missed. The variables that investigators are most likely to miss are those that measure the context (background) of the investigation.

Choice of sample

A scientific study will involve a large sample systematically constructed to ensure that it is not biased. A scientific study is likely to involve a control sample. Sample size is crucial. Researchers in management frequently use small samples. However, it is a basic rule of statistics that results based on small samples are very volatile. Another investigator using another small sample is highly likely to get different results that negate and contradict the results of the first study. Sample size is important because, as noted earlier, all measurements are subject to error. With a small sample this error does not have an adequate opportunity to cancel out. For example, with only three tosses of a coin it is not that unlikely that the error is in one direction and the result will be three heads. However, if the coin is tossed 30 times it is virtually impossible that they will all be heads: the most likely outcome is 15 heads and 15 tails.

The size of an adequate sample is determined by two main factors: the effect size and the range of differences between people. *Effect size* means roughly the same as the strength of the phenomenon studied. As would be expected, a strong phenomenon can be detected with a smaller sample than a weak one. The *range of differences* between people is a measure of how much people deviate from the average. This is usually expressed in terms of a statistic called the "standard deviation". When people differ from each other in a substantial way, a large sample is needed. When people are very similar, a small sample may be sufficient. Statisticians use complex formulae to determine the proper size for a sample. Schmidt, Hunter, and Urry (1976) calculate that a sample of 172 is needed to detect a moderately strong phenomenon. Very few studies in management have samples that meet this scientific standard. In practice, many researchers and academics adopt a rule of thumb that the minimum sample size for a scientific study is 30.

Analysis of results

The results of any investigation should be analysed rigorously. There are two main types of analysis: descriptive statistics and inferential statistics: *Descriptive statistics* give information on means, percentages and standard deviations for every variable. *Inferential statistics* give a higher level of analysis that checks whether there are relationships between two or more variables. Probably the most frequently used inferential statistics are correlations and t-tests. Some investigators analyse the data so that they produce a formula (usually a regression equation or trend-line) that states exactly how one variable is related to another. Inferential

CASE 18.4: COMPARISON OF SCIENCE IN MANAGEMENT AND PHARMACOLOGY

This case contrasts the way that the long-term effects of a drug for Parkinson's disease, L-Dopa, were evaluated scientifically (Fahn, 1999) with the famous management study *In Search of Excellence* (*ISOE*) by Tom Peters and Bob Waterman (1988). Fahn's study is thorough and scientific but by no means exceptional in its field. *ISOE* was quite exceptional in its impact on many managers. The book sold many copies and laid the foundations for Peter's subsequent career. This section is only concerned with *ISOE*'s methodology. Its origin and results are described on p. 387.

In Search of Excellence	Evaluation of L-Dopa
Choice of Variables *ISOE* included variables such as strategy, structure, systems, nature of the staff, management style, organisational skills and super-ordinate goals. However, crucially, measures of contextual factors (technology, patents, geography, trade barriers) were omitted (Guest, 1992). So, there is no way *ISOE* could be sure excellence is caused by the variables studied. Excellence might result from strong patents and strong trade barriers etc.	All variables closely related to the drug itself, the chemical formulation, the dosage rates, the improvement in the patients' health, etc. were included. The study also captured contextual variables such as patient's age, severity of illness, time since onset, etc. Consequently these variables could be ruled out as causes of any changes.
Sample 75 organisations who were selected by an ad hoc and subjective process (Guest,1992) by McKinsey consultants – on the basis on the basis of the organisations' reputation. Some companies were then, subjectively, eliminated. Eventually, 21 organisations were selected as excellent on a range of financial and other indicators. The study also included 12 companies who were considered to be "near misses". The study had only one group, the organisations deemed to be excellent. This meant that *ISOE* could not be sure whether the factors identified as important in excellent organisations were not also present in awful organisations. The samples in *ISOE* are, by no means, the worst samples in management research. Maslow constructed his hierarchy of needs on a smaller sample. Nevertheless, the *ISOE* sample is very inferior to the samples used in scientific investigations such as clinical trials.	360 participants were enrolled and divided, at random, into four groups of 120 people (high dose, medium dose, low dose and control group). This arrangement gave added power and meant that the magnitude of levels of treatment could be gauged. The study also included a "washout" period at the end of the experiment to see how patients reacted when no drug was administered.
Measurement of Variables Measurement consisted of interviews with an ad hoc grouping of senior executives and journalists. It is not known how these people were selected. Scientifically, they should be a systematic (random?) sample of employees and customers of the organisations studied. Senior executives were interviewed without the benefit of measures developed by an independent source. The reliability and validity of the information obtained was not reported. Clearly, measurement of variables falls a long way short of scientific standards. The way *ISOE* measured variables is probably poorer than most research in management.	Progress of patients was assessed using an established scale, the United Parkinson's Disease Rating Scale (UPDRS), developed by people unconnected with the study. The reliability and validity of UPDRS is reported in the scientific literature. Consequently, the investigators could not be accused of perverting their results by using a favourable standard. The L-Dopa study was also careful to avoid contamination by the Hawthorne Effect. Patients were "blind" in the sense that they did not know whether they were in the placebo group or the dosage level they were receiving. Furthermore, doctors judging their progress were also "blind" about the treatment of those they were evaluating. "Double-blind" studies of this kind are routine in scientific investigations.

In Search of Excellence	Evaluation of L-Dopa
Analysis Analysis in *ISOE* is at the descriptive level using raw counts and sometimes percentages. It rarely, it ever, gives standard deviations or uses any kind of inferential statistics.	Means and standard deviations for all variables are reported. Inferential statistics are used to check whether there were any significant differences in patients' responses to different doses. A trend-line between dose and patient reaction was also calculated.
Reporting Peters and Waterman first gave their results at a presentation to colleagues at McKinsey Consulting. After several well-received presentations they decided to publish their results in a book which was not subject to peer review.	Results of the study were submitted to the refereed journal, *Archives of Neurology*. The article was anonymously evaluated and the reviewers decided that it had sufficient scientific merit to justify publication.

statistics are usually accompanied by a level of significance – the probability that the results could have occurred by chance alone. Usually scientists only accept findings if their probability of occurring by fluke is less than 1 in 20 (less than 5 per cent).

A comparison between Peters and Waterman's study *In Search of Excellence* and Fahn's rigorous scientific study into the long-term effects of L-Dopa is given in case 18.4. It shows, beyond dispute, that management research does not always match the standards of good science. *In Search of Excellence* is by no means the worst example of management research – although it is, probably, somewhere in the bottom half. Many well-known findings are based on small samples, poor measures and inadequate analyses. Double-blind studies are virtually non-existent. You must therefore evaluate pronouncements and claims of researchers and gurus in a critical way. The aim of this chapter was not to catalogue the inadequacies of management research. It has tried to engender a critical outlook. It was noted earlier that Porter's work on strategy suggests that demanding consumers are a requirement of competitive advantage. This also applies to management research.

Activities and Further Study

 ### Essay Plans

1 With the aid of classic examples define a craze and describe the phases through which a craze is likely to pass.
2 Describe and evaluate Drucker's contribution to the understanding of management.
3 Describe and evaluate Michael Porter's contribution to the understanding of strategic management.
4 Outline the ways that apparent improvements may really be the result of chance factors.

Web Activities

1 Search the Web for more information on the work of gurus listed in Case 18.2, p. 384).
2 Surf the Web for more information on fads and crazes. Some useful sites are:

http://www.stock-market-crash.net/tulip-mania.htm (tulip-mania)

http://www.stock-market-crash.net/southsea.htm (south sea bubble)

http://www.fool.co.uk/stockideas/2004/si040203.htm (junk bond craze 1980s)

http://en.wikipedia.org/wiki/Herd_behavior

http://www.bloomberg.com/delivery/mentor/2001_fall/fall-beg-3.pdf

A good site on crashes and crazes is ***www.stock-market-crash.***

 ## Experiential Activities

1 Take ten separate coins and flip them in the air. Count the number of "tails" (fails) that result. Remove all coins that were heads. Place all the tails in a circle and say "hocus pocus" or some other incantation and breathe on each coin twice. Flip these coins again and count the number of tails. If there are fewer tails than previously, evaluate whether your incantation and breath were the cause or whether it is some other phenomenon. What is this other phenomenon called?
2 Take a recent paper published by a professor in management (preferably from your own college or university). Evaluate that paper and compare its scientific merits with the work of Peters and Fahn – see Case 18.4, p. 402.

3 Discuss with your friends which of today's' management trends will turn out to be irrational fads.

4 Discuss with your friends which of today's markets is about to crash. The housing market? China?

Careers and Management

After reading this chapter you will be able to understand the main features of careers (especially management careers) and apply the concepts to your own values, wishes and aspirations. In particular you will be able to:

1 **define** the concept of a career

2 **briefly explain** the differential approach and the developmental approach to studying careers

3 **critically evaluate** three theories of career development

4 **describe** modern changes in career structures

5 **list** at least six forms that modern careers may take

6 **describe** the characteristics of extraordinary careers

7 **explain** the concepts of career plateaux, outplacement and the psychological contract

8 **explain in detail** and apply the main stages of getting a job

9 **explain in detail** and apply the main stages of getting a promotion

By the standards of the times Henry Fortescue's career got off to a dodgy start. In 1920, at the age of 14, he started work as a trainee clerk in a government department. He disliked the work. To the dismay of everyone he quit the job after a week and went to work as a messenger in a bank. As if to make up for his early indiscretion he worked at the same bank for the next 41 years – with the exception of a few years when he was conscripted to fight a war. His steadfast work was noted by the bank's management development department, which made sure that he received proper training and experience. He was promoted almost as a matter of course. When he retired in 1960 he was a regional manager at the same bank. Henry Fortescue rarely worried about his career. There were relatively few alternative vocations. Promotion might be a little slow but it was fairly sure and the management development department would decide upon the next move and the skills he would need to develop.

Today, things are very, very different. A much wider range of jobs is available. Lifelong employment in one organisation is very unlikely. Few organisations have management development departments to guide and track individual employees. Today, an individual needs to take ownership of their own employability and navigate their own career. Bell and Straw (1989) use the metaphor of sculptures and sculptors. In the past a career was a work of art produced by other people. Now the individual is a sculptor carving out their own career. This chapter aims to help readers become proficient career sculptors. The topic is organised in six sections:

Chapter contents

19.1 Definition of Careers

Technically, "a career" is the course or progress of an object as it moves. It usually has the connotations of rapid, somewhat reckless motion as indicated by the phrases "the runaway bus careered downhill". In the context of work it has come to have two special meanings. First, the term "career" can be used as a structural property of jobs within an organisation. This usage gives rise to phrases such as "a career in the army". Second, the term "career" can be used to describe "the pattern of work-related experiences that span the course of a person's life" (Greenhaus, Callanan and Godshalk, 2000). This second definition encapsulates the notion of a person's course and progress through their working life. However, it is very constrained and does not include the more subjective aspects of a career or all its aspects. The definition by Arnold (1997) is better:

> A career is the sequence of employment-related positions, roles, activities and experiences encountered by a person.

Arnold's definition is not without its problems. It does not give sufficient emphasis to the notion that careers evolve over time (Arthur, Hall and Lawrence,1989). Combining the two strands we arrive at the definition of a career as:

> 66 A career is the evolving sequence of employment-related positions, roles, activities and experiences encountered by a person as their working life develops. 99

The breath of this definition is an advantage. It clearly puts the workplace and employment centre-stage but it does not exclude non-work positions, roles, activities and experiences. For example, a hobby mending cars would be excluded by a narrow definition of a career but it might be relevant to the work of an engineer and it would be included under the latter definition.

19.2 Theoretical Background

There are two main theoretical approaches to the subject of careers: the differential approaches and the developmental approaches (see Walsh and Osipow, 1983). In essence, the *differential approaches* are based on the fact that people differ. Furthermore, jobs differ. The characteristics of people will make them better suited to some jobs than others. Consequently, differential theorists will focus upon matching people to jobs – making sure that "square pegs" are put into "square holes". In practice, this is still the dominant approach. It has a venerable history from the time of Frank Parsons in 1909, Hugo Munsterberg in 1913 and Edward Strong in 1919. The approach is blindingly straightforward and empirical. First measure the characteristics needed by jobs, then measure the characteristics of people and help people choose jobs that match. This approach has been used with great success by vocational guidance councillors and career consultants.

The *developmental approaches* are based on the idea that people pass through stages and that their environment and their knowledge influence their progression and destination. For example, some people are ready to enter the world of work at the age of, say, 16 and have the knowledge and insight to make reasonable vocational choices. Other people of the same age are unaware of many aspects of employment and are not ready for work. The developmental approaches focus upon encouraging vocational insights and acquiring a wider knowledge. The three main developmental theories stem from the work of Super, Levinson and Schein. All were developed in the first third of the last century and may not encompass many of the recent developments in careers.

Super's career stages

Donald Super is a doyen in the field of vocational guidance. He pioneered the concept of career readiness and developed questionnaires to clarify the career readiness of teenagers. He also developed ways of improving career readiness. However, Donald Super is perhaps best known for his career stages that map out the main milestones of adult careers. Super's stages are shown in Figure 19.1

Super (see, for example, 1990) envisaged adult careers as passing through four main stages. From the age of leaving education until about the age of 27 many people explore a range of jobs without much commitment. They may change their employer and field of work several times. They may take one or more "gap sessions" where they obtain transient or seasonal employment. Super calls this stage the stage of exploration. At about the age of 27

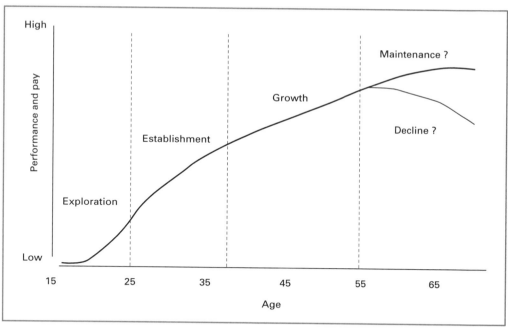

FIGURE 19.1 Super's Career Stages

people settle down into a job to which they are committed and they build up experience as individual performers in, say, a single management function. In the mid-30s people have often shown their ability and they are promoted to managing a group of people. They extend the range of their expertise into, say, two additional functions so that by the time they are 47 they will be regarded as broad-based managers who are knowledgeable in three or more functional areas. From the age of 47 the upward trajectory continues for a while but there is soon a divergence. People either continue to maintain their position or they start to decline. Those who maintain their position will expand their experience into extra functions, slowly arriving at the point when they have *some* experience in a majority of functions. Alternatively, those who decline will lose out in relative terms as the organisation and the world moves on. They will be analogous to the person who steps off an escalator that is moving onwards.

Levinson's life phases

The other major theorist about life phases was Levinson (see Levinson, 1986), who conducted extensive interviews with 40 men (and later women) and, as Figure 19.2 indicates, divided adulthood into three major phases: early, middle and late.

There are major, sometimes tumultuous, transitions between each of these phases. For example, the mid-life transition at about the age of 40 is sometimes called a "mid-life crisis". There are also minor transitions within the phases – the age 30 transition and the age 50 transition. Each of the phases has its own characteristics that have an impact on a person's career. The early adult transition involves establishing oneself as a person who is

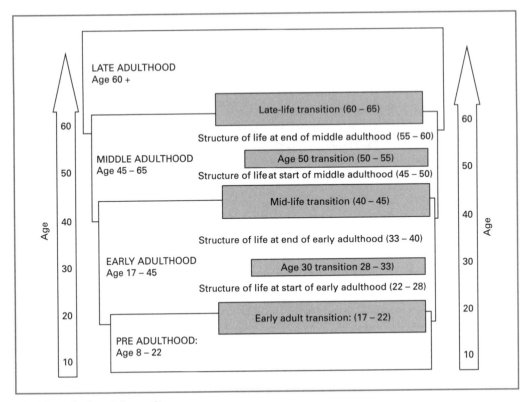

FIGURE 19.2 Levinson's Career Stages

independent from one's parents. The start of early adulthood is usually marked by the completion of education and the start of a career. There is a "minor" transition at the age of 30 where options are reviewed and there may be a career change. The latter part of early adulthood involves settling down and advancing in one's chosen career. The transition into mid-adulthood at the age of 40 is marked by a review of one's career and it may be a time of mid-life crisis. The period between the ages of 40 and 50 is often a time of consolidation and evaluation that may lead to a sense of fulfilment. The end of the mid-life phase (50 – 60) is often a very stable period leading to retirement. The final transition into late adulthood is marked by a review and reflection on one's career.

Shein's career anchors

Shein (1978) took a rather different approach based upon a longitudinal study of 44 MBA students. He found that his subjects made frequent changes and inconsistent *decisions* about their careers. In contrast, the *reasons* given for these decisions were very stable over the twelve-year period of his study. He felt that their motives, values and perceptions of their own abilities formed an anchor about which individual decisions would bob up and down and swing from side to side. Shein identified five career anchors. They were:

- **Technical competence** – an emphasis on the ability to do complex things well. Often, technical competence is exercised within a specialised area and the individual may have little interest in management.

- **Managerial competence** – an interest in pursuing a management career and rising up the corporate hierarchy to a point where they had a high degree of power and influence.

- **Security** – a desire for stability. These subjects were highly concerned with staying in the same locality or in the same community or settling down to family life.

- **Creativity** – an emphasis on the need to produce something (a company, a service, or a product) that is novel. Often, these people become entrepreneurs.

- **Independence** – the need for autonomy and freedom from the rules and regulations in big organisations.

Shein believed that one of these career anchors would become dominant and would play a pre-eminent role in shaping a person's career.

19.3 Modern Changes in Career Structures

Super, Levinson and Schein formed their ideas in middle of the last century when careers were fairly predictable and stable. One would enter a career in early adulthood and, with one or two changes, pursue that career (probably with the same employer) until retirement. However, the rate of organisational change in the 1980s and 1990s has bought about major changes in career structures. Modern careers are much less stable. Often people stay in a job for less than four years before they either change employer or the type of work they do. This means that now people can expect as many as 10 job changes and several episodes of redundancy during their career. Handy (1989) likened today's world of work to a shamrock in which there are three types of worker (Figure 19.3). There is a small group that forms an inner core of an organisation. They have permanence and stay with an organisation over long periods. They largely conform to the traditional pattern of employment. There is also a contractual fringe of people who are employed on a fee-paying basis for specific pieces of work. Often, they will be employed on a repeat-contract basis and they may do work for many organisations. Finally, there are the hired helps – people that are employed on a casual basis, when and where the need arises (see Clarke, 1992).

This relative impermanence of employment has important implications. In the past long-term employees were key organisational assets. It was in the organisation's interests to develop and improve the skills and abilities of the individuals they employed. Nowadays, this logic is less forceful. Why spend money on developing managers when, in a few year's time, they will be working for someone else. The responsibility has shifted. Today,

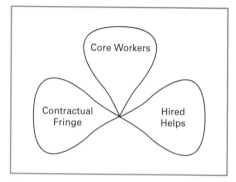

FIGURE 19.3 Handy's Shamrock

it is the individual who must ensure that their skills and experience improve so they will be able to obtain the next job or contract. People need to ensure their own "employability".

19.4 Types of Career Path

Careers can take many paths. Clark (1992) has identified eight main ones which are illustrated in Figures 19.4 to 19.6.

The *triangle* is the kind of career path followed by Henry Fortescue. One enters at the bottom of an organisation where people are promoted according to their seniority – the length of time they have worked in the organisation. Without much effort they proceed up the organisation waiting for a "tap on the shoulder" to let them know they should step forward into the next "dead man's shoes". The *ladder* is rather similar to the triangle except promotion is usually based upon some assessment of merit. The individual must put effort into climbing the organisational hierarchy. Many organisations operated in this way. However, in the 1990s many companies were "delayered" by the removal of middle-management positions. In companies where career ladders still exist, the ladders might now be missing a number of rungs. Many of their employees will be wondering if there is any possibility of promotion. The *spiral* is a relatively new kind of career path where advancement is obtained by moving upwards and outwards to a higher career in another function or even another organisation.

The *steady-state* career path is typical of many specialists. They occupy a niche within the organisation where they can apply their skills but perhaps in rather different contexts. Typical examples would be people working in biotechnology and management consultancy. A *bridge* career path has a transitory phrase that enables people to "jump" from one kind of career to another. For example, a production manager may aspire to a general management post but lacks general management experience and may also work in an organisation where there are few opportunities for advancement. In this situation, the production manager might take a post in a management consultancy where he or she can expand their experience and make contacts, which after two years will lead to a general manager position.

Clark notes that the next three career paths are relatively recent and reflect the greater uncertainties of contemporary organisational life.

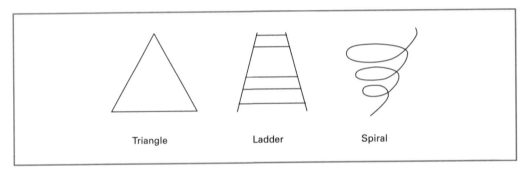

Triangle   Ladder   Spiral

FIGURE 19.4 Clark's Career Stages 1–3

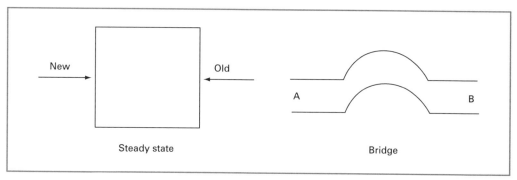

FIGURE 19.5 Clark's Career Stages 4–5

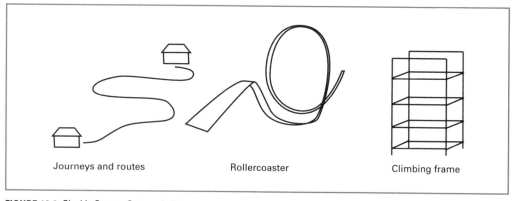

FIGURE 19.6 Clark's Career Stages 6–8
(Figures 19.4–19.6 adapted from Clark, 'Total Career Management: Strategies for Creating Management Careers' McGraw-Hill Europe. With thanks to Frances Clark.)

Nicholson and West (1988) viewed managerial careers as stories about *journeys and routes* between organisations located in different places in the world of work. The journeys of different people may vary widely. Some may follow well-known main roads. Others may follow country roads and some will end up in dead ends. Often these careers start with only vague goals and the ultimate destination is chosen while "en route". An organisation can be likened to a *climbing frame* where the bars of the ladder have all sorts of shapes and angles. This means it is possible to reach the top starting in many places and taking many different routes. The career path of the *roller coaster* is not for the faint-hearted. It is seen in fast-moving sectors where acquisitions, mergers and sell-outs are common. Roller-coaster careers move at great speed and the trajectory is not clear. There will be a swift steep climb, a swerve of direction, a precipitous plunge and perhaps a steep climb again. Entrepreneurs also often have roller coaster careers: a stunning idea – backing by venture capitalists – swift growth – employment of managers – and then overthrow by the venture capitalists and managers before having a new idea and starting another company.

Some types of careers are called *boundaryless* careers because they span many functions and departments in an organisation. Indeed, a true boundaryless career is likely to span organisations. This is often achieved by participating in collaborative projects, holding offices in professional organisations or networking with colleagues in other companies. A boundaryless career gives a wide range of experience. However, boundaryless careers have their dangers in producing someone who is a "Jack (Janet) of all trades who is master of none".

Dual careers are a relatively recent phenomenon that arises when both partners of a relationship are pursuing a career. Sometimes, the demands of careers conflict. For example, one partner's career may involve relocation to a distant city where there are few business opportunities for the other partner. Similarly, when couples have children there can be conflict in deciding whose career should be sacrificed in the interests of childcare. Resolving these conflicts can be very stressful. Often, the conflict is resolved by adopting an asynchronous approach – usually where the husband's career is given priority between the ages of 26 to 40 and the wife's career is given priority between the ages of 41 and, say, 55 (see Sekaran and Hall, 1989).

19.5 Some Facets of Careers

The literature on careers is vast and it is impossible to even summarise it in this chapter. Instead the objective will be to introduce four key facets: characteristics of extraordinary careers, career plateaux, outplacement and the psychological contract.

Characteristics of extraordinary careers

Citrin and Smith (2003) analysed the files of one of the world's leading executive search consultancies (headhunters). They also obtained completed questionnaires from over 2000 executives and they interviewed more than 300. They found that extraordinary careers shared five main characteristics:

- **Understanding one's own market value**. People with extraordinary careers had a keen understanding of what made people valuable to organisations and they had accurate appreciations of their own worth. The value of an individual to an organisation consists of two parts: potential and experience. People start their working life with a full bag of potential and an empty bag of experience. The trick, according to Citrin and Smith is to fill your bag of experience before you empty your bag of potential. Generally, experience is worth more than potential but potential gives access to experience.

- **Gaining permissions**. High-flyers are good at gaining permission from others. This is not as passive as it seems. They spot opportunities and then gain the permission of important people to exploit these opportunities. They know that the danger of operating without permission may be to be labelled an "upstart" or "a self publicist". They are also aware of the distinction between formal permission and informal permission. In the latter there is no clear reason why the initiative *cannot* be taken.

- **Benevolent leadership**. People with extraordinary carriers do not claw their way to the top: *they are carried there*. Through practising benevolent leadership they attract top talent about them and then inspire these people to produce top levels of performance.

They do this by being open, honest and willing to delegate responsibility. They are also good at aligning the goals of their team with the goals of individual members. This is in direct opposition to the common image of a successful executive: a shark or a warrior who takes no prisoners.

- **Recognising the 20/80 discretionary principal**. This is not quite the familiar 80/20 principal espoused by Pareto. In some ways it is the opposite. It is based on the fact that 80 per cent of work is predetermined and probably enshrined in a job description, result areas and targets. It is vital that the key results and targets are met. For an exceptional career, however, this is not enough – Citrin and Smith found that 95 per cent of *all* executives met their targets. What differentiated an exceptional career was the use to which the discretionary 20 per cent is put. People with exceptional careers apply the discretionary 20 per cent of the work time to carefully chosen, strategic projects that have a high profile.

- **Finding work that is compatible with one's interests and strengths**. Citrin and Smith (2003) found that successful executives were six times more likely to be in careers that could use their strengths, interests, values and "passions". Sometimes people are attracted to a profession because it offers financial rewards or it follows a family tradition. These factors may "push" them up a corporate ladder. However, there is a probability that halfway up the ladder they become dissatisfied. They then must face a difficult decision whether stay put on the wrong track or jump to a lower rung on a different ladder. Often the result is a "derailed" career.

Career plateaux

A career plateau is the point in a career when further advancement is unlikely. Unfortunately, different authors disagree on what this means in practice. For some people it is the point where further promotion is unlikely. For others it is the point where an increase in responsibility and authority is unlikely. Finally, some people interpret the career plateau at the point at which a salary increase becomes unlikely (see for example, Ference, Stoner and Warren, 1977; Nicholson 1993). It should be noted that a career plateau does not mean the same as stagnation. Plateaued managers can still experience growth arising from new commercial and technical developments. Sometimes a horizontal move or an organisational restructuring can involve the mastery of many new things. In the past, a career plateaux usually occurred in a person's late 40s or early 50s. The slimming down and de-layering of organisations has meant fewer senior management jobs. Career plateaux now occur earlier – say, from the late 30s onwards.

A career plateau can occur for a number of reasons. They are not necessarily a sign of incompetence or lack of potential. They are most likely to arise from an organisation's structure where, say, an organisational unit has been eliminated and where the number of senior posts has decreased. In these situations, the organisation is likely to retain existing staff and "ring fence" their status pay and conditions. In a minority of cases managers are plateaued because they have reached the limit of their competence but this does not necessarily mean that they are inadequate in their plateaued job.

Managers react to being plateaued in different ways. The worst reaction occurs when managers become frustrated and de-motivated. This takes a considerable toll in terms of the

CASE 19.1: A PLATEAUED CAREER

Some years ago one building society decided to move into the estate agency business and recruited an able commercial manager who had reasonable expectations of becoming the unit's Chief Executive Officer (CEO) in due course. Within six months the housing market went flat, profits in estate agency were zero so the building society sold its estate agency interests. Because it recognised the contribution the manager had made and could make in other areas of the business, the society transferred her to an equivalent post in the organisation. Although the manager's salary and status was maintained there was little hope for further advancement – she was plateaued.

individual's quality of life, organisational morale and organisational costs. Both individuals and the organisations should be alert to the symptoms of this outcome. These may take the form of prolonged periods of depression together with an increasing tendency to gossip and aggressive criticism of others. Wider symptoms include fatigue and family discord. A happier reaction occurs when a plateaued manager accepts the situation and becomes contented. Howard and Bray (1998), Ference, Stoner and Warren (1977) and Nicholson's (1993) found plateaued managers are able to develop an in-depth knowledge of their particular area. They can form a vast reservoir of tacit knowledge that helps the organisation perform well. This tacit knowledge can be passed on to younger members of the organisation via mentoring. Plateaued managers often redress their work–life balance and are happy to be relieved of the chore of jockeying for position.

Outplacement

It is quite rare for managers to lose their jobs because they are incompetent. Typically managers lose their jobs due to reorganisations, mergers, expiry of patents or a decision to move production "off shore" – they just happen to be in the wrong place at the wrong time. Since there is little or no culpability it is harsh to dismiss managers, many of whom will have given years of devoted service to the organisation, with only their statutory entitlements. Many organisations therefore give enhanced severance payments. While these payments can be a big help, they can also be heavily taxed. What a redundant manager really wants is a new job that is equal or better than their previous post.

During the 1960s (USA), 1970s (UK) and 1980s (Europe) outplacement consultancies developed in order to help executives find new jobs. Often employers provided these services out of a sense of guilt. In other cases they provided outplacement services in order to reassure employees who were to remain, and to avoid bad publicity. Where redundancy arose from a total closure of a factory it was often imperative that managers should remain to the end to ensure a proper close-down. In these circumstances it was better to pay outplacement consultants to do a lot of the work in researching the job market, preparing CVs and writing letters than have senior executives distracted by these tasks. Governments also provided outplacement by using their existing employment services or setting up "taskforces" to help workers involved in a major closure such as a shipyard or steel-mill.

The nature of outplacement services varies according to a worker's level in an organisation. In the event of a major closure a "job shop" might be established near the "factory gate" for use by manual and clerical employees. The job shop would contain a notice-board of suitable vacancies in the area, photocopying facilities and help filling in forms or writing letters. Junior managers would probably be provided with workshops where groups of people would be taught the techniques of successful job-hunting such as searching the job market, preparing CVs and attending interviews. Very senior executives would be provided with top facilities. This might include:

- A psychologist who would administer a battery of psychometric tests in order to identify their strengths and to advise on suitable employment.

- A researcher who would locate organisations that might provide suitable employment. The researcher would then produce an extensive brief about the organisation and discuss it in depth with the executive searching for a job.

- A consultant who would co-ordinate the activities of the psychologist and researcher. He or she would also advise on the preparation of the CV and practice interview tactics using closed-circuit television. If an application seemed likely to be successful, the consultant would also give advice on an appropriate salary and the means of negotiating that salary.

Today, outplacement is a mature and fully accepted aspect of human resource management.

The psychological contract

The idea of a psychological contract has been around since the 1960s. It is an unspoken understanding between an employee and their employer about what they can expect from each other – "I have promised to do this and my employer has promised me that he or she will do that". Usually the employee understands that she or he has promised effort, loyalty, trustworthiness, etc. in return for training, pay, job security and promotion from the employer. Psychological contracts in the past could be summed up by the phrase "I will give total commitment to the company and the company will look after me until I retire". Robinson and Rousseau (1994) defined the psychological contract in a more long-winded way:

> 66 An individual's belief regarding the terms and conditions of that reciprocal exchange agreement between that focal person and another party ... a belief that some form of a promise has been made and that the terms and conditions of the contract have been accepted by both parties. 99

Lawyers would regard this as a very strange contract indeed. As a contract it is bizarre in a number of ways:

- **It is rarely written down**. Only a part of the expectations on both sides are made explicit. Some of the expectations are conscious but others are subconscious and the contracting parties may not be aware of their existence.

- **It is based on perceptions**. Consequently, there are as many psychological contracts as there are employees in the organisation.

■ **The contract is dynamic and will change over time**. In a sense the psychological contract is under constant re-negotiation.

Because the psychological contract is so dissimilar to other contracts some people believe it needs to be renamed "Transitory Employee Perceptions of their Employment". This title would emphasise the subjective, individualistic and non-permanent nature of the psychological contract. Some people such as Guest (1998) complain that, in practice, we should not take the concept seriously because it involves so many variables interacting in an unknown way.

Rousseau (1995) identified two main types of psychological contract: transactional and relational. The *transactional psychological contract* is the nearest to a normal commercial contract. The worker agrees to do certain things such as work overtime or move to a new location in return for a specific reward such as extra money. Transactional psychological contracts are often seen in clearly defined jobs that are relatively short term. They tend to centre upon specific outputs and specific rewards. *Relational psychological contracts* are usually seen in long-term employees where the work is only defined in a general way. As their name implies, relational psychological contracts centre upon the way that the parties behave to each other. In the past, this was usually a paternalistic relationship where the employee would be loyal, compliant and adopt the organisation's values in return for secure employment and the knowledge that they would be looked after in times of misfortune. Modern psychological contracts where organisations can no longer offer long-term employment tend to stress a worker providing flexibility and a willingness to learn in return for high pay, the acquisition of marketable skills and a high quality of life.

Although the psychological contract implies a mutual agreement, there is usually a huge power differential between the two parties. When the crunch comes it is usually the employer's version that prevails. This leads workers to feel that the contract has been violated. This happened to large numbers of employees during the downsizing and restructuring of organisations in the 1980s and 1990s. Many workers felt cheated because, while they had kept their part of the bargain, it was widely believed that the employers had reneged on their part by increasing workloads and making many peoples' jobs redundant. In one study 54 per cent of graduates claimed that their employers have violated their psychological contracts within the first two years of employment. The areas most frequently violated included training, pay and promotion. The reactions of employees who believe that their psychological contract has been violated have been extensively researched. They experience feelings of injustice, deception or betrayal. There may be cultural differences. For example, workers in Singapore who are used to short-term contracts are less aggrieved by violations than employees in the United States. Violations of the psychological contract usually affect workers' attitudes towards their employers. It may affect their behaviour too. The most obvious response is to leave the organisation and work for another employer. Some people, probably a small minority, complain to their employers. Probably most employees adopt the third option of keeping quiet and focusing tightly on their official duties while cutting back on more discretionary behaviours such as doing extra hours. Some employees attempt to get even. Their revenge can take many forms which may include pilfering of stationery, neglecting duties that are hard to monitor, denigrating their employers in public, divulging trade secrets and even sabotage or destruction of the employer's property. Palmer (1999) gives examples of the revenge people can take.

CASE 19.2: REVENGE FOR RENEGING ON THE PSYCHOLOGICAL CONTRACT

Employees sometimes take revenge when employers renege on their psychological contract. For example, one 50-year-old from Wales tells how a new senior position was created in the service department where he had worked alone for more than four years. "I applied in writing for the new position, setting out my achievements. I was not granted even a brief interview despite the fact that I was on the premises. On the last afternoon of my resignation notice I destroyed all the test rigs I had built and the notes I had made to speed up the job. Subsequently I learned that three staff had been taken on to do the work … I had previously done myself".

Another example includes a 25-year-old publishing assistant who "rearranged" her boss's files, and did it so effectively that important documents were lost for several months. A final, ingenious example is a disgruntled word-processor operator who changed all the screens in her department to black characters on a black background. The organisation had purchased several replacement monitors before it located the real cause.

19.6 Career Toolkit: Managing Your Own Career

Previous sections have pointed out that today individuals must manage their own career and maintain their employability. This section aims to give some practical advice on two key activities: getting a job and getting promotion

Getting a job

Getting the right job is one of the most important actions in most people's lives. Yet, the process is often very haphazard. It is ironic that a great deal of advice is available on the relatively minor matter of how to invest a few hundred, or even a few thousand pounds or dollars, but little advice is given on how to invest a working life. It is doubly ironic since a lot is known about the job-finding process. Psychologists have researched the subject for a century or more and have accumulated a great deal of knowledge. The research emphasises two major points. Getting a job involves a great deal of luck and a systematic approach is necessary.

The chance element of getting a job must not be underestimated. You will have no control over who else applies for the job. For example, if six other applicants are paragons your chances will be slim. Nonetheless, for a very similar jobs advertised a fortnight later, when the six paragons are out of town attending interviews for the initial job, you may be top of the list. You will also have very little control over the interviewer. Many interviewers will not have been properly trained and their styles will vary. It is largely a matter of luck whether you are interviewed by someone with a style that suits you. Interviewers also differ in their view of the ideal candidate. For example, one officer interviewing police recruits could be looking for candidates with the deductive powers of Sherlock Holmes. A second, equally qualified officer may look for an affable personality and physical fitness. You will have no control over which one interviews you. Because so much chance is involved, you must apply for a lot of jobs so that these factors have the opportunity of cancelling each other out. You must also try to minimise the chance in factors under your control by adopting a systematic approach. This involves five stages.

Stage one: personal stocktaking

The first stage involves a cool and deliberate assessment of your strengths, style and weaknesses. This personal stocktaking is important because it ensures that you apply only for jobs which are suitable, thus allowing you to concentrate all your efforts in the direction that is most likely to bring results. An effective personal stocktaking will also prepare you for many of the questions that an interviewer might ask. A simple method of taking stock is to set aside a weekend when your social life is less hectic than usual. On Friday night start three lists:

- a list of everything that you have achieved in your life
- a list of everything you have failed
- a list of important and influential people you have met

Do not be coy. Only you and trusted friends will see the list. Include every little achievement – everything you have organised, everything you have passed, everything you have made and almost everything you have written. Keep adding new things to your list as you think of them during the weekend. People are often surprised that their "achievements list" needs several continuation sheets.

Good interviewers use a plan. The most famous is Roger's seven-point plan (see p. 104). On the Sunday afternoon find a quiet place and use the lists to help you write three sentences about yourself under each heading of the seven-point plan:

- **physical make up** such as health, physique, appearance and speech
- **attainments** such as qualifications, training received and licences
- **general intelligence**: how much you have and how much you normally use
- **special attitudes** such as ability with words, ability with numbers, ability to remember designs or ability to mend machines
- **interests and motives** such as outdoors, mathematical, scientific, mechanical, persuasive, practical, administrative or social service
- **disposition and style** such as warm-hearted, apprehensive, emotional control, conscientious, down-to-earth, imaginative, assertive or co-operative
- **home circumstances,** which include restrictions on mobility and working hours due to family life

When you have finished your stocktaking, show the sentences you have written to a trusted friend or adviser and ask for their comments. If you have difficulty in arriving at a satisfactory assessment of your strengths and weaknesses you could seek outside advice from a university or college appointments board, government careers services or private careers advisers. Be careful of your choice of private careers advisers. Ensure that they belong to the appropriate professional body such as the British Psychological Society or the Australian Psychological Association.

   The final part of the stocktaking stage is to use this information to identify a suitable career direction. Plenty of resources are available at libraries and on the Internet. When a suitable job has been identified it is prudent to take two extra steps. First, check that the industry is not in long-term decline. Second, find someone who is already doing the job, work out a spiel in advance and then contact them by telephone. Explain the position and ask the person to meet you for 20 minutes to talk about their job. Offer to buy him or her a cup of coffee. Most people will be delighted to help. They will spend longer than 20 minutes and the chances are that they will buy *you* the coffee. If this information confirms your initial choice the next stage is to find a suitable vacancy.

Stage two: finding a vacancy

Most people rely on adverts in *national newspapers* to locate professional jobs. These papers specialise in some degree. However, organisations advertising vacancies do not always follow these specialisations and a determined job hunter will scan all relevant papers. Remember four main points. First, look at every issue of a paper. Jobs are rarely advertised twice in the same newspaper. Second read all the adverts carefully. Job titles vary from one organisation to another. Do not be put off by terms such as "assistant" because an assistant in one organisation may have more responsibility and a higher salary than a manager in another organisation. Third, do not be put off if you fail to meet one of the "essential" qualifications. Firms often specify requirement and then relent when applications arrive. The main exception to this rule are stipulations for jobs in government service. Finally, follow carefully the instructions on how to apply and keep a copy of the adverts with a note of the paper and date. Similar considerations apply to local papers. Your "sweeps" of local newspapers will be more tedious because many adverts will use the condensed, lineage format. This will deter many of your competitors and you may be able to gain an advantage by using a systematic approach. A good job search will also include *trade journals, professional magazines, government recruitment agencies* and *private recruitment agencies.*

   Many job hunters overlook informal methods of finding a vacancy. At one time *personal contacts* were *the* method of finding a suitable job – friends and relatives "asked" what vacancies were available with their employer. Your network of contacts can and should be exploited. There is nothing reprehensible about looking for a job, so let contacts know that you are searching for a post. In most cases it is good idea to let them have details of your experience, qualifications and the type of work you will consider. Do not mislead them about your qualifications and experience, because this might put their reputation at risk. *Speculative applications* are surprisingly successful. You may be the only applicant who is considered because your letter arrived at the same time as a resignation and employers contact you in order to avoid the bother, delay and expense of advertising. Speculative applications also demonstrate your interest and initiative. Only target organisations which are likely to have suitable vacancies.

Stage three: making an application

It is vital to submit an excellent application. An organisation may have 100 applications for vacancy and will whittle the list down to the four or five for interview. The odds against you are higher than at any other stage in the selection process. In the initial sift, your application may only receive 45 seconds attention before it is consigned to one of three piles: probable, possible and reject. You must make sure that your key advantages stand out and can be appreciated within a few seconds. The best way to do this is to start your CV with a profile about five lines long which describe your key attributes, Once your application is in the "probable" file it will receive detailed scrutiny. If you are asked to complete an application form you should read it through very carefully and then read both the advert and the results of the personal stocktaking. Next you should draft your answers on spare paper. Only then do you complete the form. Never fill out an application form while you are eating or drinking.

Unless there is a specific request for you to complete the form in your own handwriting, word-process your answers. Never use a pen with light blue ink. Your form is almost certain to be photocopied. Light-blue ink does not photocopy well. Unless there are specific instructions to the contrary it is better to leave a section blank rather than have a whole page peppered with "none", "no experience" or "no qualifications". Give positive answers. "I am looking for a job" is a much more positive reply than "I am unemployed" and "I am seeking a new opportunity" gives a more positive image than "I am fed up with my present job". Many application forms have a section headed "any other information". This gives the opportunity to underline your strong points by repeating them in different words. Look down the list of achievements produced in your personal stocktaking and pick out any successes that are particularly relevant to the current application.

Applicants for professional or managerial jobs are frequently asked to send a curriculum vitae, which is also known as a "CV" or "Résumé". Organisations regard CVs as a good test of how well a candidate can communicate in writing. Most of the suggestions for application forms also apply to CVs. Your CV should be professionally word processed on one side of unruled A4 paper. It should not be less than 1½ sheets or more than three. Carefully read any guidance notes that your college or university or counsellor provides on the preparation of CVs. You *must* then vary the advice slightly in order to make your CV distinctive. Take great care with the layout and presentation. The content of your CV should be factual. Give dates and figures where appropriate. A final point is relevant to both application forms and CVs. Never make untruthful or misleading statements.

Make sure that a referee is aware of the points you think most relevant and tell him or her why you want that particular job and why it would be suitable. Before giving anyone's name as a referee ask their permission and check their name, initials, qualifications, job title, address and email address.

Stage four – part one: influencing organisation at interviews

It has been known for almost a century that interviewers are not very good at selecting the right person. For example, in 1929 an investigator asked twelve experienced sales managers to interview 57 applicants and rank them according to suitability. When the ranks were compared the results were appalling. One candidate was ranked first by one interviewer and last by another. Another candidate was ranked sixth and fifty-sixth. Fortunately since that time interviews have improved. Good organisations insist that any manager who interviews applicants must have special training, and interviews have a clear structure so that all candidates are asked similar questions on work-related topics. Influencing interviewers starts with careful preparation. First, try to get to know the organisation and the vacancy. Try to find out:

- the age of the organisation
- the size of the organisation (number of employees and turnover)
- its three main products or services
- its three main customers
- the location of head office and the main branches

This information can be obtained from the organisational website, reference books in the library, the organisation's accounts or from someone working for the organisation. If all else fails, get someone to telephone the organisation and "pump" the receptionist. Write the information on a small piece of card and look at it shortly before the interview.

Second, work out an answer to the inevitable question, "*why* do you want *this* job". Work out positive reasons: Because it is near home? Because it is interesting? Because it offers opportunities to extend skills? Also work out answers to the standard questions "what do you think you could bring to the organisation?" and "what do you hope to be doing in five years time" (work out a modestly ambitious answer). Sort out in your mind the details of two interests and hobbies. Fewer than two interests will be taken to indicate that you are a lifeless drip. More than two interests may be taken to indicate that you will not have enough time for serious work. Avoid dwelling upon passive or casual interests such as watching television. You should also work out an answer to the question "have you made any other applications?" ("yes but this is the one that interests me most because . . ."). A list of the 110 questions you are most likely to be asked at an interview is given in the website devoted to this book.

Many organisations use an interview technique called "situational" interviewing. The interviewers will be looking for specific competencies. You can usually work out the competencies required by reading the advert and other information very carefully. These documents will use words such as "leadership", "innovation", "persuasiveness", etc. The interviewer is properly looking for the same competencies. Think of one example where you exhibited each competency in the past. The example does not need to be grand but it does need to be realistic and true. For example, organising a holiday abroad for a group of friends would provide an acceptable example of leadership. Then, one by one go through the examples and work out:

- a short explanation of the situation that arose
- a short account of the action you took
- a short description of the results that you obtained
- a short description of the reactions of others
- a short evaluation of what you learned

The third aspect of preparation is to sort out your appearance. Pay particular attention to your grooming and hygiene. Have your hair trimmed a week before any likely interview. The style of dress is not particularly important provided it is clean and reasonably neat. On-campus interviewers are used to scruffy students but for interviewers at an organisation, especially interviews with line managers, you should be smart and formal in your dress.

Arrive five minutes early and be prepared to wait. Greet the receptionist in a relaxed but not too casual a way. Some interviewers ask the receptionists for their opinion before making a decision. When you are shown into the interview room greet the interviewer with a friendly "hello" and a smile. Wait for the interviewer to indicate where you should sit. Interviews may vary from under a quarter of an hour to over an hour. A 30 minute interview may spend two minutes on *ice-breaking and courtesies*. During this time you should smile and establish lots of our eye contact – but do not stare the interviewer in the eyes – look at the end of his or her nose! Give at least one answer that is two sentences long. The content of the sentences is not very important. It is important that you avoid one word answers such as "yes" or "no".

The interviewer will probably spend 15 minutes asking *questions to obtain information* from you. Answer honestly but positively. Avoid qualifying your answers with the words "only" or "just" – they will tend to devalue your experience. Be aware that interviews are interactive. The interviewer's questions affect your answers and, in turn, your answers affect subsequent questions. This means that interviews can get into vicious or benign circles. At all costs you should avoid getting into vicious circles. Remain calm. Remain polite. Remain pleasant and smile occasionally. Expect that some of your answers will be less than perfect but do not let this affect the way that you answer later questions. Research has shown that in most circumstances stress interviews are useless. If the interviewer uses stress tactics or gets over-argumentative, humour him or her. Remain calm. Take the style of questioning into account when deciding whether to accept a job offer. Be careful not to "knock" your present employer or university. The interviewer may think that you are the one at fault. Never criticise two past employers. Indeed, it is usually better to say something positive about your university or the people you have worked for.

In a 30-minute interview the interviewer will spend about five minutes *describing the vacancy*. Sometimes interviewers describe the vacancy before they ask you questions. However, it is slightly more usual for the vacancy to be described after the interviewer has obtained information from you. Your strategy during this stage is essentially a passive one where you indicate that the description accords with your understanding. You should do this both orally with a comment such as "I am pleased that the job is very much as I understood it would be" and with non-verbal cues such as smiles and nods of head. In theory the interviewer should spend about seven minutes asking for your questions and answering them. You *must* ask some questions but you should avoid taking a long list of questions from your pocket and tediously working your way through every one. Limit yourself to three or four questions. Try to use this time to see if the job would suit you. Phrase your questions carefully to avoid giving the impression of being "finicky". The standard questions you can ask are: "how did the vacancy arise", "what jobs are last year's intake doing now?", "what are the details of the training scheme?", "what are the opportunities to learn new skills?", "how will my work be supervised?" and "when will I be given responsibility for a significant project?". A good penultimate question is "do you have any reservations about my application?". The interviewer will probably want to be kind to your face and say something nice. His or her public commitment would then work in your favour. If the interviewer does respond with a reservation or concern, you have the opportunity to rebut it tactfully. In any event the information will be useful for other applications. Unless you have already been given the answer, your final question should be "how and when will I hear the results of my application?".

Many interviewees are surprised by how little chance they have to state their claims and explain their application. They believe that the interviewer should speak about 25 per cent of the time and that they should be given the remaining 75 per cent to prove their merits. In fact, research suggests that interviewers speaks for about 60 per cent of an interview, the interviewee speaks for about 30 per cent of the time and the remainder is spent in stony silence. If the salary is fixed there will be no room for negotiation at an interview, but, if the salary is negotiable, you will be faced with difficult decisions. Should the interviewer raise the subject of salary you will have no option but to follow the lead. However, it is probably better not to raise the question yourself. Wait until the organisation commits itself by offering you the job. You will then be in a stronger negotiating position.

Stage four – part two: ways of influencing organisations in other selection situations

So far the advice given in this section has concerned one-to-one interviews. Some organisations use different methods, which include sequence interviews, panel interviews, leaderless group discussions, presentations, in-trays and psychometric tests.

Sequence interviews are very similar to the standard interview described earlier. Sequence interviews have the advantage that your future will not depend on the whims of one person. Often the first interview will be with the organisation's personnel officer or recruitment specialist. Your second interview will be with your potential line manager. Some organisations specify the roles the two interviewers should adopt. The interviewer from the human resource department will ask questions about you as a person – your intelligence, your integrity and ability to withstand pressure, etc. The other interviewer, frequently your potential line manager, usually asks questions about your technical knowledge and competence. In many organisations you may be called back for a third interview by an organisational "grandfather" or "grandmother" – in other words, a very senior manager. If you get this far you are doing well. You will have the support of the HR department and your potential line manager. At this stage they are your allies. Your main aim is not to let them down. Ask them if they have any suggestions or if you should adopt any particular strategies. At this stage you should be pleasantly open, say something positive about the organisation and mention something good about your experiences so far. You should also say something about your aspirations to do something that will make a significant contribution to the organisation's value chain.

Some organisations use *panel interviews* where you will be questioned by several people. Generally, panel interviews are more stressful than one-to-one interviewers. Often they degenerate into rivalry between panel members to see how clever they are. Questioning in panel interviews is usually more superficial. There is only sufficient time for each member to ask two or three questions. The scope for following a theme of penetrating questions is very limited. Consequently, panel interviews entail a greater element of chance. Try to establish eye contact with each member of the panel at least twice. Try to establish who is the chair and who is the person from the HR department. They will be opinion leaders. Pay them and your potential line manager particular attention. Ensure you establish eye contact with these three role-holders. Avoid getting into arguments with obnoxious members of the panel. If all else fails, be enthusiastic and say how interesting you find the difference of opinion. Tell them how glad you on that they have raised such an important issue and then express your regrets that there is insufficient time for a thorough discussion. Similarly, avoid exclusive chats with a member of the panel who shares an interesting but irrelevant hobby such a stamp collecting, golf, yachting or taxidermy.

About 20 per cent of organisations use *leaderless group discussions* (LGDs) as a part of their selection procedures. Usually, about eight applicants are asked to discuss a general topic to which there is no right or wrong answer. Applicants are seated around a square or circular table so that there is no positional advantage. There will usually be four trained observers who sit quietly in the background noting who says what and also the reactions of other members of the group. The main thing about leaderless group discussions is to say *something* and not leave it until the last minute to blurt out your desperate contribution. If you say or do nothing you cannot gain marks on anything! If the leaderless group discussion of eight applicants lasts 40 minutes you should aim to occupy slightly more than the average "air time" – say, six or seven minutes. The main thing is to be able to break into a discussion without being rude or argumentative. You should prepare yourself with half a dozen phrases that enable you to get a word in. For example:

- "That's good. I can see that in some cases it works. But I cannot entirely agree because . . ."
- "I think that is right, but shouldn't we also consider . . ."
- "I'm glad you mentioned that because a similar thing happened to me . . ."
- "That's interesting. I'd like to hear exactly how that worked because I'm not sure if it would apply in a case where . . ."
- "What a wonderful idea. I wish I had thought of that because . . ."

Leaderless group discussions, like most meetings, have three phases. During the *opening phase* the group must establish the nature of the problem and the contributions the members can make. It is easy to prepare strategies for contributions at this stage. It is probably better to be the second person who speaks by asking a question such as "shouldn't we establish our goals?" or "how would answering this question add value to the organisation?". If this ploy has been usurped by another candidate an alternative might be to ask "shouldn't we check whether any of us has experience or information that we can use to produce a solution?". These questions are likely to establish you as a leading candidate. The *middle phase* of a group discussion is more unpredictable. You will need to adapt to the flow of the argument. Do not hesitate to make one of two suggestions yourself. They do not need to be profound but unless you make some contribution you cannot score any marks for logical thinking or generating ideas. Do not be afraid of building upon good contributions by others. An excellent ploy is to say "I think what Daniel said a few minutes ago is important. It made me think about . . .". In fact, your comments may only need a tenuous link with Daniel's previous comments! Do not speak too long yourself. When you have obtained slightly more than your "air time" try to involve others. For example, you might say "Mavis, you have not said a lot but I can see you have been thinking deeply. What is your opinion?". Mavis has probably been very unhappy at not making a contribution. She will be very grateful for your help and will probably vote for you, if necessary, at a later stage. The last phase of a group discussion involves crystallising events. Five minutes *before the end* you might say something like "our time is running out", "shouldn't we be coming to a conclusion", "the main points we have covered are . . . what do other people think" or "shouldn't we be organising our conclusions?". If there are a number of conclusions it might be wise to point out "that is a lot of recommendations. Shouldn't we put them in order of priority? Which should we put at the top of our list?". Finally, a really savvy candidate might say "we should be thinking of ways to implement our recommendations. What are the main points we should make?".

Organisations frequently ask candidates for management positions to give *presentations*. The topic may be linked to a previous exercise such as a report or a group discussion. In other cases the candidate is allowed to choose the topic. If you think you may be asked to give presentations as a part of a selection procedure you should think of a good topic in advance. Choose a topic that will allow you to demonstrate the competencies the organisation requires. A good choice is "someone I admire". You can then choose an appropriate person. For example if you were applying for a job in a voluntary organisation you could use of Albert Schweitzer or Mother Theresa and if you were applying for a job in industry you could choose Stelios Haji-Ioannou, the founder of easyJet or James Dyson. You should never choose topics such as my hobby, my pet or my house renovation. The selectors will have heard presentations on these topics many times before. Make sure that you use visual aids during your presentation. You should also make an attempt to involve the audience on at least three occasions – perhaps by asking questions or by getting them to assist in some way. Start the presentation with an anecdote or a joke that helps to focus on your topic and emphasise why people should pay attention to what you are going to say. Make sure that your presentation has a very clear structure that has about five sections. Always sum up at the end. It may be appropriate to make an explicit statement of the actions you would like people to take. Finally, remember to thank the audience for their attention.

In-tray exercises are another popular method for the selection of managers. Usually, there is a scenario such as "It is ten o'clock on the morning of Saturday 7 May 200x. Unfortunately, last night your boss was rushed to hospital for an emergency operation. The CEO has telephoned to ask you to take her place until your boss can return for work. The organisation is usually closed on Saturday but you have come into work to clear some paperwork. In exactly one hour's time you must leave for the airport in time for a flight. Your boss's personal assistant has collected together all the outstanding paperwork. As it is Saturday, no one else is at work so you must write all your instructions on the relevant documents". Candidates are then given a desk diary, an organisation chart and a sheaf of papers (memos, letters, brief reports, newspaper cuttings, invitations, etc.) that are typical of the paperwork the successful applicant might need to complete. It is generally impossible to deal with all items in the time available. It is therefore vital to quickly read through the documents and deal with them in order of priority. You should also look for links between items. You should also use the diary to ensure that you do not make commitments that clash. Finally, be sensitive to people's feelings. Consult the organisation charts to ensure that you are not cutting across responsibilities. As you jot your actions on the pieces of paper, take a few seconds to write polite comments and, if possible, add a personal touch.

Intelligence tests are used to select people for about 20 per cent of managerial posts. They are among the most accurate ways of selecting people. If you are given an intelligence test pay particular attention to the instructions and practise items. Listen carefully for any time limits. If the time limit is less than 30 minutes you must work quickly, give each question your best shot and then move on. Only double-check your answers if you have time left at the end. Then check backwards. You are most likely to have made mistakes in the last questions you have answered. Have realistic expectations. Intelligence tests are designed so no-one will be able to answer all questions. Do not get depressed or thrown out of your stride if you are unable to attempt some questions. The other candidates will be in the same boat.

Many firms use *personality tests*. Most personality tests are straightforward. Do not spend time pondering the questions deeply and looking for hidden meanings. Answer at a rate of about five or six questions per minute. Avoid giving too many answers in the middle "uncertain" box as this will give the result that you have no personality. Only about one in five answers should be in the middle position. Do not tell blatant lies in personality tests. There is often a "lie scale" which will detect your deception and your application will be eliminated out of hand. However, you do not need to be over self-critical. You are entitled to put your best foot forward.

Stage five: the offer or rejection

With any luck, if you have prepared properly and the organisation has an efficient selection system, you will be offered the job. But, if you are not successful, don't be dejected. Remember that the element of luck in selection system is never less than 35 per cent and in many cases it is a great deal more. Furthermore, the reason why you were not successful may not reflect on you at all. For example, the organisation may have been looking for someone who is sufficiently dense or desperate not to mind working alongside erratic co-workers. *You should retain your self-confidence.* However, you should spare some time for a post-mortem. Review your application to identify areas for improvement. It may be appropriate to telephone the organisation and ask them to spend a few minutes giving you feedback. Providing that you are not being too fussy your next application could be the lucky one.

The tactics of promotion

After you have been in your post for some time you may wish to be promoted. Remember, that there is no compulsion to seek advancement. It is perfectly proper to stay in a post, satisfactorily discharging duties and remaining contented with your work–life balance. Weigh up the pros and cons of promotion. A higher job is likely to bring a higher salary, higher status, possibly more excitement and probably more power. However, a higher job may also have disadvantages. If you believe that the advantages outweigh the disadvantages you can improve your chances of promotion by following eight golden rules.

Golden rule one: be in the right place – especially at the start

Being in the right place at the right time is a key ingredient of success. Look at your job from a strategic point of view. Is it in a declining trade that will be affected by technology or adverse commercial trends? Is it in a declining department or failing organisation? Is it in a declining industry? If so, think proactively about how you can change to a more promising environment. It is much easier to obtain promotion in an expanding organisation.

It is *absolutely crucial to look at your first job in a strategic way.* Look for a job which offers you challenge. Berlew and Hall (1964) indicate that success is closely correlated with the degree of challenge in an executive's first job and their success in meeting these challenges. Beware of careers with short ladders, where there are only one or two higher grades in the career structure. If you find yourself stuck in a job without much promise, consider a sideways or even a backwards move. In the early stages of a career be prepared to move on every two or three years.

Golden rule two: be a high performer

Study Citrin and Smith's (2003) five characteristics of extraordinary careers (Section 19.5). Find out the indices used to judge your success and the success of your department. Work hard and intelligently to outperform your rivals on these indices. In most organisations there will be less than a dozen key results. Do not waste your efforts on peripheral activities. However, a high performance on its own is not enough. If your work causes no trouble and seems almost effortless, people will forget that you exist or come to believe that your job is easy. Consequently the third golden rule of promotion is vital.

Golden rule three: be visible

Modern organisations are large and complex. It is difficult for senior people to know exactly who has achieved what. Quiet, efficient people tend to be overlooked. Make sure that senior people know that you exist and that they are aware of your achievements. The first stage of being visible is to know your own successes. Keep a "hero file" and a "brag sheet". Your hero file should contain any press cuttings, letters or memos of congratulation. Your brag sheet should contain a list of all your achievements. You should update both about every six months. Once you are clear about your own successes you can start communicating them to others. This needs great care and tact. Avoid overt boasting and blatantly blowing your own trumpet. Seize opportunities to show others your work in an informal way, possibly under the pretence of helping or amusing them. Avoid using the word "I". Talk instead about work activity and its outcomes, for example, "the omega project turned out well despite all the problems we encountered", or "Mrs X was very grateful for the savings we made". Never say, "I did a terrific job". Let people make their own inferences. Always keep your boss informed of what you're doing. Be visible around the organisation. Attend meetings and make your presence felt by talking to people informally, before and after meetings. Make intelligent comments and pose interesting questions during meetings. Write occasional articles or letters in your organisation's magazine or newsletter.

Golden rule four: back your boss

Rightly or wrongly your immediate boss can make or break your career. He or she will be the one who is consulted first when there is a chance of your promotion. There is a tendency, especially during the early part of a career, to be disloyal when you see the mistakes your boss makes and you feel that you could have done better. You may be tempted to point out his or her drawbacks because it may seem a way to prove your own ability. You may even receive encouragement from your boss's rivals. This is a very dangerous game. Rumours nearly always get back and your boss may never again trust you with useful information. By denigrating your boss you reduce the reputation of your unit. People are rarely promoted from units that have low reputations. Backing your boss can involve more than supporting him or her at times of organisational warfare. It can involve adopting a complementary role. Inevitably, your boss will have weaknesses. It is much more astute to help your boss overcome them. For example, volunteer to fill out reports or draft memos if your boss is not very good at these tasks. If your boss can rely on you in this way, he or she will let you substitute for him or her at meetings and functions. You will then meet people at a higher level. *Backing your boss does not require you to be a spineless "yes person".* Arrive at an implicit contract. In return for your loyalty, you should be allowed to express your own opinions confidentially. In these situations be frank, direct but always polite. If, against your advice, your boss makes the wrong decision do not gloat. Help pick up the pieces.

Golden rule five: find a sponsor

It is hard to fight the way to the top entirely on your own. Your boss may value or envy you so much that he or she is reluctant to help. A sponsor or mentor can be a great help. You can be pulled up the organisation by a patron rather than having to force your way on your own. A sponsor may endorse your credentials when you are considered for promotion. Sponsors like to pick out winners and give them an extra push. Find thoughtful little ways of occasionally doing things for your sponsor – such as forwarding and magazine article that might be of interest. Watch out for his or her achievements. It helps to make intelligent small talk when you meet informally in lifts, corridors or at meetings. Your sponsor will supplement and support the role of your boss. At promotion meetings practically every boss speaks up for their subordinate. Promotion often goes to those who have someone else who appears neutral and who corroborates what the boss says. It is a dangerous game to play your boss against your sponsor. Subtly let your sponsor know that your first loyalty is to your boss.

Golden rule six: develop your network

In this context, a network is a group of individuals who know and help each other. A network can give you access to a much wider range and information than you could obtain on your own. Belonging to a network enables you to:

- call on other's expertise
- join an information grapevine
- get known to those with power to help
- seek out new contacts

Networks do not happen on their own. *You need to put effort to create and maintain a network.* The most important thing is to join the organisation's grapevine – the informal communication system that crosses boundaries within an organisation. Be friendly and approachable to those at the heart of the grapevine. They are not always obvious people.

Cultivate contacts. Do not take them for granted. Occasionally give them snippets of information and never reveal the source of any information you use. Be prepared to spend little time asking "how things are" or "what is cooking today". The *half-hour bonus* is a key feature of developing a network. During the working day people are busy, there are lots of interruptions and it is not wise to be seen standing or sitting around chatting. However, in most organisations, there is a gathering after hours where people meet informally to discuss events. It meets at some venue: around the coffee machine, the photocopier or, perhaps, in the local club or pub. The half-hour bonus is a good time to get advice from senior managers, cultivate a sponsor or bounce ideas off people. Once a network is developed it must be maintained. Do not overwork a network. Only use contacts when you really need them. Keep some power in reserve.

Golden rule seven: learn how to influence people

Despite decades of research, Dale Carnegie's (1938) book *How to Win Friends and Influence People* remains one of the best guides on influencing skills. The most important strategy is to *avoid habitual criticism, condemnation and complaint*. Other important strategies include *avoiding becoming known as the departmental whinge*. Be genuinely *interested in people*. Remember names. Smile. Talk to people in terms of *their* interests. Above all, show respect. Remember that the only way to win an argument is to avoid it. If you lose an argument you will feel badly and probably want to get even. If you win, the other person well feel badly, and want to get even. If you are wrong, admit it openly, quickly and emphatically. Do not let people wring out a begrudging admission.

Golden rule eight: play the part

Anyone wishing promotion should act and dress like someone with potential. Others will interpret the way that you dress and act as an indication of the type of person you are. Your organisational climate needs to be taken into account. In some organisations eccentric or off-beat fashions may damage your chances. In other organisations such as a university department a uniform of washed-out jeans and a sweater might be mandatory. In a chic advertising agency people might be expected to wear something slightly outré. There is no need to be coy about deciding the impression you wish to give. Social psychologists know that, consciously or subconsciously, most people manage their impressions. One of the most important impressions you need to convey that you are efficient, reliable and confident.

It is hoped that reading about the fundamentals of management will have laid a sound basis for employment that will be both interesting and profitable. Whatever career you choose to follow, good luck!

Activities and Further Study

Essay Plans

Write plans for the following essays:

1 Compare and contrast three named theories of how careers progress.

2 How do modern careers differ from those 50 years ago?

3 What are the main features of extraordinary careers?

Web Activities

1 Use the Web to locate an employer that might offer a job you would like. Go to the career section and try to identify five competencies they would value in applicants for jobs.

2 Log on to the careers site of a local university or college. Exploit the site by touring the sections that seem relevant to you. Some good sites are:

http://www.careers.manchester.ac.uk/

http://www.ucc.ie/careers/employers.php

http://www.wits.ac.za/ccdu/career_expect.htm

http://www.careers.usyd.edu.au/students/jobsearch/jobsearch.shtml

http://www.vuw.ac.nz/st_services/careers/

http://www.smu.edu.sg/ocs/career_development.asp

http://www.asia.hobsons.com/careers_advice/job_hunting_tips

http://www.asia.hobsons.com/regional_outlook

The last site offers good advice for job hunting in Malaysia, Indonesia and China.

3 Visit some sites offering advice on CVs. Some useful sites are:

http://cv-masterclass.com/cv-demo4.html

http://www.soton.ac.uk/cas/documents/AnnaCV.pdf

http://www.alec.co.uk/cvtips/index.htm

http://www.varsity.co.nz/careers/articles.asp?id=431

Experiential Activities

1 Write three sentences about yourself under each of the headings for Roger's Seven-Point Plan.

2 Produce a CV for yourself. Make sure it starts with an easy to read, five-line profile outlining your main abilities.

3 Think of instances in the past where you exhibited intelligence, teamwork, motivation, resilience in the face of adversity and attention to detail. For each of these characteristics give a brief description of:

- the situation you faced
- the action you took
- the results that followed
- the reactions of others
- what you learned from the experience

Repeat this exercise with any characteristic that you think a specific prospective employer might want from job applicants.

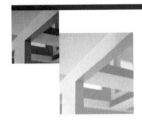

References

ACAS (Advisory, Conciliation and Arbitration Service) (1982) *Workplace Communications,* Advisory Booklet No. 8, London: ACAS.

Adair, J.G. (1984) "The Hawthorn Effect: a Reconsideration of the Methodological Artefact", *Journal of Applied Psychology,* **69** (2), 334–345.

Adams, J.S. (1965) "Inequality in Social Exchange", in L. Berkowitz, *Advances in Experimental and Social Psychology,* L. Berkowitz (ed.), New York: Academic Press.

Agnew, N.M. and J.L. Brown, (1986) "Bounded Rationality: Fallible Decisions in Unbounded Decision Space", *Behavioural Sciences,* 148–161, July.

American Marketing Association (2004) "AMA Adopts New Definition of Marketing", *Marketing News,* **15** (1), September.

Ansoff, I. (1989) *Corporate Strategy,* Harmondsworth: Penguin.

Arnold, J. (1997) *Managing Careers into the 21st Century,* London: Paul Chapman.

Arthur, M.B., D.T. Hall and B.S. Lawrence (1989) *Handbook of Career Theory.* Cambridge: Cambridge University Press.

Ashby, W.R. (1964) *Introduction to Cybernetics,* New York: Wiley.

Audit Commission (2003) *Waiting List Accuracy,* London: Audit Commission.

Australian Bureau of Statistics. (2004) *Disability, Australia,* http://www.abs.gov.au.ausstats/abs@nsf

Babakus, E., B. Cornwell, V. Mitchell and B. Schlegelmitch (2004) "Reactions to Unethical Behaviour in Six Countries", *Journal of Consumer Marketing,* **21** (4).

Baron, J.N. and D.M. Kreps, (1999) *Strategic Human Resources: Frame-Works for General Managers,* New York: Wiley.

Barrett, M. and A. Hede (2003) "Principles and Practice of Gender Diversity in Australia", in *Individual Diversity and Psychology in Organisations,* M.J. Davidson and S.L. Fielden (eds), Chichester: Wiley.

Bartlett, F.C. (1932) *Remembering: an Experimental and Social Study,* London: Cambridge University Press.

Bass, B. (1985) "Leadership: Good, Better, Best", *Organisational Dynamics,* **13** (3), 26–40.

Battles, J. (2003) "One in Five Suicides is Linked to Bullying at Work", *The Sunday Times,* **19** (9), October.

Bell, N.E. and B.M. Straw (1989) "People as Sculptors versus Sculpture: The Roles of Personality and Personal Control in Organisations", *Handbook of Career Theory,* in M.B. Arthur, D.T Hall and B.S. Lawrence (eds), Cambridge: Cambridge University Press.

Berlew, D.E. and D.T. Hall (1964) *Some Determinants of Early Managerial Success,* Working paper No 81/64, Cambridge, MA: Sloan School of Management, Massachusetts Institute of Technology.

Birch, J. (2000) Quoted in: *Management,* R.L. Daft, Fort Worth: Dryden Press.

Blake, R.R. and J.S. Mouton, (1964) *The Management Grid,* Houston, TX: Gulf Publishing Company.

Blanchard, K.H. and S. Johnson (1983) *The One Minute Manager,* London: Fontana.

Boddy, D. (2002) *Management: An Introduction,* London: Pearson Education.

Boddy, D. (2002a) *Managing Products: Building and Leading the Team,* Harlow: Financial Times Prentice Hall.

Borisoff, D. (1992) "Gender Issues in Listening", in *A Listening in Everyday Life: Personal and Professional Approach,* D. Borisoff and M. Purdy, (eds), Lanham, MD: University Press of America.

Boyatzis, R.E. (1982) *The Competent Manager: A Model for Effective Performance,* New York: Wiley.

Brigham, E. (1985) *Financial Management: Theory and Practice,* Chicago: Dryden Press.

Brigham, E.F., L.C. Gapenski and M.C. Ehrnhardt (1999) *Financial Management: Theory and Practice,* Chicago, IL: Dryden Press.

Bristow, M. (2001) "Management Competencies", Unpublished MSc Thesis, Manchester School of Management, UMIST.

Brockner, J. and B.M. Wiesenfeld (1966) "An Integrative Framework for Explaining Reactions to Decisions: Interactive Effects of Outcomes and Procedures", *Psychological Bulletin,* **120**, 189–208.

Broers, A. (2005) *The Triumph of Technology, BBC Reith Lectures 2005,* http://www.bbc.co.uk/radio4/reith2005/lecturer.shtml accessed 9/5/2005

Bromiley, P. (1999) "Debating Rationality: Nonrational Aspect of Organisational Decision-making/Rational Choice Theory and Organisational Theory; a Critique", *Academy of Management Review,* 157–159, January.

Brundtland, G. (1987) *Our Common Future: The World Commission on Environment and Development,* Oxford: Oxford University Press.

Budd J.F. Jr. (1993) "12 CEOs Found Guilty of Poor Communications", *Public Relations Quarterly,* **38** (1), 4–5.

Burns, T. and G.M. Stalker (1961) *The Management of Innovation,* London: Tavistock.

CACI (2005) *New Acorn Classification Map,* http://www.caci.co.uk/acorn/acornmap.asp

Cannell, M. (2005) *Personnel Management: A Short History,* London: CIPD, http://www.cipd.co.uk/subjects/hrpract/hrtrends/pmhist.htm

Caproni, P.J. (2005) *Management Skills for Everyday Life,* Upper Saddle River, NJ: Pearson.

Carnegie, D. (1938) *How to Win Friends and Influence People,* Tadworth, Surrey: World's Work.

Carr, A.Z. (1968) "Is Business Bluffing Ethical", *Harvard Business Review,* 143–153, January–February.

Carton, B. (1994) "At Jenny Craig Men are the Ones who Claim Sex Discrimination", *Wall Street Journal,* p. 1, p. 11, 29 November.

Cave, F.T. (2004) "Companies Internet Sales Double in a Year", *Financial Times,* p. 5, 23 November.

Central Statistics Office Ireland (2005) *Population and Vital Statistics: Population Classified by Religion and Sex 2002,* http://www.cso.ie.principalstats/cenrel1.htm

Chartered Institute of Marketing (2005) *What is Marketing? CIM's definition*, http://www.cim.co.uk/cim/dev/html/marWha.cfm, accessed 13/04/2005

Chomsky, N. (2002) *Media Control: The Spectacular Achievements of Propaganda*, New York: Seven Stories Press.

Churchill, N. (1984) "Budget Choice: Planning versus Control", *Harvard Business Review*, 150–164, July–August.

Citrin, J.M. and R.A. Smith, (2003) *The Five Patterns of Extraordinary Careers*, New York: Crown Business.

Clampitt, P. (1991) *Communicating for Managerial Effectiveness*, Newbury Park, CA: Sage.

Clark, F.A. (1992) *Total Career Management: Strategies for Creating Management Careers*, Maidenhead: McGraw-Hill Europe.

Clarke, T. and G. Salaman (1993) "Telling Tales: Management Gurus and the Construction of Managerial Identity", *Journal of Management Studies*, **35** (2), 137–161.

Clement, B. (1996) "Equality Head under Fire for 'Dictatorial' Style", *The Independent on Sunday*.

Collins, D. (2000) *Management Fads and Buzzwords*, London: Routledge.

Cringely, R.X. (1994) "When Disaster Strikes: How to Forfeit Millions in Exchange for Nothing", *Forbes Magazine*, 29 August, 60.

Crosby, P. (1979) *Quality Is Free*, New York: McGraw-Hill.

Curver, B. (2003) *Enron: Anatomy of Greed*, London: Arrow Books.

Dannemiller, K.D. and R.W. Jacobs (1992) "Changing the Way Organisations Change: A Revolution in Common Sense", *Journal of Applied Behavioural Science*, **4**, 480–498.

Dean, W.J. and M.P. Sharfman (1996) "Does Decision Process Matter? A Study of Strategic Decision Making Effectiveness", *Academy of Management Journal*, 368–396, April.

Dewson, S., J. Eccles, N.D. Tackey and A. Jackson (2000) *Guide to Measuring Soft Outcomes*, Brighton: The Institute for Employment Studies.

Diaper, G. (1990) "The Hawthorn Effect: A Fresh Examination", *Educational Studies*, **16** (3), 261–268.

Dougherty, D. and E.H. Bowman (1995) "The Effects of Organizational Downsizing on Product Innovation", *Californian Management Review*, **37** (4), 28–44.

Downes, L. (2005) "Beyond Porter", *Context Magazine*, Available (12 Jan 2005) at: http://www.contextmag.com/ setFrameRedirect.asp?src=/archives/199712/technosynthesis.asp

Drucker, P.F. (1946) *The Concept of the Corporation*, New York: Mentor.

Drucker, P.F. (1954) *The Practice of Management*, New York: Harper & Row.

Drucker, P.F. (1969) *The Age of Discontinuity*, London: Heinemann.

Drucker, P.F. (1985) *Innovation and Entrepreneurship: Practice and Principles*, London: Heinemann.

Drucker, P.F. (1994) *Post-Capitalist Society*, New York: Harperbusiness.

Drucker, P.F. (1997) "The Future That Has Already Happened", *Harvard Business Review*, **75**, 20–24.

Drucker, P.E. (1999) *Innovation and Entrepreneurship*, 2nd edn, Oxford: Butterworth-Heineman.

Drury, C. (2005) *Management Accounting for Business Decisions*, London: International Thompson Business Press.

Dubrin, A.J. (2003) *Essentials of Management*, 6th edn, Mason, OH: South-Western.

Dumaine, B. (1993) "The New Non-Manager Manager", *Fortune*, 80–84, February.

Earnshaw, J. (2003) "Management of Diversity in the UK", in *Individual Diversity and Psychology in Organisations*, M.J. Davidson and S.L. Fielden (eds), Chichester: Wiley.

Economist (2004) "The Cartel isn't Forever", *Economist,* 15 July.

Einarsen, S. (1999) "The Nature and Causes of Bullying", *International Journal of Manpower*, **20**, 16–27.

Einarsen, S. (2000) "Harassment and Bullying at Work: A Review of the Scandinavian Approach", *Aggression and Violent Behaviour*, **5** (4), 379–401.

Einarsen, S., H. Hoel, D. Zapf and C.L. Cooper (eds) (2003) *Bullying and Emotional Abuse in the Workplace: International Perspectives in Research and Practice,* London: Taylor and Francis.

EOC (2004). *Facts about Women and Men in Great Britain*, Manchester: Equal Opportunities Commission.

Fahn S. (1999) "Parkinson Disease, the Effect of Levodopa, and the ELLDOPA Trial. Earlier versus Later L-DOPA", *Archives of Neurology*, **56**, 529–535.

Federal Trade Commission (2005) *Being Frank about Search Engine Rank*, http://www.ftc.gov/bcp/conline/pubs/alerts/searchchalrt.htm, accessed on 1/02/05.

Ference, T.P., J.A.F. Stoner and E.K. Warren (1977) "Managing the Career Plateau", *Academy of Management Review*, **2**, 602–612.

Fiedler, F.E., M.M. Chemers and L. Mahar (1978) *The Leadership Match Concept,* New York: Wiley.

Fitzroy, P. (2001). *Living with Globalisation,* http://www.abc.net.au/money/curency/features/feat8.htm, accessed 8/11/2001.

Follett, M.P. (1941) *Collected Works*, New York: Harper & Row.

Follett, M.P. (1958) *New State:Group Organisation and Solution of Popular Government*, London: Longman.

Francis, R.D. (1999) *Ethics for Psychologists: A Handbook*, Leicester: British Psychological Society.

Free-definition (2005a) http://www.free-definition.com/Brand.html

Free-definition (2005b) http://www.free-definition.com/Public-Relations.html

Friedman, M. (1970) "The Social Responsibility of Business is to Increase its Profits", *New York Times*, 14 September.

GAIN (Global Auditing Information Network) (2004) *Code of Conduct of Surveys,* http://www.gain2.org/cocsum.htm

Gilliland, S.W. (1993) "The Perceived Fairness of Selection Systems: An Organisational Justice Perspective", *Academy of Management Review*, **18**, 694–734.

Gilliland, S.W. (1994) "Effects of Procedural and Distributive Justice on Reactions to a Selection System", *Journal of Applied Psychology*, **79** (6), 691–760.

Globalisation Guide (2002) Http://globalisationguide.org

Greenhaus, J.H., G.A. Callanan and V.M. Godshalk (2000) *Career Management Report*, San Diego, CA: Dryden Press.

Greenleaf, R.K. (1977) *Servant Leadership: A Journey into the Nature of Legitimate Power and Greatness*, Mahwah, NJ: Paulist Press.

Guest, D. (1992) "Right Enough to be Dangerously Wrong: An Analysis of the In Search of Excellence Phenomenon" *Human Resource Strategies*, in G. Salaman (ed.), London: Sage.

Guest, D.E. (1998) "Is the Psychological Contract Worth Taking Seriously?", *Journal of Organisational Behaviour*, **19**, 649–664.

Hackman, J.R. and G.R. Oldham (1980) *Work Redesign*, Reading, MA: Addison-Wesley.

Hage, J. and M. Aiken (1968) Organisational Interdependence and Intra-organisational Structure, *American Sociological Review*, **33**, 912–930.

Hage, J. and M. Aiken (1969) "Routine Technology, Social Structure and Organisational Goals", *Administrative Science Quarterly*, **14**, 366–375.

Hall, E.T. (1976) *Beyond Culture*, New York: Doubleday.

Hammer, M. (1995) *The Re-engineering Revolution: the Handbook*, London: Harper-Collins.

Hammer, M. (1997) *Beyond Re-engineering*, New York: Harper Business.

Handy, C. (1989) *The Age of Unreason*, London: Pan Books.

Handy, C. (2005) *Management Gurus: Michael Porter*, http://www.bbc.co.uk/worldservice/learningenglish/work/handy/transcripts/porter.pdf, accessed 10/01/2005

Hannagan, T. (2005) *Management Concepts and Practices*, Harlow: Pearson Education

Haspeslagh, P. (1982) "Portfolio Planning: uses and limitations", *Harvard Business Review*. **60**, 58–73.

Health Advantage (2004) http://www.healthadvantage-hmo.com/customer_service/terms.asp#m

Hendricks, K.B. and V.R. Singhal, (1999) *Quality Progress*, **32** (4), 35–43.

Herriot, P. (1989) "Selection as a Social Process" in *Advances in Selection and Assessment*, J.M. Smith and I.T. Robertson (eds), Chichester: Wiley.

Herriot, P. (2003) "Series Preface", in *Individual Diversity and Psychology in Organisations*, M.J. Davidson and S.L. Fielden (eds), Chichester: Wiley.

Hersey, P. and K.H. Blanchard (1982) "Leadership Style: Attitudes and Behaviours", *Training and Development Journal*, **36** (5), 50–52.

Hirschman, L. (1975) "Female–Male Difference in Conversational Interaction", in *Language and Sex Differences and Dominance*, B. Thorne and N. Henley, Rowley, MA: Newbury House.

Hoel, H., C.L. Cooper and B. Faragher (2001) "The experience of bullying in Great Britain: the impact of organisational status", *European Journal of Work and Organisational Psychology*, **10** (4), 443–465.

Hoel, H., D. Zapf and C.L. Cooper (2002) "Workplace Bullying and Stress", in *Historical and Current Perspectives On Stress and Health*, P. Perewe and D.C.Ganster (eds)., **2**, 293–333, London: Elsevier Science.

Hofstede, G. (1980) "Motivation, Leadership and Organisation: do American theories apply abroad?", *Organisational Dynamics*, **55**.

Hofstede, G. (1984) *Culture's Consequences*, Beverly Hills, CA: Sage.

Holden, L. (2001) "Organisational Communication", in *Management Concepts and Practices*, T. Hannagan, Harlow: Pearson Education.

Honey, P. (1982) *The Manual of Leadership Styles*, Maidenhead: Peter Honey.

Horngren, C.T., Foster, G. and Datar, S.M. (2002) *Cost Accounting*, Harlow: Financial Times/Prentice Hall.

House, R.J. (1971) "A Path-Goal Theory of Leader Effectiveness", *Administrative Sciences Quarterly*, **16**, 321–338.

Hovland, C.J. (1957) *The Order of Presentation in Persuasion*, New Haven, CT: Yale University Press.

Howard, A. and D.W. Bray (1988) *Managerial Lives in Transition: Advancing Age and Changing Times*, London: Guildford Press.

Huczynski, A.A. (1993). *Management Gurus: What Makes Them and How to Become One*, London: Routledge.

iboost (2005) http://www.iboost.com/promote/marketing/branding/20025e.htm

Jablin, F., L. Putham, K. Roberts and L. Porter (eds) (1987) *Handbook of Organisational Communication: an Interdisciplinary Perspective*, Newbury Park, CA: Sage.

Jaworski, B.J. and D. MacInnis (1989) "Marketing jobs and management controls: towards a framework", *Journal of Marketing Research*, **26**, 408–419.

Jay, A. (1967) *Management and Machiavelli*, New York: Holt, Reinhardt and Winston.

Kandola, R. and J. Fullerton (1994) *Managing the Mosaic: Diversity in Action*, London: Institute of Personnel and Development.

Katz, R.L. (1974) "Skills of an Effective Administrator", *Harvard Business Review*, **52**, 94.

Kay, J.P. (1996) *The Business of Economics*, Oxford: Oxford University Press.

Keen, P. (1981) "Information Systems and Organisation Change", in *Implementing New Technologies*, E. Rhodes and D. Wield (eds), Oxford: Open University Press.

Kellaway, L. (2001) "A Boast Too Far", *Financial Times*, [16] 3 December.

Kohlberg, L. (1976) "Moral Stages and Moralisation: The Cognitive–Development Perspective", in *Moral Development and Behaviour: Theory, Research and Social Issues,* New York: Holt, Rinehart & Winston.

Kolb D.A., and R. Fry (1975) "Towards an Applied Theory of Experiential Learning", in *Theories of Group Processes*, Cooper C. (ed.), New York: Wiley.

Koontz, H. (1961) "The Management Theory Jungle", *Journal of the Academy of Management*, 174–188, December.

Koontz, H. and R.W. Bradspies (1972) "Managing through Feed-forward Control", *Business Horizons*, 25–36, June.

Kotler, P. (1986) *Principles of Marketing*, 3rd edn, Englewood Cliffs, NJ: Prentice Hall.

Kotter, J.P. and J. Heskett (1992) *Corporate Culture and Performance*, New York; Free Press.

Latham, G.P. and L.M. Saari (1979) "The Effect of Holding Goal Difficulty Constant on Assigned and Participatively Set Goals", *Academy of Management Journal*, 163–168.

Lawrence, R.R. and J.W. Lorsch (1969) *Organisation and Environment*, Homewood, IL: Irwin.

Leck, J.D., D.M. Saunders and M. Charbonneau (1996) "Affirmative Action Programmes: and Organisational Justice Perceptive", *Journal of Organisational Behaviour*, **17** (1), 79–89.

Levinson, D.J. (1986) "A Conception of Adult Development", *American Psychologist*, **41** (1), 8.

Lewin, K. (1947) "Frontiers in Group Dynamics", *Human Relations*, **1**, 5–41.

Lewin, K., R. Lippit and R.K. White (1939) "Patterns of Aggressive Behaviour in Experimentally Created Social Climates", *Journal of Social Psychology*, **10**, 271–301.

Lewis, P.S., S.H. Goodman and P.M. Fandt (1995) *Management: Challenges in the 21st Century*, St Paul, MN: West Publishing Company.

Leymann, H. (1990) "Mobbing and Psychological Terror at Workplaces", *Violence and Victims*, **5**, 119–126.

Locke, E.A. (1968) "Towards a Theory of Task Motivation and Incentives", *Organisational Behaviour and Human Performance*, 3, 157–189.

Locke, E.A., K.N. Shaw, L.M. Saari and G.P. Latham (1981) "Goal setting and task performance", *Psychological Bulletin*, **90**, 225–252.

Loden, M. and J.B. Rosener (1991) *Workforce America*, Homewood, IL: McGraw-Hill.

Malcolm, C. (2000) *Who Made the First Computer?* www.dai.ed.ac.uk/homes/cam/fcomp.shtml, accessed 1/3/2005

Markillie, P. (2004) "A Perfect Market: E-commerce is Coming of Age", *The Economist*, **15**, 3–6 July.

Marks, K. (1998) "Woman Detective Wins the Payout in Sex Case", (The) *Independent*, p. 6, 17 October.

Mayo, E. (1933) *The Human Problems of an Industrial Civilization*, New York: MacMillan.

McClelland, D.C. (1971) *The Achieving Society*, New York: Irvington Publishers.

McDonald, M. (1992) *Strategic Marketing Planning*, London: Kogan Page.

McGregor, D. (1960) *The Human Side of the Enterprise*, New York: McGraw-Hill.

McLuhan, M. (1962) *The Gutenberg Galaxy*, Toronto: University of Toronto Press.

McLuhan, M. (1964) *Understanding Media*, London: Routledge and Kegan Paul.

Merchant, K.A. (1985) *Control in Business Organisations*, Marshfield, MA: Pitman.

Miceli, M.P. and J.P. Near (1994) "Whistle-blowing: Reaping the Benefits", *Academy of Management Executive*, **8** (3), 65–74.

Micklethwaite, J. and A. Wooldridge (1996) *The Witch Doctors: What the Management Gurus are Saying, Why it Matters and How to Make Sense of It*, London: Heinemann.

Miles, R.E. and C.C. Snow (1978) *Organisational Strategy, Structure and Process*, New York: McGraw-Hill.

Miller, D.S., S.E. Catt and J.R. Carlson (1996) *Fundamentals of Management: A Framework for Excellence*, St. Paul, MN: West Publishing.

Mintzberg, H.H. (1973) *The Nature of Managerial Work*, New York: Harper & Row.

Mintzberg, H.H. (1983) "The Case for Corporate Social Responsibility", *Journal of Business Strategy*, **4** (2), 3–15.

Mintzberg, H.H. (1987) "The Strategy Concept II: Another Look at Why Organisations Need Strategies", *California Management Review*, 26 January.

Mintzberg, H.H. (1994) "Rethinking Strategic Planning. Part I: Pitfalls and Fallacies", *Long Range Planning*, **27** (3), 12–21.

Morrison, A. and R. Wensley (1991) "Boxing up or Boxed in? A Short History of the Boston Consulting Group Share/Growth Matrix", *Journal of Marketing Management*, **7** (2), 105–129.

Near, J.P. (1989) "Whistle-blowing: Encourage It", *Business Horizons*, 21–25.

New Mexican (1994) "Slogans Often Lose Something in Translation", *New Mexican* 3 July, 1–2.

Nicholson, N. (1993) "Purgatory or Place of Safety? The Managerial Plateau and Organisational Age Grading", *Human Relations,* **46**, 1369–1389.

Nicholson, N. and M. West (1988) *Managerial Job Change: Men and Women in Transition*, Cambridge: Cambridge University Press.

Organisation for Economic Co-operation and Development (1989) *Predatory Pricing*, OECD: Paris.

Ouchi, W.G. (1980) "Markets, Bureaucracies and Clans", *Administrative Science Quarterly*, 129–141, March.

Packard, V. (1957) *The Hidden Persuaders*, New York: Random House.

Palmer, C. (1999) "Work: Revenge: It's Sweet but Risky", The *Observer*, 4 December 19.

Pare, T.C. (1993) "A New Model for Managing Costs", *Fortune*, **14**, 124–129, June.

Parson, H.M. (1974) "What Happened at Hawthorne?" *Science,* **183**, 922–932.

Paterson, M.G., M.A. West, R. Lawthom and S. Nickell (1997). *Impact of People Management Practices on the Business Performance*, London: Chartered Institute of Personnel and Development.

Pattison, S. (1997) *The Faith of Managers: When Management Becomes Religion,* London: Cassell.

Paulos, J. A. (1998) *Once upon a Number*, Harmondsworth: Penguin.

Penny, J.C., I.M. Hunt and W.A. Twyman (1974) "Product Testing Methodology", in *Product Management*, P. Law and C. Weinberg, New York: Harper & Row.

Peter, L.J. and R. Hull (1969) *The Peter Principle*, New York: William Morrow & Co.

Peters, T. (1995) *The Pursuit of Wow! Every Person's Guide to Topsy Turvey Times*, London: Macmillan.

Peters, T. (1997) *The Circle of Innovation: You Can't Shrink Your Way to Greatness*, London: Hodder & Stoughton.

Peters, T. and R. Waterman (1988) *In Search of Excellence*, New York: Harper & Row.

Pettinger, R. (1997) *Introduction to Management,* 2nd edn, London: Macmillan.

Pfeffer, J. (1998) *The Human Equation: Building Profits by Putting People First*, Boston, MA: Harvard University Press.

Pinder, C.C. (1984) *Work Motivation*, Glenview, IL: Scott Foresman.

Pitches, D., A. Burls and A. Fry-Smith (2003) "How to Make a Silk Purse from a Sow's Ear – A Comprehensive Review of Strategies to Optimise Data for Corrupt Managers and Incompetent Clinicians", *British Medical Journal*, **327**, 7429, 1436–1439, December.

Porter, M. (1980) *Competitive Strategy: Techniques for Analysing Industries and Competitors*, New York: Free Press.

Porter, M. (1990) *The Competitive Advantage of Nations*, London: Macmillan.

Porter, M. (1995) "The Competitive Advantage of the Inner City", *Harvard Business Review*, 153–155, May–June.

Porter, M.E. (1996) "What is strategy?", *Harvard Business Review*, 61–78, November–December.

Porter, M.E. (1998) *Competitive Advantage: Creating and Sustaining Superior Performance*, New York: Simon and Schuster.

Porter, M.E. (2001) "Strategy and the Internet", *Harvard Business Review*, 63, March.

Porter, M., K. Schwab, I.M. Sala and A. Lopez-Claros (2004) *Global Competitiveness Report 2004–2005*, Basingstoke: Palgrave Macmillan for the World Economics Forum.

Pride, W. and O.C. Farrell (2000) *Marketing: Concepts and Strategies*, Boston, MA: Houghton Mifflin.

Pugh, D.S. and D.J. Hickson (1976) *Organisation Structure in Its Context: the Aston program*, Aldershot: Gower Press.

Pyhrr, P. (1973) *Zero Base Budgeting, a Practical Management Tool for Evaluating Expenses*, New York: Wiley.

Queensland Government (2002) *Creating Safe and Fair Workplaces: Strategies to Address Workplace Harassment in Queensland*, Queensland, Australia: Queensland Government. Report available on http://www.whs.qld.gov.au/taskforces/bullying/bullyingreport.pdf

Quintessential Careers (2004) http://quintcareers.com/jobseeker_marketing_glossary.html

Randall, P. (1997) *Adult Bullying: Perpetrators and Victims*, London: Routledge.

Reilly, B.J. and J.A. DiAngelo (1990) "Communication: a Cultural System of Meaning and Values", *Human Relations*, **43**, 129–140.

Reimann, B.C. (1974) "On the Dimensional Bureaucratic Structure: an empirical reappraisal", *Administrative Science Quarterly*, 462–476.

Ricks, D.A. and A. Mahajan (1984) "Blunders in International Marketing", *Long-range Planning*, 78–85.

Robbins, S.P. and D.A. Decenzo (2001) *Fundamentals of Management*, Upper Saddle River, NJ: Prentice Hall.

Robinson, S.L. and D.M. Rousseau (1994) "Violating the Psychological Contract: Not the Exception but the Norm", *Journal of Organisational Behaviour*, **15**, 245–459.

Roethlisberger, F.J., W.J. Dixon and H.A. Wright (1939) *Management and the Worker*, Cambridge, MA: Harvard University Press.

Rogers, R. and J.E. Hunter (1991) "Impact of Management by Objectives on Organisational Productivity", *Journal of Applied Psychology*, 322–326.

Roosevelt-Thomas R.T. (1991) *Beyond Race and Gender*, New York: AMACON.

Roosevelt-Thomas R.T and M.I. Woodruff (1999) *Building a House for Diversity*, New York: AMACON.

Rosenthal, R. and L. Jacobson (1992) *Pygmalion in the Classroom: Teacher Expectation and Pupils' Intellectual Development*, New York: Irvington Publishers.

Rosenthal, R. and R.L. Rosnow (1969) *Artefacts in Behavioural Research*, New York: Academic Press.

Rousseau, D.M. (1995) *Psychological Contracts in Organisations: Understanding the Written and Unwritten Agreements,* London: Sage.

Rowe, A.J., J.D. Boulgarides and M.R. McGrath (1994) *Managerial Decisionmaking: Modules in Management Series*, Chicago, IL: SRA.

Schein, E.H. (1985) *Organisational Culture and Leadership*, C.A. San Francisco, CA: Jossey-Bass.

Schemerhorn, J.R. (2002) *Management*, 7th edn, New York: Wiley.

Schmenner, R.W. (1986) "How Can Service Businesses Survive and Prosper?", *Sloan Management Review*, 21–32, Spring.

Schmidt, F.L. and J.E. Hunter (1996) "The Validity and Utility of Selection Methods in Personnel Selection: the Practical and Theoretical Implications of 85 Years' Research Findings", *Psychological Bulletin,* **124** (2), 216–274.

Schmidt, F.L., J.E. Hunter and V.W. Urry (1976) "Statistical Power in Criterion-related Validation Studies", *Journal of Applied Psychology,* **61** (4), 473–485.

Schneider, B. (1987) "The People Make the Place", *Personnel Psychology,* **40** (3), 437–453.

Schramm, W. (1954) "How Communication Works", in *The process and Effects of Mass Communication*, W. Schramm (ed.), Urbana, IL: University of Illinois Press.

Sekaran, U. and D.T. Hall (1989) "Asynchronism in Dual-career and Family Linkages", in *Handbook of Career Theory*, M.B. Arthur, D.T Hall and B.S. Lawrence (eds), Cambridge: Cambridge University Press.

Seigne, E., I. Coyne and P. Randall (1999) *Personality Traits of the Victims of Work-place Bullying: An Irish Sample*, Ninth European Congress of Work and Organisational Psychology, May, Espoo, Finland.

Senge, P. (1990) *The Fifth Discipline: the Art and Practice of the Learning Organisation*, London: Doubleday.

Shannon, C. and W. Weaver (1949) *The Mathematical Theory of Communication*, Urbana, IL: University of Illinois Press.

Shapiro, E. (1998) *Fad Surfing in the Boardroom: Reclaiming the Courage to Manage in the Age of Instant Answers*, Oxford: Capstone.

Shaw, W.H. (1991) *Business Ethics*, Belmont, CA: Wadsworth.

Shein, E.H. (1978). *Career Dynamics: Matching Individual and Organisation Needs*, Reading, NH: Addison-Wesley.

Sheppard, B.H. and R.J. Lerwicki (1987) "Toward General Principles of Managerial Fairness", *Social Justice Research*, **1**, 161–176.

Simon, H.A. (1955) *Administrative Behaviour*, New York: Free Press.

Sinclair, C. and J. Pettifor (1991) *Companion Manual to the Code of Ethics for Canadian Psychologists*, Ottawa: Canadian Psychological Association.

Slack, N., S. Chambers, C. Harland, A. Harrisson and R. Johnston (2001) *Operations Management*, London: Financial Times Prentice Hall.

Smith, M and M. Abrahamsen (1992) "Patterns of Selection in Six Countries", *The Psychologist*, **5**, 205–207.

Smither, J.W., R.E. Millsap, R.W. Stoffey, R.R. Reilly and K. Pearlman (1996) "An Experimental Test of the Influence of Selection Procedures on Fairness Perceptions, Attitudes about the Organization and Job Pursuit Intentions", *Journal of Business and Psychology*, **10**, 297–318.

Stewart, R. (1967) *Managers and Their Jobs*, London: Macmillan.

Stone, C. (1990) "Why Shouldn't Corporations be Socially Responsible?", in *Business Ethics: Readings and Cases in Corporate Morality*, W.M. Hoffman and J.M. Moore (eds), New York: McGraw-Hill.

Super, D.E. (1990) "Career and Life Development", in *Career Choice and Development*, (2nd edn), D. Brown and L. Brooks (eds), San Francisco, CA: Jossey Bass.

Tannenbaum, R. and W.H. Schmidt (1958) "How to Choose a Leadership Pattern", *Harvard Business Review*, **36**, 95–202.

Tarbell, I. (1950) *The History of the Standard Oil Company*, New York: Peter Smith, pp. 240–41.

Taylor, F.W. (1911) *The Principles of Scientific Management*, New York: Harper and Row.

Tedeschi, R. (2004) "Trying to Reach Customers in an Era of E-Mail Suspicion", *New York Times*, 16, 6 December.

The Times (1999) "Passport to Farrago", *The Times*, 21, June 28.

Toffler, A. (1970) *Future Shock*, New York: Random House.

Towers-Perrin (1999) *Euro Rewards: Rewards, Challenges and Changes*, London: Towers Perrin.

Triandis, H.C. (1977) *Interpersonal Behaviour*, Monterey, CA: Cole.

Trompenaars, F. (1993) *Riding the Waves of Culture: Understanding Cultural Diversity in Business*, London: Nicolas Brearly Publishing.

Tyler, W.B. (1973) "Measuring Organisational Specialisation: The Concept of Role Variety", *Administrative Science Quarterly*, **18**, 383–393.

US Department of Labour (2003a) *Non-traditional Occupations for Women*, http://www.dol.gov/wb/factsheets/nontra2003.pdf, accessed 10/2/05

US Department of Labour (2003b) *20 Leading Occupations for Women*, http://www.dol.gov/wb/factsheets/20lead2003.pdf, accessed 10/2/05

Viswesvaran, C., D.S. Ones and F.L. Schmidt (1996) "Comparative Analysis of the Reliability of Job Performance Ratings", *Journal of Applied Psychology*, **81** (5), 557–574.

Vitell, S.J. and J. Muncy (1992) "Consumer Ethics: An Empirical Investigation of Factors Influencing Ethical Judgements of the Final Consumer", *Journal of Business Ethics,* **11**, 585–597.

Vroom, V.H. and A.G. Jago (1988) *The New Leadership*: *Managing Participation in Organisations*, Englewood Cliffs, NJ: Prentice-Hall.

Wade, D. (2003) "Torture of Tom Peters! Inanities", *Sunday Times*, 7, 9 February,.

Walley, L. and M. Smith (1998) *Deception in Selection*, Chichester: Wiley.

Walsh, W.B. and S.H. Osipow (1983) *Handbook of Vocational Psychology*, Hillsdale, NJ: Lawrence Erlbaum.

Weber, M. (1947) *The Theory of Social and Economic Organisations*, New York: Free Press.

Wellner, A. S. (2006) "Business was Booming, but the Richardsons were Seriously Burned Out", *Boston*, **28** (4), 52–55.

Werner, R. and V. Kumar (2002) "The Mismanagement of Customer Loyalty", *Harvard Business Review*, **80** (7), 86–97.

Wilson, E.M. (2003) "Managing Diversity: Caste and Gender Issues in Organisations in India", in *Individual Diversity and Psychology in Organisations*, M.J. Davidson and S.L. Fielden (eds), Chichester: Wiley.

Woodward, J. (1965) *Industrial Organisation*: *Theory and Practice*, Oxford: Oxford University Press.

World Bank (2005) *Women in Development*.
http/genderstats.worldbank.org/wdevelopment.pdf, accessed 10/2/05

Zadeh, L. (1965) "Fuzzy Sets", *Information and Control*, **8**, 338–352.

Index